IMPRINTS, VOICEPRINTS, AND FOOTPRINTS OF MEMORY

Society of Biblical Literature

Resources for Biblical Study

Tom Thatcher, New Testament Editor

Number 74

IMPRINTS, VOICEPRINTS, AND FOOTPRINTS OF MEMORY

COLLECTED ESSAYS OF WERNER H. KELBER

by

Werner H. Kelber

Society of Biblical Literature
Atlanta

Library of Congress Cataloging-in-Publication Data

Kelber, Werner H., author.
    Imprints, voiceprints, and footprints of memory / Werner H. Kelber.
        p. cm. — (Resources for biblical study ; number 74)
    Includes bibliographical references and index.
    ISBN ISBN 978-1-58983-892-5 (paper binding : alk. paper) — ISBN 978-1-58983-893-2 (electronic format) — ISBN 978-1-58983-894-9 (hardcover binding : alk. paper)
    1. Bible. New Testament—Criticism, interpretation, etc. I. Title. II. Series: Resources for biblical study ; no. 74.
    BS2361.3.K45 2013
    225.6—dc23   2013022942

Printed on acid-free, recycled paper conforming to
ANSI/NISO Z39.48-1992 (R1997) and ISO 9706:1994
standards for paper permanence.

In Memoriam

John Miles Foley
1947–2012

Curator's Professor of Classical Studies and English
W. H. Byler Distinguished Chair in the Humanities, University of Missouri

Founder of the journal *Oral Tradition*
Founding Director of the Center for Studies in Oral Tradition
Founding Director of the Center for eResearch

Recipient of grants and awards from the ACLS, the Guggenheim Foundation, the NEH, the Fulbright Program, and the Mellon Foundation.

At home in the ancient Greek, the Anglo-Saxon, and the Serbo-Croatian epics, Foley was the world's foremost authority in comparative oral traditions.

In his own words, he was "vitally interested in the oldest and the newest of humankind's communicative technologies, Oral Tradition and the Internet, and especially in their unexpected similarities."

Contents

Foreword

It is difficult to overestimate the significance of the work of Werner Kelber for biblical studies. His groundbreaking 1983 monograph, *The Oral and the Written Gospel*, challenged the core foundations of biblical scholarship by offering a paradigm shift of sweeping proportions. Over the last three decades he has affirmed, revised, refined, and expanded his work in conversation with others who work in the same field and who are interacting with his scholarchip. The articles and papers arranged in chronological order in this volume chart that pioneering course. Every essay makes an original contribution, even when Kelber is reviewing the work of others. I have learned an enormous amount from this opportunity to study them.

In Kelber's view, biblical scholars of early Christianity and the New Testament have not adequately taken into account the ancient media of communication. Quite the contrary, historical-critical scholarship has worked instead by using assumptions and methods of modern print culture. In Kelber's analysis, this approach represents an anachronistic understanding of the arts of communication in antiquity, resulting in flawed historical reconstructions and inadequate interpretations of biblical writings. Even more problematic, this print-media mentality has left out of account the actual ancient media of communication—a "myopia" in the way we have traditionally studied biblical cultures and texts.

Drawing on current scholarship in cultural anthropology, orality studies, memory studies, classical scholarship, psychology, and other fields, Kelber proposes a bold alternative hermeneutic that shifts the center of gravity away from a focus on texts in print-mode to a model with four interrelated components: oral speech, memory, scribality, and performance. These provide the key elements of the complex communication arts of the ancient world. In unpacking these components, Kelber discusses features of the early Christian culture of orality, the overarching significance of memory as the main storehouse of tradition, scribing and manuscripts as seen in interrelationship with orality and memory, and the importance of performance. Whereas numerous scholars have developed one or the other of these components, Kelber's body of work offers a comprehensive, innovative, and coherent theory of the ancient arts of communication that can guide our future work.

Furthermore, Kelber demonstrates how oral speech, individual and collective memory, chirographic manuscripts, and performances all served the social, political, ethical, and cultural ethos and identity of the community. To characterize the pervasiveness and importance of this cultural ethos, Kelber refers to it as the "biosphere" of a particular community. It is the life-world that a community shares and that gives a community its identity. It is the collective social memory that selects, omits, revises, adapts, re-creates, and expands the traditions to serve the needs of the community in particular times and circumstances. Within this ethos, the components of communication interrelate in various ways to create and maintain the cultural traditions that give social identity, stability, adaptability, and innovation to the community.

Also, in Kelber's view, at an even deeper level, the particular communication arts of a culture shape its individual and collective mentality in ways that are distinct from cultures with other means of communication—just as our current electronic means of communication are changing the collective ways we think and relate in the modern world. The challenge Kelber offers biblical scholarship is to overcome the mental and social assumptions of the print culture that have dominated biblical scholarship and to seek to grasp the mindset of ancient cultures, where speech, memory, and performance held priority and where the nature and function of scribal manuscripts are to be distinguished from modern print.

In making these points, Kelber deals not only with communication arts in antiquity but also with the communication media of medieval culture, premodernism, Gutenberg's print revolution, and the Reformation. In other words, these essays do not merely cover New Testament texts, history, and interpretation. They also invite readers to think about the significance of media communications across the span of Western history up to modernity. This long-range perspective serves to facilitate comparative thought by enabling readers to become aware of the modern media sensibilities that have dominated our scholarly approaches to the Bible.

Kelber makes clear that the foundational shift from a print mentality to a focus on ancient communication arts is neither an add-on nor a blind spot to be investigated with the same tools we have been using. Rather, seeing early Christianity as part of an oral-memory-scribal-performance culture represents a paradigm shift that pulls the rug from under so much of what we do and boldly proposes different presuppositions and procedures that require new tools and methods. As such, Kelber's work is revolutionary, and, as such, it is has the potential to change a great deal of biblical scholarship at the concrete level of historical reconstruction and literary interpretation. In applying the new hermeneutic, Kelber emphasizes that all the key components—oral speech, memory, scribality, and performance—were interrelated in multiple ways. Such complexity makes it necessary for us to attempt to be specific about the presence and interaction of these components in any given instance under study.

Kelber himself develops numerous examples that demonstrate how attention to the ancient media might impact our understanding of the New Testament and related writings. He offers interpretations of Mark, Paul's letters, Q, and the Gospel of Thomas, each of which manifests different configurations of the arts of communication. Kelber also shows the potential impact of the new model in several traditional historical-critical disciplines such as form criticism, source criticism, and textual criticism. He shows how these disciplines that are based on the assumptions of a print culture have led to mistaken conclusions, and he illustrates potential outcomes using alternative methods of study based on the model that employs oral, memorial, chirographic, and performative arts of communication. In the course of these arguments, Kelber reconceptualizes the model of tradition itself—not only the Gospel tradition but also the proto-Masoretic tradition of the Hebrew Bible, the early rabbinic tradition, and the Hellenistic school tradition, inviting us to discern media commonalities across all four traditions.

Whether one agrees or disagrees with every specific of Kelber's communication model or with the way he reconfigures disciplines or with his interpretations of particular works, there is no getting around the radical challenge of his work to the roots of biblical studies—his foundational critique of our anachronistic print-culture approaches and his call for another set of assumptions to guide us into a new era of biblical studies. At stake, in Kelber's view, is the historical-critical paradigm itself in its current form. In an even larger sense, it can be said that the central metaphors of Western thought are affected by this media change: text and speech, tradition and composition, authorship and reading, writing and text, memory and imagination, cognition and logic, and performance and interpretation.

Few scholars have produced works that change the landscape of biblical studies. Werner Kelber is one of them. Since the onset of Kelber's clarion call for new media foundations, many scholars have contributed to the field. They have also incorporated, expanded, engaged, and challenged Kelber's insights and proposals—in papers, conferences, seminar sections of scholarly societies, monographs and dissertations, collections of articles, websites, publishing series, and much more. This volume of collected essays represents a giant leap forward by making Kelber's work accessible in one place to a wide range of scholars, and the rippling implications left in the wake of his work will undoubtedly continue to shake the scholarly world.

David Rhoads
Professor of New Testament, Emeritus
Lutheran School of Theology at Chicago

Acknowledgments

Chapter 1 was delivered in April 1985 at a symposium hosted by the Theology Department at Marquette University on the theme of Call and Discipleship in New Testament Perspectives, then published in *Discipleship in the New Testament* (ed. Fernando F. Segovia; Philadelphia: Fortress, 1985), 24–46.

Chapter 2 was published in *Semeia* 39 (1987): 107–33. Titled *Orality, Aurality, and Biblical Narrative*, that issue was edited by Lou H. Silberman and devoted to a discussion of my book *The Oral and the Written Gospel*. The article was reprinted in revised form in *The Interpretation of Dialogue* (ed. Tullio Maranhao; Chicago: University of Chicago Press, 1990), 75–98. A French translation appeared as "Récit et Révélation: Voiler, Dévoiler at Revoiler," *Revue D'Histoire et de Philosophie Religieuses* 69 (1989): 389–410.

Chapter 3 appeared in *Semeia* 43 (1988): 1–20 (with response by Frank Kermode, 155–67).

Chapter 4 was published in the *Journal of the American Academy of Religion* 58 (1990): 69–98.

Chapter 5 was published in *Semeia* 65 (1994): 139–67.

Chapter 6 was delivered in October 1993 as the ninth annual Milman Parry and Albert Lord Lecture at the University of Missouri-Columbia. It was published in revised and expanded form in *Oral Tradition* 10/2 (1995): 409–50.

Chapter 7 appeared in the reprint of *The Oral and the Written Gospel* (Bloomington: Indiana University Press, 1997) as my response to critical reviews fourteen years after the initial publication of the volume.

Chapter 8 was delivered at the University of Natal, South Africa, in August 2000 and at the Russian Institute for Cultural Research, St. Petersburg, in June 2001. The lecture was pulished in the *Bulletin for Contextual Theology in Africa* 7/3 and 8/1 (2000–2001; double issue): 12–24, and in the series International Readings on Theory, History and Philosophy of Culture 12, in a volume titled *Ontology of Dialogue: Metaphysics and Religious Experience* (ed. Liubava Moreva; St. Petersburg: Eidos, 2002), 181–207.

Chapter 9 was delivered in October 2002 at a symposium hosted by the Evangelische Akademie, Loccum, Germany, titled "Deutungen von Wirklichkeit—erkenntnistheoretische Voraussetzungen und Geltungsanspüche religiöser und philosophischer Interpretationsmodelle." It was published in *Konstruktion von Wirklichkeit: Beiträge aus geschichts-theoretischer, philosophischer und theologischer Perspektive* (ed. Jens Schröter und Antje Eddelbüttel; Berlin: de Gruyter, 2004), 153–68.

Chapter 10 was published as "The Quest for the Historical Jesus: From the Perspectives of Medieval, Modern, and Post-Enlightenment Readings, and in View of Ancient, Oral Aesthetics," in John Dominic Crossan, Luke Timothy Johnson, and Werner H. Kelber, *The Jesus Controversy: Perspectives in Conflict* (Harrisburg, Pa.: Trinity Press International, 1999), 75–115. A revised version was delivered in June 1999 at the University of Hamburg under the title "Der historische Jesus: Bedenken zur gegenwärtigen Diskussion aus der Perspektive mittelalterlicher, moderner und postmoderner Hermeneutik." It was published in *Der historische Jesus: Tendenzen und Perspektiven der gegenwärtigen Forschung* (ed. Jens Schröter and Ralph Brucker; Berlin: de Gruyter, 2002), 15–66. A further revision was presented in April of 2004 at the University of Leuven, Belgium, under the title "The Theological Refutation, Linguistic Dilemma, and Ethical Validity of the Search for the Historical Jesus."

Chapter 11 was published in *Memory, Tradition, and Text: Uses of the Past in Early Christianity* (ed. Alan Kirk and Tom Thatcher; SemeiaSt 52; Atlanta: Society of Biblical Literature, 2005), 221–48.

Chapter 12 appeared in the form of a review essay in *Review of Biblical Literature* 9 (2007): 1–24.

Chapter 13 was published in *Saintly Influence: Edith Wyschogrod and the Possibilities of Philosophy of Religion* (ed. Eric Boynton and Martin Kavka; New York: Fordham University Press, 2009), 175–201. The piece is a contribution to the Festschrift in honor of the late Edith Wyschogrod, who served as the J. Newton Rayzor Professor of Philosophy and Religious Thought at Rice University (1992–2003) and served as president of the American Academy of Religion (1993).

Chapter 14 appeared in *Jesus in Memory: Traditions in Oral and Scribal Perspectives* (ed. Werner H. Kelber and Samuel Byrskog; Waco, Tex.: Baylor University Press, 2009), 173–206. In that volume, my essay constitutes the final, summarizing response to contributions by seven colleagues who revisit *Memory and Manuscript*, Birger Gerhardsson's landmark contribution to twentieth-century New Testament studies. Following the introductory essay (Samuel Byrskog), the contributors discuss form criticism (Christopher Tuckett), Jesus' message as oral tradition (Terence C. Mournet), the Jesus tradition in the Pauline letters (David E. Aune), "reoralizing" in the talmudic texts (Martin S. Jaffee), memory and tradition in the Hellenistic schools (Loveday Alexander), and memory (Alan Kirk)—principal themes treated in Gerhardsson's *Memory and Manuscript*. My concluding essay reflects on all seven essays as autonomous pieces and as responses to Gerhardsson's magnum opus.

Chapter 15 was delivered in April of 2008 at a conference that was part of a series of orality-literacy conferences inaugurated in 2001 in South Africa and over the years convened on three continents: Africa, Europe, and North America. This, the seventh conference in the series, was organized under the title "Oral-Scribal Dimensions of Scripture, Piety and Practice in Judaism, Christianity and Islam" and took place at Rice University, Houston, Texas. The lecture was initially published in revised form in *Oral Tradition* 25/1 (2010): 115–40, then republished in *The Interface of Orality and Writing* (ed. Annette Weissenrieder and Robert B. Coote; Tübingen: Mohr Siebeck, 2010), 71–99.

Chapter 16 was delivered on April 7, 2005, at a conference convened under the title "Walter Ong's Contribution to the Humanities at St. Louis University," celebrating the legacy of Walter J. Ong, S.J. It was published in *Language, Culture, and Identity* (ed. Sara van den Berg and Thomas M. Walsh; New York: Hampton, 2011), 49–67.

Abbreviations

Primary Sources

1 Apol.	Justin Martyr, *First Apology*
Ap. Jas.	*Apocryphon of James*
Dial. Sav.	*Dialogue of the Savior*
Did.	*Didache*
Eph.	Ignatius, *To the Ephesians*
Gos. Thom.	*Gospel of Thomas*
Hist. eccl.	Eusebius, *Historia ecclesiastica*
Inst.	Quintilian, *Institutio oratoria*

Secondary Sources

ABR	*Australian Biblical Review*
AJT	*American Journal of Theology*
AnBib	Analecta biblica
ASNU	Acta seminarii neotestamentici upsaliensis
BTB	*Biblical Theology Bulletin*
BTZ	*Berliner Theologische Zeitschrift*
CBQ	*Catholic Biblical Quarterly*
CCSL	Corpus Christianorum: Series Latina
CWS	Classics of Western Spirituality
ETL	*Ephemerides theologicae lovanienses*
FB	Forschung zur Bibel
FRLANT	Forschungen zur Religion und Literatur des Alten und Neuen Testaments
GBS	Guides to Biblical Scholarship
HvTSt	*Hervormde Teologiese Studies*
HSCL	Harvard Studies in Comparative Literature

HSCP	*Harvard Studies in Classical Philology*
HTS	Harvard Theological Studies
Int	*Interpretation*
JAAR	*Journal of the American Academy of Religion*
JBL	*Journal of Biblical Literature*
JJS	*Journal of Jewish Studies*
JR	*Journal of Religion*
JSNTSup	Journal for the Study of the New Testament Supplement Series
LCL	Loeb Classical Library
LD	Lectio divina
LTQ	*Lexington Theological Quarterly*
MoRev	*Missouri Review*
Neot	*Neotestamentica*
NTS	*New Testament Studies*
Phil	*Philologus*
PL	Patrologia latina. Edited by J.-P. Migne. 217 vols. Paris: Migne, 1844–1864.
POxy	Oxyrhynchus papyri
PTMS	Pittsburgh Theological Monograph Series
RGG	*Religion in Geschichte und Gegenwart.* Edited by K. Galling. 3rd ed. 7 vols. Tübingen: Mohr Siebeck, 1957–1965.
RHPR	*Revue d'histoire et de philosophie religieuses*
SAC	Studies in Antiquity and Christianity
SBLDS	Society of Biblical Literature Dissertation Series
SBS	Stuttgarter Bibelstudien
SBT	Studies in Biblical Theology
SemeiaSt	Semeia Studies
JSLA	Studies in Judaism in Late Antiquity
SNTSMS	Society of New Testament Studies Monograph Series
StPatr	*Studia Patristica*
TAPA	*Transactions of the American Philological Association*
TorSTh	Toronto Studies in Theology
TS	*Theological Studies*
TSAJ	Texte und Studien zum antiken Judentum
TTS	Trierer theologische Studien
USQR	*Union Seminary Quarterly Review*
WMANT	Wissenschaftliche Monographien zum Alten und Neuen Testament

WUNT	Wissenschaftliche Untersuchungen zum Neuen Testament
WW	*Word and World*
ZNW	*Zeitschrift für die neutestamentliche Wissenschaft und die Kunde der älteren Kirche*
ZTK	*Zeitschrift für Theologie und Kirche*

Introduction

> That manuscripts are different from modern printed editions is obvious
> enough. Yet only when we have spent some time among manuscripts do
> we begin to realize just how powerful this difference is.
> —John Dagenais, *The Ethics of Reading in Manuscript Culture*

> We have yet to appreciate fully the extent to which contemporary literary
> theory is founded upon an archi-typography.
> —John Dagenais, *The Ethics of Reading in Manuscript Culture*

The essays collected in this volume and arranged in the chronological order
of their composition were published between 1985 and 2011, spanning a
period of over a quarter of a century. All the pieces have previously been
published, and all have been reworked and edited. To enhance readability,
to facilitate cross-referencing, and to improve the coherence of the whole,
the sixteen chapters have been subdivided into sense units and numbered
across the volume. All essays have been written after the publication of my
earlier study *The Oral and the Written Gospel* (1983). They take their starting point from that book and seek to develop the premises initiated in it.

In the most general terms, *Imprints, Voiceprints, and Footprints of
Memory* offers analyses of the ancient world of communication as it manifested itself in voice and chirographic practices, in oral-scribal interfaces,
in compositional processes and performative activities, and in memory
both as an individual and a social phenomenon. Some essays extend the
topic of communication beyond ancient culture across the Middle Ages
and into modernity. The title articulates the core issue explored in these
essays: the dominantly typographical mediation of ancient chirographic,
oral, and memorial communication processes. Until the recent advent of
the electronic medium, the bulk of our studies of ancient biblical texts
has been processed via the print medium. Although there is little consciousness of this fact, it has influenced every aspect of modern biblical

scholarship. We tend to be least conscious of that which affects us most deeply. This volume seeks to develop a *Problembewusstsein*, a consciousness of the media problematics rooted in the authority of the modern print Bible and in the historical-critical paradigm. There is a media gap that separates by two millennia our scholarly treatment of the print Bible, processed mostly in the print medium, from the media world in which the biblical texts were composed, reoralized, and remembered. While no doubt inspired by current electronic technologies and their transformative impact on our social and political life, on consciousness and the human sensorium, these essays are intellectually indebted to the pioneering work of humanistic scholars such as Milman Parry, Frances Yates, Albert Bates Lord, Walter J. Ong, Eric Havelock, Martin Jaffee, John Dagenais, Ruth Finnegan, John Miles Foley, Elizabeth Eisenstein, Michael Giesecke, Mary Carruthers, and others who in many and diverse ways have initiated and advanced our knowledge of oral tradition specifically and of the relations between media technologies, culture, and cognition in general. In moving oral, scribal, memorial dynamics and their transformation through the print medium to a point of central reflection, the essays collected here strive after a paradigm that thematizes the materiality and aesthetics of communicative practices.

The oral-scribal-memorial-performative paradigm that is being developed in these essays poses challenges to the reigning historical, documentary, source-critical paradigm. The latter has served as the intellectual impetus for biblical scholarship since premodern times and far into postmodernism. Most of our exegetical practices and theoretical assumptions about the verbal arts in ancient, early Christian, and Jewish culture are deeply entrenched in this classic paradigm. Professional biblical scholarship has been conducting its business for over five centuries in the medium of print, and has been accustomed to experiencing the Bible as a technologically constructed objectivity. Put differently, from the perspectives developed here, the historical-critical paradigm appears culture-bound and beholden to modern media dynamics that are many centuries removed from the ancient communications culture. The first epigraph to this introduction articulates this media gap. The challenge I pose to the historical-critical paradigm is not meant to be a categorical objection to it. To the contrary. The accomplishments of the historical examination of the Bible are incontestably huge. They mark a high point of the intellectual ethos of modernity. My concern is rather that the historical-critical paradigm is not historical enough. What is advocated here is a novel sense of sensibilities that seeks to come to terms with what Foley has called "an inadequate theory of verbal art." More is involved than the correction of an imbalance. A new theory of the verbal art that is commensurate with the ancient culture of communication—that is what I have been attempting to accomplish over the past quarter of a century. The studies brought together in this volume are therefore not merely to be viewed as an embellishment or modification of conventional historical, predominantly textual studies, something to be added to the existing scholarly paradigm. Instead, these essays invite readers to examine a set of concepts that are widely viewed as a given of the historical paradigm and are often thought to require no critical reflection any more. Notions about text and speech, tradition and composition, authorship and reading, writing and text, memory and imagination, cognition and logic—central metaphors of Western thought—are all affected in the effort to rethink what in my view is a paradigm driven by a dominantly post-Gutenberg intellectualism.

Nomenclature has been a concern throughout these essays. Historical criticism by and large lacks the language to express the oral-scribal-memorial-performative dynamics of ancient word processing. I am struggling to wrest myself free from technical terms and definitions that represent typographically conditioned logic and habits, and yet I have found myself again and again slipping into the language of modernity's print medium. Ideally, the vocabulary we use must be derived from and have a direct bearing on the phenomena we observe. Nomenclature is therefore of the essence. For example, in the course of writing these essays, I have grown increasingly uneasy about the use of terms such as *text* and *textuality*, words that are loaded with assumptions derived from modern literary criticism and print technology. I now prefer *manuscript* and *scribality*, *chirography* and *scriptography*, *scriptum* and *scripta*, all terms that denote the craft of handwriting. Throughout this volume, readers will encounter the following technical terms: *equiprimordiality*: a plurality of originals as over against the single original; Jesus as *Erinnerungsfigur* (J. Assmann): a memorially engaging and accessible personage, rather than a historically retrievable and verifiable one; *archaeology of memory*: retrieval of past traditions for present identification and mythicization; *commemorative keying* (Schwartz and Kirk): a tradition's linking with archetypal figures, images, and events of the past; *reoralization*: recycling of scripts into discourse; *dedicated medium*: stylized, patterned language rooted in oral performance and designed to achieve maximal communicative effects; *mnemohistory* (J. Assmann): history as a continuous stream of rememorizing activities and processes; *damnatio memoriae*: the suppression of memory for psychological but also for political reasons; *typographic captivity*: communication and scholarship in the post-Gutenberg era conditioned and controlled by print technology; *biosphere*: tradition viewed as a live matrix of oral, scribal, memorial features and dynamics; *mouvance* (Zumthor): the recensional activity of a living manuscript culture in the process of persistent regeneration; *Traditionsbruch* (J. Assmann): a rupture in the tradition, typically after a forty years interval when (remembered) history has to yield to rememorization; *memorial threshold*: a memory crisis at the end of a generational period demanding a reconfiguration of memory; *virtuality* and *virtual text*: terms associated with the digital medium, denoting a textual reality not in the concrete, but in an electronically enhanced and transfigured sense; *scribal activism*: scribes' compositional, memorial intervention in the products of their trade; *interior visualization*: a feature of ancient rhetoric (and medieval memory theory), adverting to the interiorization of knowledge via images; *vox intexta* or *voiced texts*: scripted verbalization designed to reach its communicative realization in oral performance; *intermediality*: interaction of oral with scribal communication; *Rezitationstexte*: the nature of many ancient manuscripts to be reperformed in oral discourse; *enculturation* (the central concept in Carr's paradigm of the ancient verbal art, but employed by others as well): the educational function of ancient Near Eastern and Mediterranean manuscripts to be inculcated in people's minds and hearts; *print capitalism* (Anderson): a new cultural phenomenon in Western history characterized by the confluence of the high tech of the fifteenth century with a rapidly growing entrepreneurship; *originalism*: fascination with origin, including the search for the original saying, the original text, and so on; *les cadres sociaux* (Halbwachs) and *Bezugsrahmen* (J. Assmann): referring to a central thesis of cultural memory which postulates that the past is never directly accessible apart from memory frameworks supplied by present social experiences; *reconstructivism*: a key feature of cultural memory stating that the past has to be continually reorganized to be preserved; *loci communes* or memory places: the creation of mental spaces for the storing of knowledge (used in this book also in reference to commonplace patterns in the passion narrative).

The readers following these essays in the chronological order of their composition will observe a shift from an initial focus on literary, narratological issues towards understanding the oral-scribal-memorial-performative dynamics and a growing theoretical grasp of the subject matter.

Among the wide range of issues covered in this volume, there are four central topics to which I return repeatedly and in different intellectual contexts. The first topic is *originalism*, a term at home in jurisprudence, and a characteristic trait of the historical-critical study of the Bible. Originalism, in the words of a sitting Supreme Court justice, is "to give the text the meaning it had when it was adopted." In biblical scholarship, originalism is a defining feature of its rationality. It refers to the search for what has often been referred to as the original Greek text of the New Testament, and our efforts to recover the singular originality of Jesus' *ipsissima verba* or their *ipsissima structura*, the original text of Q, and the original version among textual variants. It is a driving force in the historical Quest, in form criticism, in text criticism, and in Q research. My argument throughout is that the search for the single origin is incompatible with the oral-scribal dynamics of the early tradition.

The notion of *the one original* reflects the experience of the print medium, a point made in the second epigraph to this introduction. As long as texts remain actively involved in a performance process, each reactivation is authentically original. We have to think the—for us exceedingly difficult—concept of multiple originals, instead of the single reference point.

Originalism is a principal impulse of the discipline of *form criticism*, the second central topic in these essays. One of the most consequential methodological principles underlying modern biblical scholarship, it is based on the premise that oral items embedded in texts are identifiable, accessible, and detachable from their contents. The discipline was initially designed to come to an understanding of the nature and processes of oral tradition, but it was early on enlisted, and, I propose, misdirected toward the Quest for the original sayings of Jesus. I argue that current orality-scribality studies compromise nearly every aspect of form criticism, including that of the detachability of oral speech, the linearity of the oral, oral-scribal tradition, and the notion of the insignificance of the Gospels' narrative poetics. I suggest that already the discipline's very own designation in terms of form criticism is misconceived, because form is a visually based concept ill-suited to capture the phenomenon of oral discourse. True to the actual processes of oral tradition, the discipline should have called itself performance criticism, in the manner in which it is presently being developed by David Rhoads. In view of the immense influence form criticism exerts over biblical scholarship, I argue the case against the discipline in detail, and in the process reiterate and enlarge my own understanding of the oral-scribal-memorial-performative paradigm.

Tradition and *Oral Tradition* is the third topic treated extensively in these essays. I am keenly aware of the nationalistic and ethnocentric connotations that have been attached to this "intriguing and appealing and sometimes treacherous concept" (Ruth Finnegan). Both terms, *oral* and *tradition*, are multivalent, and the compound *oral tradition* does not credibly lend itself to a single, simple definition. Still, Foley is right, and Finnegan would no doubt agree, that "94 percent of our historical experience depended wholly on an alternate technology, the technology of oral tradition." Writing came exceedingly late, and it was very rare for the longest part of human existence—and even print verbalization may turn out to be a mere episode. Biblical criticism has been ill-served by the neglect or misapprehension of oral tradition. The time is long past that we can dismiss it as illusionary, or, as some would have it, as campfire romanticism, or as a residue of folklore studies that are becoming extinct in the humanities. In biblical studies, the oral-scribal-memorial-performative paradigm has rapidly proliferated over the past thirty years, and the relevant scholarship has grown in historical exactness and theoretical sophistication. Still, the modern scholarly view often is that oral discourse is an appendage to writing, whereas in ancient culture, and far into the Middle Ages, the relationship was precisely the other way around: writing served the imperatives of recitation and memorization.

Oral tradition has both a synchronic and a diachronic dimension. Once writing had come into existence, oral tradition may broadly be described as a verbal-social context larger than any single papyrus or vellum-bound verbalization. For the period of late antiquity, I have introduced the concept of *biosphere*, a matrix that carries the oxygen necessary to sustain human life. Diachronically, I have throughout my writings objected to a linear, developmental concept. I suggest that the perception of an oral-scribal-oral feedback loop, rather than a chain of causalities, may approximate oral tradition more accurately than the concept of trajectory. Importantly, the medieval Church and Catholicism to this day have institutionalized tradition by placing it (along with papal and conciliar authority) on equal footing with the authority of the Bible. I also reflect on the sixteenth-century Reformers' repudiation of tradition, thereby empowering the Bible with an authority it never had achieved before in Western culture. The fateful decision, I argue with others, is closely allied with the invention of the *high tech* of the fifteenth century. I devote some space to discussing the print revolution and its impact on the role of the Bible and its interpretation. Among typography's consequences are the rise of the historical-critical paradigm, biblical literalism and fundamentalism, a notion unthinkable in ancient Christianity and the medieval church, and the Bible's commercialization, its transformation into a source of revenue and into a product that one day will be available on every night table in our hotels.

Memory, the fourth topic in this book, entered my work in the mid-1990s. Since then, my interest in the concept has steadily grown. Beginning with chapter 6, numerous aspects of memory are introduced, and various features of ancient and medieval culture are illuminated in connection with it: memory in ancient mythology, philosophy, and rhetoric (6.32), St. Augustine's meditation on memory (6.34), medieval reconceptualization of memory (6.35), memory's compositional processes (7.42), the ordeal of remembering in Judaism and Christianity (8.48–49), mnemohistory (8.50), studies on the ancient and medieval memory culture by Yates and Carruthers (9.51), early Christianity as mnemohistory, a process of constructive negotiations of (remembered) history and traditions (ch. 11), memory and violence (ch. 13)—including the passion narrative's commemorative strategies in response to a traumatic death (12.88), Gerhardsson's Memory and Manuscript (ch. 14)—including "eight faces of memory" (14.97), memory in the enculturation paradigm (15.98), the spatial model of memory (15.101), and memory and manuscript in medieval culture (15.102). Much to my own surprise, I observed in the process of editing these essays that memory had emerged as a key concept in my work. Memory is presently in the process of becoming a recognized research topic in biblical scholarship. But it is worth noting that with rare, though very distinguished, exceptions (Gerhardsson, Rodriguez, Kirk, Thatcher), memory in the past has found no place in historical criticism, in the subdisciplines of form criticism and textual criticism, and little recognition in hermeneutics. Mnemosyne, mother of the nine Muses, goddess of imagination and memory, one of the five canons of ancient rhetoric, whom Augustine counted, along with will and understanding, as one of the three powers of the soul, forces that were represented in the Trinity, "the matrix of all human temporal perception" (Carruthers), this deep space of the human mind, has played next to no role in modernity's study and interpretation of the ancient texts of the Bible. Few issues demonstrate as clearly the difference between the historical-critical paradigm and the oral-scribal-memorial-performative paradigm as the role of memory, its virtual absence in one model versus its rise to central position in the other. In these essays, I am as interested in exploring the many faces of memory as I am in considering the reasons for its demise in biblical scholarship.

Memory, not unlike tradition, is a multivalent and quintessentially interdisciplinary category, and I have taken pains to demonstrate its applicability in diverse cultural contexts. In that vein, a particular concern of mine has been to enlarge the focus on memory toward the wider field of memory, language, cognition, sense perception, and also logic—because logic is not a given, it has a history. Understood in this broadly inclusive sense, these studies on communication processes cover ancient history, run through medieval culture, and also focus on the print revolution and its impact on modernity. Among the rhetoricians, epic singers, philosophers, and theologians whose relevant thoughts have been integrated are Homer, Gorgias, Plato, Aristotle, Cicero, Eusebius, Quintilian, Origen, Augustine, Abailard, Bernard of Clairvaux, Thomas Aquinas, William of Ockham, Luther—not to forget, the blacksmith, goldsmith, artisan, printer, publisher, and entrepreneur Johannes Gutenberg. The placement of the historical-critical paradigm into this broad sweep of Western communications history is intended to facilitate comparative thought, bringing self-awareness to the modern study of the print Bible via printed texts by confronting it with ancient and medieval media sensibilities.

The treatment of one aspect of memory merits special attention. In chapter 8, I discuss four case studies that manifest poisonous acts of remembering, conflicting memories, and the ordeal of remembering. Features of the New Testament, especially their rememorizations, and aspects of New Testament scholarship itself have been, and in some ways continue to be part of, an anti-Jewish discourse. I show how the fateful verse Matt 27:25 was reimagined under social, political circumstances different from those under which they were written, triggering demonizing fantasies and murderous actions throughout Western history (8.46). As far as the Middle Ages are concerned, I use the case of the noted Barcelona Disputation of 1236 between Rabbi Moses ben Nahman and Pablo Christiani to demonstrate that their irreconcilable positions are comprehensible as a clash of cultural memories (8.47). In modern times, I interpret Elie Wiesel's novel *Night*, and its complex compositional history, as an example of the ordeal of remembering transpiring under memory's stern mandate to carry the past over into the present (8.48). I finally analyze the appropriation of the trauma of Auschwitz by Jews and Christians, Polish Jews and Polish Catholics, national and religious interests. I argue that the atrocities live on as a tragic struggle of conflicting memories and identities (8.49).

All four cases, I demonstrate, lend themselves to the application of the social or cultural memory theory.

I have found some of these case studies helpful in reconsidering the approach to the passion narrative. I conclude that the historical-critical search for source-critical precision, textual originality, accurate chronology, and for the bedrock of historical facticity misses what, I think, matters most about the sacred story: the commemorative and psychodynamic impulses that feed it. I proceed from the concept of trauma and interpret the passion narrative as a commemorative story that applies various memorial strategies to carry out the impossible objective of projecting the hideous atrocity into the present.

I have dedicated these essays to the late John Miles Foley, a shining light in the humanities, and a very dear friend of mine.

1

APOSTOLIC TRADITION AND THE FORM OF THE GOSPEL

This essay is based on three fundamental premises. One, discipleship in Mark, as in all other canonical Gospels, is inextricably linked with the literary composition and design of that Gospel. From the perspective of narrative, Markan discipleship functions as part and parcel of the Gospel's literary dynamics and causalities. Two, following the logic of the narrative, the Markan disciples are portrayed neither as entirely positive nor entirely negative characters. Their precise narrative pattern is one of parabolic role reversal, which converts them from trusted insiders to untrustworthy outsiders. This pattern culminates in the exclusion of the disciples from meeting the risen Lord. I conclude that the dissociation of the disciples from the risen Lord and hence the absence of Easter are distinctive features that contribute to the form of the Gospel. The narrative withholding of Easter creates a Gospel that is, far from being grounded in Easter faith, entirely cast in a pre-resurrectional form. In conclusion, the question is raised whether the extant form of Gospel could have arisen as an alternative model to the postresurrectional gnosticizing sayings Gospel that is grounded in the risen Jesus and his words addressed to the disciples, and operates without a narrative of Jesus' life and death.

> They [the disciples] are behaving exactly like the outsiders in the theory of parables.
> —Frank Kermode, *The Genesis of Secrecy*

1. EVOLUTIONARY VERSUS REVOLUTIONARY GENESIS OF MARK

For some time now, the theme of discipleship in Mark has attracted my attention, for nowhere in the canon does a text generate in readers as much alienation from the disciples as in this Gospel (Kelber 1972; 1974; 1979; 1983). I continue to view it as a puzzle that admits of no simple or general answer. The very oddness of the theme ought to have inspired creative explorations, whereas, in fact, it has often given rise to evasive maneuvers. The elaboration of admittedly positive features of the disciples is, of course, very much to the point. But it has not dissuaded me from holding that *the full narrative impact* of the disciples' story is a decidedly ambiguous one. The desire to muffle the effects of Markan discipleship still seems less urgent to me than the obligation to explore its fuller ramifications, for the Markan exposition of the theme is more consequential than often assumed. If I take up discipleship in Mark again, therefore, it is out of a conviction that its implications have as yet not been brought to bear upon such issues as the form of the Gospel, its connection with what preceded it, and also the role of Easter among competing early Christian traditions.

The assignation of apostolicity to the four Gospels did more than lend legitimacy to what came to be called orthodoxy. It also imposed patterns of continuity upon the early processes of the tradition. Something akin to a straight line was envisioned to lead from Jesus through his oral, apostolic successors to the Gospel. When in the eighteenth and nineteenth centuries historical scholarship commenced to probe Christian origins, the model of continuity operated within the framework of linear thinking, partly under the pressure of orthodox assumptions and partly influenced by modern intellectual disciplines, which had themselves adopted linearity as a principal hermeneutical key.

In the twentieth century, both the form critics and their challengers viewed the Gospel in direct continuity with tradition. The situation is epitomized by Rudolf Bultmann (1963)[1] and Birger Gerhardsson (1961). For Bultmann, the Gospel results from the upward causation operative in all evolutionary processes. It is assumed that tradition flows predominantly from less to more, and from simple forms to the complex construction of the Gospel. Gerhardsson suggested the existence of an authoritative λόγος τοῦ κυρίου ("word of the Lord") programmatically summed up in the speeches of Acts. They formed the basic teaching for the college of the Twelve and also for Paul. Embodying the essentials of Jesus' words and deeds from baptism to ascension, the Λόγος constituted the Gospel's genetic code inscribed into tradition from its very inception. Thus, both for Bultmann the form critic and Gerhardsson the challenger of form criti-

---

1. In view of the often-noted difficulties pertaining to the translation of Bultmann's *The History of the Synoptic Tradition*, citations are offered here from my own translation of the German original: *Die Geschichte der synoptischen Tradition* (1970).

cism, the Gospel appeared to be the natural and expected outcome of the predominantly oral, precanonical tradition.

In view of the fact that form criticism's inability to come to terms with the Gospel composition is widely recognized today, it deserves to be pointed out that Bultmann was himself torn between two potentially conflicting viewpoints. There was, on the one hand, his well-known statement that the Gospel "offers nothing in principle new, but merely completes what was already begun in the earliest, oral tradition" (1970, 347). Yet he also insisted that the "form of Gospel is first encountered in Mark; one may say that he has created it" (394). Could Mark, one must ask, become the creator of a new literary form in the Christian tradition by merely bringing oral trends to their destined culmination?

Form criticism's inadequate treatment of orality and its relation to textuality served to enhance the deeply ingrained model of continuity between tradition and Gospel. While convinced of the predominance of precanonical, Synoptic orality, form critics chose to regard the Gospel's written performance as mere transcription of oral speech. On this view, the purpose of the Gospel was consistently defined in terms of preservation of tradition. It was a position that accorded well with the classic thesis of the demise of the apostolic generation: when the living chain of apostolic transmitters of tradition was severed, it became imperative that their message be preserved in as authentic a fashion as possible. In view of the massive work undertaken by Eric A. Havelock (1963; 1978), Albert B. Lord (1960), and Walter J. Ong (1967b; 1977a; 1982) on orality, it should be obvious that form criticism paid lip service to the world of spoken words. Had form critics seriously sought to explore oral hermeneutics, as well as the processes of transformation of sounded words through textualization, they might well have concluded that preservation was not necessarily the Gospel's primary function.

Whether the appeal was to entitlement by apostolic authority, the cumulative force of tradition, the abiding effectiveness of an incipient core message, or to the impulse to stem the tide of forgetfulness—the Gospel was invariably viewed as preserver of tradition and guarantor of continuity. It was a view, moreover, that was powerfully strengthened by growing insight into the basic tenacity of linguistic and artistic conventions. No author writes independently from predecessors and without dependency on schemata, and in this sense the author is inexorably bound up with tradition. The more one recognized the force of linguistic forms and formulas, types and images, genres and styles, the less one trusted the claims to creativity. The Gospel, by this logic, was almost always perceived to stand in unbroken or evolutionary continuity with tradition.

Given the deep interiorization of the model of tradition's gradual ascent to the Gospel, the integrity of a Gospel and the novelty of its form were consistently underrated. That the Gospel could have been written for the purpose of correcting, rather than protecting, tradition was an idea whose day had not yet come.

The road toward a new appreciation of the composition of a Gospel was paved by redaction criticism and literary criticism. Above all, these disciplines demonstrated the narrative integrity of the four canonical Gospels, forcing the conclusion that a distinct authorial intentionality was operative in each of them. The arrangement and revision of traditional materials, the production of novel segments, the artistic interweaving of dramatic features, the employment of christological titles, the whole inner landscape of the narrative with setting, plot, and characters, inside views, ideological point of view, and narrative realism, and in the case of Mark—if one subscribed to Markan priority—the very form of a Gospel, all resulted from a linguistic, theological act of creation. In North American biblical scholarship, Norman Perrin took the creative literary production of Mark with utmost seriousness (1968; 1969; 1971b; 1974; 1976). Much of his Markan scholarship was designed to demonstrate that Mark's Gospel was the result of a "self-conscious ... editor, redactor, and author" (1969, 51, n. 8). But there is evidence that even Perrin did not fully realize the implications of his work as far as our understanding of the history of the tradition was concerned. He was, under the tutelage of Joachim Jeremias and Bultmann, preoccupied with myth and history and the relation between the historical Jesus versus the kerygmatic Gospel, and he never made a sustained effort at revising the gradualist, evolutionary model of tradition and Gospel. It was, however, Erhardt Güttgemanns (1979) who clearly articulated the impact of redaction criticism upon the model of the history of the Synoptic tradition: "If the gospel form is actually a language form first *created* by Mark, then we cannot simultaneously assume an immanent tendency within the tradition history of the material, which leads logically, consistently, causally, and genetically to the gospel form" (307). Güttgemanns's perception of a Gospel as "autosemantic language form" (307) carried with it the potential of overturning the time-honored, classic model of continuity with respect to tradition and Gospel. Now a Gospel could no longer be comprehended solely as product or extension of tradition, and preservation of oral materials proved inadequate as explanation for the writing of Mark. It was not tradition that, empowered by its immanent drives, emanated into the Gospel but Mark who had shaped the form of Gospel by exercising control over tradition.

Independent of Güttgemanns's theoretically conceived work, Theodore Weeden advanced our understanding of the relation of Mark's Gospel to tradition in his justly famous *Mark—Traditions in Conflict* (1971). Perhaps Weeden's most significant achievement was to introduce into Gospel studies the notion of conflicting traditions, and hence to challenge the rectilinear model of the transmission of Synoptic traditions. Henceforth, when we speak of the history of the Synoptic tradition, we ought to be mindful of *traditions* in the plural. What had long been commonplace in Pauline studies—that is, the recognition of alternate Gospels—was about to become reality for the Synoptic traditions as well. From this perspective, the Synoptic history appeared not as passive transmission of *the* Gospel, nor merely as "a process of hermeneutical translation" (Robinson 1971a, 29), but as a struggle between competing and possibly irreconcilable viewpoints. Mark's Gospel, in Weeden's view, was an active participant in the conflict between traditions and specifically designed to rebut a distinct view of Christian faith.

The basic argument of Weeden's thesis is well known. In following a principle of Hellenistic, literary hermeneutics, he focused on Mark's characters, especially the disciples, who, he claimed, hold the key to the mystery surrounding the genesis of this Gospel. The evangelist "is assiduously involved in a vendetta against the disciples. He is intent on totally discrediting them" (Weeden 1971, 50). Mark carries out the project dramatically by narrating the disciples' relationship to Jesus as one of progressive deterioration. From the initial stage of imperception of Jesus' miraculous powers, they lapse into misconceiving his messiahship, only to end in rejecting the suffering, dying Messiah. The disciples' failure is rooted in a stubborn commitment to a θεῖος ἀνήρ ("divine man") Christology that embraced a messiah in glory and power. What caused Mark to stage this extraordinary scenario was a christological controversy in his own community. It was troubled by the suffering of its members and the delay of the Parousia, when certain θεῖος ἀνήρ apostles arrived and proclaimed a Christology of power and presence. It was this heresy that necessitated Mark's Gospel. In projecting the heresy upon the disciples, and by making Jesus the spokesman of his own preferred Christology, the evangelist was able to effectively dramatize Jesus' exemplary response to the crisis.

Two obvious objections to Weeden's thesis come to mind immediately. First, the three-stage dramatization of the disciples' failure is not strictly derived from the plotted narrative. Mark's pattern of discipleship does not follow the tidy progression of unperceptiveness, misconception, and rejection. Second, the θεῖος ἀνήρ identification of the disciples is questionable. Weeden chose to examine the Markan situation in θεῖος ἀνήρ terms that were taken directly from Dieter Georgi's interpretation of 2 Corinthians (1964 [ET: 1968]). What may be obscured by such a procedure is the specificity of Mark. The problem of appropriate interpretative categories is all the more pressing since Carl R. Holladay (1977) has criticized the usefulness of θεῖος ἀνήρ for New Testament Christology. Even if Georgi's application of θεῖος ἀνήρ is judged successful in the case of 2 Corinthians, its relevance for Mark is not immediately evident.

But none of these objections must excuse us from facing up to the depth of the issue raised by Weeden. Whatever the precise narrative pattern of discipleship, did Weeden not correctly see the disciples and their ideological viewpoint discredited by the Markan Jesus? Has he not rightly sensed the total impact of the disciples' story? Yet Weeden's boldly original thesis had not persuasively come to terms with what he thought was an alternate Christian viewpoint. Such terms as *opponents, enemies,* or *heresy* are less than helpful in clarifying Mark's motivation for casting the disciples in the role of carriers of a competing viewpoint. If, in other words, the alternate tradition was carried by what Weeden calls "certain interlopers" (160), why would the evangelist see fit to tarnish the disciples—of all people!—with the burden of "heresy"? Could he not, for example, let the false prophets of Mark 13 (vv. 5–6, 21–22) play the role of adversaries? It is a tribute to Weeden's incisive mind that he has, despite deficient nomenclature, pursued the question toward what appears to be a logical conclusion. The "heresy" against which Mark wrote makes good sense if it appealed to a tradition that claimed to go back "to the disciples themselves" (Weeden 1971, 148). In other words, the "heresy" Mark challenged had invoked apostolic legitimacy.

Weeden not only broke with the evolutionary model of the genesis of Mark, but also introduced a revolutionary model in a provocative sense: Mark's Gospel arose in refutation of a perceived apostolic tradition. Therein lies the real challenge of his work, a challenge rarely understood, let alone taken up by his critics.

2. Easter's Alleged Key to Mark and the Neglect of Narrative

While the theme of discipleship has received much attention in recent Markan scholarship, its interpretation has remained a serious bone of contention. Three recent studies may serve to illustrate the scope of readings. Klemens Stock (1975) interpreted Markan discipleship in a traditional, apostolic sense. Ernest Best (1977; 1981) viewed it from a pastoral, pedagogical angle. And Günther Schmahl (1974) saw it as a function of Christology and messianic secret.

In Stock's view, the discipleship theme is designed to underscore close association with Jesus. "Being-with Jesus" (*Mit-Ihm-Sein*) is the most prominent feature of Markan discipleship. The evangelist consistently assigns to the disciples the role of appointed recipients of Jesus' message and at one particular point initiates them into the mystery of the kingdom of God. Yet being-with Jesus cannot spare them the pitfalls of apostasy. The theme of their betrayal runs almost parallel to the theme of their being-with Jesus (Stock 1975, 194). But Jesus' tireless efforts to teach the disciples and to challenge their incomprehension confirms the priority of being-with Jesus. This is so despite the fact that the disciples' flight contradicts their appointed call and brings about a complete break with Jesus. In Stock's view, Mark firmly implicates the disciples in the suspension of relations with Jesus (195). And yet, Jesus' announcement of their fall in 14:28 also contains the seed for a resumption of their being-with him. In the end, the women's Easter message extends an invitation of a reunion with Jesus, which will facilitate the disciples' apostolic mission.

Stock's book raises the question whether discipleship in Mark does in fact admit the preeminence of the motif of being-with Jesus, which subsumes and overrides the failure of the disciples. To some extent an answer will depend on a reading of the ending of Mark's Gospel. But even if one were to share Stock's preference for a happy resolution, it would have to be projected outside the given story. But is such a projection warranted in view of the absence of a narrated resolution? Given the admitted negativity of the disciples, is being-with Jesus the appropriate designation for the relation between Jesus and the disciples? Granted that the narrator characterizes the disciples both favorably and unfavorably, is there not a point in the story whence the negativity prevails, leading readers to alter their initial, positive impression?

For Ernest Best, Markan discipleship is not primarily polemical and not meant to attack some group within or outside the community. Least of all did the evangelist intend a critique of the historical disciples. Indeed, the weakness of the disciples must not be exaggerated. Their inability, for example, to come to terms with suffering and the cross compares favorably with the ruthless desire of scribes, rulers, and Pharisees to seek Jesus' death. "A failure to understand the death of Jesus is much less serious than an attempt to bring it about" (Best 1977, 394). By the same token, Jesus' rebuke of Peter is not "a personal attack on the apostle Peter but on Peter as a sample disciple who in the ultimate analysis represents Mark's community" (Best 1981, 24–25). Mark's principal motive for discipleship is thus pedagogical. "In so far as the disciples appear in a bad light it is because Mark wishes to use them as a foil" (Best 1977, 399). Their failure to understand puts Jesus in the role of enunciating the standards of Christian conduct. From him one learns what the disciples failed to learn. From him one learns also that the disciples were to be restored in the postresurrection period, which would be a source of great comfort for Mark's readers. Therefore, "if Mark wishes to show Jesus' power he must show the weakness of his disciples" (388). Rather than attacking the disciples, Mark uses the vehicle of discipleship to teach them a lesson of God's unfailing love in the face of human failure.

In a general sense, Best's pastoral, pedagogical explication recommends itself to serious consideration. In their incorrigible way of "thinking the things of men," the disciples function indeed as foils for Jesus' proclamation of the kingdom. But has Best's interpretation absorbed the full implications of Mark's story? In making all too quickly a theological virtue out of dysfunctional discipleship, he tends to blunt the narrative directives and trivialize their impact on readers (or hearers). What strikes him as "perfectly natural" (1977, 388) is hardly that at all. Mark's narrative progressively discourages its readers (or hearers) from accepting the leadership of the Twelve. Inasmuch as the Gospel's recipients find themselves disoriented from the disciples, they are also encouraged to reorient themselves, which cannot take full effect until after they have taken in the narrative down to its last word. This carefully plotted distancing of readers (or hearers) from the disciples makes it difficult to seize upon reorientation without absorbing the shock of disorientation. The history of early Christian traditions, moreover, makes it impossible not to be stunned by Markan discipleship, for the well-known Christian preference for apostolic linkage contrasts sharply with Mark's narrative incentive *not* to follow the example set by the disciples.

Günther Schmahl offers the most rigorous assessment of the disciples' negativity. With the possible exception of Peter's confession, he finds the disciples consistently lacking in perception. The explanation, he suggests, lies not in the author's intention to psychologize the disciples but rather in Christology. Functionally, failing discipleship resembles Jesus' injunctions to silence. Both themes operate so as to prevent Jesus from becoming fully known during his lifetime. This well-known Markan feature to keep Jesus "under cover" during his earthly career points toward Easter as the time of disclosure. According to this scenario, the disciples play the role of pre-Easter people, unfinished and shaky in faith. Mark's failing discipleship is, therefore, a function of a Christology grounded in Easter and the expected feature of a Gospel designed out of Easter faith.

Of the suggested explanations, Schmahl's thesis deserves our most serious reflection. His view, now widely entertained in scholarship, originated, of course, with William Wrede's (1971, 92–114, 231–36) insight into possible connections between discipleship and secrecy in Mark. For Wrede the disciples' conduct was "quite natural" (106) and entirely compatible with their high estimation in tradition; for while the bulk of the Christian tradition sanctions them in their apostolic, *postresurrectional* role, Mark chose to trace their preresurrectional career. Insofar as vision is bound to be dimmed in the *preresurrectional* status, it is with resurrection that the veil of obscurity is lifted and clarity of perception restored.

Wrede's position, resumed by Schmahl and others, is highly persuasive and appears close to the mark. But it also runs the risk of misreading Markan discipleship in the interest of a postresurrectional resolution. What comes to mind is Joseph Tyson's objection to correlating the motifs of the disciples' blindness and secrecy: "It is not as if the disciples discerned the nature of Jesus but are prohibited from broadcasting it, but it is that the disciples have a wrong conception about his nature" (1961, 261–62). Tyson has brought the issue into sharp focus: Are the disciples depicted as being excluded from understanding Jesus during his lifetime, only to be enlightened at resurrection, or are they depicted as having misunderstood the earthly Jesus so as to be excluded from meeting and representing the risen Lord?

An additional question concerns the Gospel's assumed christological genesis in an orientation toward Easter. Admittedly, the transfiguration projects fulfillment outside the story, gesturing perhaps toward the resurrection, or more plausibly toward the Parousia. But the ending of Mark's Gospel (16:8) seems less designed to assure and more to undercut the disciples' participation in the presence of the risen Lord. The disciples fail to come to terms both with his death (8:31–33; 9:31–32; 10:32–35) *and* resurrection (9:10). Consequently, they are absent during Jesus' suffering and forfeit his resurrection. Nor is it entirely certain that Easter carries full revelatory weight in Mark. The narrative is somewhat less than perfectly fitted to this conception. When the centurion, in full view of the cross, confesses that Jesus was (ἦν) Son of God (15:39), he appears to locate the cross at the summit of a messianic earthly life. The title "king," moreover, which typifies the Gospel's leading kingdom motif, does not appear until Mark 15, when it is placed over the events of the crucifixion. Those who put Jesus to death endorse the crucified Messiah out of ignorance. There is also Jesus' speaking "openly" (παρρησίᾳ) when first announcing his suffering and rising (8:31–32). This speaking in παρρησίᾳ has been identified as a hallmark of the risen Christ in gnostic Christianity. From this perspective also, Mark's use of παρρησίᾳ marks an "Easter shift," a term coined by James M. Robinson (1970, 116), which separates the risen Lord from the earthly Jesus moving toward death. The absence of a resurrection-appearance story further shifts the focus away from the resurrection toward crucifixion. The point Mark seems to be making is that Jesus' earthly life was perfected in the cross and not directly in resurrection. This does raise the question whether a Gospel that projects God's sonship upon Jesus' earthly life, making it culminate in the cross, while not reporting a resurrection appearance, has in fact grown out of Easter faith.

The question needs recasting in different terms. The absence of a resurrection appearance story gives Mark's Gospel a highly distinctive quality. One must ask whether this extraordinary feature is entirely consistent with Wrede's concealing-revealing schematization. If Mark conceals in order to reveal, why does his narrative not reveal the glory of the risen Lord? Why does he withhold from us what Matthew, Luke, and John have found impossible not to report? Why this reluctance to narrate Easter? Is he intent on keeping the risen Lord absent and silent? This line of questioning suggests that Mark's Gospel cannot immediately be assumed to have grown out of Easter faith, at least not until the issue of the unconventional absence of Easter is satisfactorily explained.

The very form of Gospel seems to militate against Mark's genesis in Easter faith. If Easter were the ground of Mark's writing, a most fitting model surely would have been the genre of the revelation dialogue (Perkins 1980), for it is difficult to find a more authentic product of Easter faith than the very genre that presents the risen Lord as revealer of sayings and donor of life. It is not inconsequential that Mark falls woefully short of this Easter genre par excellence. Indeed, the form of Mark's Gospel and the revelation dialogue appear to inhabit opposite conceptual worlds. This observation alone should caution us against uncritically endorsing the notion that Easter gave birth to the form of the orthodox Gospel.

Despite their differing readings of discipleship, the studies of Stock, Best, Schmahl, and countless others have a single hermeneutical aspect in common: *a disregard for narrative*. All fail to appreciate discipleship as an integral part of Mark's narrative. The causes for this disregard are deeply rooted in theology and hermeneutics and far from being fully explored. On the neglect of Gospel narrative, see above all the masterful study of Hans Frei (1974). Here we can only touch on two principal causes.

There is first the issue of story and history. New Testament hermeneutics has found it exceedingly difficult to appreciate the story about Jesus apart from reference to historical actuality. On the assumption that a Gospel is not merely related to but also arbitrated by Jesus' historicity, exegesis is often inclined to read the story with assistance derived from the logic of history. Despite growing insight into the linguistic web of narrative connections and strategies, this is a procedure still practiced in New Testament Gospel studies and subtly in evidence in the work of Best (1981, 20, 33–34, 164). That a Gospel lives by its own internal logic is a principle of special relevance for discipleship, which is one of the most circumspectly plotted features in Mark. It may not be amiss, therefore, to withhold credence from any theory on Markan discipleship that has not seriously attempted to decode the full narrative pattern.

A plea for storied integrity must not necessarily drive us to reduce a Gospel to an aesthetic object. This inclination to treat texts as hermetically sealed worlds owes much to what we are able to imagine as children of a venerable print culture. In the perspectives of ancient hermeneutics, however, chirographically produced texts are rarely ever fully closed. They were expected to participate in an ongoing discourse, rewording what preceded them, and subject also to reimaginings (Bruns 1982, 17–59). Each new version awakened hidden potentials and dormant competencies. This hermeneutical openness of ancient texts applies with special force to biblical material. "Scripture is something that is always turning into new versions of itself" (26). Obviously, to consider a Gospel's versional status is a far cry from relating it to the alleged historical matrix of its subject matter. Still, it is inadmissible, and hardly even possible, to grasp a Gospel's place in the ongoing hermeneutical discourse unless one has first come to terms with its rhetorical and imagistic inner landscape.

A second cause for the disregard of story relates to the hidden assumption that a Gospel functions as carrier of ideational content. Best, for example, commences his book on discipleship with Mark 8:27–10:45. Discipleship is here approached conceptually, with a view toward its pedagogical purpose, rather than consecutively, in search of progressive narration. Schmahl studies passages dealing with the "Twelve," which he divides according to appointment and mission, connection with Jesus' λόγοι and also their occurrence in the passion narrative. His is an operation that employs formal and analytical criteria irrespective of the flow of narrative. In addition, he analyzes passages that refer to disciples in a nonspecific sense, very briefly reflects on the disciples' misunderstanding, and finally turns to verses that focus on the chosen four or three. Mark's overall concept of the Twelve and of discipleship is then derived from a summary evaluation of those random passages. Stock likewise extrapolates so-called Twelve texts, dividing them into three groups: appointment texts, commissioning texts, and Jerusalem texts. Subsequently, he assesses their interrelationship apart from Mark's story before he determines their position in the story.

What typifies all these approaches is the conviction that a Gospel transports concepts and ideas that, in order to be grasped clearly, must be rescued from their narrative entanglement. Here the hermeneutic of story has been stood on its head; for story is not primarily, if at all, designed to serve as carrier of ideas—ideas, that is, that enjoy autonomy apart from the narrative ensemble. Narrativized syntax does not conceptualize, and themes have meaning only insofar as they are narrated. To analyze themes in isolation from narrative, therefore, amounts to a reduction of narrative to meaninglessness.

3. Toward a Narrative Discipleship

It is a hallmark of much recent North American work on Mark that it has avoided both historical and ideational fallacies. By way of example, Norman R. Petersen (1978; 1980) chose to treat the intrinsic poetics of this Gospel; Robert C. Tannehill (1977; 1979) studied the narrative patterns of Christology and discipleship; Thomas E. Boomershine (1974; 1981) shed light on the oral, rhetorical nature of the text, suggesting that meaning is consistently linked not with referentiality or ideation, but with rhetoric; John R. Donahue (1978 [1981]) explored Mark's parabolic dynamic; the present writer (1974; 1979; 1983) traced the narrative logic of kingdom and discipleship; and David Rhoads, together with Donald Michie (1982), composed an introduction to the narrative nature of Mark. In these instances, the Gospel's text is seen as resting not on any outside foundation but predominantly on the strength of its inner connections. If textual transparency is granted at all, it is not backward onto Jesus' history but forward to the implied reader, who is perceived to be the natural extension of the narrative.

When strictly viewed on Markan narrative terms, discipleship emerges in full view, carrying with it stark and virtually forbidding implications. The studies of Petersen and Tannehill, as well as Boomershine's recent reflections on Mark's ending, recommend themselves as entrées into the world of narrative discipleship.

Proceeding on the assumption that narrative is the art of creating time, Petersen singles out two principal plot devices: predictive, anticipatory statements that come to pass as plotted incidents later in the narrative; and predictive utterances that fail to come to pass in the narrative. Both devices "serve to create and reinforce narrative suspense" (1978, 56). The former causes short-term suspense, the latter long-term suspense. It is through these devices of prediction and fulfillment that Mark enacts discipleship. On the one hand, he introduces the disciples as privileged sharers of the mystery of the kingdom of God, while on the other hand from an early point on casting them into roles that run counter to the expectations raised about them. Since the reader is led to believe that all of Jesus' predictions will come to pass, the full weight of suspense is brought to bear on the questions of whether and when the disciples will finally live up to Jesus' expectations. This long-term suspense created by the disciples' stubborn ignorance "is resolved not in the narrative itself" but according to the predictions of Mark 9:9, 14:28, and 16:7 "in connection with a projected postresurrection meeting between Jesus and his disciples in Galilee" (Petersen 1978, 79).

Petersen's treatment of narrative time progressively closes in on the issue of discipleship, confirming its significance for the plotted story and for a time outside of story. What remains dubious is whether the scheme of prediction and fulfillment accords well with Mark's narration. It seems forcibly theological and curiously tame for a Gospel that is known less for a sense of proportionality and more for "a strong eschatological revolutionary component that rebels against order imposed from the past" (Beardslee 1970, 28). It is in any case difficult to appreciate Mark as an "irenic" theologian intent on reconciling conflicting early Christian traditions (Farmer 1982, 172–76). The most serious obstacle to Petersen's thesis is Mark's ending. Petersen has to concede that the women's failure to convey the message of life is "the one potential stumbling block" (1978, 77) to his projected postresurrectional resolution. His recent suggestion that "the narrator does not mean what he says in Mark 16:8" (1980, 162) proves embarrassing by any standard of criticism, for if Mark's ending does not fit Petersen's scheme, how true is his scheme to Mark?

For Tannehill, Markan discipleship is primarily a story of developing conflict and shifting relations between Jesus and the disciples. When initially the disciples are narrated in a positive light, the author encourages his readers to identify with them. But as their inadequacy begins to surface, and they increasingly "share the blindness of the outsiders" (Tannehill 1977, 399), the readers find themselves under pressure to choose between the disciples' way and that of Jesus. Still, Tannehill cannot bring himself to place the burden of the story's outcome entirely on the readers. He thinks, although more cautiously than Petersen, that the apocalyptic discourse in Mark 13 "anticipates a continuing role for the disciples beyond the disaster of chapter 14" (402). There is a sense in which the story of the disciples is not over, and a restored relationship appears to be at least a possibility.

Tannehill's perception of the disciples' shift from loyal followers to blind outsiders owes far more to Mark's narrative than Petersen's prediction and fulfillment scheme. What remains unclear is whether Mark 13 does indeed project a role for apostolic succession; for what the discourse *promises* is "false messiahs ["christs"] and false apostles" (13:22: ψευδόχριστοι καὶ ψευδοπροφῆται), strife and persecution, destruction and the coming of the Son of Man, and what it *demands* is preaching of the gospel, perseverance, and testimony under pressure. Far from promising the disciples a successful postresurrectional career, Mark 13 is designed to correct their false premises. The one disciple's exultation in view of the magnificent temple stones (13:1) promptly runs into Jesus' prediction of the temple's destruction, while the four disciples assumed correlation of the temple's demise with the eschaton (13:4) is subject to correction by Jesus. This corrective function of the discourse, coupled with the disciples' disastrous conduct in Jerusalem, does little to encourage readers to assume that the disciples have ceased to think in human terms. The function of Mark 13 is thus not different from the many previous teachings of Jesus, which on the story level run up against the disciples' lack of comprehension, but on the discourse level serve to supply Mark's readers (hearers) with vital information.

Boomershine's studies on Mark's ending examine the rhetorical impact of 16:8 on hearers. In his view, the recipients of the Gospel are left with signals that "pull in opposite directions" (1981, 233). While the norms associated with the women's flight and silence are strongly negative, the women's response of fear, astonishment, and trembling arouses feelings of compassion among hearers. This combination of negative performance and sympathetic characterization provokes listeners to steadily identify with the women and to reflect on their own response to the dilemma that the women confronted. Speaking to a situation of grave risks for Mark's generation, the ending encourages hearers to consider seriously the future of the Gospel's proclamation. In this way, Mark emphasizes "the same theme as the endings of the other gospels, namely, the apostolic commission to proclaim the gospel" (225).

One must ask whether Boomershine has not unduly softened the negativity of the ending. While it may be true that trembling and astonishment—the motive given for their flight—arouses a glimmer of sympathy for the women, fear—the motive for their silence—definitely does not. Earlier in the story (Mark 4:41; 9:6; 9:32; 10:33) the motif of fear contributed to the dysfunctional role of the disciples by underscoring their lack of perception. One cannot be certain, therefore, that the ending that attributes flight and fear to the women encourages progressive identification with them. Their witness of Jesus' death (15:40–41) and burial (15:47) is perceived to be positive, but already their desire to anoint the body (16:1) compares negatively with the anonymous woman's earlier anointment at Bethany (14:3–9). The women's flight, moreover (16:8: ἔφυγον), invites comparison with the disciples' earlier flight (14:50: ἔφυγον πάντες), and the motif of fear, the narrator's parting shot, serves to rank the women with the faithless disciples. Both women and disciples, therefore, receive a similar narrative treatment in Mark. In each case, initial identification with Jesus' followers is reversed by distanciation from them. If it is thus by alienation from the women, and earlier from the disciples, that Mark narrates discipleship, one cannot claim that "all four evangelists end with the theme of the apostolic commission" (Boomershine 1981, 238); for in its classic formulation, apostolic commission suggests discipleship in continuity with the Twelve, whereas Mark enforces discipleship that is discontinuous with the Twelve and also with the women.

What we witness in the studies of Petersen and Tannehill is a methodical exploration of the hermeneutic of story: the intelligibility of discipleship rests on narrative shape and development. Tannehill and Boomershine, moreover, refrain from viewing the story as a system entirely closed in on itself. They both regard discipleship as a narrative instrument that plays on and solicits readers' (or hearers') responses. It is this dual attention to narrative shape and readers' response that has informed the present writer's assessment of Markan discipleship.

4. THE PARABOLIC PATTERN OF DISCIPLESHIP

A flowering of recent publications by John Dominic Crossan (1971–72; 1973; 1975; 1976; 1978; 1979; 1980), Robert W. Funk (1966; 1975; 1982), and Paul Ricoeur (1975) has forced attention upon parable as a hermeneutical category in its own right. These scholars prepared the ground for Donahue's seminal insight into the parabolic dynamic of Mark's narrative (1978). But whereas Donahue shunned application of parabolic logic to the one theme most deeply marked by it—that is, discipleship—Tannehill in effect undertook a parabolic reading of discipleship, without, however, explicitly invoking the hermeneutic of parable. Aided by the works of Crossan, Funk, Ricoeur, Donahue, and Tannehill, I have come to recognize the parabolic pattern of Markan discipleship.

In his first public act following the proclamation of the kingdom, Jesus calls on four fishermen to follow him (Mark 1:16–20). This call is associated with a promise for the followers to become fishers of men. As the four leave their trade and families to join Jesus, a sympathetic bond is created between the faithful followers and the readers. Subsequently, the narrator promotes the readers' (hearers') identification with the disciples by strengthening the impression of an essential consensus between Jesus and the disciples. The appointment of the Twelve (3:13–19) serves to confirm our confidence, for now it is obvious that the Twelve, and among them the three, have been selected to leadership positions. To be sure, the introduction of Judas as the one "who was to betray him" (3:19) causes a crack in the structure of expectancy. But it cannot undermine faith in the reliability of the eleven; for inasmuch as Judas is singled out negatively, his case appears to be exceptional, which reinforces our positive view of the eleven.

Following his public narration of the parable of the Sower (4:1–9), Jesus withdraws from the crowds and positions the Twelve, together with a group of select ones, on the inside. As insiders they are privileged to participate in the mystery of the kingdom of God (4:10–11a). In addition to making the Twelve insiders, Jesus informs them in carefully measured terms of the characterizations of outsiders (4:11b–12). No sooner is the insider-outsider dichotomy affirmed, fully persuading us of the disciples' inside position, than Jesus questions their comprehension of the parable of the Sower, and of parables in general (4:13). The sense of reproachfulness on the part of Jesus does not seem to accord well with their position as insiders. Yet it is precisely at the point when the structure of expectancy is at its peak that the disciples' drift toward the outside is subtly set into motion.

Subsequently, Jesus, in a series of boat trips (4:35; 5:21; 6:32; 6:45; 8:10; 8:13), opens the frontier toward the Gentiles, without abandoning Jewish land, and all the way expecting the disciples to learn the paradigm of his travels. At one point he sends them out on a journey of their own (6:7–13, 30), thus living up to his earlier promise to make them fishers of men (1:17) by initiating them into apostolic successorship. And yet the logic and the purpose of Jesus' trips eludes the disciples' comprehension. Following the second trip to the Gentiles (6:45), they are in a narrative aside charged with hardness of heart (6:52), an accusation directed earlier toward hostile people in the synagogue (3:5) and later toward a group of Pharisees (10:5). If at this stage our confidence in the disciples is shaken, it will be thoroughly undermined when after the second feeding Jesus himself applies the whole catalog of outsider characteristics to the disciples: hardness of heart, lack of understanding, seeing and not seeing, and hence blindness, hearing and not hearing, and hence deafness (8:17–18). At this point the structure of expectancy is overturned.

On the way to Jerusalem, Peter's Christ confession (8:29) teases readers into taking it at face value. But as the unfolding story reveals Peter's opposition to Jesus' own confession—his first passion/resurrection prediction (8:31)—exposes Peter's "confession" as being less than adequate. Not only does Peter appear to reject a suffering Messiah, but a false sense of presence also makes him, together with James and John, misjudge the proleptic nature of the transfiguration (9:2–8). The triumvirate, moreover, exhibits unusual obtuseness in regard to the resurrection (9:9–10). Unable to perform an exorcism, the disciples default on an obligation they had earlier been able to discharge successfully (9:14–29; cf. 6:7, 13). Jesus' second passion prediction is greeted with incomprehension and fear by the disciples (9:31–32). Contrary to Jesus' wishes, the disciples obstruct the work of an accomplished exorcist (9:38–41) and rebuke children (10:13–16). Shocked over Jesus' harsh treatment of the rich young man, the disciples under the leadership of Peter point to the sacrifices they have made in following Jesus (10:28). In response, Jesus promises a new community and life (10:29–30). But this reward has a "critical edge" (Tannehill 1977, 401) to it because it is promised "with persecutions." Moreover, Jesus' last word following the qualified promise is a warning aimed at Peter and the disciples: "But many that are first will be last, and the last first" (10:31). If, as a result of the ironically qualified promise and the warning, the readers feel ambiguous about the disciples, a negative judgment soon prevails as one approaches the third passion prediction (10:32–34). Directed specifically at the Twelve, it is met with James and John's request for positions of power (10:35–40). The author, it seems, has spared little effort to sharpen the conflict between Jesus and the disciples and to thereby consolidate the outsider position of the latter.

Above, we have reflected on the function of Mark 13 in relation to discipleship. Designed to correct false premises held by the disciples, the discourse predicts disaster as well as the coming of the Son of Man, while it requests rather than promises a continuing role for the disciples. But before making a premature judgment on the disciples' postresurrectional status, it is well to remember that one "cannot judge the meaning of a story without attention to its outcome" (Tannehill 1977, 392 n. 21). There is little evidence that the disciples heed this discourse more faithfully than Jesus' previous teachings. When, for example, Jesus tells the disciples that they must bear testimony under the pressure of persecutions (13:9–13) and take heed and watch (13:33–37), he is in short-range terms anticipating a situation that the disciples will experience during his own passion. At Gethsemane the three intimates fail to wake, and fall asleep in view of Jesus' impending death (14:32–42). The immediate effect of Jesus' discourse (13:33–37) on the disciples is therefore not encouraging. Far from strengthening their future leadership positions, it corroborates their role as outsiders.

If readers (hearers) have retained a residue of confidence in the disciples, it is decisively crushed during the events surrounding the passion. Judas takes the initiative to deliver Jesus into the hands of his opponents (14:10–11). In his last words addressed to the Twelve, Jesus announces his death, the flight of the disciples, and also his return to Galilee, without, however, promising an actual Galilean reunion with the disciples (14:26–28). He will go before the disciples to Galilee, but in the context of the antecedent narrative dynamics it is entirely reasonable to ask: but will they follow him? Peter protests Jesus' announcement of the disciples' flight, which leads Jesus to refute Peter's claim and to predict his (Peter's) imminent denial. In turn, Peter refutes Jesus. Far from denying Jesus, Peter claims, he would suffer and even die with him; "and they all said the same" (14:29–31). The triumvirate falters at Gethsemane (14:32–42), Judas delivers Jesus into the hands of his executioners (14:43–46), and all desert him at the moment of arrest (14:50). Peter, the last hope, denies Jesus while the latter makes his fateful confession before the high priest (14:53–72).

After the disciples' disappearance, the women serve as vital intermediaries. One last time, hopes are aroused that the broken connection might be repaired, the message of life delivered, and the disciples reunited with the risen Lord. But inasmuch as the appearance of the women rekindles hope, their performance makes sure that that hope is dashed. While the women are indeed commissioned to carry the message of life to the disciples, they fail to carry out this vitally important task. By Mark's relentless narrative logic, therefore, the Twelve are prevented from receiving the message that is designed to get them in touch with the risen Lord. With the demise of the Twelve the structure of expectancy is firmly and irrevocably reversed, and the narrative has found its proper parabolic ending.

Frank Kermode, a literary critic and virtual outsider to New Testament Gospel studies, has confronted the issue of Markan discipleship head-on and in full light of parabolic dynamics: "They [the disciples] are behaving exactly like the outsiders in the theory of parables" (1979, 46). Indeed, the precise narrative pattern of Markan discipleship is one of parabolic role reversal: the disciples' initial role of insiders is reversed to one of outsiders.

There remains the tempting assumption of a postresurrectional reunion between Jesus and the disciples. It owes as much to a historicizing harmonization of different Gospel stories as to our natural inclination "to prefer fulfillment to disappointment, the closed to the open" (Kermode 1979, 64). But Mark's parabolic pattern intends to preclude, not promote, a postresurrectional reunion for the disciples. To postulate a closure in defiance of narrative openness is to trivialize the parabolic ending, which is designed to place the burden of disappointment and open-endedness on the readers (or hearers) of the Gospel.

5. The Narrative Withholding of Easter

Earlier we had reflected on Easter as the alleged key to the form of the Gospel and had refuted the thesis that the narrative was born out of Easter faith, moving inexorably toward the revelation of the risen Lord. Here we must come to terms with the narrative withholding of Easter. We must learn to see the ending of the discipleship narration in connection with the form of Gospel. When Jürgen Moltmann writes that "the gospels intentionally direct the gaze of Christians away from the experiences of the risen Christ and the Holy Spirit back to the earthly Jesus and his way to the cross" (1974, 54), he has described the Markan form of Gospel; for what typifies this Gospel is its exclusive cast in a preresurrectional framework. All sayings and narrative materials are singularly bound to the earthly Jesus, converging in a story in whose narrative design discipleship has a crucial stake; for insofar as discipleship culminates in the women's inability to communicate the message of life, the Gospel's ending allows but one conclusion: the inaccessibility of the risen Lord to the disciples. It is, however, precisely this nonreporting of the Lord's appearance to the disciples that sanctions the preresurrectional form of Mark. One may thus plausibly contend that the reversal of the disciples from insiders to outsiders, the women's complicity in depriving the disciples of the risen Lord, thus finalizing their outsider role, and the narrative emplotment of the preresurrectional Jesus are all complementary features in the making of the Markan form of Gospel.

If we can agree, therefore, that Mark's ending at 16:8 is by design rather than accidental, and if we can further agree that the absence of a resurrection appearance is a deliberate withholding that accords with and indeed contributes to the form of Gospel, we must concur with Moltmann that Mark's Gospel is composed to redirect Christology away from the risen Lord toward the earthly Jesus. In that case, however, those who subscribe to Markan priority will be compelled to conclude that the orthodox gospel arose not out of Easter faith itself but out of concern to deflect attention away from it.

6. The Form of Gospel versus Apostolic Tradition

Understanding the interior landscape of the text—the parabolic pattern of discipleship and its implication in the form of gospel—has brought us close to the source of Markan motivation. We saw that discipleship and its parabolic outcome were deeply connected with the narrative withholding of Easter. And yet, why Mark chose this and not any other model of discipleship, and why he deflected attention away from Easter, still leaves the question unanswered. At this point we must attend to Mark's rootedness in the depth of tradition and consider its possible function to correct what preceded it; for the answer to Markan discipleship will in the last analysis come from the history of the tradition.

My recent publication, *The Oral and the Written Gospel* (1983, 199–211), attempted a tradition-historical explanation of the Gospel as counterform to an oral tradition fraught with gnosticizing proclivities. What is striking about Mark's Gospel is a remarkably reserved attitude toward sayings, a repossession of the earthly life of Jesus that culminates in death rather than in resurrection, a withholding of the risen Lord from the disciples, and the banishment of the disciples, the initial insiders, toward the outside. Together these features appear to subvert a genre partial to sayings, the primary unit of oral speech, and partial also to the risen Lord, who continues speaking through apostolic, prophetic personalities. Keeping in mind James Robinson's observation that "gnosticism's *Gattung* begins just as regularly after the resurrection as the orthodox *Gattung* ends there" (1970, 114; 1982c, 27), the corrective function of the form of Gospel now leaps to the eye. For by withholding the resurrection, Mark undermines a crucial starting point for a genre in the tradition that is deeply indebted to the oral medium. By narrating the earthly Jesus and his death, he has countered *a Gattung* rooted in the risen Lord; and by relegating the disciples to the outside he has completed what amounts to an antigenre to the genre of a sayings Gospel.

One feels bound to revisit Weeden, who understood the tradition-historical implications of Mark's Gospel with an intuition unlike anyone I know. As noted above, he sensed in Mark's alienation of readers from the course set by the Twelve a narrative resolve to refute those who had invoked "an unimpeachable authority for their position: their kerygma was passed on to them by the disciples themselves" (1972, 162). Put simply, Mark was up against a tradition that perceived itself to be apostolic.

It is tempting to search for traces of the kind of tradition against which Mark appears to have directed his Gospel. Where in Mark itself do we encounter an oral genre that could invoke apostolicity? Among the sundry oral traditions Mark's text has absorbed, the spotlight inevitably falls on 4:1–33, the first of only two major sayings collections in Mark. The pre-Markan existence of the core of this collection is widely though not universally acknowledged (Marxsen 1955; Meagher 1979, 85–142). Here we witness Jesus as speaker of parables and sayings and the Twelve as privileged recipients. If we extricate Jesus from Mark's historicizing framework, and replace him with the risen Christ, we have in fact arrived at the genre of the revelation dialogue, or, in Robinson's terms, at the "immediate precursor to the Gospel of Thomas," where much of this material recurs (1982a, 47).

In the revelation dialogue that lies embedded in 4:1–33, we have come closest to the tradition from which Mark took major cues and in refutation of which he composed the form of Gospel. It is a tradition that sanctions the Twelve as apostolic recipients and guarantors of Jesus' λόγοι. The Jesus, moreover, who operates outside of Mark's preresurrectional framework is in all likelihood the living or resurrected Christ. Empowered by his risen status, he communicates mystery in sayings and parables. Such could well have been the tradition from which Mark learned specifically the insider role of the Twelve, as well as the riddling function of parabolic speech that may have a way of casting hearers to the outside. The gnosticizing proclivity of this revelation dialogue is immediately evident, for as carrier of secret words disclosed to the Twelve at the exclusion of outsiders, Jesus approximates the role of a gnostic redeemer, the bringer of secrecy to a chosen few. Apostolic tradition is here synonymous with esoteric knowledge.[2]

By anchoring the sayings tradition in a genre that sanctions the earthly Jesus, and by applying the outsider characteristics to the Twelve, the original insiders, Mark has defeated the authentic hermeneutical function of the sayings genre. Now the mystery of the kingdom of God no longer resides exclusively in the λόγοι of the risen Lord. For the genre of the orthodox Gospel has transformed Jesus' whole life and, above all, his death into the mystery that is accessible not to the few but to all who read (or hear) it.

---

2. For connections between gnosticism and orality, see Perkins 1980, 7–9, 32–35, 196–204.

2

INTERPRETATION OF NARRATIVE AND NARRATIVE AS INTERPRETATION: HERMENEUTICAL REFLECTIONS ON THE GOSPELS

This essay reflects on the genre of the canonical narrative Gospel from the perspective of Gospel genres, tradition, and interpretation. The first part focuses on the narrative syntax of the Gospels. While the impulse to narrate appears "natural," it is asserted that the narrative nature of the Gospels requires fresh attention. Both the long-standing neglect of narrative realism in biblical scholarship and the relatively recent appreciation of the Gospels' literary plot constructions are being considered. A second part examines the aphoristic clustering, which moves toward a nonnarrative genre of the sayings and discourse Gospels. Mark's narrative in particular is viewed as being in tension with such an aphoristic Gospel genre. The hypothesis of the Markan narrative as reinterpretation of an antecedent Gospel genre raises the issue of revisionism, a matter of signal importance in biblical hermeneutics. When in the third part the Gospel tradition is examined from the perspective of media dynamics, three orders of operation are discernible: sayings and parables as spoken communication, the genre of aphoristic and dialogue Gospel, and the narrative Gospel. The place of the so-called Secret Gospel of Mark in this model of tradition is discussed. To do justice to the narrative Gospel, both its narratological dynamics and its involvement in tradition need to be acknowledged. The Gospel functions both as "mirror" and as "window." The fourth part seeks to draw connections between the first-century Gospel narrators and the twentieth-century interpreters of Gospel narratives. Inasmuch as the Gospel constitutes interpretation itself, readers and hearers who interpret the Gospels continue hermeneutical practices pursued by the evangelists and set into motion by others before them. The encompassing condition that unites hearers, readers, and exegetes with the Gospel tradition is interpretation.

Alles Verstehen ist Auslegung.

—Hans-Georg Gadamer, *Wahrheit und Methode*

That is why in so many textual distortions we may count on finding the suppressed and abnegated material hidden away somewhere, though in an altered shape and torn out of its original connection. Only it is not always easy to recognize it.

—Sigmund Freud, *Moses and Monotheism*

... essentially, what Mark had to do was to interpret.

—Walter Ong, *Text as Interpretation: Mark and After*

There is a genuine continuity between the operations performed on their material by the evangelists, and the work of the exegetes who, for almost two millennia, have continued their labors.

—Frank Kermode, *The Genesis of Secrecy*

7. The Narrative Impulse

The art of telling stories has faithfully accompanied the human race from preliterate to postmodern times. So "natural" appears to be the impulse to narrate that one is hard put to imagine a language or culture devoid of narrative elements. The need to make scraps of life cohere in the imagination and to plot events so as to give them a semblance of coherence and sequentiality may thus reasonably be counted among the human universals. Roland Barthes was of the opinion that narrative "is simply there like life itself ... international, transhistorical, transcultural" (1977, 77). Hayden White, to whom we owe some of the most profound studies on the subject (1973; 1978), viewed narrative as "a panglobal fact of culture" (1980, 5). One may well claim, therefore, that "narrative and narration are less problems than simply data" (1980, 5). It is, however, precisely that which we take most for granted and without which we seem least able to exist that tends to elude our full attention. The very ubiquity of narrative subtly distracts us from according critical recognition to our narrative impulses and performances. We need reminding that narrative, while present like life itself, is not itself life. "No one and nothing *lives* as story" (White 1978, 111). For life, after all, does not narrate, and narrative is always artificial. Perhaps the impulse to narrate is not quite as "natural" as it seems.

In the context of ancient literary history, the canonical Gospels can hardly claim uniqueness as far as narrativity is concerned. The golden age of Hebrew narrative extended roughly from the tenth to the seventh century B.C.E. Prose narratives, especially in the form of biographies, were a standard feature of Hellenistic culture. In part at least they owed their existence to the desire to keep alive the memory of extraordinary deeds and powers that were associated with famous poets, philosophers, and rulers. It is entirely reasonable, therefore, to examine the Gospels by analogy with Greco-Roman forms of narrative (Votaw 1970; Talbert 1977; Robbins 1984). But it remains questionable whether the Gospels are fully assimilable to, and explicable by, Hellenistic narrative models, if only because the narration of a crucified Son of God was a moral, aesthetic, and literary monstrosity, contradicting Jewish, Hellenistic, Roman, and barbarian sensibilities (Hengel 1977). Appeal to Hellenistic biographies will not entirely explain the impulse to narrate the Gospel stories. One may also remember that narrative was far from being a uniform mode of expression in the early Christian tradition. Substantial parts of the canon suggest that a faithful commitment to the Christ did not perforce require a narrative genre. Moreover, a segment of noncanonical Christianity, as will be shown, appears to have been less than friendly toward narrativity. It would follow, on this view, that the nonnarrative and the antinarrative tradition in early Christianity itself does not allow us to take the narrative Gospel for granted.

Literary critics have been far from generous in acknowledging the Gospels' contribution to Western culture. The monumental three-volume set compiled by Hector Munro and Nora Kershaw Chadwick of nearly 2,400 pages in *The Growth of Literature* (1932–40), for example, makes only incidental reference to the Gospel stories. In what has justly been called a classic, Robert Scholes and Robert Kellogg's *The Nature of Narrative* (1968), the history of narrative is traced from its oral beginnings to the heights of the nineteenth- and twentieth-century realistic novel without according the Gospels a place in it. Nor are the Gospels mentioned in a recent study of the postclassical, Hellenistic birth of the novel, Thomas Hägg's *The Novel in Antiquity* (1983), which examines inter alia Philostratus's *Life of Apollonius*, the *Alexander Romances*, the apocryphal *Acts of the Apostles*, the *Pseudo-Clementines*, and various hagiographical materials. The critics' reticence to assess the Gospels' significance in literary history is all the more puzzling in that these ancient Christian stories continue to occupy a commanding position in Western culture. With the exception of the ancient Hebrew narratives, the Gospels are to this day read and recited more than any other single story composed in antiquity.

Does overfamiliarity prevent us from regarding them with fresh attention? Or does their character as sacred texts forbid an assessment in the
general context of literature? Or do the Gospels seem unpleasantly doc-
trinaire, tyrannical even? Perhaps some literary critics have considered
the Gospels the exclusive domain of biblical scholars. Whatever the reasons for the neglect, the modern breakthrough toward a literary appreciation of the Gospels is often said to have come with Erich Auerbach's
(1953, 24, 49) sensitive reading of Peter's denial in Mark. In the wake
of Auerbach, literary critics of the stature of Robert Alter (1981), Frank
Kermode (1979), and Herbert N. Schneidau (1976; 1978; 1982; 1985)
have recently turned to aspects of biblical narrative to show how these
perplexing and often disturbing texts have informed Western literature
and our sense of reality.

If until recently literary critics have left the Gospels to the biblical
specialists, they were by and large left in the lurch. For although biblical scholarship has for over two centuries subjected the Gospels to exquisite scrutiny, it has by and large failed to grasp what matters most about
them: their narrative nature. A number of approaches proved influential
in setting hermeneutical standards that discouraged coming to grips with
the narrative logic of the Gospels. One was Papias's report concerning
Mark's transcription of Petrine teachings, which was widely understood
to mean that the narrative Gospel resulted from unassimilated, uninterpreted information. Peter's historical reminiscences were assumed to be
a significant motive for the composition of the Gospels. When it was recognized—rudimentarily first by Papias and also in Luke's prologue—that
the Gospels originated out of tradition, questions concerning the relation
between Gospel and tradition tended to find an answer in the eyewitness
theory. The death of the first generation of eyewitness was assumed to have
prompted the writing of the Gospel narratives. Accordingly, a principal
function of the Gospels was to preserve the continuity of and with historical tradition. This theory lies at the root of the doctrinal, popular, and, to
some extent still academic, paradigm of a single trajectory leading from
Jesus into the historical Gospel.

Another thesis discouraging a narrative reading was biblical interpreters' inclination to distill from the Gospels an ideational or historical
core. Hans Frei (1974) has brilliantly documented the eighteenth- and
nineteenth-century's inability to come to terms with the narrative nature
of biblical hermeneutics. His examination can and should be extended
into the twentieth century because it was by and large the triumph of

historical consciousness that steadily reinforced the nonnarrative interpretation of the Gospels. Only in recent decades have biblical critics,
mostly North Americans, begun to appreciate the literary and rhetorical
dimensions of the Gospels. We have, however, at this point only taken
tentative steps toward understanding the narrative impulse in the early
Christian tradition, the nature of the narrative Gospels, and our ways of
interpreting them.

This impulse to narrate in the Christian tradition is all too often still
taken as a matter of course. The Gospels' life-to-death pattern, one of the
most common of all plot constructions, appears quintessentially like life
itself in moving toward death. What more natural beginning than birth,
and what more realistic ending than death. But no matter how natural
or realistic the narrative, artifice in Gospel composition is unmistakably
present, raising the issue not merely of represented world but also of how
it is represented.

Form criticism, for all its methodological inadequacies, succeeded in
alerting us to the significance of the tradition. If nothing else, the discipline sensitized us to the existence of a pre-Gospel history of the tradition. Yet form criticism still operated under the presupposition of relatively uncomplicated Gospel beginnings (Kelber 1983, 1–43). Bultmann
assumed that the Gospels narrated "nothing in principle new" that had
not already been said by oral tradition (1963, 321 [1970, 347]). Gerhardsson, who challenged form criticism, in effect bracketed the question of
tradition by suggesting that the core of the narrative Gospel had existed
from the very outset (1961, 208–61, 262–323). In a far more subtly executed argument, Paul Ricoeur has recently contended that the needs for
narrativization, though not the narrative Gospel itself, were inherent in
the early Christian tradition from its inception (1975). On many of these
views, the narrative impulse appears self-evident due to the facts or forces
of tradition.

8. Narrative Gospel as Corrective to the Sayings Gospel

In seeking to account for the narrative Gospel by appeal to tradition,
one tends to disregard the diversity of traditions and the divergence of
transmissional processes. Ricoeur is right in pointing to parable for the
purpose of stressing the "requirement of narration internal to the proclamation itself" (1975, 511). Indeed, the parable joins proclamation to a
story that, it has been suggested, became instrumental in the formation

of the narrative Gospel (Crossan 1975, 10, 124; 1984, 15; Donahue 1988; Kelber 1983, 117–31). Yet parable is only one element in the tradition, and commitment to narrative is only one trait of the tradition. The aphorisms of Jesus, for example, constitute nonnarrative elements, and the processes governing their transmission cannot be shown to generate the narrative Gospel. In his recent book *In Fragments* (1983), John Dominic Crossan has traced the conduct of Synoptic aphorisms as they coalesce into compounds and clusters, become attached to stories, and develop into dialogues and series of dialogues. As Crossan rightly saw, the aphoristic tendency toward clustering, dialogue, and discourse, while well recognizable in the orthodox tradition, became a decisive generic influence in what he calls the gnosticizing tradition (1983, 237, 268). What comes to mind are such documents as the *Gospel of Thomas*, the *Dialogue of the Savior*, the *Apocryphon of James*, and many others, and also Q, the sayings source, whose genre was, however, dispersed and displaced by Matthew and Luke. Is it permissible to discern in the aphoristic clustering a movement toward an alternate, a nonnarrative gospel (Kelber 1985a)?

Few noncanonical documents have as great a potential for encouraging a revision of our view of tradition as the *Gospel of Thomas*. This is all the more true if, as some have suggested, the bulk of *Thomas* is not only independent of the canonical Gospels but also antecedent to them (Koester 1983; Davies 1983, 3, passim). The *Thomas* text consists of single aphorisms, aphoristic and dialectical dialogues, and of parables, all spoken by the living Jesus. Strictly speaking, it is not a consistently composed dialogue or discourse genre, and it "lacks" a unifying narrative frame. Whether the term λόγοι in the incipit (POxy 654) was the authentic designation of *Thomas*'s genre (Robinson 1971b, 74–85), with "Gospel" being secondarily appended as subscription so as to make *Thomas* competitive with the canonical Gospels, or whether "Gospel" was the authentic term for nonnarrative *Thomas* (Vielhauer 1975, 258, 622), has yet to be decided. The fact remains that *Thomas* was perceived quite early as a distinct genre, a sayings collection, and already in its Greek version understood to be a Gospel, a *sayings Gospel* (Robinson 1971b, 76). What we observe in this case is the principle of aphoristic clustering being carried to the point of generic consummation. When viewed from the standpoint of the "*Gospel*" *of Thomas*, therefore, the aphoristic behavior to cluster among its own kind appears in a fresh light. Now one may discern in it the potential for the production of a Gospel sui generis. It is clear from this example that the needs for narrativization do not fully account for all the elements and proclivities of the tradition. The aphoristic proclamation may well have a momentum of its own toward a nonnarrative genre, the sayings Gospel.

The Nag Hammadi documents have brought into sharper focus the nature of the aphoristic processes vis-à-vis the narrative performance in emergent orthodoxy. When viewed from the canonical standpoint, it strikes one as remarkable how ill at ease all these documents are with narrative syntax. In fact, none of the fifty-two Nag Hammadi texts comes even close to the genre of the orthodox Gospel genre. Whereas the canonical Gospels commence with birth or baptism, and end with resurrection, announced or fully narrated, or with ascension, the predominant generic proclivity at Nag Hammadi is toward the sayings discourse, which stakes its authority on the teachings of the living or risen Jesus (Perkins 1980). This quite extraordinary phenomenon deserves close scrutiny not only from those interested in linguistic aspects, but from those as well who explore the social world of early Christianity. What kind of communities (or perhaps worship situations) are we to imagine that showed such conspicuous partiality toward the aphoristic genre?

Based on these observations, I have recently suggested (Kelber 1985a) that the time has come to draw a conclusion of some import for our understanding of the early Christian tradition. Henceforth, we must reckon with two Gospel genres in early Christianity, the sayings or cluster Gospel and the narrative Gospel. The sayings or cluster gospel elevated the λόγοι proclamation to generic significance, promoting a Jesus who taught and redeemed through words of wisdom. The narrative Gospel shaped a heterogeneous repertoire into biographical synthesis, favoring a Jesus who redeemed through the conduct of his life and death, followed by resurrection. Crossan (1983), on his part, proposed the existence of three Gospel genres: the cluster Gospel, the dialogue Gospel, and the narrative Gospel. As aphoristic clustering furnished the condition for the sayings or cluster Gospel, so did the aphoristic arrangement by way of comment-response or question-answer format prepare for the dialogue Gospel (*Dialogue of the Savior, Sophia of Jesus Christ*, etc.). Recognition of a duality, and perhaps even a plurality, of Gospel genres more than ever compels us to contemplate the narrative Gospel with renewed attention.

Perhaps agreement can be reached on the following four points. First, we may discern at least two, and possibly three, Gospel genres, provided it is understood that both the cluster and the dialogue Gospel arise out of aphoristic processes, and that they are for this reason closely related, whereas the narrative Gospel seems generically unrelated to the aphoristic

tradition. Second, the narrative Gospel, the one genre accepted by orthodox Christianity for canonical inclusion, appears to be the formal heir not
to the aphoristic processes, but to parable. Both in its narrative form and in
its disorienting, metaphorical proclivity, canonical Mark operates according to the hermeneutics of Jesus' parables. Third, it is tempting to speculate
that each of the two basic speech forms attributable to the historical Jesus,
the aphorism and the parable, was consummated in a Gospel of its own:
the aphorism in the sayings (and dialogue) Gospel, and the parable in the
narrative Gospel. Fourth, while the sayings (and dialogue) Gospel and the
narrative Gospel may each invoke continuity with Jesus, they grew out of
different compositional needs and transmissional processes. Such are the
differences in form, choice of materials, and Christology that it is difficult,
if not impossible, to assume direct, evolutionary connections between the
aphoristic genre and the narrative genre. They will have developed separately, and they could possibly have existed in tension with one another.

If narrativity cannot be taken for granted in the early Christian tradition, neither can the strident tone in which the narrative Gospels asserted
themselves in the canon. This point was reiterated by Elaine Pagels, who
after years of work on the Nag Hammadi texts continues to be astounded
by the polemics exhibited by the canonical Gospels: "The gospels which
came to be accepted as orthodox generally interpret Jesus traditions in
confrontational terms" (1980, 62). Her statement suggests that the Gospels' polemics are occasioned by the manner in which these narratives
relate to tradition. Preservation of traditions is not the sole purpose of
the narrative Gospels. I have recently sought to enlarge our understanding
of the connections between Mark's deeply polemical narrative dynamics
and antecedent traditions. I proposed that the canonical Gospel form had
arisen out of a conflict with the genre of the sayings Gospel (Kelber 1983,
90–139, 184–220). Mark's reserved attitude toward sayings (as compared
to Matthew, Luke, and John), the displacement of vital oral authorities (the
disciples), the banishment of the Twelve to the outside, the narrative explication exclusively of Jesus' earthly life, the narrative focus on his death, and
a withholding of the living Lord are all features antithetical to the genre
built on sayings spoken by the living or risen Jesus. In the sayings Gospel
the living Jesus alone utters the words of life, whereas in Mark death puts
an end to his speech. In terms of narrative form and focus of Christology, of principal features of dramatization, and of the rhetorical impact on
hearers/readers, the corrective function of the polemical narrative would
seem to have plausibility. Methodologically, I wished to demonstrate that

the Gospel can (and should) be read both as a coherent narrative and in relation to tradition, whereby the latter is understood not only as a process of continuity, but in terms of discontinuity as well.

James Robinson, although pursuing a somewhat different intellectual path, has arrived at remarkably similar conclusions (1970, 99–129 [1982c, 11–39]; 1982a, 40–53; 1982b, 5–37). In his view, Mark's narrative genre must be understood in the context of "the bifurcating orthodox and gnostic positions" (1970, 114 [1982c, 27]). In what he calls the "gnosticizing trajectory," the risen Christ, freed from bodily encumbrance and authorized by heavenly experiences, initiates "the time of a new hermeneutic as the time of the Spirit" (1982b, 26). Empowered by the Spirit, he speaks with authority, setting the norms of interpretation and initiating a period of higher revelation. In placing ultimacy upon the risen Christ, one tends to relegate to insignificance his earthly life "as just a lower and hence irrelevant prelude" (1970, 113 [1982c, 26]). Easter has thereby become the time differential (1982a, 48), that is, the hermeneutical turning point separating a period or hermeneutic of concealment from the time or hermeneutic of revelation. Or, as gnosticizing texts tended to put it, prior to Easter Jesus spoke in riddling parables, but at Easter the risen Christ spoke "openly [παρρησίᾳ]." "Speaking in parables" and "speaking openly" thereby became "the technical contrasting terms for designating the literal and spiritual levels of meaning ... used to distinguish the sayings of Jesus before and after Easter" (1982b, 30). Parabolic speech, moreover, can itself be typical of Christ's post-Easter instruction imparted to a group of understanding disciples (1982a, 49). Insofar as the Christ of higher, esoteric revelation became the focal point for sayings and parables revealed to a select group of initiates, the gnosticizing trajectory was on its way toward the genre of the sayings and discourse Gospel.

From the perspective of these gnosticizing proclivities Robinson finds sufficient clues in Mark to assume shifts from a post-Easter to a pre-Easter level of interpretation that are deeply connected with the genesis of the orthodox Gospel. In Mark the period of higher revelation begins when Jesus announces his first passion-resurrection prediction by speaking "openly" (παρρησίᾳ; Mark 8:32). In this case the gnosticizing "Easter shift" (1970, 111 [1982c, 29]) has been retrojected into the pre-Easter period. Consequently, the higher revelation is refocused from the parables and sayings spoken by the living Jesus to the earthly Jesus and the proclamation of his death and also resurrection. It is this orthodox emphasis on death followed by resurrection that accounts for Mark's focused narrative engagement in the passion. One might add that it also clarifies the absence and silence of the risen Christ. If death is the point of higher revelation, then the earthly Jesus has already said and accomplished all that matters. Another feature involved in shifting perspectives is the transfiguration, long suspected of being a transposed resurrection story (Bultmann 1963, 259 [1970, 278]). Robinson, endorsing the thesis, draws attention to the analogous gnosticizing type of apparition story (1970, 116–18 [1982c, 29–31]). Many gnostic Gospels are cast in the form of a luminous epiphany of the risen Lord on a mountain. Based on this analogy, the transfiguration in Mark has all the appearances of an apparition story relocated in close proximity to that Gospel's new hermeneutical turning point, the first passion-resurrection prediction.

Jesus' esoteric instruction in parables (Mark 4:1-34) likewise shows traces of a pre-Markan functioning (Robinson 1982a: 43–47). It resembles precisely the kind of higher revelation that in the gnosticizing genre is reserved for the post-Easter disciples. In Mark, however, the esoteric instruction is purposefully undermined "in that the disciples, in spite of the interpretation, remain as much in the dark as do the outsiders" (Robinson 1970, 112 [1982c, 25]). These and other observations suggest to Robinson that in Mark "Easter material is embedded back into the public ministry" (1982a, 52) with the intent to refocus or correct the gnosticizing trajectory by placing the highest revelatory premium on the earthly Jesus and his death. According to Robinson's well-known formula, "gnosticism's Gospel Gattung begins just as regularly after the resurrection as the orthodox Gattung ends there" (1970, 114 [1982c, 27]). When thus examined in the light of bifurcating traditions, the narrative Gospel presents itself as an attempt on the part of emergent orthodoxy to block the gnosticizing sayings genre and to assert itself "as a replacement for the all too ambivalent Q" (1982b, 37).

Yet another approach that arrived at a similar assessment of Mark's Gospel was undertaken by Eugene Boring (1977; 1982). He proceeded from early Christian prophecy and its modes of discourse. A distinctive feature of early Christian prophets, according to Boring, was their role as inspired spokesmen of the risen Lord. Conscious of being commissioned by the Lord, they spoke sayings in his name and on his authority. The hermeneutical rationale for prophetic speech was not, therefore, to preserve the teachings of the Jesus of the past, but to keep his voice and authority alive in the community. This study of the prophetic function of (many of) the Synoptic sayings brings Boring finally to posit his thesis concerning the genesis of the narrative Gospel. Mark carries only a little more than half as many sayings as either Matthew or Luke. Apart from the eschatological discourse, Boring can identify only five of Mark's sayings as prophetic speech (1982, 183–203). In addition, Boring sees Mark withholding all sayings from the risen Lord. The latter "is not only absent, he is silent" (1977, 377; 1982, 203). When viewed against the prophetic mode of representing Jesus' sayings as an address of the living Lord, the purpose and achievement of the narrative Gospel appears in a new light. Both Mark's paucity of sayings and scarcity of specifically prophetic sayings, and also the Gospel's ending at 16:8, which confines traditions to a strictly pre-Easter framework, find an explanation in Mark's intention to compose an alternate form to the prophetically functioning sayings tradition. His achievement was to curb the prophetic use of sayings as post-Easter revelation of the living or risen Jesus by creating the pre-Easter form that endorses the earthly Jesus.

The fact that Robinson, Boring, and my own recent work regard the narrative Gospel as a corrective to the type of sayings genre weighs all the more heavily in that we proceeded largely independently and with the aid of different methods. Robinson took his cue from William Wrede (1901 [1971]), critically advancing the latter's epochal work *Das Messiasgeheimnis in den Evangelien*, with fresh insights derived from the Nag Hammadi documents. Boring undertook a study of early Christian prophecy from its beginnings up to the formation of the narrative Gospels. My own, more theoretically conceived work developed the early Christian hermeneutics of orality versus textuality. Whether one understands the narrative Gospel as a corrective to the gnosticizing trajectory, or as an attempt to control prophetic speech and revelations, or as a rigorous application of textuality versus an oral ontology of language, all three of us view the narrative Gospel as a reaction to, or reinterpretation of, an antecedent stage in the tradition.

9. The Gospel as "Mirror" and "Window"

If we now include in our reflections the vital aspect of speech in the tradition, a model of three orders of operation suggests itself: speech, the sayings genre, and the narrative Gospel. This model is not intended to impute a sense of evolutionary ascendancy to tradition, as if it were propelled by inexorable regularity to move from speech to the sayings Gospel only to peak in narrativity. Orality, sayings Gospel, and narrative Gospel are meant to be viewed as characteristic components in the tradition, not as sequential stages in an orderly process. After all, narrativity was already entrusted to tradition with parabolic speech, and the oral medium is present throughout tradition. The sayings Gospel flourished before, concurrently with, and after the canonical Gospels; and speech remained a fertile ground all along. Indeed, the more difficult parts of the tradition to understand may be the interactions that existed not only between texts and texts, but the recycling of texts into speech—all processes little or not at all discussed in biblical scholarship. As a possible step toward clarifying the role of Gospel narrativity in the tradition, however, the model of the three orders may prove helpful.

The tradition commenced with aphorisms and parables, the two units by all accounts attributable to the historical Jesus. It would seem inescapably obvious that they are primary phenomena of speech. As such, they inhabit a world quite different from words that are fixed on papyrus to be viewed. In the oral world, aphorisms and parables operate largely on acoustic principles. They constitute speech acts, consisting of pitches and pauses, stresses and silence. "In oral speech, the sound is the sign of the meaning" (Havelock 1978, 231). Put differently, meaning is a kind of rhythmic envelope. As long as aphorism and parable function orally, one may speak of a *first order of operation*. Although it is true that written words "are on the whole far more likely to be misunderstood than spoken words are" (Ong 1967b, 115), hermeneutical complications were an inalienable part of oral tradition. Parables in particular placed into tradition from its inception the need for interpretation. Their metaphorical and withholding proclivities encouraged notions of secrecy, of insider versus outsider, and of revealing versus concealing. "Their kinship with the enigma cannot be too strongly emphasized" (Ricoeur 1975, 133). "He who has ears to hear, let him hear." But how does one hear parabolic story, and what did the parabolist intend to convey? Questions of this kind launch the process of interpretation. But in the first order of operation interpretation is not linked to fixed parable texts in the manner of Mark, who attached interpretive discourse to the parable of the Sower. The oral transaction of aphorisms and parables consists in multiple recitals, tailored to specific circumstances, without the auditors ever hearing them as departures from a binding text. In the absence of aphoristic and parabolic units one does not trade in originals and variants thereof. One knows no way of testing speech against fixed models. But the condition of interpretation exists from the outset, forcing hearers to wonder and ponder, and the parabolist to adapt and rethink.

With clustering, a *second order of operation* gets under way. Aphorisms and parables were collected and placed one next to the other in cluster arrangements or in dialogues set in slim narrative frames. Pheme Perkins, virtually the only New Testament scholar benefiting from the categories developed by Walter Ong, has suggested that the genre of the revelation dialogue still operates within the conventions of oral tradition. Indeed, many of the "gnosticizing" writings that have come to light at Nag Hammadi attracted predominantly speech material, much of which reflects "the liturgy, teaching, preaching and polemic of their respective communities" (Perkins 1980, 201). In the case of the sayings and dialogue genres, Jesus' oral proclamation, his very spoken words, had fashioned for themselves Gospels in their own right. Their primary interest was neither philosophical, nor cosmological, but soteriological. To this end they sought to retain the living voice of Jesus and to extend it into the communal present. And yet, all of this was accomplished through writing, and writing can be corrosive as far as orality's vitality is concerned. While writing retained aphorisms and parables in their oral form, a specific stage of the tradition was frozen, inviting not only reoralization but also reading and comparison, disclosing thereby the interpretive nature of the materials. Indeed, the principle of clustering is itself not in the best interest of orality because, as far as is known, oral conventions do not favor speaking in clusters of like materials. The compilation of sayings and parables, a textually contrived arrangement, can invite reflection and analysis, further heightening the impulse toward interpretation. In this second order of operation, interpretation can become a self-conscious activity. This is evident from the first saying in the *Gospel of Thomas*, which summons hearers to the task of interpretation: "Whoever finds the explanation of these words will not taste death." The 114 sayings of *Thomas* require interpretation (ἑρμηνεία), and finding it is perceived to be a matter of life and death. Despite the textual manifestations of the sayings and dialogue genres, one must be mindful of their oral functioning. The communities in which they originated did not look upon them as normative textual revelations or as textually fixed truths. While these Gospels contained the voice of Jesus, "truth is not [understood to be] definitively embodied in an inspired text. Gnostic interpretation is still the hermeneutic of an oral tradition" (Perkins 1980, 202). In different words, what mattered most was the present experience of the Christ, of the kingdom, or of wisdom.

While the second order was (inter alia) committed to the two authentic speech acts, the narrative Gospel in turn deprived aphorisms and parables of their oral status by subordinating them, together with a good deal of additional materials, to the textual ordering inside the narrative. When reflecting, therefore, on the Synoptic tradition from the perspective of its vital oral inception, something in the nature of a mutation suggests itself in the shifting from the first and second to the third order. Orality, the voice of the living Jesus, the ground and life of the tradition, and the Gospels who carried Jesus' dual proclamation were overruled by the more complex ordering of narrative textuality. It is, on this view, not entirely surprising that the *third order of operation*, the narrative configuration, asserted itself canonically in tension with the second order. Interpretation further intensified on this level. Insofar as Mark enacted an alternative to the sayings Gospel, his narrative may have accomplished the revision of a strong precursor. Ironically, Mark redescribed the second-order genre via the dynamics of parabolic reversal (Kelber 1983, 117–29). The narrative Gospel subverted conventional expectations by reversing the inside view, and placed an additional burden on its hearers/readers by forestalling closure. It was precisely this parabolic posture of the Markan narrative that called for further interpretation. Here we can see how a narrative that had already come into existence by virtue of reinterpretation was itself destined to engender more interpretation. When viewed from the perspective of tradition history, therefore, Matthew and Luke are in part at least interpretations of the interpretation (= Mark) of an interpretation (= sayings Gospel). Both Matthew and Luke domesticated the Markan narrative, blunting its parabolic edges and furnishing closure. No longer faced with Mark's task of correcting the sayings genre, they could open their Gospels more readily to aphorisms and parables. The latter, however, had to comply with the rules of their respective narrative houses. In the end, orthodoxy would disallow the sayings Gospel as a genre in its own right, and would admit the second and first order of operation into the canon only through mediation of the third order. Narrative, the most thoroughly textualized piece, emerged as the victor in the canonical ratification of the Synoptic tradition.

The time has come to include in our reflections a controversial item that, if proven authentic, further complicates our thinking about the tradition and the role of narrative within it. Our reference is to the *Secret Gospel of Mark*. Space compels us to confine the review of this intricate case to its barest essentials. The discovery of *Secret Mark* dates to 1958, when Morton Smith came across an incomplete copy of a letter of Clement of Alexandria at the Greek orthodox monastery of Mar Saba in the Judean desert (M. Smith 1973b; 1973a; 1982, 449–61). In this letter, written to an otherwise unknown Theodore, Clement cites a portion of *Secret Mark*. It concerns the story of a rich young man whom Jesus raises from the dead. Having been brought back to life, he loves Jesus and beseeches him that he might be with him. "After six days" the youth, "wearing a linen cloth over his naked body," spends a night with Jesus to be initiated into "the mystery of the Kingdom of God." Clement himself proposed that *Secret Mark* was a revision of canonical Mark, a view to some extent shared by Smith himself, if I understand him correctly (1973b, 142; 1973a, 145, 194).[1] More recently, however, first Helmut Koester (1983, 35–57) and then Crossan (1985, 91–121) have advocated a reversal of the compositional sequence: canonical Mark has revised *Secret Mark*. Canonical Mark's revision is assumed to have been motivated by the Carpocratians' interpretation, who gave the resurrection-baptismal story in *Secret Mark* a homosexual slant in the fashion of gnostic libertinism. Faced with an exceedingly delicate situation, Mark proceeded to eliminate the explosive story by dismemberment and redistribution of its parts. In other words, canonical Mark is assumed to have scattered its textual debris across his own text. The naked young man now appears at the arrest (Mark 14:51–52); the motif of love is transferred to the story of the rich man and rephrased in the sense that Jesus loved him and not the reverse (Mark 10:17, 22; cf. 10:21); the six days are connected with the transfiguration (Mark 9:2); the mystery of the kingdom is relocated after public parable (4:11); and so forth. Having thus decomposed the controversial text, canonical Mark appears to have successfully met the Carpocratian scandal, for their erotic version would henceforth give the impression of having been secondarily produced out of bits and pieces from canonical Mark. Bearing in mind that *Secret Mark* poses uncommonly labyrinthine problems that await a good deal more philological, text-critical, and historical work, we may at this stage draw four preliminary conclusions.

First, there may well have been more narrative in the tradition prior to canonical Mark. Texts are never simply created out of lived experience, least of all perhaps biblical texts, which are multifariously enmeshed

---

1. According to Morton Smith's own judgment, his *Clement of Alexandria and a Secret Gospel of Mark* is "a dreadfully complex book" (1982, 456). If I understand his central thesis correctly, *Secret Mark* is an imitation of canonical Mark, including elements, such as the baptismal-resurrection story, that were taken from a precanonical Markan Gospel.

in tradition. Indeed, it appears likely that there existed something of a Markan school tradition, as Smith had imagined it, not unlike the one we have long recognized with respect to the Johannine materials. If *Secret Mark* indeed has priority over canonical Mark, we can only speculate as to the narrative impulse of the former. Our knowledge of the history of the Synoptic tradition should caution us against assuming that in *Secret Mark* we have arrived at the narrative equivalent to the bedrock of history. As Clement himself seems to indicate, the setting of *Secret Mark* was the Alexandrian baptismal ritual.

Second, although we have known of the Gospels' involvement in tradition, canonical Mark may be more deeply and actively engaged than we ever thought possible. It can never be sufficiently stressed that fidelity to its historical subject matter cannot account for the canonical narrative in its present form. I suspect we will increasingly find dependencies and displacement features in canonical Mark that testify to his wrestling with traditions. One remembers Crossan's thesis that that canonical Mark was not only decomposing the resurrection-baptismal story of *Secret Mark*, but also redacting *Egerton Papyrus 2* (1985, 65–87) and revising the passion narrative of the *Gospel of Peter* (1985, 125–35).

Third, in all of Mark's coping with tradition, Crossan discerns the triumph of intertextuality. Yet the principle of intertextuality, far from being simply a matter of hard evidence, is also a presupposition of our media-conditioned method. Trained to interpret texts, impressed by the ubiquity of texts, and working single-mindedly with texts, we are bound to discover intertextuality. But how is one to imagine—technically, psychologically, religiously—Mark's skillful juggling of a number of written texts, using them, revising them, deconstructing them, while all along composing an impressively coherent narrative? Are we not asking canonical Mark to juggle too many balls at once? At any rate, the larger the number of traditions we find canonical Mark struggling with, the less persuasive or imaginable the principle of intertextuality becomes. If canonical Mark does interact with multiple traditions, oral apperception would seem to be a more plausible procedure. How could he have laboriously picked first from one text, then from another, revised one scrap of papyrus, decomposed and scattered another? Is he not more likely to have operated from a cultural memory that was in possession of a plurality of traditions? What to text-bound scholars appears to be tight intertextuality may in hermeneutical actuality have been free composition, "especially in antiquity, when most writers, even in citing explicitly, cited from memory" (M. Smith 1973a, 143).

Fourth, is Clement's view of the priority of canonical Mark over *Secret Mark* beyond all redemption? What if the naked young man at the arrest in canonical Mark, owing to his enigmatic presence in the narrative, gave rise to the resurrection-baptismal story in *Secret Mark* on the one hand and to the Lazarus story in John on the other? If, in different words, Mark 14:51–52 was experienced as a narrative secret, an "indeterminacy gap," then one proven way of coping with it was more narrative.

In whatever way the riddle of *Secret Mark* is finally resolved, the canonical Mark's engagement in tradition seems highly plausible. Mark's openness toward tradition and the corollary "window" reading of Gospel narrativity is currently not much in favor with those biblical critics who have embarked upon a literary examination of narrative. The study of the interior narrative world is now widely held to be incompatible with reflection on its possible involvement in tradition. To be sure, what cannot under any circumstances be questioned is the significance of our growing sensitivity to the narrative quality of the Gospels. The issue here is the tendency among literary critics of the Bible to assign priority to the literary study of narrative (Petersen 1978; Alter 1981; Polzin 1980; Culpepper 1983) vis-à-vis the historical study of its tradition and composition history. To read narrative texts *both* as "mirrors," reflecting self-contained worlds, *and* as "windows," opening upon the precanonical history, seems to be almost a violation of proper hermeneutical conduct. It is not entirely clear, however, whether biblical hermeneutics is categorically divisible into the strictly literary ("mirror") versus the tradition-historical ("window") mode of interpretation, one having precedence over the other. Murray Krieger, from whom we borrowed the metaphors of "mirror" versus "window," sought to maintain their simultaneous functioning so that meaning arises "not just through the work and not just in the work but at once through and in the work as body" (1964, 28).

Following Krieger's categorization, perhaps we can arrive at a more judicious assessment of literary criticism, if we locate "mirror" reading in the broader context of the three orders of operation outlined above. In viewing the intellectual and communications history in terms of orality, scribality, and typography, the literary criticism in the exclusively "mirror" sense, as described above, is most closely allied with typography, the phase dominated by printing. This deserves some explication. The existence of speech appears unreal when viewed from a literary perspective, because it "lacks" a visual, objectifiable presence. Oral words cannot be locked into space. They are uncontainable in formal, visual models. Bound to the authority of the speaker and inseparable from auditors, they are inevitably enmeshed in the human lifeworld. To regard spoken words as knowable in terms strictly of themselves and as operable apart from historical contextuality is a notion that has no conceivable reality in oral culture because speech cannot exist in transauthorial objectivity (Tyler 1978; Ong 1982, 5–77; Kelber 1983, 44–89). Oral discourse, as noted earlier, is rhythmically structured sound, and it acquires meaning as a contextual phenomenon. We must add here a caveat against an understanding of orality strictly in terms of sound, rhythm, acoustics, and human contextuality. Both ancient and medieval oral culture exhibited *visual* elements as well, not of course in the sense of external visualization of speech through writing, but as a form of *interior visualization* (Yates 1966). Mnemotechnics did not facilitate instant recall simply based on sound tracks drilled into the mind. The method also involved the formation of memory images, that is, heroic figures, dramatic scenes, striking places, and so on. The ideal was to express everything one wanted hearers to retain in a way that encouraged imaging. A flourishing of imagination and visions, a rich inner visualized world, was an essential part of (ancient) oral operations.

With scribality, the shift from sound to external visualization gets under way. Words written down enjoy a stable existence denied to spoken words. Demands on the *vis vivendi*, the most discriminating of the senses, intensify in scribal culture. "The eye lends distance to things, it makes them into objects" (Snell 1960, 33). Detachment, objectivity, abstraction, and introspection, all contributions to the civilizing process, benefit from the shift to spatial concretization accomplished by the scribal art. At the same time, however, the art of memory, the life of *interior visualization*, of visions and imagination, for example, the making of inner images, declines. As far as the concept of "mirror" is concerned, the notion that texts, laboriously manufactured (= handmade), relate interiorly back unto themselves, and only to themselves, is by and large still foreign to scribal hermeneutics. Contemporary scholars living in a typographically dominant civilization have rarely been trained to appreciate the ancient and medieval manuscript culture except through a consciousness shaped by the invention of printing. In her monumental work *The Printing Press as an Agent of Change* (1979), Elizabeth Eisenstein made the point that it is easier for us print-oriented people to understand orality than to grasp medieval, let alone ancient, scribality:

> The gulf that separates our experience from that of the literate elites who relied exclusively on hand-copied texts is much more difficult to fathom;

there is nothing analogous in our experience or in that of any living person within the Western world at present. The conditions of scribal culture thus have to be artificially reconstructed by recourse to history books and reference guides. Yet, for the most part, these works are more likely to conceal than to reveal the object of such a search. Scribal themes are carried forward and postprint trends are traced backward in a manner that makes it difficult to envisage the existence of a distinctive literary culture based on hand-copying. (1979, 1:9)

Hand-copied texts in scribal culture were not under the spell of the objectifying standards set by the technology of printing (Eisenstein 1979, 1:11; B. Stock 1983). Rarely, if ever, were ancient texts thought to be fully closed, and rarely, if ever, was a narrative text viewed as a hall of mirrors, reflecting nothing but internal relations. Both manufacture and use of manuscripts readily interacted with orality, be it through dictation or recitation. That most ancient manuscripts were meant to reach out toward readers, or more likely hearers, so as to influence their views and play on their emotions, is something reception theorists have discovered only recently (Iser 1974; 1978; Link 1976; Fish 1980; Jauss 1982). Yet what today we call reader-response criticism was part of a scribal hermeneutics, which by and large was still committed to the art of persuasion and unfriendly toward fully closed systems. This relative hermeneutical openness applies with special force to biblical manuscripts (Ong 1977b, 230–71; Bruns 1982, 17–59). Whether prose or poetry, epistle or narrative, wisdom or apocalypse, biblical texts aim at being heard, read, and actualized. More often than not they are the products of rewriting themselves, and in turn they can be subject to further revisions. "Scripture is something that is always turning into new versions of itself" (Bruns 1982, 26). And revising in biblical hermeneutics is not bound by modern standards of literalness, but inspired by a passion for vivification through inspiration.

With printing, technical control over words reached a state of perfection unimaginable in chirographic culture. More than ever words took on the appearance of autosemantic objectivity. "Print encouraged the mind to sense that its possessions were held in some sort of inert mental space" (Ong 1982, 132). Centuries of interiorization of typographical consciousness in the end gave birth to the Saussurian principle of integrity of language, whereby meaning is figured as relations within language and not as reference to something outside it. Both the Russian formalism and the so-called New Criticism, while originating independently, epitomized the transauthorial autonomy of texts, unthinkable without the typographic interiorization. In light of these critical disciplines, narrative was understood as a system of interrelations rather than as a product of causes. Structuralism penetrated the interior world of texts ever more deeply. With respect to narrative, the hidden structure was given priority at the expense of the plotted storyline; and genetic considerations were held to be irrelevant at worst and secondary at best as far as a proper understanding of narrative was concerned. Here we have come full circle back to our earlier observation about the hermetic, "mirror" type of literary criticism, which turns out to be a favorite child of typography. When placed in the broader context of cultural, linguistic processes, literary criticism of the formalist type appears to be flourishing at a stage in intellectual and communications history when the technologizing, objectifying impact of printing has culminated in the apotheosis of the text as a closed system. Many biblical critics who have lately adopted literary criticism adopted it in this formalist mode. We turned to it enthusiastically, though somewhat unreflectively, out of disillusionment with centuries of grossly referential hermeneutics (Frei 1974). In this situation, biblical narrative and even parable (Via 1967) were appreciated as self-referential entities, standing entirely on their own as aesthetic objects.

What bears repeating, however, is the significance of the current literary assessment of the Gospels. The analysis of the narrative nature of the Gospels is not only justifiable, but also imperative. In view of the long dominance of the historical paradigm in Gospel studies, literary criticism truly marks a Copernican revolution. But our task now is to move beyond formalism in literary theory and practice, although not in the sense of retreating to the older historical, philological model of interpretation. "A crucial test of the ability of contemporary criticism is whether it can formulate a program of literary history that uses the strengths of formalism and yet avoids its current impasse" (Hoy 1978, 9). To this end, literary critics of the Gospels should become more circumspect about the degree to which not only narrative, the object of their study, but all our ways of approaching narrative and literature are inescapably bound up with language and its technological developments. Once we learn to see distinctions between an ancient chirographically and a modern typographically informed hermeneutic, and grasp a sense of the oral apperception of ancient biblical manuscripts, might we not grow more tolerant methodologically, acknowledging the Gospels both as integral narratives *and* as narrative participants in tradition—as documents both of synchronic integrity *and* of diachronic depth? Or, to put it more provocatively, are not the Gospels both "windows" *and* "mirrors," giving us worlds that interact with themselves and the lifeworlds from which they arose and to which they speak? In any case, fear of the "referential fallacy" should not cause us to disclaim the manifold ties the Gospels have with tradition, for no text is composed in complete referential neutrality, not in antiquity, least of all in the biblical tradition.

10. Narrative Present as Displacement of the Past

As literary criticism of the Gospels commences in earnest, we should not lose sight of the well-known interrelationship between the Synoptic narratives and their wider orbit of tradition. Exclusive attention to internal, synchronic relations, we stated above, is less than faithful to scribal hermeneutics. Moreover, it may, unwittingly perhaps, introduce a false sense of foundationalism. When viewed from the diachronic perspective, the Synoptic narratives disclose their interpretive status. They came into being under the pressures of interpretation. Whatever authority they may represent, and however foundational an impression they may create, each Gospel is bound up with a process of interpretive traditioning. Given this state of affairs, anything resembling a foundational level is likely to elude us, whether it is that of history or of tradition.

The first time we encounter Gospel narrative in the full light of canonicity, we encounter it not as the ground of history or of tradition, but as a pattern of elementary tensions. Narratively, it manifests itself as a revisionist text, intent on displacing the the genre of the sayings Gospel, and perhaps other Gospels. When Robinson referred to the Synoptic transfiguration story as belonging to a tradition "suppressed in orthodox Christianity, and surviving in the New Testament only indirectly at mislocated positions" (1970, 117–18 [1982c, 30]), he was employing, quite appropriately, the language of revisionist hermeneutics: suppression, indirect survival, and mislocation. Freud, who taught us much about the mechanisms of displacement and revisionism, knew that many strong precursors will not simply vanish into the night of anonymity; their traces remain hidden in the revisionist text (Freud 1900, 117; 1939; Handelmann 1982). This is Freud's message in the third epigraph to this piece. In the *Gospel of Thomas* a strong precursor has literally returned, challenging widely held views of the traditioning process and of the rise of the narrative Gospel. Strong precursors have a way of coming back, disclosing the present as displacement of the past.

Narrative as interpretation is a concept that readily crosses boundaries we have come to take for granted. If the canonical narrative was itself born in the act of interpretation, then readers interpreting the narrative pursue an activity that is observable not only in Mark but also far back in the tradition. Whether in our time we interpret by reading or preaching, through books or commentaries, by subtle augmentation or radical revision of anteriority, we are always in the process of interpreting. Both narrator-as-interpreter and interpreters of narrative jointly partake in the embracing activity of hermeneutical translations. This hermeneutical activity, perceptively formulated by Kermode in the last epigraph to this piece, has been elevated in the first epigraph by Gadamer to the level of an epistemological principle. As such it forms the leading theme to this piece. On this view, what distinguishes the Gospels from what preceded them is not literature versus history, but rather one of interpretation turning canonical. Canonicity, far from terminating the interpretive impulse, assured survival of the narrative Gospel, thus rendering it normative for the Gospel history. Nor can a categorical distinction be drawn between the Gospels as windows vis-à-vis mirrors. Precisely because they participate in the ongoing discourse of tradition, narrative Gospels contain traces of absent others, which, while integrated in their new Gospel narratives, may serve as windows for those who know the scope of the tradition. When seen in these perspectives, therefore, opposites such as narrative versus interpretation, literary versus historical readings, and mirror versus window views of language dissolve into the single, overriding reality of interpretation. And interpretation is more than a matter of method, and more than a manifestation of madness; it is rather an essential mode of survival.

3

Narrative and Disclosure: Mechanisms of Concealing, Revealing, and Reveiling

The need to hide and disclose is manifest in every aspect of the human condition, including the mechanisms of narrative. This essay undertakes explorations of secrecy and disclosure in biblical narrative. Mark's Gospel, which has long been associated with secrecy, will serve as a an example. The first part considers Mark's alliance with secrecy, a theme developed from William Wrede to Frank Kermode and beyond. Notwithstanding the firmly established view of Markan secrecy, it is claimed that in addition and contrary to secrecy, Mark's narrative also displays a basic urge toward disclosure. The second part examines esoteric secrecy, which functions as a form of concealment that limits communication to a privileged few. A well-known example of this secrecy scenario is recognizable in Mark 4:1–34. But already Wrede realized that this particular scenario of secrecy is not limited to Mark (and John) alone but is also a notable feature in the noncanonical tradition. This prompts inquiry of secrecy in the tradition. Part 3 explicates different functions of secrecy: a strengthening of the social exclusivity of insiders, securing of privileged and confidential information, manifestation of power and authority, and preservation of knowledge. These functions help illuminate the deeper mechanisms that motivate secrecy.

The fourth part explains shifting attitudes toward secrecy in media culture. In the most general terms, dependency on secrecy diminishes as communication drifts from oral to scribal and on to typographic manifestations, lessening the oral need for secret preservation of what threatens its immaterial existence.

Based on the premise that Mark's narrative seeks to overcome more than to enforce secrecy, part 5 focuses primarily on the mechanisms of disclosure. It will be shown that the esoteric secrecy of Mark 4:1–34 is subverted in the subsequent narrative. Sundry forms of concealment scattered across the Gospel, moreover, are enjoined only to be revealed. Consideration of the role of the readers/hearers in part 6 signifies a dynamic that is irreconcilable with secrecy. The readers/hearers, it is claimed, have access not only to what is communicated, secretly or openly, to the characters in the narrative, but also to what is concealed from the latter ones. Up to a point they acquire the status of the genuine insiders. Part 7, finally, demonstrates that new secrecies arise at the very junctures where disclosure was made. The more the narrative strives to reveal, the more it becomes involved in concealments. Disclosure and secrecy condition each other reciprocally and in complex ways.

> For nothing is hidden, except to be revealed; nor has anything been secret, but that it should come to light.
>
> —Mark 4:22

> Jesus said, "I tell my mysteries to those who are worthy of my mysteries."
>
> —*Gospel of Thomas* 62

> They maintain that the Savior privately taught these same things not to all, but to certain only of his disciples who could comprehend them, and who understood what was intended by him through means of arguments, enigmas, and parables.
>
> —Irenaeus, *Adversus haereses* 2.27.2

> We are all, in a sense, experts on secrecy.
>
> —Bok, *Secrets*

> We are most unwilling to accept mystery.
>
> —Kermode, *Genesis of Secrecy*

> But the readers have never really been in the dark.
>
> —Magness, Sense and Absence

> A "gospel" is a narrative of a son of god who appears among men as a riddle inviting misunderstanding.
>
> —J. Smith, "Good News Is No News"

11. Narrative Alliances with Secrecy and Disclosure

Since William Wrede's classic study on concealment in the Gospels (1901 [1971]), narrative and secrecy are thought to be close allies in the Gospels of Mark and also John. *Messiasgeheimnis* was the code he had invented to get a significant matter into perspective. To him the term suggested a theological idea that exercised controlling influence on Mark's narrative, relegating it to *Dogmengeschichte* (1901, 131). Today few will give unqualified assent to the term "messianic secret," and fewer still subscribe to Wrede's explanation of its functioning. But the alliance of Mark's narrative with secrecy is not in doubt, and the debate about its genesis and operation continues unabated (Blevins 1981; Tuckett 1983). In our generation the issue of narrative secrecy has been revitalized by Kermode's *The Genesis of Secrecy* (1979). For him Mark serves as paradigm for the fundamental secrecy of all narrative. It was less a specific idea that accounts for the Gospel's secrecy rather than the labyrinthine property of narrativity itself, which ushers readers along meandering paths into hidden corners and unpromising dead ends. Being an insider in this situation "is only a more elaborate way of being kept outside" (1979, 27). My own work has increasingly moved toward a parabolic reading of Mark's narrative (Kelber 1983, 117–31). From my perspective, the Gospel encourages experimentation with a new logic in defiance of received opinion. Secrecy, or as I prefer to call it, mystery, results from a disorienting-reorienting narrative, which forestalls closure. Meaning is thereby not allowed to attach itself exclusively to the one, the literal sense. More recently, Williams has asserted that Mark's narrative "stands within the iconoclastic biblical tradition of paradox, irony, and abruptness" (1985, 84). On his reading, the Gospel's paratactic style is of a piece with a plot at the center of which stands the mystery of the kingdom of God (1985, 53, 90, 134). Whether one focuses on a central idea or on narrative opaqueness, on the kingdom's mystery or on parabolic plot construction, narrative and secrecy remain an issue in Mark, and perhaps for all narrative.

Not all the evidence marshaled on behalf of narrative secrecy is equally persuasive. Perhaps it is primarily to readers schooled in the more densely plotted novels of the eighteenth and nineteenth centuries that fractured surfaces and paratactic style suggest intriguing ambiguities and latent senses. It is well to remember that in the history of story there was no such thing as narrative reticence before we thought we knew what narrative plenum was. As Kermode wisely observed, "Whatever is preserved grows enigmatic" (1979, 64). Distance, both temporal and cultural, produces its own complicities with secrecy. It is thus tempting to imagine that sole emphasis on secrecy and ambiguity draws its principal inspiration from the anxieties of modernity.

In light of the foregoing it is worth noting that writing, and writing a narrative, is not in the best interest of enforcing secrecy. The best way to keep a secret is not to talk or write about it. Narrative, even though inveighing against definitional clarity, seeks to reveal more than to conceal. While it is true that our passion for narrative sequence and propriety, this deep-seated desire to finalize and fully organize life, makes us suppress narrative secrets (Kermode 1983), it is also possible that passionate attention to secrets makes us overlook narrative's desire to override secrecy. In the latter case, narrative seeks to be a natural ally of disclosure. Notwithstanding the conviction, firmly institutionalized since Wrede, that Mark has entered into a special covenant with secrecy, we shall present the view that the Gospel is also paradigmatic of narrative's basic urge toward disclosure. The bulk of this piece is about Mark's strenuous efforts at both enforcing and discrediting secrecy. To discern the forms and mechanisms of disclosure is a pre-supposition for understanding secrecy, for the crux of the matter is revealing *and* reveiling, this dual narrative attention to message and secrecy.

12. Esoteric Secrecy in Mark and Tradition

Mark 4:1–34 narrates what may well be the most intriguing and intractably difficult dramatization of secrecy in the Gospel. Despite its traditional label of esoteric secrecy, the passage furnishes a good example both for unlocking and creating secrecy.

The scene narrates Jesus' public recital of a parable, followed by his withdrawal together with "the Twelve and a few chosen ones." In response to their question concerning the parables, Jesus volunteers the solemn pronouncement: "To you has been given the mystery of the kingdom of God, but for those outside everything occurs in parables" (4:11). After disclosing additional characteristics of the outsiders (4:12), Jesus entrusts the explication of the "master parable" of the Sower (Williams 1985, 4) plus additional parables and parabolic sayings to the circle of elect ones around him. The speech is formally concluded with a narrative aside to the effect that Jesus spoke exclusively in parables, which he privately explained to his disciples (4:34).

When taken by itself this narrative scenario enacts a tightly deterministic world. The number of insiders is a limited one, restricted to the chosen few. There is no indication that newcomers might join the ranks of the insiders. Indeed, explication of the parabolic mystery appears to preclude its propagation to the outside world. Public parable and private instruction have set apart the outsiders from the insiders. The rationale for being an outsider is to remain outside and be damned so as to never get the benefit of the inside information. That is the force of what Kermode has termed "the *hina* doctrine of narrative" (1979, 33). Parable, or rather entrustment of its mystery to the chosen few, banishes all others to the outside "so that [= in order that] seeing they see but do not perceive, and hearing they hear but do not understand, lest they should turn around and be forgiven" (4:12). Inasmuch as this scenario ostracizes the outsiders, it works entirely for the benefit of the insiders. For not only are the latter favored to receive the mystery and interpretation, but they are also informed of the fate and identity of the outsiders. The insiders are thereby doubly privileged. They have received the inside information that concerns both the kingdom's parabolic mystery and the exclusion of the outsiders. They obtained access both to parable and to its hermeneutical operation. The second feature serves to heighten the first one, and together the two reinforce the status of the insiders.

It is widely assumed that Mark's narration of esoteric secrecy is not entirely an *ad hoc* composition. The feature is out of line with the canonical disposition toward publicity and proclamation of the gospel. The notion that a circle of insiders is hermetically sealed from irredeemable outsiders was not welcome news for emergent orthodoxy. What is more, the esoteric scenario constitutes a recognizable feature in the noncanonical tradition. There it had developed a distinctive profile. This brings us to consider secrecy in the tradition, although a detailed reconstruction will forever elude us. For while Mark's esoteric secrecy is quite recognizable as an entity in its own right, it has nevertheless been embedded in the Gospel's narrative project.

It is worth remembering that Wrede in his well-known study of the so-called messianic secret recognized an affinity between Mark and John, but, even more significantly, that he attributed this commonality not to direct literary dependency but to shared ideas current in the tradition (1901, 206). Today we recognize that technically Mark 4:10–34 constitutes a sayings Gospel or revelation discourse of the kind that has come to light near Nag Hammadi. A string of sayings and parables, suspended from a slim narrative frame, and linked with secrecy, is addressed to a group of privileged recipients. In the *Gospel of Thomas*, for example, "where incidentally much of this material recurs" (Robinson 1982a, 47; Koester 1980a, 114), all sayings and parables are introduced as "secret words" and entrusted to a few disciples and women. The task assigned to these privileged insiders is the interpretation of the precious words of Jesus. Interpretation more than proclamation would seem to be at least one function of the sayings Gospel.

Long before the discovery of the Coptic codices, the genre of the sayings Gospel was known through the writings of the orthodox fathers. When, for example, Irenaeus in *Against Heresies* (online version) exposed what he regarded as intolerable absurdities, he unwittingly shed light on the profile and function of the sayings model. "They [the heretics] tell us, however, that this knowledge has not been openly divulged, because all are not capable of receiving it, but has been mystically revealed by the Savior through means of parables to those qualified for understanding it" (1.3.1). Accordingly, knowledge of salvation is communicated in mystery (μυστηριωδῶς) via parabolic discourse (διὰ παραβολῶν) to those capable of comprehending it (τοῖς συνιεῖν δυναμένοις οὕτως). Irenaeus himself, on the contrary, sought to enforce what he called "the body of truth," whereby "the parables ought not to be adapted to ambiguous expressions" (2.27.1). Moreover, the heretics, according to Irenaeus, declared that "Jesus spoke in a mystery to his disciples and apostles privately" (1.25.5; ἐν μυστηρίῳ ... κατ᾽ ἰδίαν λελαληκέναι). The chosen few are here identified as the disciples and apostles, whereas Irenaeus wanted to ensure that "the parables will receive a like interpretation from all" (2.27.1). The heretics, in his view, also taught that it was "after his [= Christ's] resurrection," while he spent eighteen months on earth, and before he ascended to heaven, that he "instructed a few of his disciples, whom he knew to be capable of understanding so great mysteries" (1.30.14). For Irenaeus's most explicit repudiation of the sayings model, the reader is referred to the third epigraph of this piece. There private instruction, the exclusivity of insiders, the comprehension of certain disciples, and parabolic, riddling discourse all come together in invoking the profile of the sayings Gospel. Its resemblance to Mark's esoteric secrecy scenario is evident, and all the more so since the evangelist sums up the significance of Jesus' parabolic revelation in terms remarkably similar to those used by Irenaeus: "And he was not speaking to them without parables, but he was explaining everything privately to his own disciples" (4:34; κατ᾽ ἰδίαν δὲ τοῖς ἰδίοις μαθηταῖς ἐπέλυεν πάντα).

13. FUNCTIONS OF SECRECY

In the tradition esoteric secrecy serves important sociolinguistic functions, which give additional clues to the genre of the sayings Gospel. There are altogether three factors that contribute to esoteric secrecy.

In the first place, esoteric secrecy serves to defend and strengthen the identity of a small, distinctive group. The more restricted and distinguishable a group, the more successful the operation of esoteric secrecy. Larger, less controllable groups tend to weaken the esoteric factor (Jansen 1965, 46–47). Esoteric secrecy thrives in and on isolation. The exclusivity, therefore, of a limited group of "the Twelve and a few chosen ones" in Mark, and of disciples/apostles and women in the sayings Gospel, is an essential factor of the esoteric tradition. Second, esoteric secrecy is a guarantor of authority. Special knowledge granted to the few directly translates into categories of power and prestige. The beneficiaries of secret information and special knowledge are the carriers of authority. Reception of Jesus' secret words promotes the select few to the ranks of guardians of tradition. Their power hinges on the fact that they are privy to confidential information. Secrecy and authority feed on each other. Third, esoteric secrecy is closely allied with the possession of special knowledge. There is no secrecy without some information to be kept secret. Knowledge conveyed to a limited number of people becomes privileged information. Held by the few and withheld from all others, it fuels the basic needs of esoteric secrecy. From the perspective of the exoteric, orthodox Gospel, which promotes open proclamation, the concealment of information in esoteric secrecy could well be seen as a failure in communication. Esoteric secrecy and orthodoxy's kerygmatic impulse serve mutually exclusive interests. In the sayings Gospel the prestige of esoteric secrecy rests on the claim that an extreme minority is in possession of aphoristic and parabolic wisdom. In sum, the factors of social isolation, authority, and privileged information illuminate a large part of the mechanism of esoteric secrecy.

14. Secrecy at Media Transits

Sensitivity to media dynamics illuminates esoteric secrecy from yet another angle. Secrecy, we saw, operates against the better instincts of dissemination and diffusion. In addition to social isolation, authority, and privileged information, esoteric secrecy serves a purely conservative, pragmatic function. In her magisterial volumes *The Printing Press as an Agent of Change* (1979), Elizabeth Eisenstein has drawn persuasive parallels between early forms of information gathering and secrecy. "To be preserved intact, techniques had to be entrusted to a select group of initiates who were instructed not only in special skills but also in the 'mysteries' associated with them. Special symbols, rituals, and incantations performed the necessary function of organizing data, laying out schedules, and preserving techniques in easily memorized forms" (1:270). Secrecy or a form of censorship, if you will, could serve as mechanisms for preserving important data. In documenting links between secrecy and scribal culture, Eisenstein proceeded from the observation of the vulnerable state of scribal life. Deficient storage facilities and the perishability of writing materials, the corruption and dilution of manuscripts, drifting texts and vanishing documents all imposed a condition of vulnerability upon scribal life (1:113–15). For this reason, many forms of knowledge had to be esoteric during the age of scribes if knowledge was to survive at all (1:270). Before the advent of typographical fixity, therefore, the alliance between secrecy and preservation was a necessary and often natural one, as far as scribal culture was concerned. "The notion that valuable data could be preserved best by being made public, rather than by being kept secret, ran counter to tradition" (1:116). In short, a good way of preserving the integrity of valuable data was to withhold their publication.

Eisenstein's observations cast fresh light on the esoteric scenario of the sayings Gospel. Once we are attentive to matters of collection and preservation, secrecy can be seen as a natural mechanism for storing precious information. Valuable data are withheld from the public and guarded by the circle of initiates so as to be protected against corruption by dissemination. Knowledge is confided to the inner circle precisely for the purpose of keeping it intact. We have to do with an esoteric brotherhood and sisterhood whose plain business it is to preserve what has been imparted to it.

As far as Mark 4:1–34 is concerned, we are actually dealing with two senses of secrecy, one reinforcing the other. One sense of hiddenness is inherent in parable itself, insofar as parable displays a hermeneutic potential for mystery; hence, in the tradition parables function as bearers of the mystery of the kingdom. Appropriately, in Mark 4:1–34 this hermeneutical knowledge is directly applied to Jesus' parables, and above all to his master parable of the Sower: concealed in them is the mystery of the kingdom of God. Additionally, this mystery is secretly entrusted to the Twelve and a few chosen ones. In other words, the kingdom's mystery is itself hedged in by secrecy, which aims at protecting the kingdom's mysterious identity. This amounts to saying that esoteric secrecy in Mark is designed to protect and preserve the mystery of the kingdom by entrusting the latter to a group of insiders. In short, therefore, esoteric secrecy is the hedge built around the mystery of the kingdom.

There is a sense in which the preservative intent of enclosing parable and parabolic sayings in the esoteric scenario goes against the grain of parabolic objectives. For according to Crossan's well known typology of story (1975, 57–62), parable mystifies while myth reassures, parable undercuts structures of expectation while myth mediates structural opposites, and parable inclines toward the culture-subversive while myth genuflects before tradition. In our terms, parable is a paradigmatic instance of the open-endedness of language and signification. But parables that were placed into the scenario of esoteric secrecy have lost their power to shatter basic assumptions so as to make us vulnerable to the new logic of the kingdom. Parabolic mystery has become a safe possession in the hands of a few. But again, when parabolic discourse has come to be locked into a chapel for secret rites, and when a social world is immobilized by the irrevocable segregation of insiders versus outsiders, parables have died stillborn.

Curiously, stability is idolized and closure monumentalized on behalf of parables that were intended to invoke instability and open-endedness. Paradoxically, a world is made obvious again by conserving the very discourse that was meant to invert the obvious. In the last analysis, therefore, Mark's esoteric secrecy is a mechanism of preservation that has converted its own conservative hermeneutic into a new myth.

To point out competing tendencies in the esoteric enclosure of parabolic discourse is not to say that Mark is uncritical toward, let alone unaware of, them. Obviously, the Gospel has used the esoteric scenario as a source, not as model, for its narrative. The hermeneutical operation of the sayings genre is subsumed under the larger logic of the narrative Gospel, and the latter, we shall see, is less than sympathetic toward the parables' retreat behind the walls of esoteric secrecy.

The breaking of the secrecy code deserves as much attention as the installation of secrecy. In assessing corrosive effects on esoteric secrecy, we turn once again to Eisenstein's work. It was, in her view, the new technology of printing that undermined old alliances between secrecy and preservation prevalent in oral, chirographic culture. The preservative and duplicative powers of print, while at times amplifying and reinforcing secrecy, in the long run lessened reliance on secret knowledge and broke down secrecy barriers surrounding the crafts and trades, religious and scientific knowledge. The new reproductive technology operated against the ancient esoteric injunctions to withhold the highest truths from the public. To be sure, both secrecy and openness are integral features of the human condition. "We are all, in a sense, experts on secrecy" (Bok 1982, xv). Modern

electronic technology is used for exposing privacy and retrieving knowledge, but also for storing and concealing it. In contemporary Western civilization "the right to privacy" or the invocation of "national security" often
conflicts with "the freedom of inquiry" or "the public's right to know" (Bok
1982). None of this can diminish the validity of Eisenstein's studies concerning changing needs and attitudes toward secrecy in connection with
a shift from chirographic to typographic means of communication. Insistence on concealment seemed perfectly appropriate in reference to the
privileged few, but odd and even absurd in a culture that is nourished on
printed and speedily disseminated materials for a rapidly growing public
readership. Notwithstanding the fact that secrecy remained operational in
many guises, typographic means of publication fostered an ethos subversive to the ancient codes of privacy and privilege. Arcana were dismantled
or disclosed, and secrecy moved underground or realigned itself with different social and political forces (Eisenstein 1979, 1:272–302).

Eisenstein's observations, while amply documented with regard to
scribality and typography, apply with even greater validity to transitions
from orality to textuality. Given the nonmaterial mode of oral communication and the purely memorial storage in oral discourse, the need for limiting information to a select few would seem to be more acute with regard
to spoken than to written words. Every word written down has for the time
being at least escaped orality's insubstantial existence, while every spoken
word runs the risk of being lost unless a mechanism exists that facilitates
its preservation. In the Gospel tradition, such a mechanism is provided by
consigning sayings and parables to an authoritative body of traditionists.
Esoteric secrecy in conjunction with the sayings genre may thus well find
its most logical explanation in orality's pressing needs for preserving the
two basic speech events of the language of Jesus. In this, as in a number of
other ways, the sayings genre, while a textual production, still reflects the
ethos of an essentially oral state of the tradition (Kelber 1983, 199–203).

On Eisenstein's analogy of changing attitudes toward secrecy at the
interfaces of scribal and print culture, one may expect a diminution of esoteric secrecy already at strategic transitions from orality to scribality. Even
though scribal culture remains beholden to sundry forms of secrecy, it may
show signs of relief from the pressing needs for esoteric conservation. The
narrative Gospel, for example, mobilizes textuality, and it does so in ways
that loosen dependency on the clustering management of knowledge. It
reabsorbs and transforms the commonplace tradition of the sayings genre,
and along with it the secrecy surrounding it. Freed from preoccupation

with the sayings material, the narrative Gospel extends its imaginative recall across the spatio-temporal scope of Jesus' life and death. The drift of narrative attention is away from conserving what threatens to perish and toward reclaiming the fuller story. In brief, interpretation begins to prevail over orality's urgent need for preservation and secrecy.

15. Implosion of Secrecy Mechanisms

Mark's tendency to override the canons of esoteric secrecy is evident, for example, from the kind of wisdom confided to the insiders (4:14–32). They receive an interpretation that is less than suited for, and in fact remarkably inappropriate to, their status as recipients of esoteric knowledge. Is one to regard it entirely accidental that in the explication of the master parable (4:14–20) the seed is replaced by the word, that is, the λόγος? Accordingly, three types of recipients on whom the λόγος is wasted are contrasted with other recipients for whom the λόγος will bear threefold fruit. On this view, the λόγοι are deeply implicated in the dilemmas of their dissemination before a manifest victory is scored. This is the parable's interpretation secretly given to the insiders in reference to the mystery of the kingdom of God. Not only is the λόγος to be "sown," namely readied for publication, but the failure of its proclamation signals an essential feature of the mystery of the kingdom. The focus of secrecy has thereby been shifted from the concealment of information to the conspicuous failure of proclamation.

The remaining parables, secretly conveyed to the insiders, invoke the dynamics of secrecy and revelation, of surplus and loss. But rather than strengthening secrecy commensurate with their placement in the esoteric genre, the parables and parabolic sayings rationalize hiddenness as premise for revelation. This finds paradigmatic expression in the commentary on the lamp saying (4:21): "For nothing is hidden, except to be revealed; nor has anything been secret, but that it should come to light" (4:22). Conveyed as secret wisdom to a few, this saying deconstructs the rationale for its own secret operation. The measure-for-measure saying (4:24b) promises surplus, and the saying on "having and not having" (4:25) reiterates surplus, while pointing up the reality of loss. Contextually, these sayings suggest that those who have inside knowledge (about concealing and revealing) will be privy to revelation (as the story unfolds), while those who fail to grasp the standards set by the parabolic interpretation can in the end incur total loss. Imparted as esoteric wisdom to a few, these parabolic sayings do not merely confirm the status of the insiders, provided they comprehend the rationale of hiddenness and revelation, but they also threaten the collapse of the insiders, in case they remain deaf to the parabolic interpretation. The two concluding seed parables play variations on the theme of hiddenness and revelation. The parable of the Growing Seed narrates the inevitable process of growth from seed to harvest (4:26–29), and the parable of the Mustard Seed emphasizes the sharp disjunction between the embryonic state and the fully grown plant (4:30–32). In each case, the seed's hiddenness in the ground has the objective of manifestly rising above the ground. In both parables the wisdom secretly conveyed to the insiders anticipates a final state of openness as opposed to hiddenness.

In exposing the mechanism of secrecy and revelation, and in entertaining the possibilities of surplus gain as well as total loss, the parabolic wisdom confided to the insiders relativizes its own confidentiality, unsettles the authority of its privileged recipients, and ruptures esoteric closure. The very parables that have gained admittance into the esoteric scenario contain the seeds of its destruction. In Mark's context, esoteric secrecy is in the process of being imploded from within the confines of the sayings genre.

The seeds of deconstruction sown in the esoteric scenario (4:10–34) blossom into full life in the remainder of the narrative Gospel. For far from reaffirming the prestige of the insiders, the narrative hastens their demise. I have elsewhere shown the mechanism of role reversal (Kelber 1979, passim; 1983, 124–29; 1985a, 37–40) whereby the outsider characteristics concerning lack of understanding and having eyes but not seeing and ears but not hearing (4:12) are applied to the insiders themselves (6:52; 8:17–18). As the plot quickens to its critical moment, it retrospectively enlightens the parabolic wisdom communicated to the Twelve as a matter of grave consequence. For that wisdom, in deconstructing its own secret operation, had strained toward releasing the mystery of the kingdom from its hermetic enclosure. In other words, the secrecy-revelation mechanism conveyed through parabolic wisdom had pointed beyond its own secret mode of communication toward epiphany in the unfolding story of Jesus' life and death. Unable to follow this broader vision of the kingdom, the Twelve became outsiders in and to its unfolding dramatization, mistook the transfiguration for epiphany while escaping Jesus' cross in fear and unbelief. In thus turning the insiders into outsiders, the narrative has completed the destruction of esoteric secrecy. The notion of a distinct group of insiders in possession of confidential information has been turned inside out. In this sense, the Gospel does not at all present itself as a patron of secrecy, but rather as an ardent demythologizer of the myth of esoteric secrecy.

Outside the esoteric scenario a different type of secrecy unfolds along a longer narrative route. For the purpose of clarifying both difference and affinity between the esoteric and this other sense of secrecy, we will have to rehearse the features of the latter once again. At Capernaum Jesus does not allow the demons to speak, "because they knew him" (1:34). After having healed a leper Jesus enjoins him not to speak to anyone, but to present himself to the priest; the man, however, disobeys and spreads the news freely (1:45). At a northern lakeside setting Jesus again instructs the demons not to make him known as they pay homage to him (3:11–12). On the other hand, the demon-possessed man whose name was Legion is encouraged by Jesus himself to publicize the news of his spectacular healing (5:19). But then again Jesus gives the order to keep his greatest deed, the raising of Jairus's daughter, under cover (5:43). His journey to the area around Tyre appears to be planned as a secret operation, and yet his presence among the Gentiles becomes public knowledge (7:24). While still in Gentile territory, he forbids the proclamation of the healing of a deaf-mute, but "the more he ordered them [not to speak], the more they proceeded to proclaim" (7:36).[1] Peter's so-called confession is immediately checked by Jesus' injunction to keep it secret (8:29–30). Following his appearance on the high mountain, Jesus orders the three witnesses not to disclose the information "until the Son of man should rise from the dead" (9:9). While traveling through Galilee he wishes to remain unrecognized because (γάρ) he taught the disciples about his impending deliverance into the hands of his adversaries (9:30–31).[2] Notably, there are no discernible injunctions in the passion narrative requiring characters to refrain from proclamation.

The above-mentioned secrets differ from esoteric secrecy in at least three ways. In the first place, these secrets placed along the narrative route do not specifically cover sayings and parables. They rather relate to the

---

1. With respect to secrecy, Mark 8:26 is ambiguous. On the one hand Jesus sends the man home, while on the other he orders him not to enter the village.

2. In Mark 10:48–49 it is not Jesus but the many who order Bartimaeus to be quiet. Moreover, the beggar's confession is made in the state of blindness. From the narrator's point of view the son of David confession of blind Bartimaeus may be as dubious as that made by the followers who hail Jesus as the inaugurator of "the kingdom of our father David" (11:10).

distinctive character of Jesus. The deeds of Jesus and his identity flowing from them are the issue more than his words. Because these secrets relate to the particular character of Jesus, I shall henceforth refer to them as *identity secrets*. Second, these identity secrets are not enjoined on a select group of people, but rather on different individuals at isolated intervals. Preservation and the formation of group identity hardly lie at the root of this secrecy mechanism. Third, and perhaps most importantly, the identity mechanism is remarkably lacking in consistency. It is anything but a doctrine systematically applied to the pre-passion narrative. Not only does Jesus enforce secrecy at irregular points in the narrative, but these identity secrets are also frequently leaked. Secrecy and leaking enter into a symbiotic relationship. The leaks contribute to the growing fame of Jesus, which in turn invokes the imposition of new secrecy. The identity secrets are of a kind that cannot really be kept. Far from eclipsing Jesus' identity, they exert pressure upon the narrative toward more disclosure. The objective of this type of secrecy is thus not to remain concealed but to enhance the momentum toward unconcealment.

It is in this basic urge toward revealing, finally, that the identity secrets and esoteric secrecy, as deconstructed by Mark, converge. Despite their stated differences, they have been joined to cooperate in shaping the narrative according to a secrecy-disclosure mechanism stated in Mark 4:22: "For nothing is hidden, except to be revealed; nor has anything been secret, but that it should come to light."

With this interpretation in mind, let us return to and review the most significant proposition of secrecy in Mark—namely, Wrede's so-called *Messiasgeheimnis*. As he saw it, the secret grew out of two contradictory notions concerning Jesus' identity. On one view, Jesus became the Messiah at resurrection, while on the other his messiahship was linked already with his earthly life. What Mark did was to uphold yet conceal the earthly messianic identity so as to bring the focus on his messianic epiphany at resurrection. His achievement, therefore, was to have struck a genuine compromise between the two conflicting viewpoints. The disciples' failure was also in keeping with this design, for their blindness in the preresurrectional period was the necessary condition for their gaining sight with resurrection (Wrede 1901, 107). Mark 9:9 played the key role in shaping Wrede's understanding that the narrative had been constructed from the vantage point of resurrection, perceived to be the moment of unveiling: "He [Jesus] charged them [Peter, James, and John] to tell no one what they had seen, until the Son of Man should have risen from the dead."

This statement of Jesus "is in fact the crucial idea, the underlying point of Mark's entire approach" (1901, 67).

The immediate question posed by this explanation concerns the absence of a resurrection-appearance story. Showing next to no interest in the narrative logic of 16:1–8, Wrede postulated a "lost ending of the Gospel" (1901, 164). But work since Wrede has confirmed that the "absence" of a resurrection story is by design, and not a freak of textual history (Lohmeyer 1967, 352–60; Perrin 1971b, 44–45; Magness 1986). Rather than seeking the key to the narrative in an allegedly lost ending, one has to face up to the question of why the risen Christ was not included in the plotted narrative. One must also wonder if indeed discipleship comports squarely with the pattern of concealing and revealing, as Wrede had suggested. For to assume that the truth had been concealed from the disciples in order to be revealed to them at resurrection is to miss the narrative logic of discipleship. In point of fact, the disciples did receive all the inside information, including the vitally important one pertaining to the mechanism of secrecy and revelation. But as they were unable to follow the operation of concealment and revealing, they came to play the role of outsiders, depriving themselves of epiphany. Wrede's interpretation of 9:9, finally, poses the question of whether the luminous Christ is deferred beyond narrative time so as to strengthen his epiphanic significance, or in order to refocus on a rather different epiphany inside narrative.

If it seems the better course not to align the resurrection with epiphany, one has to look for an alternate incident inside the narrative that qualifies as genuine unveiling. Given the nature of the identity secrets, one is directed toward a narrative moment where Jesus publicly and unconditionally declares his own identity. One single verse meets this requirement: Jesus' first passion-resurrection prediction (8:31), which is characterized as a word spoken openly (8:32; καὶ παρρησίᾳ τὸν λόγον ἐλάλει). The crucially important παρρησίᾳ, a *hapax legomenon* in the narrative, signals the denouement of the secrecy-disclosure mechanism. In the perspectives of the larger narrative, identity secrets alternate with injunctions to publicize, and leaks of secrecy with nonsecrecy, leaving Jesus' identity oddly unsettled and in need of clarification. In this broader context, identity secrets and their implied mechanism of secrecy-disclosure both enhance narrative tension and in the end relax it with Jesus' open confession as the crucified one. Identity secrets, therefore, are a narrative device aimed at scoring a dramatic, a theological point. The notable decline of identity secrets after 8:31,[3] the lack of identity secrets in the passion story, and the "absence" of a resurrection story all find their explanation in the narrative epiphany at crucifixion.

Thus far we have observed that Mark's narrative, traditionally associated with messianic secrecy and mysterious language, is at least as interested in disclosure as it is in secrecy. Esoteric secrecy is demythologized. For Mark, as for Irenaeus, both representatives of emergent orthodoxy, esoteric privileging of words and persons is not acceptable. The identity secrets help negotiate the narrative suspense surrounding Jesus' identity to the point of relief that comes with his one and only open proclamation. That the latter expresses Jesus' preferred identity is confirmed by the centurion, whose confession in the face of death carries the blessing of the narrator (15:39). At this point, then, the Gospel narrative would seem to be more concerned with the demystification and disclosure of secrecy than with its preservation.

There is yet another way in which the Gospel appears to reveal more than to conceal. If we place it in the larger setting of the communications triangle of narrator, text, and reader, marks of secrecy recede to a degree that imperils the very notion of secrecy.

16. READERS/HEARERS AS INSIDERS

While narrative undoubtedly originated in oral storytelling, the technology of writing enhanced control over larger portions of language. Scribality allowed writers to accumulate words, and more words, and to coordinate them into more complex configurations. As writers positioned themselves over larger and more circumspectly designed compositions, directing narrative strategies and presiding over narrative endings, they acquired a posture of knowing. The ancient Hebrew narrators and the Gospel authors, both among the pioneers of prose fiction in the Western tradition, helped enlarge this bold notion of knowing what only God was supposed to know.

---

3. Despite disclosure at 8:31, the information disclosed to the disciples is still concealed from the crowds at large. This is the significance of the secrecy surrounding the second prediction of suffering and rising (9:30–31). This is also the reason why the third prediction is strictly limited to the twelve (10:32–33). Despite revelation at 8:31 and a notable decline of identity secrets thereafter, the narrative seeks to sustain a posture of concealment.

Narrative omniscience, as we call it today, suggests the prerogative of the storyteller to reveal the inner states of individuals, to motivate changes, to delineate temporality, and to rationalize causalities. While the characters inside the narrative have only broken threads to grasp, the narrator from his or her perspective oversees the threads coming together in a more or less purposeful design. To this situation we must now add the reader/hearer (McKnight 1985; Fowler 1983; 1984; 1985a; 1985b), who is invited to share omniscience with the narrator, and who may come to know what the characters in the narrative know only partially, or belatedly, or not at all.[4]

In the case of Mark's Gospel, the narrator has placed the readers/hearers in a position of knowing. The very first verse (in many textual versions) registers the "primacy effect" (Perry 1979, 35–64, 311–61; Rimmon-Kenan 1983, 120), conditioning readers from the outset to the protagonist's identity as the Son of God. The subsequent narrative induces them to explicate and modify this initial impression, and in the end to comply with an interpreted version of it. To some extent the readers'/hearers' journey resembles that of the disciples, the initial insiders in the narrative, who were appointed to follow Jesus in order to have their misconceptions about him overturned. Yet the readers/hearers enjoy a distinct advantage. While the disciples participate only in certain parts of the narrative, the readers/hearers get the full benefit of it. Beginning with the primacy effect they are led down the narrative path all the way to the curiously abrupt ending. The disciples are not privy to the primacy effect or to John's appearance; they are not even present at Jesus' inaugural proclamation (1:14–15). For them the inaugural proclamation is constituted by the esoteric communication of the mystery of the kingdom (4:10–34). But even in the case of esoteric secrecy, the disciples are outdistanced by the readers/hearers. While the disciples receive the inside information concerning the kingdom's mystery and the fate of the outsiders, the readers/hearers receive this same information plus the subsequent enlightenment about the true identity of the

---

4. To be sure, the concept of narrative omniscience has lost much of its usefulness for contemporary hermeneutics. We know that all narrative has properties not directly under the control of the narrator. Inevitably there are aspects, meanings, and connections that hide themselves from even the most scrupulous and self-conscious narrator. But the concept can still serve the purpose of formulating the difference in knowledge and perspective between the readers/hearers on one side and the characters in the story on the other.

outsiders. The readers/hearers are even admitted to the epiphany on the cross, the very scene from which the disciples had excluded themselves. In thus observing not only what the disciples could observe but also what had lain outside their reach, the readers/hearers progressively take on the role reserved for the disciples. This promotes the readers/hearers, together with the elusive narrator, to the status of the new insiders.

What must be borne in mind is that the readers/hearers as insiders have not become accomplices to esoteric secrecy. To be sure, to the extent that they are privileged to learn from the mistakes made by the disciples, they benefit from their exclusion to the outside. What the readers/hearers can learn in the process is that esoteric secrecy has been dismantled and that identity secrets pressure toward epiphany. These are narrative experiences that discourage membership in an esoteric brotherhood. Up to a point everyone who reads (or hears) the Gospel is invited to follow and to comprehend.

Biblical scholarship, which has barely begun to explore the narrative world of the Gospels, remains principally attracted to coherence, proportionality, and lucidity. Yet narrative does not so inevitably carry with it the view that existence is lived as an orderly and meaningful continuum. One need not be a partisan of the latest deconstructionist eccentricities to observe that narrative variously interferes with its own project. In Mark's case, narrative reveils what it was most seriously determined to reveal, leaving at its core something irreducible, a void or a mystery.

Jesus' esoteric proclamation makes the Twelve (and a few chosen ones) the privileged recipients of confidential information (4:10–32). This information pertains to the mystery of the kingdom of God, which was given (4:11: δέδοται) in parables (4:2, 10) and summed up in the master parable. Mystery, parable, and kingdom are thereby correlated. From this one may reasonably infer that the parables, epitomized by the master parable, serve as carriers of the mystery of the kingdom. The parabolic mystery of God's kingdom is at the heart of the esoteric proclamation. In addition, the insiders learn that to outsiders "everything occurs in parables" (4:11). The readers/hearers, moreover, are told that to the disciples all parabolic discourse will be explained (4:33–34). From this, and from Jesus' own remark (4:13), one may again draw the conclusion that the revised version of the master parable (4:14-20) constitutes interpretation for the insiders. What is, however, striking about this interpretation is its parabolic character. It narrates a story about differing responses to the λόγος, while withholding explanation of its nexus with the kingdom. *Le travail de l'imagination* (Ricoeur 1982) is left to the insiders, be they the disciples or the readers. Designed to interpret the master parable, its interpretation acts rather like a parable itself, withholding at least as much as it makes known. What is more, further parables are added to the parabolic interpretation (4:21–32). Presumably, they function as commentaries on the mystery that was proclaimed by way of parable in the first place. There is, of course, a rationale for explicating parable via parables. If mystery is at the heart of the proclamation, parable is its ideal mode of discourse, and parable naturally asks for more parables.

17. Insiders as Outsiders

We have arrived here at a point in the narrative where the esoteric proclamation exposes an intractability at its core. Precisely at the juncture where the narrative labors valiantly to overcome secrecy and to reveal the inside information, little is revealed beyond the promise of future revelation. For the time being the insiders are left with mystery and more parables. If it be said that to the outsiders "everything occurs in parables," it is only fair to note that the interpretation conveyed to the insiders likewise occurs in parables. Now, but only now, may we endorse Kermode's astute observation that "being an insider is only a more elaborate way of being kept outside" (1979, 27).

Despite the esoteric revealing and reveiling, the narrative continues to strive toward full disclosure. An obvious moment of unveiling comes when Jesus makes his nonparabolic confession ἐν παρρησίᾳ (Bishop 1986). Both the disciples and the readers/hearers are privy to his self-disclosure as the suffering, rising Son of Man (8:31). Both types of insiders are now groomed to anticipate the acute and fateful moment of epiphany. As for the disciples, they deprive themselves of presence at the crucifixion. It is thus left to the readers/hearers to act out their role as new insiders and to witness revelation. They are by no means unprepared for much that is to come. But they are not prepared for everything! Having had full access to the narrative information, they cannot be surprised to learn that Jesus is sentenced as blasphemer by the guardians of religion (14:64), and crucified on the charge of having made himself "king of the Jews" (15:2, 26). What does, however, come as terrifying news to us, the readers/hearers, is that Jesus dies forsaken by the God whom he had called his father (14:36; 15:34). For it is one thing to die a brutal death at the hands of the authorities, but quite a different matter to suffer the absence of God. The former had been foretold, but the latter had not. What constitutes a no less shocking revelation is the centurion's confession of Jesus' sonship of God in view of death in god-forsakenness. For it is one thing to have death reversed by the epiphany of resurrection, but quite a different matter to locate epiphany at the point of absence. The former had been foretold, but the latter had not. What finally is disclosed at the peak of a laborious narrative buildup is that revelation is not transparent. For what is revealed is not epiphany as reversal of death, but epiphany as the darkness of God's absence. The more the narrative struggles to overcome secrecy and to make disclosure, the more it reveils itself in parabolic mystery.

We, the new insiders, it was noted, have a natural advantage over the disciples, the narrative's insiders. The narrative mechanism, however, of concealing, revealing, and reveiling plays a role in showing us the limited hold we have on understanding. Granted that we are privileged witnesses of the epiphany, do we comprehend? Can one comprehend? But if one cannot understand, do we really have a "natural" advantage over the disciples?

In view of parabolic mystery at the peak of the narrative, the role reversal of the disciples from insiders to outsiders should have a chilling effect on us, the new insiders. In thinking that we are inside the narrative, we are perpetually reminded of what happens to insiders. This will not let us stay inside for long, if at all. And if we think we are inside, it is a sure sign that we are already outside.

4

In the Beginning Were the Words: The Apotheosis and Narrative Displacement of the Logos

Thematizing the philosophical/theological issue of a metaphysics of Presence, the essay brings the Fourth Gospel, viewed from the angle of orality-scribality studies, into conversation with the thought of Jacques Derrida. What justifies the conversation is a single tenet that the media approach and anti-metaphysical philosophy have in common: la voix *and* l'écriture—*although each side has developed the issues entailed in the dichotomy in very different directions. The essay does not intend to apply Derridean philosophy to the Fourth Gospel. It is meant to be a conversation between the Gospel and the philosopher. Rather than applying straightforward Derridean philosophy to the Fourth Gospel, in the sense of practicing a deconstructive reading, the essay offers a study of the Gospel refracted through deconstructive philosophy. On Derrida's terms, the* arche-Logos, *installed into privileged position as underived origin, signifies the quintessential logocentric gesture, thereby enacting precisely what the philosopher feared most about logocentrism: the consummation of desire and discourse, and the reduction of language and world to a totalizing reference point. A second feature denounced by Derrida that appears to have been dramatized in the Gospel is a metaphysics of Presence. In Johannine studies, both the Gospel's massive sayings tradition and the theme of incarnation have tempted interpreters to espouse presence, a tendency epitomized by the programmatic thesis that the* "praesentia Christi *is the centre of his [John's] proclamation" (Käsemann 1968, 15).*

In discussing the operation of aphorisms and parables, the first part of this essay postulates the impossibility of an arche-Logos *in oral discourse. Speech shows no interest in reducing the plural* λόγοι *to the single, imperial* Λόγος. *Plurality not protology, diversity not logocentric authority characterizes oral discourse. The second part makes a case for the presenting power of spoken discourse. Aphorisms and parables function efficaciously,* ad bonam et ad malam partem, *when oralized in actu and actualized in the living voice. This is a claim, however, that is strenuously disputed by Derrida. While fully recognizing that delays, hesitations, interpretive hurdles, and misunderstandings are intrinsic to oral discourse, especially to parabolic speech, the case is made here for a differentiated phenomenology of speech versus writing. The third part examines the clustering of sayings and parables in the* Gospel of Thomas *and the development of dialogues in the* Apocryphon of James. *In media terms both genres exhibit a longing for the present efficaciousness of word power, yet both disclose complications that inhibit the presence of the Word. The fourth part examines the massive sayings collection in the Fourth Gospel with a focus on the Farewell Speech. While John's sayings material is not directly derived from the* Gospel of Thomas *or the* Apocryphon of James, *there are indications that the Fourth Gospel is a beneficiary from sayings collections that extended over a wide spread in the tradition.*

The fifth part focuses on the role of the Johannine sayings in the context of the Gospel's narrative, the canonically privileged genre. Inscribed in this scribally composed space, the sayings are subordinated to a narrative logic that overrides their generic identity and function in the tradition. Here the piece agrees with Derrida's repudiation of a metaphysics of Presence. The sixth part suggests that the elevation of the singular Λόγος is not patterned after the ancient Wisdom myth, as is widely assumed, but a product of the Gospel's demonstrable tendency to move from the plurality of the λόγοι to singular Λόγος. This reduction of the λόγοι to the Λόγος is at once a concession to the potency of oral discourse and a betrayal of oral pluralism. Part 6 reflects on the Gospel's decentering of the Λόγος. In dislodging the Λόγος John administers the deconstruction of its own onto-theological origin. The Λόγος incarnated himself only to bring about a return to the origin and to logocentric essentials. In the end, it is suggested that this double gesture of antimetaphysical deconstructionism and metaphysical positivism circumscribes a logocentric circle which the Western philosophical/theological tradition has ceaselessly sought to construct and from which it has ceaselessly sought to liberate itself.

> Could Ong and Derrrida meet without hostility?
> —Moore, *Literary Criticism and the Gospels*

> We cannot utter a single deconstructive proposition which has not already slipped into the form, the logic, and the implicit postulations of precisely what it seeks to contest.

—Derrida, "Structure, Sign, and Play in the Discourse of the Human
Sciences"

To make enigmatic what one thinks one understands by the words "proximity," "immediacy," "presence" … is my final intention in this book.
—Derrida, *Of Grammatology*

Sound, bound to the present time by the fact that it exists only at the
instant when it is going out of existence, advertises presentness.
—Ong, *The Presence of the Word*

18. The Equiprimordiality of Sayings

The saying (ὁ λόγος) and the parable (ἡ παραβολή) constituted the two
formal units of Jesus' proclamation. Both were initiated orally and functioned as oral operations, and both were meant to function only secondarily as literary compositions and in literary contexts. Together they
furnished the informational and interpretational paradigms for remembrance and proclamation of the early Jesus tradition.

Speaking in sayings, whether they were called *meshalim* or λόγοι,
chriae or *sententiae*, was a proven way of managing information in antiquity. Teachers, philosophers, prophets, and scientists were accustomed to
handling knowledge in aphoristic fashion. In Jewish culture the book of
Proverbs exhibits collections of Wisdom sayings, many of which were formally designed to function independently. Fragments of Heraclitus's only
surviving work, *Peri Physeon*, consisted to a large extent of dark, riddling
sayings. Hippocrates, a founding personality of scientific medicine, left the
summation of his work in more than four hundred maxims. Brevity, rhythmic patterning, and focal intensity were characteristic aspects of ancient
sayings, including those of the Jesus tradition. All three attributes—a distinct topicality, a rhetorically impressive style, and a sharp focus—were
requirements of oral composition, which served to enhance their effectiveness vis-à-vis listeners. In short, the production of sayings was closely
attuned to the sensibilities of their hearing recipients.

The aphorism is a constricting form with its scope defined and its
boundaries drawn, and a commitment to the aphoristic genre imposed
artistic and ideological constraints upon the speaker. Formal constraints,
however, do not have to be entirely restrictive. They could also be exploited
as a source of inspiration. An effective operation of sayings, therefore,

would not be exhausted in rhetorically skilled performances, but it would also depend on using the genre to its full potential. The latter is well documented by the rich display of diverse types of sayings in the Synoptic tradition: proverbial sayings, subversive sayings, Wisdom sayings, prophetic sayings, apocalyptic sayings, ethical sayings, curses, beatitudes, and many more. Within the limitations set by the genre, diversity was desirable in order to produce maximal rhetorical effects.

Parabolic proclamation took the form of short stories, a prime instrument in oral teaching. Brevity and patternings of various kinds, a hallmark of Jesus' parables, must once again be viewed as a concession to listeners. Structurally, the parabolic repertoire of the Synoptic tradition displays considerable diversity, ranging from the ministory about the fig tree all the way to the dramatically choreographed Prodigal Son story, which divides into two separate but intertwining segments, the younger son's journey and the older son's confrontation with his father. Thematically as well, the Synoptic parables cover a broad range of experiences, introducing the mystery of hiddenness and revelation, exposing the cruelty of the human arrangement, and narrating the reversal of expectations and priorities. Like the sayings genre, the parable presented itself as a rhetorical instrument that depended for its effectiveness on the parabolist's skills to maximize its generic potentials. In keeping with oral proprieties, Jesus' parables stayed close to the human lifeworld. Up to a point hearers could recognize themselves in these stories. But in the course of a parabolic rendering the narrative realism frequently pursued a course of its own, offering, however subtly, something of a counterpoint to the social experience of the audience (Crossan 1973; Ricoeur 1975; Funk 1966, 124–222; Kelber 1983, 57–64). As the parabolic logic intruded upon the life of the hearers, disclosing a gap between narrative and social reality, the hearers found themselves at odds with the story world. Although deceptively simple, many parables did not simply reecho the world of their listeners. Rather, in telling these stories the parabolist invited audiences to come to terms with the parabolically fictionalized world and to reconsider their own world from the perspective of the storied world. Parables, in other words, were rarely, if ever, self-explanatory. They challenged hearers to examine their own constructions of the world in light of the parabolic logic, and vice versa. "He who has ears to hear, let him hear." This formula, placed at the end of a number of parables in the tradition, discloses their open-endedness toward the audience. Their real purpose lay not in themselves as finished stories but in their ability to engage hearers. Parables were not, therefore,

composed chiefly to solve the problems of remembering, storage, or retention, but rather to provoke hearers' imagination to complete the processes
begun in their storied worlds.

What typified the rendition of sayings and parables was their disposition to function as speech acts. They were not meant to be grasped as
isolated pieces, least of all as aesthetic objects. Aphoristic and parabolic
communication took place in a cultural biosphere shared by speaker and
hearers alike. It was a contextual setting that functioned as an explanatory
and interpretive matrix allowing saying and parable to plug into traditional
associations of ideas and to link up with rich and complex fields of reference. It does not mean that an oral rendition of a parable required other
parables or sayings, let alone a narrative text, as aids in interpretation. Just
as in impressionist art each picture seeks a complete encounter with viewers to achieve a single impression on them, so also did each rendition of
a saying or parable constitute a discrete utterance that was empowered by
its own logic and consistency. Each was a world-deconstructing and/or
world-constructing event, or at least the possibility thereof.

The parables' embedment in social context has important implications
for oral hermeneutics. When Jesus, the aphoristic, parabolic teacher, narrated a story at one place, and then proceeded to retell it, with modifications, at a different place, he was not in this second instance rendering
a variant of the so-called original. He was rather in both instances presenting an authentic version of the story. To Albert Lord goes the honor
of having awakened us to the fact that the epic poet never operates with
concepts such as *Urtext* or *Urwort*:

> The truth of the matter is that our own concept of "the original," of "the
> song," simply makes no sense in oral tradition. To us it seems so basic,
> so logical, since we are brought up in a society in which writing has fixed
> the norm of a stable first creation in art, that we feel there must be an
> "original" for everything. The first singing in oral tradition does not
> coincide with this concept of the "original." (Lord 1960, 101)

Even if it were possible to collect and compare all oral renditions of, let us
say, a parable, there would be no rational path leading down an evolutionary ladder to "the original version." And even if it were possible to extract
from a plurality of parabolic speech acts certain features common to all,
we would have succeeded only in creating a fictional construct. Considerations of this kind invalidate all methods and efforts that still seek to attain

the *ipsissima verba* or *ipsissima structura* of the proclamation of Jesus. Not only is this search fraught with virtually insurmountable technical difficulties, but it is, more importantly, predicated on the notion of the "one original" word, a concept nonexistent in orality. There is a sense in orality in which each performance is "an original," if not "the original." While we are inclined to search for the one "original," oral discourse deals with a plurality of "originals," and hence not at all with the single "original." Our unceasing search for the "original" message of Jesus indicates how alien and virtually inaccessible oral hermeneutics is to our textually informed consciousness. To encounter a mind receptive to the oral concept of a plurality of "originals," one has to turn to the philosophy of Heidegger, who reinvented the notion of the *Gleichursprünglichkeit*: "The phenomenon of the *equiprimordiality* of constitutive items has often been disregarded in ontology, because of a methodologically unrestrained tendency to derive everything and anything from some single 'primal ground'" (Heidegger 1962, 170).

If we are to grasp the linguistic reality of Jesus' proclamation, we may be well advised to ponder Heidegger's idea of the *Gleichursprünglichkeit* of the phenomena. Every word spoken by Jesus was equiprimordial with every other one. A thrice-proclaimed rendition of an aphorism, for example, did not yield the one "original" and two versions thereof, but rather three equiprimordial proclamations. Writing alone facilitated the possibilities to differentiate between the primary text and secondary versions.

Philosophically, the theses of Lord and Heidegger gain significance in view of Derrida's critique of the dichotomy of orality versus textuality. For it is the latter's conviction that the dualistic premise of speech versus writing, as that of all philosophical dualisms, gave rise to the problematic subordination of writing to the plentitude of speech summed up in the primordiality of the Λόγος. Inevitably, he insists, the orality-textuality dichotomy privileges the absolute Λόγος, which the Western tradition claimed to have identified (Derrrida 1976, 71). It must be pointed out, however, that oral discourse, when scrutinized from orality-literacy perspectives, discloses an interest in the enactment of λόγοι and more λόγοι, and not in their reduction to the single Λόγος. Orality does not derive itself from an *Urwort*, nor does it justify its λόγοι in relation to an *arche-Logos*. At least in this one respect, Jesus the oral performer did not operate in a logocentric manner. Indeed, what characterizes the world of oral discourse is plurality not protology, and diversity not logocentric centrality. In the beginning were the words.

19. *Arche-Logos* and *Arche*-Writing

Once Jesus, the charismatic speaker of sayings and parables, was removed by violence, how did the tradition handle his proclamation? Three modes of operation are discernible, one oral and two written: The oral-prophetic reactivation of aphorisms and parabolic stories, their clustering into sayings collections and sayings Gospels, and their inscription into narrative Gospels. Of these three procedures only the third one was acceptable to canonical Christianity.

In typical prophetic fashion early Christian speakers proclaimed sayings and parables in the name and on the authority of the one they represented (Beare 1967; Hill 1979; Boring 1982). A saying that occurs with some frequency in the tradition furnishes the rationale and legitimation for this prophetic speech function: "He who hears you [Jesus' successors] hears me [Jesus], and he who rejects you rejects me, and he who rejects me rejects him who sent me" (Luke 10:16 // Matt 10:40; cf. John 13:20; Ignatius *Eph.* 6.1; *Did.* 11.4). It is difficult to define with christological precision the authorial identity of this Jesus who manifested himself in the words spoken by his followers. Was he the preresurrectional Jesus, the risen Lord, or the returning Son of Man? Suffice it to say that he continued to function in the oral biosphere and to address hearers as a speaking authority. His *viva vox* was reenacted and his presence upheld through the vehicle of his prophetic successors. In short, the oral-prophetic speech phenomenon was a bold experiment to extend the presenting power of Jesus and his proclamation despite his absence as an earthly figure.

Apart from conjuring the authorial presence of the speaker, oral-prophetic proclamation also invested spoken words with presenting power. In John's narrative, for example, Peter acclaims Jesus as the one who holds in his possession "words of eternal life" (John 6:68: ῥήματα ζωῆς αἰωνίου ἔχεις). Words have it within their power to deliver life. Throughout the Gospel words are perceived or dramatized as exercising a dual authority: they engender life (John 5:24) and provoke strife (John 10:19); they save people from death (John 5:51–52) and effect judgment (John 12:48). Owing to their efficacious power *ad malam et ad bonam partem*, the sayings can be disregarded only with the gravest of consequences.

This perception of a dual efficaciousness of words is rooted in the oral operation of language. Speech leaves no visible traces; it is not imputable to external verification. "One cannot *analyze* oral discourse as discourse, for in order for analysis to work, it must have an object that can be dismantled and reassembled" (Tyler 1987, 104). To regard speech as knowable in terms strictly of its own linguistic self is a notion that has no reality in oral discourse. For this reason oral utterance does not exist in transauthorial and transcommunal objectivity. "The [spoken] word cannot be seen, cannot be handed about, cannot be 'broken' and reassembled" (Ong 1967b, 323). This nonobjectifiable nature of speech further suggests that spoken words are not knowable as signs divisible into signifiers and signified. The Platonic bipolarity between the sensible versus the intelligible, which typifies the character of signs, is unworkable as far as oral discourse is concerned, if only because speech does not partake in the tangibility of writing. Our sense of the disjunction between signifier and signified "is created by writing" (Tyler 1987, 20, 208). What tends to be separated in Western metaphysics into the phenomenal versus the invisibly "real" appears to exist in oral discourse as unified actuality. Because medium and referent, form and content, seem to coincide, sounded words and their subject matter are assumed to be partaking in the same level of reality. Whereas written words are visualized in space, oral words are sound, and sounded language occurs only at the moment of its oral manifestation. Speech is exclusively a present reality; it cannot exist in the past. When one encounters, therefore, in John's Gospel the notion of the authorial presence and present efficaciousness of words, one has to do with a perception of language rooted in oral sensibilities.

It is precisely this concept of the presence of the Word that has incurred Derrida's implacable vote of censure. From his perspective, full presence in terms of essence, existence, substance, consciousness, and subject is the leading motif of a hallucinatory liturgy chanted through the ages by Western philosophy, theology, anthropology, and linguistics. Built into all so-called presences, including the self-presence in and of speech, Derrida proposes, was always already differentiality. Given this differential dynamic, language, both oral and written, will not be entirely present to us, and we to it. The presence of the so-called living speech is "a central presence which has never been itself, has always already been exiled from itself into its own substitute" (Derrida 1978, 280). There is separation not only of speaker from speech, but also within the open space of speech itself. Deferment and differentiation, the conditions of writing, are thus inherent in oral discourse already. In the beginning was *arche*-writing, which is in truth "the loss of ... a self-presence which has never been given but only dreamed of and always already split, repeated, incapable of appearing to itself except in its own disappearance" (Derrida 1976, 112).

There is no disguising the fact that Derrida squarely confronts us with onto-theological strategies to bridge gaps and insinuate presence. Few have explored more keenly the high risks of language, exposing us to its dangers, deceptions, and displacements. This one must grant Derrida, as it must also be stated that his concept of *arche*-writing is bafflingly paradoxical when measured against his own intellectual principles. For a program that is built on the premise that the logocentric striving after *arche* is off limits in the space of *différance* would appear to have forfeited the right to ennoble *arche* once again and to insert it back into the philosophical discourse. No matter how skillfully Derrida assimilates *arche* to differentiality, *arche* and *différance* mix as water does with fire. To replace the *arche-Logos* with *arche*-writing is to exchange one logocentric principle for another. Heidegger's observation is to the point: "The reversal of a metaphysical statement remains a metaphysical statement" (1977, 208). Here Derrida's philosophy appears spread-eagled on metaphysics.

The specific juxtaposition of *arche* with writing, moreover, renders the object of Derrida's logocentric investment unmistakably clear. *Écriture*, in all its philosophical and linguistic implications, is metaphysically privileged. This has led some observers to comment on the ostensibly text-bound quality of Derrida's work, and others to charge him with suspicion vis-à-vis speech (Ong 1982, 165–70; Handelmann 1982, 163–78; Tyler 1987, 35–59). Indeed, Derrida has acknowledged little familiarity with the growing body of scholarship that has concerned itself with matters of oral composition and performance, discourse and dialogue, and the manifoldly tangled interactions of speech and writing. To think of speech primarily as a differential system carrying the traces of absent meanings does smack of a projection of typographic sensibilities.

Undeniably, speech already harbors alienating features. "Of course it can be maintained that even spoken words are pretenses too, in the sense that they are out of contact with the actuality they represent" (Ong 1967b, 137). Metaphoricity and metonymy are a case in point, for both proceed by way of indirection. Each constitutes a figure of speech that stands for something other than itself. Many of the Synoptic and Johannine sayings carry metaphorical implications, confirming the observation that "the oral mind is preeminently metaphorical" (Maxwell 1983, 27). Jesus' parables likewise are by definition metaphorical stories, assuming a linguistic posture whereby meaning is detached from words. Foley, moreover, has impressively described the hyperallusive, metonymic hermeneutics of oral poetics whereby speech comes to meaningful fruition not on its own terms but rather in the informing context of symbolic fields of reference (1987a; 1987b). Still, to think of the oral operation of metaphor and metonymy primarily as language of dispersion or disruption implies a lack of sensitivity to the aesthetics of oral hermeneutics. By articulating an apparent tension between two separate entities, metaphor "causes a new, hitherto unnoticed, relation of meaning to spring up between the terms that previous systems of classification had ignored or not allowed" (Ricoeur 1976b, 51). Nor will *différance* get us to the heart of the oral functioning of metonymy, for the manner in which sayings and parables draw meaning from their cultural biosphere amounts to their "metonymic fertilization" (Foley 1987b, 195) more than to deferment of meaning. In the absence of visual signifiers and spatialized verbalization, figures of indirection such as metaphor and metonymy can well work toward the presence of meaning. "Hearing engages and enforces the present as no other sense can" (Ong 1967b, 298). Perhaps more than anything else it is the commonality of space and time shared by speaker and hearers alike that effects the present transaction of oral performance in the context of collective memories.

20. THE CLUSTERING MANAGEMENT AND THE DIALOGUE GENRE: THE ISSUE OF PRESENCE

The clustering of sayings and parables was a second mode of managing the legacy of Jesus. The juxtaposition of these materials resulted in a variety of formations (Crossan 1983). Two sayings could combine into aphoristic compounds; three or more sayings and parables could coalesce into speech complexes. In the tradition this clustering management of knowledge developed in two directions. On the one hand, compounds and speech complexes, together with individual aphorisms and parables, gained entry into narrative Gospels. Such is the case, for example, with the canonical Gospels, which provided a narrative habitat for the sayings materials. On the other hand, the clustering processes of sayings and parables provided the condition for their own intrinsic genre. Such is the case, for example, with the sayings Gospel of *Thomas*. A third option, unlike the sayings Gospel and the narrative gospel, was the dialogue genre as exemplified by the *Apocryphon of James*. While alluding to some canonical sayings, it freely developed dialogues between Jesus and two disciples into a genre in its own right (Robinson 1970, 114–16; 1982c, 29–36).

What one observes in the case of the *Gospel of Thomas* is a genre at once produced by the technology of writing and yet faithful to oral interests and sensibilities. In the terminology of media studies, it constitutes an interface, bordering both on orality and textuality, and seeking a rapprochement with both.

The oral posture of the *Gospel of Thomas* manifests itself in the nature of its component parts. The genre is composed of sayings and parables (and some sayings embedded in short dialogues). This single-minded commitment to the two basic units of Jesus' language betrays an interest in preserving and/or continuing the authentic forms of his proclamation. The impression of an oral scenario is further strengthened by the identity of the speaker of these 114 sayings and parables. He is introduced as the "living Jesus." Whatever the precise christological identity implied in this designation, this "living Jesus" is clearly not meant to be an authority of the past. Not unlike Jesus the oral proclaimer himself or the orally represented Jesus of prophetic speech, the speaker in the *Gospel of Thomas* intends to function as a present authority addressing a group of male and female disciples via aphoristic and parabolic speech. What lends additional support to his oral authority is the virtual absence of a narrative syntax. Sayings and parables are juxtaposed without significant narrative connectives, which brings the bulk of the *Gospel of Thomas* into close affinity with the ancient genre of list (Kenner 1994; White 1980, 9–15; Goody 1977, 74–111; J. Smith 1982). The logic of an aggregated, additive rhetoric as over against an organization of data into linear sequentiality may be viewed as "the oral equivalent of plot" (Frawley 1987, 48–56; Ong 1967b, 84; 1982, 36–39). The summoning of the "living Jesus" and the absence of a comprehensive narrative development are intimately connected features. Writing itself puts everything into the past, and writing a narrative enhances its retrospective orientation. Unimpeded by narrative's spatiotemporal framework and in control of the discrete items of his proclamation, the "living Jesus" of the *Gospel of Thomas* seeks to elude entrapment in the past. That this is, negatively speaking, the hermeneutical strategy of the sayings Gospel is all the more likely since none of the 114 sayings and parables reflects on the religious significance of the speaker's death. Indeed, if the *Gospel of Thomas* is meant to uphold the speaking authority of the "living Jesus" and to assure life through his words, why dwell on his absence in the wake of death?

The storage of sayings and parables, the promotion of the "living Jesus," the pervasive strategy of λόγοι coordination, and the absence both of a comprehensive narrative framework and a Christology of the cross all converge in the genre's strategic design to extend the metaphysics of oral presence.

On the other hand, the *Gospel of Thomas* is unthinkable without the technology of writing. While the two basic speech forms conform to Jesus' own rhetoric, the juxtaposition of 114 separate units is unlike oral discourse. "The dominance of additivity" (Frawley 1987, 49), however much it may fall short of textuality's fuller potentials, is different from and even contrary to speech. One does not speak in lists. The clustering of like items is entirely the achievement of writing. Built into the text of the *Gospel of Thomas* is an awareness of speaking *and* writing as contributing factors to the formation of the Gospel. This is evident from the introduction, which concedes that "the secret words which the living Jesus *spoke*" were those that "Didymos Judas Thomas *wrote*" (emphasis added). But once the "secret words" spoken by the "living Jesus" were transcribed and consigned to papyrus, can they still exercise the undiminished authority of the "living Jesus"? Writing, we note, is likely to problematize one of orality's most cherished and precarious values: the presenting power of speech. As far as genre is concerned, the lack of organizational patterns in the bulk of *Gospel of Thomas*, we saw, suggested the ancient genre of list. But whereas lists have neither a beginning nor an ending, the *Gospel of Thomas* is furnished with a formal introduction, which refers to the genre in terms of "the secret words," and a formal conclusion, which sums up the 114 items as *The Gospel according to Thomas*. By its own definition, therefore, the *Gospel of Thomas* wishes to be understood as a Gospel, in all probability a sayings Gospel, and not merely as a list. The writer has imposed a single defining idea upon the whole, subordinating oral discreteness and randomness to the encompassing designation of Gospel. In principle, all sayings and parables are now subjected to this central generic focus.

Notably, the first saying issues a programmatic call, which is meant to apply to all subsequent sayings: "Whoever finds the explanation of these sayings, will not taste death" (*Gos. Thom.* 1). Redemption is thus no longer allied with oral proclamation per se, but with its interpretation. All sayings and parables are thereby united in their susceptibility to interpretation. To be sure, interpretation undoubtedly is an issue already in oral discourse as it most certainly is in the scribal medium. But the shift from the domain of auditory λόγοι to visually accessible λόγοι on papyrus prompts temporal delays, hesitations, and psychological distances that are advantageous for interpretive reflection. Interpretation, while rarely ever absent from oral performance, can become a conscious, hermeneutical activity as a result of writing. In the case of the *Gospel of Thomas*, both the oral aspirations of presence and the list's functional needs for preservation are overridden by the hermeneutical task of interpretation.

The amassment of aphorisms and parabolic stories, consciousness of their written fixation, an effort to overcome the appearance of oral randomness, as well as a programmatic interest in interpretation are all features that underscore the textual nature and self-consciousness of the *Gospel of Thomas*

Whereas the *Gospel of Thomas* presents aphoristic and parabolic sayings in discrete juxtaposition (and the sayings Gospel Q arranged its content in thematically organized speech units), the *Apocryphon of James* narrates Jesus' discourses addressed to select disciples, James and Peter. In raising questions and making comments the two engage Jesus in dialogues. The text makes reference to some canonical Jesus sayings, but it does not, in the manner of *Gospel of Thomas*, present an aggregation of discrete sayings and parables. The *Apocryphon of James* cannot therefore be said to constitute a further extension of the clustering process, although it has been argued that the text has been constructed from a composition of initially discrete sayings (Cameron 1984). Nor can the *Apocryphon of James* be viewed along the line of the narrative genre. Generically, it constitutes a dialogue genre, standing somewhere between the sayings Gospel and the narrative Gospel.

The text relates the appearance of the "Savior" to the twelve disciples after an absence of 550 days following his resurrection and prior to his ascension. The identity of the Savior will be that of the risen Lord, not unlike that of the "living Jesus" in the *Gospel of Thomas*. He encounters the disciples as they indulge in remembrances of a time past when he had spoken to each of them what they had subsequently committed to writing. This time the Savior takes Peter and James aside in order to enlighten them, inter alia, about the nature of "fullness" (salvation), the kingdom of God, life, suffering, death, cross, Satan, persecutions, about the Savior's and the disciples' preresurrectional and postresurrectional status, and other topics. On this last issue he announces:

> Henceforth, waking or sleeping, remember that you have seen the Son of Man, and spoken with him, and listened to him. Woe to those who have seen the Son of Man; blessed will they be who have not seen the Man, and they who have not consorted with him, and they who have not

spoken with him, and they who have not listened to anything from him: yours is life! (3.10–25)

At first I spoke to you in parables and you did not understand; now I speak to you openly, and you (still) do not perceive. (7.1–10)

These citations suggest a "contrast between two levels of understanding" (Robinson 1970, 115), a distinction synchronized with parabolic and open speech. It is this two-level differentiation that constitutes a major hermeneutical key to *Apocryphon of James*. The dichotomy of hiddenness versus openness explains the document's lack of interest in the preresurrectional speech of Jesus because it was veiled in parabolic obscurity, while it also defines the Savior's postresurrectional communication to the highly select group of disciples as transparent speech. On the logic of this genre, the Lord's pre-Easter words have remained hidden and/or misunderstood to such a degree that those who saw and heard the earthly Jesus are cursed, while those who did not see and heard him are blessed. The dialogues in *Apocryphon of James* are thereby characterized as postresurrectional, revelatory speech whose function it is to bring light into the darkness of a concealed or misconceived past.

From media perspectives, the *Apocryphon of James*, not unlike the *Gospel of Thomas*, carries within itself the tension between oral and scribal communication. Insofar as the text has the risen Jesus convey revelation to the two privileged disciples, it betrays a longing for present authority and the efficaciousness of word power. It is a longing that is reinforced by the virtual absence of a narrative syntax, thus keeping the Savior from being captured in the past. The reason, one may suspect, is that the language of the preresurrectional Jesus was considered veiled and obscure, hence of no lasting significance in its past mode of articulation. The opening lines of *Apocryphon of James*, moreover, describe "a situation in which scribal activity has taken place" (Cameron 1984, 129). One learns of secret books, one written in Hebrew letters, and the disciples themselves are reported to have engaged in composing books. It is also noteworthy that the Savior overrules the disciples' objection to cross and death: "Truly I say to you, none will be saved unless they believe in my cross. But those who have believed in my cross, theirs is the kingdom of God" (6.2–7).

It seems that the death of the living Jesus rather than the word power of his sayings and parables serves as the principal soteriological principle. There is finally the observation that the Savior's discourses are by no means as unambiguously lucid as one might expect. At times his speech appears shrouded in opacity, and judging from the disciples' comments and questions one may well wonder whether they always grasp what is supposed to be open, revelatory discourse. But if the so-called open language is still somewhat veiled, must it not be admitted that the hermeneutical problematic of the parabolic, pre-Easter discourse has intruded upon the post-Easter revelation? Even the conjecture that the disciples' limited comprehension serves merely as a backdrop for the readers' clear and unimpeded comprehension is not entirely to the point. For insofar as the revelation dialogues are not fully comprehended by Peter and James, they oblige the readers to involve themselves in the act of interpretation. And interpretation, once again, problematizes any claim to transparent, unmediated revelation.

Differences notwithstanding, the two examples of clustering and dialogue processes represented by the *Gospel of Thomas* and the *Apocryphon of James* partake in a common hermeneutical problematic. Both manage a composition devoid of a coherent narrative syntax. This is motivated by the desire to allow the dominical sayings to have their own say and speak directly into the present. At the same time both the sayings Gospel and the dialogue genre exhibit complications that impede, or at least complicate, the presence of the Word. In sum, the two compositions constitute interfaces between oral and textual ambitions. They are torn between the competing interests in retaining the *viva vox* of Jesus and in preserving it in writing, and also between the concealing and revealing nature of his proclamation.

21. THE JOHANNINE SAYINGS TRADITION

The sayings material embedded in the Fourth Gospel is of massive proportions (Kelber 1987a, 110–16; 1988c, 32–36). If one discounts chapter 21 as a redactional addition, approximately three-fourths of chapters 1–20 consist of sayings, dialogues, and monologues. The heaviest concentration of speech materials is located in the Farewell Discourse (John 13:31–17:26), which constitutes roughly one-fifth of the Gospel. While the isolation and identification of formerly unconnected aphorisms is a distinct possibility (K. Dewey 1980), the bulk of the Johannine sayings tradition is shaped into discourses not unlike the compositional arrangements in the *Apocryphon of James*. So impressive are the scope and formation of John's sayings that questions have been raised as to whether the Gospel could have arisen out of anthological, clustering processes, and whether these could be connected with the model of the dialogue and even the sayings Gospel. In the following we shall observe specific affinities between the Farewell Speech and the genres of the sayings Gospel and dialogue genre respectively.

The mise-en-scène of the Johannine Farewell Discourse is Jesus' last supper with his disciples and his exemplary washing of their feet. This Johannine setting designates the speech as a banquet or symposium talk addressed to the participating celebrants. Apart from the disciples there are no crowds, bystanders, or any other participants. Exclusivity of audience is one of the generic features of the sayings Gospel and dialogue genre, both of which are designed to communicate wisdom mostly to privileged male and female disciples.

In the course of the banquet talk a number of disciples ask questions, which elicit Jesus' response. Peter's inquiry into the whereabouts of Jesus' way evokes the latter's prediction of this disciple's denial (John 13:36–38). Thomas's similar question about the way is met by Jesus' self-identification as the Way (John 14:5–7). Philip wishes to see the Father, and Jesus advises him that he (Jesus) represents the Father (John 14:8–9). Judas questions Jesus' prudence to limit his revelation to the few, and Jesus responds by way of riddling indirection (John 14:22–23). Some disciples are puzzled about the meaning of a dominical saying, and Jesus offers a metaphorical, paraenetic explanation (John 16:17–24). When the disciples finally claim comprehension, Jesus in turn raises the issue of their faith (John 16:29–31). The disciples' queries and comments that engage Jesus' responses, as well as brief dialogue vignettes between Jesus and the disciples (13:36–38; 16:17–24; 16:29–33), are reminiscent of the dialogue Gospel, although in John Jesus' discourses have a tendency to evolve into monologues.

In addition to sayings, dialogues, and monologues, Jesus' last speech in a number of instances employs a sayings genre that is closely akin to the parabolic short story. Obvious examples are the stories of the true vine (John 15:1–5) and of the woman in labor (John 16:21). What is more, in reflecting on his own discourse, Jesus brings up his use of figurative speech: "these [things] I have spoken to you *en paroimiais*" (John 16:25a, 29; cf. 10:6). This reference to "figures of speech" is all the more significant in view of the fact that the Fourth Gospel does not carry any of the Synoptic parables. Their absence notwithstanding, the Johannine Jesus' last discourse does in fact consist of sayings and παροιμίαι, metaphorical short stories.

The very identity of the speaker of these sayings and παροιμίαι deserves closer attention. Reminding his disciples of the inevitability of mistreatment, Jesus declares, "And these [things] I did not say to you at the beginning, because I was with you" (John 16:4). The curious part is the explanation for his earlier silence: ὅτι μεθ᾽ ὑμῶν ἤμην. Of persecutions he did not speak to them *because* he was with them! It is as if his incarnational existence had prevented him from saying what he is now at liberty to reveal. Has he then at this point assumed the posture of the living Christ? Still more puzzling is his statement in the so-called high priestly prayer, "And I am no more in the world, and yet they themselves are in the world. ... While I was with them, I was keeping them in Thy name" (John 17:11–12). Here at the culmination of his prayer Jesus refers to his earthly career in the past tense (ὅτε ἤμην μετ᾽ αὐτῶν), speaking as one who is no longer in the world. Although the broader narrative logic has projected Jesus' glorification at his upcoming crucifixion, here he speaks as if he were already the glorified one. This christological "slippage" is all the more surprising in a narrative whose chief ideological and dramatic objective is the protagonist's incarnation. Indeed, no sooner has he asserted his freedom from the world than he appears to insist on a correction: "These [things] I speak in the world" (John 17:13: ταῦτα λαλῶ ἐν τῷ κόσμῳ). The identity of the speaker is thus ambiguous. But insofar as he claims to be no longer earthbound, he resembles the "living Jesus" or the risen Lord of the sayings and dialogue genre.

There is yet another, still greater complication lodged in the Johannine discourse. It concerns the contrast between Jesus speaking ἐν παροιμίαις and ἐν παρρησίᾳ. Earlier we noted that in John 16:25a Jesus claimed to have spoken ἐν παροιμίαις, in figurative language. To this we must now add that in the same breath Jesus anticipates a time when he will no longer be speaking ἐν παροιμίαις but rather ἐν παρρησίᾳ, that is, openly (John 16:25b). This contrasting pair, ἐν παροιμίαις (or ἐν παραβολαῖς) versus (ἐν) παρρησίᾳ, puts one in mind of distinctions made in the dialogue Gospel between the earthly Jesus speaking in figurative, parabolic language and the living, risen Lord speaking openly. The designations ἐν παροιμίαις (or ἐν παραβολαῖς) versus ἐν παρρησίᾳ must therefore be considered *termini technici*, and their occurrence in John suggests once again traces of a genre other than the narrative Gospel. What is typical for John is that he leaves the issue unresolved as to whether his Jesus in fact did speak ἐν παρρησίᾳ. The disciples think at one point that he speaks already ἐν παρρησίᾳ in the present (John 16:29: καὶ παροιμίαν οὐδεμίαν λέγεις), but their perception cannot in all instances be considered in keeping with the narrator's viewpoint.

There are, finally, a number of parallels that have been observed between certain sayings in the Johannine Farewell Discourse (and outside of it) and those in sayings and dialogue Gospels (Koester 1980a; 1980b, 119–26; 1982, 178–81; 1990, 187–200). The observed similarities do not necessarily result from direct literary Johannine dependencies on Q, *Gospel of Thomas*, *Apocryphon of James*, or the *Dialogue of the Savior*, or vice versa. What seems more likely is that John, Q, *Gospel of Thomas*, *Apocryphon of James*, and *Dialogue of the Savior* had access to similar, and perhaps interrelated, sayings formations.

The heavy concentration of speech materials in John 13:31–17:26, consisting of sayings, clusters of sayings, παροιμίαι, brief dialogue vignettes between the speaker and disciples, and monologues, the exclusivity of the audience, the partial identity of the speaker as the "living" one, use of the technical terms of speaking ἐν παροιμίαις versus ἐν παρρησίᾳ, and parallels between Johannine sayings and those in sayings and dialogue Gospels— these are all indications of affinities between the Farewell Discourse and, broadly speaking, a sayings and dialogue genre or tradition.

22. Onto-theology and the Eclipse of Presence

Aphoristic, parabolic speech, sayings, and dialogue arrangements were not allowed to stand on their own in the canon. Sayings and dialogue traditions were admitted into the company of canonically privileged texts primarily through mediation of the narrative Gospel, and not on their own generic cognizance. In the case of the Fourth Gospel a large quantity of sayings and features of a broadly identifiable discourse genre have become inscribed into the narrative composition. This is a matter of no small consequence, because the generic identity the sayings, parables, and dialogues had attained in the form of a sayings Gospel and discourse genre was thereby overruled by the narrative form. In other words, John drew on the discourse genre as a source, but refrained from following it as a model. After the oral, prophetic speech phenomenon and the formation of the sayings/dialogue genre, the narrative Gospel was now the third form by means of which the tradition managed the two units of Jesus proclamation. It was the canonically privileged mode.

Employed as source materials or freely composed, sayings and discourses were now relegated to organized narrative space. Whichever the Johannine features that were suggestive of an autonomous discourse genre, *sub specie narrationis* these turn out to be mere traces of a previous existence.

For in the narrative sequence, John 13:31–17:26 dramatizes the Farewell Discourse of a Jesus moving toward crucifixion, and not the contemporizing speech of the "living" Jesus or risen Lord. Thus a nonnarrative existence of speech materials was ruled out, and the dramatic and linguistic status of all sayings and discourses was subordinate to and determined by narrative. While both sayings and discourse genres allowed aphorisms and parables/ παροιμίαι to speak for themselves, the very ongoingness of narrative enlisted all discourse materials in a process that inhibited aspirations of oral immediacy. Narrative's plotted sequentiality engendered meaning through an unfolding process, disallowing individual sayings to have their own say.

As a matter of practical observation, texts are first and foremost dormant language, frozen in a noncommunicative state. This needs to be restated at a time when biblical hermeneutics in the wake of literary criticism is about to (re)discover the rhetorical, communicative aspects of texts. Written verbalization, we need reminding, is silent unless reactivated in the process of speaking and reading. It cannot speak for itself, or of itself. Reading is the process whereby we seek to attach meaning to visual signifiers. Readers confronted with texts find themselves in a hermeneutical situation quite different from that of hearers of words. For in the first place, orality manages to synchronize composition and communication, whereas in writing the production of the text is always separate from the actual transmission of information. Second, while speaker and hearers operate in the same informing context of symbolic reference, readers no longer share a commonality of space and time with writers. Because written language is visually given, yet by itself conceptually inanimate, it reifies the distance between language and intent, and enforces the gap between signifying manifestations and signified referents. In short, spatialized, visualized language slips into the implicit postulates of the sign that "has always been understood and determined, in its meaning, as sign of, referring to a signified, a signifier different from its signified" (Derrida 1978, 281). Precisely in this opposition between the sensible and the intelligible lies the metaphysical temptation to which our reading of texts, according to Derrida, perennially succumbs. Inevitably we privilege the signifieds above the text, attribute transcendental significance to them, imagine them as *res* and *ousia* "in the eternal presence of the divine logos and specifically in its breath" (Derrida 1976, 73). In other words, we are tempted to interpret texts phonocentrically as an oral metaphysics of presence.

Not infrequently, biblical studies and theology have succumbed precisely to this kind of temptation diagnosed by Derrida. The second epigraph to this piece quotes the philosopher's determination to repudiate a false sense of presence, which in his philosophy is defined by the harmonization of a phonocentric ontology with the materiality of texts. Nowhere is this more in evidence than in the interpretation of the Fourth Gospel. In Bultmann's reading, for example, the Johannine Jesus enters the flesh in order to manifest the presence of his divine *doxa* (1971). Kermode finds the Gospel attending to "the representation ... of the manifestations of being in a world of becoming" (1987, 453). Mack claims that the fourth evangelist created "a sense of being within a realm of absolute light and life" (1988, 358). One of the most dogmatic versions of this classic theological reading of John's Gospel has been formulated by Käsemann: "The *praesentia Christi* is the centre of his [John's] proclamation" (1967, 15). Examples of this onto-theological reading of the Fourth Gospel abound. Their common trait is a phenomenology that regards the Word of God as fully making present that of which it speaks, or rather writes. It is the kind of phenomenology that postulates something of an oral purity for Scripture, and does not take into account the theological implications of the Word's textualization. Derrida's observation that in the Western tradition "phonocentrism merges with the historical determination of the meaning of being as presence," resulting in a debasing of writing (1976, 12), finds confirmation in our habitual readings of John. It is founded on the theological rationale that abstracts ideas from their linguistic forms and formations, and treats them to the regalia of full presence. As far as textuality is concerned, therefore, Derrida's repudiation of the metaphysics of presence is not merely to the point, but long overdue. Nevertheless, it is one thing to claim with Derrida that *all language* is deferring and decentering, and quite another to claim that *texts* have deconstructive effects on oral speech and hermeneutics.

Directly or indirectly, the attribution of a metaphysics of presence to the Fourth Gospel is always linked with its central motif of incarnation. What could convey a more compelling sense of presence than the theme of the Λόγος entering into the human condition? But if presence truly was John's concern, would he not have better stayed with the oral process of prophetic speech, or with the "living," risen Lord of the sayings Gospel, or at least with the discourse genre? Does writing and a written narration about the incarnate Jesus genuinely operate in the best interest of a metaphysics of presence? Once again, our ability to do justice to the Word of God and its inscription into narrativity is burdened by metaphysical assumptions embedded in theology.

All narrative contains an active interest in the past. In creating a spatio-temporal framework, John binds all characters to historicized space and time (Ong 1977b, 230–71). The technology of writing further enhanced the inherent retrospectivity of narrative by keeping all words firmly lodged in the past. Incarnation, narrativity, and textuality, the former mediated through the vehicle of the latter two, constitute the Gospel's basic properties, and all three reinforce the pastness of Jesus. The *praesentia Christi* experienced in oral proclamation or invoked in the sayings and dialogue genre is one thing; but incarnation mediated through the technology of writing and the retrospective thrust of narrative is quite another.

The use of παροιμίαι, moreover, which discourage readers to stay on the literal level, is not limited to the Farewell Discourse. It is well known that irony, double entendre, and misunderstandings extend across the Johannine narrative (Leroy 1968; Duke 1985; Culpepper 1983, 149–202). Words often do not mean what they say, and say what they mean. There is a persistent clash between apparent and intended meanings. "To go," "to be free," "death," "to be born ἄνωθεν," "living water," and "food" all mean one thing literally while pointing toward another sense, which is the one that carries the blessing of the narrator. Theological interpreters are quick to suggest that figurative language betokens ontological signifieds, serving the aim of revelation, and hence of full presence. Johannine irony, it is said, engages readers in a process of education, raising them from the naïvetés of literalism to a level of genuine enlightenment. "Despite its apparent attempts to conceal meaning, *irony is a mode of revelatory language*" (O'Day 1986, 31). But statements of this kind tend to short-circuit the narrative workings of irony in the interest of presence. The primary observation to be made about irony is not its revelatory power, but its effectiveness in suspending meaning. For in the first place irony *prevents* meaning from being present in the clear light of consciousness. It remains to be demonstrated whether irony in fact does offer a unity of experience and whether it does generate resemblances to the point of total identification. In principle nothing prevents a narrator from letting irony do its unsettling work on the characters in the narrative and on the readers as well. One example, the narrative development of water and Spirit, must suffice to highlight irony's ability to make the readers the victims of its deferrals and reversals.

In chapter 4, a Samaritan woman and Jesus are engaged in a dialogue centering on the meaning of "water." Jesus departs from the literal sense and opens up the prospect of thinking in unaccustomed ways. The woman learns that the water Jesus has in mind is not drawn from the well, but is the "living water" (John 4:10). She further learns that Jesus himself is the dispenser of this "living water," which will prevent those who drink from ever thirsting again (John 4:13–14). While the woman remains uninformed as to the identity of the "living water," the readers learn of it at a later point. On the last day of the Feast of Tabernacles, Jesus again appeals to all those who are thirsty to come to him and drink (John 7:37–38). In a narrative aside, the "living water" is now explained in terms of the Spirit. But the very moment the figurative meaning is clarified, its narrative representation is deferred until Jesus' glorification (John 7:39). That the "hour" of glorification will coincide with the lifting up on the cross is intimated, although never fully explicated, at various points in the narrative (John 3:14; 12:23; 17:1). However well or ill the readers may be prepared to comprehend crucifixion as elevation, they are quite unprepared for Jesus' anguished cry on the cross: "I am thirsty" (John 19:28). Instead of living up to his projected role as the dispenser of the "living water," he is depicted as himself succumbing to thirst for water in the literal, physical sense. As a result, the whole narrative buildup from the literal to the figurative meaning of water is on the verge of collapse, and the expected resolution of irony is thereby turned into a stark paradox. That paradox is compounded by the narration of Jesus' giving up of the Spirit (John 19:30: παρέδωκεν τὸ πνεῦμα). Death has both subjected him to the need for water in the material sense and robbed him of the Spirit. Can this be the promised scene of elevation? The subsequent account of the piercing of Jesus' side and the issuing forth of blood as well as water (John 19:34) only heightens the paradoxical reversal of narrative expectations. Far from explicating the meaning of blood and water, the narrator has left the readers wondering what, if anything, the water coming from the dead body might have to do with the "living water" of the Spirit. Even if the readers were to decide that this water indeed represented the promised "living water," their narrative experience would still be one of paradox more than revelation. For in the end they would be faced with the paradoxical narration of life coming forth from death.

To be sure, eventually the risen Lord does function as the dispenser of the Spirit (John 20:22). Yet his status as giver of the Spirit is predicated on his abandonment of the Spirit in death. The narration of the thirsting Jesus who abandons the Spirit disallows irony to function as revelatory language meant to educate readers from the literal meaning of water to its figurative sense. Irony's revelatory course is thus obstructed by the paradoxical collapsing of death with life at the narrative culmination. Thwarted also are all notions of the efficacious powers of living speech. For if Life has to pass through the gates of death, redemption can no longer be accessible through the proclamation of words alone.

23. The *LOGOI* and the Privileging of the *LOGOS*

In absorbing a plentitude of sayings, παροιμίαι, sayings clusters, and dialogue scenes, the Gospel narrative undertook a recontextualization, not a rejection, of these materials. It operated in effect as a control mechanism, assigning all sayings, παροιμίαι, and discourses a new generic home, so as to make them function on terms dictated by the narrative. This controlling function, which the written narrative has exercised over the sayings tradition, may cast now new light on the preexistent Λόγος. Could there not be a connection between the Gospel's assimilation and regulation of a λόγοι tradition of huge proportions and its simultaneous promotion of the Λόγος?

Among the countless models invoked to explain John's preexistent Λόγος, Wisdom has for some time be the favorite candidate (R. Brown 1966, 30, 519–24; Bultmann 1971, 22–23). Clearly she provides us with a key to the principal operations of the *Logos*'s preexistence, participation in creation, entry into a hostile world, creation of the children of God, the world's incomprehension, and rejection by her own. While this myth of Wisdom's heavenly origin and descent explains the prologue to a remarkable degree, it still leaves basic questions unsettled. If John is so enthralled by Wisdom, why is it that the words σοφία and σοφός never feature in this Gospel? If it is claimed that the female σοφία could not be synchronized with Jesus—the Λόγος, of course, being male—one must point out that neither Q (Matt 11:19 // Luke 7:35) nor Paul (1 Cor 1:24) show any qualms in doing just that. This raises the larger question why the prologue introduces Jesus as Λόγος, and not as σοφία. Reference to the interchangeability of σοφία with Λόγος in Hellenistic Judaism, and to Philo's transference of σοφία attributes onto the Λόγος (Mack 1973, 96–107, 141–54) merely beg the question. Why does John perceive Jesus' entry into the darkness of the world not as Wisdom but in fact as Λόγος?

Here as elsewhere, we have grown prematurely satisfied with results obtained by the comparative method, results so eminently plausible as to distract us from a genuinely critical interrogation. For to rest content with Wisdom as *the* explanatory model is to allow the Λόγος to settle into the permanence of the Wisdom myth, and to sustain our belief in the privileged ἀρχή of the Λόγος as a theological commonplace.

Undoubtedly, the apotheosis of the Λόγος signifies *the* quintessential logocentric gesture. Installed in privileged position, the Λόγος presents himself as foundational stability, a force outside of time and prior to world. In thus elevating Jesus to the position of a transcendental signified, John has accomplished what Derrida feared most about logocentrism: the consummation of desire and discourse by reducing world and language to this prior, totalizing reference point. Viewed from this angle, the Λόγος proves himself to be a child of the archaeology of the human spirit, which always places ἀρχή or τέλος above discourse.

Concealed in the *Logos's* posture of underived origin and transcendental presence is a strong will to power, and we must ask the One who claims these categorical privileges: Whence did you acquire this privileged position? Is there no prior otherness that you are dependent on and that is concealed by your imperial status?

Elsewhere I have documented a distinct tendency in John's narrative to refocus attention from the plural to the singular (Kelber 1987b, 109–10; Braun 1968). The plural commandments (ἐντολαί) culminate in the "new commandment" (John 13:34: ἐντολὴ καινή); Jesus' many works (τὰ ἔργα) are accomplished in his work of glorification (John 17:4: τὸ ἔργον); the sign of the loaves of bread (οἱ ἄρτοι) gives rise to Jesus' self-identification as the Bread (John 6:48: ὁ ἄρτος); the disciples (οἱ μαθηταί) find ideal representation in the Beloved Disciple (John 21:7: ὁ μαθητὴς ἐκεῖνος ὃν ἠγάπα ὁ Ἰησοῦς); the sheep (τὰ πρόβατα) shall become one flock and even one shepherd (John 10:16: μία ποίμνη, εἷς ποιμήν). A reductionist movement from the plural to the singular is an intrinsic feature of the Johannine narrative. It is a distinctly imperial gesture, overriding plurality that, in media terms, is symptomatic of oral discourse and present as well in scribal traditions.

On this showing, it is tempting to assume a similar motivation for the metaphysical elevation of the singular Λόγος. A passage from the λόγοι to the Λόγος seems all the more plausible since John's deconstructive engagement in the dialogue/discourse tradition confronted him with the issue of the ownership of and authority over the λόγοι. In thus reaching beyond λόγοι and λόγοι formations, an authority is created that encompasses all the λόγοι, clusters, and discourses of λόγοι. In this manner, the replacement of Wisdom by Λόγος, and the apotheosis of the Λόγος could well be attributable to intra-Johannine dynamics.

The issue of the λόγοι and the Λόγος can be restated in terms of presence. John's deconstruction and recontextualization of the dialogue/discourse tradition brought about an eclipse of presence. Henceforth, Jesus' words are no longer those of a disembodied figure extricated from the past clinging to the present. Yet in disarming one sense of presence allied to the "living" Jesus, John introduced another and even stronger sense, the classical metaphysics of presence epitomized by the Λόγος. Sayings and discourses were now embodied in and controlled by a transcendental authority: in consequence, a logocentric primordiality has arisen from which metaphysics and metaphysical Christianity henceforth appeared thinkable.

The Λόγος of the Fourth Gospel undoubtedly presents himself as full realization of oral utterance. He epitomizes the plentitude of speech, and not a summation of written words. And yet, his preexistent authority far exceeds the bounds of what is possible and permissible in orality. Elevated to transcendental origin, the Λόγος lays claim to the purity of underived origin and to self-presence as speech. This claim is at once a concession to the potency of oral speech and a betrayal of oral pluralism, for orality, we saw, traffics in a plurality of authentic λόγοι. It cannot justify itself in reference to an *arche-Logos*, let alone conceptualize the notion of *Urwort*. This suggests that the privileging of protology vis-à-vis plurality, this logocentric reduction of the λόγοι to the Λόγος, was inspired by the mentality of *écriture*. Once we recognize the intra-Johannine dynamic between the λόγοι and the Λόγος, the latter stands therefore unmasked as a textually reinvented, monumentalized authority, and more specifically as an individualized, fantasized orality that has grown out of a process of reductionist displacements.

24. The Logocentric Circle

Once readers begin to become acquainted with the Λόγος, constructed and installed into authoritative position, they have to familiarize themselves with the abdication of his logocentric power as well. For the Fourth Gospel affirms a decentering, and it does so in dramatic fashion. While evidence for the logocentric move from the λόγοι to the Λόγος was circumstantial, dependent on narrative dynamics and features of the history of tradition, an antilogocentric thrust forms the very premise of the Gospel. Apart from installing the Λόγος, the most important function of the prologue is to engineer a decentering of the Λόγος from ἀρχή. What is announced as his "coming into the world" (John 1:9) amounts to his surrender of a privileged position in the interest of the human condition. The Λόγος is installed ἐν ἀρχῇ only to be dislodged from ἀρχή. And in decentering the

Λόγος, the Gospel administers deconstruction of its own onto-theological origin. It applies the incision at the most decisive point, namely, at its
beginning. One is inclined to think that henceforth readers/hearers are
invited to understand themselves in relation not to absolute, transcendental presence, but rather to the narrative's commencement with incarnation
and to its culmination with the crucifixion/glorification of the Λόγος.

Ruptures with centers of presence tend to unlock new modes of representation. In the case of the Fourth Gospel, the decentering of the Λόγος
sets prerogatives not only for the narrative of incarnation, but for textuality itself. Unremitting fixation on the metaphysical self-realization of the
Λόγος would not issue forth in textuality. Put less prosaically, pleromatic
self-referentiality basks in the white heat of mythology and glows in the
luminosity of its own autistic presence. If the text were to assert itself and
to survive its own invention, it had to strive to differ. And so it is in dislodging the Λόγος from his transcendental position that the text narrates
the raison d'être of its own written existence. What generates the materiality of the Gospel text is thus not the preexistent Λόγος himself, but rupture
with the logocentric origin.

It would be easy enough to overplay John's antilogocentric gesture
as a way of disposing with metaphysics. But if we think the Gospel has
overcome the onto-theological structure of metaphysics, we have not penetrated to the core dilemma it has posited for itself. For the very narrative
that grew out of a displacement of the metaphysical Λόγος is still intent
on retaining his logocentric profile. The assertion that "the Word became
flesh and we beheld his glory" (John 1:14) engenders a tension between
what has conventionally been called an incarnational versus an epiphanic
Christology. In less traditional terms, the σάρξ/δόξα dichotomy articulates
the problematics of contingency and transparency, and of the signifiers
versus the transcendental signified. The fundamental problematic has
often been rehearsed. To deliver the truth the Λόγος has to enter into the
realm of the flesh, but if he truly *becomes* flesh (σάρξ ἐγένετο), his δόξα
was to be concealed at best, and extinguished at worst. So he can either
"become flesh" and forgo glory, or reflect glory and deny the flesh.

To reconcile the irreconcilable, the narrative embarks upon the difficult and risky path of irony and metaphor, or double entendre and linguistic duplicity. A whole semiology of language is put to work to blaze a trail
from flesh to glory. The very narrative that thrives on the erasure of the
transcendental ἀρχή cultivates a signs language that aspires to pleromatic
presence. The more the text strives to enact the decentering of the Λόγος,

the more it divulges information about his preexistent origin; the more it endeavors to absorb the Λόγος, the more it enlarges his metaphysical profile. In the end, it seems as if the Λόγος incarnated himself only to bring about a return to origin and logocentric essentials. Even though signs, metaphor, and irony, as we have seen, become entangled in narratological and grammatological complications without bringing forth the pure light of transparency, it nonetheless needs to be stated that the narrative is dramatically motivated by this logocentric gesturing. It is this very struggle over the relation of opacity to transparency that accounts for a good deal of the dramatic conflict.

John's Gospel is deeply informed by this double gesture of decentering and logocentrism. We have observed the strategy of deconstructing a sense of presence that in however vague a form was still attached to the discourse genre, and of repositioning presence in absolute transcendentality; and the further strategy of decentering the Λόγος while forging a deliberately signifying narrative. In this simultaneity of deconstructionism and metaphysical positivism, John suffers the problem of language and metaphysics in search of central presence. The construction of the logocentric signified, his decomposition into narrative signifiers, and their signifying desire to reach the transcendental signified circumscribe the "logocentric circle" that the Western tradition has ceaselessly sought to construct and from which it has ceaselessly sought to liberate itself.

This is to confirm the first epigraph prefixed to this piece, according to which all linguistic significations are caught in something of a double bind. "For the *paradox* is that the metaphysical reduction of the sign needed the opposition it was reducing" (Derrida 1978, 281). Modernity manifests this paradox in the philosophical efforts of Nietzsche, Freud, Heidegger, Derrida, and many others. In antiquity, it announced itself prominently in the Fourth Gospel. For the story it dramatizes is that of the history of metaphysics and the perpetually parallel history of the deconstruction of metaphysics. For this reason the Gospel deserves pride of place in the intellectual history of the West.

5
JESUS AND TRADITION: WORDS IN TIME, WORDS IN SPACE

This essay reexamines the historical-critical paradigm that has informed our reconstruction of Jesus' message and the ensuing tradition. Whereas the focus of historical criticism has been primarily on textual evidence, that is, words committed to chirographic space and transmitted to us mostly on typographic space, the model offered here takes into account both chirographs and speech, that is, words transacted in time and in space, and also the interfaces between the two media. The resultant paradigm questions the logical/methodological procedures underlying the historical Quest and seeks to locate Jesus' message in the media context of late antiquity.

The first part expounds modern biblical scholarship as both product and beneficiary of the typographic technologizing of language, and explores the nature and function of ancient chirographs in a media environment saturated with oral communication and performances. The second part examines the modus operandi of John Dominic Crossan's study on the historical Jesus. Precisely because of the brilliance of its methodological rigor and historical, logical exactitude, the work raises the question of whether the methodology can in fact approximate the performative character of Jesus' speech. The third part seeks to situate Jesus' words in the flux of temporality, contesting the time-obviating stability suggested by the notions of ipsissimum verbum *and* ipsissima structura. *The point is not to challenge historical criticism per se, but to expose its captivity to the print medium and to restore its genuinely historical capacity. The fourth part reconceptualizes the concept of tradition, replacing the model of evolution and stratification with that of biosphere, where texts did not have firmly fixed boundaries, where speaking, not texts, did have primacy, plagiarism was a concept unknown, and in which oral and scribal media interconnected in ways that do not necessarily line up on a single trajectory. The fifth part seeks to rehabilitate media sensibilities that are commensurate with the ancient culture of communication. In place of intertextuality and processes of textual stratification a model of tradition is suggested that highlights oral and scribal means of communication, the interdependence of media and meaning, conflicting media demands, and multiple intersecting causalities. No single schematic illustration can claim to do justice to all the discrete features of tradition. However, biosphere, this essay argues, is an appropriately media-sensitive and inclusive metaphor for tradition understood as a collective, cultural memory, composed of discourse and chirographs, and shared by speakers and hearers alike.*

> What we are wrestling with, it would seem, is not just ... "oral" versus "literary," but an inadequate theory of verbal art.
>
> —Foley, *Immanent Art*

> I find it unusual for a writer to choose passages from several documentary sources as if from a buffet.
>
> —Lord, *The Gospels as Oral Traditional Literature*

> Think of how the physical reality of the book has constrained us.
>
> —Foley, *How to Read an Oral Poem*

> We moderns have poor night vision. We demand sharp outlines, unambiguous boundaries, plain definitions, lucid analyses, clear answers, and brilliant solutions.
>
> —Moore, *Mark and Luke in Poststructuralist Perspectives*

25. THE POWER OF PRINT: LINEARIZATION OF TRADITION AND REIFICATION OF TEXTS

From the perspective of media sensibilities, the academic discipline of biblical scholarship is in no small measure intertwined with typography, the technological invention that mediated both the biblical manuscripts themselves and our interpretations of them. This alliance between print technology and the academic study of the Bible has been a long and close one, although it has largely remained unrecognized by the discipline. For the past five centuries Western history, and particularly the literate elite, has managed verbal communication under the spell of the print medium. The shift from script to print has had a major part in the three historic developments that ushered in modernism—Renaissance humanism, the Protestant Reformation, and scientific rationality—and all three phenomena contributed to the rise of the historical examination of the biblical traditions. Few fields of the human enterprise were left outside the wake of the new technology of the fifteenth-century typographic revolution. Social, political, economic, and scientific thought were no less affected than artistic, educational, and religious knowledge and practices. The effects produced by the communications shift were complex and often contradictory. On the one hand, the new medium generated religious devotion among a rapidly growing readership of the Bible, while on the other hand it catered to capitalist entrepreneurship among printers and booksellers. "Print capitalism" is the term Anderson, in his celebrated book *Imagined Communities* (1983, 18), has introduced to describe the phenomenon of a growing alliance between the new medium and a rapidly developing entrepreneurship in Western Europe. Not only was the Bible at risk to be taken out of the hands of the pope and of theologians generally, but it was about to become a desirable commodity in the hands of publishers and business people. Vernacular Bible translations helped foster national identities and unity, but the Catholic-Protestant conflict, inflamed by divergent readings of the progressively disseminated print Bible, contributed to the fragmentation of Western Christendom. The decline of rhetoric and the concomitant loss of the ancient and medieval memory tradition played a part in Protestant iconoclasm, while on the other hand the new technologies of printing and engraving vastly enhanced image making in the arts as well as in scientific literature.

The two most significant features of the new technology, its duplicating and its preservative powers, exercised far-reaching effects on the perception of language and literature. Typographic fixity, something entirely unknown in ancient and medieval history, reinforced the idea of the single, original text, the base text from which departures seemed recognizable. The experience of a plurality of identical copies of the Bible, combined with a growing confusion over matters of interpretation, generated a drive for textual standardization. Notably, the designation of the *textus receptus*, the technical term for a professionally constructed and approved standard, was first used not by theologians, biblical scholars, or text critics, but by a publisher, the Elsevir Press in Holland (Eisenstein 1979, 1:338). Print, finally, took full charge of scribal space, meticulously formatting the Bible along equally spaced lines and with the aid of fully justified margins. These formatting powers of print imparted to the Bible an unprecedented sense of authority that made it possible to think of the text as standing on its own, apart from tradition and in conflict even with traditional Church authority.

Print was the medium in which modern biblical scholarship was born and raised, and from which it has acquired its formative methodological tools and habits.

Although the "unacknowledged revolution," as Eisenstein has labeled the invention of the letterpress (1979, 1:3–42), has increasingly received growing and at times intense scholarly attention, academic disciplines have rarely been in the habit of examining the impact of the print medium on their own intellectual conventions. One reason for this lack of reflective distance is that until the recent advent of the electronic media revolution, academicians have themselves on a daily basis lived and worked in and with the print medium. So deeply enmeshed in and conditioned by print texts is a significant part of humanistic disciplines that they have scarcely been aware of the powers of the medium and the effects it has exercised on their own intellectual apparatus, methods, and results.

Print depersonalized words and gave language the appearance of incontestable detachment. In the wake of the invention of the letterpress we have inherited a sense of rationality that has entered our sensibilities in dealing with biblical texts. In print culture it stands to reason that exegesis is perceived and practiced as a discipline governed by a set of methods and criteria. This rule-governed apparatus makes up the core of historical criticism, the dominant modern academic approach to the Bible.

The model of historical criticism is legitimized by appeal to the authority of reason, tested over time, and proven eminently workable. This essay, far from challenging the significance of historical criticism, raises the question of whether historical criticism is historical enough. "The fact is that logic does have a history," Walter Ong has reminded us (1977a, 208), and this essay asks whether the authority historical criticism often appeals to is the indisputable authority of Enlightenment, or whether it could be culture-bound, specifically media-bound, and a product of print culture. We need, in any case, reminding that the logic inherent in the production, formatting, and interpretation of most of the texts biblical scholars are using is removed by a media gap of centuries from handwritten papyri and scriptographic scrolls or codices. The latter represent a media world that is unthinkable without oral traditions surrounding scripts, feeding them, and emanating from them. It is, for example, considered eminently reasonable to conduct the Quest for the historical Jesus, itself a product of modern biblical scholarship, in keeping with the laws of logical consistency and by application of a logically devised classificatory apparatus. It is likewise consistent with the logic of typographic objectification and linearization to conceptualize tradition largely along the lines of transmissional, evolutionary directionality. And it makes sense in typographic culture to visualize texts and tradition as palimpsests, with layer superimposed upon layer, and stratum superseding stratum, building up to layered edifices that, if taken apart by standards of a literary, typographic diagnosis, will take us back to the single root of an evolutionary tree.

Outside of biblical studies there is a growing awareness that standards of linguistic regularity and notions of fixed verbal property are not fully suitable in chirographic culture and inapplicable for oral discourse (Coward 1988; Goody 1968, 1977; Goody and Watt 1968; Graham 1987; B. Stock 1983; 1990). The reification and neutralization of texts, while congenial to the typographic processing of language, has made us forget that ancient chirographs came to life, both from the angle of composition and from the angle of reception, in an environment saturated with verbal communication and orally performed activities. Handwritten documents did not function as strictly autonomous entities with strictly impermeable boundaries. They interacted in part and *in toto* with oral discourse and traditions. This is exceedingly difficult to understand in modernity because the methods deployed in biblical studies have tended to instill in us the notion of autonomous, individually authored texts, which grew out of texts, linked up directly with other texts, and in turn generated new texts. *We have grown accustomed to operating in a scholarly orbit, which, while uncannily depopulated and barren of emotive significance, is crowded with texts that seem to commune only with one another and in the absence of human matrix and mediation.* And yet, texts, least of all chirographically composed texts, can appropriately be understood as traffickings in one-to-one relations with other texts. The time-space links between texts are filled with dictation and recitation, acts of hearing and remembering, and a universe of vocal values, sensibilities, and actualities. Moreover, we seem to have dismissed from our thought the misunderstandings, hesitations, and silences. Forgotten also is forgetfulness. Tradition, as we like to construct it, moves with smooth perfection and in measurable textual cadences toward truths made perfect in texts. Yet it must be stated that rarely, if ever, are texts simply explicable in reference to other texts. Truths were incarnate in voices no less, and perhaps even more in voices than in texts. Not only do texts function in multiple degrees of interaction as well as in tension with social life and oral drives, but they also implement a rich diversity of phonic and rhetorical, visual and imagistic values. This "relentless domination of textuality in the scholarly mind" (Ong 1982,

10) has caused us to lose touch with human minds and memories, with the processing of language via texts *and* by word of mouth, and the interfacing of all these realities. Once we begin to think of all that has been left unthought, tradition will no longer be singularly reducible to textual transmission, and Jesus' speech no longer comprehensible in terms of the *ipsissimum verbum* or the *ipsissima structura*.

26. Jesus the Speaker Delivered unto Print

There is no end in sight to the writing of lives of the historical Jesus. A phenomenon unknown to ancient and medieval Christian piety, the life of Jesus historically comprehended was a product of the rise of historical consciousness in Western intellectual history. Ever since Hermann Samuel Reimarus inaugurated the first truly historical and critical investigation into the life of Jesus (1778), the search for the "real" Jesus has been an inalienable item on the agenda of biblical scholarship.

Since then, what came to be called the Quest has continued unabated. Believers and agnostics, scholars and novelists alike have found the challenge irresistible. Albert Schweitzer's *Quest* (1968; German original 1906) is symptomatic of the imperative claim that the Jesus of history has laid upon modern consciousness. Although uncommonly astute about the heroic but intrinsically flawed Quest of the preceding century and a half, Schweitzer himself could not resist the temptation of adding his own chapter to what he conceded had been "a constant succession of unsuccessful attempts" (6). In our own time, the Quest is carried on with undiminished enthusiasm, skill, and inventiveness. Hope for the definitive life of Jesus springs eternal. During the past quarter of a century, a large and growing number of studies on Jesus have appeared in the English-speaking world alone. Among the more prominent authors are S. G. F. Brandon (1967), Morton Smith (1978), Geza Vermes (1981), Bruce Chilton (1984), Harvey Falk (1985), E. P. Sanders (1985), Marcus J. Borg (1987), and John P. Meier (1991). Not unexpectedly, these writers confront us with a stunning plurality of portraits of Jesus. The one element of continuity that spans the history of the Quest from past to present is the resultant diversity of Jesus portraits. Precisely because each author has claimed to have given *the* accurate account of the historical Jesus, the situation is nothing short of "an academic embarrassment" (Crossan 1991, xxviii).

When in the following we direct our attention to Crossan's own work on the historical Jesus (1991; 1994a; 1994b), we do so because of all the recent books on Jesus his contribution has attracted the most intense scholarly and popular attention. It has been suggested that Crossan's Jesus is a product of the Enlightenment tradition of the lives of Jesus written among others by Gotthold Ephraim Lessing, Friedrich Schleiermacher, David Friedrich Strauss, Ernest Renan, Albrecht Ritschl, Johannes Weiss, and Joseph Klausner (Van Beeck 1994). What is symptomatic of these Enlightenment studies is that they tend to cast Jesus "as the historic proponent of the most attractive humanism imaginable" (Van Beeck 1994, 88). Indeed, Crossan's Jesus, "a peasant Jewish Cynic" (1991, 422), healer, and exorcist who practiced itinerancy and challenged his contemporaries with spiritual and economic egalitarianism, is attractive to many of us. However, Crossan's theological agenda is not the issue of this essay. What is at issue is the methodological blueprint that, it is argued, is solidly rooted in the logic of Enlightenment.

One of the most impressive features about Crossan's work is its systematic design. Few, if any, lives of Jesus have ever been constructed on so logical and reasonable a methodological basis and executed with such skillful consistency. Broadly viewed, his method rests on three pillars: a macrocosmic approach, which proceeds from a cross-cultural perspective and examines social and economic revolutions, poverty and freedom, millennialism, magic and magicians, peasant unrest and political violence, food and meals, and so on; a mesocosmic approach, which interprets these same phenomena in the Greco-Roman context of late antiquity; and a microcosmic approach, which studies the sayings of and stories about Jesus in their respective historical settings. In focusing on the third pillar of Crossan's approach, the methodological treatment of the Jesus sayings and stories, we fail to do justice to the impressive synthesis of all three approaches into an integral whole. Still, Crossan's strategy in dealing with the thesaurus of Jesus materials is fundamental to his reconstructive project. To be sure, individual components of this third approach have been in use for some time, but no one before him has deployed so judicious an apparatus of formal principles in collecting, evaluating, and classifying the available Jesus materials. His taxonomic and methodological competence has set imposing standards for the Quest.

Along with what now may be a majority of scholars, Crossan shares the conviction that the Gospels are "deliberate theological interpretations" (1991, xxx). His reconstruction, as far as the Jesus materials are concerned, is largely centered on the sayings and stories. The historian intent on writing a life of Jesus is thus confronted with materials embedded in various contexts of the tradition, that is, with "the textual problem of the Jesus tradition" (xxxi). Specifically, sayings are either retained in their essential core, adjusted to new circumstances, or newly created. In view of their entanglement in tradition, it is incumbent upon historical scholarship to "search back through those sedimented layers to find what Jesus actually said and did" (xxxi). In order to accomplish this objective, Crossan classifies the Jesus materials in terms of multiple, triple, double, and single types of attestation. Next he compiles a comprehensive inventory of Christian literary sources both inside and outside the canon. Based on chronological priority, he divides the early tradition into four strata, which are dated from 30 to 60, from 60 to 80, from 80 to 120, and from 120 to 150 c.e. Finally, he constructs a database that assigns materials of each of the four types of attestation to each stratum in the tradition. For reasons of space, Crossan's evaluation relies almost entirely on the first stratum, and in the interest of maximal objectivity he disregards single attestation even in the first stratum. Hence, plurality of independent attestation and chronological priority of stratum determine historical reliability of data. "A first-stratum complex having, say, seven-fold independent attestation must be given very, very serious consideration" (xxxii).

In treating multiple attestation in the first stratum, Crossan draws further distinctions between *sources* and *units*, *complex* and *core complex*. A saying, for example, may have four independent sources in the *Gospel of Thomas*, Mark, Matthew, and John, but six units, because Matthew and Luke each developed an additional version based on Mark (xxxiii). The compilation and juxtaposition of all the units add up to what Crossan called a "complex." Paying particular attention to the sources, for example, to plural attestation (in keeping with his choice to eliminate single attestation), Crossan then makes his final strategic decision. Rather than seeking to obtain a fully articulated wording of the saying, he proceeds to move from complex to the "core of the complex" (xxxiii). Meticulous attention to the individual units of the complex disclose certain trends and idiosyncrasies in the tradition. The resultant comparative trajectory of tradition in turn enables him to make deductions as to the plausibility of the core saying. Once a plausible core is established, additional information is ascertained by way of historical commensurability. The end result is "a common structural plot" (261), or the "single parable," or "the original image" (254). It constitutes the "core of the complex," which lies behind the complex of verifiable units.

Crossan's reconstruction of Jesus is solidly anchored in methodology. It feeds and gratifies our rational interest in method. His work is all the more persuasive to the modern reader because its methods are rigorously based on formal logic. His Quest reassures us, citizens of the age of science, in the conviction that method informed by logic produces a high ratio of assured results. The logic that drives this methodology entails efficient orderliness, systematic sharpness, and unambiguous clarity of thought. Crossan's methodological apparatus is a brilliant exercise in organization, categorization, stratification, quantification, tabulation, prioritization, and allocation in chronological order. Ordering, the methodical arrangement of items, is a favorite child of logic. Confronted with a multiplicity and multiformity of phenomena, logic administers the implementation of organizing principles. Words are sequestered and regrouped by virtue of resemblances or sequentiality. In order to be arranged systematically, items need first to be indexed. Words must therefore be categorized so as to be apportioned to divisions of classification. Stratification is one form of classification. Tradition is thereby divided into strata or layers, which are measured according to chronological gradation. By implication, tradition takes on a linear and a layered look. On the historical premise that each text has a date and belongs to this or that period, all available texts are distributed over all discernible strata. In this way texts are localized with a sense of finality, that is, appointed a fixed place in their respective strata. Furthermore, a logic of quantification is set into motion that places a high value on the numerical strength of materials. Accordingly, singular or multiple occurrences are perceived to make a difference. To further enhance analysis, words thus organized, classified, indexed, and numbered must be tabulated. Based on the combined properties of chronology and plurality, that is, remoteness in time and quantitative strength, words are then entered into a comprehensive list, placed one next to the other and cataloged according to their full indexing values. The very logic of this arrangement of words makes continuous reading or hearing supremely difficult. But the primary purpose of the entire methodological management of words is not to promote their comprehension or enjoyment. Rather, it is designed to make words serviceable to logical analysis. And the principal agent in ascertaining the one historical sense is the Baconian method of inductive reasoning, a branch of logic that infers from multiple particulars to the one singular. It is logic's most effective strategy, which, in synergistic harmony with all other devices, labors to produce the desired findings.

In Crossan's method we recognize the application of a logic that has become the discipline's dominant, although not exclusive, mode of thinking. The principal question it raises is whether Jesus, the oral performer, and the early tradition that delivered him unto writing has played by our rules. How did Jesus, speaker of aphorisms and narrator of parables, and how did those early dictators, orators, and scribes, perform and retrieve words, constitute and contextualize meaning? Were they committed, as we are, to the ethos of pure formality, linearization of thought, compartmentalization of language, stratigraphic causality, and majority rule? How did they speak, compose manuscripts, and reappropriate these spoken and written words? Are words and groupings of words really apprehensible as distinct and isolable sediments deposited at different layers in tradition? These are loaded questions, and they imply another, rather different access to ancient language and communication, and one that should be competing for our attention.

We commence by raising an issue with logic on its own terms. By what reasoning does one privilege majority rule to the complete exclusion of singularity of attestation? To take a single instance, Crossan designates the complex on "ask, seek, knock" as authentic (435): "Ask, and it will be given to you; seek, and you will find; knock, and it will be opened for you" (xiv). The judgment is made on the basis of the saying's first-stratum placement and multiple attestation. (Contrary to his own methodological decision, however, Crossan does not seem to use the saying in his reconstructive work.) While present in six independent sources (Papyrus Oxyrhynchus = Gospel of Thomas, Gospel of the Hebrews, Q, Mark, Dialogue of the Savior, and Gospel of John), it exists in seventeen units altogether (POxy: one; Gos. Thom: three; Gos. Heb.: one; Matt and Luke [= Q]: two; Mark with parallel in Matthew: two; Dial. Sav.: three; John: five). Of these seventeen units only two pairs of sayings respectively render identical versions: POxy 654: two; and Gospel of Thomas: two (corroborating the scholarly consensus that POxy represents a part of the Greek version of the Gos. Thom.), and Matt 7:78 // Luke 11:9–10, verses that represent the sayings source Q. Apart from those two exceptions, no other two versions are exactly the same. Hence, the seventeen units confront the reader with fifteen different renditions. Clearly, the complex proved to be immensely useful in and for tradition. But why must this be an argument for authenticity? In fact, the variability is so pronounced (including single stiches, double stiches, triple stiches, double assertion of triple stiches, and quadruple stiches [Gos. Thom.: seek/find, find/troubled, troubled/astonished, astonished/

ruled]) as to cast doubt upon the very idea of core stability. What we find, it seems, is difference more than identity. Is this difference comprehensible by reduction of the evidence to a structural core stability? Is not the high ratio of independent occurrences, plus the multiple deployment and the impressive variability of occurrences, evidence of the serviceability and popularity of these sayings in the tradition more than of their authenticity? The evidence neither confirms nor rules out Jesus' own utterance. But it is inadmissible to posit *as a matter of methodological principle* the iterative and adaptive behavior of tradition as ground for historical authenticity.

To be sure, reiteration and variation of words and stories must be assumed for Jesus' own proclamation as well. Multiple and in fact variable renditions are highly plausible in Jesus' own oral performance. For the oral performer repetition, be it literal or variable, is both a necessity and a virtue. But repetition is certainly demonstrable in the tradition as well. Now if *both* Jesus *and* tradition can be assumed to have operated on the principle of multiple attestation, then the principle of multiple attestation as proof of authenticity would appear to be weakened.

Equally problematic is the exclusion of single attestation from the reconstruction of Jesus' life. On what grounds do we excise singularity as a matter of principle? Knowing about the intensity of redactional and revisionist activities in the tradition, should we not attend to singular attestation with a heightened sense of curiosity? How can one justify a historical life of Jesus if its reconstruction *categorically* rules out singular attestation of sayings? All the more so since, by Crossan's own count, two-thirds of all complexes, 342 sayings altogether, have single attestation (xxxiii; 434). Moreover, his inventory of the first stratum alone has listed fifty-five complexes of single attestations. Among them he has identified twelve as "originally from Jesus (+)" (xxxiv; 441–43). This is surprising. Why exclude singularity from the evidence when twelve single attestations on the first stratum are identified as "originally from Jesus"? And why, if a number of singular attestations are in fact considered authentic, are these not used in the reconstruction of Jesus' message? Can methodological logic deliver on its promises? To be sure, singularity of utterance neither confirms nor disconfirms authenticity. But can it *as a matter of methodological principle* be dismissed from consideration altogether?

Finally, one is bound to raise the question of how one can lay claim to a historical life of Jesus if its reconstruction essentially relies on the sayings of Jesus, however well these may be contextualized in macrocosmic and mesocosmic settings. Is there a single modern historian who would base her or his primary evidence for the writing of the life of a historical figure on an extremely selective group of sayings attributed to that personage?

27. JESUS THE SPEAKER OF APHORISTIC SAYINGS AND PARABOLIC STORIES

By all accounts, Jesus was a speaker of aphoristic sayings and parabolic stories. Therefore, the modern historian, persuaded of the literary-theological nature of the Gospels and intent on coming to terms with Jesus' message, is confronted with the issue of speech. She or he must first learn that speech, in distinction from writing, is not traceable to external verification. It surrenders itself in the act of speaking. While the voicing of sayings and parables was destined to affect minds and lives of hearers, it left no externally visible residues. A text outlasts the act of writing, but spoken words exist only in the act of speaking and in the minds and memories of hearers. It is hard to escape the impression, therefore, that the words of the historical Jesus, if taken seriously as oral proclamation, are not quantifiable in any form or division; they are not accessible to us for purposes of retrieval and classification. This is a dismaying truth for those who believe that logic, based on the visual accessibility of language, must perforce yield the words of the historical Jesus.

To say that speech leaves no visible traces is to compare it negatively vis-à-vis writing. But it is a fact from which all our thinking about Jesus' proclamation must proceed. Words spoken have no quantifiable existence. Logic's critical apparatus, on the other hand, utterly depends on the external visualization, and hence permanence, of language. Logic's power to depersonalize and organize knowledge grows out of and relies on a long and intense experience with the written, printed word. But if spoken words "cannot be 'broken' and reassembled" (Ong 1967b, 323), logic cannot get a hold of the performative poetics of Jesus' proclamation. We are bound to conclude that the oral cast of his "original" words is unknowable through formal thought based on a typographically experienced logic.

Reimagining Jesus' oral poetics is a task supremely difficult because it goes against deep-set literate inclinations. When he pronounced a saying at one place, and subsequently chose to deliver it elsewhere, neither he nor his hearers could have perceived this other rendition as a secondhand version of the first one. Each saying was an autonomous speech act. And when the second rendition, delivered before a different audience, was at variance with the first one, neither the speaker nor his hearers would have construed a difference between the literal, original wording and its derivative (Lord 1960, 101, 152). No one saying was elevated to the privileged position of *ipsissimum verbum* at the expense of any other saying. In the absence of a chart arranging materials in parallel columns and a trajectory inviting comparative analysis, each saying constituted an original and authentic intention that was actualized in social contextuality. When Crossan stated that "oral sensibility and *ipsissima verba* are ... contradictions in terms" (1983, 38), he should have used the singular, *ipsissimum verbum*, which may have been what he meant to say: multiple original sayings are a fact of oral life, but the search for the single, original, correct saying is pointless. In view of the fact that the Quest for the historical Jesus is heavily based on the premise of the retrievability of the single, literal saying, Crossan's renunciation of that very premise merits wider recognition. As questers we tend to regard the concept of the *ipsissimum verbum* as an inescapably logical fact of linguistic life because biblical scholars live and work in a world of texts, each of which, we believe, must have originated in or be traceable to an *Urtext*. But when we take serious account of speech and oral performance, we learn to appreciate a poetics that cannot make sense of singular originality in the literary mode of thought. *What to scribal sensibility appear to be variables of a single Ur-saying, for oral sensibility is a plurality of authentic sayings.* When we acknowledge that orality is trafficking in *ipsissima verba*, we embrace an idea that subverts the very concept of the *ipsissimum verbum*.

When Crossan discards the specific concept of *ipsissima verba*, he does so in favor of the *ipsissima structura*, the core structure underlying multiple versions (1983, 38; 1991, xxxiii). The concept of *ipsissima structura* raises the issue of structure versus fluidity, or fixity versus flexibility, an issue long considered central to oral tradition and oral poetics. Let us first recognize that the picture of relative stability of Jesus' sayings conveyed to us in the Q passages of Matthew and Luke is not likely to be the product of oral dynamics. The striking verbal agreements between the relevant Matthean and Lukan versions are not intelligible without some kind of scribal mediation (Kloppenborg 1987, 42–51). Q has reached chirographic stability, even though, we shall see, it sought to resist and overcome it. The stability one encounters in oral tradition is not of this kind of near literalness. In oral aesthetics, stability refers to traditional story patterns, themes, and phraseology, or, to use Foley's definition, to "elements and strategies that were in place [long] before the execution of the present version" (1991, 8). The bracketing of the word "long" is ours and is intended to leave open the issue of the tradition's diachronic depth. No oral performer operates without these commonplaces, and Jesus and the tradition were no exception. In the field of orality-literacy studies, commonplace stability is conventionally assigned to oral performance or to oral-derived texts and their indebtedness to conventional features. Crossan, however, works with a stability that is neither the oral nor the textual kind. Instead, he prunes existent versions from contextual and compositional variables of tradition and assigns the resultant core complex to historical actuality. The stability Crossan seeks and uncovers is assumed to give us access to the Jesus of history. For example, the fourfold independent attestation of the saying on "Kingdom and Children" suggests an underlying "central and shocking" metaphor that goes back to Jesus (Crossan 1991, 266, 269: "These infants being suckled are like those who enter the kingdom"). The question is whether we can track our way through plural and variable sayings to the mind of Jesus by reconstructing a core complex. Must not any such reconstruction necessarily remain speculative? More importantly, are not these processes of reconstruction the result of extreme abstraction that runs counter to speech, if only because in speech verbal reality is never totalized, never fully realized, and always contextualized? Although Crossan reactualizes and individualizes the *ipsissima structura* by secondarily reinstating it into the historical matrix, the search for the common denominator underlying all existent versions operates neither on oral nor on textual principles of stability, but rather on structuralist premises. What we get is something akin to a universal grammar of the Jesus tradition. Albert Lord's dictum, although arising out of an experience with different materials, is still apropos: "We are deluded by a mirage when we try to construct an ideal form of any given song" (1960, 101). To collect and place side by side all written versions of a dominical saying and to reconstruct their core structure will give us something that had no existence in oral any more than in textual life. Even if we managed to extract a pattern common to all existing versions of a saying, we would have succeeded merely in conjuring a structuralist stability that by oral and historical standards is a fictional construct.

The search for the *ipsissimum verbum* and the *ipsissima structura* is thus based on the confidence of securing structural stability, a stability that seeks to transcend the variability of all the differences in tradition. Here we have arrived at one of the deepest desires of logic—namely, to conquer the flux of temporality and to secure time-obviating fixedness. But if we are to imagine Jesus as speaker, we will have to imagine his words being caught up in the drift of time. Sound and sounded words, proclamation and hearing, are inescapably time-bound, and "no other sensory field totally resists a holding action, stabilization, in quite this way" (Ong 1982, 32). By itself, structural stability does not get us to oral performance. At the very most, it may give us the instruments on which the music was played. But the music itself is forever beyond our audition.

The value of redundancy is axiomatic in ancient culture. Precisely what we literate people tend to shy away from, oral practitioners in antiquity and dominantly oral societies regarded as a great virtue (Peabody 1974, 4; Abrahams 1978). Repetition both on the synchronic level and in diachronic contexts found its rationale in the physical circumstances surrounding speakers and audiences (Ong 1982, 39–41). From there it permeated oral-derived and oral-dependent texts (Gray 1973). The straight, consecutive line of thought was simply not the way words were attuned to crowds and hearers of texts. Unless words and locutions were restated, and sayings and stories retold, a speaker's message would run the risk of not connecting (well) with hearers. This need for repetition applies with special force to the charismatic, itinerant speaker whose mission depended on the receptive quality of his speeches. Redundancy was an essential, rhetorical device. Addressing the same people frequently and different people deliberately, he had no choice but to communicate the message more than once. There is every reason to assume, therefore, that repeated renditions were a part of Jesus' speech habits. This point is worth stressing because our search for the *ipsissimum verbum* and the *ipsissima structura* has kept us from coping with plurality and variability.

Oral redundancy bears no resemblance to the idea of duplication associated with print. The latter takes pride in the uniformity of textual productions modeled on the original, while repetition in oral aesthetics largely consists of variation. Repetitions almost always vary, and hence are rarely literal repetitions. In face-to-face communication, the rhetorical doctrine of efficaciousness prevails over standards of exactitude (Ong 1982, 57–68), operating on a logic not of sequentiality and sameness but of reinforcement and multiple effects. It can well be expected, therefore, that repeated renditions of a saying, story, or song ever so often were not exactly identical, even if communicated by the same person. Repetition entailed variability. To put the matter differently, transmission and composition converge in oral performance (Lord 1960, 5). Although the speaker used traditional materials, she or he was composing in the process of speaking: "Each performance is more than a performance, it is a recreation" (104).

The idea was not to reproduce what was said previously, but to (re)compose so as to affect the present circumstance. In order to assure a maximum degree of resonance, speech had to adjust to different audiences to varying degrees. Once again, variability in repetition is highly pertinent to the mode of verbalization practiced by the charismatic speaker, who is anything but restricted to a single occasion or a single community or an abstract core of a message. When Jesus (re)iterated previously communicated words, ideas, and stories, he was bound, time and again, to (re) phrase his message in the interest of efficaciousness. This warrants our attention because the *ipsissimum verbum* and the *ipsissima structura*, concepts that have often defined the logic of the modern Quest, have barred from our minds the oral aesthetics of variability in repetition.

At the heart of oral poetics lies the intermingling of stability with flexibility (Peabody 1974, 96). It is perhaps the most difficult process to grasp, as Moore has intimated in the fourth epigraph to this essay, and one for which we lack a single name. We have no language capable of expressing the combined features of stability, repetition/variability, and originality—terms already shaped by textual and typographic experiences. The charismatic itinerant did not think of his multiple renditions as variables, let alone inconsistencies, because he could not associate his proclamation with a fixed model. Although traditional patterns assisted him in remembering and (re)phrasing, the idea of making changes to a traditional core that needed to be preserved was entirely foreign to him. It is only writing that exposes different versions and "favors awareness of inconsistency" (Goody and Watt 1968. 49). And it is writing that invites us to abstract from perceived changes something of an *ipsissimum verbum*, or an *ipsissima structura*, or a single core complex. "We find it difficult to grasp something that is multiform," Lord has observed, (1960, 100), and still more difficult to imagine multiformity in the proclamation of a single person. But if already in the case of the Homeric bards Lord had reason to caution us not to look "for that consistency which has become almost a fetish with literary scholars" (95), how much more does his advice apply to Jesus, whose message was ill tolerated by the establishment and rapidly mythologized by his followers. He was at once creator and re-creator of his proclamation. If we can free ourselves from the methodological principle that variability is the work of tradition and core stability typical of Jesus, we can grant him a verbal latitude broad enough to include performancial redundancy and verbal polyphony. *Jesus' proclamation was irreducible to ipsissimum verbum; it occurred in multiformity that was tantamount to multioriginality.* A thrice-narrated parable was not comprehensible in terms of a core structure and three variables thereof, but only as three equiprimordial renditions. Each rendition was an original version, and in fact *the* original version. The challenge now is to reimagine this encompassing reality that we routinely, but unreflectively, refer to as tradition.

28. Tradition: Stratification versus Biosphere

Tradition is a phenomenon as elementary and riddling as human life itself. In Christianity, Roman Catholic theology in particular has undertaken systematic efforts to conceptualize tradition, specifically its relation to Scripture (Burghardt 1951). In a nontheological sense the term is current coinage in the humanities and social sciences, above all, perhaps, in anthropology and sociology. Conventionally, when we speak of tradition and the traditional, we have in mind something that is immutable and resistant to change. Tradition as a state of immobility has received both positive and negative interpretations. Positively, it is perceived as something to fall back on in times of crisis because it prevails in the flux of history, while negatively it is viewed as the dead weight of the past that has little relevance for the present. Both the Reformation and Enlightenment advanced a sense of the polarity of tradition versus modernity. "With modernity identified with change, and by implication with the positive values associated with progress, tradition automatically came to mean the culturally changeless and historically immobile" (B. Stock 1990, 160).

In the discipline of New Testament studies the concept of tradition has been institutionalized in terms of the transmissional processes that are thought to have preceded the writing of the synoptic Gospels and John. Rather than polarizing tradition vis-à-vis modernity, the discipline has adapted tradition to the standards of modernity itself. We have interpreted early Christian processes of tradition through the horizontal timeline of history, as understood by Kant, Fichte, Hegel, Schelling, and much of modern historiography. In *The Oral and the Written Gospel* (1983, henceforth *OWG*) I questioned the dominant paradigm of the Synoptic tradition's evolutionary growth and steady incremental expansion toward the narrative Gospel (1–43). My criticism of this model was twofold. First, the model of the evolutionary growth and near-deterministic thrust of the Synoptic tradition is problematic because it has every appearance of a theoretical construct formulated by the logic of hindsight. In fact, the very designation of Synoptic tradition is problematic because it enforces the impression that all traditions preceding the Synoptic Gospels were bound to move toward and flow into these narratives. Second, the model of the evolutionary growth is also problematic because the notion of linearity, implied in that model, fails to take account of the oral, oral-scribal means of communication. Texts are given primacy over speech, and to the degree to which speaking is taken into consideration, its behavior appears to have been modeled on texts. It is noteworthy that directionality and text-centeredness, the very features that have dominated work on the early tradition, are closely interrelated phenomena. Typography, even more than chirographic culture, "encourages the habit of assimilating matter in sequences, one item after the other" (Ong 1967a, 11).

Let us commence not with the processes of transmission, but with the means of communication: orality and scribality. To us the notion of "text" conjures up a schooling system, the privacy of reading, literary competence, and above all print literacy. In antiquity, however, schooling was largely limited to upper-class boys and a few slaves employed by wealthier families; and private reading was a distinct rarity (Botha 1992a, 1992b). As for literacy, it is notoriously difficult to measure it in our own culture and more so in the distant past (Bonner 1977; Harris 1989; Graff 1987; Marrou 1956). Perhaps more importantly, it is a term that easily lends itself to anachronistic assumptions. As a general rule, reading was practiced as a reading aloud to oneself or to audiences, and hence closely allied with recitation and auditory apperception (Achtemeier 1990; Balogh 1926; Saenger 1982). "Reading and hearing" (ἀναγινώσκειν καὶ ἀκούειν or *legere et audire*) became standard phrases for an auditory reading process throughout the ancient world and far into the Middle Ages (Balogh 1926, 207). It is in this context that one must appreciate the words of introduction written by the author of Revelation: "Blessed is he who reads (ὁ ἀναγινώσκων) and those who hear (οἱ ἀκούοντες) the words of the prophecy" (1:3). The reading in this context refers to reading aloud, not to silent, private reading of single individuals. A writer either followed the dictates of a speaker, or of a script whose words she or he was likely to have uttered aloud. "Vocalized writing in antiquity was only a version of the conventional form of literary activity: dictation" (Balogh 1926, 218). Therefore, whether dictated or read aloud, texts were predominantly transacted in an oral, aural field of communication and sense perception. They "functioned as a subset of a basically oral environment, and that means that, when we turn to interpreting culture and communication of the time [of the first century c.e.], we need to be continually reminded of ... [their] orality" (Botha 1992a, 206).

Literacy, therefore, may not be an adequate term to describe the ancient media realities surrounding texts. For us the term suggests the combined skills of reading and writing. In the ancient world, a reader was a speaker or a hearer, and not necessarily a writer at all, while a scribe trained in the art of chirography was not necessarily an interested reader. Instead we should remember that papyri and manuscripts were "connected to the physical presence of people and to living speech to an extent that is consistently underestimated today" (Botha 1992a, 207). Thus in thinking about tradition, we should first imagine a world of communications in which speaking had primacy, and both the production and consumption of manuscripts grew out of the living sphere of speech.

In our discipline, tradition is virtually synonymous with textual transmission, and we tend to explicate the chain of transmission along linear and often developmental lines. There is a tendency, moreover, to imagine the process of tradition as being divisible into clearly identifiable, autonomous textual strata. This model is thinkable in a pure textual environment, where texts function in relation to other texts under the aegis of a linear, developmental governance. A telling example is the recent work on the transmissional history of the sayings Gospel of Q (Kloppenborg 1987). Commencing with Q as protobiography, Kloppenborg has retraced its history to an underlying redactional stratum composed of a *chriae* collection, which was characterized by prophetic and apocalyptic announcements, and still further back to a source of wisdom speeches, which were paraenetic in nature. Along similar lines, Koester, comparing Q and Thomas materials, has postulated an underlying sayings Gospel that must have been very primitive in nature and close to Jesus' own voice (1971b, 166–87; 1971a). One keeps going backward until one accounts for every layer as an explanation and interpretation of a prior layer. "The cartography stretches from text to text, to the last text in terra incognita" (Cartlidge 1990, 404). Or, to take our vantage point from the tradition's ἀρχή, we watch the unfolding of tradition from single sayings to sayings clusters, and from sayings Gospel to protobiography, which in turn signals the way toward the narrative Gospel.

The paradigm of the evolutionary trajectory remains the all-determining but unexamined hermeneutical underpinning. It raises a host of historical and linguistic questions. On what grounds can we define Q's generic identity as protobiography? We can know that at the outset Q situated John in the "circuit of the Jordan," setting the stage, religiously and geopolitically, for Q's message (Kloppenborg 1991, 145–60). But John's wilderness locale does not constitute a genre definition. We should also admit that Matthew and Luke saw to it that the incipit, Q's own genre designation, was erased. It is worth remembering, moreover, that it was a fluke of history, namely, Matthew's and Luke's simultaneous absorption of Q, that puts us in a position to disengage and identify Q, or parts thereof. As far as Matthew and Luke were concerned, they intended to bury Q *as genre* in their chosen narrative genres.

Are we not operating on modern standards of literary and theological consistency if we use wisdom and apocalyptic as defining criteria for separating strata in the tradition? Williams has succinctly articulated this issue: "It is ... an imposition of modern assumptions about form and genre to conclude that clusters of an identifiable type in a text represent a different stratum of redaction" (1988, 105; see also Collins 1988, 152; Horsley and Draper 1999, 61–83). Horsley's proposal that we learn to think of Q, its composition and social location, in terms of cluster formation and sequence of discourses would appear to come much closer to ancient compositional realities than stratification theories (Horsley and Draper 1999, 83–93, 195–249). His thesis that the discernment of a sapiential versus an apocalyptic stratum in Q "may be rooted more in the conceptual apparatus of modern New Testament scholarship than in the text of Q" (1991a, 196) deserves very serious attention. We must ask, moreover, to what extent has our knowledge of Thomas conditioned the allocation of wisdom materials to a first stratum of Q? Are *Gospel of Thomas* and Q traceable to a single, underlying archetype, or are they not rather collateral developments, participants in a polyphonic sayings tradition in which words intersect, replay, reconnect in ways that do not necessarily line up on a single trajectory? After all, we do not find in *Gospel of Thomas* and Q the kind of verbal agreements that persuaded us to postulate a single textual identity of Q in the background of Matthean and Lukan parallels.

Moreover, the layered concept of tradition raises questions about the adequacy of our theory of the verbal art in antiquity. Do we perhaps assume the compositional practice of successive layering without explicit reflection on matters of ancient scribality and hermeneutics? How is one to imagine, technically and chirographically, the production of a stratified text? Does the behavior of language, both oral and written, match the stratigraphic, evolutionary rationale that shapes our reconstructions of tradition?

Thinking of texts in oral contextuality, rather than in terms of literary consistency, allows us to rediscover the functional quality of ancient chirographs. The ancient world of communications exemplifies the unbound nature of all language. Fundamentally, chirographs were not perceived as having firmly fixed boundaries. Robinson's observation that the *Gospel of Thomas* not only "share[s] a fluidity of text with other non- or not-yet-canonical literature, but also a fluidity of text particularly characteristic of sayings collections where there is no train of thought or causal nexus to stabilize the text from saying to saying" (Robinson 1986b, 160–61), can be extended to cover a much larger portion of ancient scriptographic materials. In fact, the observed fluidity of text is not a generic issue per se, related to sayings collections, but an issue of the ancient media environment. Standing at the intersection with speech, any textualized saying or sayings collection, or for that matter any part of a text, could be called on to commune with the life of tradition. In part, tradition kept itself alive precisely by freely appropriating elements of chirographic culture. Nor did chirographs have temporal limitations, which would confine them to this period or that stratum. What served in the past could well be reused for the present. It would be wrong, moreover, to associate ancient texts with private authorship or ownership. For the most part, texts were viewed as constituents of a collective cultural enterprise or of a communal memory. Unrestricted by laws against plagiarism, they tended to be usable, quotable, and alterable. All this suggests a behavior quite different from stratigraphic logic, which seeks an exact determination of stages in the tradition. Only typography can seduce us into thinking in terms of tidy, closely controlled language spaces.

The observation that scribal products are embedded in the soft matrix of speech takes on special significance in the cases of Q and the *Gospel of Thomas*. In *OWG* I have suggested that Q displays "a fundamentally oral disposition" (1983, 201). Underlying many of the criticisms that have been leveled against this proposition lurks the controversial issue of Q's hermeneutical posture. Kloppenborg has emphasized the historicizing frame of Q's final version and the absence of the prophetic formula τάδε λέγει ὁ κύριος (1987, 34–37). Manifestly, it is not the exalted Lord who is speaking in Q. But is the document adequately understood as a protobiography that gives us the preresurrectional past of Jesus? As is well known, Q attributes to Jesus a mixed speaking style comprising both historicizing and contemporizing introductory formulae (Boring 1982, 179–82). To keep the problematic in focus, one should first recall that Lukan and Matthean editing, by merging Q with their narrative genres, most likely strengthened the historicizing side of the sayings Gospel. When, therefore, Luke 9:58 reads καὶ εἶπεν αὐτῷ ὁ Ἰησοῦς, and the Matthean parallel 8:20 καὶ λέγει αὐτῷ ὁ Ἰησοῦς, one is well advised to deviate from conventional "Lukan priority" and give preference to Matthew's present tense. It should furthermore be acknowledged that in many instances these formulae elude our reconstructive efforts. Comparing, for example, Luke 13:20 (Καὶ πάλιν εἶπεν) with its Matthean parallel 13:33 (Ἄλλην παραβολὴν ἐλάλησεν αὐτοῖς), one is compelled to conclude that we are dealing with a Lukan and a Matthean formulation respectively. Kloppenborg suggests that the dialectic tension between contemporizing and historicizing diction had shifted toward the latter in the last stage of the Q redaction with the addition of the temptation story (1987, 256–62), which altered the generic status of Q as a whole. In Kloppenborg's view, the effect is comparable to the displacement of words of the risen Lord into a narrative of the preresurrectional Jesus (257). However, this is precisely the kind of analogy that skews the hermeneutics of Q.

A prime characteristic of Q, negatively speaking, is the absence of the kerygma of passion and resurrection. On this we can all agree, I believe. It crucially determines the hermeneutical posture of Q in that it distinguishes it both from Mark, who narrated Jesus in his preresurrectional past culminating in crucifixion, and from the other three Gospels, which clearly distinguish between a pre-Easter and post-Easter Jesus. Not unlike the *Gospel of Thomas*, Q does not think in terms of a preresurrectional versus a postresurrectional differential at all. Tödt hits the mark in stating that "we cannot help getting the impression that it did not even occur to the members of the community which collected the sayings of Jesus in Q to distinguish between pre-Easter and post-Easter sayings, it being self-evident to them that the earthly and the risen Jesus are one and the same" (265). In other words, Jesus as historicized and presently actualized person claims one and the same authority. The "addition" of the temptation story (if we have to think in terms of redactional stages) cannot be compared with a shift from post-Easter to pre-Easter status, for Easter as a hermeneutical differential is alien to the genre of Q. Thus, far from altering the hermeneutical stance of Q, the story comports entirely with the genre's mixed style. In media perspectives, the Q community seeks to resist the stabilizing effects of writing by fusing Jesus' past with his present "because they realized the urge to continue to teach what Jesus had been teaching" (Tödt 1965, 265). Therein lies the "fundamentally oral disposition" of Q.

The media disposition of the *Gospel of Thomas* bespeaks greater complexities. The identification of the speaker with the "living Jesus" in the Gospel's incipit accommodates oral interests in a very particular sense. He is unmistakably introduced as a present and presently speaking authority. His present standing is further underscored by the absence of a thoroughgoing narrative syntax with its historicizing effects. It is doubtful whether this Jesus can be equated with the crucified/risen one of the canonical tradition, because the kerygma of death and resurrection is as alien to Thomas as it is to Q. As for Jesus' death, it need not surprise us that none of the 114 sayings of *Gospel of Thomas* reveals any interest in the subject matter. For if it is a purpose of *Gospel of Thomas* to realize the presence of Jesus as speaker of aphorisms and parables, any reflection on his death would be irrelevant, indeed, self-contradictory. A genre that is intent on extending the "living Jesus" into the present cannot at the same time propagate his absence.

As for Jesus' resurrection, *Gospel of Thomas* is not cast into the genre of a revelation discourse of the risen Christ. Sharply to the point is Koester's observation that "there are no features compelling us to understand the work as a secret revelation after the resurrection" (1971b, 167). It is therefore inadmissible to seek the rationale for the speaking posture of the "living Jesus" in the resurrection. What we do observe is a Jesus who, while consistently speaking in the past tense, continues to address the present of the Thomas community. Although de facto spatialized and in a sense frozen in time, his words are perceived to be living words that transcend spatial boundaries. As in the case of Q, we observe the phenomenon of the past and present Jesus speaking with one and the same authority.

Unlike Q, however, the *Gospel of Thomas* is further characterized by a certain amount of tension between its chirographic existence and its Jesus' speaking posture. Tension first surfaces in the incipit, which identifies "the secret sayings which the living Jesus spoke" with those that "Didymos Judas Thomas wrote." What is noticeable is a degree of self-consciousness concerning the media realities: Jesus' speech acts are meant to be presently accessible to the readers/hearers as products of writing. As articulated in the incipit, this is the media problematic that the *Gospel of Thomas* seeks to cope with by synchronizing the past of Jesus with his present. What distinguishes the words of the "living Jesus" is their oral efficaciousness; they have power to give life. And yet, life is not directly available through speech and hearing, for Thomas's Jesus imposes the arduous task of interpretation (ἑρμηνεία) upon the hearers of his words.

There are still deeper media problematics inscribed in this Gospel. Esoteric secrecy is a case in point. The *Gospel of Thomas* maintains the fictional scenario of Jesus' esoteric instruction to a privileged group of insiders, most of whom appear to be disciples. Among them Simon Peter, Matthew, Thomas, Mary, and Salome are mentioned by name. But this esoteric scene of intimate discourse conflicts with the Gospel's written identity, which extends an open invitation to all who can hear what appears to have been intended only for the few. Thus the chirograph compromised the protectionist instincts of esoteric secrecy. Spoken to the few, but written for the many, the Gospel is deeply animated by the desire to retain the *viva vox* of the "living Jesus" (Kelber 1989).

Although the tradition is available to us exclusively in texts, not all texts are intelligible on the model of intertextuality and successive layers of literary growth. The genre of the sayings Gospel illustrates the tenacity of oral drives and strategies in the tradition. This is not to deny that the genre is unthinkable, or unavailable, without the technology of writing. Sayings and parables were divorced from their speaking environment and recontextualized in a scripted arrangement. But in underwriting the validity of the aphoristic and parabolic units of Jesus' speech and in going to great lengths in extending his voice and speaking posture into the present, the genre remains at the service of basically oral sensibilities. Lest we exaggerate the media tension of *Gospel of Thomas*, we need reminding that the Gospels' oral motivation enjoyed the support of a media environment in which the boundaries between writing and speech were fluid. Benefiting from the free flow of communication that existed between chirographs and living speech, the genre could induce a sense of presence that sought to prevail over the pastness created by all writing.

Given our growing awareness of the media complexity of pre-Synoptic realities, we cannot assent to models that re-create tradition as exclusively textual processes of production, transmission, and transformation, depersonalized and diagrammatically traceable through space, any more than we can accept a reduction of tradition solely to discourse and the aesthetics of reception, untouched by literacy and transacted in primal oral purity. Brian Stock's observation that in medieval culture "oral and written traditions normally function in relation to each other" (1990, 145) will apply to the Hellenistic era as well. Writing was linked to speech in so many ways that our typographic apperception of textuality will never let us know. Our text-centrism has blinded us to imagining ways in which speech could emanate from chirographs or in turn generate writings. But once we think of tradition as interactive processes, we concede the presence of a dynamic that is other than either pure orality or pure literacy, for which we have no name and of which we have little experience.

If we conceive of tradition as a more inclusive and less tangible reality than our literate senses let us know, we must also consider the role of hearers. To be sure, words interiorized, faith engendered, doubts raised, hopes aroused, expectations reversed, and images invoked are intractable features. Vanished forever are the speakers, voices, and listeners. Reader-response criticism deserves credit for having rehabilitated the role of the reader by focusing on the rhetorical directives inscribed in texts. The ensuing shift in orientation from the mimetic to the pragmatic axis has reawakened us to the signal involvement of audiences in the work of tradition (Iser 1974; 1978; Fowler 1983; 1984; 1985a; 1985b; 1991). No doubt, interest in receptionist aesthetics "opens the way to a greater sensitivity to the oral and relational dynamics" (Coward 1988, 182) that has characterized the transaction of ancient texts. And yet in order to grasp the fuller implications of hearers' participation (not simply responses), we will in the end have to overcome our text-bound thinking and come to terms with a reality that is not encoded in texts at all. It means that we must learn to think of a large part of tradition as an extratextual phenomenon. What permitted hearers to internalize the so-called parable of the Good Samaritan, for example, was a culture shared by speaker and hearers alike. Unless hearers have some experience or knowledge of the role of priests, Levites, and Samaritans in society, or rather of their social construction, this parable will not strike a responsive chord with them. Whether hearers are Samaritans themselves, partisans of Samaritan identity, or informed by anti-Samaritan sentiments will make a difference in the way they hear the story. Shared experiences about the dangers of traveling, the social role of priests and Levites, and the ethics of charity weave a texture of cultural commonality that makes the story resonate in the hearts and minds of hearers. Tradition in this encompassing sense is a circumambient contextuality or *biosphere* in which speaker and hearers live. It includes texts and experiences transmitted through or derived from texts. But it is anything but reducible to intertextuality. *Tradition in this broadest sense is largely an ascertainable and invisible nexus of references and identities from which people draw sustenance, in which they live, and in relation to which they make sense of their lives. This invisible biosphere is at once the most elusive and foundational feature of tradition.*

The concept of tradition as biosphere suggests that the Great Divide thesis, which pits oral tradition vis-à-vis Gospel text, cannot in the end supply the answer to questions concerning tradition and Gospel. If the emphasis in *OWG* fell on that division, it was because a novel approach requires a strong thesis. It does not, however, discredit orality studies any more than it outdates examination of the role of scribality in the life of tradition. In fact, we need just such strong theses to comprehend the integrity of oral discourse versus scriptographic verbalization. To grasp the overlaps and interfaces, we have to understand the hermeneutics of speech and writing in the first place, even if they rarely, if ever, existed in a pure state.

The issue of the canonical Gospels' engagement in tradition, and tradition's relation to these Gospels, has thus remained unresolved. One reason for this state of affairs is plainly the inaccessibility of large parts of the so-called the pre-Synoptic traditions. But we are not entirely locked in ignorance either. There is what may be a prevailing view that the Gospels did not grow directly out of oral discourse any more than they originated directly in the historicity of their subject matter. Albert Lord's (1978) ingenious explication of the Gospels as oral traditional narratives has met with little approval among biblical scholars. His approach to the Synoptic Problem is entirely different from the methodological and conceptual universe in which biblical scholars work, and for this reason has remained alien to them. In light of current orality-scribality studies, however, Lord's proposal needs to be revisited. Lord's thesis aside, such are the agreements of wording and sequences of Synoptic episodes that the hands and voices of chirography cannot entirely be ruled out, especially as regards the relation of Matthew and Luke vis-à-vis Mark. To be sure, the Gospels, along with other ancient chirography, were enmeshed with speech by way of composition, recitation, and reception. But this is not to say that they are autographs of speech, that is, multiforms of essentially the same oral genre. Writing, no matter how closely allied with oral sensibilities and practices, did make a difference. Mark's parabolic narrative, for example, is clearly designed to be read to and heard by audiences, but it is not simply speech transposed into script, a rendition of an oral traditional narrative. Those are distinctions worth keeping in mind. While the Gospel invites—indeed, demands—oral performance, it is not simply the product of oral traditional composition, as has been assumed in the case of the Homeric epics.

In addition to certain literary consistencies among the Synoptic Gospels, there is the observation that Mark's Gospel provides little evidence for efforts to preserve a core tradition, that is, a traditional oral narrative. An examination of his plot dynamics, for example, his compositional intentionality, does not lead us to the assumption of an orally composed and performed narrative. We come closer to Mark's purpose if we hear the narrative not as an autograph of speech but as a hermeneutically charged transaction. In other words, the Gospel is intelligible as a narrative addressing hearers by engaging tradition selectively, but not by reappropriating it comprehensively. Crossan has proposed that Mark's Gospel came to be written as a result of multiple revisions of *Secret Mark*, *Papyrus Egerton 2* (1985), and the passion story of the *Gospel of Peter* (1988). Koester has credited Mark's narrative for having united aretological materials with the passion story (1990, 292), and he further views canonical Mark as "an abbreviated version of the Secret Gospel of Mark" (302). Robinson (1970 [1982c]), Boring (1977; 1982, 195–203), and my own work (1983, 199–211; 1987c) finally interpreted canonical Mark as a corrective to the genre of the sayings Gospel. I remain convinced that of all the traditional features Mark appears to have absorbed and revised, the sayings Gospel deserves pride of place (Kelber 1992, 42–58). The relative paucity of dominical sayings, the christological focus on the cross, the withholding of the living Lord from the disciples, the role reversal of the disciples from insiders to outsiders, the rigorously constructed pre-Easter form of the narrative, and the deconstruction of secrecy are principal features that run directly counter to the fundamentally oral disposition of the genre of the sayings Gospel. What matters here, however, is that the proposals put forth by Crossan, Koester, Robinson, Boring, and myself give us a sense both of the polyphonic nature of the pre-Synoptic tradition and of the diachronic complexity encoded in the narrative Gospel. The more complex the picture of the Gospel's plural engagements in tradition, the less plausible is the concept of the Gospel as uninterpreted fullness of what preceded it. Irrespective of the merit of each of the above proposals, it does seem demonstrable that Mark's Gospel abounds in multiple traces, plural echoes, displacement features, and revisionary strategies. No longer imaginable as the culmination of tradition's assumed evolutionary trajectory, it appears both as the beneficiary of tradition and as an interventionist text with respect to some of tradition's fundamental drives.

Those who had a hand and voice in composing the Gospel absorbed information of different kinds. "But how is one to imagine—technically, psychologically, religiously—Mark's skillful juggling of a number of texts, using them, revising them, deconstructing them, while all along composing an impressively coherent narrative?," I asked a few years ago (1987c, 120). The more numerous the materials Mark appears to be coping with, the less is this Gospel imaginable as the reworking of a single text, be it written or oral. But the principle of intertextuality also becomes increasingly implausible, unless we are prepared to locate "Mark" in a well-funded library. In the end, it seems, we cannot think of the Gospel narratives apart from their social habitat, media world, and biosphere. The Gospels were products of urban Christian communities. If we adopt Brian Stock's model of "textual communities," one may think of social settings in which certain individuals were responsible for the dictation and writing of these narratives, while the majority of the community was hearers. Considering the proliferation of the Christian movement that had already occurred with respect to the Pauline communities, one can plausibly assume the existence of a plurality of interpretive features, of rival interpretations, of a competing Gospel genre even, in those postwar communities that, in my view, authored and hosted the Gospels. Not unlike Paul, Mark had access to plural and rival features of the tradition through chirographs, oral communication derived from and filtered through chirographs, and by word of mouth. On Paul's model, moreover, we can begin to think not of unidirectional textuality or pure orality, but rather of human memory, which, while nourished in the tradition's biosphere, was perfectly capable of redescribing parts thereof.

The Gospel text once in existence was to be performed orally or celebrated liturgically, either in part or perhaps in toto. In either case, it was read aloud and reinterpreted in sermons, thus complicating tradition by a "secondary orality," one derived from and filtered through the medium of a single text. And it may also have become the springboard for new texts such as other Gospels, commentaries, and homilies yet to be written. It is in this multimedia sense that we have to imagine the workings of tradition, and in this multimedia environment that we have to place the Gospel as a defining center of community.

29. Ancient Media Sensibilities

This essay has attempted to raise consciousness about the Enlightenment parentage of the modern discipline of biblical scholarship. Throughout, the underlying, nagging question has been whether the scholarly discourse of reason accords with the hermeneutical sensibilities of late antiquity. To be sure, serious doubts about the premises of historical criticism have been raised before. From the collapse of the liberal Quest, for example, we had to learn the lesson that Gospel language and historical actuality do not correspond to each other in a one-to-one relationship. *What we have to learn additionally is that the scholarly implementation of language and our understanding of the functioning of language itself is patently culture-bound and specifically media-bound.* The search for singular originality concealed behind layers of textual encumbrances at the root of an evolutionary tree reveals much about the force of our desire but falls short of understanding the oral implementation of multioriginality in the present act of speaking. Only on paper do texts appear to relate in a one-to-one relation to other texts. The fixation on authorial intent, on language as self-legitimating discourse, on the reduction of tradition to processes of textual transmission and stratification, and on the perception of ancient chirographs as visualizable, disengaged objects opens a vast conceptual gap that separates our own typographic rationalities from ancient media sensibilities.

In reawakening consciousness about a world of tonal values, oral poetics, and speaking texts, I have attempted in this piece to summon up media sensibilities, including the time-bound nature of speech, that had informed the biblical tradition throughout ancient and medieval history. *I am persuaded that the integration of issues such as speech and the oral matrix of chirographic life, media interfaces, and the human sensorium— issues that have clearly not been given their due—matters considerably for a more adequate, indeed different, understanding of our religious past.* If we take into serious account the extensive work done on speech and writing in the last century, we can no longer reduce tradition to a history of ideas abstracted from texts and disincarnated from contexts. Instead of focusing single-mindedly on processes of transmission and text-to-text relations, we might consider reflection on the multimedia construction of meaning. Furthermore, if we can wean ourselves off of the notion that texts constitute the center of gravity in tradition, we may be able to imagine and work with a vastly broader concept of tradition and assign texts their proper place within it. There is a need as well to reexamine the editorial and source-critical theories that have fundamentally informed the work of historical criticism and to scrutinize their validity in light of ancient rhetorical and scriptographic realities. There is, lastly, but most importantly, the neglected sensory dimension in the tradition. Whereas in the logical tradition of Enlightenment, imagistic, acoustic, and emotive apperception was largely banished from the work of reason, in the ancient tradition perception was a form of imagination, for example, a form of interior visualization. It was standard epistemological experience far into the Middle Ages that word and pictures were conjoined, that the senses interacted with intelligibility, and sight and hearing served as catalysts of cognition. Instead of pure thought based on textuality, we find rhetorical discourse, chirographs soaked in the oral biosphere, interfacing media, and the play of the human sensorium, making up the cultural matrix of tradition.

6

LANGUAGE, MEMORY, AND SENSE PERCEPTION IN THE RELIGIOUS AND TECHNOLOGICAL CULTURE OF ANTIQUITY AND THE MIDDLE AGES

The first part of this, the ninth Milman Parry and Albert Lord Lecture, *locates these two scholars and their intellectual project in the broader context of the humanities. Next, the essay discusses the oral, rhetorical concept of language developed by the pre-Socratic philosopher Gorgias and contrasts it with Plato's efforts to tame rhetoric by attempting to subjugate it to logic. The third part reviews theories of memory in ancient myth and in the philosophical, rhetorical tradition (Aristotle, Cicero, Quintilian). The fourth part contextualizes Paul the apostle in the broader sweep of late antiquity's rhetorical culture. Paul's argumentative rationale, it is argued, is of an oral, rhetorical, not of a theo-logical kind. The main focus of the fifth part is St. Augustine's rapturous endorsement of memory, his assimilation of classical rhetoric to a biblically rooted scribality, and his philosophical-linguistic signs theory—all features that contributed to dominant medieval concepts of language and cognition. The sixth part explores the gradual transition in medieval history from oral, rhetorical sensibilities to a developing manuscript culture, which entailed shifts in the concepts of memory, cognition, and language. The seventh part explores the two supreme philosophical-theological achievements of medieval learning, scholasticism and nominalism, from the angle of an accelerating scribality and a growing textual database. Both St. Thomas's passion for impersonal, rational penetration of the subject matter and William of Ockham's* cognitio intuitiva, *it is argued, are beneficiaries of an established, institutionalized scribal culture. The last part summarizes the principal thesis of this essay concerning shifting roles of language, memory, and sense perception in antiquity and the Middle Ages.*

Major developments, in culture and consciousness are related, often in
unexpected intimacy, to the evolution of the word from primary orality
to its present state. But the relationships are varied and complex, with
cause and effect often difficult to distinguish.
                                    —Walter J. Ong, *Interfaces of the Word*

Omnis nostra cognitio a sensu initium habet.
                                    —St. Thomas, *Summa Theologica*

30. HOMAGE TO PARRY AND LORD

The two persons in whose honor this lecture is named were North American classicists of eminence who had acquired additional training in the
oral traditional epics of the former Yugoslavia, an achievement unequaled
among scholars of their time. Long before interdisciplinary studies had
come into scholarly and curricular vogue, Milman Parry and Albert Lord
had attained a literacy in comparative studies that was both severely academic and daringly imaginative. Almost singlehandedly, they initiated
the distinct academic field of oral traditional literature, which concerns
itself with the study of compositional, performative, and aesthetic aspects
of living oral traditions and of texts dependent on oral tradition. Strictly
speaking, the work inaugurated by Parry and Lord, and energetically carried forward by John Miles Foley, aspires to a new poetics informed by our
growing knowledge of oral tradition. By now the field has grown into a
scholarship that cuts across a wide spectrum of the humanities and social
sciences, bridging national and religious boundaries, and encompassing
the multicultural body of the human race.

Broadly speaking, the impact of Parry and Lord extends beyond the
subject matter of oral tradition. The rediscovery of a culture of speech in
the Western tradition has in turn encouraged reflection on the nature of
texts, exposing a dominantly post-Gutenberg mentality within classical,
biblical, and medieval studies. To a growing number of scholars who are
proficient in the field of oral traditional literature, it is evident that there
is something different about many of our classical texts, and our conventional reading of them, than most branches of current literary and historical criticism would let us know. Oral and orally dependent texts were
tradition-bound, variously interfacing with orality and other texts, and
deriving meaning from extratextual influences no less than from internal signification. "What we are wrestling with," Foley has suggested, "is

not just 'mechanism' versus 'aesthetics,' not just 'oral' versus 'literary,' but an inadequate theory of verbal art" (1991, 5). Eric Havelock (1963) and Walter Ong (1967b; 1982; 1983), whose work likewise came to focus on the culture of orality, pursued still broader avenues into philosophical, intellectual, and religious history. Today, the field commonly referred to as orality-literacy studies challenges us to rethink a set of concepts we thought we had known for certain. Text and intertextuality, author and tradition, reading and writing, memory and imagination, logic and cognition—these central metaphors of Western thought—are all affected by the study of oral traditions and a chirographic culture interacting with them. We begin to see—as if through a glass darkly—the broader implications of Parry and Lord's scholarship for understanding our cultural heritage.

This essay will not consider the technicalities and aesthetics of oral traditions per se. It will pay homage to Parry and Lord by developing across ancient and medieval culture some implications of the intellectual project they initiated. The broad and rather sweeping scope of the essay does not aspire to another metahistory, for this author shares postmodernism's anxiety about the futility (and vanity) of global narrative ambitions. History resists assimilation to single research paradigms. But in reinvesting imaginatively the interdisciplinary endowment of Parry and Lord, this piece seeks to identify issues of longstanding and persistent urgency resonating across the religious and technological culture of our ancient and medieval past.

31. The Emotive and Magical Powers of Speech

"Speech is a powerful ruler" (Gorgias, *Helen* 8: λόγος δυνάστης μέγας ἐστίν). With these words, the fifth-century-b.c.e. sophist, rhetor, and rhetorician Gorgias invoked what for him was the critical issue of language. Ostensibly, the idea of language he had in mind was shaped by the condition of media realities in his culture. The λόγος was perceived here neither as sign nor signification, and not as carrier of meaning or revealer of truth, but rather as a potent ruler intent on governing his subjects. Gorgias's idea of the λόγος flowed directly from the experience of oral speech. Language was perceived to be a force, orally processed and operative in relation to hearers. This theme enunciated by Gorgias has retained its hold on Western culture, bequeathing to it a myriad of linguistic, philosophical, and political problems. True to the oral, rhetorical epistemology, Gorgias advocated an approach to language that has affinity with the insights recently gained by receptionist theory. What interested him primarily about speech was not the processes of verbal composition but the aesthetics of reception. "Of λόγοι some give pain, some pleasure, some cause fear, some create boldness in hearers, and some drug and bewitch the soul by a kind of evil persuasion" (*Helen* 14: τῶν λόγων οἱ μὲν ἐλύψαν, οἱ δε ἔτερψαν, οἱ δὲ ἐφόβησαν, οἱ δὲ εἰς θάρσος κατέστησαν τοὺς ἀκούοντας, οἱ δὲ πειθοῖ τινι κακῇ τὴν ψυχὴν ἐψαρμάκευσαν καὶ ἐξεγοήτευσαν). The arousal of pain and pleasure, of fear and pity is the primary objective of the λόγοι. Among words Gorgias singled out the metered language of the poetic tradition, which effected fearsome horrors, tearful sympathies, and melancholic desires (*Helen* 9). He did not entirely dismiss the rational aspects of speech. Occasionally he would attend to speech as τέχνη, an acquirable art. But his main interest lay in the elaboration of a psychology of the emotive powers of oral communication. The efficaciousness of words meshed with the form of the soul, influencing it, molding it, and converting it. It was this affective persuasion of the soul that lies at the heart of Gorgias's theory of language.

The alliance Western culture has forged with the powers of oral speech is an addictive but uneasy one. Gorgias himself introduced the celebrated metaphor of the φάρμακον. The power of words affects the soul as the drug does the body (*Helen* 14). In speech, the processes of healing and poisoning were mysteriously mingled, swaying the psychic condition for better and for worse. Under the powerful spell of speeches, the soul was likely to be cured or deceived. The worst possible scenario, and one Gorgias was keenly aware of, was the use of words for flattery, manipulation, and the fulfillment of personal longings for power. The principal characterization of this aspect of speech was deception (ἀπάτη). It was a stigma that would cling to the powers of speech from antiquity to modernity. Pressed for an explanation for this ambiguous operation of oral language, Gorgias invoked the realm of magic and religion. The spell of words, especially poetic words, was perceived to be closely allied with magic and witchcraft (De Romilly 1975). Poetic performances, the stirrings of passion, and the conversion of the soul escaped rational probings. Divine both in origin and in their inspirational effect, they created a godlike trance (ἐνθουσιασμός) among hearers. Speech thus put into effect by accomplished oral practitioners could amount to a form of divine madness.

It bears repeating that the principal problematic of language, as viewed by Gorgias, was not meaning, but power. How did one cope with the poetic powers that drew their sustenance from divine resources? Should speech be liberated from its seductiveness and channeled into the παιδεία of truth and wisdom? How could the awesome powers of magical, inspirational speech be harnessed and integrated into a viable educational program? How destructive a force was language untamed by method and τέχνη? Clearly, the issue was that language, that is, orally produced language, manifested itself in terms of force and effect rather than with a view toward meaning, structure, or signification.

Once we recognize the importance attributed to language as power, and the duplicity of language in terms of healing and poisoning, Plato himself and his philosophical project begins to take on a novel meaning. It was Havelock's signal humanistic achievement to have relocated the master philosopher into the broad cultural context of a technological and intellectual revolution in antiquity (1963; 1978; 1982). Propelled by the invention of the "explosive technology" of the Greek alphabet (1982, 6), a literate consciousness was ushered in that challenged the millennial tradition of poeticized, recitable language—the language of power and magic. In that age of sweeping cultural changes, Plato's dialogues both accelerated the collapse of tradition-honored habits and endeavored to explore alternative ways of understanding. The philosopher lived "in the midst of this revolution, announced it and became its prophet" (Havelock 1963, vii). Poised between the ancien régime of the poets and the literate technology of a new age, he articulated a moral and intellectual program that assimilated the reorganization of culture and consciousness.

When Plato refused to admit the poets into his well-ordered state (*Republic* 605b, 607b), he pointed to the emotive and magical impact of their words. He did not mind telling his audience that what it was applauding in the theater was the conduct of a woman, whereas men had learned to retain control over their passions (*Republic* 605d, e). His chief objection, however, did not rest on the problematic linking of poetic emotions with gender, but on the issue of μίμησις. The mimetic art practiced by "friend Homer" (*Republic* 599d) and his fellow poets corrupted the soul and destroyed its rational part by fashioning phantoms removed from reality. The poeticized tradition and experience of rhythmic and emotional spells so necessary to the act of identification was a kind of "psychic poison" (Havelock 1963, 5). Plato's targets, Havelock came to realize, were the dramatic performances and the audio-visual group experience of audiences, and the degree to which this theatrical mentality indoctrinated a plurality of hearers about matters such as justice and the good. Had Homer been able to truly educate the people, he would have "possessed not the art of imitation but real knowledge" (*Republic* 600c: οὐ μιμεῖσθαι ἀλλὰ γιγνώσκειν δυνάμενος).

Plato himself lacked the temporal distance to fully appreciate the cultural, linguistic context and implications of his own tirade against the Homeric poetic tradition. It was Havelock's (1963) illuminating work on Plato that explicated μίμησις in terms of a millennial experience of oral performing and traditioning. Shaping language in rhythmic, memorable fashion and composing it via the oral processes of imitation, the poets encouraged recitation and learning through repetition, as well as emphatic participation. But as far as Plato was concerned, knowledge acquired by imitation, repetition, and empathy was of little value. What mattered was to determine "what each thing really is" (*Republic* 533b: ὃ ἔστιν ἕκαστον), which required a new type of mental activity envisioned as a conversion away from plural impressions toward the abstracted object and timeless truth. For the philosophical purpose of Platonism was "to accelerate the intellectual awakening which 'converts' the *psyche* from the many to the one, and from 'becomingness' to 'beingness'" (Havelock 1963, 258–59). This new type of intellectual activity was related to the methods of mental storage that had undergone changes since the time of the Homeric bards. Alphabetic literacy not only distanced the individual from the tribal encyclopedia but also freed the mind to entertain thoughts apart from and even against it. Plato's resentment of the poets could thus well be understood as a revolt of the literate mentality against the oral traditional hegemony of the Homeric, poetic culture.

Although Plato's philosophy was a beneficiary of the rationalizing effects brought about in part at least by the alphabetization of the Greek language and chirography, the philosopher could not bring himself to embrace the new medium as a matter of principle. While availing himself of the new chirographic technology, he lamented its corrosive effects on memory, discourse, and culture generally, basing his objections on a thoroughly oral apperception of language. Writing, far from assisting memory, implanted forgetfulness into our souls (*Phaedrus* 275a). Written words were antisocial, because they segregated themselves from living discourse. Like paintings, writings "maintain a solemn silence"; they stare at readers, telling them "just the same thing forever" (*Phaedrus* 275d: σεμνῶς πάνυ σιγᾷ ... ἓν σημαίνει μόνον ταὐτὸν ἀεί). Chirographic products were rather like children who had lost their parents and were unable to defend themselves. Plato knew that it was the inevitable fate of writings to fall into the hands of the wrong people (*Phaedrus* 275e). Writing, finally, was an unacceptable exteriorization of thought that only gave the appearance of wisdom (*Phaedrus* 275a). These were all arguments characteristic of a mind deeply versed in oral culture, distrustful of the harmful influence of writing and committed to the living, dialogical, and interiorizing powers of speech.

Poetic speech aside, what would Plato have to say about nonpoeticized, oral speech that by his time came to be called rhetoric? On this matter he joined Gorgias in denouncing speakers who "steal away our souls" (*Menexenus* 235a: γοητεύσουσιν ἡμῶν τὰς ψυχάς) with their embellished words and whose flattery sends us to the "Islands of the Blessed" (*Menexenus* 235c: μακάρων νήσοις). Rhetoric simply as a producer of persuasion was hostile to an environment that nourished discourse and dialogue. Ask any of our proficient speakers about their words, Plato exclaimed in a state of exasperation, and they will give us more speeches of the same: "Like books they cannot either answer or ask a question on their own account" (*Protagoras* 329b: ὥσπερ βιβλία οὐδὲν ἔχουσιν οὔτε ἀποκρίνασθαι οὔτε αὐτοὶ ἐρέσθαι). The "art of oratory" (*Phaedrus* 262c: λόγον ἄρα τέχνην) is no art at all if it is practiced by one who is "chasing after beliefs, instead of knowing the truth" (*Phaedrus* 262c: δόξας τεθηρευκώς). Rhetoric's basic flaw was thus its inability to enlist words in the search for truth.

Resentful of the magical powers of speech, in revolt against the poetic mentors of ancient Greece, and distrustful as well of the new technology of writing, Plato redefined the oral, rhetorical tradition in terms of dialectic. One of its objectives was to keep words alive in the flow of discourse and to forestall ideational sedimentation. Unfettered by scribal constraints and mimetic routine, dialectic availed itself of the oral mode of communication, which was flexible enough to facilitate replacement of anything with something else, should the need arise. But dialectic was now conceived as a "discourse of reason" (*Republic* 532a: διὰ τοῦ λόγου), distanced from Gorgias's magical comprehension of speech, and unthinkable without the rationalizing effects of writing. Dialectical reasoning isolated and defined subject matters, divided and subdivided them until "it reached the limit of division" (*Phaedrus* 277b: μέχρι τοῦ ἀτμήτου τέμνειν ἐπιστηθῇ). Proceeding in this analytic fashion, it aspired to lead the soul away from the particulars and toward the contemplation of "the very essence of each thing" (*Republic* 532a: ἐπ' αὐτὸ ὃ ἔστιν ἕκαστον).

One of the most revolutionary aspects of the Platonic dialectic was its ambition to arrive at the nature of things "apart from all perceptions of sense" (*Republic* 532a: ἄνευ πασῶν τῶν αἰσθήσεων). The person most likely to succeed was one whose soul was "free of all distractions such as hearing or sight or pain or pleasure of any kind" (*Phaedrus* 65c: τούτων μηδὲν παράλυπη, μήτε ἀκοὴ μήτε ὄψις μήτε ἀλγηδὼν μηδέ τις ἡδονή) and eager to pursue the truth "by applying his pure and unadulterated thought" (*Phaedrus* 66a: αὐτῇ καθ'αὑτὴν εἰλικρινεῖ τῇ διανοίᾳ χρώμενος).

The quest for knowledge was to be transacted "by thought itself" (*Republic* 532b: αὐτῇ νοήσει), as it were. The result was language no longer in keeping with the affective persuasion of words and the divine madness they created among hearers; they were diametrically opposed to the cultural mind-set of Homeric orality. Language was in the process of being transformed into a catalyst of cognition, challenging the oral powers both of emotive incitement and of rhetorical persuasion.

Viewed in the context of a cultural revolution, Plato's dialectic endeavored to forge a middle way. It sought to retain the medium of speech, while effecting its domestication in the interest of logic. As a consequence, rhetoric's "'savage' roots" were severed (Ricoeur 1977, 10), and oratory was subjected to the discipline of philosophical reasoning. Oral discourse written into the soul of the listener remained a viable procedure, but it was discourse tamed by the logical restraints of dialectical reasoning. In late antiquity and in the Middle Ages, the dialectic tradition came to be situated between rhetoric on one hand and logic on the other, whose conflictual relationship introduced a deep and enduring problematic in the Western tradition.

Plato's daring project to purify thought by the exclusion of the senses flies in the face of ancient theories of knowledge. For it was widely understood that orality and rhetoric, as well as the art of scribality, engaged the human sensorium and played the sensory register in the interest of retention, emotive incitement, and persuasion. Ong's phenomenology of culture and consciousness has furnished ample evidence of the oral affinity between sound and thought (1967b, 111–75). What must be added is that the processes of knowledge were transacted by analogy with seeing no less than with hearing. Both voice *and* vision were sense analogues for the intellect. That one should "disregard the eyes and other senses and go on to being itself in the company with truth," as Plato would have it (*Republic* 537d: ὀμμάτων καὶ τῆς ἄλλης αἰσθήσεως ... μεθιέμενος ἐπ' αὐτὸ τὸ ὂν μετ'ἀληθείας ἰέναι), remains a revolutionary but passing reference in ancient philosophical discourse. For the exclusion of the human sensorium from the pursuits of knowledge was largely unthinkable in ancient and far into medieval intellectual culture.

Indeed, Plato cannot dishabituate himself from visual metaphors altogether. His language is replete with image analogues: εἰκών, εἴδωλον, φάντασμα, ὁμοίωμα, μίμημα (Patterson 1985, 30). For example, Plato would postulate the presence of an internal painter who draws into our soul pictures of assertions we make (*Philebus* 39b). More importantly, he defined the highest form of cognition as a vision (εἶδος) of the soul liberated from all earthly chains and ready to contemplate the real and the true (*Republic* 518c–519a). To obtain this view of the good, the soul has to be converted and its vision redirected "from the world of becoming to the world of being" (*Republic* 521d: ἀπὸ τοῦ γιγνομένου ἐπὶ τὸ ὄν). Whether the vision is internalized or outer-directed, there is a form of seeing no less than hearing that serves as an agent of cognition.

32. THE MEMORY TRADITION

A locus classicus for sense perception was memory, the esteemed "treasure-house of eloquence" (Quintilian *Inst.* 11.2.1, et al.: *thesaurus eloquentiae*). Long before the art of memory was assigned a place of honor in rhetoric, its significance was already recognized in mythology. According to myth, Mnemosyne, the goddess of memory, bore Zeus nine daughters, the Muses, who personified different modes of poetry, the arts, and sciences. An imaginable female, a corporeal similitude herself, the goddess embodied memory. Her daughters, who carried the attributes of wax tablet and pencil, the flute and lyre, the tragic and comic mask, the scroll and a celestial globe, represented a civilization that was constituted by writing and music, the tragic performance and comedy as well. But whether they facilitated sound or vision, speech or writing, they always functioned as the daughters of Mnemosyne. As mother of the Muses, she was the origin of all civilized labors and a wellspring of culture. *Memory, not textuality, was the centralizing authority.* Only a civilization conscious of and dependent on oral modes of communication and thought could have produced this myth of Mnemosyne and the Muses.

From Aristotle we have received one of the earliest, strikingly philosophical testimonies to memory. His treatise *Memory and Recollection* introduced a key feature of memory, namely, the theory of images. Responding to external stimulation, memory retained a visual representation of the external object. According to this principle, all our thoughts and perceptions were deposited in memory by way of images: "We cannot think without images" (*De Memoria* 449b.30: καὶ νοεῖν οὐκ ἔστιν ἄνευ φαντάσματος). What was actually present in memory were pictures (φαντάσματα) of the real things. In principle, memory could not process understanding as a function of pure thought. Even conceptual thought, Aristotle insisted, cannot exist without mental pictures (450a.10: ἡ δὲ μνήμη καὶ ἡ τῶν νοητῶν οὐκ ἄνευ φαντάσματος ἔστιν). Apart from its mythological thematization, memory was inescapably drawn into the orbit of rhetoric. For Cicero (*De Oratore* 2.87.355–358), for the anonymous author of *Rhetorica ad Herennium* (3.16.28–24.40), and for Quintilian (*Inst.* 11.2) oratory was a subject of supreme practical value, and memory the esteemed custodian of rhetoric. In the writings of these authors the theory of memory's *imagines* and *loci* is delineated in some detail. The work of memory was conducted via images and places; these were "the stock definition to be forever repeated down the ages" (Yates 1966, 6). The challenge was to create a condition that was favorably disposed to the retention of whatever one wanted to remember. First, one had to invent figures, marks, or portraits that adhered the longest in memory. Since all images required an abode, one secondly had to employ a large number of mental places, clearly defined, in orderly arrangement and separated at measured intervals. Memory thus perceived was entirely a spatial entity, like a house divided into many rooms, and its principal operating mechanism was the storing of images in those localities. Words no less than things were thought to be transmutable into images and localizable at places, although it was often recognized that the *memoria verborum* was more difficult to accomplish than the *memoria rerum*. Thus, in the work of memory, the visual nature of mental representations was widely taken for granted. "Of all the senses, sight is the keenest," Cicero exclaimed (*De Oratore* 357: *acerrimum autem ex omnibus nostris sensibus esse sensum videndi*), extolling the cognitive superiority of vision, a theme that was going to be replayed by Aquinas, Leonardo, John Locke, and a myriad of modern thinkers. But when we consider that words such as "fantasy" (φάντασμα), "imagination" (*imago*), and "rhetoric" itself, essential components of the rhetorical model of cognition, have largely become pejorative terms in modernity, we also recognize the changes in consciousness that distance us from our ancient heritage.

The memory tradition defied all theories of pure thought and verbocentrism. Plato's penchant for disembodied thought and desensitized vision of the good notwithstanding, ancient and medieval theories and practices of language were strongly indebted to a kind of physiology of perception (Padel 1991). It was widely assumed that both hearing and seeing mediated processes of recollection and perception. In spite of a developing chirographic culture, words were still perceived to be functioning more in the biosphere of human interaction than in the tissue of intertextuality. Knowledge took its rise from the sensorium.

33. PAUL AND THE ETHOS OF RHETORIC

Augustine, practicing rhetor and trained rhetorician himself, singled out Paul as a paragon of Christian oratory: "With what a river of eloquence [his words] flow, even he who snores must notice" (*De Doctrina Christiana* 4.7.12: *quanto vero etiam eloquentiae concurrerint flumine, et qui stertit advertit*). Indeed, Paul's letters, the earliest Christian canonical literary products, operated in the mode of argumentation and with the intent of producing conviction in audiences (Bultmann 1910; Wuellner 1977; Betz 1979; Stowers 1981). If Plato was the dialectician in search of a reasonable alternative to sophistic deception and the ancien régime of oral, poetic authority, and Aristotle the analytical rhetorician making the *ars rhetorica* safe for philosophy, Paul was the practicing Jewish-Christian rhetor ever mindful of his message's reception in hearers' hearts. Academic and popular wisdom, however, unaware of the ancient recognition of Paul's rhetorical skills and identity, has frequently identified him as Christianity's first self-conscious theologian. In this role he is perceived as a thinker who developed for reflection doctrinal topics such as Christology or eschatology, and who conceptualized faith, Spirit, and works. But to perceive him in this classic theological fashion is to deliver him to the time-honored rival of rhetoric, that is, to logic. While the degree of Paul's indebtedness to Jewish, Hellenistic, or Hellenistic-Jewish culture remains subject to debate, there is a growing realization that he did not seek the truth abstracted from the pragmatics of concrete human interaction. Increasingly we learn to see him as a master in discerning the persuasive potential of current issues and concerns, and in constructing appropriate epistolary responses.

Pauline rhetoric betrays a distinctly dialogical flavor. Its reasoning, which was adverse to descriptively dispassionate thought, evolved in argumentation with others. Historical criticism has well explained the prevailing polemics in the apostolic letters as responses, not to Judaism per se, but to alternate gospel versions. Viewed from this perspective, the Pauline Letters give us insights into an early situation of multiple traditions in conflict. But there is a rhetorical rationale for Paul's mode of argumentation as well. Far from admitting of any reflection on the personality of the man, his adversarial style has grown directly out of the rhetorical culture of late antiquity. Thought and convictions in this culture were born out of assertion against opposition and in discourse with other persons. One of the best-known examples of Paul's dialogical reasoning is the diatribe. It was a device whereby imaginary and anonymous interlocutors posed questions and raised objections, which in turn provided the speaker with an opportunity to respond, correct, and state his own view on the matters in question.

The diatribe, in other words, was a rhetoric of simulated dialogue that purported to intensify contact and to lessen the distance between Paul and his audiences. Nowhere in the Pauline corpus are the interlocutory devices of the diatribe more thoroughly implemented than in Romans, the very letter that addressed a community Paul had no personal knowledge of at the time of his writing (Stowers 1981, 79–184). But it is also in Romans that the stylized nature of the diatribal discourse is most clearly in evidence. More than the other Pauline letters, this one lacks features of historical specificity. The fictionality of simulated dialogue in Romans is hardly incidental. It is designed to enhance communication in the very situation in which Paul does not seem to have access to issues of historical specificity.

A principal technique of apostolic persuasion was to adopt and revise key terms employed by his addressees. One remembers Socrates's advice given to Meno that in discourse we must employ terms "with which the questioner admits he is familiar" (*Meno* 75d: δι' ἐκείνων σῶν προσομολογῇ εἰδέναι ὁ ἐρωτώμενος). Paul's thought, as it manifests itself in his letters, proceeded in a dialectic of adoption and revision, a process that kept his language inescapably focused ad hominem. Each letter, therefore, involves readers in a different intellectual orbit and in a distinct semantic field. As a whole, the Pauline corpus presents itself as a kaleidoscopic experience, confronting readers with multiple rhetorical situations. This is a principal reason for the difficulties modern readers encounter in comprehending the apostle's letters. The casuistry of his rhetoric runs counter to theological and logical premises, prompting charges of inconsistency, even of intellectual inferiority. *But rhetoric, not logic, is the key to Paul.* In the words of Carruthers, rhetoric "does not normalize an occasion, it occasionalizes a norm" (1990, 181). If logic considers an audience at all, it thinks of a universal audience. Paul the rhetor communicates in interaction with multiple social audiences.

Dialectical features notwithstanding, Paul is more adequately viewed as belonging to the rhetorical rather than the dialectical tradition. True to the ethos of rhetoric, he shaped his message to preconceived ends. Knowing the rhetorical objective in advance, he cultivated the means of persuasion that were to attain the goal. His repeated pronouncements on the law, for example, did not move from an analysis of the human plight under the law to the solution in Christ, but rather from the experience of redemption in Christ to a reconsideration of the role of the law. Without recognizing the full import of his discovery, E. P. Sanders had in fact defined the rhetorical nature of Pauline thought when in reference to the issue of the law he coined the memorable phrase: "The solution precedes the problem" (1977, 442). Whereas a thoroughgoing dialectic is propelled by a rigorous sifting of ideas aimed at discovering truth, rhetoric "knows its conclusions in advance, and clings to them" (Ong 1983, 2). In Paul, dialectic is subsumed under rhetoric. While his argumentation is intrinsically consistent and often in keeping with midrashic norms of interpretation, it evolved out of and adhered to human life situations, and it knew its cardinal premises and conclusion in advance. The principal test of truth was loyalty to Christ, to the gospel, as well as to him, the apostolic messenger. Partiality, not objectivity, was desirable.

Paul the rhetor favored a fundamentally oral disposition toward language (Kelber 1983, 140–83). He deployed the term *gospel* predominantly in auditory contexts and exclusively in reference to the oral proclamation. To be effective, the gospel needed to be proclaimed and heard. The notion of responding to his addressees by way of a written Gospel narrative appears to have been entirely foreign to his mode of thinking. Hearing, not sight, was accorded a place of pride in his economy of the sensorium. It was the supersense that facilitated interiorization of sounded words and faith. Heart was the anthropological metaphor of human interiority and intentionality (Jewett 1971, 305–33). It was also the central receptive organ both of the Spirit (2 Cor 1:22; Gal 4:6) and the word of proclamation (Rom 10:8). Preached words, Paul insisted, entered human hearts, engendered faith, and in turn generated confession. His media advice that "faith comes from hearing" (Rom 10:17) contributed toward Christianity's historical commitment to the ancient oral-aural sense of words, a commitment that prevailed across the centuries in spite of progressively technologized transformations of language. If to Homer we owe the legacy of the "winged words" (*Iliad* 1.201, et al.: ἔπεα πτερόεντα), from Paul we have received the metaphor of the light-footed word that "runs" its course (2 Thess 3:1: ὁ λόγος τοῦ κυρίου τρέχει) across the Mediterranean οἰκουμένη, carried as it were by the apostolic feet.

As is the case with all categorizations, rhetoric illuminates principal aspects of Pauline language and thought, while simultaneously masking features that lie outside the rhetorical ethos or are in tension with it. Also present in Paul's Letters is a potentially conflictual relation with rhetoric. When in 1 Corinthians the apostle castigated the "wisdom of the world" (1:20) as a strikingly oral, rhetorical phenomenon, referring to it as the "superiority of speech and wisdom" or the "persuasiveness of wisdom" (1 Cor 2:1, 4: καθ᾽ ὑπεροχὴν λόγου ἢ σοφίας ... πειθοῖ[ς] σοφίας [λόγοις]), he sowed the seeds of a persistent Christian ambivalence about the culture of rhetoric. Unwittingly, he anticipated the later Christian distinction between a wisdom of this world (*sapientia huius saeculi*) versus the genuinely desirable spiritual wisdom (*sapientia spiritualis*). What is particularly noteworthy is that Paul was not unfamiliar with the traditional philosophical anxiety about sophistic vanities and empty eloquence. He would rather stand accused of being "unskilled in speech" (2 Cor 11:6: ἰδιώτης τῷ λόγῳ) than use the gospel's proclamation to advance his personal gain. Still, his own reservation toward the wisdom of words was based not on the philosophical urge to cleanse language of its magical roots in the dialectical search for truth, but rather on the revolutionary kerygma of the cross of Christ, which inverted human values, turning worldly wisdom into foolishness and God's foolishness into genuine wisdom (1 Cor 1:18–25).

34. From Rhetorical Pragmatism to a Theology of Signification

In the first five centuries of the common era the merits and demerits of rhetoric were subject to debate, and the compatibility of rhetoric with the Christian proclamation remained controversial. As is well known, many of the Latin and Greek fathers were trained in the art of rhetoric, and some were teachers of rhetoric themselves. Tertullian, Cyprian, the three great Cappadocians, John Chrysostom, Jerome, and above all Augustine come to mind. They assimilated rhetoric, but rarely by way of unreflective osmosis. Conscious of the linkage between medium and message, between ancient rhetorical culture and the *doctrina Christiana* (Christian teaching, not doctrine!), theologians pondered the question of whether rhetoric would compromise the gospel. Origen, a preacher and textual scholar par excellence, had little sympathy for Greek rhetoric as taught in Alexandria and Antioch (R. Smith 1974, 89–90). For others such as Cyprian, a teacher of rhetoric at Carthage, conversion was tantamount to a renunciation of pagan letters altogether (Murphy 1974, 49). "What," Tertullian asked provocatively, "has Athens to do with Jerusalem, or the Academy with the church?" (*De praescriptione: quid ergo Athenis et Hierosolmis? quid academiae et ecclesiae?*).

A matter of great consequence was the elevation of biblical texts to canonical status, creating a mode of privileged authority unknown to Greco-Roman culture. Increasingly, Christian theologians trained as rhetors and rhetoricians had to come to terms with Scripture, be it as source of a new rhetoric or as counterpoint to the old rhetoric. In tracing their Christian identity to the new authority of the Bible, they developed a homiletic mode of discourse, long established in Jewish hermeneutics. *Homily*, this Christian type of preaching, legitimated the biblical text as principal inspiration and textual guide of the proclamation. The Christian homily was thus a type of rhetoric that was "basically determined by the order of the material in the text, to which may be added material from other texts" (Kennedy 1980, 136). As a consequence, memory was often relieved of problems of invention and arrangement, and a new homiletic rhetoric evolved that was based on and filtered through the medium of the newly privileged text of the Bible.

In spite of the canonization of Scripture, which favored textuality and textually based thematic preaching to a high degree, memory was far from being ejected from the Christian tradition. Augustine himself offered a sustained meditation on the mystery of memory in the tenth book of his *Confessions*. Entirely in keeping with the tradition of ancient rhetoric, he adopted the spatial metaphor of memory, including the deposition of *imagines* at strategically placed mnemonic *loci*. He was enraptured with that vast court of memory, this "large and boundless chamber," replete with "numberless secret and inexpressible windings," "the plains and caves and caverns, innumerable and innumerably full of innumerable kinds of things." "The things themselves are not present to my senses; what is present in my memory however are their images," ready to be recalled to sight in the act of remembering. "Great is the power of memory, excessively great, o my God, a large and boundless chamber; whoever sounded the bottom thereof?" he asked exuberantly.[1] Notably, Augustine's conversion to the Bible and his prodigious chirographic activity did not diminish

---

1. *Conf.* 10.8.15: *penetrale amplum et infinitum*; 10.8.13: *qui secreti atque ineffabiles sinus eius*; 10:17.26: *campis et antris at cavernis innumerabilibus atque innumerabiliter plenis innumerabilium rerum*; 10.15.23: *res ipsae non adsunt sensibus meis; in memoria sane mea praesto sunt imagines earum*; 10.8.15: *magna ista vis est memoriae, magna nimis, deus meus, penetrale amplum et infinitum; quis ad fundum eius pervenit?*

his enthusiasm and need for the memory tradition of ancient rhetoric. Augustine belonged to a culture in which quality of thought was intricately related to the powers of remembering: "His memory, trained on classical texts, was phenomenally active. In one sermon, he could move through the whole Bible, from Paul to Genesis and back again, *via* the Psalms, piling half-verse on half-verse" (P. Brown 1967, 254). And yet, as he probed the deep space of memory, he struck out onto new ground. We note that his encomium in praise of the wonders of memory facilitated remembrance of what he had done, where he had done it, and with what feelings. As he lifted these imaged experiences into the full light of his interior vision, he came face-to-face with his own self. In this way, memory assisted him in the exploration of selfhood, a consciousness made possible by interior visualization. It seemed only sensible to ask if memory, the facilitator of consciousness, also had the power to mediate knowledge of God. Augustine had come to know God, and where else could God abide but in memory? Was God not intelligible as a memorable presence? But as Augustine traversed the vast space of his memory, he had to admit to himself that he could find neither place nor image of God. There was a sense in which his search for God arrived at the cognitive limits of the ancient art of memory. Knowing God, without finding him in his interior recesses, Augustine was compelled to reach beyond memory. "I will pass even beyond this power of mine which is called memory; yea, I will pass beyond it, that I may approach unto Thee, o sweet light. What sayest Thou to me?" (*Conf.* 10.17.26: *transibo ex hanc vim meam, quae memoria vocatur, transibo eam, et pertendam ad te, dulce lumen. Quid dicis mihi?*).

He again took up the issue of memory in *De Trinitate*, a psychological study of the Trinity unparalleled in patristics. In book 11 he developed the threefold dynamics of the mind that resemble that of the supreme Trinity. Of the many trinitarian structures he uncovered in the mind, the most important one for our purpose was that of memory, vision, and will. The perception of external impressions, internal visualization, and the concentration of the mind, while representing different properties and faculties, converged under the guidance of the will in trinitarian unity: "And so that trinity is produced from memory, from internal vision, and from the will which unites both. And when these three things are combined into one, from that combination itself they are called thought."[2] As far as memory

---

2. *De Trinitate* 11.3.36: *atque ita fit illa trinitas ex memoria, et interna visione,*

was concerned, Augustine metamorphosed the rhetorical base of mind and memory into the metaphysical realm of trinitarian psychology.

Given the high premium placed on verbal performance and modes of argumentation in Greco-Roman culture, Christianity, which was itself centrally concerned with proclamation, was compelled sooner or later to define its position in relation to classical rhetoric. The task was all the more urgent because Cicero was rapidly advancing to the status of *magister elo-quentiae* and his rhetoric becoming a cultural model for late antiquity and the Middle Ages. In spite of the fact that Christian culture increasingly embraced the Bible and popularized the homiletic style of preaching, the enduring influence of rhetoric demanded that theologians come to terms with its legacy.

No Christian writer in the first five centuries of the common era has addressed the issue of rhetoric more thoughtfully than Augustine. In *De Doctrina Christiana*, "one of the most original [books Augustine] ever wrote" (P. Brown 1967, 264), he sought to find a rapprochement between the classical institution of oratory and scriptural authority, or, perhaps more accurately, he devised a Christian hermeneutic on its own terms. Few Christians could have been more qualified for the task. From childhood on, rhetoric had been Augustine's single most important cultural influence, and yet his intellectual development took place under the aegis of a literate, increasingly biblical tradition. Indeed, his *Confessions* has been interpreted as the self-conscious construction of a conversion from an oral, rhetorical to a primarily textual culture (King 1991, 150–272).

In book 4 of this influential treatise, *De Doctrina*, Augustine assigns rhetoric a place in Christian teaching. Eloquence, he states, cannot be rejected out of hand, even though it is intimately associated with paganism. What is more, nonartistic discourse would cripple the Christian proclamation. On a number of substantial points, Augustine holds up as a model of Christian oratory "a certain eloquent man" (*De Doctrina* 4.12.27: *quidam eloquens*), who is none other than Cicero. For example, Augustine cites with approval Cicero's dictum (*De Inventione* 1.1.1) concerning the interrelationship of eloquence and wisdom (*De Doctrina* 4.5.7). In the Christian proclamation, just as in pagan speech, competent rhetoric is not without wisdom, and true wisdom is ineffective without rhetoric (4.5.7).

---

et quae utrumque copulat voluntate. Quae tria cum in unum coguntur, ab ipso coactu cogitatio dicitur.

Consistent with Ciceronian principles (*De Oratore* 1.XXXI.137), Augustine advocates three modes of proclamation, each of which entails its own particular style of speaking (*De Doctrina* 4.12.27; 4.17.34). True eloquence requires that teaching (*docere*) be done "in a subdued manner" (*parva submissa*), pleasing (*delectare*) "in a temperate manner" (*modica temperata*), and persuading (*flectere*) "in a grand manner" (*magna granditer*). And yet, Augustine does not simply plead for a Christianization of conventional Ciceronian rhetoric. *De Doctrina*, it must be remembered, is a theoretical reflection on the interpretation and teaching of a Christianity that is about to be self-consciously centered on the Bible. What distinguishes the Augustinian concept of rhetoric from classical rhetoric is the central role assigned to the Bible. The authoritative status of the Bible is assumed, and so is a biblical rhetoric intrinsic to the central book: "The great virtue of *De Doctrina Christiana* is that it made it possible for Christians to appreciate and teach eloquence without associating it with paganism" (Kennedy 1980, 159). Admittedly, the rhetoric of the Bible may fall short of the oratorical and ornamental features of pagan rhetoric, but in refraining from a more polished language, the Bible communicated what it intended to say.

If absence of sophisticated pompousness is one of the hallmarks of scriptural rhetoric, the presence of obscurity and ambiguity of meaning is another. Augustine is at pains to show how many biblical passages were written in veiled language. The separability of expression from meaning is thereby legitimized in Christian hermeneutics. As he sees it, the obscurities of biblical writings are themselves "part of a kind of eloquence" (*De Doctrina* 4.6.9: *tali eloquentiae miscenda fuerat*) designed to exercise our mental faculties in search of hidden meanings, "for what is sought with difficulty is discovered with more pleasure" (*De Doctrina* 2.6.8: *et cum aliqua difficultate quaesita multo gratius inveniri*). Consequently, the expositor's primary task is neither the demonstration of rhetorical flourishes, nor an appeal to the emotions, but a raising to consciousness of "that which lay hidden" (*De Doctrina* 4.11.9: *sed ut appareat quod latebat*). At this point, Augustine's perception of language is a world removed from Gorgias's exuberant endorsement of the magical power of words, and distanced as well from Plato's dialectical discourse of reason. *De Doctrina* does not expound the unmediated efficaciousness of spoken words any more than it makes a case for dialectical discourse, driven, but also disciplined by logic. It has more in common with Paul's misgiving concerning the wisdom of the world, although it does not share in his letters' fundamentally oral disposition toward language. What is new about Augustine's *De Doctrina* is the privileged status accorded a central text. Rhetoric is thereby transformed into a teaching of the biblical writings, a project that principally entails a search for latent meanings. In the end, Augustine's *De Doctrina*, not unlike his *Confessiones*, undertakes a painfully elaborate and intellectually meandering transit from the classical, rhetorical culture of antiquity toward a text-based, Christian hermeneutics.

It would appear that Augustine, never fully persuasive on the matter of biblical *rhetoric*, adopted a hermeneutic informed by *scribal* sensitivities. Philosophically, what concerned him most was not the efficaciousness of biblical oratory, but its character of signification. Not content with affirming the allegorical tensiveness in Scripture, he proceeded to elevate the deferring nature of language to a linguistic, theological signs theory. Postulating a distinction between sign (*signum*) and thing (*res*), he could at times attribute an astonishingly provisional value to words: "By means of words, therefore, we learn nothing but words" (*De Magistro* 11.36.5: *verbis igitur nisi verba non discimus*). The most that could be said about words was that "they serve merely to suggest that we look for realities" (*De Magistro* 9.36.2: *admonent tantum, ut quaeramus res*). All words, spoken and written, were perceived to be signs that signified the authentic *res*. Hence, "no one should consider [signs] for what they are but rather for their value as signs which signify something else" (*De Doctrina* 2.1.1: *ne quis in eis attendat quod sunt, sed potius quod signa sunt, id est, quod significant*). Words were mere prompters as it were, and "the realities that were signified were to be esteemed more highly than their signs" (*De Magistro*: 9.25.1–2: *res, quae significantur, pluris quam signa esse pendendas*). In part at least, this theory of signification was born under the pressures of scribal sensibilities. Undoubtedly, signifying deferrals were a commonplace in allegorical, metaphorical, and parabolic speech. Orality and rhetoric had long been familiar with metonymic expansiveness that resonated with the transtextual world, and with figurative language that resisted being taken at face value. However, "Augustine was the first Latin author to call words 'signs'" (Swearingen 1991, 196). What merits additional attention is his elevation of these processes of linguistic signification into a sign theory. It presumed a lifelong experience with the chirographic status of language as signs, that is, the embodiment of spoken language in a system of visual symbols. When measured against the ethos of rhetorical efficaciousness, signs were obstacles to the presenting powers of spoken words. In Augustine's theory, oral presence was deferred in the interest of a higher goal of unity. The readers of allegorical and otherwise ambiguous scriptural passages were inspired to turn over words in their minds, to move from one hint to another, and from discovery to discovery, each one opening up further depths, and ideally to arrive at the love of God and the vision of God.

In the Western tradition, Augustine's fateful distinction between signifier and signified was a major contributor to a linguistically based bipolarity of metaphysical magnitude. It was replayed in a myriad of ways, pitting exteriority against interiority, the letter against the Spirit, the sensible against the intelligible, the written text against the transcendental *Logos*, temporality against eternity, and so forth. In the end, it may be said that Augustine's assimilation of rhetoric to scribality created a kind of "metarhetoric" (Murphy 1974, 287), or perhaps more precisely, a Christian hermeneutics of communication at the heart of which lay the metaphysical nature of language. In this fashion, it made an indelible impact on medieval concepts of language, buttressing the whole medieval world of analogies and correspondences.

35. MEDIEVAL SCRIBALITY AND LATINITY

A Christian codex dated prior to 1000 C.E. depicts Pope Gregory the Great (540–604 C.E.) as interpreter of Scripture.[3] The miniature carries the title: *Pope Gregory I inspired by the Holy Spirit.* His left hand rests on an open book, which is placed on a lectern. Undoubtedly, this book represents the Holy Bible. In his right hand Gregory holds another book, which is closed. Decorated with a golden cover, it appears to be a copy of the Bible. A white dove, a symbolic representation of the Holy Spirit, sits on the right shoulder of the pope. The dove's beak is wide open and placed near the ear of Gregory: the Holy Spirit inspires the pope. Gregory's gaze is directed neither toward the viewer nor toward the books. His is a posture of auditory concentration. He is listening to the words of the dove whispered into his ear. Behind Gregory, separated by a curtain, sits a scribe. In his right hand he holds a *stilus*, a sharp slate-pencil, and in his left hand a writing tablet. With the *stilus* he points toward the dove, source of inspiration, and with his writing tablet he gestures toward the pope, possessor and mediator of Scripture. Presumably, the scribe receives the pope's dictation that had been transmitted to him through the mediation of the Spirit.

---

3. The medieval illustration was initially used by Gumbrecht and Pfeiffer (1986, 10).

Tenth-century manuscript illumination by the Master of the Registrum Gregorii, Trier 983/84. Stadtbibliothek Trier, Ms. 171a. (The author acknowledges his indebtedness to the Stadtbibliothek Trier for granting permission to republish the illustration of Pope Gregory I.)

The miniature may serve as a central metaphor both for the grand simplicity and the notable complexity of medieval linguistic and religious culture. It locates the pope center stage: he is the preeminent authority and chief interpreter of the Holy Book. Apparently, the meaning of the Bible is not self-evident. As sacred text it partakes of secrecy. For secrecy "is a way of figuring Scripture as a book of revelation which nevertheless … withholds a good portion of itself" (Bruns 1982, 18). Indeed, secrecy is an indispensable category of sacred writings (17–43). Thus, although widely understood to be the unified and unifying Word of God, the Bible was experienced as a text written in veiled language. Its authority was generally established, but its written status raised a host of interpretive questions. There is a sense, therefore, in which the miniature dramatizes the intricacies of a hermeneutical scenario surrounding the sacred text.

Encoded in the miniature are differences that call for hermeneutical mediation. The Spirit, represented by the dove and source of auditory inspiration, is once removed from the pope, twice removed from the Bibles, and thrice removed from the scribe behind the curtain. Moreover, the open book of revelation is placed side by side with the closed book of the revelation, and both Bibles are separated by a curtain from the scribe who is about to commit the pope's dictation to writing. Thus medieval Christian culture, centered on the pope, the Bible, the Spirit, and the scribe, has set into motion a process of triple mediation. Assisted by the agency of the Spirit, the pope was enabled to read and to open the closed book of the Bible, and to mediate his reading to the scribe who in turn transposed the dictation into writing, thus producing another text. The very text-centeredness of the Bible is obvious, and yet its chirographic status is innocent of the modern perception of intertextuality that imagines a devocalized environment in which texts relate impersonally to other texts. The miniature clearly conveys the impression that the connective tissue that mediated textual meaning, the Spirit's whisperings and the pope's dictation, was oral in kind.

Partially influenced by the growing dominance of the Bible, and fostered by the scribal traditions of monasticism and scholasticism, an increasing output of manuscripts was generated that lay at the basis of medieval cultural and intellectual life. Still, if one wishes to comprehend the medieval intellectual culture from the perspective of communication and shifts in communication, one must imagine trends of the type of *la longue durée*. The period roughly from the fall of Rome to the invention of printing saw a general shift from oral performance to chirographic control of writing space. Manuscripts increasingly became important tools of civilized life, and from the eleventh century onward an ever-growing scribal culture shaped the processes of learning. One must, however, guard against simplistic divides of orality versus textuality, against anachronistic notions of medieval textuality, and against facile premises concerning links between manuscript technology and the restructuring of consciousness. It bears repeating that this picture of the textualization of the medieval world is correct only on the macro level of history.

Medieval scribality was a craft that required mastery over a variety of tools and skills. The conventional scholarly image of scribes was one of dedicated copyists. The production of manuscripts was hard labor, "a seasonal activity like football" (Troll 1990, 118), but rarely of a gratifying intellectual nature. Insofar as scribes were copyists, it was often stated, they worked exclusively, or primarily, in the interest of preservation and transmission of knowledge; when they took dictation, they served as catalysts of orally dictated compositions. But whether they copied or took dictation, scribes were craftsmen, singlemindedly devoted to the hard labor of copying. Whether medieval scribes were engaged in monastic discipline or conscripted into the paid service of rulers and administrators, theirs was always hard manual labor, indeed drudgery, which did not necessarily advance their *libido sciendi* any more than it stimulated their urge for self-expression and individuation.

The above conveys an image of scribes and scribal activities that has recently been modified by Epp (1966; 2004), Ehrman (1993; 1995), Carr (2005), Parker (1997), Carruthers (1990), and Haines-Eitzen (2000). Their different approaches and emphases notwithstanding, all are agreed that scribes were active carriers of their respective traditions whose labors cannot (in all instances) be reduced to copying processes.

The effects of manuscript technology were not directly translatable into literacy. We do well to keep scribal textuality distinct from literacy. Some of the most exquisite medieval scribal productions, the illuminated Bibles, were primarily sacred artifacts, objects of ritual celebration, rather than direct sources of intellection. As a craft revolution, scribality enhanced the availability and status of manuscripts. But the literate revolution, that is, the formation of a broadly based and informed readership, did not get underway until the fifteenth and sixteenth centuries, when print technology revolutionized communications processes. In medieval culture, not only did literacy remain the privilege of few, but also reading and writing did not inevitably connect to form a literate mentality. Reading was widely practiced as an oral activity (Balogh 1926; Saenger 1982; Achtemeier 1990). To be sure, aids to visual apperception slowly increased. Punctuation as well as word and chapter divisions, initially introduced in support of oral reading, imposed a visual code upon manuscripts, a process that gradually encouraged silent copying and silent reading. Still, far into the High Middle Ages "reading was regarded as an active energetic exercise, requiring good health, and not as a passive sedentary pastime" (Saenger 1982, 382; cf. 377–82). The recipients of texts were often listeners who did not necessarily know how to write, while scribal copyists were frequently unable to comprehend what they wrote. "Reading" was linked with the dictation and recitation of texts more than with private reflection. What constituted "literate" intellectualism was thus not necessarily the combined skills of reading and writing, but rather a high degree of audiovisual apperception and memorial practices (Carruthers 1990).

Undoubtedly, the high culture of medieval learning, which excelled in formulating intricate philosophical, religious, and linguistic theses with signal keenness of intellect, was the beneficiary of a developing chirographic activity. Once ideas and experiences were enshrined in writing, they began to assume a semblance of stability, irrespective of their continued oral functioning. Once knowledge was detached from the oral traditional biosphere, it was disposed toward depersonalization and hence subject to reflection and analysis. Relentless scribal labors extended the texual base that slowly but inevitably enhanced the possibilities of comparative and critical thought. In this high intellectual culture, reflections on language, cognition, mind, and memory increasingly grew out of and were shaped by a working relationship with texts.

There was an additional feature that uniquely assisted medieval coherence and consciousness: the use of the Latin language. Medieval intellectualization owes as much, if not more, to the use of Latin as to scribal productivity (Ong 1967b, 76–79, 250–52). For at least a thousand years, roughly from the sixth to the sixteenth century, the communications culture of the Western Middle Ages was under the governing influence of Latin. *Litterati* were primarily those canonists, diplomats, administrators, and theologians who had mastered Latin—which may or may not have included the ability to read and write (B. Stock 1990, 26; Troll 1990, 112). Latin became a standard of medieval high culture and the vehicle of theological, philosophical achievements. Coleman's observation that in certain monastic circles the assiduous study of grammar "was meant to teach a way to reach heaven through latinity" (1992, 145) could well be extended to the aspirations of many clerical *litterati*: Latin was perceived to be the linguistic medium that aided in the ascent to heaven. But with the rise of ethnic, national identities, Latin either followed the concomitant upsurge in vernaculars by modulating into the Romance tongues, or it turned into learned Latin, which was "not a dead language, but a chirographically controlled language" (Ong 1967b, 78) yet lacked any broad-based social marketability. But it was precisely learned Latin's abstraction from oral life that increased its value as an ideal instrument for the academic scholarship of a culture elite. High medieval intellectual culture was thus the result not only of a rapidly increasing chirographic productivity, but also of a distinctly Latin type of literacy that flourished by its distance from the oral lifeworld.

Even though manuscripts eventually came to function as artificial memory bases in their own right, medieval scribality and Latinity neither displaced nor vacated memory. Quite the opposite. For centuries the growing body of texts only intensified and complicated demands made on memory: "Medieval culture remained profoundly memorial in nature, despite the increased use and availability of books" (Carruthers 1990, 156). Not only was there more and more material that had to be processed, and more and more authoritative voices that had to be registered and reconciled, but changing cultural circumstances also enlisted memory into new services. As far as preoccupation with memory was concerned, medieval Christian intellectualism in no way lagged behind antiquity, although memory was often exiled from its natural home in rhetoric and assimilated to new religious and epistemological tasks (Coleman 1992).

The French Cistercian reformer Bernard of Clairvaux, who represents medieval monasticism at its height, contributed to the conversion of memory from the theory of rhetoric's esteemed treasure-house of eloquence to a symbol of religious reconstruction. Steeped in the monastic experience of hard labor, prayer, and silence, he saw little meaning in memory as a depository of precious icons and *loci* that negotiated cognition and consciousness. His religious experience taught him that memory was a house that was "contaminated with intolerable filth" (*De Conversione* 4.8: *intolerabili fetore contaminat*). Into it, "as if into some cesspit runs all abomination and uncleanness" (3.4: *velut in sentinam aliquam, tota decurrit abominatio, et immunditia tota defluxit*). "Why should I not grieve for the stomach of my memory," he exclaimed, "which is congested with such foulness?" (3.4: *quidni doleam ventrem memoriae, ubi tanta congesta est putredo?*). He advised his audience to "close the windows, lock the doors, block up the openings carefully" (4.8: *claude fenestras, obsera aditus, foramina obstrue diligenter*) through which so much filth has infiltrated and clogged up memory. While Bernard was careful to state that memory itself should be left intact, he advised his hearers "to purify memory and pump out the cesspit" (15.28: *purganda scilicet memoria et exhaurienda sentina*). However brief the enticements of sensual experiences, "the memory is left with a bitter impression, and dirty footprints remain" (3.4: *memoria quaedam impressit signa memoriae, sed vestigial faeda reliquit*). These, too, should not be erased altogether, but retrained and enlisted in the service of smelling, inhaling, tasting, seeing, and hearing the delights of charity, hope, and spiritual pleasures. Memory thus reconstructed— purged and equipped with a converted sensory base—was able to facilitate the believers' gradual attainment of spiritual purity. Steeped in monastic discipline, Bernard turned memory, rhetoric's treasure-house of knowledge and Augustine's instrument of self-knowledge, into a vehicle of religious conversion.

36. St. Thomas's Model of Cognition and Ockham's *Via Moderna*

Scholasticism, one of the supreme philosophical and theological achievements of the Middle Ages, registered in different ways the cultural revolution marked by scribal productivity and Latinity. A hallmark of scholasticism's intellectual project was the compilation and juxtaposition of biblical, patristic, and philosophical authorities. The need for collecting seemingly discordant authorities is a procedure utterly foreign to us. The project was founded on the fundamental premise of the two distinct, but reconcilable, sources of truth: theology and philosophy. More is at stake here than the oral penchant for quoting authorities. The drive toward the collection and juxtaposition of authorial voices was in part at least attributable to the textualization of medieval learned culture. It was thrust upon scholastic theologians by the steady growth and growing diversity of Latin texts. The translation of Aristotle from Greek and Arabic into Latin from the tenth through the twelfth centuries had a particular bearing on this development. Here was an activity that made available systems of thought (Aristotle, Avicenna, Averroes) that were not only independent of theology, but placed a high premium on reason and rational reflection (Copleston 1993–94, 2:205–11). The compilation of discordances, the passion for weighing and comparing different opinions, the contraposition of authorities, and the desire to seek clarification amid authorial dissonance were all features traceable to a growing intellectual diversity based on a rapid enlargement of the textual database. This is precisely what the scholastic theologian Peter Abailard conceded in the prologue to *Sic et non*, a collection of seemingly contradictory authoritative statements on 150 theological issues. What necessitated his labors, he wrote, was "the very vastness of verbal materials," which "appeared to be not only in themselves different, but truly also contradictory" (*Sic et non* 1.1–2: *tanta verborum multitudine ... non solum ab invicem diversa verum etiam invicem adversa videantur*).

While driven by the conditions of a textual revolution, the scholastic method of organizing thought remained indebted to a form of dialectic. Adopting a pattern of threefold schematization, issues were isolated and discussed by way of explication of objections, argumentation of resolution, and refutation of objections (Grabman 1909–11, 1:28–54). Rather than proceeding along the lines of a sequential, discursive logic, the scholastic art of structuring thought still operated in the tradition of a disputatious dialectic. But the scholastic dialectic differed from the Platonic dialectic, which had intended to keep thought alive in the flow of living discourse. The dialectic of St. Thomas' *Summa Theologica*, for example, was characterized by a nonemotional, stylized form of thought and a severe asceticism of language. His intellectualism moved in the rarified world of intensely abstract thought. Both in its organization of thought and in the delivery of ideas, it presented itself as a paragon of supreme rationalization. In its passion for rational penetration, the *Summa* practiced argumentation in a highly formalized dialectic. It is generally acknowledged that the strategies of scholastic dialectic originated in the medieval system of academic learning (Grabman 1909–11, 1:31–32; Copleston 1993–94, 2:214–15). It was in university settings that teachers trained students by prompting them to raise objections to propositions, by directing the processes of argumentation, and by formulating final resolutions. This was the cultural context in which medieval philosophers from the tenth to the fifteenth centuries shaped the tradition of academic dialectic into an instrument of high-powered precision, composing in a Latin that was neither that of the ancients nor that of the fathers, but a Latin of a distinctly scholastic diction. However, it is typical of the harmonizing disposition of Thomas's *Summa* that the authorities were secured in tradition more than seriously challenged, that more often than not the objections raised were of a perfunctory rather than a substantive kind, and that the resolutions were anticipated in advance of the argumentation. This is but another way of saying that Thomistic dialectic, this highly formalized academic ritual that was passionately devoted to logic, was at the same time constrained by rhetorical conventions (Kinneavy 1987, 90–94). Viewed from this perspective, the scholastic method of Thomistic dialectic, anchored in logic yet beholden to rhetorical premises, carried within itself the old and unresolved conflict between rhetoric and logic.

The question of what memory was and how it collaborated with the mind had to be assimilated to the new intellectual system of scholasticism. In substance, Thomas reiterated the ancient rhetorical theory of the mnemonic *imagines* and *loci*, adding the advice that one must cleave with affection to the things to be remembered in order "to keep the shape of images intact" (Thomas Aquinas 1974, *quaestio 49: conservat integras simulacorum figuras*). Thomas fully shared the Aristotelian premise that "all our cognition takes its rise from sense perception" (Thomas Aquinas 1963, 1, *quaestio 1: omni nostra cognitio a sensu initium habet*). In his commentary on Aristotle's *De Memoria et Reminiscentia* he returned again and again to the commonplace proposition that "man cannot understand without image" (Thomas Aquinas 1875, *liber 1, lectio 2: non posit homo sine phantasmata intelligere*). In part at least, human knowing was conceived on the analogy of interior visualization; it originated in *phantasmata* or corporeal images that were situated in memory. To be sure, parts of memory had the faculty of entertaining thoughts and opinions, but in principle no human thinking could take place without some kind of imaging. Additionally, memory's imaginary perception was always of particulars; it had no grasp of universals. Owing to the scholastic axiom that "it is natural to man that he should come to the intelligible things" (the universals) "by way of the sensible things" (the particulars; Thomas Aquinas 1974, 1: *est autem naturale homini ut per sensibilia ad intelligibilia veniat*), memory and its menu of icons served as the indispensable base for all our cognitive processes. In reflection on and abstraction from the particularity of sense images, intellectual cognition came to know what was truly worth knowing: the divine universals. With Thomism, memory was thoroughly integrated into the medieval system of knowledge and faith. But it is worth noting that in the new scheme of things, memory functioned no longer in its classic oral sense as a treasure-house of eloquence, but metaphysically, as a mediator of universals and facilitator of the knowledge of God.

There was yet another, more obvious sense in which Thomas strove to disengage memory from its traditional base in rhetoric. Not content with assigning memory to the metaphysics of knowing, he also reassigned it to ethics. Memory, originally the mother of the nine Muses, had become one of eight components of prudence, the governing queen of all moral virtues. Since prudence had made it her business to secure knowledge about the future based on past or present experiences (Thomas Aquinas 1974, *quaestio* 47), and memory sought to store knowledge about the past (*quaestio* 48), prudence depended on memory. Hence, prudence and memory were expected to cooperate in the interest of discerning matters in advance so as to facilitate the right course of action. Although thoroughly familiar with the ancient and medieval disciplines of memory, Thomas refrained from commending memory as rhetoric's treasure-house of eloquence. This fact will not have come about entirely without the pressures of scribality. At a time when handwritten materials came increasingly into use, memory began to lose its ancient rhetorical rationale, and also to forfeit its base in rhetoric, Thomas recommended it as a helpmate of prudence based on considerations of practical reason (*quaestio* 47: *quod est finis practicae rationis*).

We shall conclude with a model of cognition that manifested both the height and incipient demise of scholasticism. William of Ockham, whose thought is frequently viewed in connection with the nominalism of the fourteenth and fifteenth centuries, remains "to this day the most controversial thinker of medieval intellectual history" (Klein 1960, 1556). Best known for his antirealist position in the controversy over the universals, the Franciscan friar rethought epistemology and helped clear the way for what came to be known as the *via moderna*. He was "perhaps the greatest logician of the Middle Ages" (Boehner, in Ockham 1990: xviii), whose logical brilliance, verbalized in stunningly abstract Latin, was nourished by close rapport with a flourishing scribality. At the same time, Ockham's philosophy exhibited a distinct reserve toward rhetoric, dialectic, and imagination.

It was a deeply held conviction of medieval realism that language, memory, and sense perception collaborated in the higher interest of universal knowledge. In fact, divine universals, eternally true realities, were the appropriate objective of the mind's aspirations. More than that, to universals was attributed the status of truly existent metaphysical realities. The crux of Ockham's controversial work was that it problematized the reality corresponding to universals outside the mind: "A universal is not a substance existing outside the mind in individuals and really distinct from them" (Ockham 1990, *Epistemological Problems* 6: *universale non sit aliqua substantia extra animam existens in individuis distincta realiter ab eis* [all following citations to Ockham 1990]). He refused to admit that there was anything in the experienced world that corresponded to the universality of a concept. Universality was a function of the "act of the intellect" (*Epis. Prob.* 8: *actus intellegendi*), a mental construct, or simply the manner in which the mind achieved sufficiently generalized abstractive cognition.

As a logician, Ockham was well aware that the requirements for demonstrating the being of God were exceedingly difficult to fulfill. Nonetheless, in an argument of tortured logic he undertook to prove the proposition "that God existed" (*Proof of God's Existence* 6: *quod potest demonstrari Deum esse*), while conceding all the same that God's existence "cannot be known from propositions by themselves, since in every argument something doubtful or derived from faith will be assumed" (*nec potest probari ex per se notis, quia in omni ratione accipietur aliquod dubium vel creditum*). "The unity of God," on the other hand, "cannot be evidentially proved, and cannot be proved demonstratively either" (*unitas Dei non potest evidenter probari, non potest demonstrative probari*). It was not subject to logical demonstrations of any kind, and the notion of a supreme being "we hold only by faith" (*hoc fide tantum tenemus*). On the whole, however, Ockham was more adept at demonstrating what was not demonstrable about God than in confirming his verifiable attributes.

If Ockham's preoccupation as a philosopher was to purge Christian epistemology of the metaphysics of essences, it was not because he was prompted by agnostic impulses. Nothing could be further from the truth. His philosophical intention was to immunize divine freedom and omnipotence from what he regarded as human essentialist interventions. There was no inherent necessity for anything in this world to be just as it was. So far as God was concerned, things might be different. If, therefore, the world was contingent, as Ockham thought it was, it was contingent by divine choice, and hence knowable only by its contingency.

Given this worldly contingency, Ockham held to an epistemology that presumed an autonomy of mind, memory, and cognition. Priority was assigned to *intuitive cognition*, and immediate apprehension of the particulars by intuitive cognition preceded all other modes of knowing. In Ockham's words, "A cognition which is simple, proper to a singular thing, and the first to be acquired, is an intuitive cognition" (*Epis. Prob.* 3: *cognitio simplex, propria singulari et prima tali primate est cognitio intuitiva*). Only in second-order acts of thought, the so-called abstractive cognition (*cognitio abstractiva*), could things perceived lead to the formation of images and propositions. But even these second-order mental acts relied only partially on images. Concepts and images, moreover, neither represented metaphysical essences nor invited cognitive ascent to divine universals. They were merely mental substitutions for the particulars.

Ockham's skepticism with regard to philosophical realism moved the particular, the experiential, and the contingent to the center of inquiry. Consequently, his model of language and thought focused with unprecedented force on the status and quality of distinctiveness. It was a focus that included, by implication at least, the particularity of texts. Scripture, indeed all texts, were assumed to be operating according to something akin to an intrinsic, linguistic economy, and the operations of the mind—everybody's mind—were such that they could access the internal textual logic via the *cognitio intuitiva*. Gorgias's oral theory of language, which had manifestly postulated persuasive powers over the soul, was a thing of the past. One looks in vain, moreover, for a special commitment to rhetoric. As Ockham came to view things, language was not primarily meant to arouse emotions. Furthermore, the status of memory was once again modified. Divorced from its rhetorical, metaphysical, and ethical obligations, memory became a part of abstractive cognition and subordinated to intuitive cognition. *No longer the treasure-house of eloquence, or the metaphysical abode of trinitarian psychology, or a vehicle of conversion, memory came to play the role of an almost Proustian remembering of things past.*

Most importantly, the Augustinian signs theory, which had canonized the metaphysical nature of language, was not replicated in Ockham's thought. It was not that he discarded the signs character of language, but he reintegrated it into his nonmetaphysical (not antimetaphysical) notion of cognition. The word as sign, he wrote, "does not make us know something for the first time … it only makes us know something actually which we already know habitually" (*Logical Problems* 1: *non faciat mentem venire in primam eius … sed in actualem post habitualem eiusdem*). Nowhere does one encounter in Ockham the Augustinian correspondence between *signum* and *res*. There was no discernible correspondence between the linguistic signs and the metaphysical realities. The signs character of language had become an intrinsically linguistic phenomenon transposed into intramental processes. More than that, Ockham could in a spirit almost akin to a certain notion of modernity claim that "a spoken and written term does not signify anything except by free convention" (*terminus … prolatus vel scriptus nihil significant nisi secundum voluntariam institutionem*). In postmodern linguistic terms, the relation between the signifier and the signified was an arbitrary one.

A principal feature of Ockham's model of mind and language was a mode of thought that ran counter to the universalizing thrust of Platonic, Augustinian, and scholastic philosophy. Ockham approached epistemology and theology from the side of the particular—"a change of outlook almost as epoch-making as the Copernican revolution in astronomy" (Boehner, in Ockham 1990: xxvii). In the history of humanistic thought, it was a revolution less popularly known but no less significant than the Platonic revolt against the poetic encyclopedia of ancient Greece. A certain underpinning, although by no means the single cause, of both Plato's universalist and Ockham's particularist turn was provided by the technology of chirography, which in Ockham's case was reinforced by a high-intensity Latin. When Plato aspired to the essence of things abstracted from the Homeric poetic tradition, and liberated from oral, tribal pluralism, he was aided and abetted by the alphabetic revolution in ancient Greece. In Ockham's case, it was his reliance on the inner resources of a chirographic tradition, matured to a highly stylized Latin, that fostered the mental and psychological distancing from the metaphysical superstructure. Paradoxically, it took Latin's withdrawal from life, and a penetrating reflection on the fundamental problems of logic, in order to come to the realization that the essence was in the things themselves.

That Ockham was in fact a privileged and eager beneficiary of scribal culture is well established. From the eleventh century on, manuscripts had increasingly become the working material for the cultural elite: "His whole scholarly life until 1330 was spent in the greatest of European universities, his circle the most 'bookish' of the time" (Carruthers 1990, 158). The year 1330 marked a watershed in his life. In that year he moved, in compliance with a papal ruling, to a Franciscan convent in Munich, where he lived, cut off from all major university libraries, until the end of his life in 1349. Whereas the Munich period saw the publication of distinctly political, ecclesiastical writings, virtually all of his philosophical and theological books were written prior to 1330. How important a role written materials had played in the formulation of his epistemology is underscored by the bitter complaints he issued from Munich about the unavailability of books (Carruthers 1990, 89).

Let us return to the miniature of Gregory the Great that had portrayed the authorities of the pope, the Bible, the Spirit, and the scribe in a dramatization of medieval hermeneutics. Ockham revised this drama by shifting the balance of authorities. The most consequential implication of Ockham's theology was a decentering of the pope in the interest of a sharpening of focus on the Bible, and the implementation of a *cognitio intuitiva*, an unmediated cognitive apprehension of Scripture. The text-centeredness, recognizable to a degree already in the miniature of Gregory the Great, had thereby acquired a sense of authorial objectivity. With a force unknown to previous thinkers, Ockham moved the textual authority of Scripture and its individual interpreters to center stage, anticipating events that would not come to historical fruition (and explosion) for another two centuries. For the focus on scriptural authority and the attribution of interpretive powers to individual human cognition prepared the way for a potentially conflictual relation between the authorities of the pope and the Bible.

37. SHIFTING ROLES OF LANGUAGE, MEMORY, AND SENSE PERCEPTION

In paying tribute to Milman Parry and Albert Lord, this essay has suggested degrees of connectedness between oral and chirographic incarnations of the word and the structuring of human thought. Our premise is furthest removed from the notion that language and different linguistic embodiments are comprehensible as neutral carriers of ideational freight. In the spirit of Parry and Lord, we have postulated that modes of communication were themselves potential embodiments of cognition and shapers of consciousness.

Glancing over the long haul of ancient and medieval history, we have made a set of observations concerning shifting roles of language, memory, and sense perception. Speech as divine madness was viewed as the product of a linguistic culture that was dominated by an orality largely untamed by the powers of chirography. Rhetoric, taking advantage of the technology of writing, made speech conscious of itself and also subservient to civic life. Few experiences enhanced Western text-consciousness more deeply than the canonical centering of the Bible. It helped reshape ancient rhetoric into Jewish and Christian modes of homiletics, and unleashed a seemingly unending flow of midrashic rewritings of the privileged biblical texts.

Memory, the wellspring of civilized life, was a continuing theme in ancient and medieval culture that was in fundamental ways still a memorial more than a documentary culture, notwithstanding the increasing production and availability of books. But the praxis of memory changed as different media circumstances exempted it from strictly rhetorical obligations and enlisted it into the service of ethical, metaphysical, and historical remembrance.

The fundamentally oral, rhetorical understanding of the cognitive value of the sensorium was widely shared by ancient and medieval thinkers. Plato's striving after pure, disembodied thought never found credence with a majority of thinkers. Elsewhere in ancient and medieval thought, cognition was frequently perceived to be grounded in sensory sensibilities. But a growing manuscript culture, and the possibilities it raised for detached thought, left its impact on the role of the sensorium as well. Among the cultural elite, the developing processes of medieval scribality went hand in glove with the privileging of Latin that, shaped into a finely tuned instrument for rational discourse, increasingly forfeited its marketability in a world of ethnic and vernacular ambitions.

Scholasticism's hierarchical thematization of the *sensibilia* versus the *intelligibilia* acknowledged both the foundational role of the former and the superiority of the latter. What William of Ockham set into motion was a challenge to Thomistic scholasticism, for which universals alone had been the proper object of knowledge. If what mattered were not the universals but the particulars, attention came to be refocused on the philosophically accessible, the culturally distinctive, and the chirographically available. Thus in a time of growing literacy, individual believers found themselves confronted with the internal logic of the biblical texts. The Bible as central grammatological authority was thereby reinforced in ways unheard of before. But if it was admitted that the biblical texts operated under logical laws that could be intuited by the minds of individual interpreters, then the pope's authority as preeminent interpreter of the Bible had implicitly been undermined. A whole set of far-reaching historical and theological implications came into play, increasingly text-centered implications, that reached their culmination in the sixteenth century. For in so far as the Reformers came to elevate the *sensus literalis* to the exclusion of all other senses, and to embrace the principle of *sola scriptura* vis-à-vis papal authority, and to adopt the notion of Scripture being its own interpreter (*scriptura sui interpres*), they fulfilled the legacy of the *via moderna*, a legacy principally set into motion by Ockham and his successors.

7
THE ORAL AND THE WRITTEN GOSPEL:
FOURTEEN YEARS AFTERWARD

The first part of this essay revisits my earlier study The Oral and the Written Gospel *and reviews aspects of the discussion that have centered on it during the past fourteen years. In the second part I reiterate and argue the book's principal theses: Mark's critical relation to oral tradition, the narrative poetics of the Gospel, the circumstances surrounding its composition, the construction of the passion narrative, the parabolic force of the narrative, and Paul's oral-epistolary communication viewed within a network of oral-scribal interfaces. Focusing specifically on the model of the pre-Gospel tradition in the third part, I concede greater oral-scribal complexities than previously assumed, but I reject a tight stemma model of intertextuality. The fourth part addresses the so-called Great Divide, the categorical distinction of Markan textuality from pre-Markan orality. I acknowledge the inapplicability of the Great Divide but argue that we need to think through a theoretical distinction between the properties of speech versus those of writing in order to be able to capture their interfaces and mutual reabsorptions. In the fifth part, the essay reimagines tradition, suggesting a model not of a scanning of multiple scrolls, or an oral, oral-scribal buildup toward Gospel narrativity, but of oral-scribal interactions with simultaneous accessibility to a copious cultural memory. For comparative purposes, the sixth part places the Homeric unitarians, analysts, and oralists alongside the narrative critics, the historical critics, and the advocates of the oral-scribal-memorial model in Gospel scholarship. Next, I address the issue of textualization's silencing of voice, a point I made in OWG and that drew critical responses. I suggest that there is no such thing as a textually implemented termination of speech, but a semiotic transformation, a linguistic stabilization, does occur when speech is scribalized, and the textually filtered reoralization produces something of a secondary orality. Taking up challenges to my reading of Mark in the eighth part, I caution against imposing Matthean or Lukan reading grids on the Gospel, and I expand the notion of the performative character of the Pauline letters.*

Our historical existence depended wholly on an alternate technology, the technology of oral tradition.
                                  —John Miles Foley, *How to Read an Oral Poem*

There is now greater awareness that behind any tradition, there are likely to be specific political processes and interest groups.
          —Ruth Finnegan, "Tradition, but What Tradition and for Whom?"

If studies in oral tradition could contribute to our understanding of the Gospel materials in such a way as to make possible the rewriting of Rudolf Bultmann's *The History of the Synoptic Tradition* … , this would be a major contribution.
—Charles   Talbert,   "Oral   and   Independent   or   Literary   and
                                                        Interdependent?"

38. *The Oral and the Written Gospel*
in the Context of a Growing Discourse

During the past fourteen years *The Oral and the Written Gospel* (1983, henceforth *OWG*) has helped to energize a discourse in biblical studies that focuses on the oral-chirographic communications media in early Christianity. The participants include colleagues from a variety of disciplines—orality-literacy studies, literary criticism, media studies, folklore, comparative literature, anthropology, Judaic studies, classics, theology— which gives the discussion a much-needed breadth. Largely inspired by my book and the debate it had generated, the Bible in Ancient and Modern Media group of the Society of Biblical Literature in 1987 published *Semeia* 39 under the title *Orality, Aurality, and Biblical Narrative* (Silberman 1987). Following several more years of annual discussions within a widening circle of participants, the Media group issued *Semeia* 65, titled *Orality and Textuality in Early Christian Literature* (J. Dewey 1995a), which further explored the oral-textual interfaces in the media world of early Christianity and the ancient Near East. Prodded by my colleagues' responses pro and con, I have continued to contribute to the developing discourse, and in the process refined, corrected, and enlarged my own thinking on the issues raised by a media approach to ancient (and medieval) word processing (1987a; 1987b; 1988a; 1988b; 1990; 1992; 1994a; 1994b). In short, *OWG* has taken on a life of its own in the scholarly discourse, a hermeneutical phenomenon well known to biblical and literary critics alike. Today the book communicates and resonates within this larger context. At the occasion of the republication of *OWG* by Indiana University Press, this essay seeks to recontextualize the issues raised in the current debate and articulate a response to both "bouquets and brickbats" (Silberman 1987, 1).

39. THE CENTRAL THESES OF *THE ORAL AND THE WRITTEN GOSPEL*

I commence with the principal theses developed in *OWG*. Mark, by a solid majority of biblical critics considered the earliest canonical Gospel, came into textual existence less by extension of a stream of antecedent oral traditions and more by resistance to oral drives, norms, and authorities. Part of the Gospel's sayings and storied materials, which appear to be oral in nature, were brought under the scripted control of the written narrative. Along with this recontextualization of oral traditions, the narrative dramatizes a deliberate departure from the appointed or expected carriers of Jesus' message—oral traditionists and oral authorities all of them. The logic of the narrative, *OWG* argued, appeared to be designed to construct—temporally, spatially, and thematically—a fresh beginning for the fledgling Jesus movement, which had been deeply shaken by the destruction of Jerusalem, an axial event in late antiquity. Mostly on internal narrative ground, *OWG* argued, the Gospel's composition will have to be dated after 70 C.E. As Mark viewed it, the cataclysmic loss of the center called into question the viability of the orally performed and experienced presence of the Lord, confronted his followers with the irrefutable fact of the conflagration of the temple, and rekindled their grief over the loss of Jesus. Given this situation, the Gospel did what religion does in times of crisis: it sought a new, that is, authentic, voice by returning to the origin. Thus the written narrative retrieves the life of Jesus, emancipates readers/hearers from oral conventions and authorities, reorients them toward a new place away from Jerusalem, lets the dramatization of Jesus' life culminate in a tightly constructed story of Jesus' execution, and closely connects the latter with the demise of the temple. The emphasis on his death is further strengthened by withholding the risen Lord from the disciples and women *in* the story, and from the readers/hearers *of* the story. In a challenge to one of the most deeply held premises of form criticism, *OWG* questioned the classic thesis of an early, pre-Gospel composition of the passion narrative. Linguistic, narratological, theological, and historical reasons, as developed in *OWG*, appear to point toward a later date. Moreover, Jesus' death in God-forsakenness as dramatized in the passion story will become a tragically credible model for thousands who suffered this insane brutality inflicted by the imperial power of Rome, and his vindication in and through this death will provide a rationale for those victimized before, during, and after the catastrophe of 70 c.e. The dramatic narrative of the last days, its close connection with the demise of the temple, and the fateful failure of the disciples makes Mark's passion narrative "really a story about three deaths" (*OWG* 185).

Empowering the narrative with a parabolic force, the Gospel retains continuity by remaining faithful to the authentic voice, while true to parabolic dynamics it opens up the possibility for the hearing of a new voice, which shakes hearers out of credible assumptions and confronts them with incredible options.

Paul, when viewed from the angle of orality-literacy sensibilities, presents himself as an oral traditionalist whose commitment to faith is based on oral, rhetorical grounds: "faith comes from hearing" (Rom 10:17). His own use of writing, however, facilitates a reflectively critical posture. For *writing makes a difference*. When resorting to chirographic means, even though mediated by way of dictation, Paul dissociates himself from the consequences of the enthusiastic employment of oral words in some of his communities. Pauline communication is, therefore, grounded in a complex network of oral-scribal interfaces.

Broadly, the book submits the issues of tradition and its relation to the narrative Gospel to critical examination, as well as Paul's oral/epistolary proclamation. It is precisely in these areas that scholarly discussions have ensued and critical questions have been raised.

40. THE LIFE OF THE TRADITION

In reopening the issue of tradition and Gospel, *OWG* focused attention on a classic theme extensively treated in form criticism. In the case of the canonical Gospels, the issue of tradition pertains to the assumed communication preceding these narratives. What was the tradition like out of which the Gospels have grown, and in what manner are the latter related to tradition? A frequent objection to my discussion of these issues concerns my perception of a dominantly oral nature of the pre-Markan tradition. I argued that Mark assimilated aphoristic sayings and parables, heroic stories, polarization stories, and didactic stories—materials that were patently oral in composition, although we encounter them in scripted form and resignified in a narrative plot.

The suggestion has now been made that Mark may also have made use of the so-called *Cross Gospel* for the construction of his passion narrative (Crossan 1988). This text, which is not directly accessible to us, is assumed to have flowed, subsequent to its absorption into Mark's passion narrative, via the intracanonical Gospel tradition of Matthew, Luke, and John into the postcanonical *Gospel of Peter*, from whose fragmentary text Crossan, in a masterful piece of historical, philological, and theological scholarship, has sought to disengage it. To achieve his goal, Crossan operates with a tight stemma model, which is predicated on direct textual relations between the *Cross Gospel*, Mark, Matthew, Luke, John, and the *Gospel of Peter*. In effect, he now postulates two Two-Source Hypotheses: In their pre-passion sections Matthew and Luke rely on Q and Mark, and in their passion narratives and resurrection stories on the *Cross Gospel* and Mark. In addition to making use of the *Cross Gospel*, Mark may have revised the *Egerton Papyrus 2*, one of the oldest fragments of any known Gospel, which contains Jesus materials shaped in the generic mode of discourse, controversy, miracle, and narrative (Crossan 1985, 65–87). Finally, Mark is suspected by some of having deconstructed *Secret Mark* (Koester 1983, 35–57; Crossan 1985, 91–121), parts of which were discovered in 1958 by Morton Smith in the Greek Orthodox monastery of Mar Saba in the Judean desert (1973a; 1973b; 1982, 449–61). It is noteworthy that all three texts are fragmentary. The *Cross Gospel* is a secondary, scholarly reconstruction from the fragmentary *Gospel of Peter*; *Papyrus Egerton 2* is both fragmentary and mutilated; and *Secret Mark* consists of excerpts cited in a letter of Clement of Alexandria, a second-century church father. Importantly, the pre-Markan dating of all three texts is being contested. In the case of the *Cross Gospel*, assumed to be embedded in the *Gospel of Peter*, Maurer and Schneemelcher (1987, 180–85) consider as unprovable the thesis of an ancient precanonical passion narrative that is supposed to have served as the single source both for the canonical passion and resurrection narratives and for the *Gospel of Peter*. Koester (1990, 216–40) operates with a model of the history of the passion narrative that is somewhat more loosely conceived than Crossan's tight stemma model. While he seems to want to stay clear of the designation *Cross Gospel*, he assumes, like Crossan, the existence of a precanonical passion narrative. Mark, John, and the *Gospel of Peter* have made use of it, but each independently of the others. Cartlidge and Dungan (1980, 83), on the other hand, suggest that the *Gospel of Peter* represents a form of anti-Judaism that was typical for the second century. Along similar lines, Kirk (1994) argues that the *Gospel of Peter* exhibits theological developments characteristic of later Christianity that can well be understood as further reflections on the canonical Gospels. In the case of *Papyrus Egerton 2*, both Neirynck (1985, 153–160) and independently Jeremias and Schneemelcher (1987, 82–84) have made a case for a post-Synoptic date of the text. As for *Secret Mark*, it has triggered one of the most highly charged, acrimonious debates surrounding any Gospel text in the twentieth century, with Quesnell (1975) being the first of a number of scholars making the accusation of a hoax.[1]

Despite these reservations, however, and irrespective of the outcome of the dispute over *Cross Gospel*, *Egerton Papyrus 2*, and *Secret Mark*, my view of a dominantly oral pre-Synoptic tradition may have to be modified. While I conceded that "textuality came early to the synoptic tradition" (*OWG* 210), which retold and recollected sayings of Jesus and narrated stories about him, more allowance may have to be made in favor of early textuality. This will have been the case if only because the Synoptic tradition originated and operated in the context of an already flourishing Jewish and Hellenistic culture of chirography. It is by no means unreasonable, therefore, to assume early forms of textualization in the tradition and Mark's involvement in it. But whatever textualization there was, the full range of critical activities among those early fragile papyri is not understood adequately, if at all, in terms of a tight textual rein insinuated by the stemma model.

Joanna Dewey has raised this very issue and given us a sense of how the role of texts in a dominantly oral culture may have to be imagined: "In a world as oral as the first century was, intertextuality, the use of one text by the author of another text, need not mean actual copying (literary dependence), but may mean using oral memory of written texts to create new written texts" (1995a, 54). Indeed, can one imagine the earliest phase of tradition without any recourse to oral, memorial dynamics? Foley has posed the question of tradition most provocatively: "What if traditional came actively to indicate extratextual?" (1995, 5).

---

1. Among critical assessments of Smith's thesis after the publication of this chapter, see especially Carlson (2005). For a forthcoming collection of articles on the issue, see Burke (2011).

We may, therefore, have to assume even greater complexities for the life of the pre-Markan tradition than I had postulated. The literary critic Herbert Schneidau has reminded us that Chaucer, Dante, and Aquinas, as indeed most great writers in the Western tradition, subsumed diverse texts within their own. He does not seem to have a problem with the notion that Mark tapped into multiple reservoirs: "For Mark to be diffusing several threatening texts throughout his own is not unthinkable" (1987, 136). But surely Chaucer, Dante, and Aquinas did not compose along the lines of a stemma model. The question, again, is whether the ancient tradition is properly understood as a tight web of intertextuality. Modernity seems to be comfortable with this notion. In the history of art, for example, one is reminded of the art critic Heinrich Wölfflin's often-quoted observation that all paintings owe more to other paintings than they do to nature. In reference to the verbal arts, a very similar idea is articulated by Umberto Eco: "Until then I had thought each book spoke of the things, human and divine, that lie outside books. Now I realized that not infrequently books speak of books. It is as if they spoke among themselves" (1983, 322).

Wölfflin's and Eco's observations are provocative and original, but they are also emblematic of modern and postmodern sensibilities. But whether the concepts of art interacting with art and book culture operating as a textual echo chamber are applicable to the ancient world of communications would seem to be a pertinent question.

Whatever the role of texts in the tradition, I agree that we need to part with the notion of a pre-Markan tradition that was purely oral. In *OWG* I postulated "a predominantly oral phase," while not, however, dispensing with texts altogether (23). With a majority of scholars I recognize the written existence of the sayings Gospel Q. Moreover, I suggested that "we shall never know … the precise shadings and degrees of interplay between the two media" (23). But to the extent that I have heavily focused on the oral nature of the tradition and the written Gospel's absorption and realignment of oral materials, I have unduly forced the polarity between the two media.

The force of my argument about the tradition was directed toward the form-critical premise of a development from smaller to larger units into the Gospel narrative. But the more genres and texts we assume for the tradition, and the more dependencies on and responses to oral materials we discern in Mark—that is, the more pluralistic the materials the Gospel appears to be drawing on—the less likely is the model of tradition's unidirectional and quasi-evolutionary flow into the gospel narrative. In *OWG*

I emphatically deconstructed the paradigm of the tradition's evolutionary ascent. Not unlike Jaffee, who objected to a similar conceptualization in the case of the Mishnah "as a linear culmination of early rabbinic oral tradition now breaking into written textuality for the first time" (1994, 143), I have argued that the written Gospel cannot be understood as the apex of a calculated oral drive toward the dawn of chirography. Not only does the oral, oral-scribal pre-Markan tradition ill fit the model of an evolutionary trajectory, but also the Gospel's narrative is more in control over a multi-faceted tradition than the latter is in control of the Gospel.

41. The Issue of the Great Divide

I can trace many of the critical voices raised about *OWG* to the Great Divide it has projected among readers between oral tradition and Markan textuality. There appears to be near unanimity that we should shun both the term and the implications of what has come to be referred to as the Great Divide. Cartlidge speaks on behalf of many critics when he asserts that in late antiquity "oral operations (presentation and hearing) and literary operations (reading and writing) were (1) inescapably interlocked and (2) they were communal activities. Chirographs were created for and by the community and in the service of orality" (1990, 407).

I did not myself ever use the term the Great Divide in *OWG* or elsewhere, nor was it part of our vocabulary in the late seventies and early eighties, when the book was written. Indeed, the attentive reader will observe that my understanding of tradition and Gospel is more nuanced than the label "Great Divide" may give it credit for. Nor does the fact that Mark's narrative may have been composed from oral *and* written traditions eo ipso discredit my thesis that it harbors a deep-seated animosity toward oral sensibilities—an issue to which I shall return below.

I am, however, persuaded that the strong thesis developed in *OWG* was, and to some extent still is, necessary to break theoretical ground and to challenge the chirographic-typographic hegemony that rules biblical scholarship to this day. I did want my readers to think if not about a Great Divide, then hopefully about the separate identities and communicative potentials of orality versus literacy. At the time of my writing *OWG*, the academic study of the Bible had made little allowance for voice and performance, for the role of speakers and the acts of hearing in the tradition. And whatever recognition of orality existed, it was generally incompatible with current scholarly notions of oral tradition that had been developed across the spectrum of humanistic and social sciences. To the best of my knowledge, the names of Eric A. Havelock, Walter J. Ong, Ruth Finnegan, John Miles Foley, Frances A. Yates, and Mary Carruthers, authors who have deeply influenced my thinking, were virtually unknown in biblical scholarship, and if they were known, their work was not considered relevant for the study of the Bible. An exception is Albert B. Lord, whose central theses on oral tradition and performance were introduced to the discipline by Erhardt Güttgemanns. The latter's keenly analytical critique of the form-critical concept of oral tradition was partially based on Lord's work (1979, 204–11 [1970, 143–50]). Yet Güttgemanns's work itself made little impact on German New Testament studies, and was never absorbed into US Gospel studies. In 1977 Lord directly contributed to biblical scholarship by participating in an interdisciplinary conference on the relationships among the Gospels in San Antonio (Walker 1978), in which he presented a lengthy talk titled "The Gospels as Oral Traditional Literature" (33–91). At that conference, Talbert's response (93–102) was decidedly negative, while Keck (103–22) seemed more sympathetic. But the discipline by and large has remained unresponsive to Lord's proposal.

It was in this situation that I felt I had to make a case for the singular characteristics of the human voice and its central significance in the work of the tradition in distinction from the scriptographic materiality of papyri, manuscripts, and codices. This was all the more necessary, I thought, because the form-critical concept of oral tradition, which was (and still is) dominant in biblical studies, was, in my view, unsustainable when measured against new standards set in other disciplines. As I have expressed this matter recently, even though in the "ordinary" life of language, speech and writing run together, "we need these master tropes in order to understand their interminglings, mutual reabsorptions and deconstructions" (1995b, 195). How can we comprehend oral-textual interfacings if we do not have a clear understanding of the intrinsic features of speech versus those of writing? As far as I can see, none of my critics has engaged Güttgemanns detailed argument in favor of a separate linguisticality and a differentiated treatment of the oral versus the written. In the English translation of his *Candid Questions Concerning Form Criticism* (1979), a differentiated consideration of the two media, covering more than sixty pages, ranging from J. G. Herder and W. v. Humboldt, on to folkloristics, P. Bogatyrev, R. Jakobson, and F. de Saussure, all the way to Albert Lord, concludes that "contemporary linguistics considers that between the oral and the written there are differences on all structural levels, and that means on the levels of phonology, morphology, syntax, vocabulary, and style" (197).[2]

Nevertheless, to apply the Great Divide to the life of the pre-Markan tradition versus the Gospel texts, as if they belonged to two separately definable domains, is not true to the ascertainable facts, and unlikely in the context of the ancient communications world.

But once we are forewarned about the perils of the Great Divide, our thinking about tradition needs to be equally cautious not to relapse into dominantly typographic patterns. Historical biblical scholarship, when working on the premise of a textual omnipresence, has tended to view tradition as a textual buildup of successive redactional layers or strata, and when operating on the premise of a dominantly oral trajectory has often thought of tradition as a progression from smaller to ever larger oral units. Thus while the Great Divide has now been put to rest, our model(s) of the tradition still need to be released from their typographical captivity.

42. TRADITION'S SCRIBAL, ORAL, AND MEMORIAL DYNAMICS

At this point, the task posed by orality-literacy studies is to reimagine the life of tradition, constituted by both chirographs and speech, and its relation to the Gospel's written narrative. In ancient (and medieval) media history, manuscripts functioned in an oral contextuality. By way of compositional dictation, recitation, and auditory reception, they were closely allied with the oral-aural medium. Dunn has aptly articulated the challenge before us: "To capture the blend of the fixed and the flexible, the interaction of oral and written, the interdependence of individual 'performer' and attentive audience within the Gospel traditions, in a way which truly represents the process of living tradition, is one of the great challenges still confronting researchers in this field" (1984, 21).

In addition to the oral and the written, the fixed and the flexible, and multiple interfaces, we will need to incorporate the role of memory. Dictated to a scribe and read aloud to audiences, most manuscripts were meant to be heard and hence processed in mind and memory. Handwritten papyri, scrolls and codices mediated in an oral, memorial biosphere, engaged a broader spectrum of the sensorium than the model of direct

---

2. I am aware that Jacques Derrida is opposed to precisely this viewpoint. For an engagement of orality-scribality studies with Derrida's grammatology, see ch. 4 in this volume.

text-to-text relations, processed with literary consistency, will let us know. As far as the Gospel's relation to tradition is concerned, narrative criticism has demonstrated that the Gospel is driven by multiple narrative causalities, strategies, and motivations. Events, characters, settings, thematic preoccupations, shifting relations, targeted polemics, expectations, fulfillments, nonfulfillments, and more—all function in a narrative plot that is subject to a recognizable point of view. Narrative criticism thus conceived has demonstrated that a tightly constructed model of intertextuality, projecting the Gospel as result of a skillful manipulation of literary sources, cannot serve as a satisfactory explanatory model for the Gospel's relation to tradition.

Even if a Gospel text were the product of direct copying—which none of the canonical Gospels was—its formation must have entailed in varying degrees composition in dictation and memorial apperception, essentially oral processes. I encourage the readers of *OWG* to grow comfortable with the idea that texts used for the composition of another text "were often assimilated through hearing and interior dictation more than strict copying" (23). Studies on performing medieval English scribes (Doane 1991; 1994; O'Brian O'Keeffe 1990) and on the ethnography of reading (Boyarin 1993) may prove helpful in transporting us into a scholarly paradigm of dictation, performance, writing, and reading that is quite different from analytical premises rooted in historical criticism. Contrary to the assumptions of historical criticism, a text's substantial and multifaceted investment in tradition does not necessarily suggest intertextuality in the sense of scanning through multiple, physically accessible scrolls but, more likely, accessibility to a shared *cultural memory*, which may include oral and scribal features, and compositional aspects. If Mark, not unlike many other writers, operated with a plurality of oral and written traditions, reclaiming and citing some, revising others, responding critically, even deconstructively, to the stimuli provided by various traditions, dislodging some even as he built on them and orchestrating the chorus of polyphonic voices into a narrative addressed to followers of Jesus in the period after 70, he did so not by working out of a well-stocked library, but by plugging into a copious reservoir of memories, retrieving and reshuffling what was accessible to him, textually and orally-memorially. In the end, I venture the suggestion that the Gospel composition is unthinkable without the notion of cultural memory, which serves ultimately not the preservation of remembrances per se but the preservation of the group, its social identity and self-image (J. Assmann 1992). Mark avails himself of a rich cultural memory for the purpose of securing the Christian identity for a postwar generation.

43. THE HOMERIC DEBATE

It may prove illuminating to recall the modern discussion over Homeric authorship, the formulaic nature of the Homeric tradition, and the oral-scribal quality of the *Iliad* and *Odyssey*. In its most distilled form, it may be said that the Homeric debate involved three schools of thought: the unitarians, the analysts, and the oralists. If I commence with Friedrich August Wolf, the oralist, it is not because his work marks the historical starting point of the academic study of Homer and the Homeric epics—an intellectual engagement that dates back to antiquity itself—but to make the point that interest in oral mechanisms and artistry predates Milman Parry by more than a century. It was in 1795 that the academic world was formally introduced to the idea of Homeric orality. In that year, Wolf published his *Prolegomena ad Homerum*, which developed a case for Homer as oral poet. *Then as now, it seemed preposterous to many to think of oral tradition—a medium we are apt to suppress—as having played a key role in the formative stages of the verbal art in Western civilization.* In the eighteenth and nineteenth centuries the two schools of the unitarians and the analysts took center stage in the discussion. The unitarians attributed the *Iliad* and the *Odyssey* to an individual act of craftsmanship, and paid particular attention to the literary world of the two epics. When today we commonly appreciate the two literary monuments for having inaugurated a long line of "great books," we are acting in the spirit of the unitarians. The analytic school viewed the *Iliad* and the *Odyssey* as a result of successive stages of textual growth, and, based largely on philological criteria, assumed that they had grown out of a series of editorial processes, revisions, interpolations, and redactions. The analysts enforced the rigorous implementation of what came to be called higher or historical criticism. Early in the twentieth century Milman Parry almost single-handedly laid the groundwork for a third, the oralist school, introducing the thesis of the oral techniques of Homeric verse-making (1930; 1932; 1933). Over the longest part of the twentieth century, Albert Lord, building on the work introduced by Parry and availing himself of fieldwork conducted in Bosnia-Herzegovina, brought the oralist school to broad, international recognition (1960; 1991; 1995). In our time, John Miles Foley has advanced the reading of the Homeric epics and other oral-derived texts from a technical, mechanistic assessment of Homer's metered and formulaic diction toward an artistic, aesthetic appreciation, and placed the oral theory into a fittingly global context of the epical, poetic arts (1988; 1990; 1991; 1995).

In light of the Homeric debate, one remembers that the literary-narratological approach to the Gospels, not unlike the unitarian school, focuses on the textual logic and internal causalities. Rejecting often extrinsic factors, literary criticism soon modulated into the New Criticism of the late 1930s through the 1950s, abandoning interest in authorship and bracketing the issue of tradition (Moore 1989, 7–13). To the extent that the narrative approach showed interest in the world outside the text at all, it shifted into performance criticism with a view toward the hearers/readers in front of the text. The historical-critical interpretation of the Gospels shows marked affinities with the analysts' heavily philological model. In the spirit of the analysts, tradition is imagined as a succession of developmental stages frequently executed with such clinical precision and ideational correctness so as to render its history retraceable from the Gospel on down to the earliest beginnings. In a different vein, historical criticism has attempted to identify collections of sayings, proverbs, and miracles, extrapolated from the Synoptics, the Gospel of John, and the *Gospel of Thomas*, as elements of the Gospel tradition (Koester 1971b: 158–93). And, as mentioned above, documents such as the *Cross Gospel, Egerton Papyrus 2*, and *Secret Mark* were likewise assumed to have been part of the early Gospel tradition. Equating oral with traditional, both the Homeric oralist school and Gospel form criticism assume a tradition composed of oral compositioning and performance. Whether the final, the existent text is an autograph, a direct transcription, of the oral performance tradition, or whether writing did make a difference in the transit from oral to written, is an issue that remains unresolved in both cases.

By and large, the concept of tradition in Homeric and Gospel scholarship is constructed along the lines of diachronic patterns. When in *Jesus and Tradition* I defined tradition as *biosphere* and described it as "largely an ascertainable and invisible nexus of references and identities from which people draw sustenance, in which they live, and in relation to which they make sense of their lives,"[3] I was introducing a synchronic model of tradition. Tradition, as I defined it, was the natural context shared by speaker and hearers/readers alike. The emphasis here is not on the timeline of

---

3. See chapter 5 in this volume.

cultural transmission, but on the social, cultural, oral, scribal, both visible and invisible matrix in which communication is effectuated. No doubt, a concept of tradition that is true to media realities will not be able to dispense with diachronics altogether. In the end, a model that manages to combine both the diachronic and the synchronic dynamics will do justice to the media situation.

44. Can Texts Silence Voices?

Yet another controversial point in the scholarly discussion of *OWG* concerned the media status of the Gospel and its powers vis-à-vis sounded words and voices. A new technology exercises its authority to subvert and reformulate the old medium so that "voices had to be silenced and an oral way of life subverted in order for the gospel to come into existence" (93). In this area a significant challenge was posed to my thesis concerning the status of the Gospel text and its appropriation of oral traditional speech. A text, I argued, that is as orally dependent as Mark had to silence sounded words and voices in order to assert its own textual identity. The issue here is not whether tradition is as predominantly oral as I had assumed but whether oral traditions that are textualized through the written Gospel are in fact silenced. In one of the most thoughtful review essays written on the book, David Balch suggested that I am "involved in an anachronism of about 1500 years. The text remained an oral authority. The transition from speaking to writing was not a transition from sound to silence" (1991, 192). The complexity of the issue requires a nuanced treatment.

The thesis of the silencing of oral voices is indeed misleading if stated apodictically and without qualification. Its most problematic aspect is the insinuation of a textual *termination* of oral speech per se. I clearly reject this possibility: "Obviously, it is not within the power of a text to stem the flow of oral words," I wrote in *OWG* (93). Relying on a major early work by Koester (1957), I postulated the continuation of a Synoptic orality largely untouched by (narrative) Gospel intervention until the middle of the second century. Nor am I entirely unaware of the Gospel's performative quality. Repeatedly I affirm the Gospel's parabolic genre, which is destined to be recycled into the oral medium (94, 209, 217). The full story I tell is, therefore, one of the textualization and reanimation of words. But Balch is quite right in underscoring the Gospel's oral functioning. I was not, at the time of writing the book, fully conscious of *composition in dictation*, and I was only dimly aware of cultural memory, concepts that are introduced here for the first time into the discussion. Nor did I explore the fuller implications of the lack of the visual codes of punctuation in most ancient manuscripts—a distinct feature of ancient medium history. In the absence of punctuation signs, texts were likely to be composed in conformity with a phenomenology of sound more than sight. Recently the case has been restated for vocalized writing in antiquity (Achtemeier 1990, 3–27), and a systematic approach to the grammar of sound in New Testament texts is being developed (Scott and Dean 1993; Lee and Scott 2009).

When allowance thus is made for the oral matrix and functioning of the Gospel text, the question persists whether Balch's critique does not have the effect of once again leveling the distinction between tradition and Gospel text altogether. In stating that textualization of speech did not entail "a transition from sound to silence" because "the text remained an oral authority," has he not run the risk of putting the Gospel text on equal footing with traditional speech? And if this is the case, are we not then thrown back to Bultmann's model of "an effortlessly evolutionary transition from the pre-gospel stream of tradition to the written gospel [and] his insistence on the irrelevance of a distinction between orality and literacy"? (*OWG* 6). Now it is one thing to concede that speech and writing rarely exist in distinctly separate domains and quite another to imply that a text, just like speech, is also oral authority. Notwithstanding their oral roots and function, chirographs transcribed and stabilized language in ways oral speech never could and opened it to visual inspection and unceasing efforts at interpretation. What is more, the ancients were aware of media tensions and distinctions, and they coped with them in various ways (Kelber 1994b, 206–9). A semiotic transformation in fact has occurred when speech is textualized, so that what is recycled through the medium of the Gospel's textualized narrative cannot be precisely what was spoken prior to the composition of the text—even though the pre-Gospel tradition continued to be spoken as well. I seek to capture the media differences by referring to the proclamation of the Gospel narrative as "secondary orality" in distinction from the "primary orality" of Jesus' sayings and stories untouched by Gospel textuality (1983, 217–18). In the end, I suspect, we need to move beyond concepts such as "the text as oral authority," the "silencing of speech," and "secondary orality" and to develop a more adequate linguistic apparatus that conceptualizes media interfaces, both the persistence of the oral traditional idiom in texts and its transformation through the textual register. I do not know of work better suited to this challenge than that of Foley, who has carried the discipline of orality-literacy studies to unprecedented heights of theoretical sophistication and originality (1990; 1991; 1994; 1995).

45. The Gospel's Narrative Logic

My reading of Mark's narrative, no less than my thesis about Markan textuality, has inspired strong criticism. Indeed, few aspects of the book, and of my earlier writings on the subject, have aroused as much controversy as my proposition that the oldest canonical Gospel brings the Twelve, under the leadership of Peter, into discredit, turning them from privileged insiders into disgraced outsiders. I am not the first to have recognized a Markan animus toward the disciples (Tyson 1961; Weeden 1971, 52–100; Tannehill 1977), nor was I the last. Recently, Fowler has raised our consciousness about the reading grids of Matthew and Luke that have imposed themselves as the stronger readings upon our reading of Mark (1991, 228–56). It is only when we break the hold Matthew and Luke exercised upon Mark that we discern, with Fowler's interpretive assistance, the Gospel's rhetorical strategy of moving those who were appointed to be insiders to the outside, while at the same time drawing readers into the circle of privileged insiders (256–60 and passim). What distinguishes my approach is that I develop the theme of failing discipleship, along with Mark's additional polemics against Jesus' family and early Christian prophets, into a comprehensive media thesis. Relying on Havelock's celebrated thesis about Plato's animosity toward the poets conceived as a critique of the normative, oral apparatus of Greek education (1963), I interpret Mark's polemic against the disciples, family, and prophets as an estrangement from the standard-bearers of oral tradition. I still hold this to be a sound reading in light of media sensibilities.

In reflecting on this controversial issue, I take up Boomershine's criticism, which succinctly articulates two principal objections to my thesis (1987, 47–68). A first argument suggests that the hypothesis of Mark's involvement "in an anti-Petrine polemic is historically improbable" (60). It has been my observation that those who appeal to the historical implausibility of anti-Petrine sentiments implicitly or explicitly assume Petrine composition, that is, they hold to the view that "Peter told [the Gospel narrative] and permitted it to be told about him" (60). And yet, does not the assumption of Petrine authorship fly in the face of a complex and multifaceted history of the tradition? Or, to ask the question differently, can we ever hope to retrace the complexities of the tradition to the ground level of an individual authorship? Indeed, is there such a zero level? Instead of challenging Mark's anti-Petrine outlook on the assumption of Petrine authorship, it seems more plausible to argue that Petrine authorship is least likely for what clearly is the most anti-Petrine of the canonical Gospels. This essay cannot do justice to the complexity surrounding the premise of Petrine authorship. Suffice it to say that the premise is supported by two theories, both of which originated in the early Christian tradition. One is Papias's famous statement, documented by Eusebius, concerning Mark's note-taking of Peter's preaching (*Hist. Eccl.* 3.39.15). I closely examine the passage and conclude that the ambiguity of the wording is such that it cannot bear the weight of the Petrine thesis (22–23). The second motif strengthening Petrine authorship is the apostolic eyewitness theory, the notion that the disciples/apostles, after witnessing the life of Jesus from baptism to resurrection, functioned as the initial recorders of the foundational beginnings. I propose that we open our minds to the possibility that what we are tempted to read as the historical record of the tradition's origin constitutes an essential moment in the tradition itself.

An example from the rabbinic tradition will illustrate the point. Sometime between 80 C.E. and 200 C.E. rabbinic sages developed the theory of the earwitnesses, that is, the notion that Moses verbally transmitted more or less intact to his disciples an extensive body of revealed knowledge that supplemented the written Torah. The thesis marks a point in postwar Judaism at which the tradition grows self-conscious by grounding its existence in the sacred origin and postulating unbroken continuity with the present. In a broadly analogous fashion, postwar Christianity, under the canonical initiative of Luke (Luke 1:2; Acts 1:21–22), generated the apostolic eyewitness theory, which reconnects its tradition with the sacred beginnings from which it had been rapidly growing apart. Despite differences in their respective functioning, both the rabbinic theory of earwitnessing and the Christian theory of apostolic eyewitnessing constitute moments of self-legitimation in and of the tradition.

The second argument suggests that my reading of the Markan discipleship plot is improbable on grounds of ancient media psychodynamics. When the Gospel was recited to audiences it solicited a high degree of sympathetic participation in the narrative and with its principal characters. The kind of psychological distancing I postulate is considered by some to be quite unthinkable in the realm of early Christian communication. Hence Boomershine's assertion that "Kelber has collapsed 1900 years of media development into a forty year period in the first century" (1987,

60). *Per contra* I propose that the agonistic toning of language and the narrative plotting of adversarial relations is a hallmark of oral or residually oral cultures (see especially Ong 1982, 43–45). Do we need reminding of Paul, who at least two decades prior to Mark was engaged in fierce polemics with fellow apostles, including the Jerusalem pillars? Far from admitting any reflection on the personality of Paul, his often adversarial style has grown directly out of the rhetorical culture of late antiquity. But if agonistic relations are intrinsic to oral-rhetorical aesthetics and Paul's language betrays a distinctly adversarial style, my reading of Mark's polemic against the disciples, Jesus' family, and prophets may be anything but anachronistic. Admittedly, the roles Mark plotted for the principal carriers of the early Jesus traditions contradict our historical assumptions. There is a puzzle here that summons the readers' strenuous attention, but we cannot solve it by pretending that it does not exist.

My thesis on Paul takes pains to allow for media interaction. While I devote much space to Paul "the oral traditionalist" (177), whose letters are permeated with oral sensitivities. I also describe his reaching for the "safe" ground of chirographic certainties when swamped with the consequences of enthusiastic speech. I have learned more of the performance character of the Pauline Letters (Ward 1994) and likewise of the media complexities that surround the composition, transmission, and recitation of his letters (Wire 1994). I am, moreover, fully cognizant of the importance of a greater "dialectical employment of both oral and written media" (A. Dewey 1994, 113). Still more needs to be said about Paul's "oral interpretation of Scripture" (A. Dewey 1994, 111), a phenomenon studied with exquisite care by Hays (1989). What typifies Paul's use of Scripture, according to Hays, is the extraordinary freedom he exercises with regard to the wording of scriptural citations. Unconstrained by any historical scrupulousness concerning Scripture's "authentic" meaning, the apostle "adheres neither to any single exegetical procedure, nor even to a readily specifiable inventory of procedures" (16). These are observations that need to be taken very seriously, for they suggest that Paul clearly processed Scripture memorially. The written word was, so to speak, alive in his heart and on his lips. Granted that there is in Paul's handling of the media an easy flow from chirographs to speech and back to chirographs, we should not submerge all media differences into an interactive model. There are polarities in his thought, and they lend themselves to a media interpretation. One such instance concerns his objection to the law, which in media perspectives manifests an antipathy toward the objectification and complexification of its written enactment and which contrasts with the oral gospel that engenders faith coming from hearing. In view of the fact that the "curse" of the law was frequently diagnosed in terms of its legal and legalistic authority in both Jewish-Christian and Catholic-Protestant controversies, we need to listen with renewed sensitivity to the media implications within Paul's Letters.

There is, last but not least, the issue of power and, allied with it, that of gender. I am indebted especially to Schüssler Fiorenza (1983), Wire (1990), MacDonald (1983), and Joanna Dewey (1995b, 37–65) for having educated me in this area. But it is Joanna Dewey who deserves credit for connecting gender with orality-literacy studies. Proceeding from the observation that at "every social level, women's literacy rate was lower than men's" (43), she identified the transformation from a predominantly oral to a chirographically based Christianity with a "shift to a hierarchal male leadership that upheld the patriarchal empire and family" (59). Dewey recognized that the Pauline tradition offers strong evidence in support of her thesis. One cannot help but think of the Corinthian women prophets who, speaking in the authority of the Spirit, sought independence from their marital partners (Wire) only to run up against Paul's authoritative letter of 1 Corinthians, which silenced their voices in the church and redefined their place in a hierarchically constructed society. Or one remembers the oral stories about Paul and Thecla, which represent a women's movement that subverted the patriarchal values of family, city, and empire and appears to have provoked the writings of the Pastoral Letters, which reinstituted traditional values based on male prerogatives (MacDonald). These and other examples strongly support Dewey's thesis concerning links between the deployment of writing and efforts to restrain, even suppress, women's expressed desire to live the gospel of freedom. But we need to exercise caution lest we ontologize medium-gender affinities as if media carried specific gender attributes or gender-bred proclivities. What we observe here are not psychodynamic realities that apply to gender and medium but sociolinguistic phenomena whereby, in certain situations, the elite seizes upon one medium for the purpose of exercising power and domination. When viewed from this perspective, Dewey's thesis is productive of genuinely novel insights into the Christian tradition.

The significance of *OWG*, as I see it, is not limited to the technicalities and aesthetics of oral versus written communication. In reconsidering the early Christian tradition from media perspectives, I seek to raise sensibilities that have been marginalized at best, and suppressed at worst, in more than two centuries of historical-critical scholarship. I am searching for a way out of what I perceive to be an impasse in historical biblical scholarship, which, notwithstanding its stunning accomplishments, is driven by an inadequate theory of the art of communication in the ancient world.

8

MEMORY'S DESIRE OR THE ORDEAL OF REMEMBERING:
JUDAISM AND CHRISTIANITY

*The story of how Jews and Christians have lived with, and more often
against, each other constitutes a fateful chapter in Western history. This
essay is about Jews and Christians, and the difficulties they have experienced
in living together, past and present. Memory is the guiding theme and conceptual umbrella throughout. But memory is perceived here not as individual interiority operating mnemotechnically as storage system and archival
repository, but externally as a social force imposed by religious and political frameworks. When applied to the relations between Jews and Christians,
cultural memory suggests that the two faiths are governed not by the historical past alone, but by the past as it is remembered. The memories of the
two faiths share also divide them; the history they have in common also
separates them; and the scriptural traditions that are theirs, they interpret
differently. Four chronologically unrelated case studies will explore the often
conflictual relations from the perspective of cultural memory.*

*The first part examines Matt 27:25, a verse that has left a trail of blood
in Western history. Initially operating in the intrinsically Jewish context of
Matthean social circumstances, it is subsequently reimagined as source of
demonizing fantasies when operating in different power constellations where
Christians constituted the ruling majority and Jews a marginalized minority. The second part gives an account of the famous Barcelona Disputation of
1263 between the Dominican Pablo Christiani and Rabbi Moses ben Nachman. It is argued that the dispute, apparently a conflict over differences in
scriptural interpretation, was on a deeper level a clash between two cultural
memories, each rooted in different social experiences. Moving into modernity, the third part discusses Elie Wiesel's Night, one of the programmatic
pieces of Holocaust literature. The novel's complex compositional history and
literary transformations offer insight into the operations of cultural memory*

in the face of trauma: the changing conditions of the authorial present infil-
trate the narrative so as to assimilate it to the task of commemorating the
bruta facta of the past. The fourth part recounts and contemplates a struggle
of conflicting memories over Auschwitz carried out on the site of the camp
itself. In this fashion, mobilizing entirely different and often irreconcilable
responses, the trauma of Auschwitz continues living on as a conflict-laden
mnemohistory. The fifth part, last, reflects on the concept of mnemohistory,
a memorially empowered history. It is suggested that mnemohistory neither
denies so-called factual history nor totally absorbs it, but rather expands our
concept of history. In later essays (11, §71; 13, §88) I apply insights gained
from these case studies to the passion narrative, reading it as a commemora-
tive text coping with the trauma of a violent death.

> Unlike history proper, mnemohistory is concerned not with the past as
> such, but only with the past as it is remembered.
> —Jan Assmann, *Moses the Egyptian*

> [Memory's] plastic nature stems to a large extent from the fact that it is
> reconstructed not only under the pressures exerted by the present, but
> also within particular institutional frameworks that guide selection and
> fix contours.
> —Aleida Assmann, *Cultural Memory and Western Civilization*

> commemorated past ... is not a matter of a so-called empirical past
> persisting in unelaborated form..., but a past shaped, sacralized, and
> interpreted precisely through activities of commemoration.
> —Alan Kirk and Tom Thatcher, *Jesus Tradition as Social Memory*

> The work of memory was not to re-present, not to reduplicate, but to
> construct, to deliver a place for images. Of course, the notion of memory
> as construction contrasts greatly with the assumptions of many modern
> biblical scholars.
> —Arthur J. Dewey, *The Locus for Death*

46. MATTHEW AS SOURCE OF DEMONIZING RECOLLECTIONS

Of all the verses in the New Testament, few have been more deeply implicated in the bloodstained history of Jewish-Christian relations than the

Matthean rendition of the people's response to Pilate and his declaration of his own innocence: "His [Jesus'] blood be on us and on our children" (Matt 27:25). In keeping with a Semitic idiom that the blood of someone who has been wronged will be required from the perpetrators of evil (Lev 20:9; 1 Sam 4:11; Jer 26:15), the people in Matthew's passion narrative voluntarily accept the consequences of Jesus' death. This is what the controversial verse Matt 27:25 articulates, namely, the people's self-imposed punishment, and not what it, along with other Matthean verses, came to mean in subsequent Christian culture: a warrant for genocide.

There is a broad-based scholarly opinion that Matthew's narrative mirrors a post-70 conflict between a Pharisaic, rabbinic type of Judaism and Matthew's dissident messianic Judaism (Saldarini 1991, 38–61; Hummel 1966, 26–33; Ellis 1974, 3–6). The debate between these two representatives of Judaism is rooted in the earliest period of Christian history, but it will have reached a new level of intensity in the aftermath of the colossal catastrophe of the temple's conflagration. "Thus, the Gospel of Matthew should be read along with other Jewish post-destruction literature, such as the apocalyptic works 2 Baruch, 4 Ezra, and Apocalypse of Abraham, early strata of the Mishnah, and Josephus" (Saldarini 1991, 39). Not only did Matthew, from his own perspective, operate within the boundaries of Judaism, but also the Gospel is crucially involved "in a struggle for the future of Judaism" (43). The Gospel considers itself advocating the true observance of Torah and righteousness over other interpretations, especially those of emergent rabbinic Judaism. In this context, the Gospel's vituperative language is largely designed to delegitimize Pharisaically guided Judaism, and to carve out and sanction the self-identity of its own community. In Matthew's time, the outcome over the future of postwar Judaism was still an open question, but within a short time "Matthew lost the battle for Judaism" (60). Social context and social identity are at the heart of the conflict.

Viewed in this historical context, the controversial verse Matt 27:25 in no way suggests what in fact it helped bring about in later, rather different social contexts: the shedding of Jewish blood by Christians through the centuries. There is, first of all, the issue of the identity of the people (πᾶς ὁ λαός) who invoked judgment upon themselves. In the LXX λαός predominantly signifies *people* in the sense of *nation*, which is also the connotation prevalent in Matthew. The phrase "chief priests and scribes (or elders) of the people" (Matt 2:4; 21:23; 26:3), for example, refers to the population as a collective entity. In Matt 27:24–25 the text differentiates between ὄχλος and λαός. Pilate washes his hands "before the crowd" (27:24: ἀπέναντι τοῦ ὄχλου), and the people as a whole (πᾶς ὁ λαός) declare themselves willing to accept the consequences of Jesus' death. The ὄχλος standing before Pilate pertains to the Jerusalem crowd, and the πᾶς ὁ λαός who brings judgment upon itself must be understood as the people collectively. To deal responsibly with the fateful verse, it is helpful to distinguish three senses of history. One is *the history of the subject matter*. Given the increasingly tense relations between a colonized people and imperial Rome, it is next to impossible to imagine that the Jerusalem crowds, pilgrims mostly, would insist on the crucifixion of one of their own by the despised imperialists, and frivolously invite a self-inflicted punishment (Crossan 1965). Historical power relations have been exactly reversed in the Gospel, reflecting a historical situation following the fall of Jerusalem. This brings us to the second sense of history, the *compositional setting*, which defines a period when a developing Christian identity is being constructed vis-à-vis a post-70 Judaism and in deference to Rome. A third and rather different sense of history shall be called the *narrative history* of the Gospel. What is the status of Matt 27:24 in the context of the larger narrative logic? It is often observed that the Gospel exhibits a notable preoccupation with the fate of Jerusalem, "the city of the great king" (5:35: πόλις ἐστὶν τοῦ μεγάλου βασιλέως). In the parable of the Marriage Feast (22:1–10) the king responds to the unwillingness of the invited guests to attend his son's wedding with anger: "He sent his troops and destroyed those murderers and burned their city" (22:7). The parable expounds the destruction of Jerusalem, narrated in remarkably realistic terms, as punishment for the people's disobedience. Further down in the narrative, we observe a narrative sequence of events that gives us a clue to Matthew's narrative logic and historical circumstances. The sequence commences with the seven anti-Pharisaic woes (23:1–33), which culminate in the accusation of the Pharisees persecuting and murdering "prophets, sages, and scribes" (23:34). This is followed with the announcement that the blood of the righteous will come upon them—"from the blood of righteous Abel to the blood of Zechariah son of Barachiah, whom you murdered between the sanctuary and the altar" (23:35). The Pharisaic woes are completed with the statement: "Truly, I say to you, all this will come upon this generation" (23:36: ἐπὶ τὴν γενεὰν ταύτην). The announcement of the impending judgment leads into the lament over Jerusalem (23:37–39), which again deplores the murder of the prophets and makes a veiled reference to the desolation of the temple

(23:38: ἀφίεται ὑμῖν ὁ οἶκος ὑμῶν ἔρημος). The sequence reaches its peak in Jesus' prediction of the destruction of the temple (24:1–3). Unquestionably, the narrative dramatization moves entirely within an intra-Jewish historical consciousness and does not reflect Jewish-Christian polemic. *No word here, no insinuation even, of a perpetual curse or a condemnation in perpetuity.*

While arguing from the vantage point of the Jesus movement, Matthew nevertheless joins many in post-70 Judaism who viewed the fall of Jerusalem as the temporal punishment for the sins of the people. Bringing the three senses of history together, we can now observe that the *history of the subject matter* relates to Jerusalem's temple and its destruction, the *narrative history* dramatizes a rationale for the disaster, and the *historical setting for the composition* must be assumed to have been a postwar time in history. Matthew looks back upon the physical and metaphysical disaster of the temple's conflagration, and writes in the conviction that Jesus' ominous prediction had come to fateful fruition as punishment for the sins of the people. As a matter of historical fact, the predicted judgment had come true for all to see in his generation.

In post-Matthean times, the Christians, as they came to call themselves, remembered the story of Jesus, including the controversial verse Matt 27:25, in a wider and out of a very different frame of historical reference. It would not be entirely accurate to suggest that the Gospel and its controversial verse were now read and heard out of context, and more accurate to say that the Jesus narrative came to be remembered out of a very different social context. When Christianity increasingly positioned itself as the universal religion in the empire, its custodians of memory were driven by the desire to legitimate their new religious identity vis-à-vis what to them seemed to be the old, superseded religion. From this newly gained position of power, Christian imagination reconfigured the Matthean conflict between a Pharisaic, rabbinic, and a dissident, messianic type of Judaism, this strictly intra-Jewish dissension, into an irreconcilable estrangement between the competing faiths of Christianity and Judaism. As the temple as historical reference point lost immediate historical relevance so did the intra-Jewish conflict. As far as the conflagration of the temple was concerned, it ceased to be the pivotal experience it had been in Matthean remembrance of Jewish history. The religious import of the temple's destruction signaling temporal punishment for the sins of the people was largely purged from Christian memory, and Matthew's localized setting of the people of Jerusalem was now reimagined in terms of a people who spoke on behalf of Jews everywhere and at all times. Their response to Pilate, therefore, was thought to have invited everlasting punishment upon Judaism as a whole. Given the nexus of new power constellations, with Christians constituting the ruling majority and Jews in the minority, the former arrogated to themselves a judgmental role, which far exceeded the judgment the Son of Man had been expected to administer at the end of days. Christians exhibited themselves as vengeful executioners of a people that had been branded with an eternal curse. In this manner, memory's desire to vindicate the Christian position of power both engendered a radicalized redescription of Matthew's verse that opened the way for demonizing fantasies and murderous actions. *In sum, what happened was that Christians remembered the past out of the context of a drastically altered configuration of power.*

47. MEDIEVAL CLASH OF CULTURAL MEMORIES: THE BARCELONA DISPUTATION

Throughout the Middle Ages the distinctly separate and often conflicting religious identities claimed by the two principal heirs to the biblical tradition are well documented. The following explication runs the risk of perpetuating the clichés of a normative Judaism and a normative Christianity, whereas historically there was variability on both sides on matters even as foundational as covenantal piety. With this caveat in mind, it may be said that the Jews experienced themselves as the descendants of Israel on account of the biblically documented covenantal membership. The latter entailed both the *Abrahamic Covenant*, with the promise of nation and land (Gen 12–17), and the *Mosaic Covenant*, which included the most precious gift of what came to be called the Torah, both in its written and oral form (Deut 11). Gentiles enjoyed an independently authentic covenantal relationship, the *Noahide covenant*, which governed a valid way of life (Gen 8:1–9:17). In Christian self-consciousness, the Abrahamic, patriarchal covenant ceased to be operational in its traditional Jewish sense due to the appearance of Jesus. The Abrahamic covenant came to be subordinated to the Mosaic covenant, and the promises that had been associated with the former were believed to have been consummated in Jesus, who was increasingly identified as the Messiah. In the Christian view, Jews who found themselves unable to consent to what amounted to a very novel concept of messiahship and unable to accept Jesus as the Messiah forfeited membership in what for them amounted to an unlawfully constituted covenant. Messiahship became a major bone of contention.

The faithful adherents of these two traditions might conceivably have coexisted in relative harmony were it not for two complicating factors. One was the fact that the two traditions had been rooted in and bound up with the same biblical legacy. It is one thing for two peoples to tolerate each other's ethnic and religious claims if each side traces its identity to a separate and unrelated tradition. It is quite another for two peoples to live in harmony if they disagree over the interpretation and implementation of a legacy shared by both. In the first case, the affirmation of the one religion may leave the other essentially unaffected. In the other instance, the claims of each side are bound to tread upon the sensibilities of the other. Family disputes can be more acrimonious and difficult to resolve than disagreements between two unrelated parties. A second reason for the conflictual relations was the political and legal constellation as it obtained throughout the Western Middle Ages: many, although by no means all, Jews lived as a minority in predominantly Christian countries. In virtually all instances, the rights to existence and to residence had to be secured from local, royal, and papal authorities. Neither these nor any other rights were ever grounded in inclusively and comprehensively validated constitutional agreements. Invariably Jews were subject to negotiations with and special grants accorded by those who wielded power. No matter how prominent and influential Jewish individuals may have been in local communities or at royal courts, their social status and their physical security could never be taken for granted. Coexistence was always negotiable, never a given; and coexistence on equal terms was not an option (Katz 1961, 3–23).

When in the eleventh, twelfth, and thirteenth centuries Christian Europe waged the war of the Crusades for the reconquest of the Holy Land from Muslims, the degradation, persecution, and murder of European Jews attained unprecedented heights of fury and cruelty. Jews in France and Germany in particular met with savage outbursts of pillage and murder. Aroused by national fervor, swayed by the promise of special, religious rewards, and driven by anti-Jewish as well as anti-Muslim sentiments, enthusiastic recruits by the tens of thousands rallied behind the cause of the Crusades and en route to the Holy Land indiscriminately slaughtered whole communities of Jewish inhabitants in their respective home countries. In Spain, however, the fate of Jews was quite different from that suffered by their coreligionists in France and Germany. Spanish

Christian monarchs, more than the rulers of most other European peoples, were directly confronted with the force and culture of Islam. During the centuries that saw the Crusades they were preoccupied with the consolidation of power, a process integrally linked with the ejection of the Muslims.

Ironically, Spanish Jews initially benefited from this policy, as they found themselves in a situation where their relatively high educational status and the absence of a political, social base of power were in demand. Intellectual Jews became powerful at Spanish courts, while the majority of Jewish inhabitants lived under relatively peaceful circumstances in settled communities. Thus while intolerance and brutalities toward Jews drastically intensified in most European countries during the centuries of the Crusades, this same period in Spain came to be known as the golden age for Jews. It saw an extraordinary flowering of Jewish achievements in philosophy, law, poetry grammar, and science.

This golden age came to an end with the rise of the Inquisition and the convocation of a series of public disputations between representatives of Judaism and Christianity. The Inquisition, an ecclesiastical tribunal designed to expose, define, convict, and punish heresy, was established around 1230. Initially aimed at the spread of such Christian movements as the Cathari, the Waldenses, and the Albigenses, it was increasingly disposed to implicate the Jews among those marked as heretics. Jewish-Christian disputations were a further sign that the spirit of toleration, to the extent that it had existed, was being extinguished. In official Christian parlance, the purpose of the disputations was to publicly clarify the doctrinal position of Christianity vis-à-vis Judaism. As a political reality, however, the disputations were conducted under the shadow of the Inquisition and with the implied intent of ascertaining evidence that was going to prove Jewish liability in ecclesiastical law courts. Christian theologians were inclined to posture as prosecuting attorneys vis-à-vis their Jewish counterparts. Given this situation, Jewish scholars faced a serious dilemma. If they accepted the more or less forced invitation, they found themselves confronted with Christian disputants who had stacked the ground rules, tactics, and selection of questions in a manner favorable to themselves. But if they declined participation they only aggravated the suspicion that they were concealing information, a situation that was likely to corroborate the charge of heresy (Katz 1961, 106–13). Just how risky an undertaking it was for Jews to allow themselves to be drawn into a public controversy with Christians is borne out by the Paris Disputation of 1240, the first formal discussion between medieval Jews and Christians on record. Conducted in an overtly hostile atmosphere, it was followed two years later with the confiscation and burning of the Talmud.

By contrast, the Barcelona Disputation of 1263 was conducted in a less inquisitorial atmosphere. Christians were eager to convince more than to convict. King James of Aragon, chairman of the disputation, had a reputation for relying heavily on Jews in his administration. When he received instructions from the pope to dismiss his Jewish administrators, he conveniently ignored the papal counsel. He conducted his chairmanship in the spirit of genuine intellectual curiosity and with a semblance of fairness. Still, he was subject to political pressures, including those from the Spanish church and the papacy. Moreover, it was his theologians who set the agenda and framed the questions. Also, both in Paris and in Barcelona the Christian cause was represented by a converted Jew, an apostate in the eyes of Judaism, who was thoroughly versed in Jewish sources and eager to renounce his former past. For all intents and purposes, the Barcelona Disputation was conducted under unequal conditions.

The role of the advocate of the Christian position in Barcelona was taken up by the Dominican Pablo Christiani, who was an expert in utilizing his Jewish learning to prove Christian truths from talmudic and midrashic texts. The Jewish representative was Rabbi Moses ben Nachman (Nahmanides), one of the greatest talmudic scholars of his generation, who valued reason above all—even in his writings on mysticism. In spite of a relatively conciliatory tone, the disputation amounted to an intellectual ordeal with each side burdened by assumptions, commitments, and memories that left little room for mutual understanding, let alone rapprochement (Maccoby 1982, 35–55).

In keeping with the Christian centrality of belief in the Messiah, Pablo placed messianism at the center of the disputation. For Nahmanides who held the view that the Messiah was not an intrinsic feature of the scheme of salvation—at least not in the essentialist Christian sense—the agenda must have seemed disconcerting. Why not focus on the Exodus or the Sinaitic covenant and the gift of the Torah? Messianism was a Christian preoccupation, and not, to that extent, for Judaism.

Pablo shared the Christian conviction that the corruption of humankind was such that it required rescue from its captivity in history. In personally enduring the terror of history Jesus had been able to redeem the human condition in a decisive, if preliminary sense. Nahmanides, for a variety of reasons, was unable to accept this viewpoint. For one, he remained unconvinced of any scriptural justification for the notion of a suffering Messiah. When Pablo cited an haggadic passage that seemed to him to identify Isaiah's Suffering Servant with Jesus the Messiah, Nahmanides objected by invoking the collective interpretation, a reading that identified the anonymous Suffering One with the people of Israel. Even if one were to accept a messianic reading of the passage, it had nothing to do with the historical Jesus, who had died by crucifixion at the hands of the Romans.

Second, Nahmanides's sense of history was deeply affected by his perception of the failure of messianic pretenders and the continuing suffering of humankind. "From the days of Jesus until now, the whole world has been full of violence and plundering' (Maccoby 1982, 52). Driven as he was by the memories of history, the world to him seemed thoroughly unlike the messianic era. Third, Nahmanides was informed by a different understanding of the plight of humanity and the nature of sin. Humankind, he argued, did not suffer Adam's original sin, and therefore does not live in fear of eternal damnation, nor is it in need of redemption from its cursed condition. To be sure, humans suffered the consequences of Adam's sin, but there was no such thing as inherited guilt. There lay greater human dignity in facing up to the evil in this world than in waiting for the coming of the Messiah, or in enjoying his blessings, if indeed they had been bestowed upon humankind. Once again, the Messiah in this scheme of things was perceived more as "a reward, not a necessity" (51).

The question, therefore, raised at the opening of the disputation, that is, whether the Messiah had arrived or whether he was still to come, was not an issue merely of historical verifiability. Even though the messianic question was a Christian preoccupation more than a Jewish one, it was used both by Rabbi Moses ben Nahman and by Pablo Christiani to expound the core issues of what it meant to be a Jew and a Christian: how was one to understand the human condition, the nature of sin, and the purpose of salvation?

Involved in the Barcelona dispute were also different concepts of sacred Scripture. Nahmanides could claim that even if the controversial haggadic passage were to refer to the Messiah, he was not bound by it because the Talmud contained a wealth of options that were never meant to be balanced in perfect harmony. Hence his blunt statement. "I do not believe this Aggadah" (45). In Jewish exegesis, this proposition was entirely kosher because the wealth of rabbinic learning stored in the Talmud was the accumulated wisdom of numerous rabbis who did not always agree among themselves. As far as the debate over messianism was concerned, therefore, the procedure of rejecting one passage in favor of others was by no means in violation of Jewish, talmudic hermeneutics, because the Talmud was not assumed to propound a single, dogmatic view about the Messiah. To Pablo this seemed both arbitrary and evasive. Approaching the Talmud with Christian standards of canonicity, he was puzzled by Nahmanides's avowed selectivity. Christian hermeneutics, Pablo claimed, attributed equal significance to all parts of Scripture. To such a view, Nahmanides tartly replied that Pablo himself was operating selectively, driven as he was to focus on certain passages while conveniently shutting his eyes to the plurality of options contained in the Talmud.

To complicate matters, the controversial messianic passage appeared in haggadic materials, which in Jewish exegesis operated on a plane not necessarily inferior to but quite different from halakah. As far as haggadah was concerned, truth was poetic and parabolic, and the methods applied might well be associative and intuitive, rather than strictly logical and historical. On this level of apperception, Nahmanides insisted, two contradictory statements could both be true. Nor were interpreters of the haggadic passages under any constraint to arrive at a meticulously and definitively articulated truth. Whatever else haggadah was—narrative, wisdom, lore—it was not dogmas whose function it was to save souls from damnation or, as the case may be, to condemn them. In contrast to haggadah, halakah engaged in and demanded precision. This made little sense to Pablo, who was nurtured in a tradition that held the narrative Gospels to be foundational, while Pauline antinomianism seemed to discourage halakic precisionism. Hermeneutical priorities were exactly reversed. Moreover, Jews could split hairs over the ritual purity of an oven, while Christians split hairs over the substance of the Son (whether he was similar or identical with the Father). Hence, as far as different valorizations of Scripture and different genres of Scripture were concerned, the Jew and the Christian were bound to talk at cross-purposes. Neither Nahmanides nor Pablo showed any inclination to engage in comparative reflectiveness; both were intent on saving identity.

What manifested itself at Barcelona is on one level a conflict between different notions of what constitutes binding Scripture. More significantly, it is a conflict between different interpretations of Scripture. The same scripturally encoded knowledge resulted in different expositions. Jew and Christian operated under the aegis of incompatible scriptural priorities, divergent modes of interpretation, and dissimilar theological assumptions. To all outward appearances, the figure of Abraham suggests a legacy shared by the two faiths, but in historical actuality different and conflicting memories of Israel's founding father aroused feelings of apprehension. For while in the Jewish tradition Abraham is remembered as the foundational covenanter, in Christian/Pauline understanding he is a paragon of faith who superseded and invalidated the soteriological function of the Torah. That Abraham underwent circumcision (Gen 17:23–24), moreover, is "forgotten" in the Pauline tradition. Both Nahmanides and Paolo cite scriptural passages and engage in interpretive argumentations. Undoubtedly, interpretation of texts was at stake and played a decisive role in the disputation. But Scripture is not the sole and sufficient explanatory factor. Nahmanides and Paolo performed as representatives of two religious traditions of historic dimension, and their dispute is not simply an exercise in exegetical artistry. On the surface level, selection and prioritizing, and also interpretation of texts, was a matter of exegetical and theological decision making. But again, the textual conflict is the surface level, apparent to participants and audience alike. There is a deeper sense in which different texts had long been in existence, and differing readings and interpretations had already happened in a domain that included the textual factor but was by no means limited to it. These larger and deeper frameworks within which Nahmanides and Paolo operated were made up of communally shared symbols, ritual commemorations, historical experiences, traumas, and also textual interpretations, or more precisely, remembrances of texts. To no small degree were the opposing positions taken by Nahmanides and Paolo contingent on a network of social conditions, which Halbwachs has called *cadres sociaux* and J. Assmann *kultureller Bezugsrahmen*. The Barcelona Disputation, an event comprehensible as a clash of cultural memories, cannot itself escape rememorization (Maccoby 1982, 55–75). Memories are habitually unstable. Subject to the diachronicity of time, they can reinvent themselves under changing social conditions. Both Rabbi Moses ben Nahman and Pablo Christiani composed a written account of the disputation. Not unexpectedly, their memories were at considerable variance. According to the Christian report, Nahmanides was decisively defeated. Caught in glaring inconsistencies and compelled to disavow some of his own theses, he finally departed from the scene leaving vital questions unanswered. In the Jewish report, Nahmanides prided himself on his role in drawing up the agenda, on the intrinsic correctness of his arguments, and on the demonstrated superior rationality of his faith. It is well to remember that each protagonist recorded his recollections under political pressures. Nahmanides produced his Hebrew text in a state of fearful uncertainty as to the future for himself and his community. (Following the publication of his Hebrew manuscript, he was banned for two years.) Pablo's Latin report, commissioned to be the official ecclesiastical record, was ratified and sealed by King James. Each protagonist wrote in the conviction that his document would preserve the definitive version for posterity (Maccoby 1982, 55–57). To us it is obvious that both are involved in a process of rememorization, as indeed is my own account, which has benefited from the study of Hyam Maccoby, who in turn relied on Nahmanides's text.

48. Remembering *Night*: Coping with Memory

Elie Wiesel's novel *Night* stands as a paradigmatic literary monument in memory of the twentieth-century European death camps. In part, its fame rests on the fact that it is one of the earliest narrative reports stemming from the pen of a survivor. In the West, the book first appeared in French as *La Nuit* in 1958, at a time when literary and documentary studies on the annihilation of European Jewry were virtually nonexistent. In part, its moral and literary authority is due to the powerful purity of its prose. The surface clarity of its language confronts the reader head-on, and its content appears to be directly accessible in its matter-of-factness, in spite of the painfully unbearable subject matter. And in part, the worldwide impact *Night* has achieved in informing and, as the case may be, reminding readers of the terrors of the camps results from the autobiographical nature of its genre. It applies personal names, bodies, and individualities to the unrepresentable abyss of the Shoah, and it personalizes the unassimilable. In short, *Night* is the kind of novel we ask our students to read because of its signal importance in the literature of Holocaust memoirs.

When we inquire into the compositional circumstances of a book of its kind, we are reminded that most origins, under closer scrutiny, lose their appearance of singular simplicity and unconceal complexities and plurality. Such is the case with *Night*, which has grown out of a remarkably complex literary anteriority. Like many foundational documents, it arises from and is the product of a literary history. Knowing this history informs us of the exigencies of the compositioning of memoirs dealing with a subject matter that is unrepresentable in any form or medium. *Night is a unique testimony to hell on earth, and its compositional history is testimony to the ordeal of remembering it.*

In "An Interview Unlike Any Other," Wiesel reflected on his writing of *Night* in the following words:

> I knew the role of the survivor was to testify. Only I did not know how. I lacked experience. I lacked a framework. I mistrusted the tools, the procedures. Should one say it all or hold it all back? Should one shout or whisper? Place the emphasis on those who were gone or on their heirs? How does one describe the indescribable? How does one use restraint in re-creating the fall of mankind and the eclipse of the gods? And then, how can one be sure that the words, once uttered, will not betray or distort the message they bear? So heavy was my anguish that I made a vow: not to speak, not to touch upon the essential for at least ten years. Long enough to see clearly. Long enough to learn to listen to the voices crying inside my own. Long enough to regain possession of my memory. Long enough to unite the language of man with the silence of the dead. (Wiesel 1979, 15)

From this statement one derives the impression that *Night* constitutes Wiesel's first public testimony, his elementary outcry following ten years of self-imposed silence, emotional struggle, and doubt about the feasibility of any literary rendition. Hence Robert McAfee Brown's comment in the preface to the twenty-fifth-anniversary edition of *Night*, which reminds readers that Wiesel "imposed a ten-year vow upon himself before trying to describe what had happened to him and over six million other Jews" (Wiesel 1982, v).

Contained in Wiesel's own writings, however, is a more intricate version concerning the genesis of *Night*. In his memoirs *All Rivers Run to the Sea* (1996), he reports that in 1954 he submitted for publication to Mark Turkov, a Buenos Aires–based publisher, a manuscript in Yiddish of 245 pages. It was written "feverishly, breathlessly, without rereading" on a trip to Brazil (239). Here we learn of a literary activity prior to the publication of *La Nuit*, and the impression is given that the Yiddish publication was the unedited version emanating from an act of compositional spontaneity. Yet elsewhere in his memoirs Wiesel states, "I had cut down the original manuscript from 862 pages to the 245 of the published Yiddish edition" (319). Reduced by 617 pages, the manuscript was published in 1956 (two years prior to the French edition of *La Nuit*) under the title *Un di Velt hot Geshvign* ("And the world kept silent") as volume 117 in the series *Polyishe Yidntum*. To be precise, therefore, our Western renditions of *Night* are preceded by an intense authorial/editorial activity resulting in the publication of a substantial volume in Yiddish. Wiesel encountered virtually insurmountable difficulties in getting the Yiddish version accepted by a European publisher. At that time, there was no public and little professional consciousness of the genocide. The term *Holocaust* in reference to the annihilation of European Jewry did not come into existence until the 1960s.

The 1958 French translation *La Nuit* is based on the Yiddish version of *Un di Velt hot Geshvign* but severely cut down to 158 pages. The 1960 English translation, finally, comes down to 109 pages. Thus, what the readers of that English version encounter is—contrary to Brown's introductory words—not the primal outcry following a decade of silence, but rather the literarily mediated, authorial version following an elaborate compositional, editorial, and translational history.

It took the first English publication of *Night* three years to sell the first run of three thousand copies. In 2006 it was selected into Oprah's Book Club and endorsed by Oprah Winfrey: "Required Reading for all of Humanity." By 2011 *Night* had sold six million copies and had appeared in thirty languages.

Insight into these intricate compositional, redactional, and translational negotiations of *Night* have provoked a lively controversy that included remarkably hostile responses, among them Holocaust deniers. My assessment is deeply indebted to the religiously sensitive analysis of the Yiddish and French versions by Naomi Seidman (1996). The interpretation in terms of the cultural memory and the ordeal of remembering is my own.

The title of the Yiddish version, "And the world kept silent," aptly articulates the book's leading motif expressing a towering rage, a volcanic fury over the worldwide inattention and callous lack of compassion in the face of the atrocities. From Pope Pius XII to Protestant church leaders to President Roosevelt, persons in prominent leadership positions showed next to no inclination to arouse the conscience of the world community to come to the rescue of the victims. There was, it is now well known, a host of individuals who, often at the risk of their personal lives, were engaged in unprecedented rescue missions. Granted these exceptions, those in positions of political and religious power did nothing to prevent the Holocaust, and after the war even allowed perpetrators of the crimes to carry on normal lives. This sense of rage, coupled with despair over the appropriateness of writing a memoir, is distinctly expressed in the ending of the Yiddish rendition:

One fine day I got up—with the last of my energy—and went over to the mirror that was hanging on the wall. I wanted to see myself. I had not seen myself since the ghetto. From the mirror a skeleton gazed out. Skin and bones. I saw the image of myself after my death. It was at that instance that the will to live was awakened. Without knowing why, I raised a balled-up fist and smashed the mirror, breaking the image that lived within it. And then—I fainted. From that moment on my health began to improve. I stayed in bed for a few more days, in the course of which I wrote the outline of the book you are holding in your hand, dear reader. But now, ten years after Buchenwald, I see that the world is forgetting. Germany is a sovereign state; the German army has been reborn. The bestial sadist, Ilsa Koch, is happily raising her children. War criminals stroll in the streets of Hamburg and Munich. The past has been erased, forgotten. Germans and anti-Semites persuade the world that the story of the six million Jewish martyrs is a fantasy, and the naïve world will probably believe them, if not today, then tomorrow or the next day. So I thought it would be a good idea to publish a book based on the notes I wrote in Buchenwald. I am not so naïve to believe that this book will change history or shake people's beliefs. Books no longer have the power they once had. Those who were silent yesterday will also be silent tomorrow. I often ask myself, now, ten years after Buchenwald: Was it worth breaking the mirror? Was it worth it? (Seidman 1996, 6–7)

What we learn is that Wiesel's literary activity concerning the death camps extends as far back as the year of his liberation from the Buchenwald camp. He began writing his camp experiences not ten years, but a few weeks, after American tanks had rolled into Buchenwald. He could not wait any longer, and what propelled him to turn to writing was elementary outrage and a sense of burning anger. Looking into the mirror and facing himself as one marked for—indeed, delivered unto—death, he explodes into rage and breaks the mirror, refusing to live with the image of death in himself. It was this refusal to concede to his tormentors their fondest wish to see him dead that sparked the initial impulse to write "the outline of the book." Ten years later the will to write his camp memoirs is inspired by the near-universal forgetfulness he observes all around him. Rage reinforced by the desire to stem the tide of forgetfulness impels him to undertake the larger literary project "based on the notes … [he] wrote in Buchenwald." But the Yiddish version ends in resignation and doubt over the usefulness of his book: "Was it worth breaking the mirror?"

The English version provides a somewhat different account of the events following his liberation.

> One day I was able to get up, after gathering all my strength. I wanted to see myself in the mirror hanging on the opposite wall. I had not seen myself since the ghetto. From the depths of the mirror, a corpse gazed back at me. The look in his eyes, as they stared into mine, has never left me. (Wiesel 1960, 109)

As in the Yiddish version, he stares into the mirror and sees his own image as one haunted by death; he is viewing a corpse. Unlike the Yiddish version, however, he does not smash the mirror in rage because the image of death is indelibly etched into his existence. He cannot ever outlive it. Instead of deriving the incentive for memorial writing from the obliteration of his own death image, he now recognizes that he is unable to deliver himself from his death-haunted face; he will for the rest of his life live as one who had been consigned to hell. Implied in this ending may be the notion that his forcibly acquired persona is under obligation to bear testimony to the victims. Expressly stated is only that he cannot shake his image of death. Clearly, the Yiddish version, which had articulated rage as rationale for writing his memoir, is the stronger version, which has been replaced by a softer version.

An additional example will advance a consideration of the motives that prompted Wiesel's new version. Toward the end of the Yiddish version of *Night* the reader is informed of the first action undertaken by some prisoners as they were liberated in April 1945: "Early the next day Jewish boys ran off to Weimar to steal clothing and potatoes. And to rape German girls. The historical commandment of revenge was not fulfilled" (Seidman 1996, 6).

The surviving men are explicitly described as Jewish, and the females as German. It is not just men against women, but Jews against Germans. The first gesture of liberation was one of "stealing" food and clothing. The second act was one of "raping" women. As for the issue of revenge, it is assumed that there is a historical command that obligates the victims to carry out an act of retribution for the pain that has been inflicted upon them. Stealing and raping, however, are actions that do not even come close to fulfilling the command. In spite of these expressions of liberation, the historical obligation to take revenge has remained unconsummated.

Once again the English narrative provides the gentler version: "And even when we were no longer hungry, there was still no one who thought of revenge. On the following day, some of the younger men went to Weimar to get some potatoes and clothes—and to sleep with girls. But of revenge, not a sign" (Wiesel 1982, 109).

Here the young men are involved in what appear to be far less offensive activities. They celebrate their release by going to the nearest town to procure food and clothing, and to have sex with young women. The confrontational edge of Jewish men versus German women is now blunted, as are the references to stealing and raping. Sex is a frivolous act at worst, and fun at best—or so it seems at least from the men's viewpoint. Above all, the motif of revenge has been emphatically revised, even though its authorial meaning is ambiguous. Clearly, revenge was entirely absent from the minds of the liberated men, but whether—from the authorial point of view—this is deplorable or laudable remains unstated. In either case, however, the readers are no longer reminded of a historical command to make retribution. As the French version will have it: *Mais de vengeance, pas trace* (Wiesel 1958, 174).

The reworking of the Yiddish version came about as a result of a personal negotiation of the memories that was aimed at Western readers. In the 1950s, literature on the Holocaust was still sparse in Europe and the United States. In part this was due to repressed memories and in part to sheer ignorance about the genocide, and the scale of it. There was next to no public consciousness. With rare exceptions, Western publishers were not inclined to risk their reputation on a topic that was covered by silence and promised to attract few readers.

To make the breakthrough onto the literary market in the West, Wiesel ascertained the assistance of Francois Mauriac, renowned French writer, Nobel laureate, and devout Catholic. It was on Mauriac's insistence that Wiesel agreed to break his vow of silence, or as the case will be, that he decided to revise his Yiddish manuscript for Western consumption. It was Mauriac who provided the incentive for *La Nuit*, who was its first reader, who arranged the French publisher, and who wrote the foreword to the first Western edition. It is not inappropriate to say, therefore, that inasmuch as the Yiddish version speaks to Jewish readers, the Western version is indebted to a French Catholic and composed with Western readers in mind.

In his foreword, Mauriac describes how he received Wiesel, then reporter for a Tel Aviv paper, with some apprehension because he dreaded the visits of foreign journalists. But he quickly overcame his uneasiness, and took a liking to the young reporter. In the course of their conversation, which is partially recounted in the foreword, Mauriac remembers that his wife had told him "of the trainloads of Jewish children standing at Austerlitz station." "But at the time," he claims, "we knew nothing of Nazi methods of extermination," and he confidently adds, "And who could have imagined them!" (Wiesel 1982, vii). Further into the conversation, however, in reflecting on the fate of the Jews in Wiesel's birthplace, the little Transylvanian town of Sighet, Mauriac speaks

> of the blindness [of the Jews in Sighet] in the face of a destiny from which they would still have time to flee; the inconceivable passivity with which they gave themselves up to it, deaf to the warnings and pleas of a witness who had himself escaped the massacre, and who brought the news of what he had seen with his own eyes; their refusal to believe him, taking him for a madman. (viii)

In this paragraph Mauriac addresses the topic of Jewish response to Nazi terror in ways that precariously approach the affirmation of Jewish culpability. Having exculpated himself because "we knew nothing," he insists that the Jewish population of Wiesel's childhood town should have known better.

It is truly "their" problem, Mauriac seems to be suggesting, employing an embarrassingly recognizable terminology. For those conversant with the Bible, as Mauriac was, the terminology of deafness, blindness, obstinacy, and dullness of mind invokes a classic biblical theme, initially enunciated by Isaiah (6:9–10), and frequently used in Christian texts directed against a perceived Jewish inability to grasp the mysteries surrounding Christ and the kingdom of God (Mat 13: 14-15; John 12:40; Acts 28:26-27). Employed by a Christian writer in reference to Jewish suffering, Mauriac's language speaks not for but against those murdered, and frames the horrors in terms that make the victims doubly victimized.

There is yet another way in which Mauriac's *Foreword* sets the tone, and in effect seeks to frame Wiesel's novel. He is eager to place *Night* into a profoundly theological context:

> Have we ever thought about the consequences of horror that, though less apparent, less striking than the other outrages, is yet the worst of all those of us who have faith: the death of God in the soul of a child who suddenly discovers absolute evil? (ix)

Now, the theme of the loss of faith is by no means absent from Wiesel's text. This is what the author of *Night* writes about his first night in the camp:

Never shall I forget that nocturnal silence which deprived me, for all eternity of the desire to live. Never shall I forget those moments which murdered my God and my soul and turned my dreams to dust. Never shall I forget these things, even if I am condemned to live as long as God Himself. Never. (32).

Undoubtedly, the theme of the murder of Wiesel's God is prominently displayed in *Night*. But in fairness to the novel, this theme is intricately linked with that of the murder of his people. As perceived by the terrified onlookers, God is hanging on the gallows with the two adults and the little "sad-eyed angel" (60–62). *Night* is no more a religious story purely in the sense Mauriac insinuates than it is exclusively about Wiesel's witness to the murder of his family. For it is precisely the events of the camp horrors that constitute the body of the narrative and provide the space for the enactment of God's death. In highlighting "the death of God" as central experience, Mauriac runs the risk of allowing the physical brutalities to be eclipsed by the metaphysical agony, and of letting "the soul of the child" be placed above the little boy's body at the gallows, along with the bodies of all other victims. If what centrally matters is the loss of faith, then the naked terror of the oppressors and the agonies of the oppressed are, contrary to the narrative thrust, subtly diverted to the periphery. Perhaps most importantly, the covenant with the dead, consistently sustained through the narrator's testimony, runs the risk of being seriously vitiated.

Because Wiesel's narrative presents itself as the direct and unmediated expression of an autobiographical account, the complexities of its literary anteriority easily escape attention. *So masterfully literary a piece is the novel, so powerfully direct its impact on readers, and so plenary a presence does it communicate that its antecedent transmissional history is very nearly invisible.* And yet, beginning with the first notes scribbled down in Buchenwald, followed by different Yiddish versions, and on to the severely reduced rendition of the French translation, followed by the rather brief English version, *Night* in effect made its Western appearance as product of a preceding literary history. The English version has come down to us only through intricate intertextual relays, because to a degree *Night*'s antecedent tradition is indeed an intertextual history.

Yet *Night* cannot be grasped simply in literary terms as a history of authorial, editorial, translational, and revisional operations. Encrypted in the observable facts of the compositional history is memory's desire, the driving force of *Night*'s plural literary transformations. For the composition of *Night* is an exemplary case of cultural memory and the ordeal of remembering. It is memory, propelled by the desire to preserve the past for the present and to carry recollection of the *bruta facta* forward for future remembrance, that is the root cause of *Night*'s transformational history. It is precisely because of the author's unremitting commitment to the past of the voiceless dead whose urgent claim upon the present he finds irresistible that he allows his own changing conditions to infiltrate his narration so as to engender various literary mutations. Memory and manuscript collaborate in the interest of carrying remembrance forward.

49. MEMORIAL CONFLICT OVER AUSCHWITZ

When on September 1, 1939, German troops invaded Poland, this central European country was home to the largest Jewish population in Europe, with nearly a thousand years of history rooted in Polish soil. The century and a half from 1500 to 1650, known as the golden age in Polish history, provided a particularly favorable environment for the Jewish community of the Polish-Lithuanian Commonwealth, allowing ethnic and religious entities to flourish relatively unimpeded by the imposition of religious uniformity. In the nineteenth century, Hasidism, a charismatic, revivalist version of Judaism, institutionalized itself in Poland and Galicia as a bulwark against Western modes of modernization and czarist autocracy.

In Warsaw in the 1920s approximately 442 synagogues and prayer houses existed for a community of about 350,000 people. The city's thriving Jewish community supported and maintained sports clubs, orchestras, theater companies, credit unions, orphanages, taverns, hospitals, publishing houses, choirs, and newspapers. At Warsaw kiosks, between three and five Yiddish daily papers were available. Such was the influence of the Polish Jewish community that it extended far beyond the borders of Poland. Many graduates of Polish *yeshivot* (seminaries) left their country upon graduation to found educational centers in Palestine, Western Europe, and the United States (Steinlauf 1997, 6–22).[1] Under German occupation, Poland, and in particular its Jewish culture, was transformed into a landscape of mass destruction.

---

1. Unless otherwise noted, parenthetical references in the following discussion are all to Steinlauf's study.

The death camps of Chelmno, Treblinka, Sobibor, Majdanek, Belzec, and Auschwitz-Birkenau were universes of absolute evil that came to be remembered as the epitome of Shoah. Approximately one million of the victims at Auschwitz-Birkenau were Jews, constituting roughly 90 percent of the total number of those murdered at this death camp. In 2006 no more than approximately twenty thousand Jews were living in Poland. All these figures are imprecise and open to challenge, for when it comes to human loss of such incomparable magnitude the rationality of statistics is likely to be invaded by repressed, wounded, and haunted, or, as the case may be, twisted and biased memories.

What complicates the memory of Auschwitz is that it is also the site of the martyrdom of Poland's non-Jewish and predominantly Catholic population, and of citizens of other nationalities. From 1940 to 1944 approximately 100,000 non-Jewish Poles, among them the political and cultural elite of the country, were transported to the camp to be murdered or worked to death ("Poles and Jews Feud" 1998). In addition, approximately 21,000 Romani people (also referred to as gypsies), 15,000 Soviet POWs, and 10,000–15,000 citizens of other nations died at Auschwitz. Again, all figures are entirely beyond precise verification. But it is important to remember that the Nazi terror extended to almost all Poles, not merely Polish Jews. In fact, "after the Jews and the Gypsies, [the Poles were] the most relentlessly tormented national group in Hitler's Europe" (x). It was precisely this theme of the Nazi crimes committed against the Polish people that has dominated Poland's postwar national narrative. As early as 1945 the Polish high commission in charge of the investigation of Nazi crimes in Poland gathered material on Rudolf Höss, one of the commandants of Auschwitz, to have him prosecuted. In 1947, following a formal trial, he was hanged at the very site where he had administered and supervised the atrocities.

There was, therefore, early on a Polish narrative that captured Auschwitz, monopolized it, and turned it into a monument of Polish nationalism, martyrdom, and heroic resistance. It was as if Poland's exquisitely tragic history—ceaselessly victimized by imperial powers; partitioned by Russia, Germany, and Austria; treated as a quasi-colonial people by Russia, Germany, and France; terrorized and devastated by Nazi Germany; ruled for four decades by authoritarian Communist ideologues—had found its culmination in Auschwitz. It was a narrative that was useful in legitimating modern Poland's struggle over securing borders, especially vis-à-vis Russia. "To memorialize the martyrdom of Poles at the hands of the Germans was to demonstrate the historical justice of the new political geography" (68).

Still another element that is difficult to overlook in the conflict over the memory of Auschwitz is Polish anti-Jewishness. Deeply rooted in Polish history, it was driven both by political-economic and by religious ideas, and quite frequently by an amalgam of both. Politically, anti-Jewishness was closely allied with the issue of Polish identity. Did *Polishness* include peasants, women, non-Catholics, and above all did it include Jews? To the extent that Polish identity was formulated in an inclusive sense and broadly based on modern notions of social justice, Jews were welcome as fellow patriots in a common cultural, political home. But whenever Polish national identity was defined narrowly, limiting citizenship to Polish descent and Roman Catholic faith, Jewish life and culture were at risk. In this latter case, Jewish citizens and Jewish culture were considered incompatible with and a threat to the national state. The logic of that position demanded that Jews be expelled from of all walks of Polish civilized life, including education, commerce, science, industry, and agriculture (6–14).

Quite frequently, politically motivated anti-Jewish sentiments were associated with, if not rooted in, religiously driven anti-Jewishness, the latter predominating in rural areas more than in urban centers. With Polish agriculture in permanent crisis, the large rural population was particularly vulnerable to the virus of scapegoating. It was here that the central dogma of Christian anti-Jewishness fell on fertile ground. Relentlessly propagated sermons on the Jews as Christ-killers and murderers of God poured oil on the flames of anti-Jewish sentiments and instigated a pogrom-like atmosphere, which could touch off full-scale persecutions and mass murder. Given the close connection between religious and political anti-Jewishness, and between Roman Catholic faith and Polish identity, murdering Jews could be taken to mean saving Poland.

Very little known and concealed by almost universal silence is the fact that Polish anti-Jewishness outlived the dead at Auschwitz and the other camps. Deadly hatred of Jews survived the Holocaust, and continued unabated after the liberation of Auschwitz in 1945. In the years from 1944 to 1947, between 1,500 and 2,000 Jewish people were murdered in Poland (51–52). Jewish institutions were subjected to bombings, individuals ridiculed, harassed, and beaten, and pogroms continued to play havoc with the survivors. By far the most serious pogrom took place in Kielce in 1946, where a mob attacked a residence for Holocaust survivors and murdered forty-seven persons and wounded more than one hundred. What propelled these postwar incidents was a desire to extend and prosecute the murderous logic of the death camps to its definitive conclusion. Among these postwar murderers one looks in vain for expressions of shame or at least sympathy and kindness toward the victims of the death camps.

In the last three decades of the twentieth century the two conflicting memories that are attached to the hallowed grounds of Auschwitz—Jewish martyrdom and solidarity with Polish-Christian martyrdom—erupted in open hostilities. The election in 1978 of Karol Wojtyla, archbishop of Krakow, to the supreme office in the Catholic Church focused international interest on Poland and further complicated Jewish-Christian relations in that country. While uncommonly sensitive to the Christian cancer of anti-Jewishness, Pope John Paul II also acted in ways that threatened to disrupt the incipient dialogue between Catholic Poles and Jews in his home country and elsewhere. In 1982, for example, he canonized Maximilian Kolbe, a Franciscan priest who as prisoner at Auschwitz had sacrificed his life in exchange for a fellow prisoner he did not even know personally. While the pope's eulogy was intended to put a human, indeed a Catholic, a Christian, face on Auschwitz, the discovery that Father Kolbe had been the publisher of an anti-Jewish newspaper before the war incensed Jews around the world.

The commemorative history of Auschwitz entered into a new phase when in 1984 a group of Carmelite nuns moved to Auschwitz and set up a convent on the sacred site. They were motivated in part at least by the fact that Edith Stein, a Carmelite nun who had converted from Judaism to Christianity, had been among the victims of the camp. To bear witness to the Christian martyrs and to pray for all victims, the nuns erected a twenty-foot cross in front of their home. To the Jewish community in Poland and across the world the placement of convent and cross at Auschwitz seemed alarmingly inappropriate. Growing Jewish protests and Catholic/Carmelite insistence on the right to remember Auschwitz with Christian symbols led to negotiations between the two contending parties. Begun in 1986 in Geneva and concluded the following year, the agreement stated that the convent was to be moved from the sacred ground of Auschwitz to a place nearby. But Sister Teresa, the mother superior of the convent, refused to comply, stating publicly in a Polish newspaper in 1989 that "we are not moving a single inch" (120).

What to Jewish sensibilities appeared to be yet another example of Christian anti-Jewishness, to Sister Teresa, who as a child apparently had taken food to Jewish people in hiding (169 n. 82), was a matter of Christian principle, indeed obligation, to honor Christian martyrs and to pray for all the victims of the death camp. In the end, the conflict required papal intervention. In 1993, when Jewish organizations threatened to boycott the commemoration of the fiftieth anniversary of the Warsaw uprising, Pope John Paul II, nine years after the convent had been founded, wrote a letter to the Carmelite nuns explicitly asking them to leave the hallowed grounds. That same year the Carmelite convent at Auschwitz was closed.

In addition to the Carmelite convent, the issue of the so-called papal cross deeply strained Polish-Jewish relations. That controversy erupted in 1989, when an eight-meter (twenty-six-feet) wooden cross was erected at Auschwitz. This cross, soon to be called the "papal cross," recalled a mass celebrated in 1979 by Pope John Paul II at Auschwitz in honor of 152 Polish Catholic resisters who had been executed by the Germans in 1941. In 1998 over a period of five months Catholic demonstrators surrounded the papal cross with 240 additional smaller crosses, which by 1999 had grown to nearly 300. Jewish organizations around the world expressed their outrage, and the Israeli government formally requested that Poland settle the dispute out of respect for the Jewish martyrs. To resolve the increasingly acrimonious dispute over the commemoration of Auschwitz, Mr. Kalman Sultanik, vice president of the World Jewish Congress, suggested that Auschwitz should be made an "extraterritorial" entity. Born in Poland and victim of concentration camps himself, he reasoned that this judicial act was the only way to ensure the appropriate respect for the hallowed, bloodstained site.

To Polish ears, however, Sultanik's proposal conjured up notions of national extinction because Hitler had demanded an "extraterritorial" road link from Berlin to Gdansk before invading the country in 1939. While the Polish Parliament worked under pressure toward a legal resolution, Mrs. Magdziak-Miszewska, the prime minister's special adviser on Jewish issues, pronounced that "the new crosses will go, quite soon. But the papal cross is another matter" ("Poles and Jews Feud" 1998). In 1999, shortly before the pope's eighth visit to his homeland, Polish troops, backed by police and priests, removed all crosses with the exception of the papal cross. A spokesman of the Polish episcopate expressed hope that the move would "show our maturity and moral and spiritual sensitivity to the world public." But a representative of the Simon Wiesenthal Center responded by saying there was "no compromise. The issue is not extra crosses. The issue is all crosses" ("Controversial Crosses Removed" 1999).

At the root of the controversies over convent and crosses lay conflicting modes of commemoration and starkly divergent senses of history, which made Christian presence and symbols appear in irreconcilably different perspectives. On the Catholic side, for example, the 240 crosses found their outspoken defender in Mr. Kazimierz Switon, a former member of Solidarity Union, who in the summer of 1998 took up residence in a squalid tent in Auschwitz. Speaking for many Polish Catholics, although not necessarily for the church authorities, he insisted that "we do not tell the Jews what to do in their country and they have no right to tell us what to do on our Polish soil. I will not leave until I have a written assurance from the church that these crosses, which pay tribute to the Polish victims of Auschwitz, will stand forever" ("Poles and Jews Feud" 1998). Clearly, Mr. Switon remembered and operated on a narrowly defined Polish identity: Poland belongs to Catholic Poles, and Auschwitz is, therefore, a Polish, Catholic memorial place. As he saw it, the issue of an appropriate commemoration of Auschwitz amounted to a conflict of Catholics against Jews.

The extreme Catholic view aside, the vast majority of Polish Catholics wanted the papal cross to remain at its present site in Auschwitz. They remembered that approximately three million non-Jewish Poles had been murdered during the German occupation, of whom close to 100,000 died at Auschwitz. For Polish Catholics it is, therefore, a matter of claiming the same memorial prerogatives as had been claimed by the Jews. As one Polish Catholic, Mr. Witold Urbanski, put it: "Not only Jews died in Auschwitz, and they [the Jews] have to realize that we Catholics have the same rights as them" ("Poles and Jews Feud" 1998), uncharitably separating the victims between "them" and "us." Bishop Gadaecki formulated the Catholic position only slightly more subtly in saying that "we share ... the pain of all the Jewish people. But there is the pain of the Polish people, too" ("Poles and Jews Feud" 1999), thereby implying that Polish Jews somehow were not part of the Polish people.

To Polish Catholics, the papal cross evoked intense feelings of both national and religious identity. How deeply intertwined the two identities are is obvious from the fact many crosses bore the inscription, "Only under this cross, only under this symbol, Poland is Poland, and a Pole is a Pole" ("Poles and Jews Feud" 1998). Removal of crosses, moreover, brought up memories of similar actions taken under Communist authorities, as the historian Jerzy Ledlicki explained: "The Communists removed crosses from public places, so to remove a cross today is to be an enemy of the nation" ("Poles and Jews Feud" 1998). Multiple memories intersected, some political, some religious, and many a combination of both, inducing Polish Catholics to insist on the presence of Cross and crosses at Auschwitz.

In the Jewish experience of European, and particularly of Polish history, Auschwitz has taken on a very different meaning. Indelibly impressed in Jewish consciousness is the fact that approximately one million of the victims at the Auschwitz-Birkenau camp complex were Jews, constituting about 90 percent of those murdered at the site. What Auschwitz stands for is, therefore, hardly a defense of Polish soil and national Catholic identity but a sacred remembrance mandated by all those Jewish martyrs whose voices have been silenced. If it does represent *Polishness*, it relates to the largest Jewish community in Europe and in a way also to Polish anti-Jewishness, which, fatefully combined with German anti-Jewishness, all but obliterated the country's Jewish population, and Jewish culture in Europe altogether.

In Jewish memory, moreover, Cross and crosses were attempts to Christianize Auschwitz. In the words of Mr. Ephraim Zuroff of the Simon Wiesenthal Center, it suggests "an attempt to Christianize a place of mass murder where the overwhelming number of victims were Jewish" ("Controversial Crosses Removed" 1999). But more was involved here than the dreaded Christianization of Auschwitz. In Jewish memorial experience, Cross and crosses at Auschwitz are perceived not merely as tasteless and literally "out of place," but sacrilegious. For what in the Christian experience is a symbol of redemption in Jewish memorial history has often been a symbol that has haunted Jews throughout the ages. Mr. Naftali Lavie eloquently expresses Jewish memories and sensibilities.

> My family shook with fury as they gazed upon the cross, erected on this site as if to taunt our sacred martyrs. I still remember the fears that haunted us as children, as we tried to escape the presence of the cross. In our heavily Christian communities, Catholic funeral processions were always led by a young boy holding a long metal sceptre with a cross on top. Behind the children the priest would march, reading the prayers. Any Christian passer-by meeting the procession would remove his hat, bend his knee and bow to the cross. Jewish adults knew how to handle this situation, sometimes seeking shelter in doorways to avoid confronting the cross. Children were less experienced, and were occasionally beaten when the procession passed by and they did not bend their knee before the cross. The cross continued to pursue us during the horrible period of World War II. On Sundays and Christian holidays, Jews would lock themselves in their houses in the ghetto. We took care not to get

involved with the Catholic guards who watched us when they returned from church services. We don't know what the priests preached to their flock, but by the look of anger on the faces of the God-fearing oppressors, and even more so, by the ease with which they beat us, we did not get the feeling that they were told to have pity on us. ("Auschwitz: A Fitting Site for a Christian Cross" 1989)

In view of these remembrances, to allow the cross to hover over the site of Europe's most hideous mass murder of Jews obliterated the ethnic, cultural, and religious identity of the victims and desecrated the memory of the Holocaust.

Jewish and Christian faiths, while rooted in a common biblical heritage, are distinguished by separate historical developments, and tragically separated by a history of Christian polemics and persecutions that culminated in the Holocaust. The point I am making is that the controversies surrounding the camp site at Auschwitz, not the atrocities themselves of course, can well be understood as a struggle between conflicting memories and identities. It is as *mnemohistory* that Auschwitz continues to live on, and in the case described above made ugly history. Depending on whether we are survivors or onlookers, Jews or Gentiles, Germans or Poles, we appropriate the trauma differently. Among Polish Jews and Polish Catholics the memory over the site of mass annihilation seemed irreconcilably oppositional. The cross itself, central symbol for Christians and reminder of oppression for Jews, aggravated the work of remembering as no other symbol could. Modernity's secularization of Europe notwithstanding, the cross has remained deeply encoded in European webs of cultural, religious, and political remembering. It has mobilized entirely different responses, depending on whether Polish Jews were confronted with it or Polish Catholics invoked it. It has opened old wounds, turning the work of remembering into a renewal of old anxieties and hostilities. In short, the mnemohistory of Auschwitz is testimony to the ordeal of remembering.

50. MNEMOHISTORY: BROADENING THE CONCEPT OF HISTORY

Memory, the guiding principle for this essay, illuminates aspects of Jewish-Christian relations as a conflict between two cultural identities, each living by and acting out its own memories—for better and for worse. To the extent that anti-Jewishness is rooted in religious and specifically Christian tenets, a rememorization of Matt 27:25 under changing political configurations was a significant co-contributor to a bloodstained part of Western history. The Barcelona Disputation of 1263 constitutes a rehearsing of Jewish-Christian tropes under medieval memorial conditions. The transformational literary history of Wiesel's *Night* has been viewed as having been driven by memory's desire to remember the brutal past with multiple commitments to the present and concerns for the future. Finally, as far as Auschwitz is concerned, conflict over its memory continues to make haunting history.

In *Moses the Egyptian*, Jan Assmann appears to separate history from mnemohistory: "Memory tends to inhabit the past and to furnish it with images of its own making, whereas history in its radical form of positivism tends to neutralize the past and to make it speak in its own voices, strange as they may sound" (1997, 22). A similar view is expressed in the first epigraph to this piece: mnemohistory is concerned not with the past as such, but with the past as it is remembered. I look upon this essay as an attempt to illuminate Western coping with a brutal past as mnemohistory. To my thinking, the rigorous turning toward the receptionist viewpoint that is implied in mnemohistory does not constitute a segment or a subdiscipline of history, least of all does it relativize, deny, or absorb history. Mnemohistory, I should like to suggest, broadens our concept of what history is. History broadly conceived entails the both the genocide and our attempts to memorialize it.

9

GESCHICHTE ALS KOMMUNIKATIONSGESCHICHTE: ÜBERLEGUNGEN ZUR MEDIENWISSENSCHAFT

This essay takes tentative steps toward developing a broad theoretical frame-work for media studies. The first part introduces the work of the pioneers of modern communications studies: Marcel Jousse, Walter J. Ong, Albert B. Lord, Eric A. Havelock, John Miles Foley, Ruth Finnegan, Elizabeth Eisenstein, Mary Carruthers, Jack Goody, Michael Giesecke, and Frances Yates. The second part thematizes communications history—manifested in oral efficaciousness, chirographic externalization, typographic objectification, and electronic dematerialization—as a process of rapid technologizing and increased complexification. The third part discusses intermediality, a key feature of communications history. By definition, media are perceived as mediating, interactive means of communication that are associated with culture-generative potentials. They function interactively, reabsorbing and transforming each other and generating ever more complex communications networks. At cultural thresholds (oral-scriptographic, scriptographic-print, print-electronic transits) media noticeably function as catalysts for epochal cultural, political, religious transformations. As a rule, media operate ad bonam et ad malam partem. History perceived as communications history is thereby characterized as a process both of integration, cultural advancement, and growth in consciousness, as well as alienation, cultural erosion, and loss of a sense of reality. The fourth part draws distinctions between literary criticism and critical theory on one hand and media studies on the other. Materiality of communication, the principal issue of media history, is foreign to critical theory, which is strictly text-focused and ideationally oriented. The fifth part locates communications history theologically at the transit from an Augustinian toward a Thomistic hermeneutic. For Augustine, language is characterized by the phenomenon of signification, pointing beyond itself toward the eternal res, whereas for Thomas all human cognition is grounded in the sensibilities of somatic existence. The sixth part uses the case of medieval scholasticism to illustrate the application of media theory. The dialectic method of scholasticism, it is argued, which collected and juxtaposed ancient and medieval authorities, sought to achieve a sense of clarity and orientation in the context of a chirographically engendered medieval knowledge explosion. The seventh part demonstrates the productiveness of media studies on the example of the print Bible. This first mechanically produced book in Western culture and its translations enhanced a rapidly growing readership but also caused criticism from below among increasingly educated readers. It is finally argued that the print Bible and its translations served as catalyst in the growth of national entities while simultaneously bringing dispute and disharmony that eventually led to the religious war of the seventeenth century, which devastated large parts of Europe.

> Die Materialität der Kommunikation ist in erster Linie eine Materialität ihrer Medien.
> —Jochen Schulte-Sasse, "Von der schriftlichen zur elektronischen Kultur"

> Materialitäten der Kommunikation sind ein modernes Rätsel, womöglich sogar das moderne.
> —Friedrich Kittler, "Signal—Rausch—Abstand"

> [Luther] wollte die Daten der Bibel gleichsam in einem Homecomputer unterbringen und diesen verbreiten. Nicht mehr nur das kirchliche Personal, jeder Hausvater sollte die Möglichkeit haben, sich aus der Bibel zu Hause die Informationen herauszuziehen, nach denen es ihm verlangte.
> —Michael Giesecke, *Der Buchdruck in der frühen Neuzeit*

51. WEGBEREITER DER MODERNEN KOMMUNIKATIONSFORSCHUNG

Das in den 60er Jahren des vorigen Jahrhunderts vorwiegend in der angloamerikanischen Kultur- und Humanwissenschaft aufgebrochene Kommunikationsdenken dürfte von der Suggestivkraft der gegenwärtigen Medienerfahrung nicht ganz unbeeinflusst gewesen sein. Bemerkenswerterweise sind die drei in den USA nahezu kanonisch gewordenen Werke, welche medien- und kommunikationsbewusste Kulturgeschichte betreiben, alle um 1960 herum veröffentlicht wurden: Walter J. Ongs monumentales Buch *Ramus Method, and the Decay of Dialogue* (1958), Albert Lords *The Singer of Tales* (1960), und Eric Havelocks *Preface to Plato*

(1963). Unter dem Eindruck des zunehmend mit dem Siegeszug der elektronischen Medien verbundenen technologischen Informationschubes, welcher die Transformation der modernen Lese- und Schriftkultur in die elektronisch impulsierten audio-visuellen Telekommunikationsmedien vorantrieb, begann man rückblickend geschichtliche Parallelen und epochen-geschichtliche Einschnitte (neu) wahrzunehmen. Mehr oder weniger bewusst von der gegenwärtigen elektronischen Kommunikationsrevolution beeinflusst, unternahm man es, die Materialität der Medien zu thematisieren und vergangenes Geschehen nach den Modalitäten und Trägern der Kommunikation zu befragen.

Der vorliegende Beitrag ist von dem Bewusstsein getragen, dass in der westlichen Welt, und zunehmend auf globaler Ebene, eine technisch kulturelle Umstrukturierung in Gang gekommen ist, welche an die mit der Erfindung des Printmediums im 15. und 16. Jahrhundert verbundenen revolutionären Umbrüche im religiösen, sozialen und politischen Leben der westlichen Geschichte erinnert. Heute gibt es ein nahezu globales Verständnis darüber, dass Bildschirm, Computer und Internet neuartige Forschungs- und Diskursmöglichkeiten geschaffen haben, die bislang ungeahnte oder wenig bekannte Sinndimensionen und Wirklichkeitskonstruktionen ermöglichen, und die Formen, in welchen sich Gesellschaften und Völker ein Identitätbewusstsein erschaffen, radikalen Veränderungen unterziehen.

Von der gegenwärtigen Medienrevolution inspiriert, beruft sich der vorliegende Beitrag neben den jetzt in den Human- und Sozialwissenschaften bekannten, oben benannten klassischen Werken Ongs, Lords und Havelocks auf eine Reihe von Autoren, welche den kommunikativen und medien-technischen Ansatz eingeleitet, bzw. weitergeführt haben: Marcel Jousse (1925; 1974; 1975; 1978), John Miles Foley (1985; 1900; 1991; 2002), Ruth Finnegan (1977; 1988), Elizabeth Eisenstein (1979), Mary Carruthers (1990), Jack Goody (1977), Michael Giesecke (1991), und *last but by no means least* Frances Yates (1966). Ong ist in jüngster Zeit vor allem durch seine meisterhafte Zusammenfassung der Mündlichkeits- und Schriftlichkeitsforschung vieler Generationen in *Orality and Literacy: the Technologizing of the Word* (1982; trans. into German: 1987) bekannt geworden. Bedauerlicherweise ist sein oben genanntes *magnum opus* im deutschen Sprachraum, aber auch in der anglo-amerikanischen Forschung, nur sehr geringfügig verarbeitet worden. Letzteres legte eine einzigartige sprach-, kultur- und philosophiegeschichtliche Bilanz der von dem französischen Humanisten und Philosophen Pierre de La Ramée unter dem Einfluss der

Print-Revolution inspirierten intellektuellen und pädagogischen Reform
vor. Darin analysierte Ong vor allem die zunehmende Verräumlichung
und Quantifizierung mittelalterlicher Dialektik und Logik, welche in enger
Verbindung mit einem Funktionsverlust der Rhetorik, den intellektuellen
Übergang von antiker und mittelalterlicher Geistesgeschichte zur frühen
Moderne in Europa einleitete. Bei der Erforschung der Materie hat Ong
über 750 meist lateinisch geschriebene Manuskripte in mehr als 100 europäischen akademischen Bibliotheken selektiert und katalogisiert. Lord hat
das Verdienst, auf der Grundlage jahrelanger Feldstudien im serbokroa-
tischen Sprach- und Kulturraum die homerische Frage wieder erneut ins
Spiel gebracht und dabei die Humanwissenschaften, insbesondere in den
USA, mit der kulturellen Eigenständigkeit primärer Mündlichkeit kon-
frontiert zu haben. Havelocks genialer Plato Interpretation ist es gelungen, den Philosophen am Schnittpunkt von mündlicher und schriftlicher
Sprachkultur zu verorten und dabei ein Problem, welches Humanwissenschaftler stets peinlich berührt hat, nämlich Platos Verbannung der Dich-
ter aus dem Staat, im Licht der Mediengeschichte völlig neu zu interpre-
tieren. Der französische Sprachwissenschaftler und Anthropologe Jousse,
einer der nahezu vergessenen Begründer der Mündlichkeitsforschung,
der einen Grossteil seines Lebens im Mittelosten verbrachte, entwickelte
die These der somatisch, verbo-motorischen (*verbomoteur*), in der Bilateralität des menschlichen Körpers begründeten Diktion der Mündlichkeit.
Über viele Jahre hinweg hat sich sein Lebenswerk mit der engen Verbindung von rhythmisch geformten Sprachmustern und der Bilateralität des
Körpers befasst. Foley, in gewissem Sinne in der Nachfolge Lords stehend,
hat das Meisterstück vollbracht, das epochale mündliche Erbe sowohl der
klassischen Antike und der altenglischen Traditionen wie auch der serbo-
kroatischen Kultur in breit angelegten und detailliert explizierten Werken
neu erschlossen, und dabei vergleichende Kommunikationswissenschaft
mit einer bislang in der Mündlichkeits- und Schriftlichkeitsforschung nie
dagewesenen theoretischen Finesse artikuliert zu haben. Die Anthropolo-
gin und Afrikanistin Finnegan hat das Verdienst bedeutsame, innovative
Beiträge zum Thema Mündlichkeit und Schriftlichkeit, sowie zur Multime-
dialität im allgemeinen, geleistet zu haben, die sich weit über Afrika hinaus,
auf Europa, Ozeanien und Europa erstrecken. Der Historikerin Eisenstein
ist der grosse Wurf gelungen, uns den epochalen Einfluss der Print-Revolution auf die kulturelle, politische und religiöse Geschichte der europäischen
Gesellschaft des 15. und 16. Jahrhunderts, einschliesslich der drei die frühe
Neuzeit einleitenden Bewegungen der Renaissance, der Reformation und

des naturwissenschaftlichen Denkens, in meisterhafter Ausführlichkeit vor Augen geführt zu haben. In der Mediävistik hat uns Carruthers wie kaum jemand zuvor, eine dramatisch innovative Sichtweise mittelalterlicher Manuskriptkultur eröffnet, welche sie in erstaunlich hohem Masse als eine der Gedächtniskultur zugehörige Zivilisationsstufe interpretierte. An der Schnittstelle von Geschichte und Anthropologie stehend, hat Goody den Versuch unternommen, die Konsequenzen der Alphabetisierung und der Verschriftlichung der Sprache, insbesondere den Wandel von Mündlichkeit zu Schriftlichkeit, in sozialen und politischen Zusammenhängen zu untersuchen. Giesecke hat die neben Eisensteins erwähntem Werk gegenwärtig wohl umfangreichste, auf ausserordentlichen Detailkenntnissen und hohem Abstraktionsniveau beruhende Studie über die kulturellen, wissenschaftlichen, theologischen, und politischen Implikationen des Printmediums, und dessen informationstransformierenden und speichernden Fähigkeiten vorgelegt. Auf dem Gebiet der Erforschung des Buchdrucks in der frühen Neuzeit wird sein über 900 seitiges Riesenbuch wohl lange unübertroffen bleiben. Frances Yates' Arbeit über die Rolle des Gedächtnisses in der westlichen Kultur ist in den anglo-amerikanischen Humanwissenschaften nahezu kanonisch geworden. In dem von verblüffender Originalität gekennzeichneten Werk hat sie die Geschichte der Technik und Kunst des Gedächtnisses von ihren römischen und griechischen Anfängen, durch Mittelalter und Renaissance, über Lullismus, Ramismus, Hermetik, und Giordano Bruno, bis hin zu den philosophischen Anfängen wissenschaftlicher Denkens eines Francis Bacon, Descartes, und Leibnitz geschrieben. Was einige ihrer frühen Leser zuweilen abgeschreckt haben mag, war ihre Fähigkeit, in einer bislang nie dagewesene Weise erstaunliche Verbindungen zwischen kulturwissenschaftlichen Daten, Okkultismus, und naturwissenschaftlicher Logik aufgespürt zu haben. Was all den genannten Studien gemeinsam ist, ist die Thematisierung von Medientechniken, Medienmutationen, und Gedächtnisarbeit, welche sich in ihrer Gesamtwirkung durchaus in Richtung auf ein neues Paradigma der westlichen intellektuellen und kulturellen Geschichte auswerten lassen. Geschichte, so darf man auf Grund der Lektüre dieser Studien behaupten, lässt sich als Kommunikations- oder Mediengeschichte verstehen.

52. Das Paradigma der Kommunikationsgeschichte

Prinzipiell geht das hier forschungsgeschichtlich vorgestellte Paradigma der Kommunikationsgeschichte von der Einsicht aus, dass alle Medien, nicht nur das uns in jüngster Zeit zugänglich gewordene elektronische Medium, mit gewissen kulturgenerativen Dynamiken assoziiert und potentialisiert sind. Dabei ist es geraten, von allen vereinfachenden, monokausalen Ansätzen vorsichtigen Abstand zu nehmen. Medien sind interaktiv und in vielfältigen Modalitäten katalysatorisch mit dem Kulturschaffen verflochten. Sie leisten besonders effektive und eindeutig identifizierbare Arbeit an Kulturschwellen, in geschichtlichen Phasen und Situationen, in denen die Transmission und Transmutation von kulturellen Prozessen eindrucksvoll vor aller Augen steht. Oder, um es von einer anderen Perspektive her zu formulieren, Medien erstellen die technisch-sprachlichen Rahmenbedingungen, innerhalb derer sich Erfahrungen Ausdruck verleihen, Wissen organisiert, und kollektive und individuelle Identität sich gewissermaßen seiner selbst bewusst wird. Nicht zuletzt obliegt es Medien, kognitive Fähigkeiten zu steuern, indem sie mentale Energien freisetzen, Denkmuster anregen, ausschalten oder verändern. In bezug auf Schriftlichkeit wurde der Sachverhalt von Ong in dem bekannten, prägnanten Aphorismus zum Ausdruck gebracht: *Writing restructures consciousness* (1982, 78; 78–116). Medien und Medien Transpositionen, so unsere These, können geschichtsträchtige und geschichtsfördernde Wirkungen erzielen, indem sie an politisch-sozialen, sprachlich-kulturellen und psychologisch-kognitiven Umstrukturierungen interaktiv grundlegend beteiligt sind.

Im engere Sinne beschränkt sich der Begriff der Kommunikationsmedien auf Mündlichkeit und die nachfolgenden Informationsstufen, welche durch chirographische Objektivierung, typographische Standardisierung und elektronische Entmaterialisierung gekennzeichnet sind. Im weiteren Sinne beinhaltet Kommunikationsgeschichte auch die sogenannten nonverbalen Transportmedien wie etwa Automobil, Eisenbahn und Flugzeug, welche Vorstellungen und Erfahrungen von Raum und Zeit nicht nur dissoziieren sondern auch transzendieren, und das Tempo geschichtlicher Prozesse progressiv beschleunigen. Ihnen allen kommt im Sinne der Medienfunktionen mediale, vermittelnde Bedeutsamkeit im Zivilisationsprozess zu. Die vorliegenden Überlegungen müssen sich auf die Kommunikationsmedien im engeren, sprachlichen Sinne beschränken.

Wie bereits angedeutet, lässt sich Geschichte, verstanden als Kommunikationsgeschichte, unter der Perspektive mündlicher, chirographischer (oder skriptographischer), typographischer und elektronischer Informationssysteme als einen Prozess sowohl zunehmender Technisierung wie auch progressiver Komplexifizierung verstehen. Bei der rasant zunehmende Beschleunigung geschichtlicher Prozesse und der explosionsartigen Technisierung des Mediums haben wir es mit zwei sich einander bedingenden Faktoren zu tun. Nur im oberflächlichsten Sinne darf diese so verstandene Geschichte aber als ein nach einem evolutionären Muster ablaufender Prozess verstanden werden. Es gilt zu beachten, dass jedes neue Medium früher oder später die Autoritäten des alt gewordenen Mediums zu marginalisieren, oder gar zu stürzen geneigt ist, andererseits aber im Anfangsstadium das alte Medium intensivieren kann. Zugleich muss man mit komplexen intermedialen Wechselwirkungen und Rückkoppelungseffekten rechnen. Häufig ist es gerade das Auftreten eines neuen Mediums und dessen fruchtbare Interaktion mit den vorangehenden Medien, was sich als besonders geschichtsträchtig erweist. Allerdings ist es kaum möglich, diese Interaktionen in den Griff zu bekommen, es sei denn, es besteht ein gewisses Vorverständnis über das autonome Potential eines jeden Mediums und eine generelle Einsicht in die geschichtliche Abfolge einzelner Medienstadien. Es liegt auf der Hand, dass sich in Geschichte die als Kommunikationsgeschichte verstanden wird, vielfältige Interessen und Fragen kreuzen. Aber prinzipiell darf man behaupten, dass zunehmende Technisierungs- und Komplexifizierungsprozesse der Medien für das Paradigma der Kommunikationsgeschichte konstitutive Bedeutsamkeit haben.

Was das Phänomen der Technisierung anbelangt, so wird man bereits die Schreibkultur, und nicht erst das Print-Medium in ihrer Anwendung von Werkzeugen und Materialien als eine Technologie bezeichnen dürfen, welche gesprochene Sprache nicht schlechthin auf anderer Ebene fortsetzt, sondern vielmehr in bewegungslose Materie einfriert. *Form und Funktion der oralen Kommunikation sind bei der Verschriftlichung einer radikalen Umstrukturierung unterworfen, denn nichts weniger als eine Transponierung von zeitbedingter in raumbedingte Sprache ist erfolgt.* Der sich im Sprechakt ereignende Zustand der Simultaneität von Sprecher, Kommunikation und Hörer wird dabei unterbrochen und annuliert. Autoren schreiben in der Abwesenheit von Lesern, und Leser lesen in der Abwesenheit, und meist nach dem Verscheiden, der Autoren. Im Vergleich zur oralen Sprechkultur und chirographischer Kommunikation realisierte die Drucktechnik eine bislang nie dagewesene Mechanisierung der Sprache mittels artifizieller, metallisch konstruierter Lettern. Damit war der Kommunikation eine neue Materialitätsbasis verliehen. Gutenbergs 42zeilige Vulgata-Bibel, dieses erste grosse nicht mehr manuell, sondern maschinell hergestellte, Buch in der westlichen Kultur, war das unbestrittene Paradebeispiel des High-Tech des 14. Jahrhunderts (Giesecke 1991, 67–75). Im Vergleich zur bisherigen Mediengeschichte war es das erste künstliche Buch. Ein Blick auf eine Seite der Gutenberg Bibel erweckt den Eindruck einer völligen Kontrolle über die Gestaltung des Druckraumes und einer sorgfältig ausgewogenen Proportionalität zwischen allen Lettern und Satzzeichen. Noch niemals zuvor hatte man in der Mediengeschichte Gleichheit im Sinne dieser gänzlichen Identität erlebt. Im westlichen Erfahrungshorizont hat man mit der Vorstellung gelebt, dass keine Vase völlig wie jede andere war, und keine zwei Manuskripte in allen Stücken identisch sind. Die Gutenberg Bibel erweckte aufgrund ihrer mit geradezu „zwanghafter Genauigkeit" (Giesecke 1991, 82) ausgeführten räumlichen Formatierung und Standardisierung aller Druckeinheiten den Eindruck überirdischer Schönheit. In der Tat entsprach die Gleichsetzung der Lettern, der gleichmässige Abstand zwischen Zeilen und Worten, und der rigoros standardisierte Zeilenrand dem gängigen Schönheitsideal der Renaissance: das perfekt proportionierte Verhältnis aller identisch konstruierten Einzelteile fügt sich zu einem harmonischen Ganzen zusammen. Was war das Hauptanliegen von Gutenbergs einzigartiger handwerklicher Kunstfertigkeit? Man denkt unvermittelt an die Verbreitung des Glaubens als das Hauptziel des Riesenprojektes. Doch wie die Reformatoren sehr wohl wussten: Lateinisch war keine marktfähige Sprache mehr. Gerade darum musste die Bibel, um sie unter das Volk zu bringen, alsbald in die Sprachen der neuen nationalen Einheiten übersetzt werden. Warum also unternahm Gutenberg die enorme Kapitalinvestition, die lateinische Vulgata in das neue Medium zu transponieren, und ein Riesenprojekt zu wagen, das ihn an den Rande des Ruins brachte? Es wird heute weithin angenommen, dass der Anreiz die technische und ästhetische Überlegenheit des neuen Mediums zur Schau zu stellen ein entscheidender Beweggrund seines Projektes gewesen sein muss. Sobald sich die typographische *duplicatio librorum* einmal mit rasanter Schnelligkeit über Europa verbreitete, war Glaubensverbreitung gewiss ein Hauptmotiv, aber zugleich war das religiöse Anliegen mit Unterordnung unter die Gesetze der Marktwirtschaft gepaart. Was endlich die elektronische Medialität betrifft, so ist es der Sprache dabei gelungen, sich von ihrer materiellen Gebundenheit an Raum und Zeit zu lösen und sich gewissermaßen in die Immaterialität eines ephemeren, transitorischen Seins zu bewegen. Als flimmernder Energiefluss, mehr denn je dem Einfluss des Autors entzogen, nur einen Fingerdruck vom Vergessen getrennt, transzendiert die elektronische Schrift alle bislang mit Sprache assoziierten

Raum- und Zeitvorstellungen. Es ist eine Ironie dass es gerade das elektronische Medium, dieses zutiefst in die Materialität der Technik verwickelte
Medium es ist, welches die Entmaterialisierung der Sprache, ihre Entbin-
dung von Körperlichkeit, geradezu auf die Spitze treibt.

53. Intermedialität

Was nun die sich sowohl in der Produktion wie in der Rezeption abzeich-
nenden kommunikativen Komplexifikationsprozesse anbelangt, so gilt es
zu bedenken, dass historische Medienstufen weder unverbunden nebeneinander stehen noch in diskreter Isolierung aufeinander folgen. Wie
bereits angedeutet, trifft man das Wesen der Mediengeschichte nur unge-
nügend wenn man sie als eine auf Serialität angelegte Geschichte versteht.
Vielmehr ist es entscheidend zu erkennen dass vorangehende Kommunika-
tionsformen durch neue Medientechniken nicht einfach verdrängt oder gar
ausgeschaltet werden, sondern sich in mannigfaltiger Weise bedingen und
gegenseitig interpenetrieren. Ong (1967b) hat die komplexen und oft para-
doxen Mediendynamiken mit subtiler Präzision zum Ausdruck gebracht:

> each succeeding stage does not destroy but builds on and thereby reor-
> ganizes and reinforces the preceding stage (104); a new development at
> first only exaggerates a condition which it will later eliminate (239); the
> successive stages in the development of the media can be reinforcing, ...
> even when they alter balances oft the sensorium. (282).

So ist es ratsam, über das Modell einer chronologischen Abfolge von
Medienstufen hinauszudenken und Verflechtungen verschiedener
Medientechniken, dichtere und globalere Kommunikationsnetze und
zunehmend komplexere Selektionsprozesse und Datenkompressionen in
Rechnung zu ziehen. Beispielsweise absorbierte und transformierte die
Manuskriptkultur Formen und Performanzen oralen Diskurses, wobei im
Zuge einer zunehmenden Dominanz der Printkultur der in der Antike
privilegierten Rhetorik im 17. und 18. Jahrhundert akademische Privile-
gien und die disziplinäre Eigenständigkeit aufgekündigt wurden. Und so
koexistiert im postmodernen elektronischen Zeitalter das digitale Medium
in Interaktion mit noch aus der Schriftkultur, oder gar der Mündlichkeit,
stammenden linguistischen und technischen Gepflogenheiten, wobei
überraschenderweise eine sogenannte sekundäre, elektronisch manipu-
lierte Oralität (Ong 1977a, 298–99) freigelegt wurde.

Auf lange Dauer gesehen, eröffnet sich uns somit eine Mediengeschichte zunehmender medialer Verflechtungen, kommunikativer Über-
lagerungen, linguistischer Durchkreuzungen, Rückkoppelungseffekten
und kultureller Innovationsschüben—alles Prozesse, welche dazu ange-
tan sind, den Komplexitätsgrad von geschichtlichen Abläufen und deren
historiographischer Rückerinnerung zu intensivieren, sind doch beide
unvermeidbar mit Kommunikationsmodalitäten assoziiert. Medien treten
vermittelnd bei der Schaffung von Systemen der Wissensspeicherung auf:
sie schaffen Rahmenbedingungen, innerhalb welcher Erkenntnis- und
Erinnerungsvermögen stattfinden können, sie setzen psychische und
mentale Energie frei, die in traditionellen Kommunikations und Speiche-
rungssystemen brach gelegen haben mag, sie sind vermittelnd an der Akti-
vierung des menschlichen Sensoriums beteiligt, sie tragen zu unterschied-
lichen hermeneutischen Perspektiven mit bei, sie helfen, verschiedene
Zugänge zur Vergangenheit zu bahnen und vieles mehr. Zusammenfas-
send gilt, dass die zunehmende Technisierung und technologisch manipu-
lierte Intermedialität aller Kommunikationsmedien den Geschichtsablauf
selbst, und unsere Rückerinnerung an ihn, zunehmend intensiviert, akze-
leriert und kompliziert.

Die Erfahrungen, welche unsere Generation mit dem Computer, mit
der Entwicklung der digitalen Technik und Systemintegration sammelt,
sind an früheren Medienschwellen und vorangehenden Medienstufen
zumindest ansatzweise und zum Teil mit unverkennbarer Deutlichkeit
bereits ans Licht getreten. So lassen sich Phänomene wie die Vermittlung
zunehmender Speicherkapazitäten, die Verdichtung der Kommunikationsnetze, eine Kombinierung verschiedener Medientechniken, die progressive Informations- und Datenexplosion und eine rasante Beschleunigung der Informationsvermittlung als einen geschichtlichen Prozess
verstehen, der mit der alphabetischen Erfindung erstmals in Gang gekommen war und seither seinen zunehmend labyrinthischen Lauf genommen
hat. Je länger der Weg durch die Geschichte, so dürfen wir resümieren,
umso verschlungener die Formen medialer Kommunikation und umso
vielgestaltiger die Modalitäten historiographisch-memorialer Rückbesin-
nung. Kultureller Gewinn und eindeutige Defizite sind dabei gleichermaßen zu konstatieren. Eine umfassendere und differenziertere Erschließung
der menschlichen Denk- und Handlungsräume wird um den Preis von
teilweise hohen kulturellen Verlusten erkauft. Wie von Havelock (1963)
überzeugend dargestellt, hat Plato Geschichte als Kommunikationsgeschichte lange vor uns durchlitten. Seine ernsthaften Bedenken gegenüber

der gerade ins Bewusstsein getretenen neuen Schreibkultur einerseits und
seine philosophische Zielsetzung andererseits, welche ohne chirographische Technik undenkbar gewesen wäre, sind seither symptomatisch für
die zwiespältige Mediengeschichte geworden. Es handelt sich um eine
Geschichte, die von Fortschritt, Integrationsprozessen und Erweiterung
der Erinnerungs- und Vorstellungsräume sowie von Entfremdungen, Erosion und Realitätsverlusten geprägt ist.

54. Literaturgeschichte vis-à-vis Kommunikationsgeschichte

Geschichte als Kommunikationsgeschichte steht in unverkennbarem
Gegensatz zu Geschichte als Ideengeschichte, welch letztere sich rein auf die
immateriellen, ideellen Werte und Inhalte konzentriert. Die von der Kommunikationsgeschichte geforderte Fokussierung auf Medien und Materialität ist umso· unkonventioneller, als beide Begriffe bis vor kurzem aus der
Humanwissenschaft ausgesperrt und begriffsgeschichtlich kaum erfasst
waren. In den klassischen, theologischen und philosophischen Werken
über Hermeneutik, von Schleiermacher bis hin zu Gadamer, haben Medienwissenschaft und die damit angesprochenen Begriffe von Mündlichkeit
und Schriftlichkeit, Materialität und Technologie, Körperlichkeit und Sinn-
stiftung, weder eine Stimme noch einen systematischen Ort gefunden, wie
eingehend diese Philosophen der Hermeneutik sich auch immer mit dem
Problem der Sprache befasst haben. Seit Schleiermacher ist Hermeneutik
traditionell streng text-bezogen, wobei Texte als Ideenträger ohne Berück-
sichtigung auf ihre materielle Verortung verstanden werden. Und doch
wird man Kittler (1988, 342) rechtgeben müssen, wenn er behauptet: „es
gibt erstens keinen Sinn, wie Philosophen und Hermeneuten ihn immer
nur zwischen den Zeilen gesucht zu haben, ohne physikalischen Träger. Es
gibt zum anderen aber auch keine Materialitäten, die selber Information
wären und Kommunikation herstellen könnten."
    Die oben genannten Humanisten wie Ong, Lord, Havelock, Jousse,
Foley, Finnegan, Eisenstein, Carruthers, Goody, Giesecke und andere,
die unsere konventionellen westlichen Vorstellungen von Literatur entscheidend erweitert und verändert haben, sollten der Literaturwissenschaft nicht ganz unbekannt sein, aber man kann nicht sagen, dass deren
bahnbrechenden Beiträge in bezug auf mündliche Tradition, Intermedialität, und mündlichkeitsbezogene Texte auf das literaturwissenschaft-
liche Denken entscheidend Einfluss gewonnen haben. Auch die in der
anglo-amerikanischen Literaturgeschichte als „critical theory" benannte

Schule hat sich kaum ernsthaft mit dem der Mündlichkeitsproblematik nahestehenden Gedankengut befasst. Und doch sollte man meinen, dass die Literaturwissenschaft an den Grundthesen der modernen Medienwissenschaft Interesse gezeigt haben sollte. Man denke etwa an die nun ausführlichst dokumentierte globale Reichweite oraler Kulturen und in Oralität verwurzelter Texttraditionen, die Neuerschliessung der mündlichen Traditionen nahestehenden griechischen, altenglischen und modernen serbo-kroatischen Texte, die Entdeckung, bzw. Rehabilitierung, der primären Rolle des individuellen und kollektiven Gedächtnisses in der europäischen und internationalen Geistesgeschichte, und die zunehmende Wahrnehmung der epochalen kulturellen Bedeutsamkeit von Medienschwellen von oralen zu chirographischen, und von mündlich-skriptographischen zu typographischen Kulturen—alles humanwissenschaftliche Ereignisse die folgerichtig zu neuen Einsichten in Texte hätten führen müssen. Aber wiederum muss zugestanden werden, dass die moderne literarkritische Theorie von all dem kaum Kenntnis genommen hat. Der Mündlichkeits- und Schriftlichkeitsforschung am nächsten ist wohl die sogenannte Rezeptionsgeschichte oder Rezeptionsästhetik, die Gewicht auf den Empfang und die Wahrnehmung des Textes legt, und dem vom Text gestalteten implizierten Leser grosse Aufmerksamkeit schenkt. Allerdings scheint die Rezeptionsgeschichte nicht aus der Mündlichkeits- und Schriftlichkeitsforschung hervorgewachsen, sondern aus dem literarkritischen Denken des 19. und 20. Jahrhunderts. Im allgemeinen gilt: dass literarische Texte auf ihre materiellen Grundlagen und Bedingungen befragt werden, ist deutlich mehr die Ausnahme als die Regel. So ist es nicht völlig abwegig wenn Rosenberg (1988, 111) feststellt dass „die Literaturgeschichtsschreibung unter der Dominanz der Geistesgeschichte zunehmend auf das sprachliche ‚Kunstwerk' oder ‚Wortkunstwerk' als eine geistige Entität zurückging, für deren wesentliche Züge den ökonomischen, technischen und sozialen Kommunikationsbedingungen ihrer Entstehungszeit keinerlei Bedeutung mehr beigemessen wurde." Inwieweit Verschriftlichung als solche, typographische Standardisierung und Verobjektivierung, die Formatierung der gedruckten Seite oder der flimmernde Energiefluss elektronischer Schrift die Sinnproduktion vermittelnd anzuregen imstande sein mögen, sind Gedanken, welche der literaturkritischen Forschung ferne liegen, ja, man muss sagen, ausgesprochen fremd sind.

Nun liesse sich einwenden, dass die Geschichtsschreibung angesichts ihrer historischen Topoi naturgemäss in der Materialität menschlichen

Daseins verwurzelt ist und sich daher auf materialer Ebene zu bewegen genötigt sieht. Wirtschaftliche Dynamiken und ihre Beiträge zum sozialen Wandel, Strukturen und Veränderungen politischer Entitäten, zunehmende Technisierung in der Kriegsführung, biologische Revolution in der Landwirtschaft—diese und zahllose andere Themen ˙scheinen die Historiographie unerbittlich auf den Boden sogenannter historischer Tatsachen zu verweisen. Doch das ist es nicht, was hier mit Medien und Kommunikation, Materialität und Medialität, angesprochen ist. Was vielmehr Mediengeschichte erfordert, ist eine Reflexion sowohl über die in der Geschichte herrschenden und Geschichte erzeugenden Kommunikationsmodi wie auch über die im historiographischen Reflexions- und Rezeptionsprozess selbst fungierenden Kommunikationstechniken und deren Beteiligung an der Repräsentation von Wirklichkeit. Denn so sehr White (1973) zuzustimmen ist, dass Geschichtsschreibung prinzipiell mit narrativen und rhetorischen Gattungen arbeitet, so sehr muss zusätzlich noch betont werden, dass Repräsentation von Vergangenheit prinzipiell nicht realisierbar ist, ohne dass Information und Interpretation durch bestimmte Medien gefiltert werden. Die Herausforderung besteht darin, eine tiefsitzende, humanistische Einstellung zu überwinden, Oralität, chirographische Literalität, typographische Technologie und elektronische Materialität als solche außer Acht zu lassen oder zu marginalisieren, obgleich es doch zumindest an besonderen Epochenschwellen wie dem Beginn der Alphabetisierung der griechischen Sprache, der Renaissance und Reformation oder der Postmoderne unbestreitbar klar geworden ist, dass Ideenrevolutionen und Traditionsbrüche zutiefst mit Mediendynamiken vernetzt sind. So etwa hätten die im Zusammenhang mit der technologischen Revolution des 15. und 16. Jahrhunderts bislang vorliegenden Studien die sinngebende Medialität der typographischen Technik mit kaum überzeugenderer Deutlichkeit vor Augen führen können.

55. Von Augustinischer zu Thomistischer Hermeneutik

Vielleicht lassen sich die hier angeregten Medienreflexionen theologisch so ausdrücken, dass sie eine Abwendung von augustinischer und eine Zuwendung zu thomistischer Hermeneutik implizieren. Was Augustin betrifft, so darf man als gegeben voraussetzen, dass er mit der Einführung der *signum—res* Dichotomie einen seiner wohl bedeutsamsten und einflussreichsten Beiträge zum gesamten westlichen und insbesondere christlich-theologischen Sprachdenken geleistet hat (Manetti; Engels; Markus).

Wie er vor allem in *De Doctrina Christiana* und *De Magistro* ausführte, ist mündliche und schriftliche Sprache gleichermaßen zeichenhaft angelegt, indem sie über sich hinaus auf die *res*, die dem sprachlichen *signum* entsprechenden Realitäten, hinweist. In diesem Sinne fungiert Sprache als *signum*, welches abgesehen von dem Eindruck, den es in der Sinneswahrnehmung hinterlässt, etwas entsprechend Anderes in unser Bewusstsein eintreten lässt. Wissen um diese anderen Dinge ist stets von größerer Bedeutsamkeit als die Zeichenhaftigkeit der Sprache selbst. Entsprechend dieser Theorie kommt Sprache eine transitorische Bedeutsamkeit zu. In ihrer zeichenhaften Funktion wird Sprache in einen Status der Vorläufigkeit oder Überständigkeit verwiesen, der hintan gestellt wird, sobald die *res* erreicht bzw. ins Bewusstsein getreten sind. Wir haben es mit einem Sprachverständnis zu tun, welches in seiner Zeichenhaftigkeit dem Seinsgrund der Materialität keine Aufmerksamkeit zu schenken geneigt ist.

Die Dinge sind anders im thomistischen Sprachdenken gelagert. Nach Thomas gilt, dass *omnis nostra cognitio a sensu initium habet* (1963; summa 1.1, questio 10). Demnach hat alles menschliche Denkvermögen seinen Anfang und Grund im Sensorium und der aus ihm operierenden Sinneswahrnehmungen.

In der Diktion der Moderne gesprochen, wird hier Leiblichkeit gewissermaßen als Ursprung und Sitz allen Denkvermögens und aller Sprachlichkeit angesehen. Dabei werden Zusammenhänge von sprachlicher Materialität, Sinneswahrnehmung, Gedächtnisfähigkeit und Sinnproduktion impliziert. Entsprechend dieser Theorie sind *sensibilia*, und man darf sagen: somatische Sprachbedingungen, Grund und Ausgangspunkt allen Denkens, auf die man immer erneut zurückgreift, da sie mediale und nicht transitorische Bedeutsamkeit haben.

Dass Sinnproduktion mit den technischen Bedingungen der Medien aufs engste zusammenhängt, wie etwa mit Schreibgeräten und Schriften, mit Performanz und Ritualen, mit Körperlichkeit und verschiedenartigen Dimensionen des Materialen, sind Gedanken, welche mit großem theoretischen Ernst erstmals 1987 in einem interdisziplinären Kolloquium in Dubrovnik vor einem grossen Kreis geladener Humanwissenschaftler, Biologen, Soziologen und Theaterfachleuten diskutiert wurden. Die Konferenz war von außerordentlichen Ambitionen beflügelt, wie sie Miklós Szabolcsi (1988, 910) in seinem Schlusswort zum Ausdruck brachte: „Hier fand die Suche nach einem neuen *discours* statt, denn wir alle vertraten die Ansicht, daß die alten kritischen Theorien und Lösungen nunmehr unzulänglich sind und nicht mehr zu befriedigen vermögen." Auf der Konferenz wurde

das Thema der Materialität der Kommunikation geradezu als Wegberei-
ter zu einem neuen Paradigma in den Humanwissenschaften erkoren.
Inzwischen weithin bekannt, haben die unter dem Titel *Materialität der
Kommunikation* veröffentlichten Arbeiten dennoch in den Human- und
Kulturwissenschaften nur geringfügig Eingang gefunden. Immerhin ist
es dem Kolloquium gelungen, die Problematik der Sinndimension neu zu
thematisieren, indem man Sinnprozessen in ihren kommunikativen Trägern, somatischen Modalitäten und technischen Bedingungen auf die Spur
zu kommen suchte.

56. Die scholastische Methode im Medienkontext: Peter Abälard

Die Frage, der wir uns am Schluss stellen müssen, ist die der eigentli-
chen geschichts- und kulturproduktiven Funktion der Medientechniken.
Wie lässt sich die behauptete These veranschaulichen und präzisieren,
historische Prozesse seien von den Kommunikationsmedien und deren
zunehmender Technisierung geprägt und teilweise sogar konstituiert,
und wie kann man die Funktion der Medien im Geschichtsprozess
genauer definieren?

   Ein Beispiel lässt sich vor dem Hintergrund hochmittelalterlicher
Kultur illustrieren. So eröffnet die etwa vom 12. bis 14. Jahrhundert sich
erstreckende mittelalterliche Philosophie und Theologie der Schola-
stik ungeahnte Einblicke in die mediale, kulturschaffende Funktion der
Medien. Ein charakteristisches Merkmal der scholastischen Methode war
es, biblische, patristische und philosophische Autoritäten vergleichsweise
nicht nur nebeneinander, sondern einander gegenüber zu stellen. Dieses
Zusammentragen und Vergleichen der Autoritäten ist mit der bekannten
Methodik thomistischer Dialektik verbunden, welche das Material auf der
Basis von Frage (*questio*) und Antwort (*responsio* oder *disputatio*) unter-
suchte. Es ist sicherlich richtig, dass diese Methode aus dem akademischen Unterricht des Mittelalters erwachsen ist und ihre Anwendung in
der Scholastik dazu diente, die Vernunft zur Lösung von Widersprüchen
zu aktivieren. Bekanntlich ging es letztlich darum, Vernunft und Offenba-
rung in einen theologisch vertretbaren Einklang zu bringen. All das sind
grundlegend bekannte Tatsachen, wie sie sich der traditionellen, philoso-
phiegeschichtlichen Anschauungsweise darstellen (Grabman).

   Nun lässt sich die scholastische Dialektik aber auch vom mediengeschichtlichen Gesichtspunkt aus in eine neue Perspektive einfan-

gen. So ist das Zusammentragen der Autoritäten, von den Interpreten der Heiligen Schrift und den autoritativen Entscheidungen der Päpste, Bischöfe und Konzilien bis hin zu den Vätern nicht zuletzt von Interessen geleitet, welche im Zusammenhang mit einer rapiden Intensivierung chirographischer Produktion, einem sich daraus ergebenden intellektuellen Pluralismus und einer die mittelalterliche Synthese bedrohenden Orientierungslosigkeit stehen. Die Zusammenstellung disparater Stimmen, das leidenschaftliche Abwägen und Vergleichen unterschiedlicher Aussagen, die Konfrontierung widersprüchlicher Autoritäten und der Wunsch, Klarheit in der intellektuellen Polyphonie zu finden, sind alles Erscheinungen, welche im Zusammenhang mit einer chirographischen Revolution des Hochmittelalters gesehen werden können, welche die Textbasis philosophischer und theologischer Arbeiten zunehmend verunsicherte. Peter Abälard hatte den Sachverhalt ganz klar im Prolog von *Sie et Non* zum Ausdruck gebracht: seine unter großen Mühen zustandegekommene Sammlung von 150 Vätersentenzen sei von der Unmenge von Manuskripten (*tanta verborum multitudine*) bedingt, welche untereinander nicht nur unterschiedlich, sondern sogar widersprüchlich zu sein scheinen (*non solum ab invicem diversa verum etiam invicem adversa videantur*). Nach dieser Aussage war es nicht zuletzt die *information explosion*, welche Abälard veranlasste, die Masse des Materials zu sichten, um Klarheit zu schaffen.

Natürlich war es ein Grundanliegen der Scholastik, Vernunft und Glaube in Einklang zu bringen. Überdies ist es unbestreitbar dass Format und Fragestellungen (*questiones*) in der dialektischen Methode einen rein formalen Akt darstellen, wobei die in der Tradition sicher verankerten Autoritäten nie ernsthaft in Frage gestellt zu sein scheinen. Ganz im Stile der klassischen Rhetorik scheinen die Antworten nicht stringent aus der *disputatio* entwickelt zu sein, sondern bereits implizit in der *questio* liegen bzw. in ihr vorweggenommen zu sein. Und doch handelt es sich bei Abälard um wesentlich mehr als um einen sich nach rein formalen, rhetorischen Regeln abspielenden Vorgang.

Obwohl es keineswegs bestritten werden soll, dass philosophisch gesehen die Scholastik um die Problematik von Vernunft und Glaube rang und dass rhetorisch gesehen sich das gesamte Disputationsverfahren in einem traditionsgesicherten Rahmen abwickelte, so darf von mediengeschichtlichen Gesichtspunkten aus behauptet werden, dass die dominante scholastische Thematik samt ihren benutzten Methoden und angestrebten Lösungen unausweichlich in die Medienproblematiken des Hochmittelalters verstrickt war. Es war eine Problematik, die, implizit bereits in der mittelalterlichen Kultur vorhanden, von Anbeginn der Drucktechnik beispielsweise in kritischen Stimmen laut wurde, die einem Unbehagen über Textüberschwemmung und einer damit zusammenhängenden Begriffsverwirrung Ausdruck verliehen. So lag die Schwierigkeit, eine Lösung der scholastischen Grundthematik herbeizuführen, nicht nur an einer hochbrisanten philosophisch-theologischen Grundproblematik, sondern auch an einer zunehmenden Textüberflutung, welche die der noch gängigen rhetorischen Konventionen verpflichtete Dialektik nicht gewachsen war. Theologisch-philosophische Problematik und Medienproblematiken stehen im Falle der Scholastik in einer produktiven Wechselwirkung.

57. LUTHER UND DIE TECHNISIERTE DRUCKBIBEL

Das zweite Beispiel handelt von der Print-Kultur des 15. und 16. Jahrhunderts, wobei das Hauptaugenmerk auf der gedruckten Bibel und ihrer kulturproduktiven Bedeutsamkeit liegen soll. Die durch die Druckpresse ermöglichten Vervielfältigungsprozesse führten zu einer bis dato nie dagewesenen, rasanten Verbreitung der Bibel über ganz Europa. Wie kein anderes Buch im Westen förderte die durch die Druckpresse technisierte Bibel eine Lesekultur und trug damit wesentlich zu einem rasch wachsenden Leserpublikum in Europa bei. Laien lasen, diskutierten und interpretierten nun die Bibel. Das Lesen der Bibel wurde zu einem identitätsstiftenden Merkmal der bürgerlichen Gesellschaft bis weit ins 20. Jahrhundert hinein.

Die Verbreitung der Druckbibel und ein die Heilige Schrift rezipierendes und rezitierendes Leserpublikum schufen neue Machtverhältnisse zwischen den kirchlichen Autoritäten, Luther, dem Übersetzer und Herausgeber und einem breiten Publikum. Bezeichnenderweise war Luthers Herausgabe des Neuen Testaments im September 1522 mit verletzend obszönen, antipäpstlichen Bildern ausgestattet (Edwards). Dieser Vorgang bestätigte eine Grundregel mediengeschichtlicher Dynamiken, nach welcher Repräsentanten des neuen Mediums geneigt und imstande sein können, die traditionellen Autoritäten herauszufordern und gar zu stürzen. Kaum war das Print-Medium auf den Plan getreten, benutzte Luther die durch die neue Technologie gesteigerte Autorität des Neuen Testaments, um sie gegen die des Papstes auszuspielen. Mit der Erfindung und dem Inkrafttreten des neuen Mediums begann Rom zusehends seinen Status als Zentralorgan des kirchlichen Informationssystems einzubüssen.

Das mechanische Duplikationsverfahren entwickelte sich fortan nach der ihm eigenen Gesetzmässigkeit. Drucker und Verleger sollten bald mehr Macht über die Prozesse der Bibelveröffentlichungen, der Bibelübersetzungen und den exegetischen Umgang mit der Heiligen Schrift haben als sie der Papst je besessen hatte. Nicht minder bemerkenswert ist aber, dass Luthers antipäpstliches Neues Testament alsbald im eigenen Lager auf heftige Kritik stieß, so dass er sich genötigt sah, die polemischen Bilder in den zahlreichen nachfolgenden Ausgaben wieder zu entfernen. Wären diese bildhaften Polemiken vor der Erfindung der Druckkunst erschienen, so wären sie wohl kaum über einen begrenzten Raum theologischer Spezialisten verbreitet worden. Aber das neue Medium durchbrach den esoterischen Zirkel theologischer Disputationen und Formalitäten und wandte sich erstmals an die Öffentlichkeit eines Lesepublikums, welches sich räumlich über Gebiete erstreckte, die zu einen späteren geschichtlichen Zeitpunkt Europa genannt werden sollten. In diesem, durch das Print-Medium expandierten Kommunikationsraum sah Luther die Chance, die römische Kirche als institutionelles Kontrollorgan umgehen zu können und sich in kaum je dagewesener rhetorischer Aggressivität an die breite Öffentlichkeit zu wenden. Auf der anderen Seite aber sah er sich plötzlich nicht nur theologischen Experten, sondern einem breiten Leserpublikum gegenüber, aus dem nun seinerseits kritische Stimmen zu hören waren. Zwar hatte das Print-Medium ihn in die Lage versetzt, die durch die neue Technologie verobjektivierte Autorität des Neuen Testaments in aller Öffentlichkeit gegen die alte Autorität auszuspielen, aber andererseits hatte das neue Medium in der wachsenden Leserschaft gewissermaßen den Nährboden für eine Kritik von unten geschaffen.

Die durch die Druckbibel hervorgerufenen Probleme beschränkten sich nun aber keineswegs auf den innerkirchlichen Raum. Wie nie zuvor war nun durch die technisch ermöglichte rasante Verbreitung der Bibel der Interpretation freier Raum gegeben. Theologische Dispute, bislang so weit wie möglich vom Volke fern gehalten und auf einen kleinen Kreis von Experten beschränkt, wurden nun unter das Volk getragen und brachten einen bis dahin in diesem Sinne nie gekannten, aus religiösen Disputen erwachsenden Unfrieden unter die sich herausbildenden ethnischen Volkseinheiten. Einerseits wurde nun die Print-Bibel zu einem Kristallisationspunkt der Herausbildung moderner europäischer Sprachkulturen und ethnischer Identitätsbildungen und damit zu einem bedeutsamen Gründungsmoment nationaler, europäischer Staatenbildung. Aber indem die Print-Bibel Disput und Unfrieden unter die Völker brachte war sie am Zerfall der kulturellen Einheit des Heiligen-Römischen Reiches und dessen Fragmentierung in Nationalstaaten mitbeteiligt—alles Prozesse, welche alsbald auf einen sich über 30 Jahre hin erstreckenden Religionskrieg herauslaufen sollten, der große Teile Europas der Verwüstung preisgab, wie sie in diesem Ausmaß bislang kaum bekannt gewesen war.

Die Rede kann hier nicht von einer monokausalen Begründung zunehmender religiöser Polemiken und politischer Aggressivität im 16. Jahrhundert Europas sein. Vielmehr geht es darum die signifikante Mitbeteiligung des neuen Mediums an mehr und mehr in einer breiten Öffentlichkeit ausgetragenen und politisierten Konflikten aufgrund einer nie zuvor dagewesenen Multiplikationsfähigkeit von Information zu erläutern. Von dieser Perspektive aus gesehen darf der Übergang von mittelalterlicher Kultur zur frühen Neuzeit als eine Medienschwelle bezeichnet werden, an welcher die neue Informationstechnologie kulturgenerativ *ad bonam et ad malam partem* Anteil hatte. Das Medium erscheint hier nicht als isolierter Materialitätsträger von Daten, Ideen, Potentialen, welche monokausal und deterministisch historische Dynamiken auslösen, und schon gar nicht als neutraler Agent geschichtlicher Prozesse, sondern vielmehr als zunehmend technisierte Kraft, die in produktiver Interaktion mit zahlreichen anderen kulturellen Faktoren geschichtsproduktiv wirksam wurde.

Es geht bei der Thematik von Geschichte als Kommunikationsgeschichte nicht um eine Diastase von einer medienfreien Faktizität, welche in nachfolgenden geschichtsinterpretierenden Rezeptionsprozessen versprachlicht wird. Es geht auch nicht um nicht-konstruierte Faktizität, welche interpretierenden Konstruktionen unterworfen wird. Vielmehr verstehen wir unter Kommunikationsgeschichte eine medialisierte Geschichte, bzw. die Erfahrbarkeit einer von Medien aktivierten und getragenen geschichtlichen Wirklichkeit.

10

ON THE HISTORY OF THE QUEST, OR:
THE REDUCTION OF POLYVALENCY TO SINGLE SENSE

This essay contextualizes the Quest of the historical Jesus and the composition of Lives of Jesus in a broadly sketched theological and hermeneutical context. The first part revisits the history of the Quest and its conventional classification in terms of three separate, identifiable stages. Convinced that Enlightenment seems too narrow an explanatory framework to account for the rise of the Quest, the second part deliberates the medieval hermeneutics of the Bible. The classic medieval theory of interpretation, it is argued, stated that biblical texts were amenable to multiple senses or meanings. The third part delineates the decline of medieval polyvalency and a gradual ascent of the single, literal sense, facilitated by the growing impact of the typographic medium. The fourth part compares the modern Quest with the oral proclamation of Jesus. While the former searches for the sensus literalis sive historicus, the latter operates not with the one literal, historical sense, but with a plurality of originals. The fifth part documents recent advances in textual criticism that have exposed the phenomenon of textual plurality and variability in the early scribal tradition. The sixth part critically reviews the theological challenges to the modern Quest implemented by Martin Kähler and reiterated by Luke Timothy Johnson. The seventh part points out a deep-seated irony of the Quest, which aimed at the single, historical life of Jesus and ended with a chaotic plurality of Lives of Jesus.

The critical study of the life of Jesus has been for theology a school of honesty. The world had never seen before, and will never see again, a struggle for truth so full of pain and renunciation as that of which the Lives of Jesus of the last hundred years contain the cryptic record.
—Albert Schweitzer, *The Quest of the Historical Jesus*

Historical pictures of Jesus do not take us back behind the texts; they move, as abstractions from the multifacetedness of the tradition, always in front of them.

—Jens Schröter, *Jesus and the Canon*

The quest for a single original text of the Gospels is driven by the same forces that have sought a single original saying of Jesus behind different texts of different Gospels. Both quests are dubious.

—David C. Parker, *The Living Text of the Gospels*

Das frühe Christentum war nicht an der Bewahrung des einen Ursprungs orientiert, sondern wahrte die Beziehung zu den eigenen Anfängen in Form einer freien, lebendigen Überlieferung. [Early Christianity was not oriented toward the preservation of the one origin; rather, it preserved the relation to its own beginnings in the form of a free, living tradition.]

—Jens Schröter, *Von Jesus zum Neuen Testament*

58. On the History of Questing

Albert Schweitzer's quotation cited in the epigraph above (1968, 5) has the ring of heroism paired with a sense of resignation. It sums up the author's view at the turn of the twentieth century that in terms of method the search for the historical Jesus had been a "constant succession of unsuccessful attempts" (6). Notwithstanding his own endeavor at writing a Life of Jesus, he insisted that there was "no direct method of solving the problem in its complexity" (6). To be sure, Schweitzer acknowledged that the history of the nineteenth-century Lives of Jesus research had advanced and refined theoretical reflections on the problem. More than that, historical, theological, and hermeneutical implications of the Quest had been coming into clearer view. In retrospect, it may be said that the nineteenth-century Quest significantly contributed to the clarification of issues and concepts such as myth versus history, modernity's replay of the classic theme of faith versus reason, the pervasive influence of eschatology, the issue of gospel and tradition, the so-called messianic secret, the Gospels' compositional chronology, Gospel sources and the identification of Q, the Two-Source Hypothesis, the literary configuration of the Gospels, and many more. But growing insights into historical, theological, and literary issues surrounding the Quest had not brought scholars any closer to attaining the historical truth they were looking for. Schweitzer's negative assessment and his own proposed solution notwithstanding, the Quest has continued unabated and in fact at an accelerating pace throughout the twentieth and into the twenty-first century. But it is not and cannot be the purpose of this essay to provide an inventory of the twentieth-century history of the Quest analogous to Schweitzer's review of the nineteenth-century Quest.

Today it has become customary to differentiate between three Quests, a categorization that is predicated on a broadly schematized, chronological reading of the history of the Lives of Jesus research. The initial stage of the Quest, as is widely agreed, had been designed to reconstruct Jesus' historical βίος in ways that seemed capable of correcting what was perceived to be the fetters of church dogmas.

A second stage of the Quest is generally said to have been initiated by Ernst Käsemann's mid-century challenge to the position of Bultmann, who had denied the historical Jesus a place in New Testament theology. Käsemann's often-cited 1953 Marburg talk is widely interpreted as the founding document for a post-Bultmannian stage of the Quest (1954 [1960]). However, his rightly famous document is a carefully nuanced piece that is distorted if bluntly labeled as the initiator of the second Quest. What needs to be said is that the essay unmistakably distances itself from the model of a liberal Life of Jesus.

> Ergeben sich nun nicht doch einige Schwerpunkte, von denen her man erneut, wenngleich in äußerster Vorsicht und Zurückhaltung, so etwas wie ein Leben Jesu rekonstruieren könnte? Ich würde eine solche Meinung als Missverständnis ablehnen. (1960, 212)

Käsemann's concern was clearly not a Life of Jesus based on the assumed historical *bruta facta*, but rather the articulation of and reflection on a distinctly theological/historical problem that had urgently suggested itself by the nature of the early Christian tradition. Given the acknowledged fact of multiple kerygmata, what was the relationship between the message of Jesus and its successive interpretations? He formulated the issue succinctly in the following manner: "Die Frage nach dem historischen Jesus ist legitim die Frage nach der Kontinuität des Evangeliums in der Diskontinuität der Zeiten und in der Variation des Kerygmas" (1960, 213).

Admittedly, implied in Käsemann's thesis was also the issue concerning the historical Jesus, and the author helped develop the double criterion of differentiation: what is historically reliable about the Jesus of history can be deduced from material that is neither plausible in first-century Judaism nor in an early Christian context. Based on this hermeneutical principle, he claimed that Jesus shattered the foundations of what he problematically called "Spätjudentum" (1960, 208). Still, Käsemann's essay is concerned with more comprehensive theological and hermeneutical concerns than with another Life of Jesus. The issue the essay is struggling with is that in early Christianity the risen Lord had almost entirely absorbed the earthly Jesus, while claiming the full identity of the two. How can one cope with this problem?

Shortly following Käsemann's proposal, James Robinson developed a distinctly theological program that was deeply rooted in existentialist philosophy (1959). And yet, it seems the so-called New Quest has petered out, lacking both sustaining vitality and scholarly responsiveness, while all along the tradition-honored genre of Lives of Jesus continued with undiminished strength, especially in Anglo-American scholarship.

The Third Quest was launched as the Jesus Seminar on March 12–14, 1985, at a conference of biblical scholars at Berkeley, California. Initiated and chaired by Robert W. Funk, the meeting stated the mission and set the agenda of the seminar. In an attitude abounding in exuberance and confidence, chairman Funk opened the meeting with these words: "We are about to embark on a momentous enterprise. We are going to inquire simply, rigorously after the voice of Jesus, after what he really said" (1985, 7). What has since come to be called the Third Quest was in Funk's own opening remarks characterized by five distinct features. One, aimed at Jesus' aphorisms and parables, the seminar intended to retrieve the message, not the life of Jesus. Two, the seminar utilized what were claimed to be "new and tantalizing primary sources" (8) such as the *Gospel of Thomas*, the *Apocryphon of James*, the *Dialogue of the Savior*, as well as new study tools such as more inclusive Gospel Parallels as well as newly compiled Sayings Parallels. Three, by integrating recent interpretive approaches such as parabolic hermeneutics, metaphoricity, narratology, reader-response criticism, and social description and analysis, the seminar promised an advance over the methodologies current in historical, biblical scholarship. Four, very much in the spirit of the liberal Lives of Jesus, the seminar announced a "rude and rancorous awakening" aimed at the "religious establishment" (8), which, it was asserted, had prevented scholarly findings from being disseminated to the people at large. Five, and "perhaps most important of all" (8), the seminar was designed to launch "a bonafide tradition of American New Testament scholarship" (9) representing "a startling new stage in our academic history" (9).

Rather than reviewing the three-stage categorization of the history of the Quest, this essay will seek to contextualize the phenomenon of the Quest in an uncommonly broad historical and theological context. Undoubtedly, the Quest is a child of the Enlightenment, and explorations of the logic and sensibilities of modernity have been helpful in better understanding its historical and theological distinctiveness. And yet, the matrix of modernity, the very period that gave birth to the Quest, seems too narrow an explanatory framework within which to appraise the history of the Lives of Jesus. After all, for the longest part of its history Christianity was perfectly functional without the Quest and more often than not in the absence of modernity's virtues and deficits. Theologically-philosophically, how did early Christians read the Bible, and did they deal with issues that in modernity crystallized in what came to be called the Quest? In retrospect, can one detect theological-philosophical developments that were harbingers of the modern Quest? Historically, both the progressive and the problematic significance of the Quest will become clearer if we view it in the broader context of what preceded it.

59. Medieval Plural Senses of the Bible

In his magisterial study *Jesus: An Experiment in Christology* Edward Schillebeeckx articulated the following statement: "The fact of the matter is that in the past the faithful—the Christian community, theologians, the teaching office—have seen all the New Testament traditions about Jesus as directly reflecting historical occurrences" (1979, 65).

As it stands, this judgment seems designed to ground the validity for the modern Quest in the New Testament and its receptionist history. This, however, seems to represents a view of the history of the tradition that is shaped from the vantage point of modernity and not compatible with the thrust of medieval hermeneutical proclivities.

Our reflections on medieval hermeneutics commence with Augustine, who was instrumental in setting trends for the reading of the Bible in the Western tradition (P. Brown 1967, 244–69). For him, as for most faithful throughout Christendom, the Bible was unquestionably the Word of God. This meant not only that it was divinely inspired, although authored by humans, but also that it constituted a unified communication that represented a single truth. In reading his sermons one gets the impression that the whole Bible was present in Augustine's memory. In seemingly indiscriminate fashion he roamed through the whole Bible, quoting Psalms and Gospels, Paul and Genesis, Deuteronomy and John's Apocalypse, to mention but a few biblical books. It was a citational habit that was natural to him because, in his view, all biblical texts partook of a unified whole. Grasping the books of the Bible as unified Word of God could not, however, distract Augustine from paying attention to the particularity of individual texts. He wrote homilies and commentaries on Romans, Galatians, the Psalms, the Gospel of John, and the Sermon on the Mount among others. A deeply held conviction of the unity among biblical texts was entirely compatible with a keen understanding of the textual heterogeneity in the Bible. Nor did the notion of the Bible's unified vision cause Augustine to advocate a simple, let alone literalist reading. He had no patience for literalists, that is, those who thought the Word of God was plain and obvious for all to grasp. What a misunderstanding of the Bible! How could one incarcerate the immensity of the mysteries of the Bible in the prison house of a single sense? For this was what fundamentally typified the Bible, that it was a book of inexhaustible mysteries and impenetrable complexities. How dare we in our arrogance and vanity assume that we could ever fully explore the profundities of God's Word?

Augustine reflected deeply on the reasons for scriptural intricacies and human lack of comprehension. On one hand, he suggested, it was an intrinsic characteristic of the Bible as Word of God to be veiled and inaccessible. Only if it were entirely human would the Bible be directly comprehensible and readily intelligible. It was precisely in its natural state as the Word of God that it was steeped in a sense of impenetrability. In short, Scripture's lack of immediate accessibility was primarily caused by its divinely inspired origin. There was a second reason for the mysterious incomprehensibility of the Bible, and it was specifically related to a dislocation of the human mind, documented in Genesis. Augustine viewed the fall as an event that had been both an existential and a linguistic disaster, rendering knowledge defective and the human mind incapable of grasping the fullness of biblical truth. Lack of scriptural comprehension was thus also an effect of the fall

Veiled in mystery as the Word of God, and never fully comprehensible to the imperfect human mind, the Bible also served an educational purpose. In its very complexity, it was meant to exercise the human mind, to challenge the intellect, and to encourage rational efforts and spiritual aspirations. There was, therefore, a divine pedagogy, which provided a rationale for the Bible's inexhaustibility and the readers' or hearers' inability to ever reach a full understanding.

Augustinian hermeneutics could strictly hold to a theory of the divinely inspired and unified book of the Bible while at the same time keeping entirely aloof from literalism. It was well understood: the Bible could not possibly be reduced to a single, literal sense. To the contrary, Scripture was intended to inspire hearers and readers to reach out for newer and deeper senses hidden beneath, between, or above the literal sense. Impressively articulated by Augustine in his classic work *De Doctrina Christiana*, the seven steps of scriptural hermeneutics were less a matter of strictly exegetical discernment and more of a spiritual exercise that would take the readers/hearers from the fear of God, to piety, the love of God and love of neighbor, to justice, mercy, and the vision of God all the way to a state of peace and tranquility (*Doctr. chr.* 38–40).

Augustine's conviction of the plural senses of the Bible was widely shared in the Middle Ages. To the extent that there was a general sense of hermeneutical agreement at all, the Bible was perceived to be a reservoir of plural interpretations. Its hermeneutical potential was mysteriously limitless. The classic theory of interpretation that dominated large segments of medieval Christianity espoused the fourfold meaning of biblical texts (Smalley 1952; Lubac 1959–64). It suggested that the sacred texts were amenable to four different readings: the literal or plain sense, which could be the authorial, or the historically correct one, or the grammatically and syntactically suitable understanding; the oblique or allegorical sense, which gestured toward deeper or higher meanings beyond the literal sense; the homiletic and often ethical sense; and the spiritual sense, which pointed toward higher realities. Thus was the single truth, that it was available in multiformity and accessible to multiple senses. Whether one acknowledged this fourfold sense, or merely practiced a twofold sense, or inclined toward a threefold interpretation, the spiritual sense was in all instances accorded a position of priority.

Throughout the Middle Ages, Christian hermeneutics operated with certain tropes that articulated the primacy of the spiritual sense and the subordination of the literal. One such trope was that of body and soul. Accordingly, the biblical text was conceived as the body, which contained within itself the soul. The body constituted the external, the physical part, whereas the soul was invisible, but essential. Perhaps the most influential hermeneutical trope was that of the letter and the Spirit. It was derived from 2 Cor 3:1–6, a passage in which Paul had postulated a hierarchical, indeed antithetical relationship: "for the letter killeth, but the Spirit gives life" (3:6). The verse became a proof text for hermeneutical strivings to transcend the literal, authorial, or historical sense in the interest of acceding to the allegorical, or spiritual sense.

There was in certain quarters of the High and Late Middle Ages a tendency to pay greater attention to the literal meaning by means of historical, textual, and geographical examination. In the twelfth century, for example, Hugh of the Abbey of St. Victor in Paris and his student Andrew made the literal meaning the primary subject for study by compiling chronicles, drawing maps, and producing sketches of biblical themes. Hugh objected to some of his teachers who used Paul's apodictic statement of "the letter killeth" as an excuse to place their own readings over and even against authorially intended meanings (Smalley 1952, 83–195). And he poked fun at interpreters who rushed over the literal meaning in order to arrive as rapidly as possible at the mystery of the spiritual meaning.

But the genuinely revolutionary step taken by Andrew was his pursuit of a nonchristological reading of the Old Testament. In this he proved to be a faithful disciple of the Jewish school of Rashi (1040–1105), which practiced an interpretation that had superseded the conventional halakic and haggadic readings in compiling chronological and geographical data, and resolutely opted for natural explanations of supernatural events. About Andrew's hermeneutical project Smalley wrote: "No western [Christian] commentator before him had set out to give a purely literal interpretation of the Old Testament, though many had attempted a purely spiritual one" (169). Commenting on Andrew's exegesis of the Old Testament, she remarked that "one sometimes has to rub one's eyes!" (165), observing how his imagination is so engrossed in Jewish history and tradition that he fails to pay attention to Christian interpretation. It is breathtaking to catch sight of a Christian theologian of the twelfth century reading the Old Testament in so unequivocally nonchristological a manner. And yet, in spite of their deep devotion to the literal sense, neither Hugh nor Andrew departed from the conventional notion of the subservience of the literal to the spiritual sense. The exploration of the literal sense was carried out ultimately not for its own sake but in the interest of founding as strong a basis for the spiritual sense as possible.

Entirely in accord with medieval hermeneutics, Thomas Aquinas recognized several levels of meaning in the biblical texts (Boyle 2011). He did, however, attribute particular significance to the literal sense, contributing to its further emancipation in biblical hermeneutics. As far as Scripture's literal sense was concerned, it could be studied like any other text. Resuming the distinction between the two senses, the literal and the spiritual, Thomas defined the former in terms of what in current hermeneutics would be called authorial intentionality. What human authors intended and what primary audiences comprehended was the legitimate object of study. Thomas was thereby granting considerable autonomy to the literal sense and its rational exploration. Notably, the literal sense for Thomas included metaphor. Moreover, readers/hearers may be confronted with plural, even contradictory literary senses, all of which could have been the author's intention. Distinguished from the literal sense was the spiritual sense, which was available only as a gift from God. In itself it was divided into three senses: the allegorical, the moral, and the anagogical sense. The literal and spiritual sense each could operate on its own terms without one threatening to displace the other.

William of Ockham, born in England, condemned by Pope John XXII, and who died in exile in Munich, revised and refined theories of cognition, language, and logic that were to reinforce a particular proclivity in Western intellectual history toward what came to be called nominalism, the *via moderna* that was to usher in what gradually evolved into early modernity (Klein 1960). Problematizing the traditional Augustinian notion of language as pointing toward spiritual realities, transcendental signifieds extraneous to human cognition, William of Ockham moved the particular and the contingent to the center of his philosophy. As far as the Bible and biblical exegesis were concerned, Ockham's nominalism elevated and focused on the singular status of individual texts. Holy Scripture and indeed all texts were intelligible as linguistic entities, and human cognition was capable of grasping the specificity of individual texts. Supernatural knowledge was not beyond the realm of possibilities, but it was contingent on divine intervention. "Otherwise, the logic of thought and of written and spoken language is the only certain tool of analysis we have to help us ascertain what is true, contingent and necessary" (Coleman 1992, 536). In the wake of the hermeneutical developments thus fostered by nominalism, the literal sense was increasingly and in subtle yet decisive ways both profiled and privileged.

What these very sketchy ruminations are meant to suggest is that the notion of the literal sense was not something in the Western tradition one could fall back on and invoke as a given. Schillebeeckx's contention, therefore, cited above, that in the past Christian exegesis and theology viewed New Testament traditions about Jesus as "directly reflecting historical occurrences" (1979, 65) shortcuts a complex Christian hermeneutical history that was slow in working its way toward the single, the literal, the historical sense. To the contrary, it was in a long and arduous evolutionary history that the literal sense had to emancipate itself from the presence and partial dominance of the other senses in order to eventually establish its dominance as the historical sense. Olson has captured medieval hermeneutics with unfailing precision:

> Medieval readers never have had difficulty in reading between the lines, in taking a hint, listening for allusions and nuance—in seeing a world in a grain of sand. What they had difficulty doing was just what Andrew of St. Victor was teaching his contemporaries to do, namely, capturing the meaning which is warranted by the text. (1994, 143–44)

The literal sense conceived as the historical sense was, therefore, a notion that gradually evolved in the history of reading in the West, and anything but a hermeneutical given in the Christian tradition.

60. MEDIEVAL DEVOLUTION OF THE MANY SENSES TO THE LITERAL SENSE

As far as biblical hermeneutics is concerned, the Reformation brought the ascent of the literal sense to its logical conclusion. Linking up with nominalist hermeneutics, Luther increasingly paid closer attention to the literal sense and eventually privileged it at the expense of the principle of the fourfold sense. As early as 1517 he began to distance himself from the allegorical method, while openly denouncing the patristic and medieval principle of the fourfold scriptural sense. Scripture, he insisted, in effect was an autosemantic book, self-explanatory, and, as he would articulate this matter, entirely *sui ipsius interpres*. Unimpeded by the complications and abstruseness of a fourfold hermeneutics and communicable as plain sense, the Bible was accessible to everybody who could read or hear. It therefore ceased to function as the ultimately impenetrable mystery Augustine and the medieval church had invoked and the interpretation of which had required the expertise of professional theologians and trained exegetes. Precisely what Augustine and large parts of the medieval church had frowned on was now declared normative: the text of Holy Scripture was plain and accessible to all who could read and hear. A millennium-and-a-half-long tradition of Christian biblical exegesis had been cast aside.

"We now think that Luther was wrong," Olson (1994, 154) writes matter-of-factly in his study of the conceptual and cognitive implications of writing. Indeed, Luther himself had to face up to the fact that scriptural hermeneutics was not nearly as simple as his advocacy of the *sensus literalis* appeared to suggest. For example, it was obvious to every attentive reader of the New Testament that it represented different and indeed conflicting viewpoints. To secure the notion of the unified Word of God, while simultaneously adhering to the one *sensus literalis*, Luther introduced features that were intended to influence readers' understanding and to control their readings of Scripture. To cope with biblical diversity, for example, he elevated the principle of justification by faith to a dominant position, making it the theological norm for all readers and readings of the New Testament. Texts such as the Letter to the Hebrews, the Letter of James, the Letter of Jude, and the Revelation of John, which he considered incompatible with his theological norm, were relegated to secondary status. As has often been pointed out, he in effect postulated a canon within the canon. Last but not least, he provided his numerous editions of the translated Bible with prefaces, marginal glosses, and woodcuts—all features selected and designed to sway readers' understanding of the texts. Ostensibly, the Bible was not self-explanatory, the *sensus literalis* not self-evident, and the unity of the Bible not as obvious as he claimed it was. Thus Luther had to pay the high price of a reductionist theological move and intricate exegetical devices for abandoning the tradition-honored polyvalency of the Bible in favor of the one, the *sensus literalis*. In looking back upon the history of medieval hermeneutics one is inclined to agree with Olson when he writes: "At the beginning of this [the medieval] period, texts were seen as a boundless resource from which one could take an inexhaustible supply of meanings; at the end of the period, the meaning of a text is austerely anchored in the textual evidence" (1994, 143–44).

Protestants and Catholics viewed the Lutheran *via moderna* from different perspectives. For the rapidly growing Protestant movement the Lutheran principles marked the end of medieval mystification and a check on what was perceived to be the tyranny of the professional clergy, and the potentially universal accessibility to the Bible a welcome process of democratization. To Catholics, however, the novel approach to biblical hermeneutics appeared in a different light. Steeped in the tradition of medieval exegesis, they saw in the triumph of the *via moderna* a rational degradation of the inexhaustible mysteries of the Bible and the rise of the tyranny of the single sense. The church also correctly anticipated that, notwithstanding the reduction to single sense and single norm, the Bible perceived as book accessible to all would lead to chaos because, released from church authority, the biblical texts would henceforth be read and interpreted by the many, and potentially there could be as many readings as there would be readers.

To grasp the subsequent history of the apotheosis of the *sensus literalis* it is worth remembering that for Luther the literal sense still entailed a broader hermeneutical scope than for the modern Quest. As far as the Gospels were concerned, for example, Luther apprehended them as stories narrated by the evangelists while simultaneously representing the facts of their narrated subject matter. To the Reformers and their immediate followers literal and historical readings of these (biblical) narratives were in effect entirely compatible, if not the same thing. In the words of Hans Frei: "Luther … quite naturally identified the grammatical and the historical sense of the words of the Bible. If a biblical text was obviously literal rather than allegorical or tropical, and if it was a narrative, then it was historical" (40).

In other words, Luther was still able to postulate the concurrence, or at least the correspondence, between narrated story and its historically perceived subject matter. That is to say, the narrative sequence and its assumed historical subject matter were still unified in the literal sense, which for the faithful was the Word of God.

The next decisive occurrence in the evolution of the literal sense in the interpretation of the Gospels was a rupturing of the broadly understood literal sense into a narratological, theological, or kerygmatic meaning on the one hand versus a factually representative, historical meaning on the other. The Reformers' *sensus literalis*, already the result of a notable reduction of medieval hermeneutics, was about to be reduced to the factual, historical meaning. In the era of Enlightenment, it was increasingly taken for granted that the literal sense was in fact the historical sense. If in the wake of this development, the narratively constructed and the historically conceived Jesus were no longer logically identical, then biblical hermeneutics was on its way toward a separation of story from history whereby the Jesus of history became the subject of the critical inquiry of the Quest.

In broad outline, it was this devolution of the plural senses to the one, literal sense and its growing identification of the latter with a historically plausible and verifiable reading that provided the intellectual climate in which the search for the historical Jesus came to be a possibility and for many an indispensable necessity.

61. The Quest's Reliance on the Single, Historical Sense versus the Plural, Oral Proclamation

Insofar as the modern Quest is in great measure contingent on a search for the one, historical sense of Jesus' sayings it stands squarely in the tradition of a history of the gradual devolution of the plural senses of the Bible to the single sense. Granted that the modern commitment to the *sensus literalis sive historicus* is incompatible with medieval polyvalency, is it in fact compatible with the hermeneutics of oral discourse and Jesus' own communication? In other words, how historically accurate is the Quest's insistence on founding the authentic proclamation of Jesus on the single, historical sense of his sayings?

To reacquaint ourselves with the oral hermeneutics of Jesus' proclamation is exceedingly difficult because they run counter to scholarly habits and sensibilities that have informed historical-critical research on this issue for more than two centuries. One of the great challenges is to come to terms with the fact that spoken words do not have a verifiable, detachable existence. They cannot be isolated or extrapolated, recontextualized or reassembled because they both exist and cease to exist simultaneously at the moment of their active rendition.

Let us rethink in the context of Jesus' oral proclamation the issue of the *ipsissimum verbum*, the so-called original word of Jesus, which has become a key category in the twentieth-century Quest. The Questers, it seems, have taken the *ipsissimum verbum*, the single-sense, original, historical saying to be an irrefutable fact of linguistic existence. No doubt, there has rarely been any illusion about the technical difficulties in arriving at the "original" sayings. To that end, a series of hermeneutical categories was designed and employed to overcome what appear to be insurmountable obstacles with the aim of ascertaining Jesus' verbatim "original" words, and certainty about his message itself. An inordinate amount of scholarly labor has been expended on the retrieval of what were perceived to be the authentic, "original" words of Jesus. Yet as a matter of principle, it needs to be observed that *oral discourse, the medium in which Jesus moved and communicated, is characterized by a plurality of original speech acts and not by the one, original logion. Oral proclamation is endemically plural.*

Speaking at more than one occasion and on more than one place, Jesus' delivering of speeches and stories, while conceivably the "same," will hardly have been fully identical both in impact and also wording. In addition, spoken words have no existence in isolation apart from social contextuality. In speech, social context is an essential co-contributor to meaning and comprehension, and different settings generate different performance circumstances, each requiring different audience adjustments on the part of the speaker. No matter how minimal these adjustments, neither the charismatic speaker himself nor his audience would have agreed with the view that a temporally later rendition was secondary and hence derivative, or a temporally earlier rendition a primary version and hence more "original." Differentiations such as primary versus secondary, or original versus derivative, lack any logic in oral proclamation. They are pointless and inappropriate categories. Nor would the practice, frequently employed in the Quest, of juxtaposing the sayings and stories one next to the other in order to pare off the nonessentials to arrive at the one authentic speech make any sense in oral hermeneutics. Instead, what gets us to the heart of speech and discourse is the recognition that each proclamation was perceived to be an autonomous speech act. Contrary to the Quest and its pursuit of the single "original," there exists in oral proclamation *a multiplicity of originals*. This is an intellectual concept that demands rigorous reflection because it is entirely alien to the modern, Western literary, typographic vision. What we are dealing with in this case is not simply the distinction between a singular and a plural phenomenon. Rather, the notion of the plurality and in fact *equiprimordiality* (Gleichursprünglichkeit) of speech acts, to use a Heideggerian term (1962, 131), suggests a principle altogether different from and indeed contrary to the notion of the one, "original" form pursued by the Quest. *Plurality, and in fact plurality of originals, not singular authenticity, is a key attribute of oral discourse.*

Among Questers, John Dominic Crossan, more than most of his colleagues engaged in the Quest, has exhibited an admirably differentiated appreciation of oral versus scribal sensibilities with respect to Jesus' aphoristic tradition. This awareness of the significance of the oral versus scribal mediation of Jesus' sayings is most pronounced in his earlier work on the aphorisms of Jesus, less so in his later magnum opus on the historical Jesus (1991). In his book *In Fragments: The Aphorisms of Jesus* (1983) he observed perceptively: "Scribal sensibility can conceive of *ipsissima verba* in ways utterly beyond the capacity and even the conceivability of oral imagination" (37). Above all, he suggests, scribality operates with a degree of exactitude and precision that is uncommon, if not unmanageable, in oral discourse. The communication of the latter is contingent on "a memorization primarily of structure" (37), not of content. It follows that the objective of the Quest cannot, in Crossan's view, be the retrieval of the *ipsissimum verbum*, which is incompatible with the pragmatics and aesthetics of oral proclamation, but rather that of the *ipsissima structura*. The latter, he proposes, is the characteristically representative category of oral discourse. "Oral sensibility and *ipsissima verba* are … contradictions in terms. Or, put otherwise, even if orality speaks of *ipsissima verba* it means *ipsissima structura*" (38).

How does one arrive at the *ipsissima structura* of a saying or story? To carry out his project, Crossan employs the comparative method, juxtaposing the available evidence of a given sayings unit, identifying variants, both what he terms simple, performancial and deliberate hermeneutical ones, and developing an aphoristic trajectory down to its roots, or the structural core of the sayings unit. It is this mnemonically stable, generic structure of sayings that is claimed to go back to Jesus himself. In the end, the specific meaning of that aphoristic core is determined by its secondary reinstatement in an assumed historical context.

Now, it is well known that speakers in oral cultures frequently operate with rhythmically stable, formulaic features. But does core stability itself, abstracted from the available scribal evidence, get us to the authentic performancial events? It remains questionable whether structural abstraction by itself is adequate to grasping meaning in performance. As far as the core's instatement into social contextuality is concerned, this does reflect sensitive awareness of the significance of the historical context. But is not this secondary instatement of the sayings core into social contextuality entirely a hypothetical procedure?

Performance is most frequently carried out by variation on a given theme or structure. These performancial variations can vary from small to significant all the way to the point where they may obscure the core altogether. Thus, thematization and variation of core structures, as well as pluralization of speech acts, and not abstract extrapolation of stable cores would appear to be characteristic of oral proclamation.

Crossan's Quest is to be judged as one of the most impressive of all modern Quests. But measured against the hermeneutics of orality, the pursuit of the *ipsissima structura* reflects *logic's deep desire to stem the flow of temporality and to escape plurality in order to secure a sense of permanence and stability in orality's time-conditioned medium*. If we allow the words of the charismatic itinerant to be reduced to core structures, we have accomplished an act of acute abstraction because there is no verifiable attestation for the *ipsissima structure*, neither in oral nor in scribal culture. If the *ipsissimum verbum* is one step removed from the life of the actual performance, the *ipsissima structura* is two steps removed. Returning to the broader context of the Western history of the devolution of the many senses to the single, historical sense, outlined above, the Quest manifests the apex of this development, the definitive commitment to the *sensus literalis sive historicus.*

Yet the hermeneutics and aesthetics of orality strongly suggest that Jesus' proclamation was multiform, polyvalent, and equiprimordial. It was constituted by a plurality of speech acts, representing similar or variable meanings, whereby every single proclamation was a freshly autonomous event. If we imagine Jesus as the commencement of tradition and reception history, we should not think of his proclamation in terms of foundational stability, be it in terms of the *ipsissimum verbum* or the *ipsissima structura,* but rather as a plurality of similar and disparate but always freshly autonomous words. *In the beginning were the words, not the "original" word or the single structure.* The relationship between Jesus and tradition is not, therefore, imaginable in terms of stability versus change, as Questers employing form-critical methods are inclined to assume, because oral discourse itself, whether practiced by Jesus or tradition, is characterized by multiple original speech acts with similar and different meanings.

62. Text Criticism and the Living Text of the Gospels

The concept of the one original form and sense, we observed, is out of character with much of medieval theology, and misapplied in reference to Jesus' own proclamation and oral discourse. We now turn to a state in the early Gospel tradition when Jesus' discourses shifted into writing. As a rule, the Quest, applying form-critical methodology, labored to capture and isolate this stage by way of extrapolation from the existing Gospel texts what were assumed to be identifiable materials of the tradition. It is a procedure fraught with technical difficulties and destined to result in uncertainties.

A safer and more objective procedure would seem to be an examination of the available early scribal evidence, for the papyri, uncials, and minuscules, no matter how fragmentary, fragile, or mutilated, provide us with the best, and virtually only, firm grounds for a glimpse of the early scribal life. Curiously, the Questers, almost without exception, have failed to consult and utilize the textual evidence assiduously collected and cataloged by the text critics. The hard evidence furnished by early Gospel scribality has not played a major part in the interpretation of the Gospels.

In the most general terms, textual criticism, a subdiscipline in biblical scholarship, has concerned itself with the collection, classification, and evaluation of the available manuscripts. In the discipline of New Testament studies, text criticism's objective is to catalog, review, and describe the five and a half thousand available manuscripts. While the aim of these text-critical labors traditionally has been, and continues to be, the "recovery" of the "original" text, it needs to be pointed out that the designation of "original" is increasingly used with caution, reluctance even. Additionally, textual criticism concerns itself with the historical analysis of individual manuscripts, a study of scribal culture, conscious doctrinal alterations, and other issues. Still, it is fair to say that for the longest time of its existence textual criticism has principally operated as the provider of the authoritative text.

The turn to textual criticism takes us to recent developments that have been pioneered by David Parker in a slim volume titled *The Living Text of the Gospels* (1997), which "is at risk of being overlooked owing to its simple yet significant title" (Epp 2004, 7). But something is announced in this book that, if pursued further, will issue in a significant breakthrough for textual criticism.

Parker attends both to the extant scribal tradition of the Gospels and to the issue of the "recovery" of the authentic Gospel texts. Stating categorically that "the fact that there *are* textual problems is the first and most important fact about Jesus' sayings" (76), he proceeds, not by extrapolation from the given Gospel texts in the fashion of the Questers, but by examination of the actual papyrological evidence. Reviewing some of the available manuscripts of the Gospel traditions he is struck by significant textual variations. As all scholars and attentive readers of the Gospels are aware: there are both minor and major differences among the Gospel texts. But what the manuscript tradition discloses is that there is variability among the manuscript tradition of a single Gospel, of individual sayings, and of Gospel stories. Parker's point is that acknowledgment of the degree of variation requires a serious reevaluation of the nature of the Gospel tradition and our approach to it. What the evidence points to is that the transmission of the Gospel traditions was variable rather than stable, and that it was at its most fluid especially in the early period. Variability, moreover, is more pronounced with respect to the sayings than in the narrative tradition (75). The reasons are obvious: Jesus' sayings, more than the stories about him, were of direct ethical and religious relevance for the early communities. Lacking any central authority to impose canonical uniformity on the texts, variants and different versions—if those in fact are adequate terms—were an integral part of the Gospel traditions. Given this situation, early scribal variation is not something to be contested, relegated to the critical apparatus, removed from the attention of readers altogether, judged from the perspective of the authoritative text, or, importantly, reduced to singularity. Rather, *each text form has to be accorded significance, and the intrinsic value of each variant has to be appreciated on its own terms, because each has had a life of its own in the tradition.* In full recognition of the fluidity of the early Gospel traditions, Parker wrestles with the issue of nomenclature, that is, the problem of finding a suitable language to describe the phenomenon he helped to illuminate: "The terminology which I adopt here is to characterize the text of the Gospels as free, or perhaps as living, text" (200). In turn this raises the question whether "the attempt to recover a single original text is consonant with the character of the free-manuscript tradition, or whether it is driven by external demands: in particular, those of the churches for authoritative texts … and of scholars for a sure foundation on which to build their theories" (209).

Parker has come to the conclusion that the search for the single, original text in the Gospel tradition is a dubious undertaking. To put the matter differently, the text-critical habit of evaluating variants with a view toward their suitability with respect to the "original" Gospel text has encouraged a misleading approach to tradition, for "the tradition is manifold" (212). *What is required is an appreciation of the positive aspects of multiple variants for the tradition is plural and hence not reducible to singularity.*

Parker does not seem to dismiss altogether textual criticism's traditional project of "recovering" the original Gospel text. But his concept of the Gospel tradition has influenced his understanding of the Gospel text itself. Even though textual criticism's basic working processes in the "recovery" of the "original" text are widely known, writers on ethical, historical, and theological issues drawing support from the New Testament often operate unreflectively as if they were dealing with the writers' autographs. "The importance of scrutinising this assumption," Parker writes, "cannot be stressed too highly" (7). Interestingly, the twenty-seventh edition of the *Novum Testamentum Graece* by Kurt Aland and Barbara Aland acknowledges that the Greek text of the New Testament "is a working text…; it is not to be considered as definitive, but as a stimulus for further efforts toward redefining and verifying the text of New Testament" (1993, 45).

The authoritative text is forever in the making! From Parker's perspective, not only are the Gospels the culmination of a stream of a free manuscript traditions, but they stand in a living tradition that remained fluid for centuries. Hence, "are the Gospels the kinds of texts that have originals?," he asks. At times he seems ambiguous whether there are originals, or whether the recovery of the originals "is a task that remains beyond all of us" (204). But in the third epigraph to this piece he unambiguously states that both the Quest for the original saying and the Quest for the single original Gospel are "dubious."

As early as 1983, I had argued in *The Oral and the Written Gospel* that the "concepts of original form and variants have no validity in oral life, nor does the one of *ipsissima vox*, if by that one means the authentic version over against secondary ones" (30). It turns out that my challenge to the search for the single origin was inadequate insofar as it was restricted to the oral medium. It now seems that the early scribal traditions, similar to the behavior of oral discourse, did not on the whole operate with the notion of the original form and variants thereof either. Unless one adjudicates the Gospel traditions based on the criterion of an assumed original Gospel text, one is faced with a plurality of oral and early scribal traditions that defy resolution in terms of single originality. Fixation on the one original sense misconstrues the nature and logic of the early Jesus traditions. Plurality is the proper subject of our scholarly attention, not reduction of plurality to the phantom of singularity.

In view of what today we can know about Jesus' oral proclamation and the subsequent tradition, the Quest's passionate pursuit of the single *sensus literalis sive historicus* is not as unfailingly historical a project as might be assumed. Notwithstanding the claim that the Quest is searching for the historical bedrock, and doing simply just that, its working processes will, on deeper reflection, have to be viewed as an abstraction from the multiformity of the early oral tradition and of the variability of the early scribal tradition. This is precisely the opinion expressed in an epigraph to this piece by Jens Schröter, who has grasped the inherent dilemma of the Quest more perceptively and articulated its procedures more accurately than anyone I know.

One might proceed from the insight that the "historical Jesus" represents a product of historical-critical approaches to the texts that, first of all, are reduced to *one* textual form out of which then *one* person is constructed. What is in question is not the correctness, in principle, of such an undertaking, but the claim that such images of Jesus would come closer to the person of Jesus than the early texts themselves. (2006, 121)

63. The Theological Challenge to the Modern Quest: Martin Kähler and Luke Timothy Johnson

The most thoroughgoing challenge to the modern Quest, and especially to the Jesus Seminar, did not, however, come from linguistic, hermeneutical, or media deliberations, but from a different quarter altogether. In what was essentially a theological argument, Luke Timothy Johnson subjected both the historical and the theological premises of Lives of Jesus to stringent criticism. In his book on *The Real Jesus* (1966) and in a follow-up article (1999) he articulated what has turned out to be a classic theological alternative to the historical Quest.

Reviewing recent Jesus books in the English language by John Spong (1992), A. N. Wilson (1992), Stephen Mitchell (1991), Marcus Borg (1987; 1994), John Dominic Crossan (1991; 1994a; 1994b; 1995), and Burton Mack (1988; 1993), Johnson concluded that the underlying assumption shared by all of them was that "origins define essence," and that "historical knowledge is normative for faith" (1996, 55). By this he means that in all instances, history is assumed to provide norms not only for our understanding of Jesus but also for a reform of the church as well. Yet history, he suggests, is itself a category fraught with difficult epistemological and philosophical problems, and cannot simply be taken as normative as the Questers are inclined to assume.

The premise of history's normative status reflects, in Johnson's view, the legacy of the Enlightenment, and beyond it that of Luther. For as Luther turned against tradition in his search for the historical origins, for the original language and the original gospel, so as to use historical originality as criterion to expose and correct what he perceived to be aberrations of the medieval church, so do the representatives of the current Quest seek to retrieve the historical Jesus in order to hold him up as a mirror in the face of Christianity and its perceived decline from initial greatness. History as a corrective for dogma and theology—this is the goal of the Lives of Jesus, past and present.

To accurately assess Johnson's theological position, it merits emphasizing that he poses a challenge not simply to the Third Quest, but also to modernity in theology and biblical research. Historical criticism as such, initiated in his view by Luther and reinforced by the Enlightenment, stands accused of having miscarried the message of the Bible and the proclamation of the church. There is an antimodernist slant to Johnson's position.

If we ask Johnson why the realm of history and a Jesus strictly understood within the coordinates of history cannot serve as foundation for Christian faith, we receive a series of answers. There is first the problem of the historical sources. While archaeological and textual discoveries in the twentieth century have greatly advanced our knowledge of the ancient Near Eastern world, they have, in Johnson's view, contributed next to nothing to our knowledge of Jesus. This applies with special force to the manuscript discoveries of Qumran and Nag Hammadi. "Despite all the excitement and expectation, it turns out that the canonical writings of the New Testament remain our best historical witnesses to the earliest period of the Christian movement" (89).

Second, Johnson, along with others, exhibits a sense of uneasiness about the never-ending, astoundingly divergent Lives of Jesus. "The combination of inflated claims and conflicting results should alone alert serious historians to a fundamental problem" (86). In short, the unceasing production of differing and often widely divergent Lives of Jesus reveals the absurdity of the project.

There is, third and theologically most importantly, the understanding of the person of Jesus as documented both in the New Testament and in Christian faith. Never in its millennial history, Johnson asserts, has Christian faith based itself on the historical Jesus, but always on the resurrected Lord. The Gospels are "narratives of faith" (110), are conceived and composed from the perspective of the resurrection. "Christians direct their faith not to the historical figure of Jesus but to the living Lord Jesus" (142). But if the "resurrection is the necessary and sufficient cause of the religious movement, as well as the literature it generated" (136), then the New Testament is ill suited for the project of reconstructing the historical origin with the intent of making it the basis for Christian faith.

Thus, while disclaiming the historical Jesus as basis of faith, Johnson invokes the Christ of faith as the central, unifying figure who sanctions a unified Christology as far as the writings of the New Testament are concerned. Observing a tendency in New Testament studies beginning with the Tübingen school toward a "dismemberment of literary compositions" (104), he suggests that this fragmentizing approach was a principal reason for our failure to discern unifying features. There exists, in his view, "a profound unity of understanding concerning Jesus throughout the New Testament literature" (152), so that one may claim that the canonical

Christian writings represent a "basic pattern of his [Jesus'] life" (1999, 70).
The earliest Christian literature thus exhibits "a deep consistency ... concerning the character of Jesus as Messiah," and a basic agreement as to the
character of Jesus as "the suffering servant whose death is a radical act of
obedience toward God and an expression of loving care for his followers"
(1966, 165–66).

Seeking to reverse the prevalent methodological tendency of atom-
izing, Johnson proceeds to examine the Gospels "as literary compositions"
(152), appreciating each Gospel in its own distinct narrative form (151–
58). Up to a point, therefore, Johnson may be said to be motivated by an
interest in the distinct theological profiles of a Mark, Matthew, Luke, and
John. But his deepest concern is the underlying unity beneath what he per-
ceives to be surface differences. By way of summary, he states that the Gospels' "fundamental focus is not on Jesus' wondrous deeds nor on his wise
words. Their shared focus is on the character of his life and death" (157–
58). In the last analysis, however, the central theme in each Gospel appears
to be the suffering and death, and not the life, of Jesus. As far as Mark is
concerned, his Jesus "is the suffering Son of Man" (153) and it is under
this image that everything else is subsumed. Matthew, Johnson states, "not
only agrees with Mark that the path of discipleship follows that of the suffering Messiah but deepens that understanding in terms of undergoing
persecution from outsiders, and being a lowly servant to others within the
community" (154). The situation is not any different with Luke: "The pattern of the suffering Messiah is, if anything, even more central to the plot
of the two-volume work called Luke-Acts" (155). And in the case of John,
the "passion account is no more an afterthought for the Fourth Gospel
than for the Synoptics. It is the climax that shapes the character of everything that precedes it" (157). Johnson's professed interest in the Gospels
as literary compositions encompassing Jesus' life and death notwithstanding, the observant reader of his Gospel profiles comes away with the clear
understanding that what matters in the Gospels is the passion, and everything preceding the passion has only introductory character—a notion no
doubt familiar to readers versed in modern continental theology.

Johnson's challenging alternative to the Quest is briskly and skillfully
argued, and it has all the earmarks of a theologically innovative position.
This appearance is reinforced by the fact that the name of the person who
had initiated this very position some time ago—namely, Martin Kähler—
is astonishingly absent from *The Real Jesus*. Three years later, in his follow-
up article, Johnson credited his illustrious predecessor with a footnote,

conceding that his (Johnsons's) position "bears a real resemblance to
the classic argument by Martin Kähler ... a point effectively made ... by
Sharon Dowd" (1999, 69 n. 71; Dowd 1996, 179–83).

As is generally known, in 1892 Martin Kähler formulated a programmatic thesis under the title *Der sogenannte historische Jesus und der
geschichtliche, biblische Christus* (ET: Kähler 1964). *It is Kähler's program
that Johnson, wittingly or unwittingly, has replayed in remarkable detail
more than a century later.* Deeply concerned about historical criticism and
its preoccupation with a retrieval of the historical Jesus, Kähler made the
provocative announcement that "I regard the entire Life-of-Jesus movement as a blind alley" (1964, 46). One reason for his repudiation of the
Quest was what he considered to be the excessive subjectivity of the project: "On this field people are running wild; they paint images with as much
lust for novelty and as much self-confidence as was ever exhibited in the a
priori metaphysics of the philosophers or the speculations of the theoso-
phists" (48). Hence, despite its aspirations and frequent assertions, historical research has not been able to secure core and content of Christian faith.

A second objection to the Quest was borne out of Kähler's observation
that the deepest motivation for the Lives of Jesus lay in their effort to dis-
prove or supersede the Christ of dogma. It was not history as such that the
historical Lives of Jesus seemed to be interested in, but history rather as
an instrument to be used vis-à-vis the creedal and apostolic Christ. In all
their antipathy toward Christian dogma, the authors of the Lives proved
themselves to be skilled dogmaticians. "Yet no one," Kähler noted dryly,
"can detect the hidden dogmatician so well as a person who is himself a
dogmatician" (56). In other words, trained theologians are the first ones
able to discern the theological, or antitheological, premises of the project
of the Lives of Jesus.

Third, Kähler insisted that the search for the historical Jesus behind
the Gospels was a project that was guilty of misinterpreting the function
and identity of the Gospels. These ancient narratives were "the testimonies
and confessions of believers in Christ" (92), and their principal objective
was to make present "the picture of Christ preached from and in faith, and
therefore most emphatically not the picture of an extraordinary human
being" (77). These Gospels, as Johnson comprehended them, were neither
historically valid biographies of Jesus nor psychological portraits of his
developing messianic consciousness, but rather testimonies conceived in
the encounter with Jesus as the risen Lord. Objecting to the inclination
of the Lives of Jesus to focus on the development of Jesus' consciousness,

Kähler coined the classic, oft-repeated formula that the Gospels are rather "passion narratives with extended introductions" (80 n. 11).

Fourth, the Christ represented in the Gospels is in harmony with representations elsewhere in the Bible. We find the "picture of Christ preached from and in faith" (77), or a unified "character sketch" (81), or the same "'dogmatic' character ... in the messianic sermons in the book of Acts" (83), in the Gospels, the epistles, and elsewhere in the New Testament. It is entirely justified, therefore, to speak of "the biblical picture of Christ" (84), asserting a unified vision of Jesus across New Testament writings and the apostolic creeds.

Fifth, and most importantly, Kähler demanded clarification by what authority the historical-critical method was laying claim to the articulation of theological truths. How can the uncertain results of historiography serve as basis for truth and redemption? Not only was historical research notoriously unreliable, as stated in the first objection, but also "historical facts which first have to be established by science cannot as such become experiences of faith" (74). By implication, we see here Kähler appealing to the principle of justification by faith as a means of delegitimizing the historical Quest. At this point Kähler and Johnson appeal to Luther in diametrically opposed ways. As far as Kähler was concerned, Luther provided him with the theological principle to refute the historical Lives of Jesus, whereas in Johnson's view, Luther set the precedent for the Lives of Jesus insofar as he turned Bible and tradition against the church.

In sum, it is with Kähler that a disjunction between the historical Jesus and the biblical Christ has been institutionalized both in biblical scholarship and in theology: "Christian faith and a history of Jesus repel each other like oil and water" (74). In this perspective, the historical Jesus relegated to a figure lying behind the Gospel narratives was irrelevant for Christian faith. The Gospels, on their part, came to be perceived as post-Easter testimonies designed to re-present Christ in the lives of the faithful.

Kähler's impressive alternative to the historical Quest has been of consequential significance for the direction theology has taken in the twentieth century. It dominated the premises of dialectical theology, and it continues to influence theological, biblical thought into the present. Whatever the differences in the respective theological positions of a Karl Barth, Rudolf Bultmann, and Paul Tillich (a student of Kähler), all were agreed that the basis of Christian faith was provided by the biblical Christ, and not the historical Jesus.

In the context of the history of Western theology, Johnson's *Real Jesus*, far from being a singularly innovative piece, is part of an intellectual tradition that was initiated by Kähler, deeply affected dialectical theology, and is presently reactivated in the North American discussion.

Just as we had occasion to examine and problematize the historical *ipsissimum verbum* and the *ipsissima structura* of the modern Quest, so is it incumbent upon us to examine and question the persona of the biblical Christ constructed by Johnson. The Kähler-Johnson thesis, that the Gospels are conceived and composed from the vantage point of the resurrection, or resurrection faith, is by the standards of current Gospel scholarship untenable. From diachronic, compositional perspectives, all four canonical Gospels are deeply engaged in multiple aspects of tradition. Not only do they absorb and transform traditional themes and materials, but they are also intent on resonating with current issues in communal settings. From synchronic perspectives exhibited by narrative criticism, the Gospels constitute a host of narrative constellations, including rhetorics and redundancies, plural plots and polemics, that add up to complexly woven compositions propelled by intrinsic, intersecting causalities. In view of the Gospels' manifold engagements, the thesis that they are conceived and composed from the singular perspective of the resurrection is no longer a satisfactory premise.

If we wish to encounter a Gospel genre that was constructed from the perspective of the resurrection and designed to re-present the living Lord, we need to turn our attention to the sayings and discourse Gospels of Nag Hammadi. The Jesus of these Gospels is the living or possibly risen Jesus, who, exempted from a narrative syntax and its narratively constructed temporality, embodies presence as a speaker of words of wisdom and discourse revelations. Here is a genre that comes closest to the one Kähler and Johnson have been describing: the authority rests in the living or risen Jesus who, detached from the flux of temporality, addresses words of wisdom and revelation to the present.

No less problematic is the definition of the Gospels as "passion narratives with extended introductions." Once again, narrative criticism has raised valid questions about this classic formula. Neither Kähler, nor, it must be said, Johnson appear to have a particularly developed understanding about the narrative nature of the canonical Gospels, nor have they, in a more theoretical vein, reflected on the theological implications of Gospel narrativity. Yet, when we focus our attention upon the Gospels as narratives, we observe how deeply they are constructed on a literary, dramatic logic. Among the literary and rhetorical features that aid in the construction of the Gospel narratives are arrangement and sequence of speeches and stories, threefold repetitions and duplications of various kinds, the splicing of a story into two parts that serve as frame for an intercalated story, narrative uptake of preceding themes, circumspect narrative allocation of christological titles, retrospective appropriation of words, themes and figures from the Hebrew Bible, proleptic constructions whose narrative realization lies either within or without the Gospels, plot constructions frequently characterized by conflict, psychological insights into characters, narrative asides that are exclusively aimed at the hearers and readers of the Gospels, and many more. *Once we have accustomed ourselves to reading the Gospels with sensibilities toward their narratological, rhetorical interior world, we can no longer relegate two-thirds of a Gospel merely to introduction.* From our newly gained narrative perspectives, the Kähler-Johnson formula amounts to an impermissible lack of attention to the narrative realities of the Gospels.

Undoubtedly, the narrative hermeneutics have taught us a lesson with regard to the differentiated compositional constructions of the Gospels. Such are the differences that they amount to four autonomous compositions. As soon as we concede a separate narrative identity to each Gospel, we can no longer read one Gospel through the lenses of others or fuse all four stories into one meganarrative or reduce different narrative Christologies into a single characterization. Narrative criticism has ruled out the possibility of submerging all four narrative constructions of Jesus under a single, unified picture.

"The fact that the gospels are peculiar kinds of narratives, not only theological essays, is not merely a rhetorical matter," Tracy (1987, 45) has advised us. As far as a Gospels' Christology is concerned, for example, it can no longer be limited to titles or creedal statements. If we choose to take narrative seriously as narrative, we have to come to terms with what can only be a *narrative Christology.* That is to say, the Jesus of the Gospels must be assessed both within distinct narrative microstructures, as well as in his connection with larger narrative structures stretching across the whole Gospel. Hence, from the standpoint of a literary interpretation, one has to acknowledge both the particular and the overarching narrative constructions of a Gospel. Any reduction to a simple christological formula runs the risk of ignoring a Gospel's full narrative realities.

This new consciousness about the narrative nature of the Gospels and their autonomous narrative constructions problematizes the Kähler-

Johnson hypothesis about the unified character and basic pattern of the persona of the biblical Christ. In its focus on the singular universality of the so-called biblical Christ, the Kähler-Johnson tradition has negated one of the most remarkable characteristics of the Gospels—indeed, of the writings of the New Testament—namely, the many and manifold manifestations of Christ.

64. The Modern Lives of Jesus: From the Many Senses to the Single Sense and Back to the Many Senses

In returning to the broad context of hermeneutics and theology, it may be said that both the Quest for the historical Jesus, built on the premise of singular originality, and the Kähler-Johnson thesis, concerning a uniformly constructed persona of the biblical Christ, are prompted by the desire to replace the many senses with the one sense, be it historical or theological. In stark antithesis to medieval theology and its practice of a polyvalent hermeneutics, and in departure from the ancient living Jesus tradition, both oral and scribal, the modern Quest and the Kähler-Johnson challenge to it both operate in the interest of a radical reduction of the manifold senses to the single sense, understood in one instance as the literal, historical sense and in the other as the uniform biblical, theological sense. It has been the contention of this piece that the Quest's reliance on the *ipsissimum verbum* and/or the *ipsissima structura* cannot stand up to the standards of oral hermeneutics any more than Johnson's biblical Christ is credible when measured against the New Testament evidence.

When one views the Quest from the perspective of the *longue durée* of a history of theological reflection, one cannot escape the impression of a scholarly history fraught with the deepest of ironies. In the spirit of modernity, the Quest departed from the orality and scribality of the early Jesus tradition and the home of patristic and medieval polyvalent exegesis in order to secure the firm ground of historical particularity. Viewed from these perspectives, the Quest marks the culmination of a lengthy history of the devolution of the many senses to the one sense. Now after approximately 230 years of searching for the historical Jesus, the Quest is entangled in a seemingly unceasing proliferation of both similar but also widely differing, and often contradictory, senses of the historical Jesus. While each new Jesus book is composed with the intent, and often the express claim, to put an end to the pluralism of a bewildering array of Lives of Jesus, each only contributes to and indeed intensifies our experience of pluralism. The core of the irony, therefore, is that the Quest was launched with the intent to put Christian faith on the solid foundation of the single, historical sense, only to find itself ensnared in the labyrinth of multiple senses.

But we also notice an unmistakable difference between ancient and medieval pluralism versus that of modernity. Whereas ancient and medieval polyvalency were the intended consequences of the ethos of the tradition, which was perfectly capable of integrating multiple senses in an often remarkably sophisticated hermeneutical system, modernity's plurality of the Lives of Jesus is the unintended consequence of a Quest that is strenuously focused on the pursuit of the single, historical sense and stands helpless in view of the plural results of its own project.

11

THE WORKS OF MEMORY:
CHRISTIAN ORIGINS AS MNEMOHISTORY

With regard to both its critical position and its constructive imagination, this essay seeks to gain a foothold for memory in the historical study of the New Testament. It is prompted by the conviction that we can no longer ignore oral and memorial culture in favor of textual hermeneutics. The essay commences with a reflection on the paradigmatic significance of Mnemosyne in the human and social sciences, and on the civilizing role she has played in ancient history and myth. This is followed by a brief review of modernity's exemplary representatives of memory studies: Maurice Halbwachs, Frances Yates, Mary Carruthers, Janet Coleman, Jan Assmann, and Aleida Assmann. The third part studies memory's status in the shift from oral performance to scribal verbalization. Special emphasis is placed on the concept of Traditionsbruch, *which suggests that the scribalization of oral tradition does not necessarily guarantee memorial continuity, but may entail rupture and forgetting of tradition. Next, the essay explores the myopia in biblical scholarship in the face of flourishing memory studies in current human and social sciences. Birger Gerhardsson's* Memory and Manuscript *is singled out as exceptional in introducing memory as a key concept in New Testament studies, although largely in the fashion of cold memory. The fifth part conceptualizes tradition from the perspective of oral theory and social memory. Conjointly, the two theories view tradition as a ceaseless process of rememorizations. The sixth part applies memory theory to Gospel studies. From the vantage point of media dynamics and sensibilities I raise questions—for the first time in the context of my work—about the feasibility of the Two-Source-Hypothesis.*

Jan Assmann's concept of Erinnerungsfigur *is developed: the figure of Jesus in the Gospels functions less as a historically verifiable, and more as a socially accessible and memorially persuasible personage. The compositional intent of the Gospel narratives is described as being motivated by the dynamics of social memory. For what matters most in the composition of the Gospels is the reconstitution of memories of and about Jesus in the interest of shaping present group identity. Finally, the concept of Traditionsbruch is reintroduced and applied to Mark's Gospel. Next, the concept of memory place is applied to the commemoration of Jesus' death. The passion narrative represents the circumstances surrounding the act of violence with the aid of citations and themes drawn from the Jewish tradition, to make the unrepresentable comprehensible in familiar patterns. The eighth and last part, finally, returns to biblical scholarship's damnatio memoriae. It is suggested that oral/scribal and memorial studies have the potential of reconceptualizing historical scholarship on a large scale.*

> Magna ista vis est memoriae, magna nimis, deus, penetrale amplum et infinitum. [Great is that power of memory, beyond all measure, O my God, a spacious and boundless mystery.]
>
> —St. Augustine, *Confessiones*

> Mnemosyne, said the Greeks, is the mother of the Muses; the history of the training of this most fundamental and elusive of human powers will plunge us into deep waters.
>
> —Yates, *The Art of Memory*

> Memory is the matrix of all human temporal perception.
>
> —Carruthers, *The Book of Memory*

> The Jesus tradition "cannot possibly be understood except as rooted in Israelite social memory."
>
> —Horsley, *Prominent Patterns in the Social Memory of Jesus and Friends*

65. MEMORY IN THE HUMAN SCIENCES AND IN MYTH

In the human and social sciences, the modern academic study of memory is generally acknowledged to have been initiated by the sociologist Maurice Halbwachs (1925; 1992). Virtually effaced from scholarly consciousness, he received academic acceptance only decades following his death in Buchenwald. His omnipresence in current memory studies owes much to the work of Jan Assmann, himself the author of a classic work on memory theory. In part dependent on Halbwachs and in part quite separately, memory has recently emerged as a pivotal concept in cultural studies and as a principal topic of research in the humanities and social sciences. The significance of this memory boom is twofold. On the one hand, memory has provided wide-ranging explanatory powers and conceptual insights that have proven useful for viewing central issues such as representation and cognition, identity and imagination, tradition and ritual, communication and media, and many more, in new perspectives. Certain aspects of intellectual disciplines such as history, classical studies, ancient philosophy, medieval studies, anthropology, and literary criticism, for example, have been significantly enriched as a result of memory work. On the other hand, a continually growing body of interdisciplinary studies has developed around memory, exhibiting her as a vitally integrative force that allows us to discern different and even disparate cultural phenomena and academic disciplines within a larger unifying framework. Aspects of literary and political theory, religious and art history, historiography and the cognitive sciences, for example, can plausibly be linked to memorial dynamics and in relation to communities of memory. Memory, in the words of Patrick Hutton, embodies "the quintessential interdisciplinary interest" (1993, xiii). In view of a veritable avalanche of books and articles on memory and remembering, mnemonics and memorial processes, memory images and memory places, the ethics of remembering and *damnatio memoriae*, commemoration and memory theater, one cannot escape the impression that memory has risen to a status of paradigmatic significance in the humanities and social sciences. Mnemosyne, it seems, is the topic of everyone, and no one has exclusive monopoly over her.

In this emergence of memory in the twentieth century we experience the revival of a topos that has played a major civilizing role throughout Western culture. Long before memory had been assigned a place as one of the five divisions in ancient (and medieval) rhetoric, and Quintilian had paid his respects to memory as "the treasure-house of eloquence" (*Inst.* 11.2.1 et al.), her virtues had been acknowledged by mythology. According to myth, Mnemosyne, at once the goddess of memory and of imagination, had borne Zeus nine daughters, the Muses, who personified and presided over different modes of the arts and sciences. Unmistakably, this myth of Mnemosyne and her Muses articulates the centrality of memory in human culture. As mother of the Muses, Mnemosyne was the origin of all artistic and scientific labors and the wellspring of civilization. From the perspective of that myth, it was not scribality or literary exegesis, not logic or rhetoric even, that was perceived to be the central, civilizing agency, but memory.

66. MEMORY STUDIES IN MODERNITY

Three features define the strikingly original work on *la mémoire collective* by Halbwachs, the student of Henri Bergson and Émile Durkheim. In the first place, memory was a social phenomenon, inextricably allied with group formation and identity. Benefiting from, thriving within and sustaining social settings, she was both a facilitator and the result of the socialization of human culture. Remove the life-sustaining system of group identity and confirmation, and memories wither away. Second, the process of remembering does not work purely for the benefit of retaining the past as past. That is to say, remembering is not fed primarily by the needs for preservation of the past in its state of pristine authenticity. Rather, memory selects and modifies subjects and figures of the past in order to make them serviceable to the image the community (or individuals) wishes to cultivate of itself. Socialization and memory mutually condition each other, seeking in the last analysis preservation not of the past as such but of present group identity. Third, Halbwachs developed a theory concerning the antithetical relation of memory versus history. Viewing the matter from what today may be termed a positivistic view of historiography, he held that the past begins to assert itself as historical actuality only after social groups that were thriving on the cultivation of memories had departed from the scene. Only when the past was no longer claimed and inhabited by the collective remembering of social groups could history, uncontaminated by memory's distortions, have its true say. There is a sense, therefore, in which history has to wait for its debut until it has ceased to exist in and as memory.

It remains the significant intellectual accomplishment of Halbwachs to have (re)discovered the past as remembered past and to have defined it as a social construction that consolidates the symbolic and historic group identity within the social framework (*cadres sociaux*) of the present. It is this social concept of memory that in our generation Jan Assmann and Aleida Assmann have taken up, modified, and developed—an endeavor that in turn has helped rekindle a renaissance of the thought of Halbwachs.

Pursuing aspects of memory entirely different and independent from Halbwachs, and demonstrating the integrative powers of memory, Dame Frances Yates has managed to cast within the framework of the classic theories of memory a great number of cultural events and movements, figures and themes across Western history. *The Art of Memory* (1966) traced an archival, mnemotechnical memory tradition from its ancient locus in Greek rhetoric through its medieval transformations up to the hermetic, esoteric forms it took in the Renaissance, and on to scientific modernity. In particular, Yates deserves credit for having brought to academic consciousness the phenomenon of interior visualization and the role of image-making and visually based memory practices played in cognitive processes. Defining and describing "the place of the art of memory at the great nerve centres of the European tradition" (368) allowed Yates to construct links between such diverse features and persons as the anonymous *Ad Herennium*, ancient rhetoric, Augustine, Thomas Aquinas, memory theaters, Ramism, Protestantism, hermeticism, mysticism, and last but not least the rise of the scientific method. A model of erudition and stunning originality, *The Art of Memory* is a classic in twentieth-century memory studies. Viewing history largely from the perspective of mnemotechniques and spatially constructed concepts of memory, the technique of impressing images and places in the *ars memoriae*, her book comes closest of any in modern times to the construction of a mnemohistory.

Mary Carruthers's two magisterial volumes *The Book of Memory* (1990) and *The Craft of Thought* (1998) have been on the forefront of a growing body of scholarly literature intent on enlarging and revising conventional concepts of the literary, documentary culture of the Middle Ages. Examining medieval practices of reading, writing and composing, prayer and meditation, pedagogy and visualization, the nature and habits of the medieval craft of thought, and above all the function of memory, memory training, and the neuropsychology of memory, she unfolded a religious, intellectual, and ethical culture still rooted in theories and practices that were fundamentally memorial in nature. The layout and pictorial, decorative design of manuscripts, for example, often functioned in symbiotic relations with memorial needs, and the compositional structure of texts, citational habits, and certain institutional practices are well understood, she suggested, as arising from memorial activities. Given the fact that medieval manuscript culture interfaced with oral, rhetorical, memorial needs and activities, concepts such as text and textuality, logic and cognition, authorship and textual composition did not mean in medieval intellectual life what they came to mean in typographic modernity. At the same time, however, Carruthers discovered that issues raised by modernity's deconstructionism and psychoanalytic theory had been anticipated by and sometimes lay at the heart of the medieval tradition. In sum, she concluded that the culture of late antiquity and the Middle Ages must be viewed as a predominantly memorial rather than purely documentary, textual one.

Perhaps the least-known yet philosophically and historically highly consequential work on memory and the reconstruction of the past is Janet Coleman's *Ancient and Medieval Memories* (1992). Distinguished by a superior knowledge of ancient philosophy, medieval philosophy/theology, and the cognitive sciences, the book demonstrates an uncommonly profound and subtle grasp of the relations between language, logic (cognition), and reality throughout the ancient and medieval intellectual history of the West. Ranging from classical, monastic, and Thomistic ideas all the way to Ockham's nominalist launching of the *via moderna*, and culminating in a study of modern psychological and neuropsychological theories of cognition (minus Halbwachs's sociological theory, however), Coleman has produced a hugely impressive Western intellectual history with a focus on theories and practices of (re)constructing the past.

In important ways, Coleman reasoned, ancient and medieval consciousness of the past was unlike modernity's understanding and uses of the past, so that the modern approach to the past must be viewed as representing both a recent and very particular development. Medieval theologians, philosophers, and historians, far into the twelfth and thirteenth centuries, were not inclined to entertain interests in the pastness of the past. When discordant records or voices of the past manifested themselves, medieval thinkers were more inclined to harmonize them than to plumb them for historical veracity. The past was primarily elaborated and employed in the sense that "some moral, exemplary and universal aspect of that past could be interpreted for use in the present" (299). Deep into the High Middle Ages, she claims, there existed no conceptual consciousness of the issue increasingly accentuated in emergent modernity whether we know the past in its particularity as past or whether it was accessible only as it inhabited, or we made it inhabit, our present.

Since the 1980s an interdisciplinary group of scholars under the guidance of Jan Assmann (1992) and Aleida Assmann (1999) has produced a steadily growing body of work dealing with what they term "cultural memory." One outgrowth of the group's deliberations are the two standard works by Jan Assmann, *Das kulturelle Gedächtnis* (1992), and Aleida Assmann, *Erinnerungsräume* (1999). Deeply inspired by the pioneering work of Maurice Halbwachs, they viewed memory as being inextricably tied to group and group identity. One aspect, however, that distinguishes especially the work of Jan Assmann from Halbwachs's is the latter's polarization of memory vis-à-vis history. Jan Assmann has coined the phrase "Der Mythos vom 'historischen Sinn'" (1992, 66; "The Myth of the 'Sense of History'" [2011, 50]). Interest in the past, for the most part, was and is not specifically "historical" interest but at the same time the will to achieve legitimation, justification, and reconciliation, and therefore belongs in a frame of reference that we define with remembrance, tradition, and identity. "Ich möchte daher bezweifeln, ob es so etwas wie einen historischen Sinn wirklich gibt, und halte den Begriff des kulturellen Gedächtnisses für vorsichtiger und angemessener" (67).[1] Since the presence of the past is always the result of mediated transactions, the past is neither retrievable nor preservable as a historically fresh and memorially untouched reality. "Vergangenheit steht nicht urwüchsig an, sie ist eine kulturelle Schöpfung" (48).[2] Cultural memory, in Assmann's view, is therefore the more appropriate concept for capturing human dealings with the past. For this reason, there cannot be a sharp conceptual distinction between history and memory because the past as cultural construction is never immune to, and always dependent on, memorial participation and mediation.

Yet, Assmann is careful to concede that there has existed since Herodotus (484?–425 B.C.E.) something of a theoretical curiosity, an urge for knowledge irrespective of the desire to appeal to group, to consider specific reference points, or to corroborate present identities, a consciousness, that is, to recover history on an *identitätsabstrakten* (1992, 43) tableau (43 n. 24). Within the domain of memory studies, a historiography that aims at identity neutrality would have to be assigned to the category of cold memory (1992, 43 n. 24).

Entirely in Halbwachs's sense, cultural memory for Jan Assmann functions dynamically, and not in terms of storage or archive. It undertakes the work of remembering the past by reappropriating the latter in the interest of molding and/or reimaging and/or stabilizing group identity. Identity formation is a concept that is derived from the legacy of Halbwachs, even though he himself had used the term only sparingly. Memory, according to this understanding, operates selectively, seizing on, modifying, and contextualizing topics, events, and subjects of the past in order to feed the

---

1. "I have my doubts as to whether there really is such a thing as an historical sense; the term 'cultural memory' seems more cautious and suitable" (2011, 50).

2. "The past is not a natural force, but a cultural construction" (2011, 33; my translation).

needs and define the aspirations of the group. Cultural memory, therefore, recognizes both a regressive gesture toward the past, seeking to retrieve as much of the past as seems appropriate, and an orientation toward the present (and future), preserving what is deemed to be useful at present.

While both Assmanns have discussed the interfacing of cultural memory with media dynamics (J. Assmann 1992, 87–129; A. Assmann 1999, 188–217), the principal representatives of the recent upsurge in orality-literacy studies (Lord 1960; 1991; Havelock 1963, 1978; Ong 1967b; 1977a; 1982; Goody 1968; 1977; Foley 1988; 1990; 1991; 2002) have not seriously connected with the massive work in recent memory studies. Undoubtedly, orality-literacy studies have examined the interrelations between mnemotechnics and the media. In fact, the modern discussion of orality and oral-dependent texts had its beginning in the discovery of formulaic thought structures. But it has not, to my knowledge, integrated the discourse worlds of Halbwachs, Yates, Carruthers, Coleman, the Assmanns, and others. In a widely known essay on the role written and printed texts impose on readers, fictionalizing their identity as it were, Ong (1975, 9–22), we shall see below, although not using the term *memory*, has thematized a communicative feature that is essential for the functioning of cultural memory. In view of the fact that memorial processes entail an intricate meshing of cognitive, linguistic, and social dynamics—all features that are relevant to speech, scribality, and their mutual interfacing—the dearth of reflection on memory in orality-literacy studies seems curious. Biblical scholarship no doubt can benefit not merely from orality-literacy studies and recent memory work but also, importantly, from a constructive linking of the two.

67. Memory and Media

Precisely what happens to the memorial apperception of the past in the shift from oral performance to scribal mediation is complex and difficult to describe with specificity. A number of components converge in that shift, but a crucial factor pertains to the relation between communicator and recipients, and to the communicative dynamics transacted between the two. One of the principal characteristics of the oral medium is that it actualizes itself in face-to-face performance with live audiences. "For the speaker, the audience is in front of him" (Ong 1975, 10; repr. 1977a, 56), and it is in the context of the speaker's accountability to the audience and the latter's responsiveness to the speaker that communication is processed. That is to say, communication operates within a social and intellectual frame of references that are not merely dictated by speakers' intentions but also delimited by audiences' needs and expectations as well. Given the ephemeral nature of the oral medium, it is faced both with the risk of forgetting and the task of recall. For this reason oral diction is in a special way pressured to catch the hearers' attention and to attend to their needs of remembering. Operating apart from and/or in the absence of the materiality of the scribal medium, oral discourse, if it is to succeed, has no choice but to enter into a binding contract with a mnemonically structured language. As is well known, formulaically and rhythmically shaped diction, various kinds of repetition and parallelism dominate and indeed constitute orally functioning communication. In fact, the apperception in modern times of a distinctive culture of oral style, compositioning, and performance had its beginning in the study of formularity in ancient epic language. Memory devices are deeply etched into the structure of oral discourse and knowledge. As far as oral communication in the ancient world is concerned, the mnemonic construction of oral discourse is a matter of life or death.

In the case of the scribal medium, the scribe or dictator of papyri, scrolls, or manuscripts enters into relations with recipients that differ from those that prevail in oral discourse. "For the writer, the audience is simply further away, in time or space or both" (Ong 1975, 10; repr. 1977a, 56). It is the temporal and physical distance between producer and consumer of communication that makes a notable difference in the shift from oral to scribal communication. In all instances, the authorial dictator, composer, or scribe operates in the absence of a live audience. As a result, those in charge of scribal compositioning are deprived of or, as the case may be, released from face-to-face responsiveness. In the long run, this crucial circumstance effects a lessening of direct accountability to the recipients of the message and a sense of emancipation from, or lack of commitment to, communal responsibilities. From the perspectives of memory, the agents of the production of the ancient scroll and manuscript are less bound by the strictures of mnemonic imperatives, because there is a sense in which the handwritten objects assume archival functions. This has to be conceded in spite of the fact that scroll and manuscript are usually meant to be recycled as living voice. Most certainly, scribally mediated communication in the ancient world is frequently rhetorically shaped so as to call on and affect hearers. Many ancient texts are distinguished by a varying repertoire of communicative strategies and rhetorical dynamics. But again, in the long run of literary developments, the altered state of communicative dynamics carries significant consequences for the work of memory. Produced in the absence of live audiences and thus temporarily at least exempted from immediate accountability to hearers, chirographic products can more readily dispense with mnemonic assistance.

The shift from oral to scribal communication carries a second, less obvious but equally important consequence for the role of memory. Disengagement from direct audience responsibility empowers the written documents to explore more fully their scribal potentials. Release from the immediacy of oral accountability enhances critical control over the recipients and facilitates greater freedom in the treatment of past and tradition. As far as rapport with recipients is concerned, Ong has developed the thesis that there exists in literary history a tradition of fictionalizing the readership: "The historian, the scholar or scientist, and the simple letter writer all fictionalize their audiences, casting them in a made-up role and calling on them to play the role assigned" (1975, 17; repr. 1977a, 74). Written culture intensifies the ability for separation and alienation. Most certainly, oral discourse can, and often does, challenge and recast individual and social identities as well. Much of the Jesus tradition serves as a telling example. But the point here is to acquire a hermeneutically appropriate understanding of media potentials and dynamics. In the long run of scriptographic developments, "it is only through writing that the bearer gains the necessary freedom to introduce something new, even unprecedented to the old, familiar material" (J. Assmann, 1992, 100; 2011, 84). This is noteworthy because until very recently the relation between oral tradition/authorities and the written Gospel has been conceptualized in terms of a steady flow of tradition moving toward the Gospel, intimating continuity, unbrokenness even, conceding only minimal compositional powers to Gospel scribality and thereby casting the latter into the role of cold memory. Viewing the matter of tradition and Gospel from a different perspective, Lord, in an article not sufficiently deliberated in biblical scholarship, has suggested that the Gospels are "oral traditional literature" (1978, 33–91), whereby three or four Gospels are "telling the 'same' oral traditional story" (64). Moreover, a rapidly developing literature on the rhetorical and performative character of Mark (and other biblical texts), which exhibits formidable sensitivity to media dynamics, likewise argues or implies that Mark's narrative was written not only to serve performative purposes but also in the manner it had been performed (Shiner 2003;

J. Dewey 1995a; Malbon 2002).[3] Undoubtedly, Mark, as much of ancient literature, was intended to be recycled in oral proclamation. But was the Gospel an autograph or a variant of oral narrative tradition in the sense proposed by Lord and recent performance critics? In other words, is it conceivable that that the Gospel's chirographic composition was entirely unaffected by the potentials of the scribal medium?

In view of scholarly models that espouse the unproblematic relation between oral tradition and the written Gospel, it merits restating the potential of scribality, including Gospel scribality, to disengage itself from oral imperatives, to turn a deaf ear even on the needs and expectations of live audiences, so as to undertake a productive redescription of tradition, to challenge social identities, to recommemorate the past, in short, to generate hot memory.

Jan Assmann has astutely developed the concept of *Traditionsbruch* associated with scribality that may entail risks of forgetting not known to orality (1992, 100–101, 216–17, 294–95; ET: 2011, 84–85, 194–95, 268–69): "Writing—and this for me is a crucial point—does not in itself provide continuity. On the contrary, it brings with it the risk of oblivion, of disappearance under the dust of time; thus it may often break the continuity that is integral to oral tradition" (2011: 85).[4]

The scribalization of tradition is, therefore, by no means a guarantor of continuity and stability. Scribally transacted memory may appropriate the past not necessarily in keeping with oral tradition, but in deviating from, or even rupturing with it. To be sure, a scribally mediated memory, due to scribality's storage function, gives the impression of having solved the problem of forgetting. And yet, the media complexities of the scribal medium go far beyond its function as a means merely of stemming the tide of forgetfulness. Deeper sensitivity to media hermeneutics can alert us to the phenomenon of writers' scribally enforced distance from hearers, which may enhance both the desire and the ability to break with tradition, to canonize an alternate viewpoint, and to reconfigure and

---

3. Published subsequently to this essay, see especially Rhoads 2006, part 1, 118–33, and part 2, 164–84. Most recently, see Wire 2011.

4. "Schriftlichkeit, darauf kommt es mir hier vor allem an, stellt an sich noch keine Kontinuität dar. Im Gegenteil: sie birgt Risiken des Vergessens und Verschwindens, Veraltens und Verstaubens, die der mündlichen Überlieferung fremd sind, und bedeutet oft eher Bruch als Kontinuität" (1992, 101).

thereby implement a form of forgetfulness. We shall return to the concept of *Traditionsbruch*.

68. Scholarly Myopia about Memory vis-à-vis Gerhardsson's Focus on Memory

Modernity's work on memory, which was initiated by Halbwachs and has been flourishing ever since, has (until very recently) found next to no response in New Testament scholarship. In spite of impressively productive memory work carried out in the human and social sciences, Mnemosyne is by and large not perceived to be a pressing issue in current biblical scholarship. Jens Schröter seems to be exceptional in having adopted Jan and Aleida Assmann's concept of cultural memory as a heuristic device in reading Mark, Q, and the *Gospel of Thomas* as different modalities of remembering Jesus (1997, 462–86). More recently, one of the most significant pieces of memory work has appeared in the Semeia Studies volume *Memory, Tradition, and Text*, jointly edited by Kirk and Thatcher (2005b).

Schröter's monumental volume and Semeia Studies 52 apart, the glaring disregard of memory studies is one more example of a growing isolation of biblical scholarship from the human and social sciences. How is it possible that New Testament scholarship, with one exception mentioned below, has been able to conduct its research without paying attention to the boom in memory work and disregardful of the profoundly useful explanatory categories it has produced? In the same vein, Kirk has reflected on this astounding "myopia … a problem almost uniquely of New Testament scholarship" (2005b, 1). He points to classical form criticism and its concept of tradition as having caused memory's marginalization, or, as one might call it, memory's amnesia of itself. In their jointly written essay, Kirk and Thatcher (2005a) expose the disappearance of memory as an analytical category from the work of Käsemann, Perrin, the Jesus Seminar, and above all from Bultmann's form criticism: "'Memory' has, for all practical purposes, disappeared as an analytical category in Jesus research" (27). Kirk and Thatcher's analysis of how memory fared in the work of key figures in the recent history of New Testament scholarship merits reflection. Because form criticism has dominated many of our methods and assumptions over the longest part of the twentieth century, we shall extend Kirk and Thatcher's reflections on form criticism's disconnect with memory studies.

One may single out three features that distracted classical form criticism from taking the workings and function of memory in late antiquity, and scholarly reflections on them, into serious account. One, from the outset Bultmann's form-critical project of detaching and examining orally imaginable units was premised on and oriented toward finding the original form: "The aim of form-criticism is to determine the original form of a piece of narrative, a dominical saying or a parable" (1963, 6). This programmatic intent cast Bultmann's project from its inception into a search for the origin, diverting attention away from exploring the memorial and mnemotechnical dynamics of oral tradition. Two, Bultmann's concept of the Synoptic tradition disallowed any serious consideration of memory as a dynamic, motivational force. To a considerable extent the Synoptic history was assumed to have been driven by what I have defined as the principle of "intrinsic causation" (Kelber 1983, 2–8), whereby the transmission of Jesus materials was propelled by "the immanent urge to development which lay in the tradition" (Bultmann 1963, 373). If tradition is empowered by its own evolutionary gravity, the forces of remembering in the process of traditioning would seem to be minimal at best, and irrelevant at most. Three, as is well known, it was, and to some extent still is, the form-critical premise that Mark's Gospel composition merely brought to fruition what was already lodged in tradition so that "his [Mark's] whole enterprise is explicable only in terms of the importance which the tradition itself had" (Bultmann 1963, 347). Once again, therefore, there is no place for memorial dynamics in tradition; the latter is rather mechanistically conceived as a unidirectional transmission of mostly oral materials. Nor is there a place for memorial dynamics on the level of Gospel compositioning because narrative creativity is largely limited to a channeling and fusion of forces and trends that were for the most part already inherent in the tradition that preceded the Gospel. Mark merely brought to fruition what had been well developed in tradition.

These are all features, we note, that steered form criticism away from memory's active participation both in the work of tradition and in the Gospels' composition. The notion of "the original form" is a phantom of the literary, not to say typographic, imagination and incompatible with oral hermeneutics. Once we familiarize ourselves with orality, we are in a world of plurals. Oral tradition operates with a plurality of original speech acts, which suggests a principle entirely different from and indeed antithetical to that of the one, original form (see chs. 4, §18; 5, §27; 10, §61; 14, §91; 16, §107). The concept of "intrinsic causation," moreover, misconceives the nature of the Synoptic, oral tradition. Spoken words are not subject to a forward-oriented directionality, and are in fact incomprehensible in any diagrammatic form or fashion. To be sure, spoken words are communicable from one person to another, but they do not travel in the sense of covering spatial distance that can be pictured on paper. And finally, as far as the Gospel compositions are concerned, form criticism has vastly underrated the Gospel's narrative productivity, indeed creativity, a fact widely recognized today. At this point, the exploration of the narrative poetics of the Gospels has progressed far enough to make us realize that each Gospel, far from being merely the product of dynamics in the tradition, is the result of a compositional volition, deliberately constructed plot causalities, and a distinctly focused rhetorical outreach. Our reflections on the astounding "myopia" in New Testament studies, therefore, suggest more than a failure on the part of form criticism to come to terms with memory. More, and indeed something more important, is at stake here than the absence of memory, a condition that could conceivably be remedied by integrating memorial dynamics into the work of form criticism. Put differently, the failure to make room for memory in Gospel studies is no mere oversight that could be corrected by adding the missing link to complete our conceptualization of tradition and Gospel. In depth, this scholarly "myopia" has to do with fundamental conceptual flaws inherent in form criticism, which have centrally affected the methods and assumptions of almost a century of scholarly approaches to the Gospels.

The one instance in which memory, conceived as key concept, has entered into the discourse world of New Testament scholarship was provided by Birger Gerhardsson. Aptly titled *Memory and Manuscript* (1961), his magnum opus will stand as a classic in twentieth-century biblical studies. Significantly, the very author who has shown a keen interest in memory is also deeply critical of the methods and assumptions of form criticism. Yet Gerhardsson has not benefited from the scholarship of Halbwachs and those working in his scholarly tradition either. As is well known, the author of *Memory and Manuscript* has modeled his concept of tradition and memory on Pharisaic, rabbinic Judaism in the Tannaitic and Amoraic period, dated roughly from the calamity of 70 c.e. up to the fifth century. Based on this analogy, Gerhardsson constructed a model of the early Jesus traditions in which memory assumed the role of principal facilitator of the transmissional processes. This particular affiliation of rabbinic mnemonic techniques with early Christian traditioning practices has been widely criticized. *As a rule, however, critics have failed to give Gerhardsson credit for having insisted on the centrality of memory in the early Christian tradition.* The observations by Kirk and Thatcher are, therefore, all the more commendable: "Gerhardsson's proposal resonates with social memory theory in its recognition of the constitutive nature of memory for a community" (2005a, 35). For Gerhardsson, tradition is inconceivable without memory, and vice versa.

This alignment between social memory theorists and Gerhardsson on the centrality of memory must not blur the differences that separate the concepts of memory expounded by Gerhardsson on one hand and the authors of the essays for which this piece has been written on the other (Kirk and Thatcher 2005b). Gerhardsson envisioned a near-mechanical commitment of materials to memory and an almost passive transmission by way of continual repetition. Changes that did occur in the processing of traditional items remained confined to interpretive adaptations. On the whole, the work of memory as key arbiter of tradition was, therefore, characterized by fixity, stability, and continuity, and the primary purpose of transmission was the deliberate act of communicating the legacy of Jesus for its own sake. Next to no allowance is made, on this model, for memory's active participation in the operations of tradition.

It is worth observing that the first and virtually only time memory is introduced as key concept into the modern study of Christian origins, it is presented as cold memory, highlighting its retentive function and reducing it to strictly preservative, reproductive purposes. As conceived by Gerhardsson, memory is the grand stabilizing agent in early Christian culture. Not one of the authors of the Kirk-Thatcher essay volume shares this concept of cold memory. Whereas Gerhardsson opted for an early Christian memorial culture transacted as passive transmission under the aegis of *cold memory*, the authors represented in the volume edited by Kirk and Thatcher (2005a) advocate a notion of *hot memory* propelled by active remembering and socialization (Kirk, Thatcher, Schwartz, Horsley, Hearon, A. Dewey, Masters Keightley, Esler, Wire, DeConick). As far as I can see, Kirk's statement in his introductory essay expresses a view to which all contributors seem to give their assent: "The activity of memory in articulating the past is dynamic, unceasing, *because it is wired into the ever-shifting present*" (Kirk 2005b, 10). On this view, all essayists appear to be agreed.

For two reasons Gerhardsson occupies a place at the table of memory discourse. First, as stated before, he is the one scholar of the New Testament who has secured a central place for Mnemosyne in the history of early Christian traditions. If we rightly lament the view that "a sharp distinction between 'memory' and 'tradition' is fundamental for most contemporary models of the development of primitive Christian theology and the composition history of the gospels" (Kirk and Thatcher 2005a, 25), we should likewise acknowledge that Gerhardsson is the scholar who has taken exception to this distinction. The specificity of his memory model aside, the author of *Memory and Manuscript* deserves major credit for having insisted on the inalienable synergism of memory and tradition. On this point he was right, and the form critics on the wrong track.

In particular, Gerhardsson has displayed a keen perception of the mnemonic structuring of many of Jesus' sayings. One would have thought that it was to be the first order of the form-critical project to examine the extraordinary degree to which Jesus' sayings have kept faith with heavily patterned speech, and to explore features such as alliteration; appositional equivalence; proverbial and aphoristic diction; contrasts and antitheses; synonymous, antithetical, and tautological parallelisms; rhythmic structures; and so forth—all earmarks of mnemonics, which abound in the Jesus logia. But form criticism, as we have observed, instead of focusing on the performancial style of Jesus' sayings, preoccupied itself with oral tradition and above all tradition's origin, and rapidly conceived of itself as a tool in the Quest for the proclamation of the historical Jesus. It is not normally acknowledged that Gerhardsson, more than the form critics, displayed informed sensitivity to the rhythmically and formulaically patterned diction of Jesus' sayings. To be sure, the mnemonic usability and auditory feasibility of large parts of the Jesus tradition suggested to him memorization, literal consistency, and near-passive transmission. By way of rebuttal, we emphasize, along with the essayists of the Kirk-Thatcher volume (2005b), I would like to suggest that already Jesus' own mnemonically structured speech as well as its continuing performance in the commemorative activities of his followers was subject to the constructive and reconstructive work of social memory (see ch. 10, §61). Still, in view of the widely practiced dissociation of tradition from memory, Gerhardsson deserves credit for having insisted on mnemonics at the heart of the formative stage of the Synoptic tradition. On this point he was right, and the form critics not on the right track.

Second, we should revisit and reflect on Gerhardsson's basic insight into the central role of memory in the life of tradition. At this early stage in our deliberations, let us not prematurely narrow down the range of possible memorial practices and the scope of memorial conceptualizations.

Among the concepts of memory espoused by the authors of the Kirk-Thatcher volume (2005b) memory's repetitive and recollective side may be singled out, and both deserve to be kept in mind because they constitute two classic manifestations in the memory tradition. Repetition carries forward the legacy of the past, reconstituting the past in the present, while recollection reconstructs the benefits of the past in response to the needs of the present. Manifestly, Gerhardsson has captured memory's repetitive moment, and the authors of the Kirk-Thatcher volume have sided with her recollective activities. Let us be clear: on the whole, it will be difficult to subscribe to a memorially activated tradition that carries semantically inert pieces of information across time, the whirling wheel of change, and equally difficult to deny memory's incessantly constructive ambitions to reactivate the past in the interest of current affairs.

And yet, before we opt unilaterally for a constructionist model of memory, let us keep in mind that it was precisely the interplay of the repetitive and the recollective elements that bestowed upon Mnemosyne a sense of complexity, of ambiguity even. Ever so often, memory exists in the paradoxical tension between these two aspirations: to resurrect the images of the past so as to transport them into the present, and to reconstruct the images of the past so as to adapt them to the present context. It is one of the most impressive features of Kirk's introductory essay (2005b) that while principally subscribing to memory's inclination to bring the past into alignment with the present, it also recognizes that the past may inform, guide, and constrain what we remember and act out in the present. If, therefore, we can acknowledge that in memory's work the past sets limits for and defines the scope of what is to be remembered, while the present is inclined to reactivate the past, we have actually moved beyond a strictly constructionist model. On this view, what memory will bequeath to us is contingent on a balance of revisiting and reconstructing the past. This is by no means to challenge the explicit or implied objection the contributors have raised to a model of remembering the past for the past's sake alone. As will be developed further below, *the past remembered is most often already a remembered past.* In the words of Kirk and Thatcher, the past "is not a matter of a so-called empirical past persisting in unelaborated form into the changing present of a community, but a past shaped, sacralized, and interpreted precisely through activities of commemoration" (2005a, 32 n. 1). As remembered past, it provides sociopolitical, thematic, cognitive, and linguistic patterns of what it is that is to be remembered. On this view, one may speak of memory's interplay between the

past and the present, at times attributing greater force to the remembered
past and at times to the remembering present.

69. MEMORY AND TRADITION

Interestingly, Gerhardsson (1961, 130 n. 1, 147 n. 9, 167–68) in his
magnum opus made reference to the extensive work by Marcel Jousse
(1925; 1974; 1975; 1978) on rhythm and bilateral diction in the ancient
Near East, paying close attention to the language of Jesus. But Gerhardsson did not consciously draw on and absorb Jousse's ideas so as to incorporate them into his own work. At the time of Jousse's early publications
it came as something of a shock to many of his French readers to observe
him approaching Jesus under anthropological and linguistic aspects "rigorously historical as Rabbi Ieshua of Nazareth" (Sienaert 1990, 98) who
was teaching in compliance with the oral style characteristic of his Galilean milieu. It was a central idea of Jousse's work that memory was not
accidental or supplementary to cognition in antiquity; given the predominantly oral mindset of the ancient Mediterranean culture, it was as
elementary as gravity is to the physical universe. Unfortunately, neither
Gerhardsson nor the form critics ever availed themselves of Jousse's extensive research on oral style. We are confronted with a chapter in New Testament scholarship that is fraught with irony and haunted by inexplicable
absences. Four years after Bultmann's first edition of *The History of the
Synoptic Tradition* (first published in 1921), Jousse published his seminal
work on *Études de Psychologie Linguistique: Le Style oral rhythmique et
mnémotechnique chez les verbo-moteurs* (1925), which was subsequently
followed by a series of important articles and books. In the 1920s the book
was the subject of a debate in Paris, and Milman Parry, who at that time
studied at the Sorbonne, came under the influence of Jousse's work. And
so it came that Jousse, the scholar who wrote extensively on the oral-style
method of Jesus' language, helped contribute analytical categories to the
Oral Formulaic Hypothesis developed by Milman and Lord that was to
revolutionize our comprehension of the Homeric epics. For reasons next
to impossible to fathom, Jousse's ideas have remained conspicuous by their
absence from Gospel studies generally and from form criticism in particular, the very discipline that was designed to explore orality in the early
Christian tradition.

One of the most significant features of the social-memory thesis articulated in the essay jointly authored by Kirk and Thatcher (2005a) concerns

the conceptualization of tradition. Their deliberations on the vital connection between memory and tradition deserve our most serious attention. Affirming the performance mode of tradition, they recognize close affinities between oral theory and social memory theory: "As such, 'oral tradition' and 'social memory' are essentially synonymous terms, and the connections between them should be explored by biblical scholars" (41). This interconnection between social memory and oral theory opens up a rich field for research in biblical studies. Neither one of the two theories understands tradition as a movement from stability to development, or from originality toward hermeneutical variations, or from singularity to multiformity. *Approach tradition with an exclusive interest in historical originality and you have misunderstood the operations of tradition altogether.* Affirmatively, both oral hermeneutics and social memory view tradition as a dynamic process ceaselessly engaged in the activity of reorganization and self-constitution.

According to Kirk and Thatcher, social memory connotes a stream of memorial activities, of continual rememorizations, so that what has been called tradition "is, in fact, the substance of 'memory'" (40). Integrating the two theories, one may say that tradition understood as remembering constitutes an interminable interplay of oral, scriptographic, typographic, and artistic negotiations between the past and the exigencies of the present, at times giving more weight to the past and at times to present circumstances, but always seeking to synchronize the past with the present.

Once we realize the operating force of memory, we can no longer reconstruct tradition on the basis of a secure place, immune to temporality, in the life of Jesus or in his receptionist history. Nor can one imagine tradition as an assembly-line production carrying inert items of information to be collected and objectively preserved for posterity. And the notion of tradition as a process of accretion and sedimentation is not very plausible either, because it rests on a clearly imaginable yet unrealistic developmental model. In the words of Kirk and Thatcher, the past that memory seeks to reconcile with the present "is not a matter of a so-called empirical past persisting in unelaborated form into the changing present of a community, but a past shaped, sacralized, and interpreted precisely through activities of commemoration" (2005a, 32 n. 1). It is frequently possible to observe a text negotiating the past in terms of creative rememorizations, but rarely, if at all, in terms of placing layer upon layer, or shifting from simplicity to complexity.

The *trajectory model* of tradition introduced by Robinson and Koester (1971) outlines an analytical and exegetical approach to overcome what was perceived to be a strangely immobile picture of the world of early Christianity, characterized by such terms as "background," "environment," or "context," and in their place to trace intelligible movements and sequences of theological development, which the authors termed *trajectories*. The great merit of the approach is to have redirected attention from a focus on an author's experience at the time of the textual composition toward a dynamic concept of the tradition. One question that may be asked is whether in seeking to reconstruct tradition along the line of apprehensible directionalities the trajectory model has not made transmission per se, understood in the developmental mode, the sole key to tradition. Yet transmission and transmissional directionality is not all there is to tradition. Orally transacted communication, for example, is nondirectional; it cannot be said to flow in this or that direction. Trajectories, as conceived by Robinson and Koester, are transmissional processes predominantly based on textual documentation. Memory does not seem to have been assigned a role either. From the perspective of individual as well as social memory and of oral discourse, the trajectory model, focused on textual evidence while marginalizing both oral and memorial dynamics, takes on the scepter of a somewhat abstract trafficking in intertextuality. With social memory, however, a grand motivating force is invoked that operates primarily in the interest of group formation and identity reinforcement by bridging the demands of the past with the needs of the present. The key function of mnemohistory, this memorially empowered tradition, is not transmission alone, but negotiation between a remembered or commemorated past and the contingencies of an ever-shifting present.

If one envisions tradition as a continual process of commemorating activities, can we imagine the heart of tradition as a mediation between a stable past and an ever-shifting present, or is not what we tend to refer to as past itself already caught up in rememorization? In other words, does the past have an existence as a permanently objectifiable entity outside of and exempt from memory's desires and arbitrations? In following Kirk and Thatcher, one may think of the past as correlate to social identity, being in the process of negotiations, as part and parcel of a continuous stream of memorializing processes and practices, and as an inescapable component of Halbwachs's *cadres collectifs*. In dealing with the past we are, therefore, in the words of Kirk and Thatcher, dealing with what in effect is always already a "commemorated past" (32 n. 1). Indeed, mnemohistory traffics with commemorated pasts rather than with an objectively con- stituted past. Once again, social memory and oral/scribal hermeneutics converge in insisting that the past of Jesus' proclamation is not accessible as pure, empirical commodity any more than "the original saying" exists apart from equiprimordiality. In the words of Kirk and Thatcher, "'Tradi- tion' and 'memory' are not elements of the Gospels that can be pried apart through application of particular criteria" (33). In sum, the perspectives of memory theory and of media hermeneutics, along with narrative poetics, will increasingly cast doubt on the feasibility of extrapolating "original" and "originally historical" materials with clinical precision from their tex- tually assigned locations, and construct upon their assumed historicity the edifice of tradition.

It is insightful, from this perspective, to revisit Paul's mode of nurtur- ing the memory of Jesus. The apostle is clearly misapprehended if the per- ceived absence of Jesus material in the Pauline Epistles prompts desperate scholarly attempts in search of Pauline familiarity with the historical Jesus. As Masters Keightley has persuasively demonstrated, Paul's memorial knowledge of Christ was mediated in the commemorative rituals of the Eucharist and baptism. It was there that he "met the Lord," always fresh and alive. This is entirely in accord with Paul's oral disposition toward lan- guage and presence (Kelber 1983, 140–51). The power of the gospel, the efficacious proclamation of redemption, and his experience of Christ are all rooted in profoundly oral, memorial hermeneutics.

70. Memory and the Gospels: Jesus as *Erinnerungsfigur*, *Traditionsbruch*, and Archaeology of Memory

Memory theory can be given substance through application to Gospel studies because Mnemosyne's energies and interests may well hold a vital key to the Gospels' deeper compositional and motivational forces. Ever since Heinrich J. Holtzman 140 years ago postulated a thesis that was to develop into the so-called Two-Source Hypothesis with its threefold assumption of Markan priority, autonomous Q source, and Matthean and Lukan dependencies on Mark and Q, Gospel studies have been locked in a tightly constructed scheme of a singularly textual, documentary rational- ity. *Until very recently, our methodological premises and theoretical proposi- tions, the bulk of our exegetical work, introductions to and theologies of the New Testament, all our work on the Gospels and the Jesus tradition have*

been firmly in the grip of the Two-Source Hypothesis and its predilection for
literary relations and clean source-critical explanations.

Three closely interconnected considerations may alert us to the limited plausibility of the Two-Source Hypothesis. One, recent narrative criticism has made it abundantly clear that each of the three Synoptics (and
John as well) is informed by narrative ambitions and a will to emplotment.
Ostensively, more is involved in the Gospel compositions than the use of
sources, more even than the creative use of sources. Two, the fact that each
of the three Synoptic Gospels (and John as well) is involved in plural issues
and traditions, in multiple themes and conflicts, seriously limits the usefulness, or at least the explanatory force of, the Two-Source Hypothesis
and its singularly source-critical rationality. Three, each Synoptic narrative
plot (and that of John as well) is designed both to retrieve the past while
simultaneously addressing present issues and circumstances with a view
toward the future. This would seem to be a dominant, if not the dominant, motivational force for Gospel composition, and in it we recognize
memory's favorite strategy: drawing on the past from the perspective of
the present, she seeks to legitimate the past as present. When we measure
the Two-Source Hypothesis against the inalienable insights of narrative
criticism, we cannot but observe that any kind of the mechanistic conceptualization and narrow application of the Two-Source Hypothesis seriously weakens its usefulness. The source-critical theory cannot alone, if at
all, account for the Gospels' deft handling of past and present. Given the
fact that we now can and must understand the Gospels as being driven by,
among other things, multiple narrative causalities, can we in good conscience still cling to the strictly documentary Two-Source Hypothesis, the
notion that the appropriation, revision, and conflation of literary sources
provides the single most persuasive rationale for the composition of the
Synoptic Gospels? Without doubt, it is one thing to challenge the usefulness of the Two-Source Hypothesis and quite another to question its rational applicability altogether. And yet, growing insights into the narrativity
of the Gospels, and the resultant weakening of the explanatory value of the
Two-Source Hypothesis, might in turn incline us to shift attention toward
social-memory theory. Could we bring ourselves to thinking of the Gospels, or parts thereof, ultimately as the work of memorial processes?

For some time Richard Horsley has been developing the thesis that both
Q and Mark were informed by, drawing on, and adapting cultural patterns
of Israel's historical experience. In *Whoever Hears You Hears Me* (Horsley
and Draper 1999, esp. ch. 5) he (in collaboration with Draper) developed

the thesis that the Q discourses were shaped according to ancient Israelite cultural patterns and covenant renewal structures. In *Hearing the Whole Story* (2001, esp. ch. 8) Horsley further applied this notion to Mark, suggesting that the Gospel's Jesus conducts himself both in words and actions that are designed to bring about the renewal of Israel. In keeping with these earlier studies, Horsley in his piece for the Kirk-Thatcher volume further developed the thesis that the traditional Israelite cultural pattern of the Mosaic covenant "provided a fundamental framework of organization and interpretation in Mark and Q and the movements they addressed" (2005, 75). Prominent among the Israelite themes is the well-known Elijah and Elisha double cycle of miracle stories (Mark 4:35–8:21), which carries reminiscences of Israel's popular tradition: Jesus' (Moses') crossing of the sea, Jesus' (Moses') feeding of the people, Jesus' (Moses') launching the exodus, Jesus' (Elijah's and Elisha's) healings. In thus tapping into Israel's repertoire of Mosaic covenant and Elijah/Elisha renewal themes, Mark and Q, according to Horsley, constructed part of their respective pieces in ways that deeply resonated with the people's social memory. There can be little doubt that the two sets of five Markan miracle stories, each consisting of a sea-crossing, three healings, and a feeding, carry motifs taken from Exodus and the Elijah-Elisha cycle. In all, the operation of Israelite themes and patterns in Q and Mark "was probably not derived from written texts, but rather from their continuing presence in popular Judaism and Galilean tradition" (Horsley 2005, 73). Guided by Horsley, we may, therefore, look upon the Israelite themes as residues or retrievals of the memory of ancient Israel.

But what precisely are the operations of *Mnemosyne* in this instance? Memory, we saw, invariably deals with already commemorated pasts because no past can asserts itself in the raw. She is the mediating agent that makes aspects of the past accessible to us. To this we must now add that the commemoration of foundational personages is especially apt to avail itself of interpretive frames of reference and symbolic patterns. Personages who do not seem fathomable within available categories and appear to exceed current models of comprehension make special demands on memory. Precisely in such cases, memory may fall back upon tradition-honored patterns and seize upon ancient mnemonic frames that are familiar to hearers. In other words, out-of-the-ordinary personages are especially vulnerable or, if you will, receptive to mythicization. We are here at the intersection of social memory and myth. The covenant-renewal patterns and the Elijah-Elisha motifs, discussed by Horsley as cultural patterns and motifs of Israel's historical past, remembrances of the past themselves, precisely fit Halbwachs's category of *les cadres sociaux de la mèmoire*: memory functions to sustain social formation and identity. As Jesus is cast into categories that are constitutive of Israel's identity and her relations with God, he is turned into a widely accessible and memorable *Erinnerungsfigur* (J. Assmann 1992, 200–202). As carrier of ancient values and experiences shared by the group he can now function as a believable focus of identity.

It merits our attention that in this instance we are confronted with a special mode of mediating the past. Jesus' transformation into a memorially engaging figure is accomplished not by recourse to recent memories of or about Jesus but by engagement in and application of the distant memory of the group. We encounter here what may be called the *archaeology of memory*, which operates not merely with regard to Jesus' recent past and his subsequent tradition but archaically by employment of a venerable, deep past for present identification and mythicization.

Apart from viewing certain segments of biblical texts as products of memory's desire, does it not seem plausible to view the entire Gospel as paradigmatic of memorial drives? We are not thinking here of Mark's mnemonic disposition toward oral delivery but rather of the Gospel's compositional intent as a whole as being motivated by the dynamics of social memory. Transmission for the sake of preservation or arbitration of literary sources are not the only, and not necessarily the most important, dynamics of the Gospels' composition. Even narrative emplotment, employed by multiple narrative causalities and strategies, operates in the service of a higher, an overriding goal. The deepest force driving the formation of the Gospels is the retrieval of the past for the benefit of the present. It is the ultimate objective of the Gospel composition. Remembering Jesus with a view toward the present, and not the transmission of traditions or the juggling of literary sources, provided the deepest impulse for the Gospel compositions. *What matters most in the literary, memorial composition of the Gospels is not the preservation of tradition or the negotiation of literary sources per se, but rather the reconstitution of the memories of Jesus in the interest of shaping present group identity.*

This is why the Gospel narratives as cultural memories reflect the conditions of their respective productions. To be sure, selection and organization of Gospel materials and composition of the Gospel narrative are informed by the availability of traditions and commitment to them. But the formation of the Gospels is also, and perhaps more importantly, constituted by interests and exigencies that arise from present communal settings. And if this seems an overstatement, let us modify the wording by suggesting that the Gospels are memorially driven compositions seeking to maintain a precarious balance between a simultaneous attention toward the past *and* toward the present, with a view as well toward the future. But what matters most in the literary, memorial composition of the Gospels is not preservation of tradition for the sake of preservation, but continuation of tradition for the purpose of shaping and preserving group identity. In Halbwachs's terms, the Gospels are composed from the perspective and in the context of *les cadres sociaux de la mémoire*.

At this point we can reconnect the memorial arbitration of the Gospel composition with Jan Assmann's concept of *Traditionsbruch*, a rupture in the tradition (1992, 100–101, 216–17, 294–95; ET: 2011, 84–85, 194–95, 268–69), introduced earlier in connection with media studies, and elaborated here in reference to the idea of a critical *memorial threshold*. As far as I can see, Kirk is the only scholar who has introduced Assmann's threefold concept of *Traditionsbruch, memorial threshold* (crisis of memory), and media link with writing into the study of the New Testament (2005b, 5–6).

Concretely, how does *Traditionsbruch* manifest itself in Gospel and tradition? After a period of some forty years, Assmann explains, the communicative memory is prone to approach a precarious stage: "Forty years represent a critical caesura into the collective memory, and if memory is not to be lost, it has to be transformed from biographical to cultural memory" (J. Assmann 2011, 196).[5] In the ancient experience, forty years can be the point where the generational memory ceases to function and a new group of memory carriers has to negotiate the crossing of a difficult *memorial threshold*. Classic Gospel criticism has been well aware of the generational gap, generally referred to as the passing of the eyewitnesses, but has more often than not handled it in the interest of an uninterrupted continuity of tradition. *The concept of memorial threshold suggests a reconfiguration of memories at crucial stages in mnemohistory.* One of Assmann's prime examples is the book of Deuteronomy (1992, 50–51, 212–22), fictionalized as Moses' farewell speech and addressed to the Israelites, who after forty years of wandering in the wilderness (Deut 1:4) were encamped on the plains of Moab and poised to enter the promised land. What is

---

5. "40 Jahre sind ein Einschnitt, eine Krise in der kollektiven Erinnerung. Wenn eine Erinnerung nicht verlorengehen soll, dann muss sie aus der biographischen in kulturelle Erinnerung transformiert werden" (1992, 218).

of interest to Assmann is Deuteronomy's complex interfacing with Israel's social, cultic, and memorial history. As is well known, Deuteronomy, or parts thereof, is by a broad scholarly agreement identified as "the book of the law" that was discovered in connection with King Josiah's restoration of the temple (2 Kgs 22:1–23:3) and used in the royal cultic reform. The primary objective of that reform was the centralization of the cult place, an undertaking that was meant to result in the termination of polytheism and syncretism, and the closing or destruction of numerous cult places. Josiah's forced centralization amounted to a revolution of such unprecedented harshness and terror—in some ways comparable to Akhenaten-Amenophis IV's monotheistic revolution in fourteenth-century-B.C.E. Egypt—that it generated a serious caesura in Israel's history (J. Assmann 1992, 216, also n. 44), which cried out for explanation and guidance. There lies a deep memorial significance in the fact that Deuteronomy, framed as Moses' legacy of coping with ancient Israel's *Traditionsbruch* and identity crisis following some forty years of wilderness existence, came to serve as a legitimating remembrance for another *Traditionsbruch*, Josiah's cultic revolution in the seventh century. In the wake of King Josiah's radical reform, one returned to the sacred past and the foundational figure of Moses, whose extensive farewell speech provided guidance for Israel's crisis in the seventh century. Archaeology of memory (regression into the past), commemoration of a foundational personage, memorial crisis (or memorial threshold), and media link with writing all come together in a memory thesis of considerable explanatory value.

Based on this exposition of cultural memory, is it too far-fetched to draw an analogy with the Gospel of Mark in defining and illuminating its historic location at a seminal juncture in early Christian history? As we saw above, the chirographic medium can generate the kind of distancing that is necessary to construct alternate visions in the face of extant memories, loyalties, and imperatives. If we date the Gospel some forty years after the death of the charismatic leader and in all likelihood in the aftermath of the destruction of Jerusalem in 70 C.E., one could conceivably understand the document as a narrative mediation of a threefold crisis: the death of Jesus, the devastation of Jerusalem culminating in the conflagration of the temple, and the cessation of a generation of memories and memory carriers. Could we not be dealing here with an example of a *Traditionsbruch* that, following the initial trauma of Jesus' death, was acutely compounded by a secondary dislocation some forty years later? Does not the Gospel make sense when we imagine its historical place at a point where present events severely challenged Jesus' commemorated past(s)? And could not the well-known "oddness" of Mark's Gospel be an index of a particular situation that called for a reformulation and reorientation of the collective memories of Jesus?

Ever since the historical-critical methodology has ascertained Markan priority, interpreters have (frequently) been inclined to view the Gospel in light of its assumed foundational status. If it is the earliest Gospel available, can it not be expected to carry the features of a foundational document? Both the thesis of Markan priority and the imposition of Matthean and Lukan reading grids have influenced our interpretation of Mark. But do the Gospel's uncommonly puzzling features truly fit the characteristics of a foundational text? The Gospel of Matthew would seem to come much closer to serve as base and standard for the fledgling movement that was about to develop into the church. Matthew 16:16–19, the narration of Peter's investiture, is the constitutional declaration par excellence. Hence canonical Christianity's decision to view Matthew as the first Gospel written and for this reason to place it in primary position in the canon. Now modern scholarship has by a wide margin of consensus accepted Markan priority. But again, has the priority thesis unduly influenced our readings of Mark? Is it conceivable that a Gospel as enigmatic, parabolic, and unsettled as Mark's Gospel could qualify as the primary foundational document? The oldest available Gospel no doubt, there is a sense in which it is antifoundational more than foundational. To account for the puzzling "oddness" of Mark, could the Gospel, far from constituting primary foundationalism, perhaps manifest a secondary foundation not necessarily in reaffirmation of, but as a corrective gesture vis-à-vis an antecedent tradition, narrating a reconfiguration of prior memories?

Mark's Gospel, we saw, is ill explained as the product of stable mnemonics or the repository of archivally transmitted memories, or, in my view, as direct autograph of oral traditions. Nor, we reiterate, is it simply the result of intra-Gospel processes or the calculated arbitration of literary sources. Instead, it is suggested, the Gospel's deepest compositional motivation was a regressive gesture into Jesus' recent past to recapture him as an *Erinnerungsfigur* and into Israel's *distant past* for the benefit of solidifying present group identity. One regressed into what was to become the sacred past, remembering the beginnings of the renewal movement, focusing on life and death of the charismatic leader, and one did so in narrative form that accounted for and provided guidance under new and difficult circumstances. At this point, we can return to and sharpen our earlier thesis of the Gospel composition. Granted that all remembering is a mediation of commemorated pasts with the present, *the special case of Mark suggests that we have to do with a second-order rememorization, that is, a redescription of the memories of Jesus in the wake of an excruciatingly painful Traditionsbruch that had compounded the initial trauma.*

Apart from Mark there are numerous reconfigurations of early memories in the canonical tradition of New Testament texts. One example must suffice. Esler (2005, 151–71) in an essay on collective memory in the Letter to the Hebrews united oral and memory theory in interpreting the panoply of ancestral witnesses of faith in Hebrews as product of contested memories. Chapter 11 of the letter reaches far back into Israel's remote past and revisits the figures of Abel, Enoch, Noah, Abraham, and Moses of times long gone by. As far as Abel is concerned, whom Hebrews introduces as man of faith *and* righteousness, only the latter occurs twice in Israel's tradition. The description of Enoch by the author of Hebrews as faithful, while not entirely absent from the ancestral tradition, is used very sparingly. The characterization of Noah is altered in similar fashion. The letter describes him as "an heir to the righteousness that is in accordance with faith" (Heb 11:7), but tradition has granted him only righteousness (Gen 6:9; 7:1), not faith; his attribute of perfection (Gen 6:9), moreover, is left unmentioned. In the case of Abraham, the father of Israel, his well-known righteousness is ignored in Heb 11 and retrojected back onto Abel. Moses, finally, is unknown in the tradition as a man of faith. All five personalities are introduced as paragons of faith, and thereby assimilated to the Christ movement, largely in conflict with Israel's tradition. It is Esler's contention that Hebrews' rememorization of primordial memories is "explicable within the constraints and opportunities of a residually oral culture characterized by high levels of illiteracy" (2005, 171). Far from consulting the ancient documents for purposes of textual revision, Hebrews operated memorially in oral contextuality. What we find in Hebrews 11, Esler concludes, is a rememorization of ancient traditions in the interest of establishing and reinforcing the identity of the Christ movement. Oral medium and memory, and not textual exegesis or intertextuality, lie at the heart of the processes we observe in Heb 11. As was the case with the Gospels, an archaeology of memory operates that retrieves the venerable, deep past for present identification. In J. Assmann's terms, the process of rememorization not only stabilizes and continues the past, but, in operating selectively, also generates a degree of forgetfulness, distortion even, of prior memories in the interest of constructing memory in new circumstances.

71. Commemoration of Jesus' Death

Perhaps no event in Christian origins has made greater demands on memory than Jesus' death. How is memory to deal with the massively disruptive trauma of the crucifixion? We shall not reflect here on the faith of resurrection, which is a modality of overcoming death more than a remembering of it. In the perspectives of the psychodynamics of remembering, distance is a prerequisite for facing up to the death of Jesus—the absence it induced, the silence it brought, and the psycho-chaos of grief. As far as the visual medium is concerned, it is noteworthy that depictions of the crucifixion were rare in the early Christian period. There are no crucifixion scenes in the Roman catacombs and sarcophagi, and the crucifixion is absent from a number of fourth-century passion cycles (Spier 2008, 227–36). One wonders, therefore, whether the classic form-critical principle that the passion narrative constituted one of the oldest coherent narrative pieces of the Gospel tradition, and one constructed in close proximity to the historical events, does not trivialize the ordeal of remembering the violent death. Does not, in this case, historical criticism exhibit a sense of intellectual insensitivity, failing to probe the deeper springs that motivated and fed the story of death? The relative narrative coherence of the passion narrative, implicitly or explicitly given as indication of early composition, proves first and foremost narrative competence and nothing about its date of composition, date of production, or closeness to the events narrated (Kelber 1983, 184–99). Psychodynamically, is it conceivable that the traumatic death was the first event negotiated in coherent narrative? Or does one not have to stand apart from the trauma—temporally, mentally, emotionally—so as to be able to bear and to assimilate it?

Our earlier observation that the past exists only as remembered past applies with special force to the events surrounding the crucifixion. *No event in Christian origins is less likely to be transmitted in its factual rawness, and no experience more in need of mnemonic frames and mediating patterns than Jesus' death.* The eucharistic ritual is, of course, one way of absorbing the shock effects of the execution and securing its ritual representation. The passion narrative is another way designed to mediate the violence in accessible categories. It "was not a matter of simply relating the facts," A. Dewey rightly states (2005, 14), challenging conventional lack of attention to the difficulties entailed in bringing the shocking event into narrative reality. One way of making the trauma of violence socially accessible was to tap into Israel's memorial repertoire, both recent and ancient, in search of *memory places* that were capable of localizing as well as humanizing the unrepresentable. Two scholars have contributed to the discovery of the Markan passion narrative as memory place. In a widely discussed article, Nickelsburg (1980), working in a fashion similar to Vladimir Propp's structuralism, examined narrative texts such as the Joseph stories in Gen 37–50, the story of *Ahikar*, the book of Esther, Dan 3 and 6, and Susanna, and uncovered a theme common to all of them: the Tale of the Persecution and Vindication of the Innocent One. The components of this Tale, Nickelsburg demonstrated, make up the basic structure of Mark's passion narrative. The observed commonality of the theme in a variety of narratives then prompted Nickelsburg to speak of a generic source. Following Nickelsburg, A. Dewey suggested that the tradition-honored Tale served Mark—and Matthew and Luke via Mark's mediation—as memory place on which the trauma of the crucifixion could be constructed. In his view, the Tale of the Persecution and Vindication of the Innocent One proved to be an accessible category that could serve as locus for the narrative representation of Jesus' death.

Yet another way of mediating the unspeakable was the well-known feature of tapping "a catena of ancient texts" (Kermode 1979, 104), Pss 22 and 69 in particular, which contributed significantly to the composition of the passion narrative. There is a tendency among interpreters to explicate the passion narrative's compliance with ancient biblical texts in terms of the doctrinal schematization of promise and fulfillment. Even Kermode, literary critic par excellence, thinks of the Psalm passages as "a prophecy or promise ... that will later be kept, though perhaps in unexpected ways" (106). But what if one were to approach the passion narrative with a view toward the difficulties of remembering Jesus' death, and understand the Psalm references as an "interpretive keying" (Kirk 2005a, 194; Schwartz 2005b), a mode of aligning the present to the sacred, scriptural past, thereby creating a memorial template as it were, that furnished storied components for the narration of the violence. Again, the effect was as to make the unrepresentable comprehensible within older, familiar patterns.

Even the hypothetical Q, traditionally assumed to have been silent on Jesus' death, engaged in commemorative maneuvers to mediate the passion (Kirk 2005a), although in a decidedly oblique way. In invoking Israel's commonplace of the death-of-prophets (Luke 11:49–51), an archetypical memory of violence, Q by implication has keyed Jesus' own death to the fate of prophetic personalities in Jewish history. Without expounding Jesus' crucifixion, Q has nonetheless summoned forth an ancient memory of Israel, a commemorative frame as it were, for referencing and orienting the primal violence that had traumatized the Jesus movement.

72. HISTORICAL SCHOLARSHIP'S *DAMNATIO MEMORIAE*

Biblical studies as an academic discipline is by and large the product of particular cultural developments that originated in the late Middle Ages, accelerated in Europe's premodern period, and acquired a historically identifiable profile in seventeenth- and eighteenth-century Enlightenment. Informed by nominalism's skepticism toward the transcendental signified (and a corresponding privileging of the literal sense), deeply influenced by the high tech of the fifteenth century, and spurred on by logic's (typography's logic!) imperial drive toward the formulation and implementation of method, the academic approach to the Bible increasingly came to understand itself as historical-critical scholarship.

Among the key features that typify the historical approach to the Bible, the following may be cited: the exploration of the historical conditionedness of texts both in regard to their genesis and with a view toward authorial intentionality; reliance on the literal, that is, historical, sense (*sensus literalis sive historicus*); an almost single-minded focus on texts, intertextuality, literary sources, and textual-stratification theories; interest in the production of texts more than in their consumption; and *originalism*, a fascination with questions of origin and the search for the authentic, authorial meaning of texts. The historical paradigm enjoys immense prestige and, one should say, political power in academia. And yet: in the centuries that saw the rise and flowering of historical-critical scholarship, memory has not fared well, nor has orality. But if a broad spectrum of issues related to memory and orality was intrinsic to our ancient Jewish, Greco-Roman, and Christian legacies, and to ancient Mediterranean *humanitas* at large, does not the virtual absence of memory in the historical paradigm raise questions how truly culture-bound and culture-blind it is?

During the last century, the virtual absence of memory from the historical scholarship was to no small extent correlated with the methodology and practices of form criticism. Because the methodological assumptions inherent in form criticism held sway over the longest part of biblical scholarship in the twentieth century, the critical analysis and gradual demise of the method, dramatically hastened by Güttgemanns (1970) and reinforced by growing insights both into oral, rhetorical culture and the narrative nature of the Gospels, carries far-reaching implications for the discipline. What we are wrestling with are not merely the flaws of a particular method, but the inadequacy of a theory that was fundamental to our understanding of the verbal art in biblical studies.

Separately and interactively, orality/scribality studies and social memory (and narrative criticism (in the case of the Gospels) have the potential of exposing the flaws of the historical premises of form criticism and its complicity with modernity's typographical mode of thought. Separately and interactively, orality/scribality and social memory (and narrative criticism) hold it within their powers to point in the direction of a reformulation of the historical paradigm. In the end, it may come down to an understanding of the intersections of oral, scribal, narrative, and memorial dynamics, or simply of the interfacing of memory with manuscript. But memory, we suspect, may hold the key.

12

ORALITY AND BIBLICAL SCHOLARSHIP:
SEVEN CASE STUDIES

This essay reviews seven books that treat the subject of oraliy and scribality in the Bible, talmudic literature, and world religions. All are landmark studies committed to the orality-scribality-memory-performance paradigm, and all contribute to the (re)discovery of the oral factor in ancient texts. This review essay invites readers to reevaluate the historical-critical, strictly text-focused reading of biblical and rabbinic traditions in the broader media context of ancient Near Eastern and Mediterranean communications realities.

The first part introduces the field of orality-scribality studies and the seven books under review, which have significantly contributed to the new paradigm. The second part reviews William Graham's Beyond the Written Word, *a study of the function of sacred Scripture in a broadly comparative context of the history of religion. In all major religious traditions, the author observes, the authority of Holy Writ derives from its recited, living actuality, not from its textual materiality. David Carr, whose* Writing on the Tablet of the Heart *is the subject of the third part, has introduced the conceptual model of enculturation to define the workings of the verbal arts in the ancient Near Eastern and Mediterranean world. Accordingly, the rationale of a vast majority of ancient writings was not their scripted existence per se but their internalization in people's minds and hearts. The fourth part discusses Susan Niditch's* Oral World and Written Word: Ancient Israelite Literature, *which illuminates the texts of the Hebrew Bible on a sliding scale of an oral-scribal continuum. Writing played a significant role in ancient Israel, yet biblical texts, even those that are located toward the literate end, were largely informed by an oral aesthetic. Martin Jaffee's* Torah in the Mouth, *the subject of the fifth part of this essay, illuminates the rabbinic tradition as a process of complex interpenetration of oral and scribal activities whereby the texts came to be located between recitation and reoralization. Focusing*

*specifically on the rabbinic concept of the oral Torah, the author argues that
it did not originate with the Pharisees but was the result of later reflections
in rabbinic Judaism on its own history and origin. Erhardt Güttgemanns's*
Offene Fragen zur Formgeschichte des Evangeliums, *reviewed in the sixth
part, has articulated one of the most forceful analytical challenges to the
discipline of form criticism. Based on the premise of a differentiated treatment of oral versus written communication, the book questions fundamental
form-critical premises: the model of a pre-Gospel tradition, the genesis and
nature of the narrative Gospel genre, the identification and detachability of
identifiable oral units, and the notion of "the original form" and variants
thereof. What Horsley (with Draper) has given us in* Whoever Hears You
Hears Me *in the seventh part of this essay is a study of Q as an oral-derived
text. Firmly grounded in the cultural matrix of Israel, Q consists of a series of
discourses that are designed to function in oral performance and recitation.
The eighth part, finally, discusses David Parker's* The Living Text of the Gospels, *a text-critial study of the intricacies of papyrological variability in the
early Jesus tradition. Such are the processes of the living tradition that any
assumption of or search for the single, original saying is pointless.*

> Even in the Western world only a fraction of Christians and Jews before
> the nineteenth century were able to read for themselves any part of their
> holy scriptures; only a tiny fraction of all people around the world, from
> the beginning of history to the present day, who have lived in any com-
> munity with a sacred scripture, have ever been able to read a word of
> their holy writ.
>
> —William Graham, *Beyond the Written Word*

> This study has reinforced my skepticism about text-critical attempts to
> reconstruct an eclectic ur-text of biblical books for times preceding the
> identification of authoritative reference copies against which other texts
> written in the same tradition could be corrected.
>
> —David Carr, *Writing on the Tablet of the Heart*

> While indeed there is much evidence of the increasing importance of
> reading and writing in ancient Israel, especially in commercial, military,
> and political realms, we have shown how even such texts and practices
> provide evidence not of modern literacy but of a continuum or sliding
> scale in which the aesthetics, purposes of, and attitudes to writing are
> circumscribed by an oral mentality.
>
> —Susan Niditch, *Oral World and Written Word*

What is clear is that the continuous loop of manuscript and performance had no "ground zero" at which we can isolate at a distance of many centuries an oral text or tradition as fundamental.

—Martin Jaffee, *Torah in the Mouth*

But NT (and also OT) form criticism now faces the question about the legitimacy of viewing the different variants transmitted only by "literary" means, such as a credo, the doublets of a miracle story, etc., as *form-critical* variations of an *Urfassung*, which literary criticism on methodological grounds has more and more viewed as a scholarly phantom.

—Erhardt Güttgemanns, *Candid Questions concerning Gospel Form Criticism*

All of these aspects of Mark's relation to Israelite tradition suggest that the author/story is working not from written texts but from memory/oral tradition, as were Paul and the rabbis when they referred to biblical traditions.

—Richard Horsley, *Whoever Hears You Hears Me*

There is a sense in which there is no such thing as either the New Testament or the Gospels. What is available to us is a number of reconstructions of some or all of the documents classified as belonging to the New Testament.

—David Parker, *The Living Text of the Gospels*

73. The Oral Factor and the Issue of Illiteracy

In keeping with developments in the human and social sciences, we have for some time now experienced a recovery and reconsideration of the oral factor in biblical studies. Negatively speaking what is at stake is a challenge to what Foley has called "the textualist bias of our scholarship, with its easy assimilation of all forms of verbal art to the literary-textual model" (1995, 87). This text-centered perspective has involved a sense of textual autonomy, textualization as an end in itself, texts' localization in intertextual networks, and a dominantly textual hermeneutics—all notions closely allied with the historical and literary paradigm. What the seven books reviewed in this essay, despite their different historical contexts, have in common is an understanding that many ancient texts and sacred texts globally have roots not simply in other texts but in oral tradition and cultural memory, and above all in a continuous loop of oral-scribal-memorial interactivities. The point made in studies of the Hebrew Bible

(Niditch), the New Testament (Horsley), and rabbinics (Jaffee) is that biblical and rabbinic texts are unthinkable apart from the oral factor. A fourth book, partially relying on A. Lord's empirical studies of a living oral tradition, explores the failure of New Testament scholarship to acquire a historically and theoretically adequate grasp of the oral factor and to articulate its role in Gospel studies (Güttgemanns). In the area of New Testament studies as well, a novel approach to text criticism has recently defined the early Jesus tradition in terms that are virtually analogous to oral dynamics (Parker). Significantly broadening our conceptual lens, two authors have contributed to our understanding of the essential significance of the oral factor across ancient Near Eastern and ancient Mediterranean cultures (Carr) and on the global scale of world religions, respectively (Graham).

In support of the central point made in these books are studies that have drawn our attention to the historical phenomenon of literacy, or lack thereof, in antiquity. Prominently representative of this approach is Harris's work on *Ancient Literacy* (1989), which demonstrated authoritatively that Greco-Roman antiquity was a society with limited literacy. Making allowance for different historical periods and cultural settings, for social class and stratification, for gender and changing attitudes, Harris concluded that literacy in the ancient world had been the preserve of a very small minority. As far as formal schooling was concerned, subsidies were few or nonexistent, and the education that did exist laid heavy stress on learning by heart. Moreover, access to elementary education was limited and access to rhetorical education severely restricted to a few upper class individuals. His findings, Harris rightly assumed, "will be highly unpalatable to some classical scholars" (328), and they may well serve as a corrective to the perennial dangers of idealizing our Greco-Roman legacy. But they do not really come as a surprise to those who have been working in orality-scribality studies and who understandably have been in the habit of citing Harris in support of their position.

Yet it is precisely from the viewpoint of orality-scribality sensibilities that I find the terminological framework and conceptual premise of *Ancient Literacy* susceptible to misunderstanding and distracting from a historically commensurate apprehension of the media culture of antiquity. Undoubtedly, Harris, more than most classicists, recognized the enormous significance of memory, and he repeatedly alerted his readers to the continuing power of the oral factor among Greeks and Romans. But what to my mind is problematic is the definition of literacy and semiliteracy and its correlative of illiteracy strictly in terms of reading and writing. We are dealing with our ancient legacy that knew no mass literacy and rarely considered illiteracy a problem. Three questions come to mind. Since reading and writing are defining criteria of modern Western educated people, can we assume that these skills in fact are essential marks of Greco-Roman culture? Is not the designation of illiteracy a dangerously pejorative term that runs the risk of misunderstanding the majority of ancient people, many of whom may have been orally and memorially entirely competent? Lastly, how useful are statistical data and numerical estimates about literacy versus illiteracy in telling us anything about ancient communicative practices? It is indeed astounding how frequently the term *illiteracy* turns up not only in studies of ancient literacy but in orality-scribality studies as well.

To illustrate the difficulty we have in coming to terms with the oral factor, I revisit the figure of Avdo Mededović, whose name and accomplishments reverberate through the work of Parry and Lord. A devout Muslim living in a remote village in eastern Montenegro, Avdo was one of the last of the epic singers of the Balkan Slavic tradition of oral narrative. Never able to read or write in any language, and using the *gusle*, the simplest of string instruments, and not even gifted with a particularly attractive voice, he was able to perform songs of the length of the Homeric epics. The bulk of his performances have been recorded on phonographic discs by Parry and Lord and stored in the Milman Parry Collection at the Widener Library, Harvard University. The collected materials comprise 637 recorded sides and approximately fifty-eight hours of singing (Lord 1991, 57–71). Recognizing their comparative potential, Parry and Lord developed analogies in style, type of composition, and length with the *Iliad* and the *Odyssey*, those two erratic literary boulders on the threshold of Greek literacy. Avdo, they argued, could not have accumulated and mastered performance material of such vast proportions without a tradition of long standing behind him. In view of the established analogy with Homer, the Parry-Lord argument goes, it may not be unreasonable to view him as standing in a tradition of oral, epic singing that once was practiced by Homer, oral-traditional singer himself. This is what Lord writes about Avdo Mededvic, the singer of songs: "Avdo could sing songs of about the length of Homer's *Odyssey*. An illiterate butcher in a small town of the central Balkans was equaling Homer's feat, at least in regard to length of song" (1991, 62). Obviously, Avdo, the culture hero in the Parry-Lord studies, was "illiterate" only from the perspective of our modern alphabetic competence and literate skills. Elsewhere Lord consistently refers to Avdo as "oral-traditional singer" or as "oral-traditional poet." But the fact that even Lord, one of the major figures in the study of the oral-traditional epic narrative, could refer to Avdo in terms of illiteracy proves the intellectual challenge we face in appreciating him in strictly historical terms as *an oralist who was far more accomplished in his chosen medium than most literate people are in their medium.* We will have even greater difficulty in thinking of Homer not as a sterling literary genius but as an exceptional representative of a tradition of epic singing and in viewing the *Iliad* and the *Odyssey* as oral traditional literature, pieces that we are in the habit of teaching in the Great Books course.

The case of Mededović is not meant to be directly applicable to Greco-Roman antiquity. The key issues it raises is the difficulty we face in recognizing the oral factor and acknowledging the ancient and Near Eastern media culture in terms other than our own. By way of analogy, I raise the question whether the Greco-Roman communications culture is appropriately understood in terms of literacy versus illiteracy. The Greeks and Romans, Harris confirmed, "held on to oral procedures to a greater extent than is commonly realized" (1989, 326). In that culture, what makes a person a functional member of society is not necessarily alphabetic competence but the ability to have absorbed his or her people's traditions. A person in Greco-Roman antiquity who is conversant with (parts of) Homer, the culture hero, plus local laws, medical knowledge, political declarations, lists, poems, and songs will be a fully functional citizen without the ability to read and write. Literacy versus illiteracy is not the issue it has become in the premodern and modern West.

The seven books that will be discussed in this essay all contribute to our understanding of the oral factor in written texts, and all challenge us to be alert to a sizeable blind spot in the historical and literary paradigm whose methods and sensibilities are largely derived from our continuous working with printed texts.

74. GRAHAM: *BEYOND THE WRITTEN WORD*

Although published twenty years ago, William Graham's book has remained a classic whose significance has only grown over the years. *Beyond the Written Word* (1987) does not, strictly speaking, belong to the field of oral traditional literature or orality-scribality studies. But it ranks in its pioneering spirit and intellectual acumen with the pertinent scholarship of Albert Lord, Eric Havelock, and Walter Ong, eminent humanists who have been instrumental in advancing our understanding of the oral component in the verbal arts. Graham is a historian of religion and a specialist in Islamic religious history. But the relevance of his work extends far beyond the history of religion. Biblical scholars, I suspect, will yet have to discover the intellectual fecundity of his findings. His prime concern is Scripture, or sacred texts, perceived as a general phenomenon in the major religious traditions and in the popular and scholarly practices of Western modernity. Meticulously researched, internationally documented, and written with a high degree of nuance, the book examines the overwhelmingly oral verbalization of Holy Writ in Hinduism, recitation and revelation in Muslim faith, and the audible presence and internalization of the biblical word in Christianity. Additionally, he engages principal aspects of Scripture in Judaism, Buddhism, and in numerous other religious traditions. In setting the discussion of Scripture in this broad comparative context he is able to expose concepts of the Bible that typify Western modernity. Scripture, he explains, is not primarily a literary genre, something that it has become in large measure in Western civilization, but is, when viewed in the global context of the history of religion, something more, and indeed other than, a literary genre. That is to say, whereas in Western modernity the relatively recent paradigm for Scripture is the tangible document of the print Bible, in most religious traditions, both ancient and contemporary, piety and practice are characterized by a high degree of *scriptural orality*. The latter is the key concept of Graham's study that allows for an understanding of Scripture both as written but very much as oral authority as well.

Scriptural orality, the author explains, is a dimension that has received little attention not merely because of the ephemeral quality of speech but also because modernity in the West has made the printed text the yardstick of civilized culture. Prior to the typographic revolution, the aural character of written texts, vocal reading and voiced texts, recitative and memorial powers dominated Western culture to a degree that is barely imaginable, especially for educated, literate people. To be sure, notions of the heavenly book, Buddhist adoration of physical copies of the sutras, veneration of the meticulously copied Torah, reverential treatment of texts of the Qur'an, and the deep respect extended to illuminated medieval Bibles all testify to the antiquity of the notion of the sacred book. But the sacrality of the written or even printed book was, and still is, in many religious traditions of a piece with its oral uses, be they recitation, preaching, singing, or chanting. In the West, Graham explains, the rapidly disseminated print culture did not immediately displace oral practices and sensibilities. Shifts in the human sensorium, the disappearance of rhetoric from the educational curriculum, and the emergence of the authority of the Bible independent of communicative functions and memory were slow in coming. It has to be remembered, Graham reminds us, that education in Western Europe did not accomplish mass literacy until the nineteenth century. But once the ubiquity of print textuality, combined with general literacy, "became the backbone of modern scholarship" (23), a narrowly culture-bound concept of Scripture gained ascendancy that is now shared by many across the spectrum of diverse Jewish and Christian identities: "The literalist's book religion of the Protestant fundamentalist, the conscious or unconscious image of the biblical text in the mind of the average person of whatever religious persuasion, and the liberal scholar's historical-critical understanding of he Bible's genesis are part of the same wider orientation" (48).

Graham exhibits exquisite sensibilities in drawing a vivid picture of the role of the Qur'an in Muslim society. It was in fact, he writes, his personal experience and study of the oral dimension of the Qur'an that inspired his explorations into the oral aspects of Scripture more widely. Such is the intrinsic orality and abiding oral presence of the Qur'an that it can hardly be overstated. From a very early point on, the recitative character of the Qur'an was central to Muslim perception and practice of Scripture, and Arabic—rather than vernacular translations—has remained the sacred scriptural language. Perceived as God's *ipsissima vox*, the vocally transmitted text is memorized, internalized, and repeated as divine speech, and expected to live on the lips and in the hearts of the faithful. Qur'anic recitation and cantillation manifests itself in a variety of "authentic" versions and covers a range of recitational styles, widely understood to be activities that generate blessings and forgiveness. By varying degrees and in numerous communicative modalities, the public sphere of Muslim societies is scripturally saturated: the virtual omnipresence of Qur'anic cantillation, educational memorization, Qur'anic enactments at religious events and personal festivities, the use of the Qur'an in worship, and the permeation of religious and traditional scholarly language with the vocabulary and phraseology of the Arabic Scripture. It is true, much attention is paid to the material text in the elaborately designed and illuminated copies of holy Scripture. But the developed calligraphic art notwithstanding, there always is "functional primacy of the oral text over the written one" (110). This vocal presence of Scripture predominates into the present. When in the early twentieth century something of a textus receptus was composed, the collaborative work by Muslim scholars was largely based on oral memory traditions—and hailed by Western text critical scholars as a remarkable feat of a critical edition.

Graham's discussion of Christian Scripture primarily focuses on Pachomian monasticism and the Protestant Reformation. In Pachomianism, which served as model for later Christian monastic practice and piety, the centrality of Scripture was conspicuous and scriptural presence was primarily an oral and aural one. The minds of the desert monks were disciplined by memorization, which facilitated a sustained recitation of texts. Meditation did not mean silent contemplation in the reflective, interiorized sense alone, but an exercise that included recitation *viva voce* as well. Monastic life was truly scriptural life in the sense that it was permeated, paced, and governed by the recited, living words of Scripture. Hence, memorization, meditation, and recitation implemented the oral presence of Scripture in the Pachomian communities.

The functional orality of Christian Scripture, Graham shows, did not end with the waning of the Middle Ages. The Protestant Reformers manifested profoundly oral sensibilities with respect to Scripture. *Sola scriptura* notwithstanding, Scripture remained a living presence. Martin Luther, Martin Bucer, John Calvin, and John Bunyan spoke and wrote a scripturally saturated language, not for the most part for proof-texting purposes but because they were at home in Scripture, and Scripture in them. Luther, although "the first truly prolific and widely read author of the printed word in the West" (147), was still far from viewing the printed page as silent and standing on its own.

"Does it really matter," Graham asks, "that our modern Western experience of texts may not be normative (and may even be genuinely aberrant) when seen in a larger historical perspective?" (159). Yes, it does, is his emphatic answer, as long as we rely on modern communication standards in dealing with texts that belong to a very different time in history.

The story Graham narrates is both universal and detailed, but never less than absorbing. Scriptural orality expounds a grand vision of the piety and practice of sacred Scripture. To the extent that biblical scholars have focused attention on the textual, documentary, and literary history of the Bible, Graham's work merits their close attention. Of particular interest should be the author's understanding of the theology of the biblical Word in the Reformation, a period that was instrumental in shaping what eventually came to be the historical-critical paradigm. It is at this point that I wish to add what is not necessarily a corrective to Graham's reading, but a broader hermeneutical, philosophical context in which the Reformers' undoubtedly oral sense of Scripture may be viewed. I would claim that the typographic apotheosis of the Bible deeply affected their theological thinking on matters of scriptural authority and tradition, on memory and interpretation. When we think of Luther's rejection of the medieval fourfold sense of Scripture in the interest of the one sense, his increasingly high regard for the *sensus literalis*, his repudiation of allegory and all nonliteral senses, his unprecedented elevation of *sola scriptura*, his belief in the Bible's self-interpreting capacity, the steady marginalization of memory, and, perhaps most ominously, his rejection of tradition, in the interest of a sole emphasis on Scripture, we observe a reification of the biblical text that was to create a high degree of plausibility for thinking of the Bible as standing on its own.

75. CARR: *WRITING ON THE TABLET OF THE HEART*

Carr's exceedingly ambitious book discusses ways in which people in the ancient Near Eastern world produced, worked, and lived with texts or, more specifically, ways in which writing and literature functioned orally, scribally, memorially in ancient educational contexts. *Writing on the Tablet of the Heart* (2005) is erudite at every step and broadly comparative, building on a stream of North American and international scholarship. The first part commences with the Sumero-Akkadian scribal-educational system of Mesopotamia and its modes of textual production, and then turns to Mesopotamian influence on Elam (in what is now Iran), ancient Syria, the Hittite culture in Anatolia (modern Turkey), Canaan and the Phoenician city of Ugarit, and on to Syro-Palestinian culture. This is followed by a study of Egyptian education and textuality, links between Egyptian and Sumero-Akkadian scribal cultures, and Sumero-Akkadian and Egyptian influences on Israel. This part of the book concludes with a treatment of the educational curriculum and production of cultural texts in ancient Greece, and the epigraphic and literary evidence of education in pre-Hellenistic Israel. The second part commences with an examination of education and textuality in the eastern Hellenistic world, including Egypt and Hellenistic Judaism, giving special consideration to Qumran as a model of a Second Temple Judaism that had structured communal life apart from the temple. Next, Carr takes up forms of early Jewish textuality and education linked with Sabbath observance at synagogues and no longer directly associated with the temple. The author develops a nuanced treatment of the growing consolidation of Jewish texts into the Torah-Prophets corpus, the forerunner of what came to be the Hebrew Bible. He traces this development to the early second century B.C.E., when Hasmonean policy sought to promote a Hebrew focal point for Jewish identity vis-à-vis the dominant Hellenistic educational system. In short, Carr understands the consolidation of Hebrew Scripture as a phenomenon of cultural resistance. Processes of scriptural solidification, he concludes, tend to be associated with centralized institutions of power, ranging from Mesopotamian kingdoms to the Egyptian monarchy, and from the Athenian democracy to Hasmonean Israel, and all the way to Constantinian Christianity—rabbinism's Mishnaic and talmudic scriptural consolidations, I would say, being an exception. Three streams of textual-educational cultures persist into late antiquity: Greek and Latin materials, Christian materials (including the Greek Old and New Testament), and rabbinic materials (including the Hebrew Bible). All three represented transnational entities, transcending traditional geographical and cultural boundaries.

The ancient writing culture, be it in stone, parchment, or papyrus, manifested itself in different alphabetic systems and cultural contexts. The Sumerian and Akkadian cuneiform script, incised mostly on tablets, featured elite literacy designed to train (mostly) male scribes for administrative and ritual functions. Initially devoted to the genre of lists, it later expanded toward letters, hymns, treatises, and gnomic materials. In Egypt, hieroglyphic inscriptions and cursive chirography served primarily as a means of induction into the sacral, royal bureaucratic elite. Neither in the Mesopotamian nor in Egyptian culture do we recognize an identifiable social institution that was responsible for writing, although a long tradition points to temples as locations for text collections. In ancient Greece, the principal purpose of chirographic activities shifted from the training of a scribal elite toward the formation of an aristocratic class of Greek citizens. Homer now took the place of lexical lists in Mesopotamia and of wisdom instruction in Egypt. In ancient Israel, all literate specialists were officials of some kind: scribes, kings, priests, and administrators. We observe the rise of a still fluid and growing textual curriculum, with Deuteronomy and the Mosaic Torah at the center of a temple-oriented community governed by priests. The Hellenistic period witnessed a formidable expansion of both production and consumption of texts. Gymnasia became focal points of Hellenistic culture, although literary activities at these places appear to have taken second place to athletics. In the Second Temple period, much of the indigenous textuality, including the pseudepigraphic writings, appear to have links with the temple and priestly authorities, although in Hellenistic Judaism as in Hellenistic culture generally, the use of writing and texts was no longer the privileged medium of scribal elites. Early Judaism increasingly linked scribal and educational practices with synagogal centers and nonpriestly authorities. While early Christianity rapidly turned to the codex form for Scriptures, using it in largely oral contexts, early Judaism continued to sanctify its Scriptures in scrolls, with the "Oral Torah" coming to play a central role in rabbinic culture.

A signal achievement of Carr's study is the deliberate move away from a paradigm about the ancient verbal arts that is entrenched in typographic and purely textual modes of thinking, and the construction of a model of textual production and appropriation that is firmly situated in historically suitable media contexts. Writing, texts and literacy, he suggests, have to be understood as core constituents of educational processes. From Mesopotamia to Egypt, and from Israel to Greece and into the Hellenistic period, literacy and education were closely interconnected phenomena. Indeed, literacy and education were virtually synonymous as long as it is understood that neither concept imports what it has come to mean in European and North American cultural history. Concepts derived from the contemporary experience of literacy in the West are too narrowly focused on the rudimentary ability of reading and writing. What mattered most in ancient cultures was a "broader" literacy that went beyond alphabetic competence to include training in and mastery of the tradition. A literate person was not necessarily an alphabetically skilled individual but one knowledgeable in the tradition. Education likewise entailed far more than training in the technology of writing and reading skills. The principal aim of education was the enforcement of a standardized moral, ethnic, and social consciousness, something we might call today the cultural identity of a people. In other words, the central idea of education was socialization into the elite class and increasingly, in the Hellenistic age, into a general citizenship via the (re)inforcement of a core of cultural knowledge. For this process Carr has coined the term *education-enculturation*. Most writing and texts in the ancient world served this educational function of enculturation, with the aim of inscribing on people's minds a distinct sense of social, ethical consciousness that would mark them off from others.

Given the fact that much of ancient writing was part of this *educational-enculturational project*, what was primary was the internalization of texts on people's minds and hearts. This had implications for the social role of scribes. The training of scribes predominantly occurred in family apprenticeship settings or in homes and workshops of master scribes, and far less frequently than is often assumed in schools run by professional teachers. Ideally, scribal training entailed both alphabetic skills for the purpose of (re)writing the cultural texts and the mental ingestion of these scripted materials. That is to say, scribes were expected to possess or acquire mastery of their core writings by way of memorization and recitation. Our scholarly designation of scribes, connoting strictly writing activities, is thus too limited a term to characterize the professional role and identity of ancient scribes. Memorization, scribality, and recitation were intertwined aspects of the enculturation processes, and scribes were the principal custodians of the authoritative curriculum.

The enculturation model also had implications for the composition and transmission of texts. The notion of scribes copying an extant text, or juggling multiple texts that were physically present to them is, for the most part, not a fitting model for the communication dynamics in the ancient world. Undoubtedly, texts were written down, stored, consulted, and also copied. But the core tradition was not primarily carried forward by copying of texts. Rather, scribes who were literate in the core curriculum carried texts as mental templates, using them, recasting them, and/or repeating them. They had ingested the tradition consisting of one or more than one text so as to be able to rewrite the tradition without any need for physical texts. Rewriting texts was a hallmark of enculturation processes. Biblical texts in particular bear clear marks of "recensional" activities, which have provided the basis for source and documentary theories. Carr's enculturation model suggests that "editing," "copying" and "revising," "recension," "original version" and "variants"—the nomenclature of historical-critical scholarship—seems for the most part ill-suited to come to terms with the transaction of most ancient manuscripts. Biblical texts, along with many other ancient texts, that were orally, memorially, and scribally transmitted from generation to generation Carr aptly describes as *long-duration texts*. These were texts in process, representing a fluid, mental, scribal, memorial model of transmission that challenges modern scholarly efforts at retrieving the single, authoritative, or original text.

Carr has given us a strong thesis, a conceptual model that is both comprehensive and thematically focused. Strong theses tend to be risk-taking ventures because they are intrinsically vulnerable to queries from many different angles. Should more allowance be made for processes of faithful copying of texts after all? To balance the picture, should more be said about texts such as economic, agricultural, and military records, which were preserved for pragmatic purposes as materials designed for consultation more than enculturation? How can tendencies toward standardization of texts be weighted against tradition in process of the long-duration texts? The thesis of an early dating of the consolidation of a recognizable body of Jewish texts into the Torah-Prophets corpus in the early second century B.C.E. may have to be balanced with the phenomenon of scriptural multiformity that is manifest in the Dead Sea documents. But then again, biblical studies need strong theses. In the words of Eldon Epp, "What is needed is a microscope with less power of magnification so that our field of vision is broader." Carr has given us this kind of vision that challenges biblical scholarship to reflect on the phenomenology, use, and formation of biblical texts in broader cultural settings.

76. NIDITCH: *ORAL WORLD AND WRITTEN WORD IN ISRAELITE LITERATURE*

Niditch's book is strictly focused on the Hebrew Bible, but broadly developed against the background of ancient Near Eastern cultures. While Carr operated with the educational-enculturational model, Niditch's *Oral World and Written Word in Israelite Culture* (1996) uses the concept of an *oral-literate continuum* as explanatory paradigm. Based on this model, she locates the Bible's literature either toward the literate end of the continuum, like the frequent references to the written Torah, or toward the oral end, as epitomized by Ezekiel's swallowing of the scroll (2:9–3:11), or at oral-literate interfaces, as in frequent examples to write down in order to recite (Exod 17:14–16). Niditch's major objective, therefore, is to illuminate biblical texts according to their location on the sliding scale of oral-scribal communications. It is not that writing played no role in ancient Israel, she explains, but rather that the function of writing and texts was unlike that of modern literacy. The oral-literate-continuum model postulates that literacy in ancient Israel and in traditional societies in general ought to be understood in continuity with an oral world. In that sense her model negates the Great Divide theory, which views oral and scribal dynamics in oppositional terms. In Niditch's understanding, the texts of the Hebrew Bible are variously informed by the aesthetics of orality because the "Israelites lived in an essentially oral world" (44). Written word and oral world, therefore, interact complexly and the Bible derives much of its force and effect from the dynamics of this oral-literate interplay.

While Niditch takes a cautionary approach with regard to oral compositional processes of Hebrew texts as developed by Parry and Lord, she explores, in chapters 1 and 2, what she calls "traditional Israelite aesthetics" (38). Linguistically, they manifest themselves in stylistic, phraseological, and thematic features such as repetition, recurring formulae, epithets, topoi, conventional scenes, and many more. These features, she explains, are not to be understood merely as rhetorical devices to accommodate audiences, to create strong impressions, or to profile key messages but rather as signifying elements of considerable import in creating meaning. Relying on the work of John Miles Foley, she interprets the conventional and stylized patterns as *metonymic signifiers* that tap into the larger tradition so as to bring it to the hearing of the text. In Foley's words, traditional and conventional language invokes "the ever-impinging presence of the extra-textual, summoned into the process of interpretation" (1991, 45). Obviously, this understanding of the Bible's traditional language is contrary to the work of those modern literary critics who derive meaning strictly from the internal configuration in texts. Traditional Israelite aesthetics, as perceived by Niditch (and Foley), evoke a reservoir that is deeper and larger than the particularity of any single text.

In chapters 3 and 4 Niditch examines a wide spectrum of oral-literary relations in a variety of cultural contexts ranging from the Near East and ancient Greece to medieval Europe and early twentieth-century Yugoslavia. These ethnographic parallels serve to place Israel's practice and self-understanding of writing and literacy in historical perspectives. Special attention is given to epigraphic materials, archives, and the material media of communication. Inscriptions on monuments, she states, often fulfill symbolic, religious functions more than providing service to a public readership. For example, the late eighth-century-B.C.E. inscription on the wall of the water tunnel connecting old Jerusalem with a spring to the east of the city was intended to commemorate—in the literate mode—the feat of engineering by preserving information that, however, remained inaccessible to the populace. But the inscription also belongs to the genre of graffito that is "the poor man's monument" (55), and hence closer to the oral mode. Archives and libraries (Ugarit, Ebla, Mari, Assur, Nineveh, Alexandria, Pergamum) appear to be designed for systematic long-term record keeping in the modern sense. Indeed, in some instances the archival materials give the impression of being marked for identification, consultation, and retrieval, suggesting the beginnings of our cataloging system. Some archival deposits, however, are more on the order of temporary storage places. Others lack any recognizable systematic ordering or seem to limit access to the elite. Even where archives or libraries are used for purposes of consultation, one must not immediately assume that the archived texts functioned as norms for memory and oral tradition. By no means implausible is the reverse procedure: oral tradition was perceived to be the standard on the basis of which archival texts were subject to rewriting. The writing materials (stone, ostraca [broken shards], wooden tablets, wax-coated boards, papyrus, parchment, metal, ivory) give evidence of different social circumstances and purposes for writing. Techniques of inscribing on these materials required special scribal training and skills, turning the ancient scribe into "a sort of performer" (75), once again suggesting an intriguing blending of the literary with the oral, performative mode.

In chapter 4 Niditch directs attention to the phenomenon of textual pluriformity as evidenced by the Dead Sea Scrolls and evaluated by Julio Trebolle Barrera, Emanuel Tov, and above all Eugene Ulrich. Quite possibly as late as 135 c.e. Scriptures that were eventually going to emanate into the Hebrew Bible manifested hitherto unexpected pluriformity, raising deep questions about the dating of the Masoretic textus receptus and the concept both of the "correct," authorized text and "variants." Moving beyond Niditch, I would venture to say that the scriptural pluriformity we witness in the Dead Sea Scrolls is a way, perhaps *the* way, of textual life in the Second Temple period and into the second century c.e. (see ch. 15, §99). While we are still very much in the process of assimilating the textual evidence that has been generated by the Dead Sea Scrolls, Niditch is surely right in stating that the textual multiformity exhibits "qualities of an oral register" (75).

Attitudes toward writing that are assumed by the Hebrew Bible itself are the main topic of chapters 5–7. On the one hand, writing is infused with numinous and magical qualities: the tablets of stone are written with the finger of God (Exod 31:18), investing them with special powers; the writing of names on sticks (Num 17:2–5; Ezek 37:16–17) serves to symbolize and to effect certain actions; written curses are ritualized and understood to take effect (Num 5:11–31). These and numerous other examples point to the well-known phenomenon of the oral efficaciousness of words. On the other hand, the writing of lists and genealogies, royal annals and letters, certificates and deeds approaches the literary function of record keeping, although even these documents have often retained nuances of oral dynamics. And finally, writing self-consciously operates in a dual scribal-oral role, such as the Shema (Deut 6:4–9), which is to be written on doorposts and gates, yet kept in the hearts and recited. No matter at what place on the oral-literate continuum biblical texts come to stand, they are almost always framed or colored by oral dynamics.

In conclusion, Niditch reflects on implications and applications of her studies. She advocates a reconsideration of major theories about the composition of the Hebrew Bible, foremost among them the Documentary Hypothesis regarding the Pentateuchal sources. That hypothesis, she suggests, "comes from our world and not from that of ancient Israel" (112). At the heart of it is an image like that of "Emperor Claudius of the PBS series, having his various written sources laid out before him as he chooses this verse or that, includes this tale not that, edits, elaborates, all in a library setting" (113). As regards application, Niditch hypothesizes four possible models for the genesis of the Hebrew Bible: texts originated in live performances and were written down via dictation, or orally composed but chirographically "fixed" in the interest of a pan-Israelite identity, or written in oral-traditional style, or written on the basis of an antecedent manuscript tradition. There is no single or simple trajectory that can account for the composition history of the Bible as a whole.

The author is absolutely right in arguing that all too often we assume that written manuscripts in antiquity operated like our print books. It does make a difference whether we view biblical texts from the vantage point of print-conditioned notions of textuality or in oral-traditional contexts. But my sense it that in her work, the line that distinguishes scripturality from orality is anything but clear and often a bit blurred. It is entirely appropriate to denounce the Great Divide and opt for oral-scribal interfaces, as most of the seven authors reviewed here are doing. But we will not get around articulating with a degree of precision what meets the definition of orality and of scribality. And yet, Niditch has made a bold and admirable effort at stemming the tide of a positively overpowering textual scholarship. Something is announced here and a challenge has been posed that, if pursued further, has a potential for revising substantial aspects of biblical scholarship.

77. JAFFEE: *TORAH IN THE MOUTH*

The line of thought inaugurated by Graham and pursued by Carr and Niditch is further extended in Jaffee's work *Torah in the Mouth* (2001) in Palestinian Judaism. Certainly, oral tradition and oral Torah have long been an issue in the scholarly discussion of Second Temple and rabbinic

Judaism. The oral Torah has specifically been linked with Pharisaism, while recitation and repetition of tradition are well-established features of rabbinism. Ranging widely from the last centuries of the Second Temple period to the compilation of the Talmud, benefiting from recent orality-scribality studies, and building on a close reading of texts, the author has developed a coherent and comprehensive view of the oral-literate rabbinic tradition and its perceived relation to the Mosaic Torah.

In the first part Jaffee sketches a broad scenario of the logistics of Second Temple scribalism. Palestinian scribes in that period, he writes, worked and lived with scrolls that functioned less as reference systems for information and more as memory devices for texts often already memorized. As long as the temple existed most scribes were of priestly descent and closely associated with the central administrative system. No widespread activity of lay scribes is demonstrable. As far as scribal production of scrolls was concerned, Jaffee places heavy emphasis on dictation. Scribal dictation was "a fact of life" so much so that it was fictionalized into a "rhetoric of literary authenticity" (25), which sought to validate texts by reference to the archetypal writing or dictation by revered figures such as Moses and Enoch. Hence, scrolls originated in a human voice and in turn found authentication as aural phenomena in the performative events of recitation. In this culture where scribal products were embedded in orality scribes enjoyed ample room for creative intervention; textual closure was all but nonexistent. "Scribal orality" (16) is the designation Jaffee uses to capture this Second Temple scribalism in which "the characteristic organ of the literary life was the mouth and the ear, and its main textual reservoir was the memory" (18).

At Qumran Jaffee observes the kind of "orally mediated interpretive tradition" (29) that is generally continuous with the oral-scribal dynamics he had encountered in Second Temple Judaism elsewhere. Study of the Torah, the central ritual of the community, was practiced as a collective act that required the engagement of the entire assembly. The communally centered textual appropriation proceeded in two stages. In the first stage the sacred text was read or recited aloud, and in a second stage it, or rather its recitation, became a source for explanatory discourse. Both recitation and explication, the central acts of Torah study, were thus delivered orally and apperceived aurally in communal sessions. It was, therefore, not as fixed texts per se that sacred Scripture exhibited authority but rather as an "ongoing revelation" (37) that was extended into the present. Texts in this oral-scribal media culture were perceived as both numinous and potential entities. They provided the locus of extraordinary powers, but these were powers that achieved validation in what Jaffee in a particularly felicitous phrase calls "the authoritative oral moment of textual tradition" (38). Or, put differently, the recitation reinstated the original moment of oral dictation, and the explication activated the texts' full(er) implications. Oral explication and aural appropriation were the norm, while at the same time oral activation remained firmly linked to and grounded in the sacred writings. Importantly, however, there was as yet no attempt in Second Temple communities to reflect on scribal versus oral hermeneutical procedures, let alone to differentiate the written Torah from what would be termed the oral Torah.

Finally, Jaffee addresses the often-stated thesis of a specifically Pharisaic claim on the oral Torah. His examination of the principal sources— Qumran, early Christian texts, Josephus, rabbinic literature—adduces no evidence that the idea and practice of the oral Torah originated in pre-70 Pharisaic circles. While the Qumran residents may have entertained tense relations with the "Expounders of Smooth Things"—a possible reference to Pharisees—the Dead Sea scrolls indicate nothing about a Pharisaic concept of tradition/revelation. The ancient sayings Gospel Q and the canonical Gospels have collectively developed a fairly distinct picture of the Pharisees. But apart from the fact that it is a picture drawn up in light of conflictual relations between the Jesus people and the Pharisees, these sources convey little information about the content of the Pharisaic tradition and say nothing about the significance of medium, oral or written. Josephus portrays the Pharisees as a religio-political movement that practiced scrupulous adherence to traditions anchored in the Torah, but he too remains silent on the matter of oral versus written transmission. As far as rabbinic literature is concerned, Jaffee expresses a strong caveat against assuming direct social and transmissional continuities between Pharisaism and rabbinism. The most one can say, therefore, is that the Pharisees, like most other scribal communities in the Second Temple period, participated in the prevalent oral-performative activation of texts.

In the second part Jaffee illuminates a rabbinic trajectory toward a gradual coordination of the (mostly) post-70 rabbinic traditions with the Mosaic Torah. It was a move that would culminate in the rise of the oral Torah, an entity that eventually came to share coequality with the written Torah. Following the destruction of Jerusalem and its temple, Judaism found itself in a period of reconstruction, seeking to consolidate its identity in the absence of central place. The instructional material that emerged from the early centuries of the common era was by and large oral-performative instruction, which, transcribed into written form, was finally compiled in the Mishnah and Tosefta. The emergent perception was that the memorially manageable material was transmitted by word of mouth from teacher to disciple and grounded in the personal authority of Hillel and Shammai and their circle of disciples. These two preeminent sages and their disciples were regarded as the authoritative guarantors of the rabbinic tradition. There was no indication in the earlier segments of rabbinic literature that it stemmed from ancient Mosaic origins.

The later rabbinic tradition and especially the more expansive Tosefta, the author explains, exhibit a growing discussion about the relationship between the Mosaic Torah and the rabbinic tradition associated with individual sages. How was the authority of Moses to be understood in relation to the rabbinic teachers, and what was the role of the halakic norms in relation to that of the Mosaic commandments? The underlying issue appears to have been internal rabbinic needs to obtain clarity on the origins, nature, and authority of the halakic tradition. Are rabbinic traditions already anticipated, included even, in the Mosaic revelation? How can the autonomy of the halakic tradition be preserved without undermining scriptural foundations? Several sets of correspondences between the two traditions were suggested, but no unanimity is observable. From the middle of the third century onward Tannaitic exegesis evidences statements to the effect that the rabbinic oral-performative tradition was the work of the same processes that generated Scripture or that in fact the halakic norms issued forth from the mouth of God. The purpose was to bring rabbinic tradition into closer relationship with the Sinaitic revelation. It is a tendency that culminates in the conviction that "two Torahs were given to Israel, one by mouth and one in script" (90).

The Tannaitic tendencies to link rabbinic tradition with Mosaic Scripture were further strengthened by the Amoraic sages of the third and fourth centuries. Their theories entailed the conviction that the rabbinic oral-performative tradition was by definition Torah, that it was exclusively oral in nature, that it constituted an unbroken chain of transmission from Sinai to the present, and that its covenantal efficaciousness hinged on its oral preservation and performance. The "fictionalization of rabbinic oral tradition as Torah in the Mouth" (7) had been accomplished.

Jaffee is at his most astute when he develops a model of *interpenetration or interdependence* of the rabbinic tradition. Irrespective of rabbinic self-definition, his analysis of texts suggests that rabbinic teachers drew on the oral-performative tradition for textual compositions, which in turn were subject to reoralization. There was, in short, "a continuous loop of manuscript and performance" (124) that never yields a ground zero on the basis of which "original" instructions or texts are recoverable. Pure oral tradition, uncontaminated by scribality, is as much in doubt as direct intertextuality devoid of oral-performative mediation. For example, the compositional history of the Mishnah cannot be understood as a linearly progressing oral tradition that accomplished its textual breakthrough on the level of Mishnaic redaction, but rather as a complex interaction of oral and scribal forces. I suggest that scholars of the Gospels pay particular attention to Jaffee's explanation of the relationship between Mishnah and Tosefta. While the author does not question the Toseftan literary closure after the Mishnah, he casts doubt on the compositional explanation of the Tosefta as a literary expansion and interpretation of Mishnaic materials. Instead of the widely assumed direct literary relationship he argues, on the basis of close textual readings, that both Mishnah and Tosefta independently drew on anterior oral-performative traditions. The two literary bodies are thus to be understood as separate "variant formulations" (116) rather than as literary revision of one by the other.

Finally, Jaffee explores possible rationales both for the oral-scribal media interdependency and for the apotheosis of the oral Torah. As for the former, he points to Greco-Roman rhetorical practice that was devoted to the recycling or transformation of written texts into orally manageable speeches. As far as the elevation of the oral Torah and the implied suppression of writing was concerned, the author points to the master-disciple relationship and the life-transforming experience of orally performed tradition. The concept arose from the needs of discipleship to legitimate the authority of the sages and to preserve their living instructions.

It is the very substantial achievement of Jaffee to have transposed the often intricate deliberations concerning the nature, function, and media identity of the rabbinic tradition into a new conceptual frame. My questions arise from the second part of the book, which I find not fully coordinated with the first part. Do we really need the model of Greco-Roman rhetorical education to account for the interdependence of oral and written texts in rabbinic education? Remarkably, many of the features Jaffee has described were likewise observed by Carr and Niditch within the much larger compass of the ancient Near Eastern and Mediterranean verbal arts: oral-scribal interpenetration, scribal orality, the educational locus, the absence of the "original" text, oral implementation of texts, textual variants related to recurring performances, the eminent role of memory, repetition of various kinds—although "repetition" may not be the appropriate term in the oral arts. My second question concerns what Jaffee calls the "Ideology of Orality," for example, the apotheosis of the oral Torah. This is an extraordinary feature, unparalleled, as far as I know, in the textual traditions covered by Graham, Carr, and Niditch. Jaffee is surely right in explaining it as a method of rabbinic legitimation that at a later point proved useful as a polemical tool in the Amoraic disputes with Christianity. But could we perhaps explore the oral Torah more deeply from media perspectives, a feature so well developed in the first part of the book? What is happening in a tradition that has become so consciously self-referential that it isolates, identifies, and idealizes one of its media as an entity in its own right?

78. GÜTTGEMANNS: *OFFENE FRAGEN ZUR FORMGESCHICHTE DES EVANGELIUMS*

In turning to the New Testament, and specifically to Gospel scholarship, one remembers that the issue of oral tradition has historically been the objective of form criticism. Designed to attend to the orally perceived Synoptic tradition, and to oral aspects of New Testament texts in general, the discipline has presided over much, although by no means all, of twentieth-century Gospel studies. Today form criticism is besieged by substantial challenges to its basic premises. The scholar who took the lead in developing a systematically grounded critique of form criticism was Erhardt Güttgemanns. His *Offene Fragen zur Formgeschichte des Evangeliums* (first published in 1970) ranks, in my view, among the seminal New Testament works of the twentieth century—not necessarily because of his constructive theses, some of which are questionable or unsustainable, but because of the powerfully analytical force of his criticism. Although translated in an extraordinary labor of professional dedication by William G. Doty under the title *Candid Questions Concerning Gospel Form Criticism* (1979), the work has by and large not been absorbed into the Anglo-American discussion of form criticism, redaction criticism, literary criticism, and orality-literacy studies of the Bible. James Robinson and Helmut Koester, for example, who in the United States were instrumental in espousing the Bultmannian model of form criticism as the methodological basis for Gospel studies and the history of the tradition, have, to the best of my knowledge, not engaged Güttgemanns's critical objections to the discipline.

Güttgemanns's work has to be understood by its location in the history of scholarship of the 1960s and 1970s when interest in the Gospel-tradition differential was pursued by what came to be known as redaction criticism, largely built on form-critical principles, while attention to the internal literary unity of Gospel narrativity was in the process of undermining the logic of form criticism insofar as it was built on the Gospel-tradition differential. Willi Marxsen (1956) was the first scholar to raise consciousness about the growing problematic: the form-critical model appeared to be more and more incompatible with the one that was being developed by narrative criticism. It was in this situation that Güttgemanns formulated his challenge to the Bultmannian premise of tradition's gradual buildup toward the Gospel, and the correlative practice of using the Gospels as grounds for retracing the steps of tradition. Immensely erudite, rigorously systematic, and deeply provocative, Güttgemanns articulated the first major analytical countermodel to Bultmannian form criticism and its assumptions with regard to pre-Gospel tradition and the genesis of the Gospel.

What distinguishes *Offene Fragen* from a majority of biblical studies at the time is its intense application of linguistic theory and the subjection of the historical-critical model to linguistic scrutiny. "The 'purely historical' is always transmitted by language, and it is only understandable by means of linguistic processes" (1979, 3). The motto of the book could well be: we cannot get around the facts of language because this is all we have. Güttgemanns confronts the reader with the kind of deep linguistic reflection on form-critical premises that one wishes had been undertaken by the founding fathers of that discipline. Uniquely conversant (for a New Testament scholar) in linguistic theory and ranging widely among the works of J. G. Herder, W. v. Humboldt, P. Bogatyrev, R. Jakobson, H. Bausinger, L. Lavelle, H. E. Gleason, F. de Saussure, R. H. Robins, A. Martinet, K. Bühler, K. Ammer, and numerous others, the author postulates the essential and functional difference between oral and written language. "Contemporary linguistics considers that between the oral and the written there are *differences on all structural levels*" (197). This thesis of the "structural-functional dissimilarity of 'oral' and ... 'literary' technology" (211) suggests to him that the relation between Gospel and tradition had to be more complex than the form critics had assumed and that the form of Gospel could not be derived genetically from the dynamics and processes inherent in antecedent oral tradition.

Güttgemanns's thesis has profound implications for an understanding of both Gospel and tradition. As for the Gospel, he suggests that we view it as "*an autosemantic language form*, i.e., a language form which in its 'sense' can only be explained through and by means of itself" (307). As for the pre-Gospel tradition, it occupies a territory that for the most part escapes our linguistic grasp "since the evolutionary implications of the [form-critical] method produce only false hopes and scientific phantoms" (311). If oral functions of language are different from scribal ones, if the evolutionary model of oral traditions are unprovable, and if the Gospel narrative constitutes an integral linguistic, narrative entity, then the form-critical habit of deriving oral units from the written Gospel is problematic in the extreme.

How far Güttgemanns was willing to challenge the form-critical practice of extrapolating assumed oral units from the Gospel narrative can be demonstrated in his handling of Mark's so-called passion-resurrection predictions (8:31; 9:31; 10:33–34). Discussing form-critical theories regarding the pre-Markan status of these formula-like summaries and efforts to arrive at their original form, he concludes that their perfect narrative fit inclines the argument in favor of at least Markan redaction, if not composition. Recognition of the "autosemantic" integrity of the Gospel narrative undercuts the form-critical method of identifying detachable Gospel units and using them as building blocks in the reconstruction of the so-called Synoptic tradition. About the same time, Perrin (1971b, 14–30), working without awareness of and independently from Güttgemanns, would arrive at the same conclusion: "the predictions are Markan literary productions" (28).

Still more radically, Güttgemanns struck at the heart of one of form criticism's basic assumptions about the existence and recovery of "the original form"—a thesis programmatically articulated by Bultmann. In this regard, Güttgemanns (204–211) was, to my knowledge, the first New Testament scholar to appropriate Albert Lord's empirical findings concerning oral performance and written transcription. Based on his field work on the Serbo-Croatian epic tradition, undertaken to illuminate the oral-scribal processes in the Homeric epics, Lord demonstrated that there was no such thing as "the original saying" or "the original form" of a saying. "In a sense each performance is 'an' original, if not 'the' original" (1960, 101). Moreover, if there was no such thing as an original form, or, we might more appropriately say, original performance, then there could not be variants of the assumed original form either. No matter how many, and how many different, oral performances were delivered, each oral rendition was a freshly composed speech act. Following Lord's proposition,

Güttgemanns concluded that unless we learn to understand oral speech, tradition, and genres "exclusively in terms of the creative processes of continually new performances," we have not understood the oral legacy of the Gospels (206). In my terms, an orator active in the oral performance medium is not a spokesperson of original forms, but a speaker of multiple, authentic performances.

The thesis of the fundamental linguistic differentiation between oral and written communication lies at the heart of the current Great Divide discussion, which has been conducted without reflection on, perhaps even awareness of, Güttgemanns's work. As I pointed out in the review of Niditch's work, we need to come to terms with what constitute oral versus scribal characteristics, even if, and especially if, we increasingly (and rightly) argue in favor of oral-scribal interfaces. How could we make a case for the latter unless we have demonstrated the former? Insofar as recent performative aesthetics perceive the Gospel as oral not only in its scribal status but in some instances also in its pre-Gospel manifestations, they appear to have leveled oral-scribal distinctions. In that case, the Gospel-tradition differential appears to have been obliterated altogether. But is it a plausible proposition that the Gospel composition was entirely unaffected by the chirographic medium? Clearly, the demonstration of oral-scribal interfaces is one thing, but to refrain from drawing precise distinctions between oral and scribal verbalization is another. Regardless of the outcome of the debate, some of Güttgemanns's theses are undoubtedly to the point: the autosemantic nature of the Gospel narratives, the questionable procedure of detaching alleged oral tradition units from literary contexts, the inadmissibility of the notion of the single, original rendition, and orality's trafficking in multiple authentic performances and versions.

In retrospect, one wonders whether twentieth-century scholarship on Gospels and tradition would not have developed differently if prior consideration had been given to the Gospels' interior narrative constellation before far-reaching assumptions had been made about the history of pre-Gospel traditions. Likewise, would not twentieth-century scholarship on Gospels and tradition have moved into different directions if knowledgeable consideration had been given to the nature of oral hermeneutics? Put differently, would not twentieth-century scholarship on Gospels and tradition have yielded more satisfactory results if simultaneous attention had been accorded to oral hermeneutics *and* to Gospel narrativity? Instead, we now look back on a disquieting history of form-critical scholarship that focused on oral tradition without an adequate grasp of speech and oral performance, and derived forms of assumed oral speech from Gospel texts without appropriate insights into Gospel narrativity.

Today, matters of orality and scribality present themselves in a somewhat different light than Güttgemanns had imagined. As most of the authors reviewed in this essay suggest, pure oral tradition, uninfluenced by scribality, is for the most an unlikely proposition. Equally important yet not widely recognized, however, is that pure textuality, uninfluenced by oral dynamics, and solely relying in rectilinear fashion on another text, is not a widely practiced proposition either. Manifold different oral-scribal interfaces are the rule in the ancient world of manuscript culture.

79. HORSLEY (WITH DRAPER): *WHOEVER HEARS YOU HEARS ME*

In this book Horsley (with Draper) has provided a challenging test case of the application of an oral lens to the hypothetical text Q. Treating Q (as well as Mark) as an *oral-derived text*, a definition derived from Foley and covering "works that reveal oral traditional features but have reached us only in written form" (Foley 1991, 15), the authors institute a major shift in our understanding of the ancient collection of Jesus materials.

Whoever Hears You Hears Me is motivated as much by recent developments in orality-scribality studies as it is by discomfort with mainstream Q scholarship. In the first five chapters the authors critically review previous scholarship on Q and lay out the historical, social context of the old Jesus tradition. Both theologically and methodologically, they claim, much of Q scholarship has been characterized by the application of an inadequate conceptual apparatus. A certain line of Q studies tended to reach out for universalist categories and/or to opt for an individualist concept of the kingdom, while downplaying social dynamics altogether. It is an approach that shows scholarly affinities with liberal nineteenth-century theology and its pursuit to free Jesus from perceived Jewish particularism. More recent Q studies, attending to compositional and source-critical issues, have adopted stratigraphic readings of Q that seek to demonstrate a formational division into an older *sapiential* and a secondary *apocalyptic* stage. However, Horsley argues, "If Wisdom appears in 'apocalyptic' or prophetic sayings and 'sapiential' sayings use apocalyptic language against the sages, then the criteria of categorization require critical attention" (74). In fact, Horsley views both apocalyptic and wisdom as synthetic constructs fashioned by modern New Testament scholarship (73). Prophetic would be the category most appropriate to Q. The widely used generic designation of Q as λόγοι σοφῶν is likewise deemed unacceptable, and in fact the very genre of λόγοι σοφῶν seems problematic because the many and heterogeneous materials referred to as λόγοι in Jewish, Hellenistic-Jewish, and early Christian texts cannot be forced into a single generic category (75–83).

A significant feature of the book is its rigorous focus on the social dimensions of Q. Firmly locating the ancient hypothetical text in Israel's historical matrix, the authors challenge recent interpretations that postulate Q's rejection of Israel, a thesis that failed to acknowledge the deep roots of the Q sayings and speeches in the Israelite tradition. Among the numerous Israelite references and themes Horsley identifies in Q are the restoration of the twelve tribes, exposure of the killing of prophets, Jonah's preaching, prophetic laments, Wisdom as sender of prophets, offspring of Abraham, bearing good fruit, the fire of judgment, forty days in the wilderness, indictment of Jerusalem, blessings and woes, and many more. Q stands not against but within Israel's history and society. Rather than being in conflict with Israel, Q is positioned at the point of an intra-Jewish crisis between the rulers and the ruled. Growing out of Galilean village communities, the Jesus traditions of Q are said to have taken a stance within Israel's history speaking on behalf of the Galilean and Judean peasantry against Jerusalem governed by Roman power, scribal-Pharisaic representatives, and Galilean rulers. What we find in Q, Horsley suggests, adopting the nomenclature of the political scientist and anthropologist James C. Scott, is a classic case of the little or popular tradition pitted against the great or official, Jerusalem-based tradition. In mobilizing both prophetic, revolutionary traditions long operative in Galilee and the overarching themes of the Mosaic covenant and the kingdom of God (not of King David!), Q stands in continuity with and reenacts fundamental values of Israel. In sum, the old Jesus traditions speak for a movement that aspired to the renewal (not rejection!) of Israel.

In chapters 6 through 8 Horsley and Draper develop a theory of the oral art of verbalization or, one could say, a hermeneutic of oral-derived texts. In broad agreement with a number of recent historical studies, they describe the general lack of literacy, the largely ancillary function of writing and texts in ancient Mediterranean antiquity, and the oral cultivation of ancient Israelite traditions. Writing functioned primarily as an aid to memory and in the service of oral communication, and not the other way around. Whether a text physically existed or not, and whether the genre was poetry, drama, history, or even philosophy, oral transmission and performance were predominant. In ancient Israel, scribal activity worked hand-in-glove with an intense oral, communal life. By and large, knowledge of Scripture was not obtained by reading sacred texts, and not necessarily even by listening to them as they were being read out aloud. For the most part scriptural knowledge was acquired by listening to oral recitations in the absence of textual aids because scriptural traditions were an essential part of the oral, communal repertoire. It is in this communications milieu, the authors suggest, that we have to imagine the functioning of Q. As oral-derived text (Foley 1991, 15), Q originated in oral performance to be sustained in repeated oral recitations. In other words, Q was "a libretto that was regularly performed in the early Jesus movement" (Horsley and Draper 1999, 174). The contrast, the authors point out, with the premise on which the International Q Project worked could not be more pronounced. The latter aimed at controlling and stabilizing the transmission of Jesus materials by securing what James Robinson has called "the one Q archetype. That archetype is what the scholarly community means by Q and is what the International Q Project is seeking to reconstruct" (1999, 61–62).

One of the characteristics of an oral-derived text such as Q (or Mark) is that words relate not intratextually as much as they do in reference to a wider or deeper tradition. Importantly, tradition is perceived here not in terms of transmissional processes but rather as a body of experiences, an orally recited and internalized scriptural heritage, memories, values, symbols, cultural and national identity, and so on, shared by the community. A technical terminus for tradition, perceived thus as a collectively internalized cultural legacy, is *register*, that is, idiomatic modes of verbalization and signification in which different activities, memories, experiences, ideas, and so on take on life. In each instance, the register consists not merely of a word or phrase, an idea or concept, but also of a wide range of associations that have multiple links with and often deep roots in tradition. To be effective, an oral-derived text uses terms and images that metonymically key into hearers' register by resonating extratextually with values and experiences that are immanent in tradition. An interpretation of Q will therefore seek to recover the tradition in the context of which Q was heard by summoning the register appropriate to such items as prophetic proclamation of new deliverance, Mosaic covenant renewal, mission and the sending of envoys, arrest of members and trial before authorities, sanctions on discipline and solidarity, consolation in situations of poverty, and so on. Again, tradition, conceived here not as a transmissional trajectory, but as an extratextual reservoir of a shared culture, operates as the enabling context in the production of meaning.

Following the theoretical part, Horsley and Draper demonstrate in the remaining chapters, 9 through 14, the oral functioning of key passages in Q. Instead of transmission of isolated sayings addressed to individuals, Q, they argue, functioned as a performance of discourses on issues of communal concern. As far as the actual Q text is concerned, they work with and partially present the transliterated Greek version accompanied by a translation. Both versions are divided into what are assumed to be discourse units that are marked by features characteristic of an oral-derived text: parallel lines; repetition of words, ideas, phrases, and syntactic units; stock images; mnemonic patternings; sound rhythms; paratactic constructions; and many more. Additionally, they divide Q into in stanzas, verses and lines whereby priority is given to stanzas of which verses and lines are component parts. A crucial aspect of the interpretation depends on recovery of the oral register in order to determine meanings in the performance context. For example, covenantal forms and language, prophetic woes, images and terms such as wilderness, harvest, or sheep among wolves, judgment, and Pharisees summon a larger world of meanings immanent in the tradition. On the whole, the Q discourses are defined as prophetic speech perceived to be spoken through Jesus in the present: "Whoever Hears You Hears Me" (Q 10:16). Through the performance of Q the earthly Jesus (not the exalted Lord!) continues as proclaimer of the kingdom and the renewal of Israel.

The great significance of this study is that if offers its readers a genuinely oral interpretation of a (hypothetical) text based on current theories of orality. Issues of theory and application, performance and format, history and language, social setting and oral aesthetics, register and tradition (perceived as the enabling context) are unified in a grand theory. I am sure the authors are aware of the irony that their Q text is largely based on the archetype constructed by the International Q Project, while all along the premise of Q as a single text with a single meaning is no longer tenable. In fairness, how is a translation of an oral-derived text to remain faithful to the oral metonymy and the oral register? I raise a question, moreover, as to the authors' understanding of an oral-derived text. Q, Horsley suggests, is oral in the sense that "scribes are not required for the composition of Q" (294). Foley, however, unambiguously distinguishes oral from oral-derived texts. The latter reveal oral traditional features but are the likely products of scribal composition. I reiterate the question I raised in the part on Güttgemanns with regard to the Gospels' composition: Is it plausible to think of the Q composition as having been entirely unaffected by the technology of chirography? Horsley and Draper have pushed our understanding of Q far beyond the limits of the established conventions and practices distinctive of Q research. In terms of sensitivity to oral aesthetics and hermeneutics, this study is unique in New Testament scholarship. Q in oral performance is not the objectified linguistic artifact of print culture. It is safe to say that biblical scholarship trained in the assumed certainties of strictly textual hermeneutics will find it difficult to acclimatize itself to the open-endedness and polyvalency of an oral hermeneutics.

80. PARKER: *THE LIVING TEXT OF THE GOSPELS*

I have reserved David Parker's book for last because it articulates matters of ancient scribal life in the most intellectually challenging fashion. Lurking beneath the positively conventional title are theses that, if pondered thoughtfully, confront the historical-critical paradigm of Gospel scholarship with formidable questions.

The genre of *The Living Text of the Gospels* is an intriguing one. It presents itself in the form of an introduction to text criticism, although far from offering a mere summation of the state of the discipline, "it attempts to find new departures" (xi). Chapter 1 already sets a tone that lets the reader suspect a digression from the conventional genre of introduction or handbook. The author introduces the subject of text criticism by citing the examples of Shakespeare's plays and Mozart's libretto of *The Marriage of Figaro*, this cornerstone of the operatic repertoire. In Shakespeare's case, many of his early plays exist in a number of different print versions, while the scripts of Mozart's *Figaro* consist of the autograph and additional performance copies, including the official copy of the court theater in Vienna. Both the dramatist and the composer instituted changes in rehearsals, producing differing scripts that later appeared in print format. Which version, we tend to ask, is the original one? The answer, of course, has to be that there is no single original script. For Parker, these examples are paradigmatic for the discipline of text criticism, or rather for the way in which it ought to be reconceptualized. As long as "it is assumed that there *is* an original text, the textual critic's task is very simple: to recover the original text" (6). This, of course, has by and large been the basic, although certainly not the only, fascination of the discipline: to sift through multiple textual versions in order to recover, or, as the case may be, reconstruct, the one fixed point in the tradition, namely the so-called original text.

I recognize that in recent times text critics have been guarded in using the term "the original text." And yet, the Institute for New Testament Research at Münster, Germany, on its website tells its readers that its mission "is to research the textual history of the New Testament and to reconstruct its Greek initial text." "Initial text" is not much better then "original text," and "reconstructing" the Greek text is equally misleading. *To be textually and historically accurate, we should agree that the text of the Greek New Testament has always been a* textus constructus *from Erasmus's 1516 printed edition onward, which, as is well known, the learned humanist constructed from the Greek manuscripts that were available to him at Basle University Library—medieval manuscripts representing the Byzantine text tradition—all the way to the twenty-eighth edition of the Nestle-Aland* Novum Testamentum Graece *of 2012.* Hence, Parker's provocative statement that the printed text of the New Testament "was far more a creation of northern European medieval and Renaissance technology than it was of early Christian thought" (196). He in no way dismisses the institute's mission of editing a critical text. But he is asking for greater transparency in how that mission, its objective, and its limitations are being defined.

But the quest for the so-called original text need not be the only objective of text criticism. A different and perhaps more legitimate option, Parker suggests, is to study every scrap of textual evidence *in its own right and on its own terms* and to evaluate the sum total of collected texts for the story they tell us about the early scribal tradition. Once we begin to get a sense of the startling variety of early Jesus traditions and Gospel variants, the question forces itself upon us: "Are the Gospels the kinds of texts that have originals?" (7). It is a key question Parker's book is wrestling with. Quite clearly, his book, while principally dealing with text criticism, offers more and something other than an updated summary of the current state of the discipline.

Chapter 2, still on fairly conventional grounds, discusses the classification of manuscripts according to materials, script, and contents, as well as translational versions and patristic citations, and surveys Gospel texts through the centuries from the earliest scraps of papyrus all the way to the electronic versions in CD-ROM and diskette format. In chapter 3 Parker sets alongside each other the three manuscript versions of Luke 6:1–10 (plucking heads of grain on the Sabbath and the healing of the man with a withered hand) as they exist in Codex Vaticanus (B), Codex Bezae (D), and Codex Dionysiou 10 (Ω). A thoughtful examination introduces the readers into the intricacies of manuscript variation. Many of the variants are small, minuscule even, yet cumulatively tiny changes can be more significant than one or two large ones. Can one, should one, favor a particular reading in view of the variations? The case is dramatized by the fact that "there are as many differences between D and B in Luke 6.1ff as there are between the two texts of D in Mark 2..23ff. and Luke 6.1ff" (46).

Chapters 4 and 5 examine the manuscript evidence of the Lord's Prayer and Jesus' sayings on marriage and divorce respectively. Examining the prayer in Matthew, Luke, and the *Didache*, Parker in a minute analysis of the textual evidence demonstrates the existence of the prayer in multiple divergent forms. "Behind the question 'How many texts?' is the question 'Is there a single original prayer?'" (72). Among modern text critics and, I should add, among representatives of the Quest for the historical Jesus, there is the strong determination to find the one, original version of the prayer. Parker is too impressed with the variants to want to embark on the path toward the original prayer. Sifting through the early manuscript evidence of Jesus' sayings on marriage and divorce, Parker recognizes that the problem is not simply one of explaining the (often redactional) differences between Mark 10, Matthew 5 and 19, and Luke 16. There are differences not only among these Gospel versions, as is well known, but within the manuscript tradition of each Gospel. Sometimes the differences among the manuscripts of a single Gospel are greater than those between our printed Gospel texts. Assessment of the full scribal evidence, therefore, confronts us with a quantity and quality of different renditions that go far beyond Markan, Matthean, and Lukan adaptations and are not readily explicable by a single genealogical tree that would take us back to the one root saying. "A single authoritative pronouncement," Parker writes, "is irrecoverable" (183). Perhaps one may add that the project of retrieving the single authoritative saying is not merely fraught with inextricable technical difficulties but, more importantly, incompatible with what appears to be the prevailing spirit of the early scribal tradition.

In chapters 6 through 10 Parker approaches a series of well-known problems in Gospel studies from the angle of the available scribal evidence. The textually ambiguous story of the woman taken in adultery—sometimes following John 7:52, or 7:36, or 21:25, and sometimes following Luke 21:38 or 24:53—is judged not to have been part of the oldest textual traditions. However, Parker's point is that its textually inferior status notwithstanding, its existence in the lectionaries of most denominations and in Christian consciousness generally attests to its continuous appeal.

The author concludes: "Passages do not lose their influence once they have been declared and acknowledged to be spurious" (95). So-called minor agreements between Matthew and Luke versus Mark, always a challenge to the Two Source Hypothesis, lead Parker to reflect on the quest for a strictly documentary solution to the Synoptic Problem. Advocates of the Two-Source Hypothesis, he observes, tend to envision the compositional history of the Synoptic Gospels "as though it were identical with the publishing of a printed book today" (117). Instead of assuming single-point contacts between two texts (Matthew using Mark and using Q), Parker explores the possibility of "a series of contacts between texts each of which may have changed since the previous contact" (121). The underlying conviction is that the Gospels "were not archives of traditions but living texts" (119). With regard to the issue posed by the ending of Mark, the available evidence suggests that the short ending is "the oldest form of the Gospel" (143). However, its textually superior status has (until recently) not been implemented in our readings of Mark. The fact is that the long ending "has been dominant for the reading of Mark for most of the text's history" (147). Another example Parker examines is Luke 22–24, the concluding chapters of the Gospel, which present a known textual conundrum for critics and interpreters alike. Examining the multiple textual versions of these chapters, Parker detects a tendency toward textual growth, frequently marked by harmonization and leading to the gradual loss of distinctly Lukan features. "The Gospel story continues to grow within as well as beyond the canonical pages" (174). In reviewing, finally, the textual history of the Fourth Gospel, Parker finds that there "is no manuscript evidence for either the omission of Chapter 21 or the reversal in order of Chapters 5 and 6" (177), virtually standard assumptions in the commentary literature since Bultmann. Hence to suggest the secondary status of chapter 21 and a reversal in the order of chapters 5 and 6 is to postulate a text for which we lack textual evidence.

In chapters 11 and 12 Parker expands his focus on successive scribal versions toward the materiality in which they are transmitted, thereby mutating text criticism into media criticism. The early papyrological Jesus traditions were at their most fluid in the first century of their existence: "The further back we go, the greater seems to be the degree of variation" (188). Parker places a high premium on the introduction of the codex because it facilitated inter alia comparative Gospel readings, which affected textual developments, above all harmonizations. In this sense the materiality of the codex contributed to the character of Gospel versions.

What was of the essence of the fifteen hundred years of manuscript tradition was that "every copy is different, both unique and imperfect" (188). It was print culture that conferred an unprecedented authority upon the Bible. But Parker is quick to remind us that in the desire to print the perfect, the original text, the editors constructed what must be called eclectic text versions, virtual more than real entities. The author finds it difficult to arrive at a suitable terminology to describe the new vision of the tradition. He opts for a definition of the Gospels "as a free, or perhaps as a living, text" (200).

It is easy to dismiss Parker for having drawn deeply consequential conclusions on a rather slim evidential basis. But as if to anticipate the charge, he has articulated his defense: "If the degree of variation which we have found were to exist in only one of the passages we have studied, the matter would require a serious evaluation of the nature of the tradition" (198). It is the abiding value of the book that it has contributed to a reevaluation of and new approach to the discipline of text criticism but, I dare say, to a new attitude toward the (early) Christian tradition. *I hope that Parker's studies of the early scribal life of the Jesus tradition can be brought into a fruitful collaboration with orality studies, because the* variability factor, *natural to oral tradition, now turns out to be likewise characteristic of the early scribal phase of the Gospel tradition.* In view of the theories proposed and evidence produced by Graham, Carr, Niditch, Jaffee, Güttgemanns, and Horsley and Draper, we should not be surprised about variability, multiple originality, and recurring performance in the early scribal tradition of Gospel materials, as it endeavored to flow with the flux of temporality. These phenomena, while possibly particularly pronounced in the early Jesus tradition, are well-established features of ancient communications history.

The paradigm of historical-critical scholarship has served as intellectual matrix for biblical scholarship from premodern times throughout the modern period into the present. Our assumptions about the verbal arts are for the most part indebted to and entrenched in this paradigm. It needs to be stated emphatically: the intellectual accomplishments of this paradigm have been incontestably huge, monumental even. More than that: Western modernity is unthinkable without the historical-critical examination of the Bible. But, as I stated at the outset of this review, the discovery of the oral dimension of ancient texts addresses conceptual flaws that, far from being superficial, go to the core of this paradigm. There is a palpable discrepancy between the dominantly print medium of modern scholarship and the oral-scribal communications world of its subject matter, with the former encroaching upon the latter. The seven books under review challenge us to (re)consider the Bible in its Jewish and Christian provenance, the biblical and the rabbinic tradition in the media context of the ancient Near Eastern and Mediterranean communications history.

13

MEMORY AND VIOLENCE, OR: GENEALOGIES OF REMEMBERING (IN MEMORY OF EDITH WYSCHOGROD)

This essay in memory of Edith Wyschogrod takes as its starting point the issue most insistently raised in her work: the difficulties faced by the historian and philosopher in coping with the mass exterminations of the twentieth century. The first part reviews the principal features of An Ethics of Remembering. *Focusing on Wyschogrod's central theme of memory and violence, the second part turns to the canonical passion narratives, interpreting them as memory texts that commemorated the violent death of the fallen leader and in turn generated a memorially empowered reception history—ad bonam et ad malam partem. The following four sections examine the canonical passion texts with a view toward their specific attitudes vis-à-vis Rome and Judaism. The Gospel of Mark, it is shown, exhibits distinctly pro-Roman proclivities. In the case of Matthew, attention is focused on the fateful verses 27:24–25, which raise the issue of the so-called blood curse placed on Judaism. In Luke, the pro-Roman proclivity is developed into a recognizable narrative theme, generally termed the apologia Romana. In the Fourth Gospel, it is shown how a duplicity of language, implemented by way of a carefully narrated metaphoricity and irony, is designed to lift hearers/readers from literalness to spirituality, but at the same time serves to marginalize and exclude those who have consistently been called "the Jews." The seventh part evaluates the results of the previous review of the passion texts with the assistance of cultural memory theory. It is claimed that pro-Roman and increasingly anti-Jewish tendencies are conceived from present social and historical vantage points. The eighth part resumes the discussion of Mark's passion narrative, viewing it this time with the help of memory theory. Three memory strategies are identified as being operative: the composition of memorial commonplaces, the narrative application of "interpretive keying," and the construction of causal connections between hitherto unconnected items. The ninth part evaluates the previous observation: Mark's causal connection of the death of Jesus with the conflagration of the temple. Mark, it is claimed, was the first Christian to cope with twofold trauma by constructing a causal connection between them.*

> That which can in no way be figured by *the historia rerum gestarum*, the cataclysm, a nihil whose sheer magnitude and unfigurable ethical force—a law prior to all law—resists emergence in word or image.
> —Edith Wyschogrod, *An Ethics of Remembering*

> What we celebrate under the title of founding events are, essentially, acts of violence legitimated after the fact by a precarious state of right. What was glory for some was humiliation for others. To celebration (*célébration*) on one side corresponds execration (*exécration*) on the other. In this way, symbolic wounds calling for healing are stored in the archives of the collective memory.
> —Paul Ricoeur, *Memory, History, Forgetting*

> Memory becomes a festering wound.
> —Friedrich Nietzsche, *Ecce Homo*

> But what if the text in question were ethically flawed? What if it were misogynistic, say, or anti-Jewish?
> —Stephen D. Moore, *Poststructuralism and the New Testament*

81. FROM INEFFABILITY TO LANGUAGE

Three interrelated features may be said to characterize the work of Edith Wyschogrod. There is first an interdisciplinary drive to rise above institutionally sanctioned boundaries and to retrieve intellectual categories from their disciplinary captivity so as to reconfigure them in novel contexts. It is this desire and the ability to bring widely differing genres, discourses, and traditionally separate intellectual orbits into productive coalitions that has increasingly distinguished her writings. This interfacing of philosophy and theology, psychoanalysis and science, literary criticism and linguistics, architecture and the arts, media studies and above all ethics is carried off with a high degree of learning and refinement. Undoubtedly, the intellectual agility she has mastered and the philosophical voice that has distinctly become her own are the product of prolonged reflection, of hesitancy even.

Second, from the beginning of her writing career to the present, her work is deeply informed, not to say haunted, by the mass exterminations of the twentieth century that were sui generis. In her words, "The ethical question of our age [is] the death-event, and the death-worlds intrinsic to it" (2009, 247). Underlying her philosophical work is the conviction that the very magnitude of the organized mass murder of peoples that epitomizes the necropolis of the twentieth century, has, or ought to have, altered all our philosophical, psychological, religious and ethical assumptions about and perspectives on the human condition. Undoubtedly, the challenge she poses runs up against, inter alia, autonomous intellectual agendas and their entrenched disciplinary *Eigengesetzlichkeit*.

Third, in following Emmanuel Levinas, she has made the ethics of alterity a pillar of her own philosophy. Driven by the ethical passion for the Other and a corollary respect for difference, more perhaps than by virtue of intrinsically linguistic, literary rationales, she shares postmodernism's anxiety about totalizing imperatives and the imposition of sameness in religion, politics, science, culture—everywhere. Time and again, her thought has explicated the self not as a monadic, self-contained subject and not as an integrally rational and cognitive self, but rather as a corporeal, social self who discovers her or his identity in the face of the Other. Undoubtedly, the concept of self that her work calls into question is one founded on the myth of individual autochthony and one that in the modern Western world is increasingly implemented in terms of economic production and consumption.

In *An Ethics of Remembering* (1998), which marks a culmination point in her ethical/philosophical work, Wyschogrod has pondered with her customary acuteness and sympathetic generosity the role of the contemporary historian and the moral responsibilities and quandaries he or she faces both in a general epistemological sense and specifically in view of a history disfigured by institutionalized mass murder.

As far as the grounds of knowledge are concerned, there is the general issue all historians are confronted with, namely, the irrecoverable nature of the past. Is it not a truism that the past cannot be brought back in all its lived actualities? More than that, is it not accurate to state that the past seems lost beyond retrieval? Given this claim, how can one speak for the past and remember it, let alone retrieve it? What is it that we are doing when we bring the past into present articulation so as to carry it forward into the future? Then there are the well-known predicaments faced by representational epistemology, for example, the unreliability of memory, the precarious state of sources, unceasing interpretive difficulties, in short, the issue that language cannot make actuality transparent in terms of factual correctness. To put this issue in terms coined by Ricoeur, does not "the fundamental vulnerability of memory" result from "the relation between the absence of the thing remembered and its presence in the mode of representation"? (2004, 57–58). Given the demise of a positivistic episte-mology, how can linguistic articulation do justice to what Wyschogrod refers to as the *historia rerum gestarum*? How does one take the step from ineffability to language, and should or could one aim at a mode of lan-guage that transcends the representational impulse? Specifically in view of the totalization of evil in modernity, can words be attached to the ter-rors? How does the historian deal with "the genocidal catastrophes of the twentieth and twenty-first centuries, which cannot yet must be thought" (Wyschogrod 2009, 245)? In a different vein, is there something still to be said in favor of the polarity of fact versus fiction? Or, if we come to under-stand representation as necessarily constructed and fictional, how does the inevitability of a fictionalized element in representation square with the urgency of telling the truth about the past? Can fiction be distinguished from lie? What does it mean and what does it take to tell the truth about the past?

Today's historian, moreover, finds herself or himself consciously living and operating at a medium transit, an experience that heightens sensi-bilities toward modes and materialities of communication and their com-plicity in our construction of the past. Looking back on previous media stages—the age of the voice, the period of the scribal visualization of lan-guage, the typographic revolution, which turned language into mechanical reproductions—historians today find themselves caught in the web of an electronically manipulated communications culture that reduces knowl-edge to information and information ultimately to numbers "in confor-mity with the Pythagorean principle that the world is made of numbers" (Wyschogrod 1998, 16). How are the digitization processes in the current culture of globalizing electronic technologies and commodity distribution systems influencing both the commitment to and the representation of the past? How do television, computer, cellular phones, and an ever-growing number of electronic communication devices change both transmission and perception of past events, and hence our narratives of them?

As the title of Wyschogrod's major philosophical work indicates, the historian's treatment of the past is inextricably linked with memory and remembering, memory images and memory places, mnemonics and commemoration, and predominantly with an ethics of remembering—all topoi that once were perceived to be central to civilizing developments in Western civilization, and lately have risen again to the status of paradigmatic significance in the humanities and social sciences. If one holds with Aristotle that "all remembering implies lapse of time" (Aristotle 1957: *On Memory and Recollection* 449b31: διὸ μετὰ χρόνου πᾶσα μνήμη), remembering is of a piece with time, or our constructions of it, and indeed inextricably enveloped in temporality. When the historian aspires to the dream of recovering the past, he or she has to confront his or her subject matter's inextricable implication in the flow of lived time, and at the same time deal with one's own diachronocity, the historian's very own lived time. And in reclaiming past events, does one perceive time as a continuous homogeneous flow or as evolutionary trajectory, or in punctiform fashion, to mention but a few among numerous alternatives?

Those who have made it their particular objective to write about the death events and passionately wish to recover and retain knowledge of this immediately past century's mass murders, initiated and organized by state governments, by institutions and individuals alike, are faced with exquisitely difficult challenges. The linguistic, philosophical issue of the demise of representational epistemology aside, how can the unrepresentable cataclysms of history ever be re-presented? The paradox is a stark and searing one: what cannot be shown and what can hardly be articulated is precisely what, on ethical grounds, ought to be shown and said. Is the mass annihilation to be mediated through the organizing effects of narrative, or the intellectualizing efforts of philosophy, or the aestheticizing impact of artifacts, or the moralizing deliberations of ethics, or the anesthetizing effects of solipsistic meditation? Ethically, can and should the historian be "both the narrator of events and litigant for the powerless"? (Wyschogrod 1998, 248). In short, how can the historian manifest her or his "eros for the dead" (xiii), this responsibility toward those who have been rendered mute? How can this "passion for the dead others who are voiceless" (38) be transposed in language? What stance does the reporter take and from what place does she or he speak? Is there such a position "from within the cataclysm" (70), and if so, will one gain a hearing, an understanding even by speaking from within, if it were possible? Is one to rely on witnesses in the face of diverse and discordant testimonial affirmations, and what assurances can be given that the testimonies are trustworthy? How do oral testimonies of survivors differ from memoirs committed to writing? "Covenanted to the dead" (10) as our historian is, how can she or he fulfill her or his covenantal promise truthfully and with a passion for moral rectitude?

For the survivors, death, far from bringing closure, marks the inaugurating occasion for processes of rememorizations. Put differently: for those not (yet) consumed by extinction, the death of the countless has every appearance of being a traumatic yet memorially profound, productive experience. It is not surprising, therefore, that human efforts to revisit the violence of the past and to work through the trauma of death traditionally enlist the works of memory. Whether it is by dint of historiography, of narrative, of art, or of psychoanalysis that we seek to repossess the past and call back its dead, memorial methods and practices invariably infiltrate our historical, fictional, artistic, and psychoanalytic endeavors. A sharp conceptual distinction, therefore, between narrative, history, art, and psychoanalysis vis-à-vis memory is not necessarily warranted. Driven by the desire to connect with the dead, memory comes into its own, as it were, acting out the role it seems destined to play in the face of death. Hence Wyschogrod's strong claim on behalf of the role of memory as regards the ethical responsibilities of the historian to address and bring to consciousness the mass extermination of peoples, events that have gravely stained the twentieth century.

Highlighting memory and memorial responses to the cataclysms and their victims, Wyschogrod pondered a series of concepts of memorial practices, ranging from mnemotechnical and archival to neurological all the way to computational models. What memorial practices does the historian appropriate and how does she or he implement them? If so-called facticity and what is memorially recalled are not homologous, what is it that is being remembered? To what extent do present experiences infiltrate our recollections of the past? What are the processes of remembering and those of forgetting? Precisely how are remembering and forgetting correlated? When is forgetting epistemologically meaningful, therapeutic even, and when is it dishonorable, immoral even? Is the content of what is forgotten irretrievably lost, or is memory—to use the spatial model, broadly conventional in antiquity—conceivable as a chamber whose *magna vis* and intricate vastness had moved Augustine to rhapsodic excitation in the tenth book of his *Confessions*? Or, still abiding by the spatial model, should memory be thought of as a crypt, a reservoir of dead images that need to be reactivated, or as an impenetrable labyrinth, a blur of indistinguishable sensations? Remembering the dead, especially those victimized by state-ordered decrees, by imperial brutalities, or as a result of crass casualness, is bound to be an agonizingly painful experience. Hence, if one is to remember the wounds suffered by and the humiliations inflicted upon the Other, can one occupy a station where one "neither ignores nor is overwhelmed by the cataclysm" (213)? Is there a possibility to bring sense to the senseless without letting one's emotions being carried away toward a new discourse of intolerance? And still on the issue of emotions, dare we duplicate affect in remembering the pained torments of the victims? May one rely on the ambiguities of metaphoricity or on the anesthetizing effects of understatement, or do "the claims of alterity demand nothing less than a crying out, a shriek of protest" (178)?

In this piece, which is to honor Edith Wyschogrod, the point it not, and cannot be, to take up and respond to each of the issues raised in *An Ethics of Remembering*. The very least of our objectives is—to use an intellectually and ethically irresponsible phrase—to bring closure to questions many of which are simply not amenable to representation in any medium and not amenable to analytic answers of any kind. This is Wyschogrod's point in the first epigraph to this essay. Indeed, the construction of closure would betray the victims of the traumas of the twentieth century, the incalculability of the horrors and the unmitigated darkness of *Night* in the face of which all human responses seem pointless. Instead, what this essay intends is to take into serious account the issues raised in Wyschogrod's work by allowing it to encourage a set of sensibilities, an aesthetic of psychodynamics and a memorial intelligibility that connects with trauma, so as to encourage a newly refracted reading of a primary genre of early Christian texts, the passion narratives of the Gospels.

82. Remembering as Remedy and Poison

The passion narratives that are here under consideration are foundational to Christian identity and canonical with respect to their scriptural status. Their reception history is characterized by what I will call a fateful double complicity. On the one hand, these narratives operated as generators of a deeply felt piety and faith, and as media for musical and artistic representations of great dramatic power and aesthetic brilliance. On the other hand, the passion texts and their pictorial, choral, and instrumental representations could act as perpetrators of terror, persecution, and bloodshed. Sometimes hostilities among hearers and viewers were generated as a result of bluntly polemical interpretations and provocative expositions. But the mechanism of polemics also operated in more subtle ways. Seemingly minor artistic features and casual verbal insinuations could instill or reinforce feelings of anti-Jewish sentiments. More often than not, however, responses grew out of hearers' and viewers' present cultural contexts that were saturated with hurtful polemics and biased commonplaces, a whole set of anti-Jewish ideas, imaginations, and attributes. It was what Maurice Halbwachs has called *les cadres sociaux de la mémoire* that in significant ways came to nourish the reception history.

To illustrate this memorially empowered response mechanism, one may think less of overtly aggressive interpretations and representations, but of the impact of universally celebrated pieces of art: Johann Sebastian Bach's *Passion according to St. Matthew*, Matthias Grünewald's *Isenheim Altar* in the Musée d'Unterlinden in Colmar, France, Salvador Dali's *Crucifixion* and El Greco's *Christ Carrying the Cross*, to name but a few of the most prominent exemplars. By Western reckoning at least, these are artistic commemorations of unquestionable magnificence. It may justly be said that they do not convey anti-Jewish sentiments, or at least not in as overt a fashion as, for example, the medieval passion plays that found their most popular expression both in the performative style and moral insensitivity exhibited in the Oberammergau dramatizations. Nor are the above-mentioned masterpieces as subtly complicit in anti-Jewish sentiments as Mel Gibson's *The Passion of the Christ*. But whatever the degree of anti-Jewish sentiments that these commemorative works of musical and pictorial representation may or may not convey, they inevitably come to be heard and viewed within webs of cultural, religious, and political remembering that mobilize a range of diverse responses. Always in remembering, people's own present and, more deeply, their history of remembering, affects the desire to preserve the past and infiltrates remembrances of it. Depending on one's particular memorial experiences, symbols that are central and unifying to some can be the cause of rather different—indeed, oppositional—memories to others, generating a remembering of one against the Other. The cross, for example, a central symbol of redemption in Christianity, and the dramatized center of the passion narratives, can in Jewish recollection be viewed as a symbol that has haunted Jews throughout the ages. Even the commemorative passion masterpieces may receive an equivocal reception. What for one faith conjures up memories of self-giving sacrifice on behalf of the Other for the other faith may bring back memories of brutalizing actions taken against its own. In part at least, the dual reception is due to viewers' and auditors' personal and collective genealogies of memories.

We may, however, keep in mind that this double complicity in the reception of the passion stories to a degree already resides in the canonical passion texts themselves, although, again, it is nourished in *les cadres sociaux de la mémoire* of hearers and readers. To the extent that both redemption and rejection, *célébration* and *exécration*, to invoke terms taken from Ricoeur's epigraph to this piece, are in various degrees already inscribed in these inaugurating texts, the duplicitous history of their remembering is but an extension of initial narrative impulses. Hence something of a fateful coherence exists between the inaugural narratives and a subsequent history of representation and remembrance. Viewed in this manner, the lines of demarcation between the master narratives and their memorial representations are all the more blurred if, as will be shown, the passion texts themselves are products of cultural memory and significantly fed by motivations and aspirations surrounding their compositional settings.

Remembering the killing of the charismatic leader, these stories, in the most general sense, strive to make sense of the events surrounding the crucifixion, and they manifestly do so from present perspectives. This is why their narrative dramatization, above all the power relations among the principal protagonists and the roles they played in Jesus' execution, are infiltrated by experiences and partialities which are those of the authorial, compositional present. The differentiation, therefore, between the canonical passion texts on one hand and their oral, literary, and artistic reception history on the other, masks their memorial commonality, that is, the fact that they all participate in a commonly shared history of memorializing activities, a genealogy of remembering that reaches into the deep past and extends into the receptionist present. To be sure, from the perspective of canonicity, the four passion stories are the foundational master narratives that are secondarily interpreted and reinterpreted in a subsequent reception history. No doubt, as Jan Assmann has reminded us, canonicity breathes enhanced normativity into texts, enabling them to conquer and control variance (J. Assmann 1992, 123–24: *Bändigung der Varianz*; ET: 2011 104–5). No doubt, the author has captured a primary aspect of canon and canonicity. But Assmann would likewise be the first to concede that the so-called postcanonical history invariably shows that even canonized texts, no matter how unbending their authority was and was meant to be, are never fully controllable. From the perspective of memory, the distinction between canonical and postcanonical textual identity is of little consequence, if not misleading. Memorially speaking, the passion narratives are memory texts themselves that endeavored to commemorate the death of the fallen leader, and in turn generated memorially empowered verbal and artistic responses.

83. MARK: PRO-ROMAN PROCLIVITIES

In turning to the passion narrative in Mark, we remember that text-critical examinations of the available manuscript tradition "reach the conclusion … that the oldest form of the Gospel is the Short Ending" (Parker 1997, 143). We are dealing, therefore, with a passion narrative that lacks a resurrection appearance story, although this is an inappropriate assessment formulated from the perspective of the other three canonical Gospels. The reading grids of Matthew, Luke, and John aside, Mark does not "lack" anything. As it stands, a sense of unrelieved gloom is hovering over Mark's rendition of Jesus' violent death.

In this review on Mark, as in the following segments on the other canonical Gospels, those features are being examined that contribute to the duplicitous history of remembering. In the case of the Markan passion narrative the high priest and Pilate function in parallel fashion in the twin trials (Mark 14:55–65; 15:2–15). Both ask Jesus about his messianic identity (14:61; 15:2), both encounter Jesus' silence (14:61; 15:5), and both receive a qualifying or indirect answer (14:62; 15:2). But this is where the similarities end. The high priest and the priestly establishment seem determined to gain Jesus' conviction so as to put him to death (14:55). They persuade the crowds to plead for his execution and to have a man (of probably revolutionary violence) released in his place. Pilate, on the other hand, is a more complex figure. Although he sees through the high priestly motivation (15:10), he yields to the pressure put on him by the crowds, has the man of violence (Barabbas) released, and has Jesus turned over to his executioners (15:15), but he acts to please the crowds and against his own better judgment (15:6–9) and unconvinced of Jesus' culpability (15:14). He "wonders" (15:5) while Jesus is alive, and, following crucifixion and death, he "wonders" (15:44) whether Jesus is already dead. Subsequently Pilate grants the request of "a respected member of the council" (15:43), who dares approach him (τολμήσας εἰσῆλθεν), to honor Jesus with a dignified burial (15:42–46). Thus while Jesus' own high priest and the priestly establishment press indictment and conviction, Pilate, representative of the imperial, foreign power, mistrusts the priestly motivation (15:10) and seeks to save the life of Jesus.

This particular plot development reaches its point of culmination in the "testimony" of the Roman centurion. Observing the manner of Jesus' dying and the circumstances surrounding his death, he makes what amounts to a confession: "Truly, this man was Son of God" (15:39). In the overall plot construction two features add special weight to this testimony. One, the "Son of God" designation carries the blessing of the Markan narrator. Programmatically located by the narrator (in some manuscripts) in 1:1, and announced by the heavenly voice both at baptism (1:11) and transfiguration (9:7), it is, apart from the high priest's question asked at his interrogation (14:61), invoked only by the unclean spirits (5:7; 3:11) who speak the "truth" out of ignorance. Two, the centurion's "testimony" constitutes not merely the "correct" confession but also the only "correct" confession made by a human being in the Gospel. In character with the Markan plot logic, the disciples who should have made this confession fail to make it. They abandon Jesus at the outset of his last and fateful journey into Jerusalem, while the man in charge of the execution paradoxically pronounces the "confession" that was theirs to make.

The rhetorical impact of this narration is to incline Christian hearers/ readers sympathetically toward Pilate and still more so toward the centurion over and against the high priest. While the narrator unmistakably speaks for and takes the place of the victim, he also sides with the Roman authorities against the high priestly establishment on the issue of moral and judicial responsibility. This pro-Roman proclivity injected an element of forgetfulness, distortion even, into Christian memory, the repercussions of which will be felt throughout the Jewish-Christian memorial history of the passion texts.

84. Matthew: The Killing of the Righteous One(s)

In regard to the passion text in Matthew, few biblical statements have left more bloodstained traces in the history of Jewish and Christian remembering than "all the people's" response to Pilate that "his [Jesus'] blood be on us and our on children" (Matt 27:25). In the subsequent history of Christian rememorization of the Matthean passion narrative, this verse, or rather, a particular reading of this verse, came to function as a contributing factor to the shedding of Jewish blood at the hands of Christians through the centuries.

In the Matthean context, the identity of "all the people" (πᾶς ὁ λαός) who invoke judgment upon themselves requires examination. In the

LXX the prevailing meaning of λαός is people in the collective sense of nation. In Matt 27:24–25 a distinction is made between ὄχλος and λαός. Pilate, declaring his innocence with regard to the shedding of Jesus' blood, washes his hands "before the crowd" (27:24: ἀπέναντι τοῦ ὄχλου), whereupon "the people as a whole" (or "all the people": 27:25: πᾶς ὁ λαός) pronounce themselves ready and willing to accept the consequences of Jesus' death. Both in keeping with the Matthean narrative logic and in the larger linguistic context, it is entirely reasonable to identify the ὄχλος with the people assembled locally in Jerusalem before Pilate's judgment seat, and πᾶς ὁ λαός in the sense of nation.

The fateful, fatal verses, Matt 27:24–25, will have to be understood strictly within the context of the Gospel's narrative logic—all the more so since subsequent interpretations operated from a rather different context of later Jewish-Christian power relations. Jerusalem and its temple are an issue in Matthew, and the destruction of the holy place by the Romans has left more tangible traces in this Gospel than in Mark. In the parable of the Wedding Banquet (Matt 22:1–14) those who have been invited to join the festivities fail to follow the king's invitation. Enraged by their lack of response, the king orders his troops to move in, and they "destroyed those murderers, and burned their city" (Matt 22:7). The devastation of Jerusalem, and the conflagration of its temple, is here realistically articulated and explicated in terms of a punishment for the disobedience of murderous people. The circumstances of the murders and the identity of their victims are spelled out in remarkable detail in the culmination of the seven anti-Pharisaic woes (Matt 23:1–36), an attack directed against a well-established group of leaders in Israel: "Therefore I send you prophets, sages, and scribes, some of whom you will kill and crucify, and some you will flog in your synagogues and pursue from town to town, so that upon you may come all the righteous blood shed on earth, from righteous Abel to the blood of Zechariah, son of Barachiah, whom you murdered between the sanctuary and the altar" (Matt 23:34–35).

We encounter here the well-known Jewish topos of the killing of the prophets and the murder of the righteous ones, a distinct preoccupation of Matthew: they always kill the best of our people. The concluding sentence of the anti-Pharisaic woes expresses a dire warning that the blood of the righteous will come to haunt the people: "Truly I say to you, all this will come upon this generation" (Matt 23:36: ἀμὴν λέγω ὑμῖν, ἥξει ταῦτα πάντα ἐπὶ τὴν γενεὰν ταύτην). The understanding of "this generation" is a critical and consequential one. By way of example, in his commentary on

Matthew Eduard Schweizer expresses the view that "by 'this generation' Matthew means not just the first generation after Jesus but all the generations of Judaism that reject him" (1975, 458). Formulations of this kind call for special caution on the part of the reader. There needs to be full consciousness of the fact that Schweizer, along with interpreters before and after him, in effect has introduced the notion of an eternal curse being placed upon Judaism. The author belongs to a generation of scholars who were not versed in narrative criticism, the discipline that pays close attention to interior narrative causalities long before assumptions are made about a text's referential outreach. In the Matthean narrative context the announcement of the impending doom to be inflicted "upon this generation" is immediately followed by Jesus' lament over Jerusalem, which once more deplores the killing of prophets and the stoning of those sent to the city (23:37–39), which leads directly into Jesus' prediction of the destruction of the city's temple (24:1–2). We therefore recognize the following narrative sequence: anti-Pharisaic woes—exposure of the murdered victims: prophets, sages, and scribes, including Abel and Zechariah—the blood of the righteous will come upon the murderers—anticipation of punishment of "this generation"—lament over Jerusalem and anticipation of its desolation—prediction of the destruction of the temple. This intratextual sequence of developments is entirely plausible within an intra-Jewish context.

There is a widely shared scholarly opinion that the experience of a post-70 conflict between a Pharisaic, rabbinic form of Judaism and Matthew's dissident messianic Judaism has deeply infiltrated the Gospel narrative (Saldarini 1991, 38–61; Hummel 1966, 26–33; Ellis 1974, 3–6). The composition of the Gospel, it is likewise understood, is to be dated in the time after the temple's calamitous conflagration in 70 C.E. Like many in post-70 Judaism, Matthew viewed the fall of Jerusalem and the conflagration of the temple as the temporal punishment for the disobedience of the people (Stone 1981; Henze 2012). Looking back on the physical and metaphysical disaster of the temple's demise, he writes in the conviction that Jesus' ominous prediction had come to fateful fulfillment for his own generation.

The catastrophe forced the issue of Jewish identity with exceptional intensity, setting national-religious interests against one another, and driving religious, political parties to compete over the soul of Israel. In that context, "the Gospel of Matthew should be read along with other Jewish post-destruction literature, such as the apocalyptic works of 2 Baruch, 4 Ezra, and Apocalypse of Abraham, early strata of the Mishnah, and Josephus"

(Saldarini 1991, 39). Matthew, from his perspective, is critically involved "in a struggle for the future of Judaism" (43). Locked in an intra-Jewish conflict of identity, the Gospel advocates a messianically motivated observance of the Torah, indeed a Torah radicalization combined with a rigorous sense of righteousness in opposition to rabbinic, Pharisaic Torah observance. In this context, the Gospel's vituperative anti-Pharisaic language is largely designed to delegitimate Pharisaically guided Judaism, and to legitimize its own brand of messianically inspired Torah observance. In Matthew's time, the outcome over the future of postwar Judaism was still an open question, but within a short time "Matthew lost the battle over Judaism" (60).

The Matthean antagonism toward Pharisaism is entirely comprehensible as an intra-Jewish conflict. After all, the dissenting community of Qumran was likewise involved in a conflict with the Pharisees (Jaffee 2001, 39–44). But when Christianity began to position itself as the absolute religion in the Western and Eastern Hemispheres, its custodians of memory were driven by the desire to legitimate their increasingly universal Christian claims vis-à-vis what was now judged to be the old, superseded religion. The result was a Christian reconfiguration of Matthew's intra-Jewish dispute in universalist terms. *Matthew's dramatization of a conflict between a Pharisaic, rabbinic, and his own dissident, messianic type of Judaism in later times was metamorphosed into an irreconcilable estrangement between Christianity and Judaism.*

In this new historical context, the intra-Jewish configuration that was mirrored in the Matthean narrative fell into oblivion. With the temple conflagration receding into an ever-more-distant past, its demise ceased to be understood as a pivotal watershed that had been perceived as temporal punishment for the murders of Israel's very best ones. For all intents and purposes, Matthew's Jerusalem localization and the momentous religious import of the fall of the temple were eclipsed in conformity with Christianity's universal claims and ambitions. Matthew's localized setting of the people of Jerusalem and of people at a particular time was now reimagined in terms of a people who had spoken on behalf of Jews everywhere and at all times, and their response to Pilate was thought to have invited an ever-lasting punishment upon Judaism as a whole. Given the nexus of new power constellations, with Christians constituting the majority and Jews in the extreme minority, the former arrogated to themselves the role of vengeful executioners of a people who, in their view, had been branded with an eternal curse. In this manner, memory's desire to redescribe the Matthean passion story with a view toward vindicating the Christian position of universal power paved the way for demonizing fantasies and murderous actions.

85. LUKE: *APOLOGIA ROMANA*

More than any other canonical Gospel, Luke has foregrounded the demise of Jerusalem and its temple. His narrative refers to the military siege and destruction of the city in historically graphic terms: Jerusalem is "surrounded by armies" (Luke 21:20); the "enemies will set up ramparts [around it] and surround [it], and hem [it] in on every side, and crush [it] to the ground" (19:43–44). The city will be "trampled on by the Gentiles" (21:24), and people "will fall by the edge of the sword" (21:24). But in spite of Luke's historical alertness to Rome's overwhelming military power and the tragic affliction of the population of Jerusalem, his Gospel issues neither complaint nor criticism concerning Roman brutalities and refrains from holding Roman military and political authorities responsible for the people's suffering. The Gospel's critical lament is over Jerusalem and its people because they did not recognize "the things that make for peace" (Luke 19:42: τὰ πρὸς εἰρήνην), and not about imperial brutalities. The fault, Luke argues, lies with the city and its citizens who habitually killed prophetic messengers (13:34) and missed the appropriate time (καιρός) of God's visitation (19:44).

Notably, Luke abides by the Markan pattern of absorbing the destruction of city and temple into the narration of Jesus' life and death, instead of relocating the catastrophe, as would appear historically logical, into his (Luke's) second volume. Like Matthew and Mark, Luke constructs close narrative links between Jesus and the fate of the city. Over and above the lament over Jerusalem (13:34–35), narrated also in Matthew (23:37-39) but not in Mark, and Jesus' prediction of the destruction of the temple (Luke 21:6; Mark 13:2; Matt 24: 2), Luke alone introduces two more lament scenes: Jesus weeping over Jerusalem (Luke 19:41–44) and his grieving over the daughters of Jerusalem (Luke 23:27–31). Both scenes are located in the passion narrative, one at Jesus' entry into the city and one on the way to the crucifixion, thereby closely connecting his fate with that of the city—both being doomed. Undoubtedly, Luke is in possession of detailed knowledge about the demise of Jerusalem, and the mass extermination of its people, yet his narrative logic is not driven as much by passion for the dead as by a conventional, religious rationale: the sins of the people were the root cause of their demise.

Luke's traditional theme of the culpability of the people interacts with the theme of the apologia Romana, *creating a theological reasoning that was to become programmatic in Christian memory.* As narrated by Luke, the twin issues of Roman taxation and Jewish messiahship are linked together in bringing Jesus to trial. When brought before Pilate, the charge against him is that "we found this man perverting our nation, forbidding us to pay taxes to the emperor, and saying that he himself is the Messiah, a king" (23:2). Kingship, messianism, revolution, and Roman taxation constitute the core of the indictment, a potent political charge that is designed to secure the death sentence. Luke, although not unaware of Pilate's gross insensitivity toward particular ethnic, religious groups (Luke 13:1), nevertheless goes further than either Mark or Matthew toward promoting the Roman governor into a model Christian. Pilate responds not once, but three times: there was no basis for the charges (Luke 23:4), Jesus was not guilty (Luke 23:14), and there is, therefore, no judicial basis for pronouncing the death sentence (Luke 23:22). This is the first time in Christian memory that the formal charge of political culpability has been brought against Jesus—only to be dismissed, and dismissed by the principal Roman authority in charge of the case. Henceforth, the *apologia Romana* is firmly entrenched in Christian memory.

After Pilate has pronounced Jesus innocent, Luke will not have the latter tortured by Roman soldiers. In Mark, Pilate has Jesus flogged (Mark 15:15) before he turns him over to the soldiers (οἱ στρατιῶται), who in turn mock and humiliate him (Mark 15:16–20). Matthew narrates a very similar scenario (Matt 27:27–31). Hence, both in Mark and in Mathew, Jesus twice undergoes physical and mental suffering on the instruction of Pilate and by Roman hands. In Luke, however, Roman soldiers verbally abuse Jesus while on the cross (Luke 23:36), but neither they nor Pilate will subject him to physical or mental degradation prior to his execution. Pilate intends to have him flogged, but he yields to the crowds, who demand crucifixion (Luke 23:22–23). Those who arrested Jesus are "the chief priests, the officers to the temple police, and the elders" (Luke 22:52), those who mock and beat him in the courtyard of the high priest's house are "the men holding him" (Luke 22:63–65). The Lukan plot construction is a harbinger of things to come in Christian commemoration: the culpability for Jesus' suffering and death is increasingly transferred from Roman to Jewish authorities, and eventually to the Jewish people at large. Luke's *apologia Romana* reaches its peak with the centurion, the Roman official in charge of the execution, who, when viewing Jesus' death, pronounces him righteous or, legally speaking, innocent (23:47: ὄντως ὁ ἄνθρωπος οὗτος δίκαιος ἦν). As far as Luke is concerned, therefore, Jesus' death was a judicial error forced upon the Romans by the Jewish authorities and crowds in Jerusalem.

In seeking to make a case for the compatibility of the new religion with Rome, Luke is aware that he needs to address the controversial issue of Jesus' political culpability. Crucifixion by the Romans made Zealotic criminality eminently plausible. The Gospel concedes that the charge of revolutionary involvement and political culpability was indeed an issue and the principal reason for the hearing before Pilate. But Luke's *apologia* is so contrived a construction that it strains not only historical plausibility, but narrative logic as well. Whereas the people view Jesus as a political revolutionary and want to see him executed, Pilate, the man in charge of imperial law and order, does not. On the other hand, the people demand the release of a political revolutionary, Barabbas, who, Luke emphasizes, "had been put in prison for an insurrection in the city, and for murder" (23:19). Thus Luke's Pilate not only sentences a man whom he considers innocent of the charge of messianic, Zealotic culpability, but he also lends support to insurrectionism by giving in to the people's pressure in ordering the release of Barabbas, a known Zealotic insurrectionist.

In view of Luke's sympathy toward Gentile culture and Roman power, the ending of his two-volume work is particularly revealing and gives us a clue to his narrative perspective. In Acts Paul the apostle is described as a Roman citizen by birth (Acts 22:25–27; 23:27) who is being hounded by the Jewish community and authorities, who stands accused of being "an agitator among all the Jews throughout the world" (Acts 24:5), and has been subject to a Jewish assassination attempt (Acts 23:12–15; 25:3). By contrast, the Roman governor Felix treats Paul generously while he is in custody (Acts 24:23), and the Roman governor Festus approves his appeal to the Roman emperor (Acts 25:12). The Jewish king Agrippa II—educated in Rome, in support of Vespasian's and Titus's military campaign against Jerusalem, and rewarded for his devotion to the Roman imperial cause in Rome—stands ready to set Paul free, had it not been for the fact that he had appealed to the emperor. After his arrival in Rome, Paul spends two years in the capital proclaiming the gospel. His appeal never comes to fruition, but he preaches the gospel without interference on the part of the authorities (28:30–31). His historically very plausible violent death under the government of emperor Nero is never mentioned. Viewed from the angle of narrative construction, this is a revealing ending because

Luke's second volume, as all narrative, entails to some degree a plotting backward from its anticipated ending. This *interior retrospectivity* (Ong 1977b, 240–53) implies that both Gospel and Acts are constructed with a view toward and from the viewpoint of the city of Rome, which Paul had reached at the end of Acts. In other words, Luke designed his two volumes from the perspective of a Christianity that had to be sensitive to its existence and survival in the capital of the empire.

86. John: Metaphysical Aspirations and the Fate of the Other

When Clement of Alexandria espoused the idea that the author of the fourth canonical Gospel, encouraged by his friends and prompted by the Spirit, "composed a spiritual Gospel" (πνευματικὸν ποιῆσαι εὐαγγέλιον), the early church father intended to draw a distinction between the Johannine narrative and the other three canonical Gospels. Whereas the Synoptics had grasped the "corporeal things" (τὰ σωματικά), the Gospel of John had come into existence under the special guidance of the Spirit (Eusebius, *Hist. eccl.* 6.14.5–10). There is no denying that the Fourth Gospel entertains a high estimation of the Spirit, if only because—unlike any other canonical or noncanonical Gospel—John developed the figure of the Paraclete, who sustains the presence of the Spirit in the absence of Jesus. Clement and the tradition he relied upon had rightly sensed the spiritual, indeed metaphysical, underpinnings of the Gospel.

There is, however, a growing awareness of an aspect seemingly at odds with the Gospel's spirituality: its anti-Jewishness. Even Raymond Brown, a mainline interpreter of the Gospel, concedes that "in setting up a contrast between Christian and Jew, John may well be the strongest among the Gospels" (1966, lxx).[1] That would be a cautious understatement of a matter of gravity. Not infrequently exegesis has been inclined to belittle and rationalize the issue, and reluctant to acknowledge that the animosity John exhibits toward the Jews is in conflict with its spirituality and theological profundity. Should it not be possible to isolate and excise the unspiritual elements in the interest of highlighting the Gospel's spiritual and ethical grandeur? Tempting as this proposition might be, it will be suggested here that John's spirituality and its anti-Jewish animus are tragically intertwined

---

1. Space does not permit discussion of an intra-Johannine conflict reflected in the narrative (Woll 1981; Kelber 1987a; Thatcher 2005).

features. Antipathy toward the Jews and philosophical ambition are concurrent phenomena in this Gospel. *This is another way of saying that the Gospel's anti-Jewish sentiments, far from being a regrettable deviation from its spiritual core, are an essential component of its metaphysical agenda.*

Reaching back to the beginning of beginnings, to a state outside of time and prior to creation, the Johannine prologue lodges the Λόγος in foundational primordiality (John 1:1: Ἐν ἀρχῇ). In what appears to be a strikingly logocentric gesture, the Gospel shows forth its metaphysical ambition. Yet it is a metaphysical ambition that is complicated from the outset. The noteworthy feature about the metaphysical Λόγος is not its absolute transcendence and undifferentiated identity, but a status of ambiguity. In being both "with God" (John 1:1: πρὸς τὸν θεόν) and "God" (John 1:1: θεὸς ἦν), the Λόγος, in almost classical fashion, manifests difference in identity. Inscribed into the logic of identity is the irrepressible nature of difference. From the beginning, therefore, the Gospel creates a dilemma for the Λόγος that has a critical bearing on the subsequent narrative and its readers.

As the Λόγος embarks on his earthly career, he chooses the status of incarnation, which enlarges his difference from divinity. But inasmuch as he differs, he simultaneously seeks to retain his identity from above, for as the Gospel time and again asserts, the Λόγος who enters into the flesh does so for the purpose of manifesting his glory. The Jesus who submits to spatio-temporal conditions never tires of pleading his unity with the heavenly Father. In principle, therefore, the Λόγος, once descended into the status of humanity, acts out a problematic that had been inscribed ἐν ἀρχῇ. But the transfer to earth has magnified the dilemma into one of above versus below, glory versus flesh, and transcendence versus contingency. The status of the incarnate Λόγος, initially articulated in terms of *being God* and simultaneously *being with God*, is now more accurately defined as divinely incarnate—seeking to retain the glory while being naturalized in the flesh.

How does the Gospel take up this central dilemma, deal with it, negotiate it, attempt to resolve it? Its principal hermeneutical tool seems to be a linguistic duality, a twofold structuring of language that is enacted in both the narrative and the discourse sections of the Gospel. Upon entering into the condition of the flesh, the Λόγος speaks words that are both in conformity with worldly intelligibility and in excess of it. This is the linguistic trait of the double entendres that characterize Johannine language, including a whole semiology of symbols and signifying features. It serves to dramatize a differential quality of communication, giving rise to tensions between apparent and intended meanings, and eliciting ascending moves from corporeality to transcendence. In the ebb and flow of the narrative, John's metaphoric language seeks to make room for the literal while at the same encouraging transcendence in pursuit of spiritual aspirations. In short, insofar as both narrative and discourses embolden hearers/readers to let themselves be "lifted up" from literalness to spirituality, they operate in the interest of the Gospel's metaphysical agenda.

In the perspective of most contemporary practitioners of the narratological approach to the Gospel, John's double entendres and the corollary misunderstandings engage hearers/readers in a process of education. Through symbolization and consequent misunderstandings, it is suggested, the narrative enables them "to ascend again and again to the higher plateau of meaning" (Culpepper 1983, 199) so as to rise from the naïvetés of literalness to genuine enlightenment. In this way, the recurrence of misunderstandings that arise primarily over the ambiguities of language seem calculated to usher hearers/readers into the circle of privileged insiders.

Lest we grow overly confident in assuming that linguistic duality, irony, and the whole scheme of signification—as if by a fiat of language—"sweetens and spices the fellowship between reader and narrator" (Culpepper 1983, 180), we need reminding that ironic double-talk can well serve as mode of marginalization and as a means of exclusion. In the philosophical tradition, it was Kierkegaard who had viewed irony less as a catalyst of illumination and more as an instrument of destruction (1965; original Danish, 1841). For him, the Socratic execution of the pedagogy of irony was "exclusively negative" (232) in carrying out a "destructive activity" (236). "Thus irony is the brand, the two-edged sword, which he [Socrates] wielded over Hellas like a destroying angel" (234). If the example of Kierkegaard seems far-fetched, it may at the very least serve to make us mindful of irony's potential in acting not necessarily as a benign educator, but also as perpetrator of negativity, of cruelty even.

Where there are insiders, there also are those who are cast to the outside. As the Johannine Gospel dramatizes its persistently dichotomous plot, "the Jews" are the ultimate victims. Their exclusion is coexistent with the metaphysical aspirations of the narrative. Whether the protagonist strives to carry the burden of the flesh while manifesting glory, or the discourses address audiences from below while seeking to communicate a truth from above, or the narrative opens the space of signifying differences in gesturing toward the metaphysical signified—the narratological, linguistic, and theological enactment of this Johannine agenda coexists with and indeed feeds on the marginalization, indeed the demonization (John 8:44) of "the Jews." The more metaphor and irony are doing their divisive work, the more are characters in the narrative marginalized, above all "the Jews."

In anticipating the crucifixion, "the Jews" are barred from the *Aufhebung*, this central event of lifting the whole plot of double entendres onto a new level of synthesis. Three times the Johannine Jesus speaks in mysteriously metaphorical language about his death in terms of being "lifted up" (John 3:14: ὑψωθῆναι; 8:28: ὑψώσητε; 12:32: ὑψωθῶ). At the third and last time, the veil of obscurity is slightly drawn aside and a hint is given of the double meaning of *Aufhebung*, conceding access to the transcending ascent, which is to coincide with the moment of fateful lifting up onto the cross (John 12:33). To the crowd, however, the dual signification of being "lifted up" remains unintelligible. Since the Messiah is to remain forever on earth, his presence is unambiguously terrestrial, and the thought of his death, let alone the paradoxical sublation of his death on the cross, is irreconcilable with his identity (John 12:34).

As in Matthew, so also in John has the experience of an intra-Jewish conflict between a synagogal community (possibly connected to the Jamnia Academy) and John's dissident messianic community deeply infiltrated the narrative. J. Louis Martyn (1979), more than anyone, has illuminated the Gospel's social setting and its assimilation into the narrative. And, as was the case with Matthew, that conflict has to be dated in the postwar years following the physical and metaphysical trauma of the temple's destruction, a period marked by intense struggles over religious, ethnic, and cultural identities. At issue in John is neither the Torah nor the Gentiles, but commitment to the messiahship of Jesus, the role of Moses (especially his identity as Prophet Messiah based on Deut 18:15, 18), and the status of signs (miracles) in relation to messiahship. Unlike Matthew, John polemicizes not primarily against the Pharisees as a distinct group within Judaism but against "the Jews" collectively. Seventy times the hearers/readers are alerted to the designation of "the Jews" in John's Gospel (over against five or six occurrences in the three Synoptics altogether). Moreover, the Johannine use of ἀποσυνάγωγος ποιεῖν/γένηται (9:22; 12:42; 16:2), a *hapax legomenon* with no known use prior to or outside of the Fourth Gospel, reflects the experience of an expulsion from the synagogue. Hence, what commenced as a local, intra-Jewish conflict appears to have deteriorated into a schism, a separation into two communities espousing different and opposing religious identities.

The Gospel's language of double entendre, we saw, is meant to place hearers/readers of the narrative on the royal road to unity with the Father. But again, it is precisely this linguistic duplicity that plays havoc with the welfare of the Other. In this intricately metaphorical and ambitiously metaphysical narrative "the Jews" by and large remain stuck on the literal level, unable to lift themselves up to the spiritual level. Undoubtedly, the difficulties inscribed in John's metaphysical agenda affect all characters in the narrative and its hearers/readers as well. But no one faces greater obstacles than "the Jews" because the metaphorical plot dynamics are primarily played out against them. In this sense the Gospel has created the precondition for the fateful Christian supersessionism which asserted that Judaism was in carnal servitude to the letter, "taking signs of spiritual things for the things themselves" (Augustine, *De doctrina Christiana* 3.6).

87. The Present Pressed into the Service of Remembering the Past

In sum, we see the four canonical passion texts redescribing a past event by variously resorting to and arguing from present experiences. *The past is pressed into the service of the present, just as the horizon of present experience serves as frame of reference for the narration of a past event.* In this respect, the passion texts operate precisely according to the norms of cultural memory as defined by Jan Assmann (who in turn is indebted to Maurice Halbwachs). Defining reconstructivism (*Rekonstruktivität*), a key element of cultural memory theory, Assmann writes: "Memory, then, works through reconstruction. The past cannot be preserved by itself. It is continually in the process of being reorganized according to the changes taking place in the frame of reference of each successive present" (2011, 27; 1992, 41–42).

What this suggests is that neither the canonical passion narratives themselves nor their subsequent history of verbal and artistic representation can preserve the past as "pure" past. In all instances, the past is preserved as a remembered past, and this remembering takes place within social frames of present references. These *Bezugsrahmen*, or, to use Halbwachs's term, *cadres sociaux*, which frame and organize remembering, are subject to continuous alterations due to ever-changing present circumstances (Halbwachs 1925). It is noteworthy that the dramatic element of double complicity, which in John's case on one hand facilitates the ascent to enlightenment and transcendence and on the other hand breeds marginalization, antagonism, and demonization, enters the passion texts primarily as a result of changing social frames of present references. In the Fourth Gospel, the present *cadres sociaux de la mémoire* reflect tense relations between emergent Jewish and Christian identities in postwar circumstances. As a result, the language of these Christian foundational narratives increasingly runs the risk of projecting an identity of the Other as a target for violence. As we saw, once invaded by double complicity that is spurred by present experiences, the passion texts in turn inspire an interpretive remembering that likewise continues to be influenced by people's personal and collective memories. In this way, the commemorative passion narratives and their subsequent memorial representations constitute a single, duplicitous mnemohistory or a long haul of genealogies of remembering—for better and for worse.

88. Mark Again: Remembering Violence

Until the recent arrival of literary, narratological criticism, interpretations of the passion texts (and of the Gospels at large) were predominantly the prerogative of historical criticism. Among the key issues that have typified the historical-critical approach to the passion texts, the following may be cited: Markan authorship; an assumed pre-Markan passion narrative; the text's compositional history, postulating one or two pre-Markan stages in the tradition; assumed ideational shifts in the text's compositional history, from a Jewish toward a Gentile-oriented stage, or from a martyrological narration to a theological conception, or from a historically grounded account to legendary embellishments; traditions before, after, and in Mark; the generic identity of the passion text; literary relations among the three Synoptic passion texts; the literary and religious differences among the four canonical passion texts; possible relations between the passion in Mark and the *Gospel of Peter*; discrepancies between Synoptic and Johannine chronologies; the historicity of the trial before the Jewish establishment; the accusation, in that trial, that Jesus pronounced a threat against the temple; the hearing before the Roman governor; judicial questions with respect to trial and hearing, in particular the legal authority of the Sanhedrin; the law of amnesty used to procure the release of Barabbas; the chronology of Jesus' death: day, month, and year; comparison of the Last Supper traditions in Paul and the Synoptic narratives; Jesus' own understanding of his death; the passion narrative's theological framing, and in particular what has been termed its royal Christology. These and numerous other topoi have played a significant role in the interpretation of the passion texts.

These are all matters of central importance to the passion narratives—when viewed through the lenses of the historical-critical paradigm. The issues raised, the approaches taken, and the results obtained are born out of, and in turn reinforce, what seem to be perfectly settled perspectives. And yet, should we not perhaps more accurately say that the issues raised, the approaches taken, and the results obtained are framed from the perspective of the paradigm's very particular understanding of history and historical criticism? *Is not the historical-critical paradigm's application of* critical thought *more correctly described as an engagement in* habits of critical thought, *and has not the paradigm's intellectuality been nourished from distinctive premises about the nature of ancient texts, the life of tradition, compositional practices, the role of sources, and about historical processes?* Once the historical-critical method had gained control over the text in compliance with the norms by which it views and treats all forms of the verbal art in antiquity, the conditions for understanding were assumed to have been met. Within the confines of the historical paradigm, this procedure seems entirely reasonable. What we are describing here is the triumph of the model of truth as literary, generic, compositional, source-critical, chronological, and historical correctness.

Yet I cannot but be struck by a certain aridity in our historical appreciation of the passion narrative, of all narratives, and by something of an affective void in our interpretations. We are, after all, dealing with the story of a violent death, a sacred story in Christian faith, commemorated in sacrament and liturgy, and celebrated in the artistic media. It is maintained here that the search for authentic textuality and textual originality, for accurate chronology, for the bedrock of facticity, and comparative literary analysis fails to connect with the commemorative and psychodynamic impulses that feed the narrative. At the very least, the historical-critical paradigm falls short of probing the deeper springs that motivate and nourish the narratives of death.

In apprehending the passion narratives as commemorative texts, interpretation proceeds from the concept of trauma, ever mindful of the fact that the founding event was an act of gross violence, in the sense this has been articulated by Ricoeur in an epigraph to this essay. Such is the monstrosity of that event that it must have posed severe challenges to all modes of representation and commemoration: one cannot verbally communicate the unvarnished, unedited terror in its factual rawness. Little wonder that Roman authors, while virtually unanimous that crucifixion was horrific business, exercised reticence in writing about it. "Crucifixion was widespread and frequent, above all in Roman times, but the cultured literary world wanted to have nothing to do with it, and as a rule kept quiet about it" (Hengel 1977, 38). Caesar, Lucretius, Virgil, Statius, the younger Pliny, Aulus Gellius, Horace, Tacitus, and many others were either silent or exceedingly restrained in giving any account of the Roman death penalty. There is hardly any reference to it in any of the numerous inscriptions etched onto enduring materials like stone. Least of all is it possible to find principled objections to crucifixion in Roman sources. "This means, however, that the relative scarcity of references to crucifixions in antiquity, and their fortuitousness, are less a historical problem than an aesthetic one, connected with the sociology of literature," writes Hengel (38). Perhaps one should add that the relative silence about the ghastly matter was a moral problem as well, testifying to the failure of the intelligentsia and all those in positions of power to arouse the conscience of the people.

Proceeding from the concept of trauma prompts the question of how the transposition of an act of gross violence onto the arena of language could be accomplished, and how emotional wounds can be healed, or at least treated. How is this "exhibitionist act of political violence" (Kirk 2005a, 192) made accessible to hearers/readers by writing it up, or better, by writing about it? Apart from death's ritualization in the Last Supper, can this founding event of violence be commemorated in any narrative form? A fundamental strategy of cultural memory is the fusion of (recollections of) the past with social experiences in the present. We have observed this habitual procedure throughout this essay, and we have detailed its efficaciousness *ad bonam et ad malam partem*. By drawing on the past from the perspectives of the present, one retains not the past itself, but a re-created, freshly remembered past. One principal memory strategy, therefore, is to refuse to let past history ever fully define present identity and those who are engaged in the work of remembering.

In what follows, three more memory strategies will be elaborated that are operative in Mark's passion narrative. One feature concerns the construction of a "memory place" that provides a safely familiar habitat for what seems utterly unrepresentable. A second feature is called "interpretive keying," which in the most general terms suggests scanning of the past in search of meaning for the present. In Gospel studies it specifically refers to the retrieval of scriptural references as interpretive "keys" in the formation of the narrative. The third feature seeks to cope with the traumas of history and its disrupting effects by devising causal connections and a sense of normative coherence. What all three strategies—memory place, interpretive keying, and construction of causal connections—have in common is a mode of encoding "the festering wound" (*die eiternde Wunde*) to use Nietzsche's poignant expression cited in an epigraph to this essay, in older, familiar patterns and in a network of newly constructed causalities so as to make violence both comprehensible and in a sense bearable.

Concerning memory places, the scholarly realization of a commonplace pattern underlying the Markan passion text has been a matter of growing realization via the studies of Lothar Ruppert (1972a; 1972b; 1973), George Nickelsburg (1980), Burton Mack (1988), and Arthur Dewey (2005). In the 1970s Ruppert published a series of books that offered a comprehensive survey of the motif of the offended, assaulted, and persecuted righteous one(s). Covering nearly a millennium of Jewish scribal productivity, ranging from the Hebrew Bible and the Septuagint, across Hellenistic-Jewish, Qumran, and apocalyptic literature, he observed and traced a number of trajectories of the motif of the *passio iusti* or *justorum* through the centuries. While Ruppert's work remained strangely inconclusive in its limited focus on the accumulation of occurrences of the motif in their respective semantic fields, it has nonetheless succeeded in uncovering a widely dispersed and tradition-honored complex of standard features associated with the sufferings of the righteous one(s). Nickelsburg was far less reticent in drawing firm and bold conclusions. Confining his investigation to a smaller number of comparative texts, he argued that the motif of the rescue and vindication of a persecuted innocent person or persons (156) had been emplotted in the Markan passion text. Moreover, what for Ruppert was a motif for Nickelsburg was a genre, in fact a "literary genre" (163), which, owing to its discrepancy with Markan redaction, was "best explained by the hypothesis that [it] ... derive[s] from a pre-Markan passion narrative" (183). Assuredly, the latter assumption represents a thinking in the register of the documentary paradigm, which is habitually prone to solving interpretive issues textually and ever so often by reference to a hidden text behind the text. But Nickelsburg considerably advanced thinking about the motif of the *passio iusti* and its implication for our understanding of Mark's passion text. Mack (1988), while generally—although not in all details—agreeing with Nickelsburg's assessment of the existence of the motif in Mark, refrained from tracing it to the assumed pre-Markan history of the passion text. If I understand him correctly, his overall argument is in favor not of a pre-Markan passion narrative but of the Gospel's plot coherence and overall compositional logic. The Gospel's compositional achievement was the employment of the motif of the persecuted innocent one, who, Mack claims, is "wisdom's child" (269). In turn, it served as the basis for the construction of a merger of the early Jesus traditions with the Hellenistic Christ myth (273–76). Unaware of the wide-ranging dispersion of the motif as demonstrated by Ruppert, Mack chose to return to an old theory concerning Mark's theological, compositional achievement. Here we see how a potentially promising approach is forced back into the Bultmannian model of the genesis of the Gospel (Bultmann 1970, 372–73; 1963, 346–47)—a model for which there is next to no evidence.

We owe to A. Dewey (2005) the beginnings of a thoroughgoing rethinking of basic assumptions about and approaches to Mark's passion text. While he is, like Mack, unaware of Ruppert's extensive research on the ancient passion motif, he acknowledges Nickelsburg's identification of the motif and its location in Mark (122). The theme of the suffering innocent one provides "the overarching story pattern" for Mark's passion text (127). Dewey's achievement is to link the commonplace pattern in the Markan passion narrative with memory theory. Inspired by Carruthers's studies on memory in medieval culture (1998), he proposed that the construction, or more precisely the *inventio*, of a commonplace pattern in the narrative commemoration of Jesus' death was precisely the kind of device one could expect from memory's operations. "The work of memory was not to re-present, not to reduplicate, but to construct, to deliver a place for images" (126) that could serve as a habitat for the trauma. In short, memory's principal objective was "not simply a matter of recalling the death of Jesus," but "to 'invent' a *locus* for his death on which one can perform the craft of memory" (127). Invention, I add, is not to be assimilated to falsehood and untruth, but rather to creation and construction. One of rhetoric's favorite attributes, *inventio* denotes not the invention of something entirely new, but rather the (re)discovery of what Dewey calls "a commonplace" (126). It is a felicitous choice since it denotes a technical term in rhetoric (*loci communes*). It signifies both a set of traditional features and a localization that, in Mark's case, could serve as setting for the founding event of violence. For Dewey, therefore, memory theory supplies the rationale for the commonplace pattern of the *passio iusti* in Mark, a motif, as Ruppert has shown, widely known in tradition and hence usable for the mediation of a trauma. In this way, Nickelsburg's literary genre and Mack's wisdom story have been transposed into a memory bed that was to bring the unthinkable event of violence into accord with a familiar, almost normative pattern. In other words, the commonplace pattern of the *passio iusti* serves to "normalize" Jesus' death and to make him a memorially accessible *Erinnerungsfigur*, or "memory figure" (J. Assmann 1992, 200–202; 2011, 179–81).

Dewey is fully conscious that the memory thesis has placed scholarly deliberations of the Markan passion text on a new footing: "The notion of memory as construction contrasts greatly with the assumptions of many modern biblical scholars" (2005, 126). We remember the issues cited at the beginning of this essay that have typified the historical paradigm and its approach to the passion text. From Dewey's perspective, questions that arose out of historical criticism do "not even begin to touch on how ancient memory worked" (128). I had observed that the commemoration of Jesus' death labors under the predicament of representation: how can the virtually incommunicable founding event of violence be represented in verbal narrative form? This can now be qualified in terms of memory theory. The passion text may well contend with the problematic of a narrative rendition of the initial trauma. But a formulation of the matter in terms of a representational theory may still be too closely tied in with modernity's literary as well as historical sensibilities. For memory's objective, it turns out, is not primarily the representation of reality in keeping with the aesthetics of literature (as Auerbach [1953] has so brilliantly argued), nor the narration of trauma within the confining boundaries of historiography. Dewey's most significant theoretical accomplishment was to recognize that memory's primary impulse was heuristic, inventive, and constructive rather than representative, mimetic, or reproductive. To that end, it devised a narrative sepulcher of Jesus' death by tapping into the cultural reservoir in search of a topos capable of localizing and humanizing what was deemed unspeakable as well as indescribable.

Concerning interpretive keying, it is well known that large segments of Mark's passion narrative are suffused with and even constructed on citations, paraphrases, echoes, and imagery from Hebrew Scripture. Primarily psalms of lamentation (22; 31; 41; 49; 69) but also Isa 53, Zech 13, and Dan 7 were complicit in the composition of the sacred text. Among principal Markan passion motifs that are composed on the basis of scriptural resources are the following: conspiracy to kill, betrayal by friends, desertion or dispersion of followers, grief unto death, false witnesses, false accusers, silence before accusers, Son of Man confession, mocking

by adversaries, dividing of garments, derision of onlookers, cry of der-
eliction, vinegar for thirst, and others. Exegetical tendencies to explain
the phenomenon have been of a midrashic or an apologetic kind. Strictly
speaking, however, the diffusion of and allusion to scriptural references
across the passion text bears no resemblance to midrash's moral, homi-
letical, and allegorical explication of scriptural stories that had become
clouded by the passage of time. Interpretive keying serves constructive,
not explicatory ends. Nor does the observed phenomenon conform to passion apologetic, widely employed in both explicit and subliminal fashion
to view scriptural references as proof texts, which are sometimes assumed
to have on *passion testimonia*, a collection of "Old Testament" texts. Their
designed purpose was to "prove" that the passion was the realization of
scripturally grounded prophecies. On this view, the evidence was pressed
into the schematization of promise and fulfillment. Apologetics is by far
the preferred mode of explanation. Even Frank Kermode, literary critic
par excellence, was of the opinion that Ps 22 "is clearly a source, or, if
you prefer, a prophecy or promise of incidents in the historical Passion
Narrative" (1979, 106). But the promise-fulfillment schematization, while
certainly present in New Testament texts, has to be enlisted with greater
caution. Burdened with tradition-honored doctrinal tenets, the scheme
tends to divert attention away from the deeper motivations of what are
perceived to be citational habits, scriptural references, echoes, and imagery. That the promise-fulfillment pattern is definitely not applicable to
Mark is a cautionary lesson that has been taught us by Suhl (1965). In
an impressively argued study devoted to the function of scriptural citations and references in Mark, the author demonstrated that Scripture in
that Gospel is a "traditionelle Grösse" (166) understood to be revelation
that operates as source of inspiration and narrative interpretation. The
specific reason for Mark to refrain from the doctrinal schematization,
Suhl claimed, was that for the first Gospel time was not yet sufficiently
stretched into a temporal duration to allow for differentiation in terms
of present promise and future fulfillment. Unless one reads Mark's passion narrative under the smothering embrace of his powerful successors,
Matthew and Luke, his so-called scriptural references, far from being subservient to an overriding promise-fulfillment thematization, are integral
elements of the passion narrative.

Two features specifically merit attention with regard to Mark's use
of Scripture. To begin with, almost none of the passages under consideration are introduced with a citation formula. They are—for the most

part—not identified as "scriptural" and for this reason do not, and do not wish to, alert hearers/readers to their origination in Scripture. It is the modern editor and scriptural specialist who lifts these passages from their narrative contexts. Fowler (1991) has perceptively described and diagnosed the phenomenon:

> We can observe the effort made in critical editions of the Greek text of the New Testament or in translations of the New Testament to pin down quotations from and allusions to the Jewish Scriptures. We use italics, quotation marks, indentation, and elaborate cross-reference systems to set off scriptural echoes from the rest of the text, thereby revealing our "anxiety of influence." Only literate-visualist moderns worry so about giving proper credit to antecedent texts; only we strive so to achieve originality and to avoid plagiarism. (88)

The only additional editorial device I would add is renditions in bold font, a favorite convention of the *Nestle-Aland Novum Testamentum Graece*. For the most part, therefore, we conclude, the so-called scriptural citations, references, imagery, and echoes are not perceived to be that at all. They are enmeshed in the narrative and indistinguishable as scriptural sources.

Second, all the so-called scriptural passages lend support to and enhance the commonplace structure of the *passio iusti*. They are, we must now say, an integral part of memory's observed construction of the commonplace framework that underlies the passion text. Rather than viewing them as scriptural citations or midrashic explications or proof texts, one should see them as part of the work of *inventio*, memory's search of topoi for a normative locus to place the story of Jesus' death. Both compositionally and thematically, therefore, the issue of the commonplace pattern and the so-called scriptural passages are one and the same phenomenon. Here we have arrived at the primary enigma of the memorial phenomenon: its extensive appropriation of traditional topoi and its constructive skills in the formation of the passion text. In it we recognize the technique of what Kirk (2005a, 194), relying on Schwartz (2000, 225–32), has termed "interpretive keying," whereby widely familiar, even archetypal language is reclaimed to serve as key to understanding the excesses of violence within older, established frames. In the case of Mark's passion text, the ample use of traditional topoi has converted Jesus into a what above we have described as a recognizable and communicative *Erinnerungsfigur* (J. Assmann 1992, 200–202; 2011, 179–81).

Overall, the etymology of re-membering and re-collecting meaning-fully portrays the compositional rationale of Mark's passion narrative. For what the text reflects and demonstrates is not an explication of prior texts any more than the articulation of promises made in the sacred past, but the retrieval of dispersed items into a new memory bed.

The third memory strategy we recognize in Mark's passion text pertains to the temple motif, or, as it should more aptly be called, the anti-temple motif. It is clearly not part of the *passio iusti* commonplace pattern. One may see in the narration of Jesus' actions undertaken in the temple at the occasion of his second entry into the city (Mark 11:15–19) a reminiscence of a historical event that took place during the end of his life. However, insofar as the destruction of the temple is the central issue in the temple dramatization, we recognize once more the Gospel's memorial disposition to reconstruct the past from its own post-70 vantage point. Memory's constructive achievement is evident in the connection of the antitemple motif with the death of Jesus, thereby providing a narrative rationale for hitherto unconnected traumas of history.

In Mark's passion, Jesus enters Jerusalem three times, on three successive days. In each instance, his entry into the city amounts to an entry into the temple (11:11, 15, 27). At his first entry he undertakes a survey of the temple, then leaves for the place from which he had departed (11:11). The second entry is conventionally associated with the so-called cleansing of the temple. However, Mark's plot frames the temple incident (11:15–19) with the cursing of the fig tree story (11:12–14, 20–22), suggesting more serious implications than a mere "cleansing." Mark's well-known framing device establishes a connection between the framing stories concerning the fig tree and the framed story concerning the temple. Accordingly, the fig tree stands for the temple and the dead tree symbolizes the temple. The third journey into the city takes Jesus once again into the temple (11:27), making it (12:35, 41) the locale for controversial teachings directed toward the guardians of the temple and the guarantors of tradition. Notably, none of the three temple visits is associated with prayer and worship. Having symbolically identified the temple with the dead fig tree and dissociated himself from all authorities associated with the temple, Jesus exits the temple for the last time (13:1), never to return to it, and promptly announces its physical destruction (13:2). This announcement marks a preliminary culmination of his persistent antitemple activity.

Additionally, the narrative establishes a close connection between Jesus' antitemple mission and the plot on his life. The initial death plot (resuming the programmatic announcement in 3:16) is reported in reaction to Jesus' symbolic cursing of the fig tree (11:18). The plan to kill him is reiterated by the temple authorities when he identifies himself with the rejected cornerstone (12:12). Following Jesus' announcement of the destruction of the temple (and subsequent communication regarding a coming time of war and bloodshed) the death plot is made known for the third time (14:1). Within the broader structure of the passion text, therefore, a link is made between the death of the temple and the death of Jesus.

Not surprisingly, the issue of the temple surfaces in the trial and at the hour of death. In the hearing before the high priestly assembly Jesus' pronouncement concerning the temple is introduced as evidence against him. The charge is that he was heard saying: "I will destroy this temple made with hands" (14:58), an accusation repeated by the passersby at the crucifixion (15:29). But the witnesses are immediately refuted as giving false and inconsistent testimony and the passersby are discredited as adversaries. In the context of the narrative logic, Jesus is the opponent of the temple who symbolically enacts and announces its downfall, but is not the agent of its destruction. The final culmination of the antitemple motif is reached with the rending of the temple curtain at the moment of death (15:38). The interpretation of the incident is controversial. Either the veil is in front of the holy of holies and its tearing asunder facilitates universal access or the tearing from top to bottom symbolizes the destruction of the temple. Three observations incline the interpretation toward the latter meaning (Donahue 1973, 201–3). In Josephus and the LXX, ναός, the term used in 15:38, is never used to designate the holy of holies. In Mark, ναός is also used both by the false witnesses (14:58) and the mocking passersby (15:29) in reference to the temple building. In the narrative context, the rending of the curtain brings the antitemple motif to the point of culmination. At this point the narrator has synchronized the death of the temple and the death of Jesus.

So densely is the temple motif integrated into the narrative realism and so persuasive is its reality effect that interpreters rarely step back to reflect on Mark's constructive achievement. Yet *Mark is the first Christian who faced up to the challenge of coping with the two principal traumas suffered in the foundational period: the death of Jesus and the destruction of the temple. The gospel's principal mechanism in dealing with the traumas was to construct a causal linkage between them.* Jesus anticipated, even precipitated, the temple conflagration, and in part it was in the process of his mission against the temple that he was destroyed himself.

89. MEMORY'S MEDIATION OF TWO TRAUMAS

Mark's passion text came to be written under the aegis of a twofold death. The challenge was not to face death as the great equalizer who levels all destinies, but to confront the historical specificity of two traumas: the death of the just one and the death of the Holy City. There is lurking beneath the narrative surface a sense of poignant absence. One possible way of understanding the passion text, therefore, is to view it as the work of mourning, seeking to mediate conciliation with the twofold loss.

More precisely, the passion narrative is the work of memory. Inciting the powers of memory, the twofold trauma proved to be a memorially productive experience. Remembering in this context is best understood not as repetition and not strictly as updating but as a new realization of the past. The narrated past was thereby constructed as a remembered past or, put differently, the past was memorialized to facilitate remembering so as to better serve both present and future.

A principal strategy in coping with the aporias of representation was the construction of a normative pattern made up of commonplaces that pertained to the sufferings of the just one. This memory place is not a locus in the topographical sense but something in the nature of a grid of relevant topoi. It is clearly a place of memory and not of history, although it is endowed with the remarkable capacity to generate an immense genealogy of rememberings.

One can understand the history of the passion text, a memory text itself, along with the subsequent history of continuous rememberings as mnemohistory. *But mnemohistory, while empowered by memory, denotes not simply a history of memory in the abstract, but rather an intricate interweaving of memory with history. It is history that breeds memories of the past, which are nourished by present history and in turn interact with present history and generate more memories.* History begets memories, which beget more history and more memories. *In this sense, the concept of mnemohistory occupies the position formerly held by tradition.*

Throughout mnemohistory present historical experience is an active coproducer in the formation of memories. As Christianity sought accommodation with the Roman imperial power structure and relations between Jews and Christians grew more tense, memories of the passion texts accentuated certain aspects at the expense of others. The specificity of the anti-temple motif was increasingly subsumed under the emergent theme of the anti-Jewish polemic. And so it followed that instead of serving as an antidote to violence, the memories of the victim of violence came to generate further violence.

14

THE WORK OF BIRGER GERHARDSSON IN PERSPECTIVE

Half a century after Birger Gerhardsson wrote Memory and Manuscript, *a monument to twentieth-century biblical scholarship, seven colleagues joined together to revisit and reassess the author's academic accomplishments. Their studies were published in a volume titled* Jesus in Memory *(Byrskog and Kelber 2009). They selected six topics of importance in New Testament, rabbinic, and Hellenistic studies that have been the focus of Gerhardsson's attention or have been suggested by him as subject for further inquiry. Samuel Byrskog and I served as editors of the volume, and the former also contributed the introduction, which reviews Gerhardsson's academic career and scholarly significance. The topics and contributors to* Jesus in Memory *are "Form Criticism" (Christopher Tuckett), "The Jesus Tradition as Oral Tradition" (Terence C. Mournet), "Jesus Tradition and the Pauline Letters" (David E. Aune), "Honi the Circler in Manuscript and Memory: An Experiment in "Re-Oralizing" the Talmudic Text" (Martin S. Jaffee), "Memory and Tradition in Hellenistic Schools" (Loveday Alexander), and "Memory" (Alan Kirk). The following is my concluding essay, which covers an array of issues pertaining to early Christian, rabbinic, and Hellenistic traditions. It summarizes the preceding contributions and their interactions with Gerhardsson, and seeks to move the discussion forward.*

In the first part I locate Gerhardsson's Memory and Manuscript *in the context of New Testament and rabbinic studies, and I articulate the rationale for revisiting the author's masterpiece. In the second part, on the discipline of form criticism, I agree with Tuckett that Gerhardsson's critical stance vis-à-vis form criticism is more relevant today than ever. I take the position that major aspects of Gerhardsson's view of the early Jesus tradition are entirely in keeping with ancient communications dynamics, and superior to those developed by form criticism. In the third part I take up Gerhardsson's model of the Synoptic tradition and Mournet's reflections on it. Among the features under discussion are transmission via formal teacher-disciple relationship (didactic model), the concept of eyewitnesses, rote memoriation, and oral-scribal intermediality. In the fourth part I seek to carry forward the issue of the Jesus tradition in Paul in response to Gerhardsson and via Aune's deliberations. The principal point I make here is that Paul appears to have been processing Jesus sayings in a living tradition in which the scope of what would constitute the early Jesus tradition was still in the making. Next I review Gerhardsson's model of the oral, scribal, memorial operations of the rabbinic tradition—along with rabbinic studies by Jacob Neusner, Peter Schäfer, Elizabeth Alexander, and Steven D. Fraade— and carried forward in* Jesus in Memory *by Martin Jaffee. When viewed in this broadly sketched context of rabbinic studies, Gerhardsson's model of rabbinics, it is claimed, has stood the test of time rather well. In the sixth part I discuss Loveday Alexander's study on the reminiscenses or memories (ἀπομνημονεύματα) tradition and the anecdotal and sayings (χρεῖαι) literature, taking up some of Gerhardsson's suggestions in* Memory and Manuscript. *Alexander's emphasis is on the generic flexibility and multipurpose status of these traditions, observations that need to be taken into account in devising a model of the Synoptic tradition. In part seven I reflect on the larger implications of Alexander's work. Broadly viewed, the Hellenistic school tradition, the rabbinic tradition, and the early Jesus tradition share cultural commonalities that cut across ancient Mediterranean history. The eighth part of the essay is devoted to a discussion of memory, a principal topic in Gerhardsson's work and further elaborated by Kirk in* Jesus in Memory. *In the conclusion to this essay, I develop eight ways in which memory was operative in the Gospel tradition.*

> I do not believe that there is any simple answer to the question concerning the origins of the gospel tradition.
> —Birger Gerhardsson, *Memory and Manuscript*

> The greater part of the ancient literature is intended for the ears as much as, if not more than, the eyes.
> —Birger Gerhardsson, *Memory and Manuscript*

> The study of the Torah is, according to a typical rabbinic mode of expression, "a work of the mouth."
> —Birger Gerhardsson, *Memory and Manuscript*

> To Gerhardsson goes the lion's share of the credit for placing the oral-performative dimension of rabbinic literature at the center of the study of this literary corpus.
> —Martin Jaffee, "Honi the Circler in Manuscript and Memory"

The reinstatement of memory as a core activity in the construction of early Christianity is one of the lasting contributions of Gerhardsson's work.
—Loveday Alexander, "Memory and Tradition in the Hellenistic Schools"

Among the some 5,400 Greek manuscripts of New Testament texts, for example, no two are identical; more relevant, perhaps, is the fact that some fifty-two extant manuscripts that can be dated to the period from the second century to the fourth exhibit more differences and variations than the thousands of later manuscripts.
—Kim Haines-Eitzen, *Guardians of Letters*

90. Revisiting *Memory and Manuscript*

The status of New Testament studies at the outset of the twenty-first century is impressively different from what it was in the late 1950s and early 1960s, when Gerhardsson wrote *Memory and Manuscript* (1961; repr. 1998). However, humanistic scholarship, including biblical studies, is ill perceived as steady growth and systematic advances in knowledge in the sense that it would allow us to simply slough off all academic work of the past as irrelevant and dead matter. To say that biblical scholarship does not conduct itself as an upward spiral toward ever-greater enlightenment but rather as a complex interfacing of present with past states of learning is to acknowledge that with genuine advances in knowledge come transformations of ostensibly assured results, challenges to what we thought we had known for certain, and rediscoveries of what had long existed in the intellectual tradition but had slipped our scholarly consciousness. This insight applies with special relevance to the work of Gerhardsson. Recent developments in the study of orality, scribality, and memory and the bearing they have on biblical and rabbinic scholarship, as well as a growing understanding of communication and education in Hellenistic culture, prompted us to revisit Gerhardsson's work and to reacquaint ourselves with some of is principal features.

In the previous discussion of *Memory and Manuscript*, no issue has drawn greater attention than the assumed backdating of rabbinic transmissional practices into the Second Temple period and their application to the early Jesus tradition. Ever since Morton Smith (1963) had made this the central point in his critical appraisal of Gerhardsson's magnum opus, reviews have revisited this subject again and again, sometimes singling it out as the sole criterion by which to judge the author's work. By now the issue has been further explicated by Gerhardsson (1991; 2005) and clarified by Byrskog in the introduction to *Jesus in Memory* (Byrskog 2009, 1–20), while the critical assessment of *Memory and Manuscript* itself has been revoked by Jacob Neusner in his foreword to the reprint of the book (Neusner 1998, xxv–xlvi; 1997, 171–94). One can, therefore, proceed with the understanding that Gerhardsson's rabbinic approach is just that, "an example, a model, a possibility" (Neusner 1998, xxv), or, as Mournet (2009, 47) put it, the model furthered "new heuristic categories that enabled the Jesus tradition to be approached through new … lenses." At the time of the composition of *Memory and Manuscript* Gerhardsson's mastery of rabbinics was almost unique among New Testament scholars. But a unique possibility to engage Gospel and rabbinic studies comparatively was largely missed as far as New Testament scholarship was concerned. To this day, however, the study of the Gospel traditions in the context of Second Temple oral-scribal culture of communications and with a view toward post-70 rabbinism remains a promising undertaking, as will be shown below. But any further discussion of the specific topic of a back-dating of rabbinic techniques has become a moot point, all the more so since the heavy focus on this issue has had the effect of eclipsing other, more significant features of Gerhardsson's work.

91. Form Criticism:
The Original Oral Form versus Oral-Scribal Interfaces

What matters at this point is to remember once again that a cardinal point in Gerhardsson's work is to propose an alternative to the form-critical paradigm of Gospel origins. He developed a paradigm of tradition and Gospel in the face of what Byrskog has rightly called "the most influential scholarly agenda at the time" (2009, 10), the discipline of form criticism, which for the longest part of the twentieth century was the reigning methodology in Gospel studies and eventually in biblical scholarship at large. Tuckett, author of the first essay in *Jesus in Memory* (2009, 21–38), is therefore quite correct in calling Gerhardsson's magnum opus "highly courageous" and indeed "seminal in opening up and generating debate and discussion in important areas" (10). Not surprisingly, form critics were among the most vociferous critics of *Memory and Manuscript*, who in making the rabbinic (back)dating the central issue managed to deflect the author's objections to their own form-critical project. As far as I can see, Gerhardsson never developed his position vis-à-vis form criticism systematically and in a single piece. The closest he came to a methodical articulation of his critical appraisal of the reigning discipline was an enumeration of ten points in "Der Weg der Evangelientradition" (1983, 98–101; trans. 1991; repr. 2001). Tuckett has registered some of Gerhardsson's major objections and added a fair number of his own. The conceptual and linguistic flaws of form criticism are systematically treated in 16.107 in this volume. In view of what appears to be a growing discontent not only in Anglo-American scholarship, but on the European continent as well (Güttgemanns 1979), Gerhardsson's critical position vis-à-vis form criticism today is far more relevant than the form critics were willing to concede half a century ago. The value of his own alternative model quite apart, it needs to be acknowledged that in light of the current discussion and from a retrospective vantage point many of his observations and reservations concerning form criticism are well taken and often to the point.

To do justice to Gerhardsson's concept of the Synoptic tradition, three interconnected features need to be taken into consideration. There is, first, his contribution to a conceptualization of the origin and mechanisms of the early Jesus tradition. It is a subject that, not unlike his application of the rabbinic tradition, has met with much criticism, overshadowing highly commendable aspects of his work. To begin with, conveniently ignored is Gerhardsson's rather adroit treatment of the issue of originality: how does one capture and conceive of the commencement of the Jesus tradition in the ebb and flow of history? In view of large parts of the preceding scholarly discussion of his work, it may come somewhat as a surprise to read that it is "not possible historically to understand the origins of [the] early Christian tradition by beginning with the *preaching* of the primitive Church" (1961, 324). Even more astonishing, however, is his follow-up statement: "Nor is it possible to begin with Jesus" (324). And there is, finally, the assertion that Jesus' sayings "have been used for many different purposes" and appear "in different contexts" so that it is "often extremely difficult to decide the 'original' meaning of a saying of Jesus which has become separated from its situation" (332). One needs to compare this with form criticism's basic objective, programmatically formulated by Bultmann: "The aim of form-criticism is to determine the original form of a piece of narrative, a dominical saying or a parable. In the process we learn to distinguish secondary additions and forms, and these in turn lead to important results for the history of the tradition" (Bultmann 1963, 6 [1970, 7]).

It bears remembering that form criticism's primary objective is the so-called original form (*die ursprüngliche Form*), which is claimed to be accessible through a process of elimination of so-called secondary features. *It was with form criticism that biblical scholarship's fixation on originality became methodologically legitimated.* Gerhardsson's skepticism concerning the retrievability of "the 'original' meaning," although not consciously arising from orality studies and not systematically developed, nonetheless reflects appropriate insights into the variable employment of Jesus sayings in the tradition. Not only are his sayings and stories inescapably "'remembered,' repeated, expounded and applied" (1961, 332) in different historical settings, but his message was from the start bound up with what Gerhardsson calls the "Torah tradition" (324), broadly understood as Judaism's oral and scribal legacy. In view of recent theories about an analogy of the historical Jesus to Hellenistic Cynicism (Betz 1994), the emphasis on Jewish culture and background seems more relevant than ever. Mournet rightly observes: "Gerhardsson's work reawakened awareness of the Jesus tradition's thoroughgoing indebtedness to Judaism and Jewish pedagogical practices which were present within the Gospel texts all along" (2009, 48). On the specific issue of "the original form" and "the original meaning," then, two rather different models of thought are apparent. There is, on one hand, the form-critical search for the narrow and "pure" base from which to trace secondary developments of the tradition, and on the other Gerhardsson's situational concept, which is far less concerned with "the original" form or meaning of a saying, and more insightful about a saying's interfacing with an already-existing tradition.

There is, second, Gerhardsson's firm grasp of the oral property and forces of tradition. Elsewhere I have expressed my appreciation for the author's exquisitely sensitive study of the oral dynamics and mechanisms that empowered the tradition (Kelber 1983, 13). Whether his explorations pertained to the auditory function of much of ancient literature; the concept of language as sound; the oral principle of arranging materials by association; the practice of recitation, repetition, and memorization; the significance of imitation in the relation between teacher and pupil—these and other aspects have all contributed to a communications model that is largely in keeping with what today we know about the verbal arts in the ancient world. As far as oral sensibilities are concerned, Gerhardsson has taken the early Jesus tradition out of the scholarly web of intertextuality by elucidating features that form criticism should have displayed but unaccountably failed to. In short, on the matter of the oral property and forces of the tradition, form criticism could have greatly benefited from his work.

Gerhardsson has, third, advanced an explanatory model that was suited to demonstrate the concreteness of the traditioning processes and the actual techniques that were operative in the production, transmission, and reception of the tradition. This is once again an area where form criticism appeared to be rather reticent, exhibiting little curiosity about the physical nature of manuscripts, copying processes, learning mechanisms, reading and recitation, and next to no interest in memory. The form critics, Gerhardsson rightly observed, "give only vague hints as to how the early Christian gospel tradition was transmitted, technically speaking" (1961, 14). In placing emphasis on what he called the "material tradition" (2001, 104–5), a matter today called the "materiality of communication," he fostered sensibilities that stand at the center of current media and communications studies.

In sum, Gerhardsson projected mechanisms of the tradition in ways that have next to nothing in common with the still pervasive form-critical notion of a linear, indeed evolutionary, progression of smaller units into larger entities. Nor are the Gospel authors, as form criticism suggested, correctly identified as mere collectors or editors. Mark, Gerhardsson states, "certainly was a pioneer" (2001, 134), an assertion unthinkable in Bultmann's *History of the Synoptic Tradition*, although Gerhardsson quickly qualifies his statement by adding in italicized font that "*his* [Mark's] *achievement was hardly very creative*" (134). Last but not least, Gerhardsson posited that up to the middle of the second century the Gospels "function to all appearances mainly orally" (1961, 202), a view, daring no doubt at the time of writing his magnum opus, but one that is widely shared today by performance criticism. *It needs to be acknowledged that on a number of rather substantive points Gerhardsson's model of the origin and mechanisms of the early Jesus tradition serves not merely as a corrective to the form-critical paradigm, but as a superior alternative to it.*

92. THE SYNOPTIC JESUS TRADITION:
THE ISSUE OF THE DIDACTIC MODEL

As current scholarship extricates itself from form-critical premises and gropes after an adequate model of the Synoptic tradition, seeking ways in which voice and text cooperated in generating meaning as event more than meaning as content, it faces new and formidable challenges. Let us begin with Gerhardsson's model of the early Jesus tradition. He distances himself from the form-critical model by elevating the role of individuals as carriers of the tradition. Form criticism, he rightly observed, had failed to assign individuals a role in the transmission of the tradition. In the initial stage, he observed, Jesus himself was the principal authority and the Twelve the leading traditionists in the transmission of the Jesus' message. The apostles were initiated into the role of bearers of the tradition by observing Jesus' mode of living and by listening to, repeating, and memorizing his words. Adopting the principle of imitation, the apostles practiced a lifestyle that had been pursued by other followers of Jewish and Hellenistic teachers and schools. There is a high degree of plausibility that the apostles "presented their preaching and teaching in the form of an eyewitness account" (1961, 283). As far as Jesus' speech was concerned, it comprised aphoristic and narrative *meshalim* that were conspicuous by "*their laconicism and brevity*" (2005, 11). Lacking the kind of verbosity that "is characteristic of much popular narration" (11), his diction suggests that it originated and was carried forward in deliberate and programmatic teaching situations. In other words, we must think of transmission as a "conscious, technical act of instruction" (2001, 23). *Gerhardsson's concept of the traditioning process may therefore appropriately be called a "didactic model."*

For Gerhardsson, memory in the form of mechanical memorization was central to Jesus' mode of teaching and that of his followers. Transmission was transacted for the sake of preservation so that what was being preserved was marked by relatively stable verbal properties. One is, moreover, dealing with an "institutional" and "intraecclesiastical" (2001, 105–7, 131) tradition that proceeded from and was largely controlled by "the leading *collegium* in the Jerusalem church" (1961, 331). Due to the relative stability and formality of the transmission, there was "an obvious unity, constancy, and continuity in the Jesus tradition" (2001, 35). Changes undoubtedly did occur in the course of transmission. Gerhardsson has perceptively and in much detail studied the "aphoristic meshalim and the narrative meshalim" (1991, 266), and the changes they underwent in their narrative contexts (1991). But alterations were more in the nature of "*interpretive adaptations*" (2001, 53): "Creativity did not have a free reign when the narrative meshalim of Jesus were transmitted and used—and new ones created— in the Church during the time between Jesus and the evangelists" (1991, 301). Communal needs did color the tradition, but they did not create it. As far as the Gospels were concerned, they can generally be understood as the written editions of Jesus' teachings and of eyewitness reports, all of which existed in organic unity with tradition. Last but not least, Gerhardsson observed that "Jesus and his disciples did not live within an oral society" (2005, 13), which explains why the Jesus tradition is permeated with words and motifs taken from the Hebrew Bible. Centuries of living with sacred texts had left a deep imprint on Jewish life and culture, and it was Judaism rooted in textual tradition that served as the primary source for Jesus' discourse practices.

In his discussion of Gerhardsson's didactic model, Mournet, author of the second essay in *Jesus in Memory* (2009, 39–61), introduced what he termed the *orality model*, which originated in the work of Kenneth Bailey (1976; 1980; 1991; 1995) and is largely based on studies by Dunn (2003a; 2003b) and Mournet (2005) himself. My own model, which has grown out of what is sometimes referred to as the Anglo-American oralist school, and which I have called the orality-scribality-memory approach, identifies more closely with the work of Albert Lord (1960; 1978), Walter Ong (1967b; 1977a; 1982), Havelock (1963; 1978), and Foley (1988; 1991; 2002), all authors mentioned with approval by Mournet. The similarity between the orality and the orality-scribality-memory models is a fairly close one, while commonalities with Gerhardsson's didactic model are evident as well.

As far as Gerhardsson's concept of eyewitnesses is concerned, it has recently received substantial confirmation through studies by Byrskog (2002) and Bauckham (2006). Byrskog gave an exquisitely informed and detailed account of *autopsy* (eyewitnessing information processing) in Greek and Roman historiography, the results of which served him as comparative basis for eyewitness transmission in early Christian texts. Bauckham, relying on early patristic sources and internal Gospel evidence, argued for a close association between an official body of apostolic eyewitnesses and the Gospel tradition, especially Mark and John. In my view, the individual identity of carriers of the tradition and the correlate notion of eyewitnesses, especially in the earliest period, is not merely plausible, but entirely commonsensical. Luke's reference to αὐτόπται (1:2) would seem to be evidence for early traditionists who were acknowledged to have been eyewitnesses. The question is this: Are Gospel materials identifiable in reference to an individual carrier? Can we, for example, distinguish a given group of sayings and/or parables as Petrine tradition? Byrskog concedes: "A search through the Markan narrative, which is most likely to include items of eyewitnesses, brings rather meagre results. It is impossible to verify any large amount of Petrine chreiai" (2009, 297).

It is noteworthy that Papias (as related by Eusebius, relying on a report by a presbyter), in describing Mark's role in the composition of the Gospel, never mentions the concept of eyewitness, but twice refers to remembrance: "He wrote down accurately whatsoever he remembered" (ὅσα ἐμνημόνευσεν, ἀκριβῶς ἔγραψεν), and again; "writing down things as he remembered them" (ἔνια γράψας ὡς ἀπεμνημόνευσεν) (*Hist. eccl.* 3.39.15). Memory, not eyewitnesses, seems to be the key as far as Papias's understanding of the composition of Mark's Gospel was concerned. More will be said below on Justin Martyr's association of memory as a generic designation with the Gospels.

All three models strongly assert the role of memory in proclamation and traditioning processes. In this they part company with classic form criticism, which had next to no formal role assigned to memorial dynamics. The rise of memory in the scholarly assessment of the Synoptic tradition is evident. What is at issue is whether in the early Jesus tradition memory can be construed as more or less mechanical memorization that operated in a semi-institutional framework so as to secure the stability of communication. Specifically, all three schools acknowledge the importance of mnemotechnics in the Synoptic tradition. That much of the early Jesus tradition is structured by demonstrable rhetorical features to fashion appeal to audiences is incontestable. But the existence of an aphoristic tradition shaped by mnemonic devices cannot in itself be proof of the kind of formal transmissional processes envisioned by Gerhardsson. Mournet takes a reserved position toward formal didactic settings and consciously controlled transmissional processes: "Certainly not every social context in which Jesus was involved was formal and revolved around intentional didactic activity" (2009, 57). But we will see below that Loveday Alexander, based on her study of the Hellenistic school tradition, strongly affirms Gerhardsson's model of teacher and his followers providing the social, didactic matrix for the processing of tradition. In recent times, Crossan (1983) and Aune (1991) have offered comprehensive and meticulous analyses of Jesus' aphorisms culled from the Synoptic tradition, including Q, the Gospel of John, the *Gospel of Thomas*, and the Apostolic Fathers. Crossan's is a rigorous form-critical examination that focuses both on the earliest recoverable version and on the transmissional processes of the aphorisms. His study compiled an inventory of 133 aphoristic items. Aune, heir to the legacy of Crossan's work on aphorisms, drew up an inventory of 167 items, reviewing all issues that are basic to the study of the early Christian aphoristic tradition: the function of aphorisms in the life of Jesus and in the early tradition, their generic identity, methodological considerations, their morphology, various types and forms, and compositional tendencies. It is noteworthy that neither Crossan nor Aune saw any reason to make a case for rote memorization in formal educational settings. It is well understood that folkloric and anthropological studies have shown that rote memorization is a fact, and can be an important fact, in oral tradition (Finnegan 1977, 73–80). But the likelihood for the phenomenon to have existed in the early Jesus tradition seems to me to be a meager one.

A matter of long-standing dispute, and one related to memory, is that of flexibility versus fixity in the Synoptic tradition. There is general agreement that a combination of both may come closest to doing justice to the workings of the tradition, whereby the didactic model is leaning toward fixity, Mournet is opting for a mediating "informal controlled" model, and the orality-scribality-memory model is favoring flexibility. However, the question I wish to raise is whether flexibility versus stability was in fact recognized as an issue by the early carriers of the tradition. Did they frame their experience and practice of the tradition in terms of change versus invariability? It is well understood: efforts to regulate tradition and to secure its reliability, or parts thereof, are written all over the face of its history. The formation of the canon would be a principal instrument to control ideational and scribal pluralism. The issue here is the early Jesus tradition. Parker's study (1997), which is based on the hard data of the earliest papyrological evidence of the Gospel tradition, discovered a good deal of fluidity: "The terminology which I adopt here is to characterise the text of the Gospels as free, or perhaps as a living text" (1997, 200). Once we acknowledge the existence of the early *living text*, we should not then project the dichotomy of flexibility versus stability into the observed phenomenon. Again: flexibility versus fixity will be later concerns in the tradition, and a preoccupation of modernity. Given the evidence, the appropriate historical question is: What was the rationale for the "living text"? The answer is to be found in the manner in which large parts of ancient culture, including the early Jesus tradition, perceived language. *The nature and function of language was pragmatic rather than preservative, focusing on efficaciousness more than on signification and construction of meaning.* Interestingly, contemporary reader-response criticism in its consumer and recipient-oriented focus amounts to a rediscovery of the ancient pragmatic role of language (Fowler 1991; Tompkins 1980). The point of the early Jesus tradition, we summarize, did not seem to have been to strive for fixity any more than it was to aspire to flexibility, but rather to articulate the tradition so as to achieve maximal effects on hearers.

Above we remarked on Gerhardsson's understanding of the oral nature of the tradition. To grasp his concept of language comprehensively, we need to add that the early tradition, in Gerhardsson's view, was "both oral and written" (1961, 202). "For several decades," he writes, "the tradition concerning Christ appears to have been carried orally," while at the same time one "began within the Church to write down parts of the tradition" (202). More to the point, what was distinctive about the relation of oral versus written words was that the latter "were hardly more than an aid to oral presentation, declamations" (2001, 119). Writings, in other words, functioned less as autonomous, silent objects because even "the *written* word is a vocal word" (113). This applies to copying processes as well: "Even the copyists used to read vocally when they copied" (113). And scripted words were vocal not only in the sense of being subject to reoralization but in the sense as well of standing in need of oral support and explication. Sharply formulated, we may say that *verba scripta* by themselves had no credible linguistic standing.

In an early review of Gerhardsson's magnum opus I made critical reference to his "blurring of oral and written dynamics" (1983, 10). I now recognize that his objection to my criticism is fully justified (Gerhardsson 2001, 116–17). With others I have come to understand that the interface of oral and scribal dynamics was a hallmark not merely of Second Temple and early Judaism, but also of the ancient Near Eastern and ancient Mediterranean communications world at large. I do point out, however, that intermediality was a polymorphous phenomenon, comprising numerous possible interactive dynamics.

This brings us, finally, back to the nature of the Synoptic tradition. If oral-scribal interfaces were the norm, tradition can no longer be conceptualized as a purely oral communication. *We cannot imagine tradition as a purely oral phenomenon, followed by a purely textual stage, nor can we think of it as an incremental progression from smaller to larger units along developmental lines encouraged by form criticism.* The new paradigm of media interactivity, or intermediality, suggests that notions of "pure" orality versus "pure" scribality fail to capture the communicative dynamics of the Gospel tradition. Aune properly acknowledged that "the interplay between oral and written transmission of the Jesus tradition was an extraordinarily complex phenomenon which will probably never be satisfactorily unraveled" (1991, 240). There cannot be a diagrammatic, visually imaginable design that could serve as a model commensurate to the oral, scribal, memorial, performative operations of the Synoptic tradition.

Gerhardsson himself has no illusions about the numerous unresolved issues that still lie ahead of us. Far from considering the case closed, he has kept the discussion open by raising a series of stimulating questions (2001, 129–30). In that spirit, I shall conclude the issue of the Synoptic tradition by raising a few questions of my own. If "an Apostle was an *eyewitness*" (1961, 281), was not his witnessing bound to turn into remembering? Is it imaginable to invoke apostolic eyewitnessing (280–84) without consideration of memory? We will return to this issue below. How can we match the Gospels' narrative causalities with the notion that these narratives are the result of and basically structured by apostolic preaching? In other words: Can narrative critics and proponents of a strongly developed eyewitness theory ever find common ground? Do the concessions Gerhardsson made to changes in the Jesus tradition, to revisionist activities on the Gospel's narrative level, and to textual variants (2001, 56, 79; 2005, 16), including his acknowledgment that Luke "obviously provides a highly simplified, tendentious, and stylized picture of a complicated historical process" (2001, 50), soften or undercut his didactic model? Does our growing knowledge of the narrative competence of the Gospels still permit us to extricate orally identifiable items from the scribal composition? Should one agree with Güttgemanns's characterization of the pre-Gospel tradition as "das 'urgeschichtliche' Dunkel" (1970, 195; 1979, 304: "the 'pre-historical' Obscurity") whose retrieval forever escape our grasp? Have the proponents of the didactic model, the orality model, and the orality-scribality-memory model come to terms with performance as key feature in tradition? Are we still, overtly or perhaps subliminally, captive to the notion of unilinear, unidirectional transmission processes? Have the three models assimilated memory, not merely in its mnemotechnical sense, but as a social, cultural force? Could we assent to the notion of the inseparability of tradition from memory, featuring the former as a process of memorializing activities? How do recent claims that Mark is a thoroughly oral text (Botha 1991; J. Dewey 1989; 1991; 1992; 1994; 2004; Horsley and Draper 1999, 53–78; Lee and Scott 2009; Malbon 2002; Shiner 2003; Wire 2011), perhaps compositionally and certainly performancially, square with the idea of a pre-Gospel, oral, oral-scribal tradition from which Mark may have drawn? More precisely, does the view of Mark as oral *composition* still require allegiance to the thesis of a pre-Synoptic history of oral, oral-scribal *tradition*? (On this see also below Neusner's understanding of the oral form of the Mishnah and the issue of a premishnaic oral tradition.) Gerhardsson's basic question remains a valid one: "How do we imagine that Mark, Matthew, Luke, John—let me call them so—actually proceeded, when they produced their famous books?" (2001, 60).

In the end, one should not underestimate the degree to which authorial setting and cultural prevalence can exercise influence on nearly every aspect of historical inquiry, including the preference for one model over the other. Does the model of relative stability aspire to escape from the corrosive effects of time, seeking quasi-religious transcendence beyond the reach of temporality? Or, is the model of a *living text* and relative adaptability conceived under the impact of modernity's fast-paced communications world and its predilection for change?

93. THE JESUS TRADITION IN PAUL: TRANSMISSION IN PROGRESS

The issue of Paul and orality entails two different, but not entirely unrelated, features. One part comprises the broad area of the oral composition and delivery of the apostolic letters, the role of epistolary emissaries, Pauline authorship in an oral-scribal communications environment, the function of amanuenses, the apostolic parousia or Paul's oral presence, the citation of Scripture, the oral/rhetorical style and diction of the epistolary communication, the agonistic conflict with competing apostolic figures, appeal to oral tradition and authorities, and many more (J. Dewey 1995b; Botha 1992b). The other part relates to Paul's transmission of the Jesus tradition. Aune, author of the third essay in *Jesus in Memory* (2009, 63–86), reviewed a number of studies, including Gerhardsson's own contribution, on the issue of the Jesus traditions, or lack thereof, in Paul's Letters. He concluded with a novel way of linking Paul's epistolary literature with memory. The letters, he argued, initially functioned as *aides-mémoire*, providing a summation of Pauline data for local communities, and at a later stage became *lieux de mémoire*, serving as sources in the process of rememorization. In the following, I will, proceeding from Gerhardsson's contribution, seek to carry the discussion forward.

Gerhardsson's model suggests that Paul relied on a twofold source of revelation: the Jewish Scriptures and tradition. As far as reference to tradition (παράδοσις, παραδόσεις) in the Pauline Letters was concerned, it consisted for Gerhardsson in "a body of authoritative material" (1961, 290), the core of which was provided by "sayings of, and about, Christ" (295). Gerhardsson refers to it as "the gospel tradition" (295). It was this tradition that formed "a foundation and a focus" (301) for the apostle, and it, rather than abstract principles, informed a good deal of his teaching. In Ger-hardsson's view, Paul had received this "gospel tradition" from "the college of Apostles in Jerusalem" (300; see also 296–97, 306, 321) or, to be more precise, from Jesus via the college of the apostles. Among Gerhardsson's arguments in favor of the apostolic Jerusalem origin of the "the gospel tradition," two merit attention. One, concerning Paul's fifteen-days' visit with Peter in Jerusalem, Gerhardsson translates the rationale for the trip, ἱστορῆσαι Κηφᾶν, in the sense of "to get information from Kephas" (Gal 1:18) (297–98). Two, as is well known, the confessional formula concerning Christ's death and resurrection in 1 Cor 15:3–8 is defined as a tradition received and transmitted in a formal, technical sense (v. 3: παρέδωκα γὰρ ὑμῖν ἐν πρώτοις, ὃ καὶ παρέλαβον). Gerhardsson proposes that each line of the formula represents a passage in the Gospel's passion narrative: the death, the burial, the resurrection on the third day, the appearance of the risen Lord to Peter, the appearance to the Twelve and to the others in chronological order (299–300). There is "good reason to suppose that he [Paul] derived this tradition … from the college of Apostles in Jerusalem" (300).

In the larger context of scholarship, Gerhardsson's Pauline thesis could well be understood as an antithesis to an influential segment of the *religionsgeschichtliche Schule* (Bousset 1970 [German ed. 1913]; Reitzenstein 1978 [German ed. 1910]), which drove a wedge between Jesus and what was considered to be the Hellenistic Paul. Whether Gerhardsson was conscious of his position vis-à-vis the *religionsgeschichtliche Schule* (and its influence on Bultmann) or not, he clearly endeavored to (re)confirm continuity between Paul and Jesus, "the Apostle's doctrinal authority" (311). No doubt, Gerhardsson is correct in affirming that the apostle has access to a tradition of Jesus' words and confessional formulae (1 Cor 11:23–26; 15:3–5). As for the historical starting point of these traditions, it has to be said that tracing the precise point of origin for oral traditions is fraught with difficulties, and often impossible.

Since it is in Paul's epistolary literature that we encounter Jesus sayings for the first time in writing, their employment merits scrutiny. In 1 Thess 4:15 the apostle cites a dominical saying (ἐν λόγῳ κυρίου) about the fate of the dead and the living in relation to the coming of the Lord. All other dominical sayings occur in 1 Corinthians. The preponderance of Jesus sayings in that epistle is a special issue to which we shall return below. Here we will discuss their specific authorization. First Corinthians 7:10–11 communicates a command of the Lord (ὁ κύριος) on the issue of divorce,

9:14 conveys the Lord's instruction (οὕτως καὶ ὁ κύριος διέταξεν) on remuneration of apostles, and 11:23–26 submits a formulation of the Lord's Supper as a tradition received from the Lord (ἀπὸ τοῦ κυρίου). Moreover, in 1 Cor 7:25 Paul makes the point that concerning the virgins he was not in possession of a dominical saying (ἐπιταγὴν τοῦ κυρίου οὐκ ἔχω).

As has often been observed, Paul consistently introduces the Jesus material, including his statement about the unavailability of a dominical saying, by appeal to the authority of the Lord (ὁ κύριος). It would seem to be a reasonable assumption to view the association of the Jesus tradition with the Lord as intentional. A key to understanding the significance of this use of κύριος lies in Paul's framing of the institution of the Lord's Supper (1 Cor 11:23–26). In this ritual tradition he draws a subtle distinction between "the Lord Jesus" (ὁ κύριος Ἰησοῦς) and "the Lord" (ὁ κύριος). The person who initiated the breaking of the bread and the drinking of the cup "in the night when he was betrayed" is identified as "the Lord Jesus." He is the earthly Jesus who presided over the last meal at the end of his life and maintains his presence as Lord in continuing eucharistic celebrations. In the ritual, therefore, he functions as "the Lord Jesus" who embodies his past and present authority. But as far as the tradition of the last Supper is concerned, Paul has "received it from the Lord" (παρέλαβον ἀπὸ τοῦ κυρίου). This carefully drawn differentiation between Jesus and the Lord suggests that the Jesus tradition, far from being bound to the earthly, let alone the historical, Jesus is being legitimated by the Lord, who continues to exercise his authority in the presence. Or, more precisely, the tradition is sanctioned by Jesus only insofar as he has assumed the authority of the living Lord. Based on very similar observations, Jens Schröter has drawn consequences that are entirely appropriate for an understanding of the operation of the Jesus tradition in Paul.

> When Paul, in these passages, always refers to the Lord (kyrios) but never speaks of the "word of Jesus," it shows that he understands the "words of the Lord" to be a teaching legitimated by the Risen and Exalted One that is made concrete in various situations through the apostles and prophets. His intention is thus not to hand on, word for word, what was spoken by the earthly Jesus but to connect to a tradition grounded in the authority of the Lord as the basis for Christian teaching. (2006, 109 [2005, 187]).

Schröter's view is that Paul's perception of the authority the κύριος has assumed over the Jesus sayings points not in the direction of the historical Jesus, who is the concern of modernity's historical methods and critical mentality, but toward what he calls—very much in accord with what above we have observed to have been Parker's conclusion—a free, living tradition: "Early Christianity and the early church understood the Jesus tradition from the beginning to be a free and living tradition" (Schröter 2006, 120 [2005, 199]).

Gerhardsson is not, of course, unaware of the signal importance of the κύριος in the apostle's experience, and he is sensitive to the differential relation between Jesus and the Lord in Paul's Letters. However, his evaluation of the evidence puts a different emphasis on Paul's affirmation of Jesus versus the Lord, which does not result in the concept of a living tradition. When Gerhardsson stated that the "earthly Jesus, too, was Paul's Lord (κύριος)," he meant to say that "Paul did not consider that what the earthly Jesus had said and done had been cancelled out by the cross and resurrection" (1961, 309). The emphasis is on the earthly Jesus so as to make sure that the correct transmission of his sayings is in no way eclipsed by the authority of the Lord. Schröter reads the evidence differently. "In instances," he writes, "involving words that originated with the earthly Jesus, Paul is interested in the fact they are Jesus' words only insofar as the earthly Jesus is also the one raised and exalted by God" (2006, 109 [2005, 187]). The emphasis here is on the present Lord to make certain that it is he, and not solely the earthly Jesus, who continues to legitimate the living tradition.

If we ask how precisely the living tradition worked, Paul's own dealing with the Jesus sayings deserves another look. In 1 Thess 4:15 he explicates the word of the Lord about the dead and the living by following up with a detailed apocalyptic scenario about the Lord's coming (1 Thess 4:16–18). In 1 Cor 7:10–11, after citing a command on divorce, issued not by him but by the Lord (v. 10: οὐκ ἐγώ ἀλλὰ ὁ κύριος), he adds a rather differentiated amendment (1 Cor 7:12–16), which, he declares, was issued by him, not by the Lord (1 Cor 7:12: λέγω ἐγώ, οὐχ ὁ κύριος), explicating the command in the case of marital relations between believers and unbelievers. In 1 Cor 9:14 Paul expounds a command of the Lord that pertained to apostolic remuneration only to dissociate himself as far as his own apostolic lifestyle is concerned (1 Cor 9:15–18). Gerhardsson readily acknowledges the significance of Paul's decision on this matter, writing: "Paul thus relinquished the right, bestowed by the Lord himself, 'to live off the gospel'" (1961, 319). Could one perhaps suggest that rather than "relinquishing the right" Paul de facto overruled what he himself had perceived to be a command of the Lord (1 Cor 9:14: ὁ κύριος διέταξεν)? Moreover, the apostle does not seem to have a problem offering in one and the same epistle a version of the Lord's Supper (1 Cor 10:16) that is at variance with the very one he had received from the Lord (1 Cor 11:23–25). This is nothing short of astonishing since it is fair to assume that ritualized verbalization generally inclined toward greater fixity. We conclude that in the few cases where Paul introduced Jesus materials he explicated and amended sayings, set his authority apart from that of the Lord, and in fact overruled a command of the Lord in one instance. Do we not have evidence here of Paul operating in the spirit and context of a living tradition? Again, Gerhardsson fully recognizes that Paul's employment of both the Jewish Scripture and of the Jesus tradition "take[s] account of both solid and fluid elements," and he has no doubt that "we must reckon with material having a more powerfully accentuated normative standing, and material having less emphatic authority (according to Paul himself)" (1961, 303). Yet in the end, Gerhardsson's assessment is that "Paul subjects himself to the tradition from the Lord, and regards what Jesus bound as being bound indeed" (320). But does the evidence encourage this very conclusion? *Could one not interpret Paul's dealing with the tradition in the sense that he remembered Jesus' sayings not in the interest of upholding their stability or their flexibility, nor to enforce greater or lesser authority, but for the purpose of reactivating them so as to apply them to current situations? It would seem that the Jesus tradition in Paul, far from being "bound," appears to have operated as a living tradition.*

The operation of the Jesus tradition aside, there remains the "perennial issue" of "the apparent neglect of Jesus traditions in the Pauline letters" (Aune 2009, 75). Why is it that the apostle does not seem to have felt greater urgency to resort to Jesus material so as to ground his message in what Gerhardsson has termed "the Apostle's doctrinal authority"? (1961, 311). Two closely interrelated features are frequently cited to solve the problem. One is the thesis, endorsed by many who have attended to the issue, that Paul could assume prior knowledge of the words of Jesus among his addressees. Gerhardsson himself subscribed to this suggestion: "[Paul] always expressly assumes in his epistles that the basic authoritative tradition has already been passed *on at an earlier stage* by himself, when the congregations in question were founded" (291, 295). This argument from silence is, second, sometimes buttressed with reference to the numerous allusions to Jesus sayings in Paul. With respect to the allusions, Aune observed: "The view that Paul alludes to Jesus traditions almost unconsciously is one of the major solutions to the problem of the apparent neglect of Jesus traditions in Paul" (2009, 75). These allusions, I suggest, deserve careful scrutiny, less for what they reveal about Paul's knowledge of Jesus sayings and more for the valuable insight they offer us into the workings of the tradition. The more obvious allusions and their matching sayings in the Synoptic traditions (and in Hebrew Scripture) are as follows:

- The saying on mountain-moving faith (1 Cor 13:2) appears in Mark 11:22-23 and Matt 17:20.
- The call to be at peace (1 Thess 5:13) is used in Mark 9:50 and Matt 5:9.
- The blessing of the persecutors (Rom 12:14) has an analogy in Matt 5:44.
- The statement regarding uncleanness (Rom 14:14) is similar to Matt 15:11.
- The council regarding the sudden coming to the Lord (1 Thess 5:2, 4) is echoed in Matt 24:43.
- The saying about kindness to enemies (Rom 12:20), a citation from Prov 25:21, figures in Matt 5:44 // Luke 6:27, 35 as the commandment to love one's enemies.

The most important point about these Synoptic allusions in Paul is that none of them is identified as a Jesus saying. Their analogy to Jesus sayings is obvious to us only because we can trace and identify them by chapter and verse in our printed Gospel texts. But as far as we know, narrative Gospels were not available to Paul and his communities. While Paul undeniably had access to Jesus traditions, it is far from certain whether he was consciously alluding to Jesus sayings and/or whether the hearers of his letters were able to recognize the voice of Jesus in these allusions. Or, more succinctly, we cannot be sure that in the Pauline communities this material was meant to be and in fact was known as Jesus sayings or as allusions to Jesus sayings. The allusions to Jesus sayings in Paul are allusions only in hindsight. What we can say with certainty is that a number of topics in the Pauline sphere came to be identified as Jesus sayings in what modern scholarship has conventionally called the Synoptic tradition. Once we formulate the evidence in this manner, we have reformulated the issue traditionally referred to as that of the paucity of Jesus sayings in Paul. Instead, what the evidence seems to suggest is the existence of a very fluid, a living tradition. It is highly likely that the latter existed in the oral medium, or in close oral-scribal intermediality. Taking both the Pauline and the Synoptic evidence into consideration, we conclude that not only was the tradition of Jesus sayings subject to reactivation and revision, but the boundaries of the Jesus tradition were pliable and (as yet) not unalterably fixed. Schröter, once again, has seen this very clearly.

> Even before the origins of the Gospels there was a sphere of tradition made up of words of Jesus, early Christian teaching authorized by the Lord, *topoi* from Jewish-Hellenistic ethics, and citations from scripture. Within this sphere, out of which primitive Christianity created its own tradition ... the distinction between "genuine" words of Jesus and other traditions played no part at all. (2006, 110 [2005, 188])

We must not, therefore, operate with too firmly established a concept of the early Jesus tradition and assume that it has existed as a fully formed and authorially identified entity. *In the Pauline sphere of influence at least, the scope and identity of the tradition was as yet not fully determined and in a sense still in the making.* Viewed from this perspective, one needs to accentuate an often unacknowledged function of the narrative Gospel: to locate sayings materials within the literary frame of Jesus' life and thus firmly fix their authorship as that of the earthly Jesus.

We will, finally, turn our attention once more to the preponderance of Jesus sayings in 1 Corinthians. James Robinson has developed the thesis of an existent tradition of Jesus sayings in the Corinthian community among those who challenged the Pauline version of the gospel (1971a, 37–46; 1971b, 71–113). The thesis was supported by Helmut Koester (1971b, 186–87), among others, and substantially elaborated by Heinz-Wolfgang Kuhn (1970). One need not agree with Robinson's cross-cultural trajectory of a *Gattung* of wisdom sayings ranging from Second Temple Judaism to Hellenistic Gnosticism, but the unusual emergence of *sophia* and Paul's challenge to it in 1 Corinthians is certainly noteworthy. Could it be that the relative frequency of Jesus sayings in 1 Corinthians, Paul's polemically articulated reconceptualization of wisdom via a theology of the cross, and his extension of resurrection hope toward the living *and the deceased*, to cite only three distinct features of the epistle, were directed toward those who employed Jesus sayings in proclaiming wisdom made perfect in the present arrival of the kingdom and the realization of personal resurrection of the living? This would also explain Paul's peculiarly defensive posture that in certain cases he was not in possession of a saying of the Lord (1 Cor 7:12, 25), directed toward those who played out Jesus' authority against the apostle. If in fact knowledge of Jesus sayings had been communicated to the Corinthian community without the mediation of Paul, we will have to imagine a model of significant spread and diversification for the operation of the Jesus tradition. In that case, a simple sayings trajectory from Jesus through the apostles to Paul will not do justice to what were far more diverse channels of communication. Nor must we imagine an uncontested, straightforward line of transmission. From a very early point in the tradition, the transmission of Jesus sayings was deeply implicated in competing struggles over interpretation and authentication.

94. THE RABBINIC TRADITION:
PERFORMATIVE PRACTICE, ORAL AESTHETIC, AND PEDAGOGIC DESIGN

One of Gerhardsson's abiding achievements is the detailed attention he has paid to rabbinic Judaism in conjunction with his work on the early Jesus tradition. His rabbinic scholarship merits the highest commendation both for its singular erudition and for its deep insightfulness. The issue of rabbinic dating in his scholarship aside, the comparison of rabbinic processes of transmission with those of the early Jesus tradition is as relevant a project today as it was fifty years ago. Indeed, it was one of the unfortunate responses to *Memory and Manuscript* that form criticism chose to pay very little, if any, attention to the rabbinic tradition. Challenging Gerhardsson on the dating of the rabbinic tradition, form critics by and large felt certain to have settled the issue of rabbinism and continued to disregard rabbinics in its model of the early Jesus tradition. As a result, the discipline of form criticism ran the risk of developing a culturally rather isolated model of the tradition. Often overlooked by Gerhardsson's critics is the fact that his work on the role of oral learning and memorial techniques in the formation and transmission of rabbinic tradition has by and large received the respect of rabbinic scholarship. By way of example, I refer the reader to Jaffee's epigraph to this essay, which expresses his appreciation for Gerhardsson's contribution to rabbinic studies.

As will be shown below, recent scholarship in rabbinics, including Jaffee's own innovative contribution (1994; 2001; 2009), has illuminated dynamics and mechanisms in the rabbinic tradition that ought to attract and engage the close attention of New Testament scholars. Whatever the specific interpretations of both the early Jesus and the rabbinic tradition, it needs to be acknowledged that in principle Gerhardsson's academic engagement of rabbinics merits applause rather than criticism.

The most significant value of Gerhardsson's study of rabbinic Judaism in the Tannaitic and Amoraic periods has to be seen in his comprehensive and sensitive elaboration of the oral, scribal, memorial operations of the tradition. The first part of *Memory and Manuscript* treats the written and the oral Torah in detail and with a broad vision, encompassing both Scripture and what was carried forward orally on the mishnaic and talmudic levels. As far as the conflict between Pharisees and Sadducees, and their attitude toward oral and written Torah, was concerned, Gerhardsson reiterated the conventional thesis. The Pharisees, while "hardly opposed to writing in principle, ... preserved an archaic practice ... the transmission of the oral Torah" (1961, 158). "The Sadducees," by contrast, "denied—in theory—the fully normative standing of the oral customary Law" (22). Oral versus written was thus a contributing factor to their well-known internal controversy. The so-called oral Torah was for the most part "formulated in quite a fixed way" (79), aspiring to the virtues of verbal brevity and conciseness. Though predominantly verbalized in compliance with oral principles, the oral Torah operated in close affiliation with Scripture interpretation and was in the beginning processed midrashically, in interaction with the written Torah, until at a later period it developed independently. Because the rabbinic material was both orally fixed and subject to interpretation, both scripturally related and recited memorially, it must by and large "be classified as oral text material" (80). In principle, therefore, it can be reasonably affirmed that Gerhardsson envisioned rabbinic Judaism in its mishnaic and talmudic manifestation not as a purely literary phenomenon any more than as a purely oral performance culture, but as literature empowered both by oral and textual dynamics. In whatever form the oral-textual dynamics are specifically conceptualized, the premise of oral-textual interfacing enjoys the full support of current orality-literacy studies and large parts of rabbinic scholarship (E. Alexander 2006).

Gerhardsson's model has not always been appreciated, let alone recognized, for the claims it has and has not made. It is often asserted that he solely advocated the preservative instincts of the tradition. Yet while preservation for him is a key feature of transmission, it does by no means, in his thinking, define the tradition on all counts. In their entirety, he suggested, the traditional texts of the oral Torah were characterized both by conservation of the authentic wording and by a general mobility of the tradition. On the one hand, the oral texts were recited again and again by skilled professional traditionists, repeated by their pupils, corrected once more by teachers until the wording was learned by heart. In these processes, the chief concern was the faithful and flawless preservation of the what Gerhardsson termed "*condensed memory-texts*" (141). On the other hand, repeated and memorized as the rabbinic traditions were, they were also accompanied by and subject to expository processes, whereby "continual interpretation gives constant rise to newly concentrated text material" (80). In this fashion, the sacred texts, while fixed and memorized, were also susceptible to augmentation by interpretation and growth until the body of collections was systematized and given final form in the Mishnah—those very traditions that the Tannaim came to know by heart. While envisioning processes of growth, Gerhardsson did not force tradition into a linear let alone evolutionary pattern. For him tradition consistently remained contextualized in situations of recitation and memorization. Basically, he advocated an educational, not an evolutionary theory. Thus far from defining the tradition wholly in terms of strictly verbatim retention and transmission, Gerhardsson's model is empowered by repetition and interpretation, memorization and augmentation. In whatever form stability and flexibility are nuanced and specifically conceptualized, the premise of both preservative and dynamic trends in the tradition is well established in his work. In its entirety, therefore, Gerhardsson's model of rabbinic history is one of a tradition in motion.

Among the models of tradition that have been advanced since *Memory and Manuscript*, Neusner's documentary hypothesis ranks at the top in terms of sheer volume and magnitude of detailed analyses (1979; 1987; 1995). His thesis proceeds from the premise that each of the principal books of rabbinic Judaism—Mishnah, Tosefta, and the Talmudim *Yerushalmi* and *Bavli*—is characterized by an internal integrity that gives voice to coherent points of view. Hence, every single rabbinic document has to be studied as an entity unto itself "essentially out of all relationship to the other documents of the larger canon of authoritative and holy books of Judaism" (1995, 21). When thus examined on its own terms, the Mishnah consistently exhibits stylized formulations, fixed and identifiable commonplace patterns both in its smallest component parts and in its intermediate divisions that are largely made up of conglomerates of the individual units. Additionally, the Mishnah displays literary and ideational traits that evidence redactional activities, shaping the mass of separate materials into a logical and syllogistic whole.

The kind of mnemonic characteristics that are observable with regard to the Mishnah—and not the Tosefta and the Talmudim—confirm that "Mishnah is Oral Torah" (1979, 60), a designation that requires careful explication. To begin with, it signifies that the Mishnah undoubtedly carries materials, even ancient traditions, from earlier generations, that exhibit precise and striking mnemonic patterning. Clearly, that material and the Mishnah in its final form were designed to facilitate oral transmission, recitation, and memorization. But the claim that the Mishnah is a profoundly oral document does not (necessarily) force the conclusion that it is the product of an (identifiable) history of oral tradition. Here Neusner proposes that the oral composition, or reshaping, of the mishnaic materials presents itself as an integral whole that has been accomplished in writing by the authors of the final version: "The bulk of the [mishnaic] document has been formulated all at once, and not in an incremental, linear process extending into the remote past" (1995, 31). (Above I have raised the question whether the thesis of an oral, compositional identity of the Gospel of Mark still requires allegiance to the thesis of a pre-Synoptic, oral-scribal tradition.) In the context of questioning a premishnaic oral tradition, Neusner also challenged the widely assumed thesis concerning the Pharisees as possessors and curators of oral traditions apart from Scripture. When guided by Josephus and the Gospels, he suggested, one should not have assumed Pharisaic cultivation of an expressly oral tradition (1979, 69–75). In the absence of a demonstrable oral tradition, therefore, the Mishnah itself is oral Torah as far as its composition is concerned, but it cannot, in its final form, be understood as (the product of) oral tradition.

In the course of problematizing the notion of an oral, premishnaic tradition, Neusner also expressed disapproval of Gerhardsson's concept of tradition. The latter, he explained, has made "the most extreme claim" about "originally orally composed and orally transmitted materials" of the rabbinic tradition (63 n. 3). But in view of our analysis of Gerhardsson's model of tradition, it is an open question whether Neusner has grasped it in its entirety. What can be affirmed with certitude is that Neusner's model is more heavily weighted toward a literary analysis, and Gerhardsson's more toward oral performance culture.

A rather different approach to rabbinic literature has been proposed by Peter Schäfer (1986; 1988). If Gerhardsson advocated an oral, pedagogical model, and Neusner a literary, synchronic one, it was Schäfer's insight that textual criticism, albeit a critically revised form of it, provided a key to appreciating the nature and dynamics of the rabbinic tradition. Intensive studies of the *Hekhalot* literature (1988) took him to the center of questions that, while by no means unacknowledged in rabbinic scholarship, had, in his view, not been given adequate consideration. Recognition of the enormous fluctuation and complexities of the status of *Hekhalot* manuscripts convinced Schäfer that one was dealing with a genre of literature that "proves to be astonishingly unstable" (1986, 149). Hence his reasoning that the convention of operating on the basis of a critical edition, the so-called textus receptus accompanied by an apparatus of variants, was incommensurate with the manuscript evidence that had been reassembled over lengthy periods of time in ever new literary configurations. Among the principal conclusions Schäfer has drawn with regard to the *Hekhalot* tradition, the following two seem to be of special significance: "Divergent settings of a tradition are therefore not to be reduced to assumed 'original' forms but have to be respected as autonomous stages of the development. … Any edition of texts of Hekhalot literature has to take into consideration that the *one* text is an illusion" (1988, 16).

In other words, if the *Hekhalot* manuscripts reached the stage of standardization "very late or not at all" (1986, 149), then the text-critically sanctioned procedure of building interpretation solely on the so-called textus receptus was running the risk of overlooking, suppressing even, the realities of the tradition as manifested by the manuscript evidence.

Textual criticism perceived in this fashion, Schäfer proposed, is applicable to rabbinic literature as a whole (1986). As long as one treats Mishnah, Tosefta, midrashim, and the Talmudim *Yerushalmi* and *Bavli* as stable entities, one has failed to take account of the bulk of manuscript traditions that has sustained rabbinic life and piety over the centuries. Instead of placing the major rabbinic works in a closed frame of reference one ought to reach behind the final redactions and familiarize oneself with the "open text-continuum" (150) of rabbinic literature. This, however, will require that text criticism "must rid itself of the odium of the whimsical scholar constantly in quest of the 'better' reading and finally buried under his collection of variants" (151). For what should truly matter in text criticism is not the identification and marginalization of variants of the assumed static text, but rather "the documentation and description of a dynamic manuscript tradition" (151). It, and it alone, can be the presupposition for a historically more realistic assessment of the nature of the rabbinic tradition. One senses in the work of Schäfer the makings of a profoundly mobile paradigm of rabbinic literature, one that is in tension with the synchronic model yet deeply sensitive to the actual life of the tradition.

The case for textual variability and oral-scribal pluriformity has now been made for four separate traditions: the proto-Masoretic tradition of the Hebrew Bible, the early Jesus tradition (both in Paul and in the Gospels), the early rabbinic tradition, and the Hellenistic school tradition. Regarding the proto-Masoretic tradition, see Ulrich (1999; cf. ch. 15, §99); regarding the early Jesus tradition, see Epp (2004; 2007) and Parker (1997; see also ch. 4, §18; 5, §27; 10, §§61–62; 12, §80; 14, §§91, 96); regarding the rabbinic tradition, see Jaffee (1994; 2001; 2009; ch. 12, §77), E. Alexander (2009), and Schäfer (1988); and regarding the Hellenistic school tradition, see L. Alexander (ch. 14, §95). As far as I can see, scholars working in one tradition arrived at their conclusion without input from colleagues working in any of the other traditions. As developed by Ulrich, Epp, Parker, Jaffee, E. Alexander, Schäfer, and L. Alexander, the four traditions have three characteristics in common: One, textual variability and pluriformity applies to all four traditions. In chapter 15, §99 we will define this phenomenon as the *mouvance* of tradition. Two, all our four traditions are processed by way of oral-scribal intermediality, although the precise dynamics of media interfacing can vary considerably. Three, by implication these scholars who have developed a concept of the tradition's variability and mobility have, explicitly or by implication, problematized the text-critical project of constructing the one, original text.

While Schäfer has set his gaze on textual traditions that lie behind the final redaction, Steven Fraade looks forward to the text's receptionist implications and to readers'/hearers' engagement in interpretation. His principal book, *From Tradition to Commentary* (1991), conducts an inquiry into the oldest extant, midrashic commentary on Deuteronomy. Three features characterize the directions into which Fraade's reading is taking rabbinic scholarship: (1) a hermeneutical appreciation of the "formal and substantive heterogeneity" (63) of the commentary tradition, (2) an explication of the commentary as a "performative medium" (19), and (3) the commentary's function as "transformative work" (22). On the first point, Fraade has raised the heterogeneous and sometimes discordant copiousness of midrashic meanings and perspectives to a level of heightened hermeneutical consciousness. Discursive and fragmentary as the interpretations are, they are woven "on the loom of Scripture itself" (65), so that the fixed text of Deuteronomy still can be assumed "to have been a commonly held cultural possession" (64). Second, as "performative medium" the commentary aspired not simply to transmit correct information but also to engage the students in the unfinished process of interpretation. Poring over and absorbing the multiple midrashic versions, the

Torah students were engaged "in the reconstructive and redemptive work of its interpretation" (21), advancing it, though never fully completing it. And third, the internalization and actualization of the midrashic network of interpretations was understood to generate transformative effects upon the rabbinic sages and their students. "In a sense, as they work through the commentary the commentary works through them" (21). Fraade has moved rabbinics a long way toward the recognition of a performative practice and oral aesthetic. Certainly, oral Torah and oral tradition, recitation and repetition, have long been central issues in rabbinic scholarship. But it is Fraade's achievement to have skillfully integrated the resources of current hermeneutical, literary, and communicative theory into a compelling thesis about the *Sifre*. The commentary—and the rabbinic commentary tradition in general—operates dialogically and interactively as an "oral circulatory system of study and teaching" (21) and in "the multivocality of a received yet restless tradition" (18). Historical criticism's elevation of the text as a cultural icon with a fixed, uniform, and autosemantic integrity is thereby severely challenged.

Jaffee, the author of the fourth essay in *Jesus in Memory* (2009, 87–111), is widely known for his book *Torah in the Mouth* (2001), published forty years after Gerhardsson's *Memory and Manuscript* and, like Gerhardsson's magnum opus, a classic in rabbinic scholarship. With *Torah in the Mouth*, Jaffee has succeeded in detailing a comprehensive and infinitely complex theory of the oral, performative nature of rabbinic literature, ranging widely from Mishnah and Tosefta through midrashic compilations all the way to the two massive literary bodies of the *Yerushalmi* and *Bavli* Talmuds. Benefitting from current orality-scribality studies, Jaffee set before us a "model of interpenetration or interdependence of oral and written textual formations" (2001, 101). Briefly, the model suggests that texts "enjoyed an essentially oral cultural life" (124) by being continuously *reoralized*—one of Jaffee's consequential terms—while the recitation in turn derived from and was shaped by scribal skills. It is difficult, therefore, "to posit a rabbinic tradition of 'pure' orally transmitted discourse prior to the Mishnah" (101), and more reasonable to think of "the continuous loop of manuscript and performance [which] had no 'ground zero' at which we can isolate ... an oral text or tradition as fundamental" (124). Orality unaffected by scribality is therefore as much in doubt as unadulterated scribality devoid of oral-performative mediation. Instead, Jaffee's model covers the oral dimension of scribal literacy and the performative and interpretive dimension of scribes and reciters alike, the vital role assigned to memory, including memorization processes, and generally projects a tradition in motion. Like Neusner, Jaffee disavows any specifically Pharisaic claim on the oral Torah. The evidence will not support the thesis of the Pharisees as guardians of the oral Torah. The most one can say is that the Pharisees, like most other Jewish communities in the Second Temple period, participated in the prevalent oral-performative transaction of texts. In distinction from the conventional thesis about the Pharisaic identification with the oral Torah, Jaffee moves the discussion in a rather different direction. The book's title, *Torah in the Mouth*, denotes his key idea. By the second, early third century c.e., he writes, tension in rabbinic culture surfaced between the sages' teachings and the Mosaic revelation of Scripture. To ward off the risk of splitting the tradition into two separate sources of revelation, *torah* emerged as the designation suited for mediation between the Mosaic Torah and the sages' oral-performative tradition. Gradually, both traditions came to be considered *torah*, the rabbinic *Torah in the mouth* no less than the Mosaic *Torah in script*. In this way, *torah* "has made room for the co-existence of Scripture and rabbinic tradition within a comprehensive body of authoritative learning that transcends both" (87). Torah in the mouth, Jaffee writes, is therefore explicable as an "ideological construction" (84) that served to integrate the rabbinic corpus into a comprehensive chain of tradition covering the First and Second Temple periods and culminating with the third-century Rabbi Gamaliel III. In its entirety, the concept was an "effective apologia defending the continuity of rabbinic teachings with the teaching of Israel's greatest prophet" (84). It is tempting to suggest a comparative examination of the rabbinic model with the apostolic model, which was to surface early on in the Jesus tradition. In both cases, it seems, we may speak of the *construction of tradition*, that is, the emergence of concepts that would henceforth dominate the way in which the two faiths would think of, live in, and practice their respective traditions.

In his contribution to *Jesus in Memory* Jaffee makes "an experiment in 're-oralizing' the talmudic text" (2009, 110) of Honi the Circler, a second-century holy man. In keeping with his model of an oral-scribal interfacing, he postulates a history of reperforming and rewriting the text whereby earlier renditions are not (necessarily) being sloughed off. More than many, Jaffee deeply probes the intricacies of oral-scribal interfaces. Large parts of rabbinic literature were retrieved from "a primary performance setting of face-to-face study" (89), written by the rabbinic text makers, the sages, "so to speak, with their ears" (90), who were not copying the texts as much as they were "rehearsing them in memory" (90). Performativity rather than intertextuality stands at the center of rabbinic "text-processing" activities.

In this situation, "the oralist textual scholar" faces the task of "rehearsing" and "restaging" the oral-performative milieu of the textualized tradition (90). To accomplish the objective, Jaffee reproduced the text of Honi the Circler in two versions. One is the English translation of the printed facsimile without cues to assist readers how to vocalize text. The second version breaks up the text into a series of small "breath-units." In addition, he used different typefaces to represent different performative moments. Using standard source- and redaction-critical methods, typefaces in italic, plain, and boldfaced plain letters stand for Tannaitic (ca. early third century), Amoraic (mid-third through late fifth century), and Stammaitic performative phases or moments respectively. In this manner, Jaffee attempted to effect the orchestration of a symphony of voices that invites readers to hear the voices the text has neutralized while simultaneously securing the conditions for their recovery. Unlike form criticism, which sought to isolate assumed oral units, and different from Neusner's synchronic analysis of separate text units, Jaffee attempts to retrieve the diachronic performance history in and from the final text.

Elizabeth Shanks Alexander (2006), further developing Jaffee's approach, used the oral conceptual lens to focus not, or not exclusively, on the transmissional processes of the Mishnah, the foundational document of rabbinic Judaism, but primarily on its "performative effect," trying "to imagine what would result from performing its material" (169). Developing a concept of the ancient tradents of early rabbinic materials as active shapers rather than passive carriers of the tradition, she concluded that the pedagogical benefit of the mishnaic performances lay not merely in the transmission of content but in "imparting a method of legal analysis" (171) that trained students to practice modes of legal analysis of their own. Alexander's model is thus a deeply educational one.

When recent rabbinic scholarship is thus aligned and surveyed in this manner, Gerhardsson's accomplishment shows up rather well. No doubt, since the writing and publications of *Memory and Manuscript*, knowledge in Second Temple scribalism and in the oral-scribal literature and dynamics of Mishnah, Tosefta, and the Talmudim has been advanced in ways that extend, correct, and at times supplant his model. Inevitably, his work has been winnowed by ongoing rabbinic scholarship and outpaced by time itself. What is, however, remarkable is the extent to which his fundamental premise of the oral, memorial dynamics as root condition of rabbinic Judaism has stood the test of time.

95. The Hellenistic School Tradition:
Texts between Performance and Reoralization

While Gerhardsson's work is closely allied with rabbinic scholarship, his intellectual curiosity reaches far beyond rabbinics and the early Jesus tradition. *Memory and Manuscript* is shot through with references to traditions outside of rabbinic culture: he adverts to relations between Jewish and Hellenistic school traditions; wonders about the role of reading, writing, recitation, and repetition in cultic and noncultic contexts among Jews, Greeks, and Romans; and poses questions about methods of teaching and transmission of knowledge in philosophical schools. Regarding his principal topic of memory, he inquires to what extent Judaism was influenced by Hellenism, and concludes that the significance of memory broadly extended beyond Judaism across all of classical antiquity, and he clearly recognizes that the rabbinic techniques of memorization are to be located and understood in the broader context of ancient educational practices (1961, 76–77, 100, 126, 150, 158, 163).

Loveday Alexander, the author of the fifth essay in *Jesus in Memory* (2009, 113–53), has followed up Gerhardsson's hints to examine features of the philosophical and rhetorical school traditions in order to ascertain to what extent the Hellenistic cultural context can illuminate the rise of the Gospel tradition. Her principal attention is focused on the genre of the *reminiscences* or *memories* (ἀπομνημονεύματα) and on *anecdotes* or *sayings* (χρεῖαι). Ἀπομνημονεύματα τῶν ἀποστόλων ("memoirs of the apostles"), it is well known, was the designation Justin (*1 Apol.* 66.3) around 156 c.e. attached to the Gospels. In doing so, he associated memory as a generic designation with the Gospels, and shaped the Gospel traditions early on into the form of memory. The term is at home in Hellenistic culture and part of an ἀπομνημονεύματα literature, represented, among others, by Xenophon, Ariston, Persaeus, Lynceus of Samos, Zeno, Dioscourides, and Favorinus. As far as the χρεῖαι tradition was concerned, it associated anecdotes, episodic narrative units, and sayings that were deemed useful for life to a person of prominence. The vast and varied repertoire of the anecdotal tradition functioned, in Alexander's understanding, "as cultural databanks" (124), an essential resource on which public speakers, philosophers, and rhetoricians could draw for educational purposes. Both the Gospels' designation as ἀπομνημονεύματα and the χρεῖαι materials, well established in the Synoptic Gospel and *Gospel of Thomas*, enhance the comparative relevance of Alexander's explorations.

The usage of both ἀπομνημονεύματα and of χρεῖαι is inherently fluid, and Alexander cautions against "over-refinement of generic types perpetuated by the form critics in a mistaken deference to the definitions of Greek rhetoric" (144). The ἀπομνημονεύματα literature is not fully categorized as a single genre. Trained as many New Testament scholars still are in the hard and fast categories of form criticism, it may be difficult to appreciate the vast and varied repertoire of the anecdotal compositions and the degree of generic fluidity that can mutate into a range of formations and serve multiple purposes. Anecdotes and maxims, and collections and combinations of these speech units, were subject to a great deal of variation. I wonder, from this perspective, whether it could not have been an objective of rhetoric and rhetorical handbooks to tame the uncontrolled state of language, to impose definitional discipline upon speech and scribal activities, to standardize communication, and, in a word, to categorize orality. The question this raises for Gospel scholarship is whether the form-critical categories (biographical apophthegms, scholastic dialogues, controversy dialogues, prophetic, apocalyptic and wisdom sayings, etc.), which have been subjected to ever more subtle rhetorical refinements, are not running the risk of overdetermining the Synoptic history to the point where they threaten to obstruct the lifeblood of the tradition.

In view of the variegated nature of the anecdotal tradition, it is not surprising that it serves a wide spectrum of different purposes. One obvious incentive for the collection and citation of anecdotes was the preservation of biographical information. But, Alexander writes, one must not think of the ἀπομνημονεύματα exclusively serving the interests and aspirations of the cultural elite. Entertainment, gossip, polemics, and sheer curiosity were often a desirable objective. "Nothing is more powerful in cultural bonding than a shared joke" (145). In short, "the anecdotal tradition was a treasury of cultural memory, passed on in a variety of locations" (134). In my view, the issue of the multipurpose anecdotal tradition raises for Gospel form criticism the question of whether the conventionally assumed one-to-one correspondences between oral form and setting in life is a realistic proposition. What is emphasized in current orality-scribality studies is that "context matters" (Foley 2002, 79). But context is understood not only as a narrowly definable social context, but also in the broader sense of *register* (26, 114–17). When addressing an audience, the speaker not only operates within a social context, but she or he connects with, plays on, and is responsive to the so-called register, that is, a cultural *lingua franca* that is more than a strictly social or linguistic phenomenon and includes values and symbols, memories and experiences shared by speaker and hearers alike. Alexander's portrait of the multipurpose status and multiple settings of the Hellenistic anecdotal tradition ought to be taken to heart as we seek to construct a model of the Synoptic tradition.

Granted the generic fluidity and multipurpose nature of the ἀπομνημονεύματα and χρεῖαι literature, there is one predominant context, and it is education and the Hellenistic school tradition. The composition and sheer endless reoralization of the materials served as key instrument in the processes of the Hellenistic παιδεία. They were being "worked and reworked at all levels of the educational system" (L. Alexander 2009, 146). On a surface level, they functioned to provide assistance in finding one's way through the vagaries of living. But this does not get us to the heart of their educational mission. Rehearsing the deeds and sayings of persons of prominence brought their ethics and values, their quick-wittedness and mental agility, their wisdom and experience before the ears of the audience. In this sense, the anecdotal tradition provided fundamental building blocks in the construction of μίμησις, a projection of "exemplary types (παραδείγματα) presented for emulation at every stage of ancient education" (145). In sum, the anecdotal tradition was a contributing factor to cultural memory that encouraged hearers to identify themselves as a people with a common tradition and shared values.

While the ἀπομνημονεύματα can gravitate toward a documentary, philological status, they never ceased to function as primary vehicles for oral delivery. In fact, the anecdotal material was "never without its performative context" (135). Alexander sets herself apart from earlier generations of classical scholarship that were inclined to approach the material from a dominantly literary perspective: "Issues of orality have scarcely begun to impact the study of the anecdotal tradition" (133). Working not with a model of textuality focused exclusively on written and mostly print materials, but with an oral-scribal-memorial-performative model, she exhibits unique sensibilities toward design and function of the ἀπομνημονεύματα and χρεῖαι tradition. "The anecdote collection," she elegantly writes, "is perched on the cusp between orality and writing" (122). All items of the tradition are ceaselessly involved in vital processes of writing and rewriting, reoralization, and internalization to the point where "there is no such thing as a 'final form'" (151). The borders between script and voice are entirely porous. Texts, she reasons, are but "a fleeting moment between performance and re-oralization" (149). Rarely has there been a more apt description of the status of texts in an oral performance culture that took immense pride in verbal craftsmanship.

And then, there is always memory. With respect to the ἀπομνημονεύματα and χρεῖαι literature, Alexander's focus is heavily on the relation between tradition and memory, much in the sense as Gerhardsson had elaborated this matter with respect to the rabbinic and early Jesus traditions. In an educational culture where remembering is the foundation of knowledge, memory is a key factor in accessing, organizing, inculcating, and reciting the anecdotes. For the most part, the tradition preserved was "a memory of 'gist' rather than of exact verbal recall" (136, 152). Rote memorization definitely had a place in the school tradition, but more often remembering was an active process of internalization and mental assimilation. The tradition's unceasing process of reoralization, rescripting, and rememorization suggests that the textual status of the ἀπομνημονεύματα and χρεῖαι was operative as a potentiality in need of implementation in performance and actualization in people's minds and memories. In sum, Alexander's contribution to *Jesus in Memory* has admirably succeeded in capturing the media dynamics of the Hellenistic school tradition and in reorienting the media sensibilities of those of us who are in the habit of treating texts as end products with a sense of verbal finality.

96. The Oral-Scribal Traditions: Instantiations of Broader Commonalities

To what extent, we asked above, can the Hellenistic school tradition illuminate the early Gospel tradition? Broadly, Gerhardsson was correct, Alexander states, in affirming a *phenomenology of memory and tradition* shared by the Hellenistic school tradition, the rabbinic tradition, and by the early Jesus tradition as well. Her judgment is informed by an enlightened understanding of comparative scholarship. The traditions are not to be viewed as rival models, nor are the similarities a matter of "borrowing" or "influence." Rather, one should understand each tradition "as a particular instantiation of the broader formational patterns that can be observed right across the ancient Mediterranean world" (2009, 141–42). The implications Alexander has drawn for Gospel and tradition are illuminating and not without surprises. If the vast and variegated processing of the ἀπομνημονεύματα and χρεῖαι has anything to tell us about the

Synoptic tradition, it is that the latter will not lend itself to firmly established generic definitions and to dependable patterns. The form-critical
premise regarding rule-governed relations between characteristic speech
units and specific social contexts remains puzzling. The Hellenistic school
tradition does not support this concept, nor, I should add, is it a theorem
known in orality-scribality studies generally.

   *Throughout Alexander's study we are reminded that tradition is a pro-
cess that cannot be reduced to products.* Moreover, any kind of evolutionary pattern should henceforth be dismissed from any and all models of
the early Jesus tradition. There is no reason to underwrite the correctness of "the widespread assumption in gospel studies that 'sayings tradition' automatically predates 'biographical anecdotes'" (144). Nor are the
more compressed χρεῖαι in the *Gospel of Thomas* necessarily evidence of
their chronological priority over the more elaborate forms in the Synoptic
Gospels. To the contrary, the pressures in the educational system could
produce more compression over time, and the papyrological data of the
ἀπομνημονεύματα suggest that larger forms were in circulation at an earlier
date (144). The presence of biographical elements in the formation of Q,
moreover, is entirely within the realm of the Hellenistic ἀπομνημονεύματα
tradition. The teacher-disciple model as one specific social context for
Jesus' teachings finds ample confirmation in the Hellenistic school tradition. More surprisingly, perhaps, the anecdotal tradition offers no encour-
agement for the (often unstated) premise that the individual sayings and
stories had to collect into a sequential narrative as if by a law of nature.
Indeed, "there were a thousand and one other things you could do with
anecdotes, and weaving them together into a connected narrative was by
no means the most obvious" (125–26). Form criticism's premise of a quasi-
evolutionary flow into the narrative Gospel is thus once more powerfully
disconfirmed. In fact, the formation of the *bios* genre enjoyed a rather
low priority in the ἀπομνημονεύματα tradition. Last but by no means least,
Alexander finds it difficult to arrive at a biographical narrative model that
matches the generally more complex Gospel narratives. Coming from an
expert in the Hellenistic school tradition, this is a significant conclusion,
and one that weighs all the more heavily if we remember that the *bios*
genre is nonexistent in the rabbinic tradition. This is not, of course, to
make a case for the uniqueness, let alone superiority, of the narrative Gospels in any kind of ideological or theological sense. But it does suggest
that Alexander may well be right in proposing that the formation of the
Gospels should be "considered as a creative outworking of the ideology of

the Jesus movement in its own right, and may owe as much to the Bible as to the Greek biography" (150).

97. THE EIGHT FACES OF MEMORY: *FONS ET ORIGO* OF CIVILIZED LIFE

Among the numerous features that distinguish Gerhardsson's work, one achievement looms larger than all others: his boldness in making memory a centerpiece both of the rabbinic and the early Jesus tradition. Byrskog has rightly extolled the powers enjoyed by and the virtues attributed to Mnemosyne: first among the Muses, goddess and fountain of life, mother of all civilized activities, essential link to the past, indispensable tool in successful oration and persuasion, and many more (Byrskog 2009, 1–3). Gerhardsson's persistent deliberation of memory, and the inseparable bond of memory and tradition, thus enjoys the strong backing of ancient history and of large segments of modernity's human sciences as well. Yet the significance of his elevation of memory to "a dominant research paradigm" (Kirk 2009, 155) is not fully appreciated unless one is mindful of the virtual absence of memory in much of twentieth-century studies of Gospel and tradition. With very rare exceptions in recent times—Gerhardsson being the most prominent example—memory in the discipline of biblical scholarship was virtually nobody's business. Gerhardsson's was a lonely voice while the form critics, who appeared to signal the way of the future, failed in taking his memory work to heart. "The disappearance of memory as an analytical category in biblical studies," wrote Kirk in a recent programmatic essay on memory, "may be attributed to a number of factors, most significantly the effects of form criticism" (2005b, 29). It is indeed the case that the work of Bultmann and the discipline of form criticism displayed next to no sustained reflection on, let alone application of, the role of memory to tradition. The reason, one suspects, is that form criticism failed to devise a conceptual apparatus commensurate with oral, spoken words. Virtually from the start, its principal focus was on securing the original form of a saying or story, and not on the rhetorical, performative, memorial aspects of speech. Whereas form criticism operated, in Byrskog's words, with the effect to "dissolve the ancient relationship between memory and tradition" (2009, 4), Gerhardsson was working exactly in the opposite direction: he explored the intricate relations between memory and tradition. To be sure, the actual mechanics of memory are certainly debatable, but it needs to be acknowledged that Gerhardsson's work exhibits a keen perception of memory, without which any concept of tradition in the ancient world remains unrealistic.

While from a strictly disciplinary perspective the virtual absence of memory can thus be closely allied with form criticism, the roots of the demise are sunk firmly in Western intellectual history. It is helpful to remember that memory has a history, extending into the deep past, a fact to which Byrskog has once more alerted us in his introduction to the subject in *Jesus in Memory* (2009, 1–20). If we catch an outline of this history, in however sketchy a fashion, we may be able to contextualize more broadly memory's demise, and biblical scholarship's complicity with it. Widely viewed as a centralizing authority of civilized life in ancient and to some extent medieval culture, memory was (along with invention [*inventio*], arrangement [*dispositio*], style [*elocutio*], and delivery [*pronuntiatio*]) one of the five canons of rhetoric. Under the influence of, among other things, a growing chirographic culture it was slowly but steadily deprived of its privileged status, and relegated to auxiliary functions in the ethical, metaphysical, and eventually the historical disciplines. In medieval culture, memory became integrated into prayer, meditation, and moral philosophy, until early modernism and modernity itself increasingly privileged logic—typographically grounded logic—over against memory and rhetoric. The rise of premodernism, viewed from humanistic and not scientific perspectives, is the subject of Walter Ong's (1958) unparalleled magnum opus on the French philosopher, logician, and educational reformer Pierre de la Ramée, convert to Protestantism from Catholicism and victim of the St. Bartholomew's Day Massacre, who reorganized and streamlined "the whole of knowledge and indeed of the human lifeworld" (ix). Deconstructing Aristotelian scholasticism, he "encouraged thinking in terms of models conceived of as existing in space and apprehended by sight, rather than in terms of voice and hearing" (280). His dialectic shifted rhetoric's auditory pole toward the diagrammatic and the visually representable. "Ramus," Ong writes matter-of-factly, "can dispense with memory" (280), at least with memory in its traditional sense of dependence on sound recall. Divested of its honorable position as *fons et origo* of civilization, memory was thus steadily denigrated to a peripheral position. This sweeping sketch of memory's trajectory could be a salutary lesson for biblical scholarship to locate itself, its methods of reasoning, and its *damnatio memoriae*, in the context of broader intellectual developments in the West. Put differently: *when the academic discipline of biblical studies sided with modernity in the form of adopting historical criticism it did so*

*by paying a price. It embraced the documentary revolution for which tradi-
tion was synonymous with texts (mostly printed texts), and it imagined a
textually, that is, typographically constructed tradition, which was deemed
operational without recourse to memory.*

All contributors to the volume *Jesus in Memory*, including Byrskog,
author of the volume's introduction, have acknowledged Gerhardsson's signal achievement in elevating memory to central position and
in making it a key agent in the formation of tradition. Kirk, the author
of the sixth essay in *Jesus in Memory* (2009, 155–72), has devoted his
whole contribution to the topic of memory. In fundamental ways, he
writes, Gerhardsson was ahead of his time. In assigning to memory a
vitally pervasive function, and in fact *the* crucial operational role in tradition, he anticipated developments in the social sciences and humanities, "where memory has become a dominant research paradigm" (155).
By the same token, Kirk suggests that Gerhardsson's model of memory
and tradition represented an "over-determination by the properties of
the written medium" (165). The author of *Memory and Manuscript*,
so Kirk's principal concern, operates with a "fixed-text memorization
model" (159), although, Kirk concedes, he "takes full cognizance of the
phenomenon of variation" (170). Just as Gerhardsson's concept of textuality appears overdetermined, so, Kirk reasons, is his working hypothesis
of oral dynamics and oral genres underdeveloped. On the whole, Kirk
approaches memory and tradition from a different angle than Gerhardsson. Tradition, he argues, has to be responsive to changing social realities or else it falls into oblivion. Given that premise, he finds the work
of Halbwachs, Schwartz, Jan Assmann, and others helpful who have
illuminated memory as a social phenomenon. Given memory's interfacing with social realities, the often observed variations and modifications
in the Synoptic tradition are therefore not be seen as difficulties to be
explained or excused for, but as "a core property of the gospel tradition"
(171). Memory, viewed from the angle of social life, operates productively, not iteratively. "Memory is a constructive, … artificing faculty that
compounds memory artifacts out of the flux of pertinent experience"
(169). In sum, Kirk takes the view that the past cannot in its full sense be
retrieved without memory's transformative powers.

Precisely how was memory implicated in the operations of the Gospel
tradition? Proceeding from the premise that one cannot grasp the full range
of memory's activities unless one recovers the *multiple acts* of memorial
mediation, I will approach the issue by developing *eight faces of memory*.

First, there exists a direct nexus between memory and Jesus' words of teaching. Memory is a mediating agent between temporally separate renditions of words spoken by Jesus himself. When we detect sameness between two or more performance units, we think "repetition." There can be no doubt that "repetition" is a hallmark of oral culture. But in a performance culture where a recurring rendition is of the same status as any prior or subsequent proclamation, "repetition" in the sense of something already said, and hence of diminished authenticity, may not adequately capture the phenomenon. I have introduced the term *equiprimordiality* (chs. 4, §18; 10, §61; 11, §69) to define the phenomenon of multiple authentic renditions of the same (or different) communication, and I now claim that we cannot think the performance processes of equiprimordiality without memory. When Jesus reactivated his earlier messages, he was confronted with an interval of time that had elapsed between prior delivery and present actualization. Whenever a time differential occurs in oral tradition, memory enters to reconnect with the past. The memorial mode in that case was not that of a search for items lost in the past, nor for items present in the tradition, but rather a remembering something—in however conscious or unconscious a manner—that had already been in the mind of the speaker.

Second, another nexus exists between Jesus' words and the tradition of his people. We are in the habit of thinking of him as the solitary starting point of tradition. It is a notion that the Quest has continued to reinforce in its Herculean efforts to isolate *ipsissima verba* as the basis of his proclamation and the foundation of the Synoptic tradition. As was pointed out above, Gerhardsson did not share this concept of a ground-zero origin of the tradition. To reiterate his observation, Jesus' teachings were bound up with the "Torah tradition," suggesting his dependence on and engagement in the oral and scribal legacy of Judaism. Although cast in his own diction and in response to current affairs, his stories and maxims nonetheless drew from and responded to the Torah tradition. If, therefore, we keep cultural contextuality in mind—as we must in all oral performative settings—we may say that he was feeding on and living in the memories of his tradition, not necessarily as he had read and studied it, but more likely as he had heard, pondered, and recited it, and as he was living in it. In other words, *we are bound to imagine Jesus as being enmeshed in the memories of his people.*

A third memorial aspect concerns the oral-rhetorical construction of Jesus' parabolic and aphoristic tradition. It is symptomatic of oral performance that it does not possess durative powers because it operates without attachment to any form of materiality. Words spoken are entirely on the plane of immateriality. For this reason, mnemonic structuring is not simply an aesthetic embellishment or an additional bonus for aphoristic and parabolic speech. It is rather built into the compositional status and modus operandi of Jesus' discourse with the aim of lightening the burden of remembering. Mnemonics is the life of oral tradition; you cannot have oral tradition without memory.

Fourth, apart from words spoken by Jesus, the tradition carries stories about him, such as the miracle stories. These are, it is well known, tightly constructed and thematically compact narrative units that have been iso-lated and generically classified by form criticism. The question is whether these sparingly constructed items are the result of oral, memorial economiz-ing, or whether they represent a textual tightening of a once live oral culture. Clearly, they are not examples of "ordinary discourse" any more than the Homeric language exhibits "ordinary discourse." We are dealing here with what is called a *dedicated medium* (Foley 1995, 16, 53, 56, passim), namely, a stylized, "artificial" language rooted in oral performance and dedicated to a highly efficient communicative economy unknown in daily speech and conventional literature alike. We may thus look on the densely constructed miracle stories, and other tightly formalized items in the Synoptic tradition, as footprints of memory, if not authentic children of memory.

The mnemonic structuring of the "dedicated medium," it is gener-ally affirmed, is intended for oral proclamation and acoustic appercep-tion. Here we will add to the well-known feature of the vocal property of oral-derived texts, the oral feature of visual appeal and apperception. By way of example, the parables accommodate hearers to *reimage* their storied worlds. In strictly historical readings, the pictorial vividness of the parables is often appreciated as an exemplary faithfulness to the facts of Galilean rural life. An interpretation of this kind represents historical-critical consciousness and concern to match or compare texts with the history of their subject matter. But when we approach parabolic discourse from the viewpoint of media dynamics, paying attention to cognition and the human sensorium, we may conclude that they encourage *interior visualization*, inviting hearers to internalize the stories pictorially. Both Mary Carruthers (1990) and Janet Coleman (1992) have treated in exqui-site detail interior visualization, a central feature of knowledge in ancient rhetoric and medieval theology/philosophy.[1] Memory-images or word

---

1. A superior study of the subject is King 1991.

pictures, variously referred to as *simulacrum*, or *imago*, or *phantasia sive imago* were a central feature of the ancient composing imagination (image making) "whereby things are presented to our *animus* with such vividness that they seem actually before our eyes" (Quintilian *Inst.* 6.2.29).

Fifth, as long as tradition was carried orally, memory was an operational component of communication. Apart from the miracle stories, all items communicated orally had to be subject to mnemonic structuring. Whether people listened to Jesus himself or to apostolic and prophetic followers, the message always had be processed memorially. Even if eyewitnesses played a role in the earliest tradition, memory could not have been absent from their witness. No matter how close they had been to the facts of history, their testimony was bound to be filtered through memory. They testified as they remembered what they had seen and heard. And if in fact rote iteration featured in the early tradition, it was the work of memory at its most intense: special mental faculties had to be trained and implemented. Prodigious memory feats, of which there are numerous examples in ancient and medieval culture, were a case of engaging the mind's retentive functions to its fullest iterative capacity. For the most part, I suspect, memory in the early communication of oral Gospel materials was a process of internalization and mental assimilation prompted and processed by the *dedicated* structuring and the mnemonic cues provided by the tradition.

Sixth, we turn attention to the nexus between memory and the early scribal (oral-scribal) tradition. Recent advances in textual criticism, pioneered above all by Parker (1997; 2008, 173–84 [see also ch. 12, §80]) and Epp (2004; 2007), have abandoned, or at least partially abandoned, text criticism's search for and privileging of the "original text," this assumed fixed point in the tradition. Entailed in the new approach is a critique both of the role of the so-called critical edition of the Greek text of the New Testament and of text criticism's skewed way of evaluating the available evidence for an understanding of the early tradition. "Regrettably, the critical text at the top of the page, at least for many users of the Greek New Testament, represents an authoritative result that can be taken over and used without further consideration" (Epp 2007, 298). Instead of evaluating the papyrological evidence with a single-minded view toward the construction of a standard text, Parker and Epp have chosen to take each scribal variation seriously on its own terms. In focusing on the papyrological, fact-specific evidence rather than on the construction of the so-called original text, they have paved the way for a historical understanding of the early tradition that is consistent with the evidence on the ground without "postjudging" it from the perspective of typographically constructed norm. The new approach has arrived at a significant conclusion. Parker has demonstrated that the early papyrological Jesus tradition was characterized by considerable fluidity. In his words, "the most remarkable thing about that period [the earliest centuries] is the great diversity between the witnesses" (1997, 188). Very similarly, Epp has expressed regret that our *critical editions* relegate "the profusion of variants in the early period [up to 300]" (2007, 285) to the bottom of the page, "the netherworld," as he calls the critical apparatus, whose inferior position "mutes their voices and suppresses their narratives" (297). Since the papyrological evidence on the ground does not take us back to the period usually designated for the Synoptic tradition, the relevance of Parker and Epp's observations for the earliest period might be challenged—were it not for Parker's additional judgment that "the further back we go, the greater seems to be the degree of variation" (1997, 188), and again "the greatest amount of textual variation in the New Testament took place before the year 200" (2008, 183), and also for Epp's observation that "there is greater diversity among the texts in the first few centuries of Christianity than in later periods" (2007, 294). In other words, on the basis of the available evidence we can trace a plausible trajectory back to the very beginnings and postulate a high degree of textual variability.

How do we evaluate the papyrological variability, and what is its nexus with memory? The behavior of these earliest Christian papyri tells us something about communication and intermediality in the early communities. *I am struck by the fact that the early Christian papyrological samples functioned in ways that are analogous to the early oral tradition.* As was the case with the oral performances, the very nature of the early scribal tradition is constituted by variables and multiforms. As was the case with the oral performances, the early scribal tradition does not differentiate between primary and secondary, "original" and derivative, or second-best texts. Those are differentiations drawn by modern scholarship in the interest of securing access to the assumed authentic text. But as interpretation of the scribal evidence from a new perspective is now beginning to demonstrate, one should not speak of the "original" version any more than of "variants" thereof, because "variants" suggest derivation from some kind of standard authority or normative baseline. As was the case with the early oral tradition, the early scribal tradition, rightly understood, is likewise characterized by equiprimordiality of its multiple authentic versions. And finally, and most significantly, as was the case with the early performative culture, the early scribal tradition, notwithstanding its chirographic materiality, seeks to stay with the flux of temporality by way of social adaptability. Epp (2004), in his meticulous study of the Oxyrhynchus papyri has documented their role in worship, liturgy, and everyday life. As was the case with oral tradition, so also was social contextuality a codeterminer of the work of scribality. In this we recognize the dynamics of social memory, which allows the present to enter into the construction of the tradition.

Having posited the oral, memorial character of the early Christian papyri, what can we now say about the compositional milieu of that tradition? How precisely can we imagine the role of memory in connection with scribal activities? It is not inconceivable that conventional iconographical depictions of scribes, often surrounded by one or more other texts, bent over their reading desks in the process of producing texts has overdetermined our imagination about ancient scribal practices one-sidedly toward the textual, copying pole. Richard Horsley (2007) has recently reviewed the intellectual, social, and political role of scribes in Second Temple Judaism and argued that they were frequently high-profile figures who functioned as professional counselors and administrators because they possessed the requisite communications skills as few people did. Even if their role in the political and administrative sphere were exaggerated, their role in the area of communication and education is certain. As scribal experts and in command of scribal learning, they were the guardians of the cultural repertoire. "The training and professional practice of scribes was devoted to learning and cultivating in memory the various texts of the cultural tradition" (Horsley 2007, 104). In the case of scribes dealing with the Jesus tradition, knowledge of that tradition could well be assumed. That is to say that scribes were not simply copying the Jesus sayings with their eyes fixed on the papyri, but rehearsing them in their minds so as to configure, or reconfigure them with the conditions of their own time and place in view. One could well speak of the performative character of their labors, indicating that scribal activity entailed mnemonic and memorial participation. I am aware that "simple" copying represent a significant aspect of the work of the tradition. But these are procedures that have been emphasized to the virtual exclusion of memorial activities. *Memory has had no business in textual criticism any more than it did in historical criticism generally.* And yet, "in antiquity and the medieval world," Kirk (2009, 162) has observed, "manuscript was adjunct to memory." Perhaps no one in recent years has devoted more focused attention to scribal activities in the early Christian tradition than Kim Haines-Eitzen (2000). Her basic premise is that the scribes who processed the early papyrological tradition "were not mere 'copyists,'" but rather persons "whose contexts—ideological, theological, social, geographical—were unavoidably interwoven with their practices of copying written texts" (129). They made an intellectual, religious investment in their writings, because what they wrote mattered to them. The copyists of the early Christian papyri were therefore not simply producers "but also the users of this literature" (17). Viewing scribality and its products more from the angle of Christian doctrine, Bart Ehrman (1993; 2005) has likewise subscribed to the concept of the activist role of scribes, but I find his notions of orthodox corruption, misquotation, and forgery unnecessarily judgmental and overtly sensational. On my view, the scribality of many, although by no means all, of the early papyri is inseparable from memorial, compositional activities. To varying degrees, memory cooperated in the compositional processes of the papyri. Scribes' intervention in the products of their trade is a cultural phenomenon. It has been found in French medieval literature (Zumthor, see ch. 15, §99) and in Spanish medieval literature (Dagenais, see ch. 16, §106), and I have argued its existence in four different traditions of late antiquity: the proto-Masoretic tradition, the early Jesus tradition, the rabbinic tradition, and the Hellenistic school tradition. We are therefore justified in calling it a transcultural phenomenon. Ehrman's findings in early Christian literature are therefore entirely in keeping with the widely observed *mouvance* of tradition. *In fact, they mark the heartbeat of the tradition's mouvance.* To relegate scribal activism to theological aberration or ethical ineptutude is tantamount to a category mistake.

Seventh, there is a nexus between memory and the death of Jesus narrated in the passion narrative. Since I have elsewhere (see chs. 11, §71; 13, §88) developed this aspect, I limit the argument to a succinct summation. I proceeded from the assumption that psychodynamically Mark faced the challenge of literarily representing Jesus' execution (as well as the destruction of the temple). *Memory is of the past, and memory of death is remembering the darkest side of the past.* What is required in extreme situations of this kind is mediation, mediating agents, and mediating processes. *Cultural memory*, as developed by Halbwachs (1925; 1992; 1997) and J. Assmann (1992 [2011]), furnishes the theoretical means for conceptualizing the mediation of the past. "The subject of memory," Assmann writes, "is and always was the individual who nevertheless depends on the 'frame' to organize this memory" (2011, 22). The past is never directly accessible, cultural memory informs us, least of all the raw facts of a crucifixion. What is required in this case is a referential framework, a *Bezugsrahmen* (35–37), or what Halbwachs has called the *cadres sociaux*, to locate, organize, assimilate, and thereby transform the events of the past. Such a frame of reference does indeed exist in the passion narrative. It has been the achievement of Ruppert (1972a; 1972b; 1973) to have identified the widely known theme of the *passio iusti* (the *Tale of the Persecution and Vindication of the Innocent One*), which George Nickelsburg (1980) has defined as the generic narrative substructure of Mark's passion narrative, and which Arthur Dewey (2005) subsequently interpreted as a memory place. In the terms of cultural memory, the *passio iusti* served as the *Bezugsrahmen* that frames the execution within a widely familiar pattern so as to "normalize" the traumatic event for hearers and readers alike. Apart from Dewey, it was Kirk and Thatcher who fully recognized the memorial construction of the passion narrative: "Mark's Passion story … is memory in the irreducible shape of the commemorating community's social and cultural frameworks" (2005a, 37). Memory's tradition-honored memorial pattern designed to bring the unimaginable in accord with the familiar is a very long distance removed from the conventional historical-critical concept of truth as literary, compositional, source-critical, and chronological correctness.

Eighth, it is conceivable to think of the Gospel composition in its entirety ultimately as work of memorial processes. Elsewhere (see ch. 11, §70) I have given three reasons that in their aggregate seem to me to weaken the usefulness and plausibility of the Two-Source Hypothesis. Overall, the explanatory powers of the Two-Source Hypothesis, in most instances a dominantly textual theory, are increasingly being challenged. To make, by contrast, a case for the role of cultural memory in the formation of the Gospels is to cultivate extratextual sensibilities, and to think of a cultural tissue at once more copious and elusive than our linear perception of literary sources will allow. The deepest impulse driving the memorial composition of the Gospels is the retrieval of the past, not for the purpose of preserving the past, but for the benefit of the present. Transmission for the sake of preservation is not the only, or even most important, function of memory. Rather than aspiring to preserve the precious past as past, the cultural memory that we see operating in the formation of the Gospels proceeds from the present because it seeks to legitimate the past as present. By drawing on the past from the perspective of the present, one arrives not at the past itself but at a re-created new past.

This is why *the Gospel narratives as cultural memories always reflect the conditions of their production*. Selection, organization, and composition of materials are informed not predominantly by responsibility vis-à-vis the past, but more by ethical, communicative, and rhetorical accountability toward the present. And if this seems an exaggerated view, let us modify the wording by claiming that the Gospels as memorially composed texts seek to maintain an impossible balance between a simultaneous responsibility toward the past *and* toward the present, with a view as well toward the future. But it remains to be said that while the modern scholar is brought up on the inviolate authority of texts and their relation to other texts, ancient and medieval thinkers were more interested in the dynamics of reception and internalization.

The essays in *Jesus in Memory* strike pathways through a vast area of subjects and open rich fields of research. Given the numerous disciplines and topics that are being discussed, the editors' fondest wish is that they will succeed in initiating dialogue between the various academic positions and subdisciplines: narrative criticism, the eyewitness theory, rhetoric, orality, form criticism, current media studies, comparative studies of early Christianity, rabbinic studies, Hellenistic studies, the psychodynamics of the human sensorium, and always the role of memory in every one of these disciplinary approaches. That would be the most fitting tribute to Birger Gerhardsson, whose keen sense of the voiced nature of ancient texts and the prominent role of memory in the tradition has pointed a clear way for the future in biblical studies.

15

The History of the Closure of Biblical Texts

For some time now my work in biblical studies has examined the power of the media in our ancient and medieval past, and in the very different communications cultures of early modernism and modernity. All along my concern has been to probe the sensibilities and potentials associated with oral speech and tradition, oral-scribal intermediality, the early papyrological tradition, memorially empowered communication dynamics, the developing chirographic culture, the growing documentary intellectualism, and modern print culture. I have devoted particular attention to the ways in which oral discourse, scribality, and the print medium, along with their manifold intermedial entanglements, influence cognitive faculties, structure communication and thought processes, alter modes of discourse, organize formatting techniques both in the mind and on material surfaces, and reinforce, complexify, and even deconstruct reasoning processes. Time and again, I have highlighted the pervasive influence of print and the magnitude of what I have termed the typographic captivity of historical-critical scholarship of the Bible. Throughout I have explored print's authoritative influence over basic features of the discipline: our ritualized habits of reading and writing, our editorial practices, the methodological tools we apply to the explication of texts, and our assumptions about ancient word processing, oral and textual compositioning, and the nature of tradition.

Mindful of the power of the media, this essay sketches an overview of the history of biblical texts from their oral and papyrological beginnings all the way to their triumphant apotheosis in print culture. In macrohistorical perspectives, a trajectory will be observed that runs from oral and scribal multiformity, verbal polyvalency, and oral, memorial sensibilities—allied all along with intermedial complexities—toward a steadily growing chirographic control over the material surface of texts, and culminating in the near-autonomous authority of the print Bible.

The first part discusses the enculturation *paradigm, that is, the interiorization of texts in people's minds and hearts in ancient Near Eastern,*

Greco-Roman, Jewish, and early Christian culture. Introducing the paradigm of mouvance, the second part discusses the textual pluriformity and scribal fluidity of the early manuscript tradition of the Hebrew Bible and the papyrological early Jesus tradition. The proposal is submitted that these two traditions, along with the early rabbinic tradition and the Hellenistic school tradition, operate on the model of mouvance in the global media context of ancient Near Eastern and Mediterranean enculturation processes. The third part treats the technological, chirographic inventions of codex and canon, assessing their status in the media environement of late antiquity. Fourth, the essay explains Origen's Hexapla and Eusebius's Canon Tables as manifestations of textual rationalization. The fifth part places the medieval Bible in the communications web of written records, memorial apperception and compositioning, oral recitation, and homiletic exposition. The sixth part views the print Bible both as beneficiary and as catalyst of the modern world of print capitalism.

> Technology exercises its most significant effects and its most real presence not in the external world but within the mind, within consciousness.
> —Walter J. Ong, "Technology outside Us and inside Us"

> Streng genommen sollte man für das Mittelalter ... nur von *den* Bibeln anstatt von *der* Bibel sprechen. Die Standardbibel ist erst das Produkt der frühen Neuzeit. [Strictly speaking, as far as the Middle Ages are concerned, ... one should speak of *the Bibles* instead of *the Bible.* The standard Bible is only the product of early modernity.]
> —Michael Giesecke, *Der Buchdruck in der frühen Neuzeit*

> Frequent consultation of indices, thumbing books to pick up previously marked passages, writing citations on to parchment slips, even "scissors-and-paste" composition—have all been presumed by medievalists to have been the methods by which scholarship was conducted during this period.
> —Mary Carruthers, *The Book of Memory*

> Peter Ramus ... attempted to replace the earlier techniques of memory with new ones based upon "dialectical order," a "method," a "logic" resting on the analytical study of texts, which ... owes a great deal to the diffusion of printed texts and the reproduction of charts by means of the newly invented typography.

> —Jack Goody, *The Domestication of the Savage Mind*

98. The Enculturation Paradigm

Writing and print, as well as electronic devices, Ong has proposed, are technologies that produce effects in the sensible world outside us but also affect the way our minds work (1992a). Handwriting slowly undermined and partially replaced a predominantly oral lifeworld, print drastically altered all major aspects of Western civilization, and the electronic medium is well on the way to ushering in a transformation of global dimensions. These are external changes, well known and plainly in view, especially at epochal threshold events such as the alphabetic revolution in ancient Greece around 700 B.C.E. (Havelock 1981), or the fifteenth-century shift from script to print (Eisenstein 1979)—occurrences that scarcely left a single sphere of human activities untouched. But, and this is Ong's point, we have not been sufficiently aware of the depths to which media technologies have penetrated the human mind and psyche. Granted the impact of "the technologies of writing, print, and electronics" (Ong 1992a) on cognition and consciousness, the challenge he has posed is understanding their operation within us.

Elsewhere I have treated the impact of the scribal medium on the human sensorium, on medieval reading and learning practices, on cognition and hermeneutics (chs. 6, §§35–37; 9, §56). What I will discuss in the following is the issue of interiorization itself. How does interiorizarion work in the case of exteriorized scripted words? When chirographically produced knowledge is internalized, what are the processes whereby scripted words before the eyes of readers become part of the interior self?

In the oral medium, communication is entirely a process of interiority. Strictly, oral verbalization operates without any physical, material assistance. As long as it stays within the confines of its own medium, it manages perfectly without recourse to material maintenance. It is well understood that oral discourse is of necessity enmeshed in the human lifeworld, and that feedback from writing to speech is an ever-present actuality. And yet, its operations proceeding from one person's interior self are manifest only in another person's interior self. To all outward appearances, speech communicates unassisted by script. Obviously, retention, retrieval, and organization of knowledge are all issues that have to be faced in oral tradition. But interiority itself is a given. Oral discourse is always an interpersonal communication, conversing from interiority to interiority. Orality, one may say, is personalized interiority.

Once we move to the textual medium, interiorization becomes an issue, because now we are confronted with materially secured words, and with verbal realities, which, while originating from mind and consciousness, are located outside of mind and consciousness. Unless reactivated, scripted words are mute, standing by themselves, and exhibiting a physical integrity of their own. Already the writing of a papyrus ensures a status of verbal stability to the scripted words. While voiced words flow with the stream of time, the *vox intexta* pretends to withstand the test of time. This is not to revive the settled issue of the Great Divide, but to claim that a shift from aural incorporeality to scribal stability, however fragile, temporary, and orally based, is an integral feature of oral-scribal phenomenology.

A significant contribution to our understanding the interiorization processes in the communications world of ancient cultures has been presented to us by David Carr in his hugely ambitious book *Writing on the Tablet of the Heart* (2005; see also ch. 12, §75). Covering a series of civilizations ranging from Mesopotamia to Egypt, from Israel to Greece and extending into the Hellenistic period, including early Jewish and Christian traditions, and intent on learning how they processed their cultural legacies, Carr has introduced the so-called enculturation paradigm into the discussion. It has a social and a mental component, and the two join into a single explanatory unit. Essential to the paradigm is a cognitive mastery of the tradition on the part of the elites—primarily scribes, priests, and teachers. (Kings rarely achieved mastery over the tradition.) "The ideal, at least, was the writing of the tradition 'on the tablet of the heart,' whether or not many people in a given time achieved that ideal" (288).

Precisely, how are we to understand this interior writing? Those who performed scribal tasks were not merely trained in the mechanics of writing but socialized into a whole system of values. A key aspect of the enculturation paradigm is that the carriers of their people's legacy often had to have prior familiarity with the text "in order to be able to fluidly 'read' it from the highly reader-unfriendly manuscript" (4). This knowledge of the cultural lore, the long-duration texts, as Carr has called them, was acquired by memorization and reinforced by performance. Writing what were often *Rezitationstexte* was inseparable from their performative actualization, and recitation was symbiotically allied with scribality. Those engaged in writing the tradition's texts were thus part of a whole system of oral-scribal-memorial-recitational interfacing activities. The principal objective was moral formation and education largely of the cultural elite, but gradually also of a nonliterate broader public, and eventually of urban citizens in the Hellenistic world. Education here is understood not simply in the narrow sense of schooling, but in the wider sense of socialization. The fact is not ignored that literal copying was a recognized practice, nor is it overlooked that texts were used for a number of purposes other than educational as well. Detailed allowance is made for cultural particularities. In fact, *Writing on the Tablet of the Heart* is strictly speaking a comparative study of the function of long-duration texts in a wide range of ancient civilizations. But the book also exhibits a remarkable gift for synthesis. Across different civilizations, so Carr's main point, the common denominator of the bulk of these texts is their operation as core curricula in oral-scribal-memorial-recitational communicative practices.

For our purpose, two features deserve special recognition: the role of scribes and the centrality of memory. *Carr has deconstructed the image of scribes as intellectually passive copyists in favor of cultural activists, and he has transformed the business of scribality from an activity preoccupied with the chirographic medium into one that enlisted all available media potentialities.* As far as memory is concerned, he writes that "the mind stood at the center of the often discussed oral-written interface" (6). Memory, not texts, constituted the power center of the ancient media world, functioning as source of recitation, retention, and composition all at once. Interiorization, while specifically a mental, memorial phenomenon, depended on and was operative in the larger context of the ancient media world.

Carr's enculturation paradigm has no counterpart in today's Western world of communications, and it is, I should like to claim, unlike notions of word processing that characterize much of the historical-critical study of the Bible. Recitation and memorization, essential features in Carr's communications model, are still largely unacknowledged in the historical-critical paradigm, and the oral-performative dimension is still regularly bypassed. Perhaps most significantly, Carr has shifted the emphasis from text to mind and memory—the very features that are conspicuous by their absence in historical criticism.

99. The *Mouvance* of Tradition

With Carr's global portrait of the ancient media world in mind, we now turn specifically to the Jewish and early Christian traditioning processes. I commence with reflections on the genesis of the Masoretic textus receptus, the normative text of the Hebrew Bible. When we study the Hebrew Bible we are handed the Masoretic Text, and when we learn elementary

Hebrew, we are confronted with Tiberian Hebrew, the linguistic system of the Masoretic scholars who produced the text between the seventh and tenth century C.E. All biblical scholars, Jews and Christians alike, grow up on the Masoretic textus receptus, a text, moreover, that was reproduced numerous times in carefully handwritten copies. We are all familiar with the conventional picture, prevalent in many introductions to the Bible, of a Jewish scribe bent over his manuscript while copying the Torah. Judging from the pictorially depicted intense concentration of the scribe he is copying the sacred Scripture in a meticulous fashion. This picture of the scribal expert, reinforced by its reproduction in countless print text books, continues to influence the conventional understanding of Judaism as a religion not merely of the book but also of the scrupulously reproduced book. Sensibility to oral-scribal dynamics may modify and will certainly complicate this picture.

It is well known that prior to the discovery of the Dead Sea Scrolls no single manuscript of the Hebrew Bible/Old Testament existed that was older than the ninth century C.E. With the availability of the Dead Sea Scrolls we have been unexpectedly projected back to an early state in the making of what came to be the Hebrew Bible. Written roughly between the first century B.C.E. and the first century C.E., these Scrolls are a millennium removed from what used to be the oldest available copy of the Masoretic text. A forgotten past has been lifted into historical consciousness. With it a world of scholarly inquiry has been opened up that cleared the way for new dimensions of understanding.

Interestingly, scholarship has had some difficulty in coming to realistic terms with the new textual evidence that continues to come forth from examinations of the scrolls. How deeply scholarship was beholden to conventional habits of thought may be demonstrated by the example of the famous Isaiah scroll, one of the best-preserved among the Dead Sea manuscripts. Burrows (1955), eminent representative of the first generation of Qumran experts, observed a remarkable agreement between the ancient Isaiah scroll and its Masoretic textual version. In some cases, where the Isaiah scroll differed from the textus receptus (in terms of orthography, morphology, and lexical items), he postulated copying mistakes that pointed to an inferior textual quality of the ancient scroll. In other cases, he judged variants of the ancient scroll to be superior and adopted them as a means of amending and improving the Masoretic standard. In either case, therefore, he was inclined to evaluate the ancient Isaiah scroll not so much as a text in its own right, but rather from the perspective of the established standard of the textus receptus, displaying a desire to demonstrate that the Isaiah scroll "confirms the antiquity and authenticity of the Masoretic text" (314). In short, he had made the Masoretic textus receptus, a text that is between seven and eleven centuries removed from the date of the Qumran text, the norm and criterion for his scholarly judgments.

Burrows's eminent textual scholarship, one recognizes in retrospect, operated under distinct text-critical and theological premises. As far as text criticism was concerned, he held that its primary objective was "to detect and eliminate errors in the text as it has come down to us, and so to restore, as nearly as possible, what was originally written by the authors of the books" (301). In other words, text criticism, in his view, was designed to recover the original text. It is a premise ill-suited, we shall see, to comprehending and appreciating the copious nature of the manuscript evidence of the Hebrew Bible. Theologically, he insisted that in spite of the fact that the transmission of scriptural texts has "not come down to us through the centuries unchanged," the "essential truth and the will of God revealed in the Bible, however, have been preserved unchanged through all the vicissitudes in the transmission of the text" (320). This, too, represents a position that is not well suited to face up to the nature of the tradition as it now manifests itself in light of the evidence procured by the Dead Sea Scrolls. Burrows's premises generated an optical illusion that made us see the newly discovered textual material for something other than it really was.

As more and more variables of biblical texts were identified at Qumran, the notion of a Masoretic text existing in the period roughly of the first century B.C.E. was increasingly called into question. There is no question that at Qumran scribes copied manuscripts as accurately as humanly possible. But a sense of an active transcription of tradition was difficult to overlook. Textual pluriformity had to be accounted for not as aberration from the assumed normative text, but rather as a phenomenon sui generis. Few experts have taken this insight more seriously than Eugene Ulrich (1999), the chief editor of the Qumran scrolls. Far from disregarding, explaining away, or rationalizing textual variability, he, along with others, has moved it to center stage: "The question dominating the discussion of the history of the biblical text is how to explain the pluriformity observable in the biblical manuscripts from Qumran, the MT, and the versions" (80). Textual pluriformity has become a dominant issue.

The scholarly assimilation of the new textual evidence is still very much in progress. As a result of some fifty years of intense academic labors, however, a number of points seem certain. One, the textual variability observed in many of the Dead Sea Scrolls is not specific to the Qumran community but appears to be typical of Judaism in the Second Temple period. Along with the Dead Sea Scrolls, the textual evidence of the Samaritan Pentateuch, the Septuagint, the New Testament, and Josephus in his dealings with scriptural materials "demonstrate[s] bountifully that there were variable literary editions of the books of Scripture in the Second Temple period" (9–10). As far as the ancient scriptural traditions are concerned, variability does not represent an exceptional behavior, but *a* and perhaps *the* norm. *Two, one needs to exercise caution in stigmatizing so-called variants as secondary, aberrant, deficient, wild, or nonbiblical. All too often, these are judgments based on the criterion of later standards of (assumed) normativity.* Textual pluriformity was a given and an acceptable way of textual life. Three, as far as we can look into the scribal activities at Qumran, we do not detect critical and specifically text-critical efforts in the sense of comparing and selecting so-called variants for the purpose of arriving at a norm. The community appears to have lived in textual pluriformity. Four, there is no evidence for the Masoretic textus receptus's having achieved the status of normativity in the Second Temple period. Textual pluriformity was a way of life at a time when both the early Jesus and the rabbinic traditions were in their formative stages, and it was, we shall see, symptomatic of both of them. Five, *not only is the text-critical search for "the original text" fraught with technical, philological difficulties, but also, and more importantly, it jars with the textual realities on the ground.* Ulrich has been forthright in challenging text criticism's principal preoccupation: "Should not the object of the text criticism of the Hebrew Bible be, not the single (and textually arbitrary?) collection of Masoretic texts of individual books, but the organic, developing, pluriform Hebrew text—different for each book—such as the evidence indicates?" (15). Six, just as many of us have come to question the notion of "normative Judaism" prior to the Bar Kokhba revolt, so will we now have to be skeptical about the concept of a single "normative biblical text" in that period. Seven, the consequences of Roman imperialism and colonialization of Palestine were devastating: the destruction of Qumran in 68 C.E., the destruction of the Jerusalem temple in 70 C.E., conquest of Masada in 74 C.E., the Roman crushing of the last revolt of the Jewish-Roman War (132–135 C.E.). The political realities and ambitions at the time were anything but conducive to sustained scholarly labors aimed at accomplishing a standard text. Eight, given the observed pluriformity of texts, some of which eventually came to be canonized and at a later stage standardized, we may have to reconsider our view of the work of scribes. Many do not seem to have been mere copyists, although they were that too, but creative traditionists as well. This is the point where the picture of scribes meticulously copying the Torah needs to be (re)viewed in a broader media context. Nine, clearly there is in Second Temple Judaism broad reference to the Law, and the Law and the Prophets, but we should not think of them as "biblical," let alone canonical authorities, as if "the Bible" in its canonized sense had already been in existence. In the words of James Barr, "The time of the Bible was a time when the Bible was not yet there" (1983, 1). Not only was "the Bible" not in existence, but also at Qumran, Enochic literature was no less important than Deuteronomy, and Jubilees just as vital as Isaiah. Ten, we can be certain that in the Second Temple period two or three textual editions of, for example, the Pentateuch were in circulation. In that case, canonization and standardization is in the making. But when we accord these editions canonical or semicanonical status we are probably making retrospective judgments, reconfiguring history according to later developments and categories.

Perhaps the newly acquired Qumran evidence may prompt us to reconceptualize the relationship between the Masoretic norm and scriptural (rather than biblical) traditions.

Instead of imagining a densely intertextual web with the Masoretic Text at center stage and scriptural manuscripts gravitating around and toward it, we should envision multiple scriptural versions, including those representative of and allied to what came to be the Masoretic norm, finding their hermeneutical rationale in recitation, explication, and memorization, with some texts, for example the Pentateuch and prophetic literature, being in the process of assuming authoritative, though not canonical, significance.

By and large the discipline of biblical studies lacks descriptive terminology and technical nomenclature that is commensurate with ancient media realities. It is difficult to arrive at historically appropriate language that captures the dynamics of the phenomenon of textual variability and pluriformity. I have found the designation of *mouvance* helpful in describing a significant portion of the Jewish tradition in Second Temple Judaism (and in the early Jesus tradition, and other traditions as well).

The term was initially coined by the medievalist Paul Zumthor (1990), who applied it to the manuscript tradition of French medieval poetry. His usage was based on the observation of a high level of textual variation in medieval texts involving not only modifications of dialect and wording but also more substantial rewritings and the loss, replacement, or rearrangement of whole sections of a piece. French medieval poetic material spread both temporally and geographically, "not merely by virtue of the text's physical movements as it circulates in manuscripts or in the mouths of reciters and is handed down to posterity, but also as a result of an essential instability in medieval texts themselves" (Zumthor 1990, 45–46). Textual mobility and authorial anonymity can, in Zumthor's view, be regarded as connected features. Anonymity suggested that a text was not tied to individual authorship, hence nobody's intellectual property, and for this reason free to be subject to recurrent rewritings.

By analogy, ancient Mediterranean traditions, including the early manuscript traditions of the Hebrew Bible and the early Jesus traditions, may be understood on the model of *mouvance*, that is, as a living tradition in the process of persistent regeneration. I view the above-mentioned enculturation paradigm as a broadly designed media model that captures the oral-scribal-memorial-recitational-performative practices, while I regard the *mouvance* paradigm as a subcategory that pertains to the specific phenomenon of textual variability and pluriformity.

It is in the broader context of enculturation and within the narrower confines of *mouvance* that the early Jesus tradition will have to be located. At various points in the preceding chapters (4, §18; 5, §27; 10, §61) I have developed the *equiprimoridality* of the oral Jesus tradition and its orally empowered papyrological pluriformity. Here it will suffice to summarize our findings. The oral proclamation of Jesus and that of oral tradents is characterized by multiple renditions, each claiming authenticity and in fact originality. We therefore have to reckon with a plurality of originals, or a tradition of equiprimordial versions. Both the search for single originality and the concept of variants thereof are pointless in oral tradition. There is no one original from which variants could deviate. The early papyrological tradition likewise enacts itself by way of textual mobility or fluidity. Terminology again is important. For example, references to the tradition as being "unstable," or lacking in "fixity" and "realiability" misjudges it by standards of preservative stability that are foreign to it. Mouvance *is the heart of the early tradition. The greater the relevance of Jesus' sayings, the greater the urge* not *to preserve them literally.* To be faithful to his words meant to keep them in balance with communal life, its needs and aspirations. The behavior of the early papyrological tradition has thus all the appearances of being empowered by oral dynamics and performative sensibilities (ch. 14, §96). *Text criticism's assumption of a foundational text at the beginning fails to comprehend that oral and scribal pluriformity governs the behavior of the tradition in its initial stages and that something akin to a foundational text comes into existence at later stages.*

We have identified four separate traditions (ch. 14, §§92–95) that operate on the model of *mouvance* in the global media context of ancient Near Eastern and Mediterranean enculturation processes: the proto-Masoretic tradition discussed above, the early Jesus tradition (4, §18; 5, §27; 10, §62; 12, §80; 14, §92), the early rabbinic tradition (12, §77; 14, §94), and the Hellenistic school tradtion (14, §95). When set against the background of the ancient Near Eastern and Mediterranean culture of communication, the oral-scribal, performative, memorial dynamics of these four traditions make good sense: by and large they were embedded in an oral biosphere that was distinguished by various degrees of diversity, mutability, and regenerability of its oral and written contents. It was a dominant operative logic of these traditions to reactivate (not to repeat) themselves rather than to reach for closure. To comprehend their behavior, we should think of recurrent performativity rather than intertextuality. Thus when the historical paradigm discovers textual stratification, postulating literary sources, one should perhaps in many, although not, of course, in all instances, more aptly speak of compositional phases characteristic of the process of rewriting culturally significant traditions.

100. CODEX: WRITING COMING INTO ITS OWN; CANON: ENTROPY CURTAILED

Information is a property of materiality, and materiality a catalyst of information. Media "are informed materiality or materialized information" (Giesecke 1991, 38: Medien "sind informierte Materie oder materialisierte Information"). This reciprocity of information with diverse modes of materiality is an elementary aspect of communication. In communicative processes the properties of one change those of the other. Exchange of information is "by its nature never onesided and monocausal, but reciprocal and based on the feedback mechanism" (37: "sind von Natur aus niemals einseitig und monokausal, sondern wechselseitig und rückgekoppelt").

Undoubtedly, the well-documented early use of the codex in the Christian tradition resulted from changes in information processing and a technological innovation that in turn was instrumental in ushering in wide-ranging cultural changes. Many of these changes were slow in coming and not immediately effective. On the macrolevel the codex instituted the book format and paved the way for the media transfer from the scriptographic to the typographic book. Two interrelated but distinct charcacteristics associated with the codex are storage capacity and accessibility. In providing a storage place for depositing lengthy texts and a potentially large number of manuscripts, the codex surpassed the physical capacity of the scroll. Looking at the new situation from the angle of memory, we may say that the new facility enhanced the potential for exteriorizing knowledge outside of the interior self. This in turn was to have an effect on memory. The more knowledge became available externally, the more memorial processes were weakened, or obsolete, or restructured. Memory places located interiorly had to make room for physical memory places on physically spatialized surfaces. In terms of accessibility, the codex inaugurated the shift from the awkward scrolling of the roll to the easier page-turning experience. One can open a codex at the desired place almost instantaneously without having to scroll all the preceding pages.

The combined impact of storage capacity and accessibility had a more subtle, less widely acknowledged impact on the verbal art and human consciousness. Compared with the scroll, the codex provided a more stable material surface and new insights into the practicability of writing space, features that invited bolder experimentation with the newly constructed chirographic space. Below we shall observe how techniques of formatting and arrangement were on the rise, which, combined with the page-turning practice, were suited to encourage the making of grids and tabular charts, even cross-referencing, all habits that in turn affected the perception of the nature of texts and the notion of textually perceived traditions. Thus in taking advantage of the new format, the codex created opportunities for textuality exploring its own potentials and more and more coming into its own.

Canon and canonicity is a topic that has for some time now commanded wide-ranging interest in biblical studies, in the history of religion, and more recently in literary criticism (Zahn 1889–92; Leipoldt 1907–8; Kümmel 1965, 334–58; Gamble 1985; A. and J. Assmann 1987; J. Assmann 1992, 103–29 [2011, 87–110]; Metzger 1997; Hallberg 1983). The making of the canon of the Hebrew Bible is roughly dated between 200 B.C.E. and 200 C.E. One needs to keep in mind that the canonization of both the Jewish and the Christian Bible was a process that extended over centuries. Any dating with greater precision is difficult. The greatest difficulty in determining canonicity lies in the observed variability and pluriformity of the textual tradition of the Bible. More importantly, even after a cluster of texts, such as the Law and the Prophets, reached authoritative status, one still faces the issue of textual pluriformity. For example, when the Law and the Prophets reached authoritative status, but existed in textual pluriformity, can we speak of canonicity? The Christian canon reached a semblance of agreed uniformity only in the fourth century, but a dogmatic articulation of canon and canonical authority did not occur until the Council of Trent (1546 C.E.). In the case of the Christian canon, something of a scholarly consensus about the criteria and rationale for canonicity appears to have been reached. Among the criteria, apostolicity, orthodoxy, and customary usage of texts are cited by many. The reasons for canon formation are usually seen in a defense against Marcionism, Gnosticism, and Montanism. One notes that the overall argument falls along the lines of orthodoxy versus heresy, categories that are no longer quite fashionable in current historical scholarship.

From a broadly cultural perspective one might suggest that the canon formation, both in Judaism and in Christianity, has to be understood against the background of the ideational and textual pluralism that we have observed as being characteristic of Second Temple Judaism. Jan Assmann (1992, 103–29) has seen this quite clearly. The need for canonicity, he reasons, arises out of the experience of an excessive textual pluralism and lack of ideational uniformity that threaten the raison d'etre of the tradition. In that situation, the canon responds to "the need to rein in the principle that 'anything goes'; we fear loss of meaning through entropy" (2011, 105; 1992, 123: "ein Bedürfnis, zu verhindern, dass 'anything goes', eine Angst vor Sinnverlust durch Entropie"). The selective privileging of texts, therefore, manifests a will to curtail entropy, that tendency, lodged in the tradition, toward diffusion and exhaustion of energy. To define this particular canonical function, Assmann has coined the phrase of the "Bändigung der Varianz" (2011, 105; 1992, 123), a taming of the phenomenon of variance. From this perspective, one may view the canon as a means of safeguarding tradition by strictly defining its boundaries, and thereby (re)asserting the cultural identity of a people. Canonicity thus understood signified an approach to cope with pluriformity and variability via selectivity and exclusivity. It is meant to secure cultural identity, but it did so, and this is a central point of this essay, at the price of closing the textual borders. Viewed against the *mouvance* of the Jewish and Christian textual tradition, the creation of the canon marks a principally authoritative and unmistakably reductive move. The canonical intentions were only slowly and partially implemented, and the canon would never in full measure succeed to prevail over cultural pluralism. To be sure, it was print technology that was capable of enshrining the canonical body of the tradition in unprecedented authority. But print likewise was the medium that brokle down cultural barriers and created an environment inhospitable to canonical rationality. In the end, canon and canonical boundaries turned out to be an unsustainable imposition on history, assuredly so in print, and without doubt in the electronic age.

101. ORIGEN'S *HEXAPLA*: SCRIPTOGRAPHIC DATABANK; EUSEBIUS'S *CANON TABLES*: ANCIENT CONCORDANCE

In highlighting early triumphs of textual rationality, we turn to Origen's *Hexapla* and Eusebius's *Canon Tables*. In a recent study titled *Christianity and the Transformation of the Book* Anthony Grafton and Megan Williams (2006) have shown particular sensitivity to the media dimension of scroll and codex, moving far beyond conventional philological and theological concerns. Giving careful account of Origen's *Hexapla*, they call it "one of the greatest single monuments of Roman scholarship, and the first serious product of the application to Christian culture of the tools of Greek philology and criticism" (131). Without exaggeration one may call it the most colossal textual production in antiquity. In the perspectives we have been developing, the *Hexapla* is a prime example of a sophisticated utilization of the potentials of the codex by way of experimenting with format and layout, and implementing new forms of textual arrangements. The result, in the words of Grafton and Williams, is a "milestone in the history of the book," even though "its form, its contents, and above all its purpose remains unclear" (87).

As the titular designation implies, the *Hexapla* was a codex, or rather a series of approximately sixty codices, which arranged six different versions of the Jewish Bible in parallel, vertical columns: the Hebrew version, the Greek transliteration of the Hebrew rendition, the Greek versions of Aquila (a proselyte to Judaism), of Symmachus (an Ebionite), the Septuagint (LXX), and Theodotion's version (a Hellenistic Jew), in that order. There is now broad agreement that what prompted the massive project of the *Hexapla* was the conundrum of textual pluriformity that Origen encountered. "The reason for the Hexapla," states Ulrich, "was that the multiplicity of texts and text traditions proved problematic for one espousing the principle that, because the text was inspired, there must be a single text of the Bible" (1999, 225). Grafton and Williams express themselves more cautiously: "Only in its original context of almost unlimited textual and translational variety can we fully appreciate the nature and function of the Hexapla" (2006, 130).

Yet granted textual pluriformity and variability, precisely how is one to understand and appreciate the rationale for constructing the *Hexapla*? What did Origen intend to accomplish by undertaking a textual enterprise of such colossal proportions? We recognize that he was himself not as well informed about the pluriformity of textual versions and traditions as we are from our retrospective vantage today. He assumed, for example, that the Hebrew text type was identical with that from which the LXX had been translated, whereas current scholarship suggests that neither the LXX nor the Masoretic text are homogeneous, and that the textual character in both traditions changes from book to book. But Origen was sufficiently aware of textual pluriformity of biblical texts to embark on the intellectually demanding, economically expensive, and physically grueling work of selecting, reproducing, and collating six versions of the Jewish Bible. Indeed, "The complex *mise-en-page* of the Hexaplaric columns must have presented significant logistical challenges to the scribes who created and reproduced them" (105). Scholars generally share the view that Origen's principal purpose was a text that could serve as reliable basis both for Christians themselves and for their disputes with the Jews. While this may well have been Origen's ultimate objective, it is not directly evident from the *Hexaplaric* arrangement. As a matter of fact, constructing a single text is precisely what he did not do. Rather than composing a standard text, Origen exposed his readers to textual pluriformity, albeit on a reduced scale. Could one perhaps interpret Origen's masterpiece the way Eusebius appears to have read it: as a realistic concession to the fact that no single authoritative text could be reconstructed? In the words of Grafton and Williams, "Eusebius read the Hexapla as Origen meant it to be read: as a treasury of exegetical materials, some of them perplexing, rather than an effort to provide a stable, perfect text of the Bible" (170). In the end, it seems, it was left to readers to sort things out for themselves.

Be that as it may, in juxtaposing texts, one next to the other, and in inviting comparative readings across six different versions of the same text Origen constructed a textual databank that constituted a virtual countermodel to the *mouvance* of the performative tradition.

Origen's innovative use of parallel columns in his *Hexapla* appears to have provided Eusebius with a model for his *Canon Tables* (Nordenfalk 1938). These represent one of the most intricate layouts of writing space ever formatted in the ancient communications world. In unprecedented ways, diagrammatical organization, numerical structures, and architectural designs were imposed upon the Gospel texts. In conjunction with the *Canon Tables* Eusebius had divided the texts of the four Gospels into sections and then furnished each section with a number as well as a reference to its location in the tables. These consisted of ten columns, each carrying the section numbers marked on the margin of the Gospel texts. In all, table 1 numbered the sections common to all four Gospels; tables 2 to 4 those sections common to three Gospels; tables 5 to 9 those common to two Gospels; and table 10 listed section numbers with no apparent parallels. No text was presented, only numbers. These were written vertically in the so-called *intercolumnia*, the spaces between the columns. Something else altogether was in play here than an innovative layout of texts—namely, the mathematization of texts. A numerical grid had been imposed, and by virtue of its numbering index an entirely new approach to the Gospels texts was introduced. What Eusebius and his staff of secretaries and notaries had constructed was a strictly quantifying, systematic environment of extreme logical severity and total artificiality. Deliberately abstracted from narrative logic and subjected to analytical logic, the *Canon Tables* had no basis in the real life of the Gospels, nor did they leave any room for social engagement, for participation in the oral-scribal-oral loop, or for compositional involvement in memorial processes. No wonder Grafton and Williams entertain the view that Eusebius was anticipating aspects of the modern library system. His experimentation with systems of information storage, they write, "represented as brilliant, and as radical, a set of new methods for the organization and retrieval of information as the nineteenth-century card catalogue and filing systems would in their turn" (230). Paying close attention to the operational intent of the newly constructed information system, we might say that it functioned rather like a concordance not of words but of numerical data that facilitated horizontal cross-referencing and comparative readings across the four Gospel texts.

How can one account for Eusebius's rigid but ingenious formatting of writing space in a world of oral-scribal-memorial-recitational information processing? We cannot hold typography responsible for it. Carruthers (1990), in discussing the *Canon Tables*, has devoted particular attention to the pictorial, architectural design of the layout. The use of arched columns decorated with birds and floral motifs, the creation of columnal space, and various other architectural features were "representing a classical facade" (93). These were all traits, Carruthers observes, reminiscent of the ancient and medieval model of memory, which was spatially and in fact architecturally constructed. As reestablished for us in a classic study by Frances Yates (1966), and now further developed by Carruthers (1990), the art or technique of remembering was practiced in walking through mental places in a building and looking for stored items in different rooms. In the case of the *Canon Tables* Carruthers suspects a projection of the well-known memorial use of spatial designs, grids, rooms, and architectural format from a three-dimensional mental location to the two-dimensional flat surface of writing space (129). Linearily formatted pages were thus a memory design that had long been in mental existence before its appearance on the physical page. How far back in history can we trace the pictorial memory design? Carruthers relies on the judgment of Nordenfalk, one of the foremost experts on book illumination in late antiquity and the early medieval period, who had suggested "an Egyptian or at least Near Eastern source for the Eusebian layout" (1938, 320 n. 150). Linearily and pictorially formatted patterns of thought may thus have been in existence from earliest times in history.

All this has important implications for media studies. Linear formalization, the use of grids, and spatial patterning for organizing thought—all abstractions from the human lifeworld—are not the invention of typography. There does seem to be a sense in which the mind has been programmed for this kind of thinking. *We cannot think of the typographic medium, or of any of the other media, as having interfered with or colonized the human mind in the fashion of foreign intruders. What typography, and all other media, accomplished was a (re)activation of potentialities that were already in mind and memory.* Media, on this view, are catalysts that mediate between mind and materiality.

102. Memory and Manuscript

From later perspectives, it is evident that codex and canon, *Hexapla* and *Canon Tables* were harbingers of things to come. At the time, however, the cultural potential for the new formatting techniques provided by the codex was far from being fully explored. It was a matter of centuries for the scribal medium to optimize its material resources, and for human consciousness to interiorize scribal technology. The immense textual

compilations accomplished by Origen and Eusebius were peak performances standing out in a culture that by and large remained heavily
beholden to oral, scribal, and memorial modi operandi.

As suggested above, codex and canon did not immediately translate
into a universally acknowledged authority of the Bible as a single, unified
book. To the extent that textual uniformity was an essential component of
the authoritative Bible, medieval manuscript culture, even though it had
advanced beyond the scribal technology of the Second Temple period, was
by its very nature not qualified to produce identical copies because it was
"of the essence of a manuscript culture that every copy is different, both
unique and imperfect" (Parker 1997, 188).

Moreover, throughout patristic and medieval times the Bible was
operational more often in plural form than as solitary authority. Collections of the Minor Prophets, for example, or a clustering of the Psalms into
the Psalter, and of the Gospels into Gospel books enjoyed broad usage.
Missals, breviaries, and lectionaries, widely used as service books in the
medieval church, tended to disperse biblical texts into *lectiones*. There was
a sense, therefore, in which *the biblical tradition in the Middle Ages was
experienced more as a collection of many books and a plurality of auditions
than as a single text between two covers.*

One will further have to remember that for the longest part of its existence the Bible was largely present in the lives of the people as an oral
authority: proclaimed, homiletically interpreted, listened to, and internalized. Nor did the oral proclamation always emanate from the Bible itself.
The Book of Hours (Duffy 2006: 42), for example, composed of psalms
and biblical quotations, was often a household's sole book, known from
memory by millions and recited aloud at each of the eight traditional
monastic hours of the day. Duffy's claim is thus very much to the point: "If
we are to understand the point of contact between people and the written
word [of the Bible] in the late Middle Ages, there is no more fundamental
text than the *Book of Hours*" (42). While the chirographic Bible was rare in
the hands of laypeople, some of its contents existed via the Book of Hours
in the hearts of millions.

Last but not least, the Bible's authority coexisted on equal footing
with that of the councils and the oral and written tradition. On theological grounds, the medieval church operated with a plurality of authorities.
For a millennium and a half, therefore, there was no such thing as the sole
authority of the Bible in Western Christendom. It was only with print technology, and accompanying theological developments, that a standardized

text and duplication of that text was a feasible proposition. *Sola Scriptura, we may safely assert, was a concept technically unworkable and theologically unthinkable prior to the invention of printing.*

The oral authority of the Bible brings us to the phenomenon of memory. Credit for the influential force of memory in Western civilization goes to Yates (1966) and Carruthers (1990). It was the signal accomplishment of Yates (1966) to have constructed in *The Art of Memory* (1966) a historical narrative of the driving force of *memoria* ranging from *Ad Herennium* (first century B.C.E.) through hermeticism and esotericism up to the birth of the scientific method in Bacon, Descartes, and Leibnitz. In *The Book of Memory* Carruthers almost single-handedly reconceptualized the philologically focused academic field of medieval studies. For our purpose, Carruthers is of special importance. Her central thesis states that medieval culture was a memorial culture—memorial not in the sense of remembering death but of bringing the past back to life. *Memoria* and *inventio*, two of the five canons of rhetoric, were closely interacting forces in medieval (and ancient) culture. One cannot exist without the other. Memory, therefore, was not simply a retentive, iterative property, but a re-collective, even calculative potency. Composition was understood to be a memorial activity, and memory was the ability to find and recombine what had been stored mentally. Memory, in short, was both the retentive capacity and the compositional faculty of the mind. If we can trust contemporary sources, St. Thomas composed his monumental *Summa theologica* mentally, with minimal, if any, recourse to texts (Carruthers 1990, 5; see also ch. 6, §36). It was by no means uncommon for people to have instant recall of biblical texts, whether they had memorized them from start to finish, or whether they were in command of selective passages, or merely knew a series of aphorisms and stories. Augustine stands for many theologians who were entirely comfortable in combining the rigors of the manuscript culture with the demands of memory (ch. 6, §34). Peter Brown (1967) has vividly described his bookish environment: "On the shelves, in the little cupboards that were the book-cases of Late Roman men, there lay ninety-three of his own works, made up of two hundred and thirty-two little books, sheafs of his letters, and, perhaps covers crammed with anthologies of his sermons, taken down by the stenographers of his admirers" (428). But the man who surrounded himself with books, many of which he had composed himself, was persuaded that the quality of his intellect was intricately linked to the powers of memory (see ch. 6, §34). Augustine's competence in and cultivation of memory was not only essential for his retention of knowledge and mental compositioning, but also, in the end, for the quality of his thought. *Memory and manuscript interacted in ways we can hardly imagine today.*

Still, there were intellectual developments afoot that would anticipate the eventual demise of memory. Albertus Magnus (ca. 1200–60) and St. Thomas Aquinas (1225–74), whose intellectual activities were memorially empowered to an extent entirely unfathomable for us, nonetheless chose to disconnect memory from rhetoric and to associate it with prudence. In this they anticipated the work of Petrus Ramus (1515–1572), who associated memory with dialectic, by some three hundred years. In the broader context of Western intellectual history, those were moves that shifted memory from its oral, rhetorical pole to the pragmatic, logical pole.

For more than a millennium, roughly from the time of the sack of Rome (410 C.E.) to the invention of printing (ca. 1455 C.E.), a general shift from oral, rhetorical sensibilities to a developing chirographic control over the organization and growth of knowledge is observable. Manuscripts increasingly became important tools of civilized life, and from the eleventh century onward an ever-growing scribal culture shaped the processes of learning. Brian Stock (1983) has documented the world of communications and cultural transformations in the High Middle Ages. It is a complex story. Oral-scribal-memorial interfacing dynamics constituted "not one but rather many models, all moving at different velocities and in different orbits" (34). There was the high culture of the papacy and monasticism, of chanceries and diplomacy, of jurisdiction and above all of scholasticism. Undoubtedly, those were elite circles that excelled in thinking and formulating complex philosophical, theological, legal, and linguistic ideas often with signal keenness of intellect. Theirs was a culture of written records that both benefited from and contributed to the developing chirographic communication. But one must guard against facile premises concerning links between a developing medieval documentary life and a restructuring of consciousness. The processes entailed in the interiorization of medieval scribalism are intricate, raising deep questions regarding the interfacing of the materiality of language and knowledge with mind and memory. In the most general terms, however, it seems fair to say that relentless scribal labors enhanced the textual base of knowledge; that knowledge, insofar as it was managed by a working relationship with manuscripts, was apt to become detached from the oral, traditional biosphere; that in the minds of the literate elite, "oral tradition became identified with illiteracy" (12); and that knowledge processed scribally would foster comparative and critical thought. But it needs to be restated that this mutual interpenetration of scribal technology and human thought is observable predominantly among the chirographic elite.

Thus while professional scribality began to exercise effects on mind and consciousness, and the Bible became the most studied book in the West, a book whose language and contents permeated medieval language, literacy still remained the privilege of few, and reading and writing did not instantaneously result in literate intellectualism. And this is the other part of the complex medieval communications world: the chirographic technology was, and continued to be, tedious, backbreaking business (Troll 1990). By typographical standards, writing one letter after the next, and word after word, was exceedingly slow work, and the time spent on completing a manuscript of average length was inordinate. And so was the price of a manuscript. The copying of existing manuscripts aside, the manufacture of new texts was usually the result of a division of labor. There was the *dictator* or intellectual initiator of a text, who was frequently unable to write himself or herself. There was, second, the *scriptor*, who in taking dictation may or may not have had an intellectual grasp of what she or he was writing. Moreover, medieval Bibles for the most part did not have chapter and verse division. It was only around 1200 c.e. that the first chapter divisions were introduced into biblical manuscripts, and around 1500 c.e. that biblical texts began to be atomized into individually numbered sections or even verses. *Neither the rabbis nor Augustine, neither Maimonides nor Thomas Aquinas ever cited and appropriated the Bible the way typographic folks do.*

Standing in a complex communications web of chirographic technology, memorial activities, oral recitation, and homiletic exposition, the Bible was anything but a closed book with a single sense. Augustine's hermeneutics, for example, could strictly hold to the theory of a divinely inspired and unified book of the Bible while at the same abhorring literalism. Along with many theologians in the Middle Ages he subscribed to the notion of the plural senses of the Bible (see ch. 10, §59). Such was the nature of truth that it comprised multiple senses. Orr's (2007) conclusion about the notion of the literalism of the Bible is, therefore, entirely to the point: "Christianity did not, for most of its history, insist on anything like literal interpretation of scripture. ... Literalism, at least as a dominant view, appeared surprisingly late in the history of Christianity, and in the wake of the Reformation and the Counter-Reformation" (35). And the fifteenth and sixteenth centuries, the period of the church reforms, we shall see, coincided with the invention and rapid domination of the print medium.

103. THE WORD MADE PRINT:
THE TYPOGRAPHIC APOTHEOSIS OF THE BIBLE

There were intellectual forces at work in medieval culture that directed the focus toward texts and developed a textually grounded theo-logic to unprecedented heights. Impelled by skepticism toward philosophical realism, the notion of universal verities existing outside the mind, William of Ockham shifted philosophical-theological attention to contingency and distinctiveness, including the particularity of texts (see chs. 6, §36; 10, §59; Adams 1987; Leff 1975). Scripture came to be perceived as operating in accordance with its own internal logic, which was accessible via the *cognitio intuitiva*. From the perspective of media sensibilities, we observe an intellectualism that is at home in the prevailing chirographic culture and, however unconsciously, exploited its inner resources. In nominalism, of which Ockham was a prominent representative, the notion began to assert itself that the full potential of texts was to be found not primarily in their metaphysical referentiality, proclamatory outreach, or reception but rather in their internal textual economy. With Ockham, the closure of the biblical text was about to receive a hermeneutical, indeed theological, justification. That premise of the closed text was soon to receive powerful technological support through the print medium.

Between 1452 and 1455 C.E. Johannes Gutenberg produced the first print Bible, universally known as the forty-two-line Bible. It is not immediately obvious why he selected a book as monumental in scope as the Bible to implement a technology that was very much in its infancy. At first glance, print's technical effects of duplication appear to point to the propagation of faith as the principal objective. But many arguments speak against it. The casting of close to three-hundred different characters was labor-intensive and hiked up the price of the print Bible. Moreover, Latin, the language of the Vulgate, was no longer marketable; few people could actually read the Latin print Bible. Last but not least, Gutenberg's undertaking was not a commissioned project and for this reason required vast capital investments. Analogous to developments we observe at the launching of the electronic medium, the print medium effected the entrée of a large-scale entrepreneurship into the communications world. *Capitalism took hold of the new medium with a vengeance.* A new culture was coming into existence that merged the new medium with entrepreneurship, and technology with the profit motive, a phenomenon for which Benedict Anderson has coined the fitting term "print capitalism" (1983, 18, passim).

In Gutenberg's case, the print Bible brought its master no economic profit whatsoever. As is well know, he died a poor man, enmeshed in lawsuits and unable to pay his debts (Ruppel 1993; Kapr 1996).

To the viewers and readers of the first major machine-made book in Western civilization, the most striking feature was sameness and pro-portionality. Prior to the invention of printing, sameness in this sense of complete identity had never been experienced. No one jar was like the other, and no two manuscripts were quite alike. The copies of Gutenberg's two-volume Vulgate represented models of stunning sameness, setting the highest standards of calligraphic virtuosity. By virtue of their unprec-edented spatial formatting and finality of precision they expressed a sense of unearthly beauty. Giesecke (1991) has suggested that aesthetics, in par-ticular the Renaissance ideal of beauty in the sense of complete propor-tionality, must have been uppermost on the mind of Gutenberg.[1]

Owing to the duplicating effects of typography, textual pluriformity was now being effectively challenged by the ideal of uniformity. Theology and biblical scholarship were increasingly operating in a media environ-ment that was losing touch with Jewish and Christian textual pluriformity. One was approaching a time when the *mouvance* of tradition was viewed as something that had to be remedied text-critically, or one was beginning to lose sight of it altogether. In short, the notion of *mouvance* was being suppressed and supplanted by what was to become the icon of typographic stability. Moreover, the Bible's complete standardization, combined with its breathtaking beauty, projected a never-before-visualized model of author-ity (see ch. 16, §106). Indeed, it was in part at least a result of the techni-cally facilitated uniformity that contributed to the Bible's unprecedented authority. But again, it was an authority that was accomplished at the price of isolating the Bible from its biosphere. The printed pages, in all their per-fectly proportioned beauty, created the impression that sacred Scripture was closed off in a world of its own, uniformly spatialized, consummately linearized, and perfectly marginalized, a world, that is, where in the words of Alberti any alteration of any kind would only distort the harmony. Now,

---

1. Giesecke (1991, 141–43) cites a programmatic statement concerning the Renaissance ideal of beauty by the Italian art historian and architect Leo Battista Alberti (1404–1472) in *De Re Aedificatoria*: "Beauty is a harmony of all component parts, in whichever medium they are represented, juxtaposed with such a sense of proportionality and connectivity that nothing could be added or altered that would not distort it" (my trans. of Giesecke).

but only now, was it possible not merely to conceptualize the premise of *sola scriptura*, but to visualize it spatially.

It is often pointed out that the Protestant Reformers still exhibited profoundly oral sensibilities with respect to Scripture. *Sola scriptura* notwithstanding, Scripture remained a living presence for all of them. Martin Luther, Martin Bucer, John Calvin, Thomas Cranmer, William Tyndale, and others spoke and wrote a scripturally saturated language because they were at home in Scripture and Scripture in them. Their respective theological positions remained fully cognizant of and sympathetic to the power of oral proclamation. Luther never viewed his vernacular translation simply as a linguistic feat, but rather as a Pentecostal reenactment of the bestowal of the Spirit (Newman 1985). The presence of scriptural orality in the theology of the Reformers cannot be in doubt.

Equally significant, however, was the influence of the print medium (Newman 1985). The typographic apotheosis of the Bible deeply affected the Reformers' theological thinking on scriptural authority, tradition, memory, interpretation, and numerous other features. Seven developments, all of them in varying degrees bound up with the new medium, were instrumental in having a corrosive impact on the oral-scribal, memorial world of verbalization. One, the rejection of the fourfold sense of the Bible aided and abetted the rationale for the closure of biblical texts. Two, the increasingly high regard for the *sensus literalis* jeopardized the hermeneutical pluralism cultivated by the medieval church. Three, the repudiation of allegory—the very figure that generated worlds of correspondences—contributed to reducing biblical interpretation to intratextual literalism. Four, the unprecedented elevation of the Bible to *sola scriptura* conjured up the notion of the Bible as a freestanding, monolithic artifact detached from tradition. Five, what came to be called the Protestant principle of Scripture, namely, Luther's *scriptura sui ipsius interpres*, had the effect of closing the Bible into its own interior textual landscape. As Giesecke describes the assumed operation of the Bible: "The fountain gushes forth all by itself. All one need to do is drink from it" (1991, 163: "Der Brunnen sprudelt von sich selbst, man muss nur noch trinken"). Of course it was, he writes, wishful thinking (*ein Wunschbild*), but symptomatic of the conviction of the Bible's hermeneutic self-sufficiency. Six, the steady marginalization of memory effected a shifting of the interpretation of the Bible toward a fully textualized, documentary model. Seven, and perhaps most ominously, the rejection of tradition, this larger-than-textual life of communal memory, disconnected biblical texts both from their vital sustenance and their performance arena. To be sure, some of these features had been anticipated, implicitly or explicitly, in the manuscript culture of ancient and medieval theology, and especially in nominalism's *via moderna* of the fourteenth and fifteenth centuries. One cannot make print the sole determinant of these developments. But the word made print, namely, the inauguration of the medium that "is comfortable only with finality" (Ong 1982, 132), heavily contributed toward viewing the Bible as a closed book, or, better perhaps, toward fantasizing it as a closed book. Typography was a major, although not the only, factor that effectively reified the biblical texts and generated a high degree of plausibility for thinking of the Bible as an authority that was entirely objective and standing on its own.

No doubt, these are profoundly consequential developments not only with respect to the status and interpretation of the Bible but for Western intellectual history in general. To begin with, the unprecedented elevation of the authority of Scripture was accomplished at the price of depriving it and its interpretation of the oxygen of tradition. Second, the Bible's newly acquired authority was to no small degree based on the systematically formatted typographic space, which encouraged new habits of reading and understanding. Third, and most significantly, the systematic reification of the Bible's typographic authority and the tendency of something approaching a general readership was a complex process that will not allow for a simple explanation in terms of progressivism. *Media invariably operate* ad bonam et ad malam partem. James Simpson (2007) has recently developed the thesis that the Reformers were the protagonists not (merely) of modern liberalism but of fundamentalism as well, and he has linked the rise of literal, historical reading of the Bible with the rapidly dominant power of the high tech of the fifteenth century. Along similar lines, Elizabeth Eisenstein has asked us to imagine not merely the trajectory of humanism, Renaissance, and Reformation toward Enlightenment and modernity, but to acknowledge other trajectories as well. Fundamentalism in the sense of the literal interpretation and inerrancy of the Bible, she observes, while strictly speaking a late nineteenth- and twentieth-century Protestant, North American phenomenon, was in the age of Erasmus "just beginning to assume its modern form" (1979, 1:366). Unless we recognize these connections, she states, "the appearance of fundamentalism in the age of Darwin or the holding of the Scopes trial in the age of Ford become almost completely inexplicable" (440). For Eisenstein, author of *The Printing Press as an Agent of Change*, the genesis of sixteenth-century fundamentalism is definitely allied with the printing press and its impact on the formatting, reading, and interpreting of the Bible. On the whole, however, she carefully balances her assessment of print's effect on religious culture: "The impact of printing on the Western scriptural faith thus pointed in two quite opposite directions—toward 'Erasmian' trends and ultimately higher criticism and modernism, and toward more rigid orthodoxy culminating in literal fundamentalism and Bible Belts" (366–67).

Luther, it is well known, was fully conscious of the unprecedented potential of the print medium: "Typography is the final and at the same time the greatest gift, for through it God wanted to make known to the whole earth the mandate of the true religion at the end of the world and to pour it out in all languages. It surely is the last, inextinguishable flame of the world."[2] We know that he was in possession of print copies of Johann Reuchlin's De Rudimentis Hebraicis, of a Hebrew Bible (first published by the North Italian Jewish Soncino press in 1488) and of Erasmus's Greek New Testament. To a large extent, therefore, his translation project was carried out with the assistance and on the basis of print materials. Additionally, he utilized printed copies of the Bible and the New Testament as tools for proclamation, propaganda, and polemic. But he could not have anticipated the full impact the print Bible would have on the religious, social, and political landscape of Europe. No medium escapes the law of unintended consequences, and the print medium is no exception.

The print Bible was by no means the unmixed blessing that its inventor and many of its promoters had envisioned. It was the first modern mass-produced industrial commodity, and the first best seller in Western civilization. On one level, the rapid dissemination of the vernacular print Bible raised literacy to a level never before seen in Europe and created a steadily growing readership of unimaginable proportions. In media terms, it was Luther's aspiration to locate a home computer that carried the basic data of Christian faith in every branch of the institutional church, in every monastery and convent, and in every household as well (Giesecke 1991, 245). Moreover, general accessibility to the Bible posed a

---

2. The citation is from Luther's Tischreden, written down by Nikolaus Medler (1532) and cited by Giesecke (1991, 163 and 727 n. 167): "Typographia postrem est donum et idem maximum, per eam enim Deus toti terrarum orbi voluit negotium verae religionis in fine mundi innotescere ac in omnes linguas transfundi. Ultima sana flamma mundi inextinguibilis."

challenge to authoritative control over the Bible and fostered democratic instincts about scriptural ownership and rights to interpretation. On a different level, however, "the infallibility of the printed word as opposed to the 'instability of script' was recognized even by contemporaries as a fiction" (Newman 1985, 101). The serious malaise that was affecting the print business, Newman observed, was of a twofold kind: "First: printers were hasty and negligent in the practice of their trade. Second: they were concerned above all with the pursuit of profits" (102). Luther himself was increasingly disturbed that "his" printed Bible had been pirated to the point where ever more printed texts of ever poorer quality were in circulation: "I do not recognize my own books ... here there is something left out, there something set incorrectly, there forged, there not proofread" (110). In other words, the very medium that was capable of standardizing the text had set into motion a process of accelerated reproduction and rapid commercialization that resulted in textual inaccuracies. But in the mechanical medium, textual errors were likely to be multiplied a hundredfold and a thousandfold. One is bound to ask: Did the new medium recapitulate, perhaps even aggravate, textual pluriformity, the very condition it had set out to overcome?

The globalizing tendencies inherent in typography were making themselves felt not only in the rapid dissemination of standardized copies, and of flawed copies as well, but also in conflicting interpretations. Notwithstanding its typographical orderliness, the ever more widely publicized content of the Bible became a bone of fierce contention. Among a steadily growing readership, the biblical texts were exposed to unprecedented scrutiny. Inevitably, scriptural discrepancies came to light. But whereas in chirographic culture, theological controversies stayed confined to a small circle of theological experts, in print culture, disputes went public across regional and national boundaries. In this way, the new medium marketed dissension and deepened disagreements.

Last but not least, vernacular Bibles became the rallying points for national aspirations, demarcating linguistic and ethnic boundaries, and contributing to the rise of nation states. "It is no accident that nationalism and mass literacy have developed together" (Eisenstein 1979, 363). While the new medium thus gave momentum to national languages and identities, it also helped draw new lines of religious and national division, and strongly exacerbated Catholic-Protestant polemics. Eisenstein has articulated typography's unintended implication in the dissolution of Latin Christianity and the fragmentation of Europe, provocatively asserting that

"Gutenberg's invention probably contributed more to destroying Christian concord and inflaming religious warfare than any of the so-called arts of war ever did" (319).

16

THE WORK OF WALTER J. ONG
AND BIBLICAL SCHOLARSHIP

The relevance of Walter Ong's work has rightly been claimed to encompass the full range of the humanities and social sciences, and to extend to the so-called hard sciences that shape our technological world. His studies of the development of logic along the lines of the linguistic and technological evolution from primary orality through writing and print to the electronic culture has yielded what amounts to an impressive phenomenology of communication, culture, and consciousness that productively connects with virtually every division of human learning. In view of the intellectual fecundity and wide-ranging applicability of Ong's thought it seems odd that his work has not—with rare exceptions—significantly influenced the ancient and tradition-honored discipline of biblical scholarship. Why is it that his studies on language, mind, and thought, which exhibit vast knowledge of and exquisite sensitivity to the Bible and its immense and boundlessly intricate receptionist history, have left the academic discipline of biblical studies largely unaffected? This essay in memory of Walter Ong seeks both to account for this situation and to argue for the abiding relevance of his thought for biblical studies, biblical narrative, and the oral-textual psychodynamics of the Bible.

The first part gives a brief overview of Ong's intellectual profile as Renaissance historian, Jesuit priest, and author of the monumental Ramus, Method and the Decay of Dialogue. *The second part defines key features of the historical-critical paradigm and locates modern biblical scholarship at the confluence of Ramism, Renaissance humanism, Protestantism, and typography. Ong's intellectual orbit of an oral-scribal phenomenology, cognition, and media studies is described as being critically distanced from the textual, documentary model of biblical scholarship. To demonstrate the alienation of the historical-critical paradigm from the oral-scribal-memorial world of antiquity, the third part examines the media identity of the Greek New Testament. It is defined as a virtual text, a typographically mediated and transformed text that has arisen out of an ongoing elimination process of ancient witnesses. The fourth part takes a critical look at form criticism, a foundational methodology of the historical-critical paradigm. Ten characteristic features are identified, and it is demonstrated that Ong's phenomenology of orality-literacy problematizes all of them. The fifth part pleads for consideration of Ong's work, which is deemed highly relevant for modern biblical scholarship.*

The definitive breakthrough in scriptural studies, I believe, is yet to come.
—Walter J. Ong, "Maranatha: Death and Life in the Text of the Book"

One of the reasons for reflection on the spoken word, the word as sound, is of course not to reject the later media, but to understand them, too, better.
—Walter J. Ong, *The Presence of the Word*

Writing and print isolate the individual or, if you prefer, liberate him from the tribe.
—Walter J. Ong, *The Presence of the Word*

104. Ong's Intellectual Profile

Although a restlessly interdisciplinary mind, Ong was strictly speaking an expert in the literary and intellectual history of the Renaissance, and not a biblical scholar. To many he was known as one of the world's experts on comparative media studies or media ecology, as it is called today, but to those who knew him closely he seemed to be in a category all by himself. As far as his intellectual persona is concerned, he managed to assimilate deep introspection with a sometimes astonishing pragmatism, and a limitless curiosity about virtually all aspects of human knowledge with an unfailing commitment to Christian faith and the church. He never applied his circumspectly developed expertise in orality, scribality, and typography to a methodical treatment of the Bible or to any particular aspect of its heterogeneous literature, nor did he pay sustained attention to the exegetical minutiae or hermeneutical discussions that make up the life of the incalculably immense and ever-growing body of biblical scholarship. Yet his work is dotted with intriguing and often profound insights into the Bible, both from the perspective of orality-literacy studies (aural assimilation, tribal memory, oral substratum, changing sensoria, rhetoric, interiority, corpuscular epistemology, Bible reading and divisiveness, textual criticism and philology, etc.) and of theology (incarnation, presence, Holy Spirit, *fides ex auditu*, inspiration, Eucharist, Trinity, economy of revelation, etc.). Moreover, his intense concentration on the *word* as speech event, his rethinking of textuality from the vantage point of orality, and his development of the implications of his media work for human culture and consciousness have given us a theoretical framework that is highly suitable for a revitalization and revision of assumptions, methods, and practices that govern current biblical scholarship. Indeed, I venture the claim that, given more time to let Ong's work be absorbed by the guild of Scripture scholars, few academic fields will be more profoundly affected by his ideas on the verbal arts as biblical scholarship.

To properly assess the work and person of Walter Ong, one has to take into account that he was a Catholic priest, the only priest ever elected to the presidency of the Modern Language Association of America (1978), and a member of the Society of Jesus. Three principal characteristics may be associated with his Jesuit identity. One, he was a man of stupendous learning, unimaginable and indeed unimagined in today's humanities. His definitive bibliography, meticulously compiled by the late Thomas M. Walsh with the assistance of M. Kathleen Schroeder comprises 434 items, not counting (frequently revised) reprints and a never-ending stream of translations (Berg and Walsh 2011, 185–250). Two, standing in the legacy of the Aristotelian-Thomistic tradition, the human sensorium, above all auditory and visual perceptiveness, occupied a central role in his thought. Ong's magnum opus on Pierre de la Ramée (1958) describes in exhaustive detail and with meticulous philosophical exactitude the latter's intellectual contribution to the rise of premodernism. As Ong elaborates it, Ramée's system of thought was marked by a logic of quantification and airtight systematization, a knowledge arranged in tidily drawn charts and tables, increased use of spatial patterns, language conceived to be locked in space, closed-pattern thinking, the dichotomization of knowledge, and knowledge treated as commodity (as information or data, we would say today)—all developments that amounted to a restructuring of the human sensorium from its oral-aural form toward a more visualist form. Ong therefore had a keenly philosophical understanding of where the modern mind came from in promoting a system that "furthered the elimination of sound and voice from man's understanding of the intellectual world and helped create within the human spirit itself the silences of a spatialized universe" (Ong 1958, 318). Three, he succeeded admirably in synthesizing Catholic universalism with secular globalism in developing a broadly designed phenomenology of human culture and consciousness. All closed-model thinking of the kind Ong had encountered and studied in the work of Pierre de la Ramée was suspect in his eyes because he believed in the inevitable openness of human thought and discourse. Along with his Jesuit friend, the paleologist and geologist Teilhard de Chardin, he envisioned a universal worldview, an aspiration that included his growing interest in cosmology. When asked how he would like to be remembered, he replied that it had been his aim to "further understanding of the relationships between verbal as well as other types of human expression and the total evolution of the cosmos that we human beings are part of and are still learning more and more about daily" (Kleine and Gale 1996, 83).

Two articles come to mind that deal exclusively with biblical texts, each written from the viewpoint of varied oral-textual interlockings. One is his well-known "Maranatha: Death and Life in the Text of the Book" (1977b, 230–71). The essay is a deeply original and hence genuinely Ongian, or, as he himself and his students might put it, "Onglish" contribution to the textual and in particular narrative nature of the Bible. To be sure, his sensitive elaboration of the retrospective orientation of narrative, the artificiality of plot, and the futurity of biblical texts are issues that are by no means unknown to literary and biblical scholars. However, the subtle but precise differentiation between retrospective proclivities in oral discourse versus those in textually managed verbal arrangements is vintage Ong. Above all, there is his beautifully developed and substantiated central thesis concerning connections between textuality and death. There are thousands of references pointing to connections between writing and death, he observed. Among the numerous examples he cites are 2 Cor 3:6 ("the letter kills, but the Spirit gives life"), Longfellow ("books are sepulchres of thought"), Bacon ("libraries, which are the shrines where all the relics of the ancient saints, full of true virtue, … are preserved and imposed"). While associations of writing with death are not readily accessible to the historical, literary analysis of texts, they are nonetheless "manifold and inescapable" (240). The essay probes the psychodynamics (a favorite word of Ong) of textual-oral interfaces and touches on the deeper structures underlying biblical texts. Characteristically Ongian, the author moves beyond, or rather below, what is demonstrable via conventional literary and historical-critical tools. He was himself entirely aware of the singularity of his thesis: "The connections here [between life, death and the Word of God] do not leap to the eye. Conscious acknowledgement of their presence may meet with resistance, for what we are dealing with are connections operating well below the ordinary threshold of consciousness, in the unconscious or subconscious realms of the psyche" (1977b, 261).

Indeed, his perception seems almost mystically attuned to stirrings far below the threshold of conscious awareness. Little wonder that the article has made next to no impact on our academic studies of the Bible because it raises sensibilities that have remained unknown and unexplored in biblical scholarship.

Ong's second contribution to an oral-literacy understanding of the Bible is "Text as Interpretation: Mark and After" (1992b, 191–210), a review essay of *The Oral and the Written Gospel*. Ong, the Catholic thinker, thoroughly conscious of the significance of tradition, and conceptualizing tradition in terms of oral-textual-oral dynamics, had no problem with my locating Mark at an oral-scribal interface: "Essentially what Mark had to do was to interpret," he writes (1992b, 194). From the perspective of media dynamics, the early Jesus tradition was distressingly complex: "Oral materials are textualized, the textual materials then freely circulated orally, with or without some textual control conjoined to oral control, and then are reprocessed from orality into text again" (208). Moreover, oral utterance is inescapably contextualized: Jesus "spoke in every case in a context of real concerns of real people in real social structures" (197). Put more theoretically, verbal *and* extraverbal elements cooperate in the construction of the message's meaning. Given tradition's complexity and orality's social contextuality, the aspiration to want to retrieve the "original" utterance is, Ong writes forthrightly, "quixotic" (196). As if the debate over the Great Divide had never taken place, he makes reference to "the antithetical relationship of textuality and orality" (200), and to "the subversion of orality by writing" (202). Mark, therefore, in his view, while "residually oral," is not oral composition but a "chirographic organization of the kerygma" (198). Finally, drawing on Brian Stock's concept of a "textual community" (1983, 90, passim), he ventured a definition of the church in media terms, bringing the full force of media complexities into play, and stating that "this oral-textual-oral-textual-oral interpretive community is the Church" (208). He concludes by observing that "the work of understanding is just beginning" (210).

Clearly, Ong's thought inhabits an intellectual universe that is quite different from current historical-critical studies. To forestall any possible misunderstanding, it is worth pointing out that his intellectual position and his critique of biblical scholarship have nothing in common with the early twentieth-century conflict between a largely Protestant modernism and a predominantly Catholic antimodernism over the right approach to biblical interpretation. In that conflict, Catholicism's objections to the so-called historical criticism of the Bible were modified in the 1943 encyclical *Divino Afflante Spiritu* (*Inspired by the Divine Spirit*), the Magna Carta of Catholic biblical studies issued by Pope Pius XII and further developed in the Dogmatic Constitution on Divine Revelation, *Dei Verbum* (*The Word of God*) issued by Pope Paul VI at the twenty-first Ecumenical Council, popularly called Vatican II (1961–65) (Donahue 1993). Ong's intellectual bent and disciplinary preoccupations betray no overt interest in or influence by this historic dispute.

Ong did raise objections to aspects of current biblical scholarship, but his criticism grew entirely out of his very own thought world of communications and the verbal arts. He once told me in a private conversation that "you biblical folks will be the very last ones to catch on," and then he added with a twinkle in his eyes: "because you are the most bookish people of all." This characteristic statement arose from his expert knowledge of orality-literacy studies, familiarity, although not close acquaintance, with biblical scholarship, and most significantly deep insights into the rise and nature of modern intellectual thought. Equipped with a learned understanding of Ramist philosophy and its forced divorce from Aristotelian-Thomistic medievalism, he understood the core of modernity better than most, both its assets but also its liabilities, and he was therefore able to locate intellectually the historical-critical scholarship of the Bible far more perceptively than biblical scholarship itself has been able to critically assess its procedures and objectives in a broader cultural context. Plainly, his concern was not that modern biblical studies was heavily secularized and had failed to make room for the agency of the Spirit in human affairs and in an orally-textually mediated tradition. His objections came from a very different direction. Modern biblical studies, in his view, was dominated by an excessive confidence in words-in-space and driven by a sense of domination by textuality, and a lack of sensibility toward the oral-aural operation and apperception of biblical words; they had lost touch with the oral substratum and rhetorical outreach of many biblical texts, and generally had little awareness of the multiple oral-textual interfaces residing in the Bible as a whole. *By implication, his diagnosis was that the historical-critical scholarship of the Bible was a genuine child of Ramism, as he had come to know it. We literate children of the typographic age suffer from a "cultural squint"*

because we have allowed "the communications media of our own culture [to]
impose themselves on us surreptitiously as absolutes with crippling effects."
Ours is a "disability [that] has interfered with our understanding of the
nature of the Bible, with its massive oral underpinnings, and of the very
nature of language itself" (1967b, 20–21). These are harshly critical words.
To comprehend the fuller implications of Ong's criticism we need to grasp
a sense of the intellectual profile of modern biblical scholarship. In that
process, we shall apply and extend Ong's media criticism of the historical-
critical approach to the Bible.

105. THE HISTORICAL-CRITICAL PARADIGM

The academic discipline of the historical-critical examination of the Bible
is by and large the result of an alliance of three cultural constellations or
intellectual developments that arose in the late Middle Ages and came to
fruition in the fifteenth and sixteenth centuries: Ramism, Renaissance
humanism, and Protestantism. The link connecting all three movements,
shaping them into what came to be premodernism, was print technology. Humanism, which reinvigorated philology and philosophy; Ramism,
which carried out a drastic educational reform; and Protestantism, which
initiated a religious revolution, eagerly embraced the new medium and
immeasurably benefited from its technological innovation. *Very broadly*
sketched, it was in this humanistic, Ramist, Protestant, typographic cultural
context that a premodern and developing modern intellectualism began to
prepare the ground on which the philological, documentary, historical exam-
ination of the Bible, the print Bible, was to take root.

Among the key features that typify the historical criticism of the Bible,
the following may be cited: the construction of a chronological framework
that proved serviceable as backbone for the reconstruction of the history of Christian origins; a circumspectly designed methodology for the
classification and interpretation of texts; a rapidly increasing reliance on
the printed text in response to the triumph of typography in the fifteenth
century; a reduction of the medieval plural senses to the one historical
sense (*sensus literalis sive historicus*); the exploration of the historical conditionedness of texts, reading them both in the context of their historical
genesis and predominantly with a view toward authorial intentionality;
the text-critical construction of so-called critical editions, more often than
not in the interest of securing the "original text"; the recovery of sources
that were deemed usable for the purpose of recovering oral and literary

antecedent stages in the tradition; a tendency to imagine tradition, even oral tradition, on the model of a linear sequentiality and often along the straight line of an evolutionary ascent; interest in the production of texts more than in their consumption; a general focus on texts, intertextuality, and textual stratifications more than on orality and oral/scribal interfaces (form criticism notwithstanding); and a fascination with questions of origins, including the singular originality of Jesus' *ipsissima verba* or the *ipsissima structura* presumed to be recoverable from given texts; and many more. This historical-critical paradigm has served as the intellectual matrix for a biblical scholarship that was a significant contributor to premodernism, and has extended its influence far into the present. Its intellectual accomplishments have been very significant. Western modernity is unthinkable without the immense body of historical, literary scholarship devoted to the critical analysis of the Bible. More to the point: *the critical analysis of the Bible and the historical reconstruction of early Christian history should be seen as a hallmark of the intellectual ethos of modernity.*

106. The Greek Text of the New Testament: *Textus Constructus* versus *Textus Receptus*

Only very recently under the buildup of growing media sensitivities has consciousness been raised in some quarters about connections between the historical-critical paradigm and the rapidly emerging print culture of the fifteenth and sixteenth centuries. We need to be mindful of the fact that for the most part biblical scholarship's theories about the ancient verbal arts (the functioning of texts and speech, as well as notions about authorship, text, tradition, composition, and others) have been deeply entrenched in this paradigm. By the same token, many of the notions that flourished under the aegis of the typographic medium (individual authorship, authorial property, production of entirely identical texts, rigidly formatted texts furnished with punctuation marks, construction of "critical editions," and others) had no place in the ancient media culture. And yet, it is not the chirographic culture as much as the print Bible, the first major, mechanically produced book in Western civilization, that has served, and continues to serve, as the centerpiece of modernity's biblical scholarship. Many of our historical methods and assumptions about biblical texts, about intertextuality, about tradition, both oral and scribal, originated in the analysis and interpretation of these typographically objectified and monumentalized biblical texts.

The textual authority of the Bible on which historical scholarship relies and from which it derives basic insights into early Christian history and tradition appears to be a matter of such settled scholarly disposition that we are likely to forget that in media terms it is the product of typographic technology. Such is the academic prestige of the Greek text of the New Testament that one easily loses sight of the fact that it is entirely the creation of the medium of modernity. Parker (1997, 196) has articulated this point with the necessary historical precision: "That a Greek New Testament contains what it does is so natural to us that we need to be particularly careful to remember how much more a theoretical than a real entity the Greek New Testament was, until the invention of printing. It was far more a creation of northern European medieval and Renaissance technology than it was of early Christian thought."

The only change in words I would suggest is the replacement of the description of the Greek New Testament as being "more a theoretical than a real entity" with the definition of *virtual text*. *Virtuality*, a term associated with the new digital medium, denotes a real but electronically transfigured and enhanced model of actuality. In that sense, the Greek New Testament is a virtual text, that is, a real but typographically mediated and transformed text. More is at stake here. Not only is it a text constructed by the high tech of the fifteenth century, which has dominated modernity ever since, but it is also a text continuously in the making. As is well known, the Greek New Testament is the product of an ongoing process of selection from a number of manuscripts and from a vast and growing pool of textual variants. We will not go wrong, therefore, to claim that the Greek text of the New Testament is an eclectic or composite text. Obviously, this is not new information for biblical scholars. I am treading on familiar ground. But I question whether the implications of the Greek text's construction have been sufficiently internalized in scholarship. The Greek text, I reiterate, both in its modern typographic identity and in its ongoing compositional selectivity is a text that has never existed before, most certainly not during the ancient and medieval centuries of oral, chirographic, performative communication. It is entirely the constructed product of modernity's dominant medium and of typographically facilitated and accelerated selection processes. *Textus receptus* has been the designation used for the approved standard Greek text of the New Testament. It is a term that was "first employed not by a church synod, but by the Leiden branch of the Dutch publishing firm of Elsevier, as a blurb" (Eisenstein 1979, 1:338). That is to say, not only the typographically steadily "improved" Greek text but also the designation for it in terms of *textus receptus* were nonexistent in the ancient and medieval history of the Latin West and the Greek East. The term did not enter the vocabulary until the early seventeenth century, at a time when the typographic medium and its transformative, constructive powers were in full gear. The term *textus receptus* itself is, therefore, a creation of premodernism and the new typographic medium. The noteworthy fact that the technical term appeared in the light of print for the first time in the form of a commercial blurb, to "advertise the merits ... of Erasmus' version" of the New Testament (338 n. 112) ultimately suggests "print capitalism" (Anderson 1983, 18, passim) as its social background and matrix. As far as the designation of *textus receptus* is concerned, it conjures up an unproblematic history of the tradition, which retained and passed on what had been received, and it masks the plurality and heterogeneity of the tradition. *Textus receptus*, therefore, in reference to the Greek New Testament *has been a misleading and inaccurate term. It represents the interests, not least the commercial interests, and the claims, not to say pretensions, of modernity and of its typographic mind-set. The historically accurate designation for the Greek New Testament is* textus constructus, not textus receptus.

Undeniably, composite texts are by no means the sole prerogative of the typographic medium. Ancient and medieval New Testament manuscripts were often textual composites or conflated texts, and most had absorbed both written sources and oral traditions. But the process of a systematic, typographically (and more recently electronically) facilitated, and (by very few people) controlled elimination of so-called variants is an altogether modern phenomenon. The *textus constructus*, I reiterate, is a predominantly premodern, modern commodity, and the result of a process that in this efficiency is difficult to imagine any time before that. Indeed, what is remarkable about the early period of chirographically Gospel traditions is their considerable textual variability (ch. 14). Stabilization was a gradual process and still a far cry from what in the early seventeenth century came to be called the *textus receptus. The stated or implied claim, therefore, that the Greek text of the New Testament is in the process of steadily being "improved" in the sense of taking us further back to the beginnings must be judged historically inaccurate.*

Difficulties of the kind we encounter in the construction of a standard Greek text of the New Testament are by no means unknown in other humanistic disciplines. In the area of medieval, and specifically Spanish medieval, manuscript culture, John Dagenais (1994) has struggled with those very text-critical issues.[1] More than anyone I know he has probed the rationale and in fact the morality at work in the elimination processes that produce the victorious finalist in the form of the "critical edition." Given the existence of "tens of thousands of medieval manuscripts," what is the rationale, Dagenais asked, for marginalizing, discarding, and categorizing them into lists of variants, instead of appreciating them "as living witnesses to the dynamic, chaotic, error-fraught world of medieval literary life that we have preferred to view till now through the smoked glass of critical editions" (xviii). And Dagenais continues: "What is the intellectual value (and cultural significance) of taking a text that was written and read in a variety of forms in numerous medieval manuscripts and transforming it into a single printed book?" (xvi). Medievalism, he concludes, is "the only discipline I can think of that takes as its first move the suppression of its evidence" (xviii). *But medievalism is not the only discipline that has transformed history into virtuality, all the while claiming to be closest to the pulse of history.* The analogy with the New Testament manuscripts and their subjection to a severe elimination process leaps to the eye. The New Testament exists, partially but also completely, in more manuscripts than any other ancient work: it is preserved in over 5,400 complete or fragmented Greek manuscripts. What is the rationale of relegating the majority of these hard data to the margins in the interest of constructing the *virtual* text—which in turn is allowed to serve as arbiter in the elimination process? How far has modernity's historical-critical scholarship removed itself from the oral, chirographic realities of ancient and medieval culture?

The materiality of the Bible as an unalterably authoritative, single book is a notion so thoroughly internalized that we need reminding that this kind of authority was not fully established until its texts had been metamorphosed via the medium of typography. It was only with printing that a text approaching something of a standard type as well as duplication and dissemination of what now were fully identical copies of the standard type was a feasible proposition. It is, of course, entirely correct to point to the codex and its well-documented use at an early stage in Christianity, to the emergence of canon and a canonical mentality and, in the West, to the triumph of the printed Vulgate as features inclining toward the stabilization of biblical texts and the centralization of biblical authority. All three

---

1. I owe reference to John Dagenais's *The Ethics of Reading in Manuscript Culture* to Rachel Fulton Brown, a graduate of Rice University and now an associate professor of medieval history in the Department of History at the University of Chicago.

factors were principal forces in advancing the authority of the one-volume Bible. However, the production of the fourth-fifth-century codices of Sinaiticus, Alexandrinus, Vaticanus, and Ephraemi Rescriptus carrying the whole Bible were not the rule in manuscript culture, and the composition of fifty copies of the Bible ordered by Emperor Constantine was a highly exceptional event, feasible and affordable only because mandated by imperial decree. "Complete Greek Bibles, even complete New Testaments, were very rare," Parker writes (1997, 195). The price of producing a single Bible was prohibitive, and once in existence, few could read it. Moreover, theological rationales and religious practice tended to foster preferences for certain biblical books over others. For all practical purposes, the medieval Bible was experienced more as a corpus of many books than as a single text between two covers.

For centuries the Bible manifested itself to a very large extent as an oral authority, proclaimed to and heard by the people. Moreover, early appeals to *Tradition*, both oral and written, as an authority coequal to that of *Scripture* prepared the way for what later came to be codified as the two sources of revelation. Church councils varied in terms of judicial status and deliberative outreach, but conciliar decrees could be of historic significance, extending and, some might argue, eclipsing the authority of the Bible. The First Ecumenical Council of Nicaea (325 c.e.) is a case in point. For a millennium and a half, the notion of the sole authority of the Bible was therefore nonexistent and pointless in Western Christendom.

In addition to theological reasons, there was undeniably a pragmatic reason for this relative lack of singular biblical authority, or more precisely, for this—by later print standards—somewhat diffuse and unfocused notion of biblical authority. Textual uniformity, an essential ingredient for the acceptance of the Bible as a single, authoritative book, was not the forte of manuscript culture. It simply was not within the power of chirography to produce one single standard type. To say that prior to printing the Bible existed in scribal multiformity is to make the point that no manuscript, not even biblical manuscript, was exactly like any other. It was only with print technology that a standardized Bible and the dissemination of a virtually limitless number of fully identical copies became an attainable objective. The duplicating and commercializing effects of the print medium and of its technological showpiece, the print Bible, enhanced the authority of the latter in ways it had never enjoyed before. As Parker notes, "The discovery that it was possible to produce hundreds of identical copies led to a new confidence in the book's [i.e., the Bible's] authority, and with it the assumption that the identical copies represented an authoritative edition" (189). It was the typographically standardized Bible, the first major mechanically produced book of early modernity, that served as midwife to the birth of modern biblical scholarship, and ever since has provided the authoritative textual basis for the philological, historical, and theological examination of the Bible.

The notion of complete sameness generated by typography manifested itself not merely in identical Bible copies but in the internal proportionality of each individual print Bible. Nothing quite like it had ever been experienced in the Western history of communications. Aesthetics was a concern uppermost in the mind of Gutenberg (Giesecke 1991, 134–46). To be sure, the chirographically produced medieval manuscripts were already showpieces of aesthetic perfection, and, as is well known, Gutenberg used manuscripts as models for his project. He scrutinized page layout, individual letter types, the composition of color in illuminated manuscripts, specifically the application of gold, the making of parchment, and numerous other technical attributes. But he did so with a conscious view toward surpassing medieval chirography via the new technology. His goal was not primarily a speedy reproduction and mass distribution, and the propagation of faith, as one might assume as a matter of course. His forty-two-line Bible was entirely unsuitable for propagandistic purposes. Not only was it beyond the reach of virtually anybody to acquire and possess the priceless masterpiece, but also its Latin text communicated a language that was rapidly falling out of vogue in Europe. Gutenberg was a superior technician and craftsman, and his deepest aspiration was to produce a technically perfect and aesthetically superior Bible. Owing to the typographically accomplished sameness of the Bible, an artistically executed internal proportionality, a perfectly executed layout, a rigidly methodical formatting of the text, and the ability to produce a potentially infinite number of totally identical exemplars, all these attributes contributed to the authority of the print Bible, which was rapidly recognized to be technically superior over the chirographic Bible.

Historical-critical scholarship has, for most of its history, but without full intellectual reflection, tended to apply to ancient scribality and its multiple oral-scribal interfaces literary theories that were acquired from observations made largely on typographically constructed, modern texts. As a result, modern biblical scholarship has run the risk of being vulnerable to the charge of a cultural and specifically media anachronism. Put differently: *From the perspective of media studies, the historical-critical paradigm is rooted in a post-Gutenberg intellectualism and is therefore patently culture-bound and specifically media-bound.* Biblical scholarship has justly claimed that it ranks—along with classical philology—among the oldest and methodologically most developed academic disciplines. Yet we may eventually come to see the historical-critical scholarship of the Bible not (or no longer) as a kind of unerring force that is justified simply by being practiced, but rather as an element, a phase as it were, in the receptionist history of the Bible. Eventually we may become aware that the historical paradigm insofar as it originated in an intensely close working relationship with the print Bible and flourished (until recently) in a steadily growing typographic environment is culturally quite different from the predominantly oral-scribal, memorial, performative environment in which biblical texts were composed and in which they functioned. It is this discrepancy between the communications world of modern biblical scholarship and that in which its subject matter arose and operated that Ong had in mind when he expressed exasperation about that scholarship.

107. Form Criticism: Miscarriage of Oral Psychodynamics and Inattention to Narrative Poetics

What complicates an assessment of the historical-critical paradigm and its role in the interpretation of the Bible is the fact that it *did* make ample room for orality and oral tradition. Despite the paradigm's intense fixation on texts and intertextual relations, its practitioners, far from steering clear of orality, developed a methodology to account for and deal with the Bible's oral matrix, residues, and tradition. The methodology and discipline of form criticism, initially applied by Hermann Gunkel to the Hebrew Bible/Old Testament, was subsequently developed by New Testament scholars Rudolf Bultmann, Martin Dibelius, and Karl Ludwig Schmidt, who concerned themselves with orality in the New Testament in general and with the Synoptic tradition in particular. In the case of the Synoptic tradition, form criticism postulated that oral tradition lay behind the Gospels of Mark, Matthew, and Luke, and were recoverable with methodological precision. Today one can retrospectively claim that form criticism was one of the most significant methodological principles underlying twentieth-century biblical scholarship.

The following ten features—all of which, we shall see, need to be problematized today—may be said to be constitutive of form criticism. One:

designed to explore oral style and speech in the Gospels and other biblical texts, form criticism chose to operate with the concept of speech form. Hence the method's formal designation. The *concept of form* is visually based, and sight has "a propensity to take vision as a perfectly adequate analogue for intellectual knowing" (Ong 1977a, 123). From the outset, speech, the explicit objective of form criticism, was thereby nudged into a direction of objectifiable visualization. Two: the Gospels and other biblical texts were understood to be carriers of *identifiable oral items*, usually small units such as sayings or short stories that were deemed detachable from their textual environment so as to be studied in isolation. Three: form criticism was preoccupied with the search for *the original form*, as it had been programmatically articulated by Bultmann: "The aim of form criticism is to determine the original form of a piece of narrative, a dominical saying or a parable. In the process we learn to distinguish secondary additions and forms, and these in turn lead to important results for the history of the tradition" (1963, 6 [1970, 7]). By pruning existent versions of isolated oral units from what were perceived to be secondary contextual additions and contextual compositions, one strove to arrive at the original form of sayings or stories. Four: because form criticism was defined and practiced as the discipline that was capable of recovering "the original form" of Jesus' sayings and parables, it was almost from its inception transformed into a project that stood at the service of the Quest for Jesus' *ipsissima verba*, or as it came to be reformulated more recently, the *ipsissima structura* of Jesus' sayings. While Bultmann retained a keen interest in utilizing form criticism as a means of reconstructing the nature and processes of the early Jesus tradition, subsequent form-critical work rapidly utilized the method as *an auxiliary instrument for the historical Quest*. Five: form criticism postulated *a predictable correlation between characteristic speech forms and social settings*. The assumption was that distinct "settings in life" corresponded to distinct forms of speech just as clearly definable speech forms were linguistically drawn to, or generated by, clearly definable social contexts. Because of this interrelationship between oral and social life, form criticism claimed to be able to recover the social and in particular the religious life of early Christian communities. Six: form critics tended to either disregard linguistic and sensory distinctions between oral versus scribal dynamics and processes, or to positively advocate the irrelevance of such a differentiation. The latter position was taken by Bultmann, who in reflecting on developments in the tradition proposed that it was "immaterial [*nebensächlich*] whether the oral or written tradition has been responsible; there exists no difference in principle" (1963, 87). Seven: in its deal-ings with oral tradition, form criticism invariably operated with a model of *linear transmissional processes*. Either explicitly or implicitly, tradition was conceived as a chain of verbal transmissions in the sense of transporting words forward from one person to another, and from one place to the next, in ways that were visually imaginable as quasi-linear directionality. Eight: implicitly the linearity of tradition was understood in *evolutionary terms*. The predominant trends in oral tradition were from smaller to larger and from simple to more complex units, thus facilitating the analytical reverse procedure of retracing tradition by eliminating what were perceived to be secondary embellishments back to the original form. Nine: as far as the relationship between oral tradition and the written Gospel (of Mark) was concerned, form criticism postulated a smooth and unproblematic transi-tion from one medium to the other. In keeping with the principle of what I have termed *intrinsic causation* (Kelber 1983 [1997], 4), the evolutionary tradition grew and exerted pressure toward complexification so that Mark's project in part at least "has grown out of the immanent urge to develop-ment which lay in the tradition" (Bultmann 1963, 373); the Gospel "only completes what was begun in the oral tradition" (321). The written Gospel, he argued, must therefore "be considered in organic connection with the history of the material as it lay before the evangelist" (321). Ten: as far as the significance of the Gospel is concerned, it is for form criticism to a very large extent *a product of tradition*. For this reason the claim is made that Mark's literary and religious profile is inherited rather than self-made. This is a judgment that was famously articulated in Bultmann's statement that from the perspective of the antecedent tradition, the composition of the Gospel "involves in principle nothing new" (321). It is a thesis that was reiterated as late as 1990 by Helmut Koester: "Mark is primarily a faithful collector" (289; see also 286).

What makes Ong's work so powerfully pertinent for biblical scholar-ship is the fact that orality-literacy studies, the field to which he made magisterial contributions, problematizes virtually every single assump-tion of form criticism. In the long run, form criticism, the basic method and subdiscipline of twentieth-century biblical scholarship, is not likely to escape the challenge posed by orality-literary studies, especially by the latter's application to the oral, scribal, memorial, and performative aspects of the Synoptic tradition and the Gospels.

The new perspectives obtained by orality-literacy studies render each of the ten characteristic features of form criticism problematic at a minimum and untenable in most instances. One: Ong persistently reminds us that spoken words "are occurrences, events" (1982, 31), "sounded, and hence power-driven" (32) and never assimilable to spatial surfaces. By opting for form as its key concept, form criticism immediately nudged its thinking on orality and oral tradition in the direction of stable, objectifiable language, that is, toward a literary paradigm. It now seems that form criticism, in choosing its foundational category and in designating its disciplinary approach, was misdirected from its very inception. *Instead of form, the normative category should have been performance*, which suggests an event that is linguistically incomplete and contingent on communicative and social contexts.

Two: it is one thing to state that Gospel texts interact in multiple ways with oral tradition, yet quite another to claim that oral units are detachable from the text and subject to focused study. The latter was, and is, the generally accepted form-critical procedure that many of us have been following over the years. And yet, can there be some such thing as detachable speech? Today orality-literacy studies compels us to claim much less. We need to recall and take seriously Ong's observation that, strictly speaking, *orally verbalized words cannot be externalized in any mode of representation*: "A [spoken] word can live only while actually issuing from the interior, physical and psychic, of the living individual. As soon as it has passed to the exterior, it perishes" (1992d, 69).

Dedicated to the recovery of speech forms, the discipline of form criticism needs to bear in mind that speech is sound that "is not simply perishable but essentially evanescent, and it is sensed as evanescent" (Ong 1982, 32), and is therefore irretrievable in any textual mode. Moreover, recent literary work on the Gospels has demonstrated their coherent plot structures. What were once perceived to be detachable, oral items can now be understood as integral parts of the narrative unit. Even though the Gospels, as most ancient manuscripts, were calibrated for oral delivery and auditory reception, the awareness of narrative unity renders the postulate of autonomous, orally functioning, detachable units increasingly problematic. None of this, of course, is to challenge the concept of a living oral tradition in early Christianity. The point is that practitioners of form criticism should guard against our easy acceptance of the concept of detachable, oral units.

Three: the critical postulate about the original form in relation to which secondary and tertiary versions are attestable profoundly misconceives the functioning of oral verbalization. There is, on one hand, the evanescent quality of spoken words that renders futile the project of differentiating secondary and tertiary versions from the primary one. No textual basis exists on which to make judgments of this kind. No less important is the observation, well known in orality-literacy studies, that spoken words "never occur alone, in a context simply of words" (Ong 1982, 101). The social context in which speech is enmeshed, to which it responds, and from which it receives relevant cues is an all-important contributor to oral performance. Ong has formulated this idea as follows: "Each oral utterance emerges from a situation that is more than verbal: a certain person or persons at this time situated in living relationship with a certain other person or persons. The repetition of oral utterance is itself not context-free" (1992b, 196).

Put differently, no matter how many different oral performances, or how many repeat performances of a saying or a parable Jesus transacted, each rendition was freshly composed, and none was intelligible as a variant of the so-called original. Neither the speaker himself nor his audience would ever have thought of differentiating between primary oral wording and its secondary or tertiary derivations. Albert Lord had pointed out that "each performance is 'an' original, if not 'the' original" (1960, 101). From its very inception, therefore, that is, beginning with Jesus the oral performer himself, *the so-called Synoptic tradition is constituted by plural originals, and not by singular originality.* The heart and ethos of oral tradition consists of multiple originality.

(Four:) assuming the existence of "the original form" of Jesus sayings and taking for granted that it was recoverable by means of critical methods, the practitioners of the discipline turned it almost from its inception into an auxiliary instrument of the Quest for the historical Jesus. And yet, the concept of "the original" and its variants entirely misses oral hermeneutics. To repeat: no matter how many times Jesus narrated the so-called parable of the Sower or how many times he spoke the saying about seeking and finding, each rendition was *an* original and in fact *the* original. The method of form criticism applied to the Jesus tradition in search of the one, single origin *operated with a concept of origin that not only was to remain forever inaccessible, but also, in the form it was imagined, never existed.* Rather than allowing itself to become an instrument in the search for Jesus' so-called *ipsissima verba*, form criticism would have been well advised to develop an oral hermeneutics, a model of oral performance, or rather of composition and transmission in performance, and, above all, a genuine model of an oral and oral-scribal (as well as memorial) tradition.

Five: spoken words function in live social contexts in a way written words do not. The Gospels quite appropriately represent this understanding by locating Jesus' aphoristic and parabolic tradition in the historical particularity of social contexts. Yet it must be kept in mind that each of these Gospel contexts is not a live oral setting but a textually narrated one. In the historical, social context, sayings address and respond to live audiences, whereas in the narrative context, sayings are first and foremost responsible to the Gospel's immediate written narrative environment. Writing, mostly created in isolation, has a tendency to isolate its product from live discourse. It turns itself into a second-level participant in dialogue, its actualization being postponed in time, subject to reading or reoralization of its basically inert text. The actualization of a text is always delayed and variable, depending on the situation of reader or performer. Voice, by contrast, is programmed for personal interaction and is entirely wrapped in social contextuality. Again, Ong saw this very clearly: "Both Jesus' oral sayings and the oral memory of them were always contextual, though they of course could have universal relevance" (1992b, 197). Granted the coexistence, indeed interaction, of orally verbalized speech and social setting, form criticism's premise of a predictable correspondence between characteristic speech forms and specific social contexts remains puzzling. This is not a theorem known in current orality-literacy studies. What is emphasized is the importance of context: "Across a wide spectrum, context matters" (Foley 2002, 79). But for Foley, context is understood not in a narrowly defined social sense, but in a broader sense of a *lingua franca*, that is, of cultural commonalities shared by speaker and hearers alike. Specifically adverting to the force of contextuality, Foley has articulated what has become a classic formulation in orality-literacy studies: "Oral poetry works like language, only more so" (2002, 18, passim). Word power is actualized not by the mere delivery of words as such, but by multiple interactions with social contexts. Ong understood the issue of the correlation between speech and social context in the same manner when he wrote that "the meaning of each oral utterance [of Jesus' sayings] had to be gathered from the extraverbal as well as the verbal components" (1992b, 196). These are issues raised by current orality-literacy studies and they are a world apart from the kind of correspondences that form criticism assumed to exist between oral and social life.

Six: in principle, form criticism's trivialization of any distinction between oral and scribal communication is untenable. Ong has devoted a substantial part of his life's work to developing just that: a noetics and psychodynamics of orality vis-à-vis the technology of writing and textuality. Orality-literacy studies has been contested both from many directions and manifold points of view. A frequent objection, raised both from

anthropological and Derridean perspectives, states that Ong's differentiation of an oral versus a literary phenomenology has idealized the former
at the expense of the latter. It is an objection that, in my view, cannot be
sustained. On the matter of oral psychodynamics Ong has unequivocally
declared that "orality is not an ideal, and never was" (1982, 175). And on
the matter of writing and textuality he proposed that while there existed
multiple interactions between textual and oral verbalization, literate civilization was in fundamental ways an advance over oral cultures: "To say
writing is artificial is not to condemn it but to praise it. ... Technologies
are artificial, but—paradox again—artificiality is natural to human beings.
Technology, properly interiorized, does not degrade human life but on the
contrary enhances it" (82–83).

Writing for Ong is a technology, and "all major advances in consciousness depend on technological transformations and implementations of the
word" (1977b, 42). *There are few contemporary humanistic thinkers of stature who have succeeded quite like Ong has in making sense of the technological inventions of writing, print, and electronic verbalization within the
framework of a phenomenology of human consciousness and culture.*

To be sure, as far as the media realities of ancient communications
culture are concerned, *chirographically crafted manuscripts and oral verbalization tended to operate interactively*, with scribality more often than
not variously contingent on speech, and handwritten documents bent on
being heard rather than viewed. But the point to remember is that the
particularities of those interactive relations must remain unknown and
unknowable without a prior understanding of the distinctive characteristics of oral versus scribal communication.

Elsewhere (10.62; 14.17) I have developed the observation that the
early papyrological Jesus tradition, when viewed from media perspectives,
functioned analogously to oral dynamics. Notwithstanding its scripted existence, it evidently sought to stay with the flux of time by way of social adaptability. Do we not have here a complete blurring of oral-scribal attributes?
Not completely. Once transcribed onto papyrus, scribal versions enjoyed,
or were stuck with, the relative stability of a materially documented existence denied to oral speech. Unless reoralized or rewritten, their written
existence consisted of "only marks on the surface," which had the advantage
of outlasting speech (Ong 1977a, 234), and the potential of assuming an
archival status ready to become part of the developing textual tradition.

Seven: the notion of oral tradition operating along the line of transmissional processes is visually imaginable but orally unworkable. The very

idea of "'line' is obviously a text-based concept" (Ong 1982, 61). Spoken words transpire at the moment of their vocalization without any demonstrable existence beyond their utterance except in people's minds and memories. Existing in time, and never in space, speech cannot be conceptualized on any spatial model, least of all on a model of directionality. As Ong stated programmatically, spoken words have "not even a trajectory" (Ong 1982, 31). There is no way to hold on to them for the purpose of organizing them in linear patterns.

What complicates the media culture in early Christianity is that this culture is not primarily oral. *One cannot, therefore, realistically imagine the early Jesus tradition as exclusively scribal in composition and transcription any more than one can entertain the idea of a discourse world of primal, oral purity untouched by scribality.* Oral and scribal verbalizations operated in multiple interactions with each other. *Intermediality* is the technical term for this phenomenon. The Jesus papyri mentioned above, for example, were handwritten records embedded in oral contextuality both on account of their social adaptability and by virtue of their being recycled back into oral proclamation. But *it is not possible to attribute to these oral-scribal interfaces a sense of purposeful directionality.* Words moved in and out of the two media in relation to audiences in social settings; speech could emanate from chirographs and in turn generate writings; what served in the past could well be reused in the present. In this media environment, oral-scribal entities acted both as chirographs and as performative possibilities/actualities, as matters of record and of recall. But nowhere was there a single controlling agency that aligned all oral-scribal traditions toward a demonstrable, single orientation, least of all a linearly conceived trajectory.

Eight, along with the above-mentioned notions of the linearity of "transmissional processes" and "original form," the idea of tradition as an evolutionary form helped generate a paradigm of the tradition that is impressive by its intellectual and imaginable persuasiveness. That oral and oral-scribal communication proceeds incrementally, from smaller to ever larger units, endows tradition with a measurable pattern that seems both logical and imaginable. Indeed, much of current scholarship on Gospel and tradition, including the Quest for the historical Jesus, is deeply committed to an evolutionary trajectory. The latter has remained the subtle, or not so subtle, determining, but unexamined, philosophical underpinning of Gospel scholarship.

If evolution has as its intrinsic rationale an unfolding and emergence of a completed form that in some sense was immanent in the originary state, then orality-literacy studies are not conscious of any such design. We still lack a model of the early Jesus tradition that is commensurate with the media realities of the ancient communications world. The processes we have observed prohibit us from thinking of chains of causalities that would allow us to isolate something of a primal cause, the "ground zero" that marked the origin and starting point of the tradition. We will come closer to an understanding of tradition if we think of *a feedback mechanism of interactive oral and scribal communications dynamics, of manuscript and performance, always interfacing with social variables to which communication relates and that in turn impinge on the processes of the tradition.* These are dynamics that are in no way suggestive of evolutionary proclivities.

Nine: on the matter of Gospel and tradition, form criticism was inclined to give major credit to tradition and very little to the Gospel composition. Having grown out of "the immanent urge to development" in tradition, the Gospel, largely a product of tradition, seemed to be the result of a calculated oral trajectory toward a chirographic epiphany. Hence, the postulate that the antecedent history of the tradition constituted the defining matrix for the narrative Gospel, and that in relation to tradition the Gospel produced "in principle nothing new" (Bultmann 1963, 321). Form criticism had great difficulties acknowledging inventive, productive, and memorial activities on the level of Gospel composition.

The notion of internal pressures propelling oral tradition toward Gospel textuality is once again an appealing theory, but not grounded in linguistic actualities. No rule in orality-literary studies, or indeed in literary criticism, states that oral tradition by virtue of intrinsic pressures is destined sooner or later to mutate into textuality. Again, the very notion of causalities intrinsic to oral communication misses the point, because it conceptualizes oral and oral-scribal tradition as an abstraction apart from contextuality. *Tradition is inextricably tied in with social variables and social register, and it is this social context that exerts pressures and not causalities that are intrinsic to oral-scribal communication per se.*

Ten: the idea of the Gospel as mere product of tradition founders not only on a proper understanding of tradition but on an adequate grasp of the Gospel as well. During the last five decades, biblical scholars have approached the Gospels with a particular sensitivity toward literary, narrative competencies. These literary explorations have progressed far enough that we can now speak of the narrative poetics of a Mark, a Matthew, a Luke, and a John. There is a deliberate and creative imagination at work in the formation of these Gospels that gives each of them a distinct narrative profile.

These distinct narrative points of view are mediated by thematic, rhetorical, and literary devices such as the conscious arrangement of episodes, distinct plot causalities, the casting and typecasting of characters, framing devices of various kinds, ring compositions and intercalations, strategies of misunderstanding and role reversal, multiple forms of redundancies, pointedly executed polemics, topological-geographical configurations, and many more.

Once one allows for the Gospels' narrative intentionality, that is, their ability to score dramatic points, to channel discernible values, and to dramatize corrective views, the thesis that the Gospels are solely products of tradition loses its explanatory force. This is by no means to deny the Gospels' complex roots in the diachronic depth of tradition. But it is internal narrative causalities more than causalities assumed to be intrinsic to tradition that play a formative role in the Gospel compositions. *The weight of tradition notwithstanding, in the last analysis it is a compositional, narrative volition that is molding tradition, and not vice versa, that holds responsibility for the final narrative form of the Gospels.*

108. Epilogue: Rediscovery of Lost Sensibilities

It was the intent of this essay to plead for recognition of the significance of the work of Walter Ong for biblical and especially New Testament studies. My understanding of the current status of the academic study of the New Testament and Christian Origins, and of the work of Ong, and my acquaintance with what I now refer to as *orality-scribality-memory-performance criticism* have convinced me that Ong's critical assessment has much bearing on the state of biblical scholarship.

It may be useful to recapitulate three principal propositions put forward in this essay. One, I have come to realize that the historical-critical paradigm is entrenched in a post-Gutenberg intellectualism and locked in what may be called a typographic captivity. Two, the high tech of the fifteenth century and the rapidly disseminated print culture throughout the fifteenth and sixteenth centuries was an agent of hitherto unparalleled changes in all walks of life in Western history. Three, a gaping gulf separates the typographic culture and print mentality, in which modern New Testament scholarship is rooted from the scriptographic culture of its subject matter. "Scribal themes are carried forward, post-print trends are traced backward" (Eisenstein 1979, 1:9) in a manner that makes it exceedingly difficult to reimagine a culture that was driven by word-power, speech events, interior visualization, hand-copying, rememoriza-tion activities, composition-in-dictation, and many more. Given this state of affairs, Ong's critical insights seem powerfully relevant.

The phenomenology of orality-scribality studies brings significant challenges to biblical scholarship and raises a host of questions for the discipline. Undoubtedly, the novel perspectives will have to be put on a firmer theoretical footing and amplified across all texts and traditions of early Christianity.

The recovery of lost sensibilities will require a threefold effort. One, a deep reflectiveness on the critical habits and premises of the discipline would seem to be urgent and indispensable business. I have found it useful to locate the academic study of the Bible in the broadest possible context of Western cultural history, and I learned much about the discipline and its Ramist, typographic technifications by studying (apart from Ong's book on Ramus) Eisenstein's two-volume set *The Printing Press as an Agent of Change* (1979) and Giesecke's monumental tome *Der Buchdruck in der frühen Neuzeit* (1991). Two, I do not think we will succeed in converting the historical-critical paradigm into the oral-scribal-memorial-perfor-mative paradigm unless we acquaint ourselves with the studies by Lord, Havelock, Finnegan, Foley, Carruthers, Yates, Coleman, and of course Ong, among others. Three, the challenge before us requires a strenuously applied self-criticism to extricate ourselves from acquired habits, meth-odological convictions, and intellectual mentalities. My analysis of the project of form criticism and of the construction of the Greek text of the New Testament were meant to demonstrate both the discipline's ingrained typographic captivity and the fruitfulness of the media approach.

WORKS CITED

ANCIENT AND MEDIEVAL SOURCES

Abailard, Peter. 1977. *Sic and Non: A Critical Edition*. Edited by Blanche B. Boyer and Richard McKeon. Fascicles 1–4. Chicago: University of Chicago Press.

Ad Herennium. 1954. Translated by H. Caplan. LCL 403. Cambridge: Harvard University Press.

Aristotle. On Memory and Recollection. 1957. Pages 283–307 in *On the Soul. Parva Naturalia. On Breath*. Translated by W. S. Hett. LCL 288. Cambridge: Harvard University Press.

———. 1973. *De Sensu and De Memoria*. Translated by George Robert Thomson Ross. New York: Arno Press.

Augustine. 1861a. *De Doctrina Christiana*. PL 34:15–122.

———. 1861b. *De Trinitate*. PL 42:819–1098.

———. 1873. *On the Trinity*. Translated by Arthur West Haddan. The Works of Aurelius Augustine, Bishop of Hippo 2. Edited by Marcus Dods. Edinburgh: T&T Clark.

———. 1958. *On Christian Doctrine (De Doctrina Christiana)*. Translated by D. W. Robertson. Library of Liberal Arts. New York and London: Macmillan.

———. 1970. *De Magistro*. CCSL. Pars 2. Turnhout: Brepols.

———. 1981. *S. Aureli Augustini Confessionum*. Edited by Martin Skutella. Stuttgart: Teubner.

Bernard of Clairvaux. 1862. *Sermo de Conversione*. PL 182:833–56.

———. 1987. *Selected Works*. Translated by G. R. Evans. CWS. Mahwah, N.J.: Paulist.

Cicero. *On the Orator: Books 1–2*. 1942. Translated by E. W. Sutton and H. Rackham. LCL 348. Cambridge: Harvard University Press.

———. *On Invention. The Best Kind of Orator. Topics*. 1960. Translated by H. M. Hubbell. LCL 386. Cambridge: Harvard University Press, 1960.

Eusebius. *Ecclesiastical History, Books 1–5*. 1932. Translated by Kirsopp Lake. LCL 153. London: Heinemann; New York: Putnam's.

Gorgias. 1989. *Reden, Fragmente und Testimonien*. Edited by Thomas Buchheim. Hamburg: Meiner.

Homer. 1960. *The Iliad: Books I–XII*. Edited by Walter Leaf. 2nd ed. Amsterdam: Hakkert.

————. 1976. *The Iliad of Homer*. Translated by Richmond Lattimore. Chicago: University of Chicago Press.

Justin Martyr. 1949. *The First Apology, The Second Apology, Dialogue with Trypho, Exhortation to the Greeks, Discourse to the Greeks, The Monarchy, or The Rule of God*. FC 6. New York: Christian Heritage.

Ockham, William of. 1990. *Philosophical Writings*. Translated by Philotheus Boehner. Indianapolis and Cambridge: Hackett.

Philostratus. *Life of Apollonis of Tyana, Books 1–4*. 2005a. Translated by Christopher P. Jones. LCL 16. Cambridge: Harvard University Press.

————. *Life of Apollonis of Tyana, Books 5–8*. 2005b. Translated by Christopher P. Jones. LCL 17. Cambridge: Harvard University Press.

Plato. 1859–63. *Platonis Dialogi*. Vols. 1–4. Edited by Karl Friderich Hermann.

————. 1961. *The Collected Dialogues of Plato*. Edited by Edith Hamilton and Huntington Cairns. Bollingen Series 71. Princeton: Princeton University Press.

Quintilian. *Institutio Oratoria*. 1922. Translated by H. E. Butler. LCL 4. London: Heineman; New York: Putnam's.

Tertullian. 1954. *De Praescriptione Haereticorum*. CCSL. Tertulliani Opera, Pars 1. Turnhout: Brepols.

Thomas Aquinas. 1875. *De Memoria et Reminiscentia*. Opera Omnia 24. Edited by Stanislai Eduardi Frettè. Paris: Ludovicum Vivés.

————. 1963. *Summa Theologiae*. Vol. 1, *Christian Theology*. Translated by Thomas Gilby. Cambridge: Blackfriars; New York: McGraw-Hill; London: Eyre & Spottiswoode.

————. 1974. *Summa Theologiae*. Vol. 36, *Prudence*. Translated by Thomas Gilby. Cambridge: Blackfriars; New York: McGraw-Hil; London: Eyre & Spottiswoode.

CONTEMPORARY SOURCES

Abrahams, Roger D. 1978. *License to Repeat and Be Predictable*. Folklore Preprint Series. Indiana University, 6.3:1–13.

Achtemeier, Paul J. 1990. *Omne Verbum Sonat*: The New Testament and the Oral Environment of Late Western Antiquity. *JBL* 109:3–27.

Adams, M. McCord. 1987. *William of Ockham*. 2 Vols. Notre Dame, Ind.: University of Notre Dame Press.

Aland, Kurt, and Barbara Aland, eds. 1993. *Novum Testamentum Graece*. 27th ed. Stuttgart: Württemberg Bible Society.

Alexander, Elizabeth Shanks. 2006. *Transmitting Mishnah: The Shaping Influence of Oral Tradition*. Cambridge: Cambridge University Press.

Alexander, Loveday. 2009. Memory and Tradition in the Hellenistic Schools. Pages 113–53 in *Jesus in Memory: Traditions in Oral and Scribal Perpsectives*. Edited by Werner H. Kelber and Samuel Byrskog. Waco, Tex.: Baylor University Press.

Alter, Robert. 1981. *The Art of Biblical Narrative*. New York: Basic Books.

Anderson, Benedict. 1983. *Imagined Communities: Reflections on the Origin and Spread of Nationalism*. Rev. ed. London/New York: Verso, 2006.

Assmann, Aleida. 1999. *Erinnerungsräume. Formen und Wandlungen des kulturellen Gedächtnisses*. Munich: Beck. ET: *Cultural Memory and Western Civilization: Functions, Media, Archives*. Translated with David Henry Wilson. New York: Cambridge University Press, 2011.

Assmann, Aleida, and Jan, eds. 1987. *Kanon und Zensur. Archäologie der literarischen Kommunikation II*. Munich: Wilhelm Fink.

Assmann, Jan. 1992. *Das kulturelle Gedächtnis. Schrift, Erinnerung und politische Identität in frühen Hochkulturen*. Munich: Beck. ET: see J. Assmann 2011.

———. 1997. *Moses the Egyptian: The Memory of Egypt in Western Monotheism*. Cambridge: Harvard University Press. Translated as *Moses der Ägypter: Erinnerung einer Gedächtnisspur*. Munich: Hanser, 1998.

———. 2000. *Religion und Gedächtnis*. Munich: Beck.

———. 2011. *Cultural Memory and Early Civilization: Writing, Remembrance and Political Imagination*. Translated with David Henry Wilson. New York: Cambridge University Press.

Auerbach, Erich. 1953. *Mimesis: The Representation of Reality in Western Literature*. Translated by Willard R. Trask. Princeton: Princeton University Press.

Aune, David E. 1991. Oral Tradition and the Aphorisms of Jesus. Pages 211–65 in *Jesus and the Oral Gospel Tradition*. Edited by Henry Wansbrough. JSNTSup 64. Sheffield: Sheffield Academic Press.

———. 2009. Jesus Tradition and the Pauline Letters. Pages 63–86 in *Jesus in Memory: Traditions in Oral and Scribal Perspectives*. Edited by Werner H. Kelber and Samuel Byrskog. Waco, Tex.: Baylor University Press.

Bailey, Kenneth E. 1976. *Poet and Peasant: A Literary-Cultural Approach to the Parables in Luke*. Grand Rapids: Eerdmans.

———. 1980. *Through Peasant Eyes*. Grand Rapids: Eerdmans.

———. 1991. Informal Controlled Oral Tradition and the Synoptic Gospels. *AJT* 5/1: 34–54.

———. 1995. Informal Controlled Oral Tradition and the Synoptic Tradition. *Themelios* 20/2:4–11.

Balch, David. L. 1991. The Canon: Adaptable and Stable, Oral and Written, Critical Questions for Kelber and Riesner. *Foundations and Facets Forum* 7:183–205.

Balogh, Joseph. 1926. Voces Paginarum. *Phil* 82:84–109, 202–40.

Barr, James. 1983. *Holy Scripture: Canon, Authority, Criticism*. Philadelphia: Westminster.

Barthes, Roland. 1977. *Image—Music—Text*. New York: Hill & Wang.

Bauckham, Richard. 2006. *Jesus and the Eyewitnesses: The Gospels as Eyewitness Testimony*. Grand Rapids: Erdmans.

Beardslee, William A. 1970. *Literary Criticism of the New Testament*. GBS, NT series. Philadelphia: Fortress.

Beare, Frank W. 1967. Sayings of the Risen Jesus in the Synoptic Tradition: An Inquiry into Their Origin and Significance. Pages 161–81 in *Christian History and Interpretation*. Edited by W. R. Farmer, C. F. D. Moule, and R. R. Niebuhr. Cambridge: Cambridge University Press.

Berg, Sara van den, and Thomas M. Walsh, eds. 2011. *Language, Culture, and Identity: The Legacy of Walter J. Ong, S.J.* New York: Hampton.

Berkovits, Eliezer. 1973. The Historical Context of the Holocaust. Pages 86–113 in *Faith after the Holocaust*. New York: Ktav.

Best, Ernest. 1977. The Role of the Disciples in Mark. *NTS* 23:377–401.

———. 1981. *Following Jesus: Discipleship in the Gospel of Mark.* JSNTSup 4. Sheffield: JSOT Press.

Betz, Hans Dieter. 1979. *Galatians: A Commentary on Paul's Letter to the Churches in Galatia.* Hermeneia. Philadelphia: Fortress Press.

———. 1994. Jesus and the Cynics: Survey and Analysis of a Hypothesis. *JR* 74:453–75.

Bishop, Jonathan. 1986. Parable and *Parrhesia* in Mark. *Int* 40:39–52.

Blevins, James L. 1981. *The Messianic Secret in Markan Research, 1901–1976.* Washington, D.C.: University Press of America.

Bok, Sissela. 1982. *Secrets: On the Ethics of Concealment and Revelation.* New York: Pantheon.

Bonner, Stanley Frederick. 1977. *Education in Ancient Rome: From the Elder Cato to the Younger Pliny.* Berkeley and Los Angeles: University of California Press.

Boomershine, Thomas E. 1974. *Mark the Storyteller: A Rhetorical-Critical Investigation of Mark's Passion and Resurrection Narrative.* Ph.D. diss., Union Theological Seminary.

———. 1981. Mark 16:8 and the Apostolic Commission. *JBL* 100:225–39.

———. 1987. Peter's Denial as Polemic or Confession: The Implications of Media Criticism for Biblical Hermeneutics. *Semeia* 39:47–68.

———. 1988. *Story Journey: An Invitation to the Gospel as Storytelling.* Nashville: Abingdon.

Borg, Marcus J. 1987. *Jesus: A New Vision: Spirit, Culture, and the Life of Discipleship.* San Francisco: Harper & Row.

———. 1994. *Meeting Jesus Again for the First Time: The Historical Jesus and the Heart of Contemporary Faith.* San Francisco: HarperSanFrancisco.

Boring, M. Eugene. 1977. The Paucity of Sayings in Mark: A Hypothesis. Pages 371–77 in *SBL Seminar Papers, 1977.* Missoula, Mont.: Scholars Press.

———. 1982. *Sayings of the Risen Jesus: Christian Prophecy in the Synoptic Tradition.* SNTSMS 46. Cambridge: Cambridge University Press.

Botha, Pieter J. J. 1991. Mark's Story as Oral Traditional Literature: Rethinking the Transmission of Some Traditions about Jesus. *HvTSt* 47:304–31.

———. 1992a. Greco-Roman Literacy as Setting for New Testament Writings. *Neot* 26:195–215.

———. 1992b. Letter Writing and Oral Communication in Antiquity: Suggested Implications for the Interpretation of Paul's Letter to the Galatians. *Scriptura* 42:17–34.

———. 2012. *Orality and Literacy in Early Christianity.* Biblical Performance Criticism Series 5. Eugene, Ore.: Cascade.

Bousset, Wilhelm. 1970. *Kyrios Christos: A History of the Belief in Christ from the Beginnings of Christianity to Irenaeus.* Nashville: Abingdon. German ed., 1913.

Boyarin, Jonathan, ed. 1993. *The Ethnography of Reading.* Berkeley and Los Angeles: University of California Press.

Boyle, John F. 2011. St. Thomas Aquinas and Sacred Scripture. Online: http://www3. nd.edu/~afreddos/papers/Taqandss.htm.

Brandon, S. G. F. 1967. *Jesus and the Zealots: A Study of the Political Factor in Primitive Christianity*. New York: Scribner's.

Braun, F.-M. 1968. La Réduction du Pluriel au Singulier dans l'Evangile et la Première Lettre de Jean. *NTS* 24:40–67.

Brown, Peter Robert Lamont. 1967. *Augustine of Hippo: A Biography*. London: Faber and Faber. 2nd ed. Berkeley and Los Angeles: University of California Press, 2000.

Brown, Raymond E. 1966. *The Gospel According to John. I–Xii*. Vol. 1. Anchor Bible 29. Garden City, N.Y.: Doubleday.

Bruns, Gerald L. 1982. *Inventions: Writing, Textuality, and Understanding in Literary History*. New Haven: Yale University Press.

Bultmann, Rudolf. 1910. *Der Stil der paulinischen Predigt und die kynisch-stoische Diatribe*. Göttingen: Huth, 1910. Repr., FRLANT 13. Göttingen: Vandenhoeck & Ruprecht, 1984.

———. 1963. *The History of the Synoptic Tradition*. Translated by John Marsh. New York: Harper & Row.

———. 1970. *Die Geschichte der Synoptischen Tradition*. 8th ed. FRLANT 29, NS 12. Göttingen: Vandenhoeck & Ruprecht.

———. 1971. *The Gospel of John*. Translated by G. R. Beasley-Murray et al. Philadelphia: Westminster.

Burghardt, Walter J. 1951. The Catholic Concept of Tradition. *Proceedings of the Sixth Annual Convention of the Catholic Theological Society of America* 6:42–76.

Burke, Tony, ed. 2011. *Ancient Gospel or Modern Forgery? The Secret Gospel of Mark in Debate*. Eugene, Ore.: Cascade.

Burrows, Millar. 1955. *The Dead Sea Scrolls*. New York: Viking.

Byrskog, Samuel. 2002. *Story as History—History as Story: The Gospel Tradition in the Context of Ancient Oral History*. WUNT 123. Tübingen: Mohr Siebeck.

———. 2009. Introduction. Pages 1-20 in *Jesus in Memory: Traditions Oral and Scribal Perspectives*. Edited by Werner H. Kelber and Samuel Byrskog. Waco, Tex: Baylor University Press.

Byrskog, Samuel, and Werner Kelber, eds. 2009. *Jesus in Memory: Traditions in Oral and Scribal Perspectives*. Waco, Tex.: Baylor University Press.

Cameron, Ron. 1984. *Sayings Traditions in the Apocryphon of James*. HTS 34. Philadelphia: Fortress.

Carlson, Stephen C. 2005. *The Gospel Hoax: Morton Smith's Invention of Secret Mark*. Waco, Tex.: Baylor University Press.

Carr, David M. 2005. *Writing on the Tablet of the Heart: Origins of Scripture and Literature*. Oxford: Oxford University Press.

Carruthers, Mary. 1990. *The Book of Memory: A Study of Memory in Medieval Culture*. Cambridge: Cambridge University Press.

———. 1998. *The Craft of Thought: Meditation, Rhetoric, and the Making of Images, 400–1200*. Cambridge: Cambridge University Press.

Cartlidge, David R. 1990. Combien d'unités avez-vous de trois à quatre? What Do We

Mean by Intertextuality in Early Christian Studies? Pages 400–411 in *SBL Seminar Papers, 1990*. Atlanta: Scholars Press.

Cartlidge, David R., and David L. Dungan, eds. 1980. *Documents for the Study of the Gospels*. Philadelphia: Fortress.

Chadwick, H. Munro, and Nora K. Chadwick. 1932–40. *The Growth of Literature*. 3 vols. Cambridge: Cambridge University Press.

Chilton, Bruce D. 1984. *A Galilean Rabbi and His Bible: Jesus' Use of the Interpreted Scripture of His Time*. Wilmington: Glazier.

Coleman, Janet. 1992. *Ancient and Medieval Memories: Studies in the Reconstruction of the Past*. Cambridge: Cambridge University Press.

Collins, Adela Yarbro. 1988. Narrative, History, and Gospel. *Semeia* 43:145–53.

Copleston, Frederick. 1993–94. *A History of Philosophy*. 9 vols. New York: Image.

Coward, Harold. 1988. *Sacred Word and Sacred Text: Scripture in Word Religions*. Maryknoll, N.Y.: Orbis.

Crossan, John Dominic. 1965. Anti-Semitism and the Gospel. *TS* 26:189–214.

———. 1971–72. Parable and Example in the Teaching of Jesus. *NTS* 18:285–307.

———. 1973. *In Parables: The Challenge of the Historical Jesus*. New York: Harper & Row.

———. 1975. *The Dark Interval: Towards a Theology of Story*. Niles, Ill.: Argus.

———. 1976. *Raid on the Articulate: Comic Eschatology in Jesus and Borges*. New York: Harper & Row.

———. 1978. A Form for Absence: The Markan Creation of Gospel. *Semeia* 12:41–55.

———. 1979. *Finding Is the First Act: Trove Folktales and Jesus' Treasure Parable*. SemeiaSt 9. Philadelphia: Fortress.

———. 1980. *Cliffs of Fall: Paradox and Polyvalence in the Parables of Jesus*. New York: Seabury.

———. 1983. *In Fragments: The Aphorisms of Jesus*. San Francisco: Harper & Row.

———. 1984. Language and Creativity. Jesus as Aphorist and Parabler. Paper presented at SBL/AAR/ASOR Annual Meeting. Chicago, Ill.

———. 1985. *Four Other Gospels: Shadows on the Contours of Canon*. Minneapolis: Winston.

———. 1988. *The Cross That Spoke: The Origins of the Passion Narrative*. San Francisco: Harper & Row.

———. 1991. *The Historical Jesus: The Life of a Mediterranean Jewish Peasant*. San Francisco: HarperSanFrancisco.

———. 1994a. *The Essential Jesus*. San Francisco: HarperSanFrancisco.

———. 1994b. *Jesus: A Revolutionary Biography*. San Francisco: HarperSanFrancisco.

———. 1995. *Who Killed Jesus? Exposing the Roots of Anti- Semitism in the Gospel Story of the Death of Jesus*. San Francisco: HarperSanFrancisco.

Culpepper, R. Alan. 1983. *Anatomy of the Fourth Gospel: A Study in Literary Design*. Philadelphia: Fortress.

Dagenais, John. 1994. *The Ethics of Reading in Manuscript Culture: Glossing the Libro de Buen Amor*. Princeton: Princeton University Press.

Davies, Stevan L. 1983. *The Gospel of Thomas and Christian Wisdom*. New York: Seabury.

De Romilly, Jacqueline. 1975. *Magic and Rhetoric in Ancient Greece.* Cambridge: Harvard University Press.

Dean, Margaret E. 1966. A Grammar of Sound in Greek Texts. Now published as A Grammar of Sound in Greek Texts: Toward a Method for Mapping the Echoes of Speech in Writing. *ABR* 44 (1996): 53–70.

DeConick, April D. 2005. Reading the Gospel of Thomas as Repository of Early Christian Communal Memory. Pages 207–20 in Kirk and Thatcher 2005b.

Derrida, Jacques. 1976. *Of Grammatology.* Translated by Gayatri Chakravorty Spivak. Baltimore: Johns Hopkins University Press.

———. 1978. Structure, Sign, and Play in the Discourse of the Human Sciences. Pages 278–93 in *Writing and Difference.* Translated by Alan Bass. Chicago: University of Chicago Press.

———. 1981. *Positions.* Translated by Alan Bass. Chicago: University of Chicago Press.

Dewey, Arthur J. 1994. A Re-Hearing of Romans 10:1-15. *Semeia* 65:109–27.

———. 2005. The Locus for Death: Social Memory and the Passion Narratives. Pages 119–28 in Kirk and Thatcher 2005b.

Dewey, Joanna. 1989. Oral Methods of Structuring Narrative in Mark. *Int* 43:32–44.

———. 1991. Mark as Interwoven Tapestry: Forecasts and Echoes for a Listening Audience. *CBQ* 52:221–36.

———. 1992. Mark as Aural Narrative: Structures as Clues to Understanding. *STRev* 36:45–56.

———. 1994. The Gospel of Mark as Oral/Aural Event: Implications for Interpretation. Pages 145–63 in *The New Literary Criticism and the New Testament.* Edited by Elizabeth Struthers Malbon and Edgar V. McKnight. Sheffield: Sheffield University Press.

———. ed. 1995a. *Orality and Textuality in Early Christian Literature. Semeia* 65. Atlanta: Society of Biblical Literature.

———. 1995b. Textuality in an Oral Culture: A Survey of the Pauline Traditions. *Semeia* 65:37–65.

———. 2004. Mark—A Really Good Oral Story: Is That Why the Gospel of Mark Survived? *JBL* 123:495–507.

Dewey, K. E. 1980. *Paroimiai* in the Gospel of John. *Semeia* 17:81–100.

Doane, A. N. 1991. Oral Texts, Intertexts, and Intratexts: Editing Old English. Pages 75–113 in *Influence and Intertextuality In Literary History.* Edited by Jay Clayton and Eric Rothstein. Madison: University of Wisconsin Press.

———. 1994. Performance as a Constitutive Category in the Editing of Anglo-Saxon Poetic Texts. *Oral Tradition* 9:420–39.

Donahue, John R. 1973. *Are You the Christ? The Trial Narrativ in the Gospel of Mark.* SBLDS 10. Missoula: Society of Biblical Literature.

———. 1978. Jesus as the Parable of God in the Gospel of Mark. *Int* 32:369–86. Repr. as pages 148–67 in *Interpreting the Gospels.* Edited by J. L. Mays. Philadelphia: Fortress, 1981.

———. 1988. *The Gospel in Parable: Metaphor, Narrative, and Theology in the Synoptic Gospels.* Minneapolis: Fortress.

———. 1993. The Bible in Roman Catholicism since Divino Afflante Spiritu. *WW* 13/4:404–13.

Dowd, Sharon. 1996. Review of Luke Timothy Johnson, *The Real Jesus*. *LTQ* 31/2:179–83.

Duffy, Eamon. 2006. *Marking the Hours: English People and their Prayers, 1240–1570*. New Haven: Yale University Press.

Duke, Paul. 1985. *Irony in the Fourth Gospel*. Atlanta: John Knox.

Dunn, James D. G. 1984. Testing the Foundations: Current Trends in New Testament Studies. Inaugural Lecture. Durham: University of Durham.

———. 2003a. Altering the Default Setting: Re-envisaging the Early Transmission of the Jesus Tradition. *NTS* 49:139–75.

———. 2003b. *Jesus Remembered*. Grand Rapids: Eerdmans.

Eco, Umberto. 1983. *The Name of the Rose*. Translated by William Weaver. San Diego: Harcourt Brace Jovanovich.

Edwards, Mark U. 1994. *Printing, Propaganda, and Martin Luther*. Berkeley and Los Angeles: University of California Press.

Ehrman, Bart D. 1993. *The Orthodox Corruption of Scripture: The Effect of Early Christological Controversies on the Text of the New Testament*. New York: Oxford University Press.

———. 1995. The Text as Window: New Testament Manuscripts and the Social History of Early Christianity. Pages 361–79 in *The Text of the New Testament in Contemporary Research : Essays on the Status Quaestionis*. Edited by Bart D. Ehrman and Michael W. Homes. Grand Rapids: Eerdmans.

———. 2005. *Misquoting Jesus: The Story behind Who Changed the Bible and Why*. New York: HarperCollins.

Eisenstein, Elizabeth L. 1979. *The Printing Press as an Agent of Change: Communications and Cultural Transformations in Early-Modern Europe*. 2 vols. Cambridge: Cambridge University Press.

Ellis, Peter F. 1974. *Matthew: His Mind and His Message*. Collegeville, Minn.: Liturgical Press.

Engels, J. 1962. La doctrine du signe chez Augustine. *StPatr* 6:366–73.

Epp, Eldon Jay. 1966. *The Theological Tendency of Codex Bezae Cantabrigiensis in Acts*. Cambridge: Cambridge University Press.

———. 2004. The Oxyrchynchus New Testament Papyri: "Not without Honor Except in Their Hometown"? *JBL* 123:5–55.

———. 2007. It's All About Variants: A Variant-Conscious Approach to New Testament Criticism. *HTR* 100:275–308.

Esler, Philip F. 2005. Collective Memory and Hebrews 11: Outlining a New Investigative Framework. Pages 151–71 in Kirk and Thatcher 2005b.

Falk, Harvey. 1985. *Jesus the Pharisee: A New Look at the Jewishness of Jesus*. Mahwah, N.J.: Paulist.

Farmer, William R. 1982. *Jesus and the Gospel: Tradition, Scripture, and Canon*. Philadelphia: Fortress.

Finnegan, Ruth. 1977. *Oral Poetry: Its Nature, Significance and Social Context*. Cambridge: Cambridge University Press.

——. 1988. *Literacy and Orality: Studies in the Technology of Communication*. Oxford: Blackwell.

——. 1991. Tradition, but What Tradition and for Whom? The Milman Parry Lecture on Oral Tradition for 1989–90. *Oral Tradition* 6/1:104–24.

——. 2007. *The Oral and Beyond: Doing Things with Words in Africa*. Oxford: James Currey.

Fish, Stanley. 1980. *Is There a Text in This Class? The Authority of Interpretive Communities*. Cambridge: Harvard University Press.

Fishbane, Michael A. 1987. *Judaism: Revelation and Traditions*. San Francisco: Harper & Row.

Foley, John Miles, ed. 1985. *Comparative Research on Oral Traditions: A Memorial for Milman Parry*. Columbus, Ohio: Slavica.

——. 1987a. Man, Muse, and Story: Psychohistorical Patterns in Oral Epic Poetry. *Oral Tradition* 2:91–107.

——. 1987b. Reading the Oral Traditional Text: Aesthetics of Creation and Response. Pages 185–212 in *Comparative Research on Oral Traditions: A Memorial for Milman Parry*. Columbus, Ohio: Slavica.

——. 1988. *The Theory of Oral Composition: History and Methodology*. Bloomington: Indiana University Press.

——. 1990. *Traditional Oral Epic: The Odyssey, Beowulf, and the Serbo-Croatian Return Song*. Berkeley and Los Angeles: University of California Press.

——. 1991. *Immanent Art: From Structure to Meaning in Traditional Oral Epic*. Bloomington: Indiana University Press.

——. 1994. Words in Tradition, Words in Text: A Response. *Semeia* 65:169–80.

——. 1995. *The Singer of Tales in Performance*. Bloomington: Indiana University Press.

——. 2002. *How to Read an Oral Poem*. Urbana and Chicago: University of Illinois Press.

Fortna, Robert T. 1970. *The Gopel of Signs: A Reconstruction of the Narrative Source Underlying the Fourth Gospel*. SNTSMS 11. Cambridge: Cambridge University Press.

Fowler, Robert M. 1983. Who Is "the Reader" of Mark's Gospel? Pages 31–53 in *SBL Seminar Papers, 1983*. Edited by Kent H. Richards. Chico, Calif.: Scholars Press.

——. 1984. Thoughts on the History of Reading Mark's Gospel. *Proceedings: Eastern Great Lakes Biblical Society and Midwest SBL* 4:120–30.

——. 1985a. The Rhetoric of Indirection in the Gospel of Mark. *Proceedings: Eastern Great Lakes Biblical Society and Midwest SBL* 5:47–56.

——. 1985b. Who Is "the Reader" in Reader Response Criticism? *Semeia* 31:5–23.

——. 1991. *Let the Reader Understand: Reader-Response Criticism and the Gospel of Mark*. Minneapolis: Fortress.

Fraade, Steven D. 1991. *From Tradition to Commentary: Torah and Its Interpretation in the Midrash Sifre to Deuteronomy*. Albany: State University of New York Press.

Frawley, William. 1987. *Text and Epistemology*. Norwood, N.J.: Ablex.

Frei, Hans. 1974. *The Eclipse of Biblical Narrative: A Study in Eighteenth and Nineteenth Century Hermeneutics*. New Haven: Yale University Press.

Freud, Sigmund. 1900. *Die Traumdeutung*. Leipzig and Vienna: Franz Deuticke. ET: *The Interpretation of Dreams*. New York: John Wiley & Sons, 1961.

———. 1939. *Moses and Monotheism*. Translated by Katherine Jones. New York: Vintage.

Funk, Robert W. 1966. *Language, Hermeneutic, and the Word of God: The Problem of Language in the New Testament and Contemporary Theology*. New York: Harper & Row.

———. 1975. *Jesus as Precursor*. Semeia Studies 2. Philadelphia: Fortress, 1975. Repr., Missoula, Mont.: Scholars Press, 1979.

———. 1982. *Parables and Presence: Forms of the New Testament Tradition*. Philadelphia: Fortress.

———. 1985. The Issue of Jesus. *Forum* 1/1:7–12.

Gadamer, Hans-Georg. 1960. *Wahrheit und Methode. Grundzüge einer philosophischen Hermeneutik*. Tübingen: Mohr Siebeck.

Gamble, Harry Y. 1985. *The New Testament Canon: Its Making and Meaning*. Philadelphia: Fortress.

Georgi, Dieter. 1964. *Die Gegner des Paulus im 2. Korintherbrief: Studien zur Religiösen Propaganda in der Spätantike*. WMANT 11. Neukirchen-Vluyn: Neukirchener. ET: Philadelphia: Fortress, 1968.

Gerhardsson, Birger. 1961. *Memory and Manuscript: Oral Tradition and Written Transmission in Rabbinic Judaism and Early Christianity*. ASNU 22. Lund: Gleerup; Copenhagen: Ejnar Munksgaard. Repr., foreword by Jacob Neusner, Grand Rapids: Eerdmans, 1998.

———. 1983. Der Weg der Evangelientradition. Pages 79–102 in *Das Evangelium und die Evangelien. Vorträge vom Tübinger Symposium 1982*. WUNT 28. Tübingen: Mohr Siebeck. ET: The Path of the Gospel Tradition. Pages 75–96 in *The Gospel and the Gospels*. Edited by Peter Stuhlmacher. Grand Rapids: Eerdmans, 1991. Repr. in *The Reliability of the Gospel Tradition*. Peabody, Mass.: Hendrickson, 2001.

———. 1991. Iluminating the Kingdom: Narrative Meshalim in the Synoptic Gospels. Pages 266–309 in *Jesus and the Oral Gospel Tradition*. Edited by Henry Wansbrough. JSNTSup 64. Sheffield: Sheffield University Press.

———. 2001. *The Reliability of the Gospel Tradition*. Peabody: Hendrickson.

———. 2005. The Secret of the Transmission of the Unwritten Jesus Tradition. *NTS* 51:1–18.

Giesecke, Michael. 1991. *Der Buchdruck in der frühen Neuzeit. Eine historische Fallstudie über die Durchsetzung neuer Informations- und Kommunikationstechnologien*. Frankfurt am Main: Suhrkamp.

Gillard, F. D. 1993. More Silent Reading in Antiquity: *non omne verbum sonat. JBL* 112:689–94.

Goody, Jack. 1968. *Literacy in Traditional Societies*. Cambridge: Cambridge University Press.

———. 1977. *The Domestication of the Savage Mind*. Cambridge: Cambridge University Press.

Goody, Jack, and Ian Watt. 1968. The Consequences of Literacy. Pages 27–68 in *Literacy in Traditional Societies*. Edited by Jack Goody. Cambridge: Cambridge University Press.

Grabmann, Martin. 1909–11. *Die Geschichte der scholastischen Methode*. 2 vols. Berlin: Akademie. Repr., Berlin: Akademie, 1956.

Graff, H. J. 1987. *The Legacies of Literacy: Continuities and Contradictions in Western Culture*. Bloomington: Indiana University Press.

Grafton, Anthony. 1983–93. *Joseph Saliger: A Study in the History of Classical Scholarship*. 2 Vols. Oxford-Warburg Studies. Oxford: Oxford University Press.

Grafton, Anthony, and Megan Williams. 2006. *Christianity and the Transformation of the Book: Origen, Eusebius, and the Library of Caesarea*. Cambridge: Belknap Press of Harvard University Press.

Graham, William. 1987. *Beyond the Written Word: Oral Aspects of Scripture in the History of Religion*. Cambridge: Cambridge University Press.

Gray, Benison. 1973. Repetition in Oral Literature. *Journal of American Folklore* 84:289–303.

Gumbrecht, Hans Ulrich, and K. Ludwig Pfeiffer, eds. 1986. *Stil. Geschichten und Funktionen eines kulturwissenschaftlichen Diskurselements*. Suhrkamp-Taschenbuch Wissenschaft 633. Frankfurt am Main: Suhrkamp.

———. 1988. *Materialität der Kommunikation*. Suhrkamp-Taschenbuch Wissenschaft 750. Frankfurt/Main: Suhrkamp.

———. 1993. *Schrift*. Materialität der Zeichen. Reihe A, Band 12. München: Fink.

Güttgemanns, Erhardt. 1979. *Candid Questions Concerning Form Criticism: A Methodological Sketch of the Fundamental Problematics of Form and Redaction Criticism*. Translated by William G. Doty. PTMS 26. Pittsburgh: Pickwick. German original, Munich: Kaiser, 1970.

Hägg, Thomas. 1983. *The Novel in Antiquity*. Berkeley: University of California Press.

Haines-Eitzen, Kim. 2000. *Guardians of Letters: Literacy, Power, and the Transmitters of Early Christian Literature*. New York: Oxford University Press.

Halbwachs, Maurice. 1925. *Les cadres sociaux de la mémoire*. Étude de mémoire collective. Paris: Alcan.

———. 1941. *La topographie légendaire des évangiles en Terre Sainte*. Paris: Colin. 2nd ed. 1971.

———. 1992. *On Collective Memory*. Edited and translated by Lewis A. Coser. Chicago: University of Chicago Press.

———. 1997. *La Mémoire Collective*. Edited by Gerard Namer and Marie Jaisson. Rev. ed. Paris: Michel.

Hallberg, Robert von, ed. 1983. *Canons*. Chicago: University of Chicago Press.

Handelmann, Susan A. 1982. *The Slayers of Moses: The Emergence of Rabbinic Interpretation in Modern Literary Theory*. Albany: State University of New York Press.

Harris, William V. 1989. *Ancient Literacy*. Cambridge: Harvard University Press.

Havelock, Eric A. 1963. *Preface to Plato*. Cambridge: Harvard University Press.

———. 1978. *The Greek Concept of Justice: From Its Shadow in Homer to Its Substance in Plato*. Cambridge: Harvard University Press.

———. 1982. *The Literate Revolution in Greece and Its Cultural Consequences*. Princeton: Princeton University Press.

Hays, Richard B. 1989. *Echoes of Scripture in the Letters of Paul*. New Haven: Yale University Press.

Hearon, Holly. 2005. The Story of "the Woman Who Anointed Jesus" as Social Memory: A Methodological Proposal for the Study of Tradition as Memory. Pages 99–118 in Kirk and Thatcher 2005b.

Heidegger, Martin. 1962. *Being and Time*. Translated by John Macquarrie and Edward Robinson. New York: Harper & Row. 16th ed. Tübingen: Niemeyer, 1986. First German ed., 1927.

———. 1977. Letter on Humanism. Pages 193–242 in *Basic Writings*. Edited by David F. Krell. New York: Harper & Row. Original German, 1946.

Hengel, Martin. 1977. *Crucifixion in the Ancient World and the Folly of the Message of the Cross*. Translated by John Bowden. Philadelphia: Fortress.

Henze, Matthias. 2012. Jewish and Christian Responses to the Roman Destruction of the Temple. Lecture presented at the University of Queensland. Brisbane, Queensland, Australia.

Hill, David. 1979. *New Testament Prophecy*. Atlanta: John Knox.

Holladay, Carl R. 1977. *Theios Aner in Hellenistic Judaism: A Critique of the Use of This Category in New Testament Christology*. SBLDS 40. Missoula, Mont.: Scholars Press.

Horsley, Richard A. 1991. *Logoi Propheton?* Reflections on the Genre of Q. Pages 195–209 in *The Future of Early Christianity*. Edited by Birger A. Pearson. Minneapolis: Fortress.

———. 2001. *Hearing the Whole Story: The Politics of Plot in Mark's Gospel*. Louisville: Westminster John Knox.

———. 2005. Prominent Patterns in the Social Memory of Jesus and Friends. Pages 57–78 in Kirk and Thatcher 2005b.

———. 2007. *Scribes, Visionaries and the Politics of Second Temple Judaism*. Louisville: Westminster John Knox.

Horsley, Richard A., with Jonathan A. Draper. 1999. *Whoever Hears You Hears Me: Prophets, Performance, and Tradition in Q*. Harrisburg, Pa.: Trinity Press International.

Hoy, David Couzens. 1978. *The Critical Circle: Literature and History in Contemporary Hermeneutics*. Berkeley and Los Angeles: University of California Press.

Hummel, Reinhart. 1966. *Die Auseinandersetzung zwischen Kirche und Judentum im Matthäusevangelium*. Munich: Kaiser.

Hutton, Patrick H. 1993. *History as an Art of Memory*. Hanover, N.H.: University Press of New England.

Iser, Wolfgang. 1974. *The Implied Reader: Patterns of Communication in Prose Fiction from Bunyan to Beckett*. Baltimore: Johns Hopkins University Press.

———. 1978 *The Act of Reading: A Theory of Aesthetic Response*. Baltimore: Johns Hopkins University Press. German original, 1976.

Jaffee, S. Martin. 1994. Writing and Rabbinic Oral Tradition: On Mishnaic Narrative, Lists, and Mnemonics. *Journal of Jewish Thought and Philosophy* 4:123–46.

———. 2001. *Torah in the Mouth: Writing and Oral Tradition in Palestinian Judaism, 200 BCE–400 CE*. Oxford: Oxford University Press.

———. 2009. Honi the Circler in Manuscript and Memory. Pages 87–111 in *Jesus in Memory: Traditions in Oral and Scribal Perspectives*. Edited by Werner H. Kelber and Samuel Byrskog. Waco, Tex.: Baylor University Press.

Jansen, W. Hugh. 1965. The Esoteric-Exoteric Factor in Folklore. Pages 43–51 in *The Study of Folklore*. Edited by Alan Dundes. Englewood Cliffs, N.J.: Prentice Hall.

Jauss, Hans Robert. 1982. *Toward an Aesthetic of Reception*. Minneapolis: University of Minnesota Press.

Jeremias, Joachim, and Wilhelm Schneemelcher. 1987. Papyrus Egerton 2. Pages 82–84 in *Neutestamentliche Apokryphen*. Edited by Wilhelm Schneemelcher. 5th ed. Tübingen: Mohr Siebeck.

Jewett, Robert. 1971. *Paul's Anthropological Terms: A Study of Their Use in Conflict Settings*. Leiden: Brill.

Johnson, Luke Timothy. 1996. *The Real Jesus: The Misguided Quest for the Historical Jesus and the Truth of the Traditional Gospels*. San Francisco: HarperSanFrancisco.

———. 1999. The Humanity of Jesus: What's at Stake in the Quest for the Historical Jesus. Pages 48–74 in *The Jesus Controversy: Perspectives in Conflict*. Harrisburg, Pa.: Trinity Press International.

Jousse, Marcel. 1925. *Études de Psychologie Linguistique : Le Style oral, rhythmique et mnémotechnique chez les Verbo-moteurs*. Paris: Beauchesne.

———. 1974. *L'anthropologie du geste*. Paris: Gallimard.

———. 1975. *La Manducation de la Parole*. Paris: Gallimard.

———. 1978. *Le Parlant, la Parole, et le Souffle*. Paris: Gallimard.

Kähler, Martin. 1964. *The So-Called Historical Jesus and the Historic, Biblical Christ*. Translated by Carl E. Braaten. Philadelphia: Fortress. German original: *Der sogenannte historische Jesus und der geschichtliche, biblische Christus*. Leipzig: Deichert, 1892.

Kapr, Albert. 1996. *Johannes Gutenberg: The Man and His Invention*. Translated by Douglas Martin. Brookfield: Scolar Press.

Käsemann, Ernst. 1954. Das Problem des historischen Jesus. *ZTK* 51:125–53. Repr. as pages 187–214 in vol. 1 of *Exegetische Versuche und Besinnungen*. 2nd ed. Göttingen: Vandenhoeck & Ruprecht, 1960.

———. 1968. *The Testament of Jesus: A Study of the Gospel of John in the Light of Chapter 17*. Philadelphia: Fortress.

Katz, Jacob. 1961. *Exclusiveness and Tolerance: Jewish-Gentile Relations in Medieval and Modern Times*. West Orange, N.J.: Behrman House.

Keck, Leander E. 1975. Oral Traditional Literature and the Gospels: The Seminar. Pages 103–22 in *The Relationships among the Gospels: An Interdisciplinary Dialogue*. Edited by William O. Walker Jr. San Antonio: Trinity University Press.

Kelber, Werner H. 1972. Mark 14:32-42: Gethsemane. Passion Christology and Discipleship Failure. *ZNW* 63:166–87.

———. 1974. *The Kingdom in Mark: A New Place and a New Time*. Philadelphia: Fortress.

———. 1976. The Hour of the Son of Man and the Temptation of the Disciples. Pages 41–60 in *The Passion in Mark: Studies on Mark 14–16*. Edited by Werner H. Kelber. Philadelphia: Fortress.

———. 1979. *Mark's Story of Jesus*. Philadelphia: Fortress.

———. 1983. *The Oral and the Written Gospel: The Hermeneutics of Speaking and Writing in the Synoptic Tradition, Mark, Paul, and Q*. Foreword by Walter J. Ong. Philadelphia: Fortress. Repr., Bloomington: Indiana University Press, 1997. French trans.: Paris: Cerf, 1990.

———. 1985a. Apostolic Tradition and the Form of the Gospel. Pages 24–46 in *Discipleship in the New Testament*. Philadelphia: Fortress. Repr. as ch. 1 in this volume.

———. 1985b. From Aphorism to Sayings Gospel, and from Parable to Narrative Gospel. *Foundations and Facets Forum* 1:23–30.

———. 1987a. The Authority of the Word in St. John's Gospel: Charismatic Speech, Narrative Text, Logocentric Metaphysics. Festschrift for Walter J. Ong. *Oral Tradition* 2/1:108–31.

———. 1987b. Biblical Hermeneutics and the Ancient Art of Communication: A Response. *Semeia* 39:97–105.

———. 1987c. Narrative as Interpretation and Interpretation of Narrative: Hermeneutical Reflections on the Gospels. *Semeia* 39:107–33. Repr. as pages 75–98 in *The Interpretation of Dialogue*. Edited by Tullio Maranhao. Chicago: University of Chicago Press, 1990. Repr. as ch. 2 in this volume.

———. 1988a. Die Fleischwerdung des Wortes in der Körperlichkeit des Textes. Pages 31–42 in *Materialität der Kommunikation*. Edited by Hans Ulrich Gumbrecht and K. Ludwig Pfeiffer. Frankfurt am Main: Suhrkamp.

———. 1988b. Narrative and Disclosure: Mechanisms of Concealing, Revealing, and Reveiling. *Semeia* 43:1–20. Repr. as ch. 3 in this volume.

———. 1989. Sayings Collection and Sayings Gospel: A Study in the Clustering Management of Knowledge. *Language and Communication* (issue in memory of Eric A. Havelock) 9:213–24.

———. 1990. In the Beginning Were the Words: The Apotheosis and Narrative Displacement of the Logos. *JAAR* 53:69–98. Repr. as ch. 4 in this volume.

———. 1992. Die Anfangsprozesse der Verschriftlichung im Frühchristentum. In *ANRW* 26.1:3–62. Edited by Wolfgang Haase and Hildegard Temporini. Berlin: de Gruyter.

———. 1995a. Jesus and Tradition: Words in Time, Words in Space. *Semeia* 65:139–67. Repr. as ch. 5 in this volume.

———. 1995b. Modalities of Communication, Cognition, and Physiology of Perception: Orality, Rhetoric, Scribality. *Semeia* 65:193–216.

———. 1996. Metaphysics and Marginality in John. Pages 129–54 in *What Is John? Readers and Readings of the Fourth Gospel*. Edited by Fernando F. Segovia. Atlanta: Scholars Press.

———. 2002. The Case of the Gospels: Memory's Desire and the Limits of Historical Criticism. *Oral Tradition* 17/1:55–86.

———. 2008. The Oral-Scribal-Memorial Arts of Communication in Early Christianity. Pages 235–62 in *Jesus, the Voice, and the Text: Beyond the Oral and the Written Gospel*. Edited by Tom Thatcher. Waco, Tex.: Baylor University Press.

———. 2011. The Work of Walter Ong and Biblical Scholarship. Pages 49–67 in *Language, Culture, and Idenity: The Legacy of Walter J. Ong, S.J.* Edited by Sara van den Berg and Thomas M. Walsh. New York: Hampton.

Kelber, Werner H., and Samuel Byrskog, eds. 2009. *Jesus in Memory: Traditions in Oral and Scribal Perspectives*. Waco, Tex.: Baylor University Press.

Kennedy, George A. 1978. *Greek Rhetoric Under Christian Emperors*. Princeton: Princeton University Press.

———. 1980. *Classical Rhetoric and Its Christian and Secular Tradition from Ancient to Modern Times*. Chapel Hill: University of North Carolina Press.

Kenner, Hugh. 1994. *Flaubert, Joyce and Beckett: The Stoic Comedians*. Boston: Beacon.

Kermode, Frank. 1979. *The Genesis of Secrecy: On the Interpretation of Narrative*. Cambridge: Harvard University Press.

———. 1983. Secrets and Narrative Sequence. Pages 133–55 in *The Art of Telling: Essays on Fiction*. Cambridge: Harvard University Press.

———. 1987. John. Pages 440–66 in *The Literary Guide to the Bible*. Edited by Robert Alter and Frank Kermode. Cambridge: Harvard University Press.

Kierkegaard, Søren. 1965. *The Concept of Irony: With Constant Reference to Socrates*. Translated by Lee M. Capel. Bloomington: Indiana University Press. Danish original: *Begrebet Ironi*, 1841.

King, Nathalia. 1991. The Mind's Eye and the Forms of Thought: Classical Rhetoric and the Composition of Augustine's *Confessions*. PhD diss., New York University.

Kinneavy, James L. 1987. *Greek Rhetorical Origins of Christian Faith*. New York: Oxford University Press.

Kirk, Alan. 1994. Examining Priorities: Another Look at the *Gospel of Peter's* Relationship to the New Testament Gospels. *NTS* 40:572–95.

———. 2005a. The Memory of Violence and the Death of Jesus in Q. Pages 191–206 in Kirk and Thatcher 2005b.

———. 2005b. Social and Cultural Memory. Pages 1–24 in Kirk and Thatcher 2005b.

———. 2009. Memory. Pages 155–72 in *Jesus in Memory: Traditions in Oral and Scribal Perpsectives*. Edited by Werner H. Kelber and Samuel Byrskog. Waco, Tex.: Baylor University Press.

Kirk, Alan, and Tom Thatcher. 2005a. Jesus Tradition as Social Memory. Pages 25-42 in Kirk and Thatcher 2005b.

———, eds. 2005b. *Memory, Tradition, and Text: Uses of the Past in Early Christianity*. SemeiaSt 52. Atlanta: Society of Biblical Literature.

Kittler, Friedrich. 1987. Signal—Rausch—Abstand. Pages 342–59 in *Materialität der Kommunikation*. Edited by Hans Ulrich Gumbrecht and K. Ludwig Pfeiffer. Frankfurt am Main: Suhrkamp.

Klein, J. 1960. Ockham Wilhelm von (1285-1449). In *RGG* 4:1556–62.

Kleine, Michael, and Fredric Gale. 1996. The Elusive Presence of the Word: An Interview with Walter Ong. *Composition Forum* 7:65–86.

Kloppenborg, John S. 1987. *Formation of Q: Trajectories in Ancient Wisdom Collections*. SAC. Philadelphia: Fortress.

———. 1991. City and Wasteland: Narrative World and the Beginning of the Sayings Gospel (Q). *Semeia* 52:145–60.

Koester, Helmut. 1957. Synoptische Überlieferung bei den Apostolischen Vätern. Berlin: Akademie.

———. 1971a. The Historical Jesus: Some Comments and Thoughts on Norman Perrin's *Rediscovering the Teaching of Jesus*. Pages 123–36 in *Christology and a Modern Pilgrimage: A Discussion with Norman Perrin*. Edited by Hans Dieter Betz. Claremont, Calif.: New Testament Colloquium.

———. 1971b. One Jesus and Four Primitive Gospels. Pages 158–204 in *Trajectories Through Early Christianity*. Philadelphia: Fortress.

———. 1980a. Apocryphal and Canonical Gospels. *HTR* 73:105–30.

———. 1980b. Gnostic Writings as Witnesses for the Development of the Sayings Tradition. Pages 239–61 in *The Rediscovery of Gnosticism*. Edited by B. Layton. Leiden: Brill.

———. 1982. *Introduction to the New Testament.* Vol. 2. Philadelphia: Fortress; Berlin: de Gruyter.

———. 1983. History and Development of Mark's Gospel (From Mark to Secret Mark and "Canonical Mark"). Pages 35–57 in *Colloquy on New Testament Studies: A Time for Reappraisal and Fresh Approaches*. Macon, Ga.: Mercer University Press.

———. 1990. *Ancient Christian Gospels: Their History and Development.* Philadelphia: Trinity Press International; London: SCM.

Krieger, Murray. 1964. *A Window to Criticism: Shakespeare's Sonnets and Modern Poetics.* Princeton: Princeton University Press.

Kuhn, Heinz-Wolfgang. 1970. Der irdische Jesus bei Paulus als traditionsgeschichtliches und theologisches Problem. *ZTK* 67:295–320.

Kümmel, Werner Georg. 1965. *Introduction to the New Testament.* Edited and translated by A. J. Mattill. 14th ed. Nashville: Abingdon.

Lee, Margaret Ellen, and Bernard Brandon Scott. 2009. *Sound Mapping the New Testament.* Salem, Ore.: Polebridge.

Leff, Gordon. 1975. *William of Ockham: The Metamorphosis of Scholastic Discourse.* Manchester: Manchester University Press.

Leipoldt, Johannes. 1907–8. *Geschichte des Neutestamentlichen Kanons.* 2 Vols. Leipzig: Hinrichs'sche.

Leroy, Herbert. 1968. *Rätsel und Missverständnis. Ein Beitrag zur Formgeschichte des Johannesevangeliums.* Bonn: Hanstein.

Levinas, Emmanuel. 1994. Judaism and Christianity. Pages 161–66 in *The Time of the Nations*. Bloomington: Indiana University Press.

Link, Hannelore. 1976. *Rezeptionsforschung: Eine Einführung in Methoden und Probleme.* Stuttgart: Kohlhammer.

Lohmeyer, Ernst. 1967. *Das Evangelium nach Markus.* 17th ed. Göttingen: Vandenhoeck & Ruprecht.

Lord, Albert B. 1960. *The Singer of Tales.* HSCL 24. Cambridge: Harvard University Press. Repr., New York: Atheneum, 1968. 2nd ed. edited by Stephen A. Mitchel and Gregory Nagy. Cambridge: Harvard University Press, 2000.

———. 1978. The Gospels as Oral Traditional Literature. Pages 33–91 in *The Relationships among the Gospels: An Interdisciplinary Dialogue*. Edited by William O. Walker Jr. San Antonio: Trinity University Press.

———. 1991. *Epic Singers and Oral Tradition*. Ithaca, N.Y.: Cornell University Press.

———. 1995. *The Singer Resumes the Tale*. Ithaca, N.Y.: Cornell University Press.

Lubac, Henri de. 1959–64. *Exégèse Médiévale: Les Quatres Sens de l'Écriture*. 4 vols. Paris: Aubier.

Maccoby, Hyam, ed. 1982. The Barcelona Disputation. Pages 39–75 in *Judaism on Trial: Jewish-Christian Disputations in the Middle Ages*. Rutherford, N.J.: Fairleigh Dickinson University Press; London: Associated University Presses.

MacDonald, Dennis Ronald. 1983. *The Legend and the Apostle: the Battle for Paul in Story and Canon*. Philadelphia: Westminster.

Mack, Burton L. 1973. *Logos und Sophia. Untersuchungen zur Weisheitstheologie im hellenistischen Judentum*. Göttingen: Vandenhoeck & Ruprecht.

———. 1993. *The Lost Gospel: The Book of Q and Christian Origins*. San Francisco: HarperSanFrancisco.

———. 1988. *A Myth of Innocence: Mark and Christian Origins*. Philadelphia: Fortress.

Magness, J. Lee. 1986. *Sense and Absence: Structure and Suspension in the Ending of Mark's Gospel*. Atlanta: Scholars Press.

Malbon, Elizabeth Struthers. 2002. *Hearing Mark: A Listener's Guide*. Valley Forge, Pa.: Trinity Press International.

Manetti, Giovanni. 1993. *Theories of the Sign in Classical Antiquity*. Translated by Christine Richardson. Bloomington: Indiana University Press.

Markus, R. A. 1957. St. Augustine on Signs. *Phronesis* 2:60–83.

Marrou, Henri-Irénée. 1956. *A History of Education in Antiquity*. Translated by George Lamb. New York: Sheed and Ward.

Martyn, J. Louis. 1977. *History and Theology in the Fourth Gospel*. 2nd ed. Nashville: Abingdon.

Marxsen, Willi. 1955. Redaktionsgeschichtliche Erklärung der sogenannten Parabeltheorie des Markus. *ZTK* 52:255–71.

———. 1956. *Der Evangelist Markus. Studien zur Redaktionsgeschichte des Evangeliums*. Göttingen: Vandenhoeck & Ruprecht. ET: *Mark the Evangelist: Studies on the Redaction History of the Gospel*. Translated by James Boyce et al. Nashville: Abingdon, 1969.

Maurer, Christian, and Wilhelm Schneemelcher. 1987. Petrusevangelium. Pages 180–88 in *Neutestamentliche Apokryphen*. Edited by Wilhelm Schneemelcher. 5th ed. Tübingen: Mohr Siebeck.

Maxwell, Kevin B. 1983. *Bemba Myth and Ritual: The Impact of Literacy on an Oral Culture*. New York: Lang.

McKnight, Edgar V. 1985. *The Bible and the Reader: An Introduction to Literary Criticism*. Philadelphia: Fortress.

Meagher, John C. 1979. *Clumsy Construction in Mark's Gospel: A Critique of Form and Redaktionsgeschichte*. TorSTh 3. New York: Mellen.

Meier, John P. 1991. *A Marginal Jew: Rethinking the Historical Jesus*. New York: Doubleday.

Merkel, H. 1986. Das "geheime Evangelium" nach Markus. Pages 89–92 in *Neutestamentliche Apokryphen*. Edited by Wilhelm Schneemelcher. 5th ed. Tübingen: Mohr Siebeck.

Metzger, Bruce M. 1997. *The Canon of the New Testament: Its Origin, Development, and Significance*. Oxford: Oxford University Press.

Minette de Tillesse, G. 1986. *Le Secret Messianique dans l'Évangile de Mar*. LD 47. Paris: Cerf.

Mitchell, Stephen. 1991. *The Gospel according to Jesus*. New York: HarperCollins.

Moltmann, Jürgen. 1974. *The Crucified God: The Cross of Christ as the Foundation and Criticism of Christian Theology*. Translated by R. A. Wilson and John Bowden. New York: Harper & Row.

Moore, Stephen D. 1989. *Literary Criticism and the Gospels: The Theoretical Challenge*. New Haven: Yale University Press.

———. 1992. *Mark and Luke in Poststructuralist Perspectives: Jesus Begins to Write*. New Haven: Yale University Press.

———. 1994. *Poststructuralism and the New Testament: Derrida and Foucault at the Foot of the Cross*. Minneapolis: Fortress.

Mournet, Terence C. 2005. *Oral Tradition and Literary Dependency: Variability and Stability in the Synoptic Tradition and Q*. WUNT 2/195. Tübingen: Mohr Siebeck.

———. 2009. The Jesus Tradition as Oral Tradition. Pages 39–61 in *Jesus in Memory: Traditions in Oral and Scribal Perspectives*. Edited by Werner H. Kelber and Samuel Byrskog. Waco, Tex.: Baylor University Press.

Müller, Jan-Dirk. 1986. Der Körper des Buchs. Zum Medienwechsel zwischen Handschrift und Druck. Pages 203–17 in *Materialität der Kommunikation*. Edited by Hans Ulrich Gumbrecht & K. Ludwig Pfeiffer. Frankfurt am Main: Suhrkamp.

Murphy, James J. 1974. *Rhetoric in the Middle Ages: A History of Rhetorical Theory from Saint Augustine to the Renaissance*. Berkeley and Los Angeles: University of California Press.

Neirynck, Frans 1985. Papyrus Egerton 2 and the Healing of the Leper. *ETL* 61:153–60.

Neusner, Jacob. 1979. Oral Torah and Oral Tradition: Defining the Problematic. Pages 59–75 in idem, *Method and Meaning in Ancient Judaism*. Chico, Calif.: Scholars Press.

———. 1987. *Oral Tradition in Judaism: the Case of the Mishnah*. New York: Garland.

———. 1995. *The Documentary Foundation of Rabbinic Culture: Mopping Up after Debates with Gerald L. Bruns, S. J. D. Cohen, Arnold Maria Goldberg, Susan Handelman, Christine Hayes, James Kugel, Peter Schaefer, Eliezer Segal, E. P. Sanders, and Lawrence H. Schiffman*. South Florida Studies in the History of Judaism 113. Atlanta: Scholars Press.

———. 1997. Gerhardsson's Memory and Manuscript Revisited: Introduction to a New Edition. *Approaches to Ancient Judaism* NS 12:171–94.

———. 1998. Foreword to *Memory and Manuscript: Oral Tradition and Written Transmission in Rabbinic Judaism and Early Christianity*; with, *Tradition and Transmission in Early Christianity*, by Birger Gerhardsson. Grand Rapids: Eerdmans.

Newman, Jane O. 1985. The Word Made Print: Luther's 1522 New Testament in an Age of Mechanical Reproduction. *Representations* 11:95–133.

Nickelsburg, George E. 1980. The Genre and Function of the Markan Passion Narrative. *HTR* 73:153–84.

Niditch, Susan. 1996. *Oral World and Written Word: Ancient Israelite Literature*. Lousiville: Westminster John Knox.

Nietzsche, Friedrich. 2005. *Ecce Homo*. Munich: Beck, 2005. Written 1888, published 1908.

Nirenberg, David. 2013. *Anti-Judaism: The Western Tradition*. New York: W. W. Norton.

Nordenfalk, Carl. 1938. *Die spätantiken Kanontafeln. Kunstgeschichtliche Studien über die eusebianische Evangelien-konkordanz*. 2 Vols. Göteborg: Isacson.

O'Brian O'Keeffe, Katherine. 1990. *Visible Song: Transitional Literacy in Old English Verse*. Cambridge: Cambridge University Press.

O'Day, Gail R. 1986. *Revelation in the Fourth Gospel: Narrative Mode and Theological Claim*. Philadelphia: Fortress.

Olson, David R. 1994. *The World on Paper: The Conceptual and Cognitive Implications of Writing and Reading*. Cambridge: Cambridge University Press.

Ong, Walter J. 1958. *Ramus, Method and the Decay of Dialogue: From the Art of Discourse to the Art of Reason*. Cambridge: Harvard University Press. Repr., Farrar, Strauss & Giroux, 1974; Harvard University Press, 1983; University of Chicago Press, 2004.

———. 1967a. *In the Human Grain: Further Explorations of Contemporary Culture*. New York: Macmillan.

———. 1967b. *The Presence of the Word: Some Prolegomena for Cultural and Religious History*. New Haven: Yale University Press. Repr., Minneapolis: University of Minnesota Press, 1981.

———. 1975. The Writer's Audience Is Always a Fiction. *PMLA* 90:9–21. Repr. as pages 53–81 in *Interfaces of the Word: Studies in the Evolution of Consciousness and Culture*. Ithaca, N.Y.: Cornell University Press.

———. 1977a. *Interfaces of the Word: Studies in the Evolution of Consciousness and Culture*. Ithaca, N.Y.: Cornell University Press.

———. 1977b. Maranatha: Death and Life in the Text of the Book. Pages 230–71 in *Interfaces of the Word: Studies in the Evolution of Consciousness and Culture*. Ithaca, N.Y.: Cornell University Press.

———. 1982. *Orality and Literacy: The Technologizing of the Word*. London and New York: Methuen. Repr., London and New York: Routledge, 1988.

———. 1983. Foreword to *The Present State of Scholarship in Historical and Contemporary Rhetoric*. Edited by Winifred Bryan Horner. Columbia: University of Missouri Press.

———. 1992a. Technology outside Us and inside Us. Pages 189–208 in *Selected Essays and Studies*. Vol. 1 of *Faith and Contexts*. Edited by Thomas J. Farrell and Paul A. Soukup. Atlanta: Scholars Press. Originally published in *Communio: International Catholic Review* 5/2 (1978): 100–121.

———. 1992b. Text as Interpretation: Mark and After. Pages 191–210 in *Supplementary Studies*. Vol. 2 of *Faith and Contexts*. Edited by Thomas J. Farrell and Paul A. Soukup. Atlanta: Scholars Press. Originally published as pages 147–69 in *Oral*

Tradition in Literature. Edited by John Miles Foley. Columbia: University of Missouri Press. Repr. in *Semeia* 39: *Orality, Aurality, and Biblical Narrative* (1987): 7–26.

———. 1992c. Voice and the Opening of Closed Systems. Pages 162–90 in *Supplementary Studies.* Vol. 2 of *Faith and Contexts.* Edited by Thomas J. Farrell and Paul A. Soukup. Atlanta: Scholars Press. Originally published as pages 305–41 in *Interfaces of the Word: Studies in the Evolution of Consciousness and Culture.* Ithaca, N.Y.: Cornell University Press, 1977.

———. 1992d. Voice as Summons for Belief: Literature, Faith, and Divided Self. Pages 68–84 in *Supplementary Studies.* Vol. 2 of *Faith and Contexts.* Edited by Thomas J. Farrell and Paul A. Soukup. Atlanta: Scholars Press. Originally published in *Thought* (1958): 43–61.

Padel, Ruth. 1991. *In and Out of the Mind: Greek Images of the Tragic Self.* Princeton: Princeton University Press.

Pagels, Elaine. 1980. The Orthodox Against the Gnostics: Confrontation and Interiority in Early Christianity. Pages 61–73 in *The Other Side of God: A Polarity in World Religion.* Edited by Peter L. Berger. Garden City, N.Y.: Anchor Doubleday.

Parker, David C. 1997. *The Living Text of the Gospels.* Cambridge: Cambridge University Press.

———. 2008. Scribal Tendencies and the Mechanics of Book Production. Pages 173–84 in *Textual Variation: Theological and Social Tendencies.* Edited by D. C. Parker and H. A. G. Houghton. Piscataway, N.J.: Gorgias.

Parry, Adam, ed. 1970. *The Making of Homeric Verse: Collected Papers of Milman Parry.* Oxford: Clarendon.

Parry, Milman. 1930. Studies in the Epic Technique of Oral Verse-Making I: Homer and Homeric Style. *HSCP* 41:73–147.

———. 1932. Studies in the Epic Technique of Oral Verse-Making: II: The Homeric Language as the Language of Oral Poetry. *HSCP* 43:1–50.

———. 1933. Whole Formulaic Verses in Greek and Southslavic Heroic Songs. *TAPA* 64:179–97.

Patterson, Richard. 1985. *Image and Reality in Plato's Metaphysics.* Indianapolis: Hackett.

Peabody, Berkeley. 1974. *The Winged Word: A Study in the Technique of Ancient Greek Oral Composition as Seen Principally Through Hesiod's Works and Days.* Albany: State University of New York Press.

Perkins, Pheme. 1980. *The Gnostic Dialogue: The Early Church and the Crisis of Gnosticism.* New York: Paulist.

Perrin, Norman. 1968. The Creative Use of the Son of Man Traditions by Mark. *USQR* 23:357–65.

———. 1969. *What Is Redaction Criticism?* Philadelphia: Fortress.

———. 1971a. The Christology of Mark: A Study in Methodology. *JR* 51:173–87.

———. 1971b. Towards an Interpretation of the Gospel of Mark. Pages 1–71 In *Christology and a Modern Pilgrimage.* Edited by Hans Dieter Betz. Claremont: New Testament Colloquium.

———. 1974. *A Modern Pilgrimage in New Testament Christology*. Philadelphia: Fortress.

———. 1976. The Interpretation of the Gospel of Mark. *Int* 30:115–24.

Perry, Menakhem. 1979. Literary Dynamics: How the Order of a Text Creates Its Meaning. *Poetics Today* 1:35–64, 311–61.

Petersen, Norman R. 1978. *Literary Criticism for New Testament Critics*. GBS. Philadelphia: Fortress.

———. 1980. When Is the End Not the End? Literary Reflections on the Ending of Mark's Narrative. *Int* 34:151–66.

Polzin, Robert. 1980. *Moses and the Deuteronomist: A Literary Study of the Deuteronomic History*. New York: Seabury.

Quesnell, Quentin. 1975. The Gospel Hoax: Morton Smith's Invention of Secret Mark. *CBQ* 37:48–67.

Reimarus, Hermann Samuel. 1778. Von dem Zwecke Jesu und seiner Jünger. Pages 254–376 in *Gotthold Ephraim Lessing , Gesammelte Werke 8*. Berlin: Aufbau. ET: Pages 59–269 in *Reimarus: Fragments*. Edited by Charles H. Talbert. Translated by Ralph S. Fraser. Philadelphia: Fortress.

Reitzenstein, Richard. 1978. *Hellenistic Mystery-Religions: Their Basic Ideas and Significance*. PTMS 15. Pittsburgh: Pickwick Press. Original German, 1910.

Rhoads, David M. 2006. Performance Criticism: An Emerging Methodology in Second Testament Studies. *BTB* 36/4: part 1: 118–33; part 2: 164–84.

Rhoads, David M., and Donald Michie. 1982. *Mark as Story: An Introduction to the Narrative of a Gospel*. Philadelphia: Fortress.

Ricoeur, Paul. 1975. Biblical Hermeneutics. *Semeia* 4:27–148.

———. 1976a. From Proclamation to Narrative. *JR* 64:501–12.

———. 1976b. *Interpretation Theory: Discourse and Surplus of Meaning*. Fort Worth: Texas Christian University Press.

———. 1977. *The Rule of Metaphor: Multi-disciplinary Studies of the Creation of Meaning in Language*. Translated by Robert Czerny et al. Toronto: University of Toronto Press.

———. 1982. La Bible et L'Imagination. *RHPR* (Hommage à Roger Mehl) 62:339–60.

———. 2000. *La Mémoire, l'Histoire, l'Oubli*. Paris: Cerf. ET: see Ricoeur 2004.

———. 2004. *Memory, History, Forgetting*. Translated by Kathleen Blamey and David Pellauer. Chicago: University of Chicago Press, 2004.

Rimmon-Kenan, Shlomith. 1983. *Narrative Fiction: Contemporary Poetics*. New York: Methuen.

Robbins, Vernon K. 1984. *Jesus the Teacher: A Socio-Rhetorical Interpretation of Mark*. Philadelphia: Fortress.

Robinson, James M. 1957. *The Problem of History in Mark*. SBT 21. London: SCM.

———. 1959. *A New Quest of the Historical Jesus*. London: SCM.

———. 1970. On the Gattung of Mark (and John). Pages 1:99–129 in *Jesus and Man's Hope*. Edited by Dikran Y. Hadidian. Pittsburgh: Pittsburgh Theological Seminary. Repr. as pages 11–39 in *The Problem of History In Mark and Other Marcan Studies*. Philadelphia: Fortress, 1982.

———. 1971a. Kerygma and History in the New Testament. Pages 20–70 in *Trajectories through Early Christianity*. Philadelphia: Fortress.

———. 1971b. LOGOI SOPHON. On the Gattung of Q. Pages 71–113 in *Trajectories through Early Christianity*. Philadelphia: Fortress.

———. 1982a. Gnosticism and the New Testament. Pages 40–53 in *The Problem of History in Mark and other Marcan Studies*. Philadelphia: Fortress.

———. 1982b. Jesus: From Easter to Valentinus (or to the Apostles' Creed). *JBL* 101: 5–37.

———. 1982c. On the Gattung of Mark (and John). Pages 11–39 in *The Problem of History in Mark and Other Marcan Studies*. Philadelphia: Fortress.

———. 1986a. The Gospel as Narrative. Pages 97–112 in *The Bible and the Narrative Tradition*. Edited by Frank McConnell. New York: Oxford University Press.

———. 1986b. On Bridging the Gulf from Q to the Gospel of Thomas (or vice versa). Pages 127–75 in *Nag Hammadi, Gnosticism and Early Christianity*. Edited by Charles W. Hedrick and Robert Hodgson Jr. Peabody, Mass.: Hendrickson.

———. 1999. A Written Greek Sayings Cluster Older than Q: A Vestige. *HTR* 92:61–77.

Robinson, James M., ed. 1977. *The Nag Hammadi Library in English*. San Francisco: Harper & Row.

Robinson, James M., and Helmut Koester, eds. 1971. *Trajectories through Early Christianity*. Philadelphia: Fortress.

Rodriguez, Rafael. 2010. *Structuring Early Christian Memory: Jesus in Tradition, Performance, and Text*. Library of New Testament Studies 407. New York: T&T Clark.

Rosenberg, Rainer. 1987. Die Sublimierung der Literaturgeschichte oder: ihre Reinigung von den Materialitäten der Kommunikation. Pages 107–38 in *Materialität der Kommunikation*. Edited by Hans Ulrich Gumbrecht und K. Ludwig Pfeiffer. Frankfurt am Main: Suhrkamp.

Ruether, Rosemary. 1972. The Pharisees in First-Century Judaism. *The Ecumenist* 11:1–7.

Ruppel, Aloys. 1939. *Johannes Gutenberg: sein Leben und sein Werk*. Berlin: Mann. Repr., 1947.

Ruppert, Lothar. 1972a. *Der leidende Gerechte: eine motivgeschichtliche Untersuchung zum Alten Testament und zwischentestamentlichen Judentum*. FB 5. Würzburg: Echter.

———. 1972b. *Jesus, der leidende Gerechte?* SBS 59. Stuttgart: KBW.

———. 1973. *Der leidende Gerechte und seine Feinde: Eine Wortfelduntersuchung*. Würzburg: Echter.

Saenger, Paul. 1982. Silent Reading: Its Impact on Late Medieval Script and Society. *Viator* 13:367–414.

Saldarini, Anthony J. 1991. The Gospel of Matthew and Jewish-Christian Conflict. Pages 38–61 in *Social History of the Matthean Community: Cross-Disciplinary Approaches*. Edited by David L. Balch. Minneapolis: Fortress.

Sanders, E. P. 1977. *Paul and Palestinian Judaism: A Comparison of Patterns of Religion*. Philadelphia: Fortress Press.

———. 1985. *Jesus and Judaism*. Philadelphia: Fortress.

Schäfer, Peter. 1986. Research into Rabbinic Literature: An Attempt to Define the Status Quaestionis. *JJS* 37:139–52.

———. 1988. *Hekhalot-Studien*. TSAJ 19. Tübingen: Mohr Siebeck.

Schillebeeckx, Edward. 1979. *Jesus: An Experiment in Christology*. Translated by Hubert Hoskins. New York: Seabury.

Schmahl, Günther. 1974. *Die Zwölf im Markusevangelium. Eine redaktionsgeschichtliche Untersuchung*. TTS 30. Trier: Paulinus.

Schneidau, Herbert N. 1976. *Sacred Discontent: The Bible and Western Tradition*. Baton Rouge: Louisiana State University Press.

———. 1978. For Interpretation. *MoRev* 1:70–88.

———. 1982. The Word against the Word: Derrida on Textuality. *Semeia* 23:5–28.

———. 1985. Literary Relations among the Gospels: Harmony or Conflict. *Studies in the Literary Imagination* 18:17–32.

———. 1987. Let the Reader Understand. *Semeia* 39:135–45.

Scholes, Robert, and Robert Kellogg. 1967. *The Nature of Narrative*. London: Oxford University Press.

Schröter, Jens. 1997. *Erinnerung an Jesu Worte. Studien zur Rezeption der Logienüberlieferung in Markus, Q und Thomas*. WMANT 76. Neukirchen-Vluyn: Neukirchener.

———. 2006. Jesus and the Canon: The Early Jesus Traditions in the Context of the Origins of the New Testament Canon. Pages 104–22 in *Performing the Gospel: Orality, Memory, and Mark*. Edited by Richard A. Horsley, Jonathan A. Draper, and John Miles Foley. Minneapolis: Fortress. German ed. in *BTZ* 22/2 (2005): 181–201.

———. 2007. *Von Jesus zum Neuen Testament. Studien zur urchristlichen Theologiegeschichte und zur Entstehung des neutestamentlichen Kanons*. Tübingen: Mohr Siebeck.

Schulte-Sasse, Jochen. 1988. Von der schriftlichen zur elektronischen Kultur: Über neuere Wechselbeziehungen zwischen Medien- Geschichte und Kulturgeschichte. Pages 429–53 in *Materialität der Kommunikation*. Edited by Hans Ulrich Gumbrecht and K. Ludwig Pfeiffer. Frankfurt am Main: Suhrkamp.

Schüssler Fiorenza, Elisabeth. 1983. *In Memory of Her: A Feminist Theological Reconstruction of Christian Origins*. New York: Crossroad.

Schwartz, Barry. 2000. *Abraham Lincoln and the Forge of National Memory*. Chicago: University of Chicago Press.

———. 2005a. Christian Origins: Historical Truth and Social Memory. Pages 43–56 in Kirk and Thatcher 2005b.

———. 2005b. Jesus in First-Century Memory: Origins as MnemoHistory—A Response. Pages 249–61 in Kirk and Thatcher 2005b.

Schweitzer, Albert. 1968. *The Quest of the Historical Jesus: A Critical Study of Its Progress from Reimarus to Wrede*. Introduced by James M. Robinson. Translated by W. Montgomery. New York: Macmillan. German original: *Von Reimarus zu Wrede: Geschichte der Leben-Jesu Forschung*. Tübingen: Mohr Siebeck, 1906. [6th German ed: *Geschichte der Leben-Jesu Forschung*. Tübingen: Mohr Siebeck, 1951].

Schweizer, Eduard. 1975. *The Good News according to Matthew*. Atlanta: John Knox.

Scott, Bernard, and Margaret Dean. 1993. A Sound Map of the Sermon on the Mount. Pages 672–725 in *SBL Seminar Papers, 1993*. Edited by Eugene H. Lovering Jr. Atlanta: Scholars Press. Repr. in *Treasures Old and New: Recent Contributions to Matthean Studies*. Edited by David Bauer and Mark Allan Powell. Atlanta: Scholars Press, 1995.

Segal, Charles P. 1995. Gorgias and the Psychology of the Logos. *HSCP* 66:99–155.

Seidman, Naomi. 1996. Elie Wiesel and the Scandal of Jewish Rage. *Jewish Social Studies* 3/1:1–19.

Shiner, Whitney. 2003. *Proclaiming the Gospel: First-Century Performance of Mark*. Harrisburg, Pa.: Trinity Press International.

Sienaert, Edgar Richard. 1990. Marcel Jousse: The Oral Style and the Anthropology of Gesture. *Oral Tradition* 5/1:91–106.

Silberman, Lou H., ed. 1987. *Orality, Aurality and Biblical Narrative*. Semeia 39. Decatur: Scholars Press.

Simpson, James. 2007. *Burning to Read: English Fundamentalism and Its Reformation Opponents*. Cambridge: Belknap Press of Harvard University Press.

Smalley, Beryl. 1952. *The Study of the Bible in the Middle Ages*. Oxford: Basil Blackwell.

Smith, Jonathan Z. 1978. Good News Is No News: Aretalogy and Gospel. SJLA 23. Leiden: Brill.

———. 1982. Sacred Persistence: Toward a Redescription of Canon. Pages 36–52 in *Imagining Religion: From Babylon to Jonestown*. Chicago: University of Chicago Press.

Smith, Morton. 1963. A Comparison of Early Christian and Early Rabbinic Tradition. *JBL* 82:169–76.

———. 1973a. *Clement of Alexandria and a Secret Gospel of Mark*. Cambridge: Harvard University Press.

———. 1973b. *The Secret Gospel: The Discovery and Interpretation of the Secret Gospel According to Mark*. New York: Harper & Row.

———. 1978. *Jesus the Magician: Charlatan or Son of God?* San Francisco: Harper & Row.

———. 1982. Clement of Alexandria and Secret Mark: The Score at the End of the First Decade. *HTR* 75:449–61.

Smith, Robert. 1973. *The Art of Rhetoric in Alexandria: Its Theory and Practice in the Ancient World*. The Hague: Nijhoff.

Snell, Bruno. 1960. *The Discovery of the Mind: The Greek Origins of European Thought*. New York: Harper & Row.

Soloveitschik, Joseph B. 1964. Confrontation. *Tradition: A Journal of Orthodox Jewish Thought* 6:17–29.

Spier, Jeffrey, ed. 2008. *Picturing the Bible: The Earliest Christian Art*. New Haven: Yale University Press.

Spong, John. 1992. *Born of a Woman: A Bishop Rethinks the Birth of Jesus*. San Francisco: HarperSanFrancisco.

Steinlauf, Michael C. 1997. *Bondage to the Dead: Poland and the Memory of the Holocaust*. Syracuse: Syracuse University Press.

Stock, Brian. 1983. *The Implications of Literacy. Written Language and Models of Interpretation in the Eleventh and Twelfth Centuries*. Princeton: Princeton University Press.

———. 1990. *Listening for the Text: On the Uses of the Past*. Baltimore: Johns Hopkins University Press.

Stock, Klemens. 1975. *Boten aus dem Mit-Ihm-Sein. Das Verhältnis zwischen Jesus und den Zwölf nach Markus*. AnBib 70. Rome: Biblical Institute Press.

Stone, Michael E. 1981. Reactions to Destructions of the Second Temple. *Journal for the Study of Judaism* 12/2: 195–204.

Stoneman, Richard, ed. and trans. 1991. *The Greek Alexander Romance*. New York: Penguin.

Stowers, Stanley Kent. 1981. *The Diatribe and Paul's Letter to the Romans*. SBLDS 57. Chico, CA: Scholars Press.

Suhl, Alfred. 1965. *Die Funktion der alttestamentlichen Zitate und Anspielungen im Markusevangelium*. Gütersloh: Mohn.

Swearingen, C. Jan. 1991. *Rhetoric and Irony: Western Literacy and Western Lies*. New York: Oxford University Press.

Szabolcsi, Miklós. 1988. Neue Ernsthaftigkeit. Pages 909–13 in *Materialität der Kommunikation*. Edited by Hans Ulrich Gumbrecht and K. Ludwig Pfeiffer. Frankfurt am Main: Suhrkamp.

Talbert, Charles H. 1977. *What Is a Gospel? The Genre of the Canonical Gospels*. Philadelphia: Fortress.

———. 1978. Oral and Independent or Literary and Interdependent? A Response to Albert B. Lord. Pages 93–102 in *The Relationships among the Gospels: An Interdisciplinary Dialogue*. Edited by William O. Walker Jr. San Antonio: Trinity University Press.

Tannehill, Robert C. 1977. The Disciples in Mark: The Functions of a Narrative Role. *JR* 57:386–405.

———. 1979. The Gospel of Mark as Narrative Christology. *Semeia* 16:57–95.

Thatcher, Tom. 2005. Why John Wrote a Gospel: Memory and History in an Early Christian Community. Pages 79–97 in Kirk and Thatcher 2005b.

———. 2006. *Why John Wrote a Gospel: Jesus—Memory—History*. Louisville: Westminster John Knox.

Tödt, Heinz Eduard. 1965. *The Son of Man in the Synoptic Tradition*. Translated by Dorothea M. Barton. Philadelphia: Westminster.

Tompkins, Jane P. 1980. *Reader-Response Criticism: From Formalism to Post-structuralism*. Baltimore: Johns Hopkins University Press.

Tracy, David. 1987. *Plurality and Ambiguity: Hermeneutics, Religion, Hope*. San Francisco: Harper & Row.

Troll, Denise A. 1990. The Illiterate Mode of Written Communication: The Work of the Medieval Scribe. Pages 96–125 in *Oral and Written Communication: Historical Approaches*. Edited by Richard Leo Enos. Newbury Park, Calif.: Sage.

Tuckett, Christopher, ed. 1983. *The Messianic Secret*. Philadelphia: Fortress.

———. 2009. Form Criticism. Pages 21–38 in *Jesus in Memory: Traditions in Oral and Scribal Perspectives*. Waco, Tex.: Baylor University Press.

Tyler, Stephen A. 1978. *The Said and the Unsaid: Mind, Meaning, and Culture.* New York: Academic Press.

———. 1986. On Being Out of Words. *Cultural Anthropology* 1:131–37.

———. 1987. *The Unspeakable: Discourse, Dialogue, und Rhetoric in the Postmodern World.* Madison: University of Wisconsin Press.

Tyson, Joseph B. 1961. The Blindness of the Disciples in Mark. *JBL* 80:261–68.

Ulrich, Eugene. 1999. *The Dead Sea Scrolls and the Origins of the Bible.* Grand Rapids: Eerdmans.

Van Beeck, Frans Jozef. 1994. The Quest of the Historical Jesus: Origins, Achievements, and the Specter of Diminishing Returns. Pages 83–99 in *Jesus and Faith: A Conversation on the Work of John Dominic Crossan.* Edited by Jeffrey Carlson and Robert A. Ludwig. Maryknoll, N.Y.: Orbis.

Vermes, Geza. 1981. *Jesus the Jew.* Rev. ed. Philadelphia: Fortress.

Via, Dan O. 1967. *The Parables: Their Literary and Existential Dimension.* Philadelphia: Fortress.

———. 1975. *Kerygma and Comedy in the New Testament: A Structuralist Approach to Hermeneutic.* Philadelphia: Fortress.

Vielhauer, Philipp. 1975. *Geschichte der urchristlichen Literatur.* Berlin: de Gruyter.

Votaw, Clyde Weber. 1970. *The Gospels and Contemporary Biographies in the Greco-Roman World.* Philadelphia: Fortress.

Walker, William O., Jr., ed. 1978. *The Relationships among the Gospels: An Interdisciplinary Dialogue.* San Antonio: Trinity University Press.

Ward, Richard F. 1994. Pauline Voice and Presence as Strategic Communication. *Semeia* 65:95–107.

Weeden, Theodore J. 1971. *Mark—Traditions in Conflict.* Philadelphia: Fortress.

White, Hayden. 1973. *Metahistory: The Historical Imagination in Nineteenth-Century Europe.* Baltimore: Johns Hopkins University Press.

———. 1978. *Tropics of Discourse: Essays in Cultural Criticism.* Baltimore: Johns Hopkins University Press.

———. 1980. The Value of Narrativity in the Representation of Reality. *Critical Inquiry* 7:5–27.

Wiesel, Elie. 1956. *Un di velt hot geshvign.* Poylishe Yidntum 117. Buenos Aires: Tsentral-Farband fun Poylishe Yidn in Argentine.

———. 1958. *La Nuit.* Paris: Minuit.

———. 1979. An Interview Unlike Any Other. Pages 14–26 in *A Jew Today.* Translated by Marion Wiesel. New York: Random House.

———. 1982. *Night.* New York: Bantam, 1960.

———. 1996. *All Rivers Run to the Sea: Memoirs.* Vol. 1. London: HarperCollins.

Williams, James G. 1985. *Gospel Against Parable: Mark's Language of Mystery.* Bible and Literature Series 12. Decator: Almond Press.

———. 1988. Parable and Chreia: From Q to Narrative Gospel. *Semeia* 43:85–114.

Wilson, A. N. 1992. *Jesus: A Life.* London: Sinclair-Stevenson.

Wire, Antoinette Clark. 1990. *The Corinthian Women Prophets: A Reconstruction through Paul's Rhetoric.* Minneapolis: Fortress.

———. 1994. Performance, Politics, and Power: A Response. *Semeia* 65:129–35.

———. 2005. Jewish Birth Prophecy Stories and Women's Social Memory. Pages 173–89 in Kirk and Thatcher 2005b.

———. 2011. *The Case for Mark Composed in Performance*. Biblical Performance Criticism Series 3. Eugene, Ore.: Cascade.

Wolf, Friedrich August. 1985. *Prolegomena to Homer*. Princeton: Princeton University Press. Translated by Anthony Grafton, Glenn W. Most, and James E. G. Zetzel. Originally published as *Prolegomena ad Homerum*, 1795.

Woll, D. Bruce. 1981. *Johannine Christianity in Conflict: Authority, Rank, and Succession in the First Farewell Discourse*. SBLDS 60. Chico, Calif.: Scholars Press.

Wrede, William. 1901. *Das Messiasgeheimnis in den Evangelien. Zugleich ein Beitrag zum Verständnis des Markusevangeliums*. Göttingen: Vandenhoeck & Ruprecht. ET: *The Messianic Secret*. Translated by J. C. G. Greig. Cambridge: Clarke, 1971.

Wuellner, Wilhelm. 1977. Paul's Rhetoric of Argumentation in Romans: An Alternative to the Donfried-Karris Debate Over Romans. *CBQ* 38:330–51. Repr. as pages 152–74 in *The Romans Debate*. Edited by K. P. Donfried. Minneapolis: Augsburg. 2nd ed., pages 128–46 in Peabody, Mass.: Hendrickson, 1991.

Wyschogrod, Edith. 1998. *An Ethics of Remembering: History, Heterology, and the Nameless Others*. Chicago: University of Chicago Press.

———. 2009. An Exercise in Upbuilding. Pages 241–59 in *Saintly Influence: Edith Wyschogrod and the Possibilities of Philosophy of Religion*. Edited by Eric Boynton and Martin Kavka. New York: Fordham University Press.

Yates, Frances A. 1966. *The Art of Memory*. Chicago: University of Chicago Press.

Zahn, Theodor von. 1889–92. *Geschichte des Neutestamentlichen Kanons*. 2 Vols. Erlangen: Deichert.

Zumthor, Paul. 1990. *Oral Poetry: An Introduction*. Minneapolis: University of Minnesota Press.

NEWSPAPER ARTICLES

Auschwitz: A Fitting Site for a Christian Cross. 1989. *Jerusalem Post*. September 19.

Chief Rabbi Is Asking a Favor of "Mr. Pope." 1999. *New York Times*. June 12.

Controversial Crosses Removed from Lot Bordering Auschwitz. 1999. *Buffalo News*. May 29.

Nirenberg, David. Anti-Judaism as Critical Theory. *Chronicle of Higher Eduication*. January 28, 2013.

Orr, H. Allen. 2007. A Religion for Darwinians? Review of *Living with Darwin: Evolution, Design, and the Future of Faith*, by Philip Kitcher. New York: Oxford University Press, 2007. *New York Times*. August 16, 2007.

Poles and Jews Feud about Crosses at Auschwitz. 1998. *New York Times*. December 20.

Polish Catholic Indicted for Instigating Auschwitz Dispute. 1999. *Jerusalem Post*. March 2.

Pope Urged to Remove Camp Cross. 1999. *Los Angeles Times*. June 12.

Index of Ancient Documents

Index of Authors

Index of Names and Subjects

CPSIA information can be obtained at www.ICGtesting.com
Printed in the USA
BVOW08s0040311013

335127BV00002B/34/P